Common Culture

Reading and Writing About American Popular Culture

Common Culture

Reading and Writing About American Popular Culture

SEVENTH EDITION

Edited by

Michael Petracca
Madeleine Sorapure
University of California at Santa Barbara

PEARSON

Boston Columbus Indianapolis New York San Francisco Upper Saddle River
Amsterdam Cape Town Dubai London Madrid Milan Munich Paris Montreal Toronto
Delhi Mexico City Sao Paulo Sydney Hong Kong Seoul Singapore Taipei Tokyo

Senior Editor: Brad Potthoff
Editorial Assistant: Nancy C. Lee
Senior Supplements Editor: Donna Campion
Senior Marketing Manager: Sandra McGuire
Senior Media Producer: Stefanie Liebman
Associate Managing Editor: Bayani Mendoza de Leon
Project Coordination, Text Design, and Electronic Page Makeup: PreMediaGlobal
Operations Specialist: Mary Ann Gloriande
Art Director, Cover: John Callahan
Cover Designer: Laura Shaw
Cover Images: (clockwise from top right) © Kristian Dowling/PictureGroup; © Olivier Douliery/PictureGroup; © Tetra Images/Roberstock; © Robert Llewellyn/Superstock, Copyright Media Bakery/Photononstop Images/Till Jacket

Credits and acknowledgments borrowed from other sources and reproduced, with permission, in this textbook appear on pages 566–569.

Library of Congress Cataloging-in-Publication Data

Common culture : reading and writing about American popular culture / [compiled] by Michael Petracca, Madeleine Sorapure.—7th ed.
p. cm.
Includes bibliographical references and index.
ISBN-13: 978-0-205-17178-1
ISBN-10: 0-205-17178-8
1. Popular culture—United States. 2. United States—Social life and customs—1971- 3. United States—Civilization—1970- 4. Popular culture—Study and teaching—United States. 5. United States—social life and customs—1971—Study and teaching. 6. United States—Civilization—1970—Study and teaching. I. Petracca, Michael, 1947- II. Sorapure, Madeleine.
E169.Z83C65 2011
973.924—dc22

2011015706

1 2 3 4 5 6 7 8 9 10—STP/RRD—14 13 12 11

ISBN-13: 978-0-205-17178-1
ISBN-10: 0-205-17178-8

To Lisa and Eric, Jade and Leif, Corinne and Ben and the as-yet-unnamed New Addition, and Annie and Beth . . . my extended aquatic family

—M.P.

For my daughter Sophia, from whom I will learn much about popular culture (and much else) in the coming years.

—M.S.

Contents

Preface

When we started teaching composition courses that examined television, pop music, movies, and other media-generated artifacts, we looked for a text that would cover a full range of topics in the field of popular culture from a variety of theoretical perspectives. We discovered that no satisfactory text existed, and therefore we began putting together assignments and reading materials to meet our needs. From this compilation *Common Culture* emerged.

The more we've taught writing courses based on popular culture, the more convinced we've become that such courses are especially appealing for students and effective in improving their critical thinking, reading, and writing skills. Students come into the writing classroom already immersed in the culture of YouTube, the iPhone, and the Wii. The advantage, then, is that we don't have to "sell" the subject matter of the course and can concentrate on the task at hand—namely, teaching students to think critically and to write clear and effective prose. Obviously, a course that panders to the lowest common denominator of students' taste would be a mindless, unproductive enterprise for all concerned. However, the underlying philosophy of a pop culture–based writing course is this: By reading, thinking, and writing about material they find inherently interesting, students develop their critical and analytical skills—skills which are, of course, crucial to their success in college.

Although students are already familiar with the many aspects of popular culture, few have directed sustained, critical thought to its influence or implications—that is, to what shopping malls might tell them about contemporary culture or to what they've actually learned from watching *Dancing with the Stars*. Because television shows, advertisements, and music videos, for example, are highly crafted artifacts, they are particularly susceptible to analysis; and because so much in contemporary culture is open to interpretation and controversy, students enjoy the opportunity to articulate and argue for their own interpretations of objects and institutions in the world around them.

Although popular culture is undeniably a sexy (or, at least, lively) subject, it has also, in the past two decade, become accepted as a legitimate object of academic discourse. While some may contend that it's frivolous to write a dissertation on *Buffy the Vampire Slayer*, most scholars recognize the importance of studying the artifacts and institutions of contemporary life. Popular culture is a rich field of study, drawing in researchers from a variety of disciplines. Because it is also a very inviting field of study for students, a textbook that addresses this subject in a comprehensive and challenging way will be especially appealing both to them and to their writing teachers.

Common Culture, seventh edition, contains an introductory chapter that walks students through one assignment—in this case, focusing on the Barbie doll—with step-by-step instruction in reading carefully and writing effectively. The chapters that follow open with a relevant and catchy cultural artifact (for example, a cartoon, an ad, an album cover) that leads into a reader-friendly, informative introduction; a selection of engaging essays on an issue of current interest in the field of pop culture; carefully constructed reading and discussion questions; and writing assignments after each reading and at the end of the chapter. This edition also contains sections on visual literacy and conducting research on popular culture, along with a selection of color and black-and-white images that students can analyze and enjoy.

Common Culture approaches the field of popular culture by dividing it into its constituent parts. The book contains chapters on advertising, television, music, technology, sports, and movies. Most of the chapters are divided into two parts: the first presents essays that address the topic generally, while the second offers essays that explore a specific aspect of the topic in depth. For example, in the chapter on advertising, the essays in the first group discuss theories and strategies of advertising, while later essays explore developments and possible future directions in the field of advertising.

We've purposely chosen readings that are accessible and thought-provoking, while avoiding those that are excessively theoretical or jargon-ridden. The forty-six readings in this book, twenty-four of which are new to the seventh edition, have the added advantage of serving as good models for students' own writing; they demonstrate a range of rhetorical approaches, such as exposition, analysis, and argumentation, and they offer varying levels of sophistication and difficulty in terms of content and style. Similarly, the suggested discussion and writing topics, including a "Thinking Rhetorically" prompt with each selection, move from relatively basic concerns to tasks that require a greater degree of critical skill. Because of this range, instructors using *Common Culture* can easily adapt the book to meet the specific needs of their students.

SUPPLEMENTARY MATERIAL FOR INSTRUCTORS AND STUDENTS

For more details on these supplements, available for college adoptions, please contact your Prentice Hall representative.

Instructor's Manual

A comprehensive Instructor's Manual is available in print and online and includes sample syllabi, teaching tips, and other information. Please contact your Pearson representative for access.

MyCompLab

MyCompLab empowers student writers and facilitates writing instruction by uniquely integrating a composing space and assessment tools with **market-leading instruction, multimedia tutorials, and exercises for writing, grammar and research.**

Students can use MyCompLab on their own, benefiting from self-paced diagnostics and a personal study plan that recommends the instruction and practice each student needs to improve her writing skills. The composing space and its integrated resources, tools, and services (such as online tutoring) are also available to each student as he writes.

MyCompLab is an eminently flexible application that instructors can use in ways that best complement their course and teaching style. They can recommend it to students for self-study, set up courses to track student progress, or leverage the power of administrative features to be more effective and save time. The assignment builder and commenting tools, **developed specifically for writing instruction, bring instructors closer to their student writers, make managing assignments and evaluating papers more efficient, and put powerful assessment within reach. Students receive feedback within the context of their own writing, which encourages critical thinking and revision and helps them to develop skills based on their individual needs.**

Learn more at www.mycomplab.com.

ACKNOWLEDGMENTS

As California instructors, and therefore participants in the growth-and-awareness movement, we'd like first to thank each other for never straying from the path of psychic goodwill and harmony, and then to thank the universe for raining beneficence and light upon this project. And while on the subject of beneficence and light, we'd like to thank the editorial teams who have helped shepherd all of the previous editions of *Common Culture*, with special thanks to our current editorial team—especially Brad Potthoff and Nancy Lee—for their expert assistance with this edition.

We also want to thank Muriel Zimmerman, Judith Kirscht, and Susan McLeod, former directors of the Writing Program at UCSB, for lending moral and intellectual support to the project in its various editions. Madeleine would like to thank Bob Samuels for his many delightful contributions to the cause of *Common Culture*. Michael continues to shower Jan Ingram with bonus megadollars for her unflagging support of this project at its inception. In addition, we extend our thanks to the following reviewers: Gareth Euridge, Tallahassee Community College; Judith Hauser, Des Moines Area Community College; Shepherd M. Jenks, Jr., Central New Mexico Community College; Melissa Miller-Waters, Houston Community College–Northwest; Lisa Owens, Malcolm X College; James W. Scannell, Middle Tennessee State University; and Mallory Young, Tarleton State University.

Michael Petracca

Madeleine Sorapure

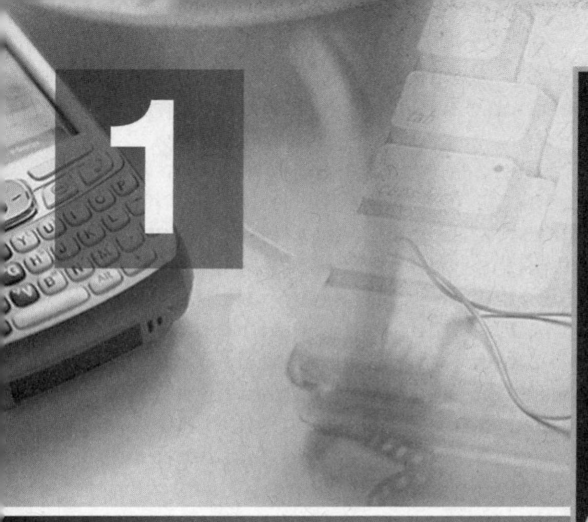

1

Reading and Writing About American Popular Culture

iPhone.
CSI.
Lucky Brand.
Caesar's Palace.
Tiger Woods.
MySpace.
The Daily Show.
The World Series of Poker.
The White Stripes.

If any of these names and phrases sound familiar—and it would be a great surprise if some didn't—it's because we spend our lives immersed in popular culture. There's no escaping it. Like hydrogen atoms and common cold viruses, pop culture is everywhere. You absorb it at home watching television, listening to the stereo, or reading a magazine or newspaper; passing billboards or listening to the radio on the street; chatting over coffee at work or having a burger with friends; going out to movies and dance clubs, health spas, fast-food restaurants, shopping malls, and sports arenas; even noticing the graffiti that glares out at you on building facades and highway overpasses.

In fact, unless you're isolated in a mountaintop cave, you can hardly avoid the influence of popular culture. Television, radio, newspapers, and magazines shape your ideas and behavior; like family, friends, and school, pop culture is part of your learning environment, supplying ready-made images, ideas, and patterns of behavior that you draw from, consciously or unconsciously, as you live your daily life. Exactly how you learn and just what you learn may not be all that certain, but it is undeniable that popular culture is one of your most powerful teachers.

One reason to study popular culture is that by paying closer attention to this daily bombardment of information you can think more critically about how it affects you and others. You may start by asking relatively simple questions—"Do I really need my breath to be 'Mentos fresh and full of life'?"—and work your way to far more significant ones—"How can we keep young women from starving themselves in their desire to conform to the images they see in advertisements?" Analyzing pop culture with a critical eye allows you to begin to free yourself from the manipulation of the media; it is an important step toward living an examined life.

WHAT IS POPULAR CULTURE?

What do we mean by popular culture? The term may at first seem contradictory. *Popular,* in its broadest sense, means "of the people," while we often associate *culture* with refinement and intellectual superiority, "the best which has been thought and said," as Matthew Arnold put it. We might ask how culture, traditionally reserved for the elite, the educated, and the upper class, can simultaneously belong to the common mass of humanity.

One way to resolve this seeming dilemma is to think of culture in an anthropological sense, as the distinct practices, artifacts, institutions, customs, and values of a particular social group. This is the way, for instance, that we distinguish the culture of the United States in the early twenty-first century from the culture of our great grandparents or from that of societies in other times and places.

We can also define popular culture by distinguishing it from its counterparts: *high culture* and *folk culture.*

High culture consists of the artifacts traditionally considered worthy of study by university academics and other educated people: classical music by composers such as Beethoven and Brahms; "fine" art from the impressionists and expressionists; literature and philosophy written by the likes of Shakespeare and Sartre.

At the other end of the spectrum, folk culture refers to artifacts created by a specific community or ethnic group, usually a relatively isolated nontechnological society, such as the pygmies of Africa's Ituri Forest or certain communities in our own Appalachian Mountains. While high culture is primarily preserved and studied in the academy, folk culture is generally transmitted through oral communication; both, however, place a high value on tradition, on artifacts produced in the past, and on the shared history of the community.

By contrast, popular culture encompasses the most immediate and contemporary elements in our lives—elements that are often subject to rapid changes in a highly technological world in which people are brought closer and closer by the ubiquitous mass media. Pop culture offers a common ground as the most visible and pervasive level of culture in a given society. If the Metropolitan Opera House represents high culture, then Madison Square Garden represents pop. If the carefully crafted knives used in Asian cooking rely on a folk tradition, then the Veg-O-Matic is their pop counterpart.

Several other terms help us establish a working definition of popular culture. *Mass culture* refers to information we receive through print and electronic media. While mass culture is often denigrated as juvenile or "low," it has to be treated as an important component of popular culture by virtue of the immense size of its audience. The terms *subculture* and *counterculture,* on the other hand, suggest a desire to resist the pressures, implied or explicit, to conform to a common culture. Subcultures are specific segments of society outside the core of dominant culture. Minority groups in the United States might be called subcultures, just as certain groups such as artists, homosexuals, lawyers, or teenagers can be thought of as having cultural markers distinct from the broader culture. A counterculture, on the other hand, is a group or movement that defines itself specifically as opposing or subverting the dominant culture. Hippies of the 1960s and punk rockers of the 1980s defined themselves as countercultural groups.

Although we may place ourselves in specific folk or high cultures, subcultures, or countercultures, we are still aware of and immersed in the broader popular culture simply by virtue of living in society. As Edward Jay Whetmore notes,[1] "Popular culture represents a common

[1]Whetmore, Edward Jay. *Mediamerica: Form, Content, and Consequence of Mass Communication.* Belmont, CA: Wadsworth, 1989.

denominator, something that cuts across most economic, social, and educational barriers." If the notion of culture reflects a certain degree of social stratification and differentiation, then popular culture represents the elements of everyday life, the artifacts and institutions shared by a society, and a body of common knowledge.

Another distinguishing characteristic of popular culture is its transitory nature. New images appear on our TV screens, replacing the popular images of years or seasons before; new phrases supersede former favorites in our popular lexicon; unknown entertainers become celebrities overnight, while others fade just as quickly from the spotlight. Beyoncé takes the place of Britney, who took the place of Madonna, who took the place of Gidget. *The Bachelor* replaces *A Change of Heart*, which replaced *Studs*, which replaced *Singled Out*, which took over from *The Dating Game;* the expression "Just do it!" was for the 1990s and 2000s what "Ring around the collar!" was for the 1970s.

Interestingly, if an icon of popular culture survives, it can often make the leap into high culture. For example, Wilkie Collins's nineteenth-century horror stories were read as avidly as Stephen King's novels are today. His works survive among today's elite audiences but are virtually unknown to most popular audiences. We might ask then, what of contemporary popular culture might survive beyond the immediate here and now and ultimately speak to future audiences at a higher, more specialized level?

What, then, is pop culture? Although it's notoriously difficult to define, some elements of a definition emerge from this discussion: pop culture is the shared knowledge and practices of a specific group at a specific time. Because of its commonality, pop culture both reflects and influences people's way of life; because it is linked to a specific time and place, pop culture is transitory, subject to change, and often an initiator of change.

WHY STUDY POPULAR CULTURE?

Though pop culture is increasingly accepted as a legitimate object of academic inquiry, educators still debate whether it should be studied. Some critics contend that it would be more valuable to study the products of high culture—Shakespeare rather than Spielberg, Eliot rather than Elvis. Their arguments often center on the issue of *quality,* as they assert that pop culture, transitory and often trendy, lacks the lasting value and strong artistic merit of high culture. Further, they argue that, because pop appeals to a mass audience rather than an educated elite, it is necessarily of low quality, no better than average. Although few critics of pop culture deny its pervasive influence, many argue that this influence should be considered negative, and they point to the violence and sexual explicitness of song lyrics, television programs, and movies, as well as to the triviality and downright foolishness of many popular trends. Pop culture debases us, these critics contend, turning us into passive recipients of low-quality goods, distracting us from higher pursuits.

It's important to note that very few proponents of pop culture—pop cultists, as Marshall Fishwick[2] calls them—take a wholesale, uncritical approach and approve all things popular. Many, for example, accept the argument that products with mass appeal are often qualitatively inferior to those intended for an educated, elite audience. However, pop cultists remind us that the gap between the two isn't always so wide; that the same basic activities of creation, refinement, and reception are involved in both popular and high culture; and that, as we've noted, the "popular" works of one era can become the "classics" of another.

Moreover, pop cultists argue for the validity of studying MTV, *The National Enquirer,* video games, and the Miss America Pageant because such mass phenomena serve as a kind of mirror in which we can discern much about ourselves. George Lipsitz,[3] for instance, suggests that "perhaps the most important facts about people have always been encoded within the ordinary and the commonplace." And as Ray Browne,[4] a noted scholar of pop culture, puts it, "Popular culture is a very important segment of our society. The contemporary scene is holding us up to ourselves to see; it can tell us who we are, what we are, and why."

We see reflected in pop culture certain standards and commonly held beliefs about beauty, success, love, or justice. We also see reflected there important social contradictions and conflicts—the tension between races, genders, or generations, for example. To find out about ourselves, then, we can turn to our own popular products and pastimes.

Another argument for studying popular culture focuses on the important influence it exerts on us. The media and other pop culture components are part of the fund of ideas and images that inform our daily activities, sometimes exerting a more compelling influence than family or friends, school or work. When we play sports, we mimic the gestures and movements of professional athletes; we learn to dance

[2]Browne, Ray B., and Marshall Fishwick. *Symbiosis: Popular Culture and Other Fields.* Bowling Green, OH: Bowling Green University Press, 1988.

[3]Lipsitz, George. *Time Passages: Collective Memory and American Popular Culture.* Minneapolis: University of Minnesota Press, 1990.

[4]Browne, Ray B., and Marshall Fishwick. *Symbiosis: Popular Culture and Other Fields.* Bowling Green, OH: Bowling Green University Press, 1988.

from the videos on MTV; we even name our children after popular television characters. More importantly, we discover role models; we learn lessons about villainy and heroism, love and relationships, acceptable and unacceptable behavior; we see interactions with people from other cultures. Even if popular culture is merely low-quality amusement or a means of escaping the demands of the "real" world, it delivers important messages that we may internalize and later act on—for better or for worse. We should examine and analyze pop culture, then, in order to assess—and sometimes resist—its influences.

The readings and assignments in *Common Culture* give you the chance to explore these issues and determine for yourself the role of popular culture in shaping society and in shaping you as an individual. The book includes chapters on important components of popular culture: advertising, television, music, technology, sports, and movies. You may already know quite a lot about some of these topics, and you may have relatively little interest in or exposure to others. Either way, as an engaged participant or a disinterested observer, you can bring your critical skills to bear on phenomena of the contemporary world. The readings and assignments encourage you to observe carefully, to question, and to construct and defend your own interpretations of some of the institutions and events, the beliefs and practices, the media and the messages in your everyday life.

Before beginning, we will look at methods of reading and writing that will help you participate fully and critically in reaching the goals of this book.

ACTIVE READING

We've discussed the importance of paying attention to the "common culture" that surrounds you in order to recognize its meanings and influences on your life. In this section, we present specific reading strategies that you can apply both to pop culture and to the essays in this book. Whether you're watching TV or reading an essay about TV, the habit of active, engaged interpretation will make the experience much more worthwhile. While you may have been encouraged to be an active reader of print material, the essays throughout this book also encourage you to be an active reader of the culture around you, including the images in which popular culture immerses you. We use the term *reading* here to apply both to texts and images, although in a later section we suggest specific strategies for reading and interpreting images.

There's a crucial difference between passively receiving and actively reading. Passively ingesting information requires very little effort or interest, and it gives very little in terms of reward or stimulation. Active reading demands more of your time, effort, and thought, but it is ultimately much more useful in helping you develop a better understanding of ideas.

Although reading a text or an image is generally a solitary activity, it helps to think of active reading as a discussion or dialogue with another person. You look and listen carefully; you compare what the person tells you to what you already know; you question statements that strike you as complicated, confusing, or incorrect; you identify ideas that are particularly interesting and important to you; you respond with ideas of your own. As a result of your active participation, you come away with new insights and a clearer sense of your own position. You may even be stimulated to seek out more information from other sources in order to clarify your thoughts.

When you read actively—whether printed texts or visual products of popular culture—you use very similar strategies, questioning and responding and speculating about what you're reading. You are no longer a disinterested bystander simply "listening in"; rather you are a participant who is energetically engaged with an author's ideas.

Strategies for Actively Reading a Text

Active reading involves a number of specific stages and strategies. In the **preparatory** stage, you develop a general sense of what the essay will be about. In the **reading** stage, you begin the actual dialogue with the author by paying close attention to what he or she has written, identifying key points, responding to certain ideas, and asking questions. Next comes the **rereading** stage, in which you go back through the essay to get a clear and firm understanding of what you've read. Finally, in the **reviewing** stage, you take time to draw conclusions, evaluate the author's position, and develop your own responses; often you'll want to go back to the essay and read certain sections even more carefully or to turn to other sources to help you formulate your response. In the actual practice of active reading, these four stages circle back on one another as well as spiral outward, prompting you to do further reading and exploration.

As you see, actively reading a text is quite different from passively receiving or consuming information. By reading actively, you'll be able to clarify and develop your own ideas and your responses to the influences operating on you in your everyday life. You can become a more proficient and accomplished writer, increasing the range and precision of your vocabulary, using different options for constructing sentences and paragraphs, creating different stylistic effects, and, in general, improving your "feel" for written language.

An Active Reading Casebook: Three Selections About Barbie

This section includes three reading selections—a poem and two essays about the Barbie doll—that demonstrate the strategies of active reading and suggest the kind of reading you'll be doing in later chapters. In the color insert at the center of the book, you will find two images of Barbie (p. CI-1) that you can interpret using strategies discussed in the "Reading Images" section.

We've chosen to begin with a look at Barbie because of her longevity, popularity, and cultural significance. Since her "birth" in 1959, Barbie has achieved celebrity status in U.S. culture and, indeed, worldwide. More than one billion Barbies have been sold in the last forty-five years, and Barbie products continue to bring in over a billion dollars every year for Mattel, Inc., her owner and America's biggest toy company. Placed head to toe, all of the Barbies and friends sold since 1959 would circle the earth three and a half times. Barbie lives in nearly every U.S. and Canadian household that includes children and in more than 140 other countries as well. In addition to her extensive accessories and her many friends (among them, her boyfriend, Ken, and her African American pal, Shani), Barbie has her own magazine and fan club and her own corps of press agents, advertising executives, and "personal secretaries" to answer her fan mail. Versace, Dolce & Gabbana, Vera Wang, Gucci, Yves St. Laurent, and Bill Blass have designed clothes especially for her; Tiffany created a sterling silver version of Barbie; and for one week in 1974, a segment of New York City's Times Square became "Barbie Boulevard" to mark her twenty-fifth birthday.

For three decades, girls (and curious little boys, as well) have been playing with and learning from Barbie, and thus she serves as an important force in conveying cultural values and attitudes. Barbie's influence is undeniable, but opinions vary as to the quality of that influence on the children who play with her and on the adults they become. Barbie's critics argue that her influence has been largely detrimental, that her improbable measurements (36-18-33), her even more improbable hair, and her inexhaustible supply of clothes and accessories help perpetuate an inappropriate model of women's interests and lives. However, defenders argue that her influence has been positive, at least in part. They point out that Barbie has recently had careers such as corporate executive, airline pilot, medical doctor, animal rights activist, and even presidential candidate, offering girls a chance to envision themselves being successful in the working world. Although Barbie's wedding dress is one of her most popular outfits, she's never officially married Ken (or G.I. Joe), and she remains a single, independent career woman, providing, some observers say, an alternative to the view that women's primary roles are as wives and mothers.

You can see that Barbie has served as a symbolic reference point for broader debates about femininity and masculinity, about beauty and success, about consumerism and lifestyle in our culture. Barbie is a good example of the way elements of popular culture can be interpreted in order to reveal some fundamental aspects of our society.

While reading this background information on Barbie, you may be thinking of your own experience as a child playing with Barbie or with other dolls and toys, and speculating about their formative influence on you. If so, you've begun to prepare for reading, by orienting yourself to the topic, by exploring your own ideas and experiences, and by thinking about the issues at hand.

Preparing to Read Let's turn now to our first selection, a poem about Barbie written by Hilary Tham. All the readings in this book are accompanied by headnotes, which briefly explain what the reading is about and give some background information on the author. In this sense, headnotes are like the front and back covers of many books, providing an overview of what will follow and serving as the place to begin thinking about the topic. Here is the headnote for the poem "Barbie's Shoes":

> Our first selection is a poem by Hilary Tham. Tham was born in Kelang, Malaysia, and currently lives in Virginia with her husband and three daughters. She teaches creative writing in high schools and has published several books of poetry, including *No Gods Today, Paper Boats, Bad Names for Women,* and *Tigerbone Wine.*

You can get an idea of what to expect from the poem both by reading the headnote and by recalling what you know about poetry in general. The headnote tells you that Hilary Tham is originally from Malaysia and now lives in the United States. You might conclude from this information that Tham brings a dual perspective to the Barbie doll and other features of U.S. pop culture. The headnote also points out that Tham has three daughters and teaches high school students. Before you read the poem, then, you might speculate on how being a mother and a teacher would influence Tham's thoughts about the Barbie doll.

Reading and Annotating In the reading stage, one of the most useful strategies you can use is *annotating* the text. When you annotate, you use a pencil or pen to mark key words and phrases in the text and to write questions and responses in the margins. You underline words that you need to look up in a dictionary and phrases that you find particularly interesting, forceful, important, questionable, or confusing. You also record your reactions, thoughts, questions, and ideas in the margins. By annotating in this way, you keep track of what the author is saying and of what you're thinking as you read.

Here are one student's annotations of Tham's poem . . . but keep in mind that your annotations would probably identify different elements as particularly important.

Barbie's Shoes
HILARY THAM

I'm down in the basement
sorting Barbie's shoes.
    sequin pumps, satin courts,
    western boots, Reebok sneakers,
    glass slippers, ice-skates, thongs.
All will fit the dainty, forever arched
feet of any one Barbie: Sweet Spring
    Glitter-Eyed, Peaches and Cream,
    a Brazilian, Russian, Swiss, Hong Kong
    Hispanic or Mexican, Nigerian
    or Black Barbie. All are cast
in the same mold, same rubbery,
impossible embodiment of male fantasy
with carefully measured
    doses of melanin to make
    a Caucasian Barbie,
        Polynesian Barbie
        African-American Barbie.
Everyone knows that she is the same
Barbie and worthy of the American Dream
House, the Corvette, opera gloves, a
hundred pairs of shoes to step into. If only
the differently colored men and women we know
could be like Barbie, always smiling, eyes
wide with admiration, even when we yank
off an arm with a hard-to-take-off dress.
Barbie's shoes, so easily lost, mismatched,
useless; they end up, like our prejudices,
in the basement, forgotten as spiders
sticking webs in our darkest corners,
we are amazed we have them still.

Why the basement?

Different shoes show Barbie's many activities

Barbies are different But also the same

Barbie = American Dream

Simile: Barbie's shoes are like our prejudices— forgotten, but still there, in the basement, like spider webs.

Rereading After you read and annotate the poem, your task is to fully understand it and formulate your own response to it. Many students close the book after just the first reading without realizing that the next two stages, rereading and reviewing, are crucial to discovering the significance of what they have read.

In the rereading stage, you go back through the poem and the annotations in order to develop a good understanding of the writer's ideas. Then you begin to articulate those ideas—in your own words. Here's an example drawn from the earlier annotation of "Barbie Shoes."

> I'm really drawn to the simile in the last few lines: that Barbie's shoes are "like our prejudices, / in the basement, forgotten as spiders / sticking webs in our darkest corners, / we are amazed we have them still." Tham is saying that Barbie's shoes are more than just tiny plastic footwear. They represent prejudices which we think we've thrown away but in fact still have in our "basements" (our subconscious thoughts?). And by comparing these prejudices to spiders' webs "in our darkest corners," perhaps Tham is suggesting that our prejudices still "catch" things; they still operate in our lives even if we've forgotten them or don't see them.

With ideas like these as a starting point, you can go back through the entire poem and begin to formulate a response to other key ideas and phrases: the list of Barbie's shoes; the list of different nationalities and ethnicities of Barbie dolls; the idea that all Barbies are in some way the same; the suggestion that Barbie represents the American Dream. Rereading like this will surely provoke further questions about the poem. For instance, why does Tham make a point of mentioning the many different types of Barbies? In what ways are these differences only superficial and unrealistic? And what does Tham mean when she writes, "If only / the differently colored men and women we know / could be like Barbie, always smiling, even when we yank / off an arm. . . ."? You know that Tham is being ironic, since we don't generally yank arms off other people, but what point is she making in this comparison, and how does it relate to her ideas about prejudice?

These kinds of questions lead you to reread the poem, clarifying your understanding and finding further meanings in it. After each essay in this book there are similar sorts of reading questions that will help you explore the ideas you've read about. We also encourage you to develop your own questions about what you read to focus your exploration on those points that you find most interesting, important, or controversial.

Reviewing After rereading, questioning, and exploring the writer's ideas in detail, you should take time to summarize what you've learned. Here is a student's summary of her analysis of "Barbie's Shoes."

1. Tham suggests that Barbie's shoes are like prejudices (forgotten, seemingly lost, down in the basement, "useless" and "mismatched"); why can't we just throw them out? Why are they still in the basement?

2. Why does Barbie have so many shoes?! Perhaps Tham is implying that we have an equal number of seemingly insignificant prejudices, one for every occasion, even.
3. Tham points out that there are many different kinds of Barbie dolls (Caucasian, Polynesian, African American) but all are "worthy of the American Dream House." In this sense, Barbies are all the same. So does Barbie influence us to overlook the real differences in women's lives? We're not dolls, after all, and although we're all worthy of success and accomplishment, we don't all get the same chances.
4. Tham describes Barbie as the "impossible embodiment of male fantasy." How is this observation related to the rest of the poem? Could she be saying that this fantasy is related to prejudice?

Such questions and tentative answers can help you begin to formulate your own interpretation of and complete response to what you've read.

Reading Pop Cultural Criticism In the previous discussion, we used Hilary Tham's poem as our example because poetry can pack so much meaning into the space of relatively few words. In the chapters that follow, you won't be reading poems, but rather articles, essays, and chapters of books, most of which fall into one of two categories. The first we might call *pop cultural criticism;* this includes the kind of pieces written for general audiences of popular magazines and mass market books. Typically these reflect a particular social perspective—whether traditionalist or cutting edge, conservative or liberal, pro or anticapitalist—and are often written in response to a particular issue or phenomenon reported in the media.

The following piece by John Leo is an example of pop cultural criticism. As you read, practice the strategies that we've discussed. Begin by considering the headnote and what it suggests about Leo's perspective and purpose, then underline important passages in the essay and jot down your thoughts, responses, and questions in the margins.

The Indignation of Barbie
JOHN LEO

John Leo's "The Indignation of Barbie" was first published in U.S. News & World Report in 1992. Leo, a conservative journalist and social commentator, writes about the controversy surrounding the talking Barbie doll produced by Mattel in the early 1990s. Among Talking Barbie's repertoire of phrases was "Math class is tough," viewed by some feminists and professional women as discouraging girls from pursuing the subject. Here, Leo imagines a dialogue with Barbie, in which the talking doll defends herself against charges that she's a "prefeminist bimbo."

Barbie will probably survive, but the truth is, she's in a lot of trouble. It seems that the new Teen Talk Barbie, the first talking Barbie in 20 years, has shocked many feminists with a loose-lipped comment about girls and math. Each $25 doll speaks four of 270 programmed one-liners. In one of those messages, Barbie says, "Math class is tough." This was a big error. She should have said, "Math is particularly easy if you're a girl, despite the heavy shackles of proven test bias and male patriarchal oppression." 1

Because of this lapse from correctness, the head of the American Association of University Women is severely peeved with Barbie, and you can no longer invite both of them to the same party. Other feminists and math teachers have weighed in with their own dudgeon. 2

Since this is Barbie's darkest hour, I placed a phone call out to Mattel, Inc. in California to see how the famous long-haired, long-legged forerunner of Ivana Trump was holding up. To my astonishment, they put me right through to Barbie herself. 3

"Barbie, it's me," I said. As the father of three girls, I have shopped for 35 to 40 Barbies over the years, including doctor Barbie, ballerina Barbie, television news reporter Barbie, African-American Barbie, animal-rights Barbie, and Barbie's shower, which takes two days to construct and makes the average father feel like a bumbling voyeur. So I figured that Barbie would know me. 4

Barbie spoke: "Do you want to go for a pizza? Let's go to the mall. Do you have a crush on anyone? Teaching kids is great. Computers make homework fun!" 5

In a flash I realized that Barbie was stonewalling. These were not spontaneous comments at all. They were just the prerecorded messages that she was forced to say, probably under pressure from those heartless, controlling patriarchs at Mattel. 6

Subtle rebuttal. At the same time, I began to appreciate Barbie's characteristic subtlety; by reminding me that she was recommending the educational use of computers to young girls, she was, in effect, stoutly rebutting the charge of antifeminist backlash among talking toys. I had to admit it was pretty effective. 7

So I pleaded with her to speak honestly and clear her name. I heard a telltale rustle of satin, and then she spoke. "You're the one who took three days to put my shower together. That was ugly." 8

"Two days," I said, gently correcting the world-famous plastic figurine. I asked her about the harsh words of Sharon Schuster, the awfully upset head of the AAUW. Schuster had said, "The message is a negative one for girls, telling them they can't do well in math, and that perpetuates a stereotype." 9

"That's a crock," Barbie replied. "Just because a course is tough or challenging doesn't mean my girls can't do it. Weren't your daughters a 10 little apprehensive about math?" I admitted that they were. "Well, how did they do?" "Top of the class," I replied brightly.

"Then tell Sharon Schuster to stop arguing with dolls and go get a life." Her remark was an amazement. This was not roller-skating Barbie or perfume-wearing Barbie. It was the real thing: in-your-face tough-talking Barbie. 11

"The first time I open my mouth after 20 years, and what happens? I get squelched by a bunch of women." At this point, I mentioned that my friend M. G. Lord, the syndicated columnist who is doing a book on Barbie, is firmly on her side. M. G. told me: "Math class *is* tough, but it doesn't mean you have to drop out and go to cosmetology school. These people are projecting a lot of fears onto Barbie." 12

Barbie was grateful. "Thank M. G. and tell her I look forward to her biography of me. And tell her that if she ever fails in life, she can always become head of the AAUW." That remark may have been a trifle sharp, I said. "Well," said Barbie, "I'm just tired of taking all this guff from women's groups. They're scapegoating the wrong girl. I'll match feminist credentials with any of them. I worked my way up from candy striper to doctor. I was a stewardess in the '60s, and now I'm a pilot. Ken is one of my flight attendants. You can buy me as Olympic athlete, astronaut and executive." 13

Barbie was on a roll now. I was writing furiously to keep up. "This summer they put out a presidential candidate Barbie, and two days later, Ross Perot withdrew. Figure it out," she said. "As far back as 1984, my ad slogan was, 'We girls can do anything.' I've done more than any other doll to turn girls into achievers, and still they treat me as a prefeminist bimbo. What's wrong with the women's movement?" 14

I knew enough not to touch that one. Besides, it's a very short column. But I was struck by her comment that Ken was now employed as a flight attendant. "Didn't he used to be a corporate executive?" I asked. "We're not voting for Bush again," she replied bitterly. 15

Then I heard a muffled side comment: "Ken! Be careful with those dishes." I said I felt bad about Ken's comedown, but Barbie brought me back to reality: "Remember," she said, "he's only an accessory." This was tough to take, but the issue was settled. Barbie is indeed a feminist. Over to you, Sharon Schuster. 16

As you first read Leo's essay, his technique of personifying the doll as an "in-your-face tough-talking Barbie" is most striking and allows him to humorously present a talking Barbie who seemingly speaks up for herself. In rereading you can see even more clearly Leo's purpose: he uses Barbie's "voice" to offer his own defense of her influence and significance. Moreover, ultimately he is making fun of feminists' "projecting a lot of fears onto Barbie," since she herself derisively asks, "What's wrong with the women's movement?" When Leo has Barbie "say" that she's "done more than any other doll to turn girls into achievers," it's clear that Leo himself agrees and feels that Barbie critics should lighten up.

As a reviewing activity, you might write down your thoughts about the following questions and discuss them with your group or class:

1. Do you agree that Barbie has "done more than any other doll to turn girls into achievers" (paragraph 14)?
2. Do you think Leo's use of humor contributes to the effect of his essay?
3. According to Leo, what is the relationship between Barbie and Ken? Do you agree with Leo's ideas?
4. If you could give speech to Barbie, what would you have her say?

Reading Academic Analysis In addition to pop cultural criticism, this book provides essays on pop cultural phenomena written not for a general audience, but by academics primarily for other academics. Generally published in academic journals or in collections from scholarly presses, these essays often present the results of extensive research or provide a very close, detailed, and original analysis of the subject at hand. You might find them more difficult than the pieces of pop cultural criticism, but in many ways they are closer to the kind of writing that will be expected of you in many of your college courses.

Note that, while "objective" in tone, academic cultural analysis generally reflects a particular interpretive framework, which may be ideological (e.g., feminist or Marxist) or methodological (e.g., semiotic, structuralist, or quantitative) or some combination of the two. These frameworks will be discussed in more detail in the headnotes to individual readings.

The following excerpt from an essay by Marilyn Ferris Motz is an example of academic cultural analysis, written from a perspective that might be called "feminist–historical." As you read the headnote and the essay itself, apply the strategies we've discussed: familiarize yourself with Motz's view and with the topic as it's presented in the headnote, then read the essay carefully and make your own annotations in the text and in the margins.

"Seen Through Rose-Tinted Glasses:" The Barbie Doll in American Society

Marilyn Ferris Motz

Originally published in a longer form in The Popular Culture Reader, *Marilyn Motz's "'Seen Through Rose-Tinted Glasses': The Barbie Doll in American Society," takes its title from a 1983 Barbie sticker album marketed by Mattel: "If you stay close to your friend Barbie, life will always be seen through rose-tinted glasses." In her essay, however, Motz suggests that Barbie has other messages for us and that the doll's influence is more problematic, especially for children. Pointing out that several generations of girls have learned cultural values and norms from playing with Barbie, Motz focuses on the fact that, although Barbie has changed through the years to keep up with changes in the "baby boom" generation, the doll and her accessories still convey an outdated image of women's circumstances and interests.*

A 1983 Barbie sticker album copyrighted by Mattel describes Barbie:

As beautiful as any model, she is also an excellent sportswoman. In fact, Barbie is seen as a typical young lady of the twentieth century, who knows how to appreciate beautiful things and, at the same time, live life to the fullest. To most girls, she appears as the ideal elder sister who manages to do all those wonderful things that they can only dream of. With her fashionable wardrobe and constant journeys to exciting places all over the world, the adventures of Barbie offer a glimpse of what they might achieve one day. If Barbie has a message at all for us, it is to ignore the gloomy outlook of others and concentrate on all those carefree days of youth. Whatever lies in store will come sooner or later. If you stay close to your friend Barbie, life will always be seen through rose-tinted glasses. 1

Most owners of Barbie dolls are girls between the ages of three and eleven years of age. A Mattel survey shows that by the late 1960s, the median age for Barbie doll play had dropped from age ten to age six (Rakstis 30). Younger children find it difficult to manipulate the relatively small dolls, although Mattel created "My First Barbie," that ostensibly was easier for young children to handle and dress. Although some boys admit to playing with Ken, or even Barbie, Barbie doll play seems to be confined largely to girls. 2

Like all small figures and models, Barbie, at 11 1/2 inches high, has the appeal of the miniature. Most people are fascinated with objects recreated on a smaller scale, whether they are model airplanes, electric trains, dollhouse furnishings, or doll clothes. Miniatures give us a sense of control over our environment, a factor that is particularly important for children, to whom the real world is several sizes too large. In playing with a Barbie doll, a girl can control the action, can be omnipotent in a miniature world of her own creation. 3

When a girl plays with a baby doll, she becomes in her fantasy the doll's mother. She talks directly to the doll, entering into the play as an actor in her own right. When playing with a Barbie doll, on the other hand, the girl usually "becomes" Barbie. She manipulates Barbie, Ken and the other dolls, speaking for them and moving them around a miniature environment in which she herself cannot participate. Through the Barbie doll, then, a preadolescent can engage in role-playing activities. She can imitate adult female behavior, dress and speech and can participate vicariously in dating and other social activities, thus allaying 4 some of her anxieties by practicing the way she will act in various situations. In consultation with the friends with whom she plays, a girl can establish the limits of acceptable behavior for a young woman and explore the possibilities and consequences of exceeding those limits.

The girl playing with a Barbie doll can envision herself with a mature female body. "Growing-Up Skipper," first produced in 1975, grew taller and developed small breasts when her arms were rotated, focusing attention on the bodily changes associated with puberty. Of course, until the end of puberty, girls do not know the ultimate size and shape their bodies will assume, factors they realize will affect the way others will view and treat them. Perhaps Barbie dolls assuage girls' curiosity over the appearance of the adult female body, of which many have only limited knowledge, and allay anxiety over their own impending bodily development. 5

Through Barbie's interaction with Ken, girls also can explore their anxieties about future relationships with men. Even the least attractive and least popular girl can achieve, by "becoming" Barbie, instant popularity in a fantasy world. No matter how clumsy or impoverished she is in real life, she can ride a horse or lounge by the side of the pool in a world undisturbed by the presence of parents or other authority figures. The creator of the Barbie doll, Ruth Handler, claims that "these dolls become an extension of the girls. Through the doll each child dreams of what she would like to be" (Zinsser, "Barbie" 73). If Barbie does enable a girl to dream "of what she would like to be," then what dreams and goals does the doll encourage? With this question, some of the negative aspects of the Barbie doll emerge. 6

The clothes and other objects in Barbie's world lead the girl playing with Barbie to stress Barbie's leisure activities and emphasize the importance of physical appearance. The shape of the doll, its clothes and the focus on dating activities present sexual attractiveness as a key to popularity and therefore to happiness. Finally, Barbie is a consumer. She demands product after product, and the packaging and advertising imply that Barbie, as well as her owner, can be made happy if only she wears the right clothes and owns the right products. Barbie conveys the message that, as the saying goes, a woman can never be too rich or too thin. The Barbie doll did not create these attitudes. Nor will the doll insidiously instill these values in girls whose total upbringing emphasizes other factors. An individual girl can, of course, create with her own doll any sort of behavior and activities she chooses. Still, the products available for the doll tend to direct play along certain lines. Barbie represents an image, and a rather unflattering one, of American women. It is the extent to which this image fits our existing cultural expectations that explains the popularity of the Barbie doll. . . . 7

As an icon, Barbie not only reflects traditional, outdated roles for women; she and Ken also represent, in exaggerated form, characteristics of American society as a whole. Through playing with these dolls, children learn to act out in miniature the way they see adults behave in real life and in the media. The dolls themselves and the accessories provided for them direct this play, teaching children to consume and conform, to seek fun and popularity above all else. 8

Thorstein Veblen wrote in 1899 that America had become a nation of "conspicuous consumers." We buy objects, he wrote, not because we need them but because we want others to know we can afford them. We want our consumption to be conspicuous or obvious to others. The more useless the object, the more it reflects the excess wealth the owner can afford to waste. In the days before designer labels, Veblen wrote that changing fashions represent an opportunity for the affluent to show that they can afford to waste money by disposing of usable clothing and replacing it with new, faddish styles that will in turn be discarded after a few years or even months of wear (Veblen 60–131). 9

Sociologist David Riesman wrote in 1950 that Americans have become consumers whose social status is determined not only by what they can afford to buy but also by the degree to which their taste in objects of consumption conforms to that of their peers. Taste, in other words, becomes a matter of assessing the popularity of an item with others rather than judging on the basis of one's personal preference. Children, according to Riesman, undergo a process of "taste socialization," of learning to determine "with skill and sensitivity the probable tastes of the others" and then to adopt these tastes as their own. Riesman writes that "today the future occupation of all moppets is to be skilled consumers" (94, 96, 101). This skill lies not in selecting durable or useful products but in selecting popular, socially acceptable products that indicate the owner's conformity to standards of taste and knowledge of current fashion. 10

The Barbie doll teaches a child to conform to fashion in her consumption. She learns that each activity requires appropriate attire and that outfits that may at first glance appear to be interchangeable are slightly different from one another. In the real world, what seems to be a vast array of merchandise actually is a large collection of similar products. The consumer must make marginal distinctions between nearly identical products, many of which have different status values. The child playing with a Barbie doll learns to detect these nuances. Barbie's clothes, for instance, come in three lines: a budget line, a medium-priced line, and a designer line. Consumption itself becomes an activity to be practiced. From 1959 to 1964, Mattel produced a "Suburban Shopper" outfit. In 1976 the "Fashion Plaza" appeared on the market. This store consisted of four departments connected by a moving escalator. As mass-produced clothing made fashion accessible to all classes of Americans, the Barbie doll was one of the means by which girls learned to make the subtle fashion distinctions that would guarantee the proper personal appearances. 11

Barbie must also keep pace with all the newest fashion and leisure trends. Barbie's pony tail of 1959 gave way to a Jackie Kennedy style "Bubble-cut" in the early 1960s and to long straight hair in the 1970s. "Ken-A-Go-Go" of 1960s had a Beatle wig, guitar and microphone, while the "Now Look Ken" of the 1970s had shoulder-length hair and wore a leisure suit (Leavy 102). In the early 1970s, Ken grew a detachable beard. In 1971 Mattel provided Barbie and Ken with a motorized stage 12 on which to dance in their fringed clothes, while Barbie's athletic activities, limited to skiing, skating, fishing, skydiving and tennis in the 1960s, expanded to include backpacking, jogging, bicycling, gymnastics and sailing in the 1970s. On the shelves in the early 1980s were Western outfits, designer jeans, and Rocker Barbie dressed in neon colors and playing an electric guitar. In 1991 Rollerblade Barbie was introduced.

Barbie clearly is, and always has been, a conspicuous consumer. 13 Aside from her lavish wardrobe, Barbie has several houses complete with furnishings, a Ferrari and a '57 Chevy. She has at various times owned a yacht and several other boats, as well as a painted van called the "Beach Bus." Through Barbie, families who cannot afford such luxury items in real life can compete in miniature. In her early years, Barbie owned a genuine mink coat. In the ultimate display of uselessness, Barbie's dog once owned a corduroy velvet jacket, net tutu, hat, sunglasses and earmuffs. Barbie's creators deny that Barbie's life is devoted to consumption. "These things shouldn't be thought of as possessions," according to Ruth Handler. "They are props that enable a child to get into play situations" (Zinsser 73). Whether possessions or props, however, the objects furnished with the Barbie doll help create play situations, and those situations focus on consumption and leisure.

A perusal of the shelves of Barbie paraphernalia in the Midwest 14 Toys "R" Us store reveals not a single item of clothing suitable for an executive office. Mattel did produce a doctor's outfit (1973) and astronaut suit (1965 and 1986) for Barbie, but the clothes failed to sell. According to Mattel's marketing manager, "We only kept the doctor's uniform in the line as long as we did because public relations begged us to give them something they could point to as progress" in avoiding stereotyped roles for women (Leavy 102). In the 1960s, Mattel produced "all the elegant accessories" for the patio including a telephone, television, radio, fashion magazines and a photograph of Barbie and Ken (Zinsser 72). The "Busy Barbie," created in 1972, had hands that could grasp objects and came equipped with a telephone, television, record player, "soda set" with two glasses and a travel case. Apparently Barbie kept busy only with leisure activities; she seems unable to grasp a book or a pen. When Barbie went to college in the 1970s, her "campus" consisted only of a dormitory room, soda shop (with phone booth), football stadium and drive-in movie (Zinsser 72). In the 1980s, Barbie traveled in her camper, rode her horse, played with her dog and cat, swam in her pool and lounged in her bubble bath (both with real water).

The Barbie doll of the 1980s presents a curiously mixed message. 15 The astronaut Barbie wore a pink space suit with puffed sleeves. The executive Barbie wore a hot pink suit and a broad-brimmed straw hat, and she carried a pink briefcase in which to keep her gold credit card. Lest girls think Barbie is all work and no play, the jacket could be removed, the pink and white spectator pumps replaced with high-heeled sandals, and the skirt reversed to form a spangled and frilly evening dress. Barbie may try her hand at high-status occupations, but her appearance does not suggest competence and professionalism. In a story in *Barbie* magazine (Summer 1985) Barbie is a journalist reporting on lost treasure in the Yucatan. She spends her time "catching some rays" and listening to music, however, while her dog discovers the lost treasure. Barbie is appropriately rewarded with a guest spot on a television talk show! Although Barbie is shown in a professional occupation and even has her own computer, her success is attributed to good luck rather than her own (nonexistent) efforts. She reaps the rewards of success without having had to work for it; indeed, it is her passivity and pleasure-seeking (could we even say laziness) that allows her dog to discover the gold. Even at work, Barbie leads a life of leisure.

Veblen wrote that America, unlike Europe, lacked a hereditary aristocracy of families that were able to live on the interest produced by inherited wealth. In America, Veblen wrote, even the wealthiest men were self-made capitalists who earned their own livings. Since these men were too busy to enjoy leisure and spend money themselves, they delegated these tasks to their wives and daughters. By supporting a wife and daughters who earned no money but spent lavishly, a man could prove his financial success to his neighbors. Therefore, according to Veblen, affluent women were forced into the role of consumers, establishing the social status of the family by the clothes and other items they bought and the leisure activities in which they engaged (Veblen 44–131). 16

Fashions of the time, such as long skirts, immobilized women, making it difficult for them to perform physical labor, while ideals of beauty that included soft pale hands and faces precluded manual work or outdoor activities for upper-class women. To confer status, Veblen writes, clothing "should not only be expensive, but it should also make plain to all observers that the wearer is not engaged in any kind of productive employment." According to Veblen, "the dress of women goes even farther than that of men in the way of demonstrating the wearer's abstinence from productive labor." The high heel, he notes, "makes any, even the simplest and most necessary manual work extremely difficult," and thus is a constant reminder that the woman is "the economic dependent of the man—that, perhaps in a highly idealized sense, she still is the man's chattel" (Veblen 120–21, 129). . . . 17

Despite changes in the lives and expectations of real women, Barbie remains essentially the woman described by Veblen in the 1890s, excluded from the world of work with its attendant sense of achievement, forced to live a life based on leisure activities, personal appearance, the accumulation of possessions and the search for popularity. While large numbers of women reject this role, Barbie embraces it. The Barbie doll serves as an icon that symbolically conveys to children and adults the measures of success in modern America: wealth, beauty, popularity and leisure. 18

Suggestions for Further Reading

Leavy, Jane. "Is There a Barbie Doll in Your Past?" *Ms.* Sept. 1979.

Rakstis, Ted. "Debate in the Doll House." *Today's Health* Dec. 1970.

Riesman, David, Nathan Glazer, and Reual Denney. *The Lonely Crowd: A Study of the Changing American Character.* Garden City, NY: Doubleday Anchor, 1950.

Veblen, Thorstein. *The Theory of the Leisure Class.* 1899. New York: Mentor, 1953.

Zinsser, William K. "Barbie Is a Million Dollar Doll." *Saturday Evening Post* 12 Dec. 1964: 72–73.

As you can see from Motz's essay, academic cultural analysis can present you with much information and many ideas to digest. A useful rereading activity is to go through the text and highlight its main points by writing a one- or two-page summary of it. Then in the reviewing stage, you can use your summary to draw your own conclusions and formulate your own responses to the writer's ideas. To do so with Motz's essay, you might use the following questions as starting points:

1. In what ways do you think fashion dolls like Barbie provide a different play experience for children than "baby dolls"? Do you think one type of doll is "healthier" or more appropriate than the other?
2. To what extent do you think Thorstein Veblen's comments on status and consumerism in American society (paragraph 9) still apply today? Do you agree with Motz that Barbie contributes to the promotion of "conspicuous consumption"?
3. If Motz is right that Barbie represents an outdated and potentially detrimental image of women's lives, why do you think the doll continues to sell more and more successfully every year?
4. To what extent do you think that the values represented by Barbie—"wealth, beauty, popularity and leisure" (18)—are still central to success in America?

Ultimately, your goal as a reader in this course will most likely be to prepare yourself to complete specific writing assignments. In the "Writing Process" section, we will present the process one writing student went through in composing an essay requested in the following assignment:

> What do you see as the significance of the Barbie doll in contemporary American culture? How are your ideas related to those of Tham, Leo, and Motz in the selections presented here?

READING IMAGES

Before turning to this assignment, however, we will address strategies you can use to read images effectively. In many ways, the four-step process we just described for reading texts—Preparing to Read, Reading and Annotating, Rereading, and Reviewing—applies to images as well. There are some differences, though, as we discuss below.

Preparing to Read

With both text and image, it is wise to begin by getting an idea of what to expect, a first impression. Just as you read the headnote in order to get an introduction to an essay or poem, so too can you read the information that surrounds the image. Next to a painting in a museum, for instance, you'll often find information about the work: the name of the artist, the dates he or she lived, the date the work was completed, the media used in the work (oils, watercolor, paper, etc.), the dimensions of the work.

But outside of a museum, images are often presented to you without this kind of helpful, orienting information. In these instances, which are of course far more common in the world of popular culture, an important strategy to prepare yourself before diving in to interpret the image is to look at the context in which the image occurs. Is it an advertisement you're being asked to analyze? If so, what magazine is the ad in? What is the typical audience of this magazine? On what page of the magazine is the ad found (in the expensive beginning pages or in the more modestly priced pages toward the end of the magazine)? Is it a Web site you're interpreting? If so, who is the author of the site? Who is its audience? What is the purpose of the site? When was the site last updated?

These questions of context can orient you in the same way that headnotes can: they give you a general sense of what to expect. Moreover, knowing the context, and especially the audience and purpose of an image, can guide your subsequent interpretation by helping you determine why certain features are present or absent in the image.

Finally in the "Preparing to Read" stage, you should think about your initial impressions of the image you're analyzing. What key features do you notice immediately? What mood or feeling does the image evoke in you? What immediate response do you have to the image?

Let's turn to a specific example and begin with the "Preparing to Read" process. Take a look at the image of Barbie at the top of page CI-1. As you can see from the information included below the image, the photographer is Aaron Goodman and the caption for the image is "Barbie and Ken Branding." This information gets you started on your analysis of the image, particularly with the idea of "branding" mentioned in the caption. The fact that the image is created by a photographer indicates, in this instance, that it is a composite of many photographs that generate a not-quite realistic image of Barbie and Ken in New York City's Times Square.

As you think about determining the audience and purpose of this image, you might consider the fact that it doesn't seem to be officially sponsored or endorsed by Mattel, Inc., Barbie's creator. We can assume that the primary purpose of the information and images generated by

Mattel would be to promote its products. If you take a look at Barbie's official Web site (*www.barbie.com*), for example, you can assume that everything included there has the ultimate function of selling Barbie dolls to little girls and their parents. Aaron Goodman's image, by contrast, doesn't have this promotional purpose; rather, it is more likely to be driven by aesthetic goals or intended to deliver a critical interpretation of Barbie.

What's your first impression of this image? What strikes you as most immediately noticeable about it? We can put it in one word: brands! We count at least seventeen identifiable brand names and/or logos competing for space in this image. Let's move on now to the next step, in which you take a closer look at the details of the image and begin interpreting it.

Reading and Annotating

Unless you own the image that you're interpreting, it would probably be a good idea to refrain from annotating (that is, writing on it). You can get into some trouble doing this, particularly in places like the Metropolitan Museum of Art. Instead, annotating becomes a process of note-taking, and reading becomes a process of looking. Put simply, look at the image and take notes.

But that's putting it too simply. What should you look at in an image, and what sort of notes should you take?

One of the major differences between text and image is that a text generally presents information in a sequential and linear manner; there's usually no question about where you should begin reading and, having read one word, it's not usually difficult to decide what word you should read next. With images (and here we're speaking only of still images and not videos, commercials, or other kinds of sequenced images), everything is presented simultaneously so that you can begin and end where you choose and your eyes can follow different paths through the image. Having said that, though, it's also the case that images often try to draw your attention to a certain place, a focus point. This focus point is often relevant in understanding the key messages of the image.

What is the focus point of the Barbie image? For us, it's Barbie herself. It seems fairly obvious that Barbie would be the key element in an image with the caption "Barbie and Ken Branding," but what details in the image can we find to support this claim? Here's where the qualities of *arrangement* and *dimension* come into play. The arrangement (or placement) of elements in the image clearly draws our attention to Barbie. Although the center is the key focus point in many images, in this case Barbie's placement closest to the viewer makes us notice her first. Dimension (or proportion) also draws our attention to Barbie because she is larger than any other object in the image. In fact, she's unnaturally large, as is Ken; it's difficult to imagine them cramming themselves into the taxicab that's right alongside them. So here again, evidence in the image supports a (fairly obvious) claim that the focus of the image is Barbie herself.

It's often helpful to imagine alternative arrangements and dimensions for images that you're analyzing in order to register the impact of the image as it is. For instance, what if the placement of Ken and Barbie were switched in this image? That would place Barbie in the center, but it would also make her significantly smaller than Ken, and perhaps would even suggest that she's tagging along after him or is subordinate to him. Envisioning this alternative, we can see all the more clearly that placement gives Barbie primary importance. In terms of dimension, what if Barbie and Ken were realistically sized? The taxi and car would become more important elements of the image, and the "Times Square" background might threaten to overwhelm them. As it is, Barbie and Ken are disproportionately large in order to draw attention to their significance in the image.

Continuing to look at the image and to take notes, we might next turn to the remarkable number of brand names and logos and try to determine why they're there and how they contribute to the meaning of the image. While the real Times Square certainly has many billboards and advertisements, a photograph of it wouldn't show so many legible, identifiable, and well-placed brand names. Clearly, Aaron Goodman created this composite photograph with brands and branding in mind. But what is the relation between Barbie and all of the other brands in the image? The *perspective* of the image suggests that Barbie and Ken are in the forefront of a world composed almost entirely of consumer goods. Perspective is often a helpful category to use in analyzing images. The perspective essentially situates the viewer, defining the relation of the viewer to the image: are you positioned above or below the objects in the image? Are you on the outside looking in (implying perhaps that you're excluded or don't belong)? In this case, the perspective asks you to see Barbie and Ken first, and then to see brand names and consumerism all around them. Carrying her Coke, her Gap bag, and her American Express Card, Barbie is clearly in her element.

Rereading

Having looked carefully at the image and taken notes on its focus, arrangement, dimension, and perspective, the next step is to articulate the ideas you've developed. Making statements about the image and writing down questions you have about it will compel you to look at it even more closely, clarifying your understanding and finding further meanings.

Based on the information discussed above, a general statement about the image might be that it promotes an idea of Barbie as a key player in an overwhelmingly consumerist world. Given the fact that many little girls play with Barbie, the image may be suggesting that Barbie initiates girls into this consumerist culture. Indeed, perhaps the image is implying that just as girls collect Barbie's clothes and accessories, grownups continue this collecting by buying other name brand products.

But some questions remain. For instance, what is the significance of the fact that the image evokes Times Square as its setting? What connotations does Times Square have for Barbie, for branding, and for consumerism? Concerning the *colors* and *contrasts* of elements in the image, why do red, white, and blue seem to be the predominant colors (along with yellow in the taxi and the Kodak sign on the left side of the image)? How would the meaning of the image be changed if the colors were mostly browns, greens, or purples? Taken together with the Times Square reference, is the image suggesting a strong connection between Barbie, consumer brands, and the American lifestyle? Finally, the *medium* of the image can be an important component of its meaning. In this case, the composite photograph created by Goodman suggests both the realism of photography (which captures how people and places actually look) and the complete artificiality of this particular scene (with Barbie and Ken figured as real people walking in a distorted version of New York). In what ways might this interplay of reality and illusion be related to the meaning of the image?

Reviewing

So we've examined the image, taken notes, looked at the image again, asked questions, and formulated some ideas and some questions about it. In the final stage, take the time to summarize what you've learned. Perhaps you can do this in the form of a statement about what you think the image means, or perhaps it's more effective to write about what strategies the image uses to convey its messages. In either case, you'll be prepared if you're asked to write about the image or to include an analysis of it with an analysis of a text.

Before concluding this section and turning to the writing process, take a look at the second Barbie image we've selected at the bottom of page CI-1. Follow the same steps described above in reading this image:

1. Take a look at the explanatory information and decide on the context of the image. Who is its audience, and what is its purpose? Note your first impressions of the image.
2. Read the image by noting where your eyes are initially drawn; why is this focal point important to the message of the image?

Note other important features of the image: color, dimension, contrast, perspective, arrangement, shape, and medium. What reasons can you determine for the choices the artist made in these areas?

3. Write down a statement or two that you think explains the meaning of the image, along with any questions you still have about it. Examine it carefully to see what elements you have previously missed.
4. Summarize what you think are the messages and strategies of this image.

We think that one of the most enjoyable parts of studying popular culture is gaining expertise in interpreting the images that bombard us every day, from all angles, from many media. This composite photograph of Barbie gives us a lot to think about in terms of what the doll symbolizes for American culture.

At the end of the introductory chapter and scattered throughout *Common Culture,* you'll find more images upon which you can exercise your interpretative powers. They are drawn from magazines, posters, the Web, and other sources, and they comment on the themes of the chapters of this text: advertising, television, music, technology, sports, and movies. In a highly visual culture like ours, these images serve as "readings" that supplement and provide a different perspective on the more traditional reading materials in each chapter.

THE WRITING PROCESS

Frequently, when an instructor gives a writing assignment—for example, "Write an essay exploring the significance of the Barbie doll in contemporary American culture"—students experience a type of mini-panic: producing a focused, coherent, informative, and logically developed paper seems a monumental task. Some students may be overwhelmed by the many ideas swirling around in their heads, worrying they won't be able to put them into coherent order. Others may think they won't have enough to say about a given topic and complain, "How long does the paper have to be? How can I come up with four pages?"

However, there's really no reason to panic. Just as there are definable activities in the active process of reading, so the writing process can be broken down into four discrete stages: **prewriting, drafting, distancing,** and **revising.** Taking it a step at a time can make writing an essay a manageable and productive experience.

Prewriting

The first stage of the essay-writing process should be especially invigorating and stress-free, since at this point you don't have to worry about making your prose grammatically sound, logically organized, or convincing to a reader. All you have to do is write whatever comes into your head regarding your topic so that you can discover the beginnings of ideas and phrasings that may be developed in the drafting stage and ultimately massaged into an acceptable form of academic writing.

Writers use a number of prewriting strategies to generate ideas and happy turns of phrase. Experiment with all of these to discover which of them "click" in terms of how you think and which help you most productively get your ideas down on paper. Most writers rely more heavily on one or two of these prewriting strategies, depending on their own styles and dispositions; it's a matter of individual preference. If you're a spontaneous, organic sort of person, for example, you might spend more time freewriting. On the other hand, if you have a more logical, mathematical mind, you might gravitate naturally to outlining and do very little freewriting. There's no right or wrong way to prewrite: it comes down to whatever works best for you. But what's best usually involves some combination of the three following techniques.

Freewriting This prewriting strategy lets your mind wander, as minds will, while you record whatever occurs to you. Just write, write, write, with no judgment about the validity, usefulness, grammatical correctness, or literary merit of the words you're putting down. The only requirement is that you write nonstop, either on paper or a word processor, for a manageable period of time, say, fifteen minutes without a break.

Your freewriting can be open—that is, it can be pure, stream-of-consciousness writing in which you "stay in the present moment" and record every thought, sense impression, disturbing sound—or it can be focused on a specific topic, such as Barbie dolls. When freewriting in preparation for writing an essay, it's frequently helpful to keep in mind a central question, either one from your instructor's original topic assignment or one sparked by your own curiosity, so that your freewritten material will be useful when you start composing your actual essay. Here is a typical focused freewrite on the subject of Barbie dolls written by a student in response to the writing assignment quoted earlier:

> *Toys: what did you want as a child vs. what you were given? I don't know, but I wanted cars and ended up with Barbie Corvette. Brother got G.I. Joe, Tonka trucks, I got talking Barbie, Barbie playhouse, Corvette.*

B. served as model for ideal female figure, and now that ideal is depicted in magazines. I guess that represents a kind of perpetuation of this image: girls raised on Barbie ? cycle continues w/images in the media. The I = ideal image of women in America seems to be let's see: white, flawless, flat nose, wide eyes, that kind of thing. Whatever, it's clear that Barbie creates unreal expectations for women.

Yeah! her figure would be inhuman if a real person had it—they would probably die! If she puts on jogging shoes, Barbie stands sloped because she's designed for high heels . . . so it seems as though Barbie is clearly designed for display rather than real activity, let alone profession.

Display literature (written stuff) on Barbie packages—she's not interested in doctoring nurse, etc.; just having money, cars, looking good, taking trips etc. Re: tech—women think computers are "fun." Re: math—women supposedly aren't good at it. Barbie reinforces these stereotypes—and lots more—in girls

Changes in society? discuss for concl.?

Clustering Clustering is especially useful for discovering relationships between ideas, impressions, and facts. As a prewriting activity, it falls between freewriting and outlining in that it's usually more focused than freewriting but less logically structured than an outline.

To prewrite by clustering, begin by writing down a word or central phrase in the center of a clean sheet of paper. In the case of the Barbie doll assignment, for example, you would probably start by writing "Barbie" in the middle of the page, and then drawing a circle around it. Having written and circled this central word or phrase, you can then jot down relevant facts, concrete examples, interesting ideas, and so on. Cluster these around the circled word, like this:

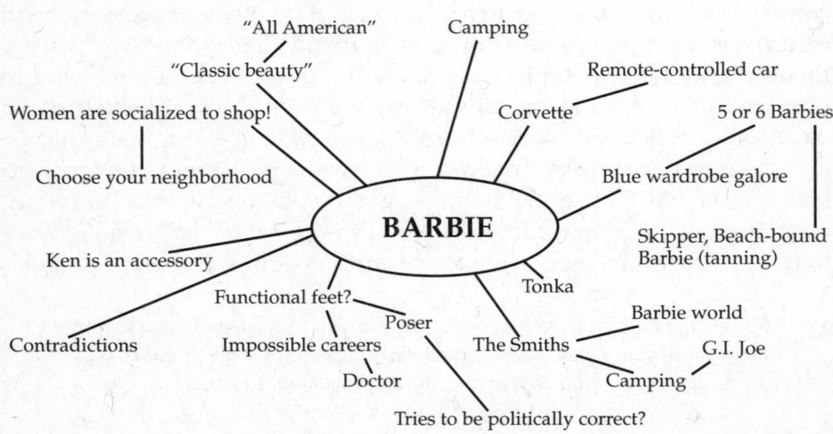

Frequently, one or more of your random jottings will serve as a new central word—as a jumping-off point for a new cluster of ideas. Later on, when you're drafting, you can use these clustered "nodes" as the basis for supporting paragraphs in the body of your essay.

Outlining If you have a rough idea of what the main points of your paper will be, outlining is an extremely useful prewriting technique in that it helps you plan the overall structure for your paper and often generates new ideas about your topic. There are several different types of outlines, most notably scratch, sentence, and topic outlines.

For a *scratch outline,* you list your intended points in a very tentative order, one that may only reflect the fact that you don't yet know in what order you want to put your supporting ideas. A scratch outline might not even suggest which subordinating points are most important to developing your thesis. For this reason, scratch outlines are most useful early in the prewriting phase, as a means of generating ideas as well as beginning to organize your thoughts logically. In fact, if you have not yet arrived at a thesis for your paper, one may emerge in the process of listing all your main and subordinate points and then reviewing that list to discover which of those ideas is the most central and important.

As you think more about your essay and come up with new ideas and supporting evidence, you will almost certainly revise your scratch outline to make it more detailed and conventionally formatted with numbered and lettered headings and subheads. A *topic outline* presents items in key words or brief phrases, rather than sentences, and frequently features no indentation. A *sentence outline* is even more developed than a topic outline in that it describes the listed items in complete sentences, each of which is essentially a subtopic for a supporting paragraph. In fact, sentence outlines, when fully developed, can contain most of the supporting information you're going to present in your essay and can therefore be extremely useful tools during the prewriting process.

Developing her freewritten material about Barbie into an outline, our student writer sketched out the following:

I. Introduction

A. Discuss my own experience with toys while growing up: parents "let" me play with Tonka trucks, but they gave me a Barbie Corvette when I wanted a race car.

B. Discuss social shaping of gender roles generally.

C. Working thesis: Significance of Barbie in American society is that although people say women have "come a long way" and that there are new expectations, this is not really true. If it were, Barbie, depicted as mere sexual, leisure seeking consumer, could not be accepted.

II. *The media see that people—especially young ones—need role models, and manufacture products to fill the following needs.*
   A. *Childhood: Barbie.*
      1. *Barbie presents a totally unrealistic female body as a role model for young women.*
      2. *This role-modeling is crucial in young women's psychological development, because little girls role-play with Barbie, taking her actions as their own.*
   B. *Pre-teen: Models in Seventeen magazine.*
   C. *Teen: Vogue and Mademoiselle.*
   D. *Adult: Cosmopolitan, Victoria's Secret lingerie models, advertisements in mainstream magazines.*

III. *The popularity of Barbie depicts the entrenched nature of traditional female roles.*
   A. *The change toward women's equality is not something that is deemed beneficial by everyone, such as the religious ultra-right.*
   B. *People purchasing Barbie either:*
      1. *Don't see the image that's being perpetuated; or*
      2. *Respect those values and want to pass them on to their children.*
   C. *Significance in popular culture of Barbie is that she illustrates inconsistencies between changing social roles (women and minorities) and the concepts we are teaching youngsters.*
   D. *Although the makers of Barbie make a superficial attempt at updating her, Barbie depicts traditional women absorbed in leisure, consumption, and beauty.*
      1. *Barbie completely reinforces old role expectations.*
      2. *Barbie in the '90s can have a career (she has some doctor outfits, I think), but she isn't ever functional in that career. The emphasis is still on leisure.*

IV. *The Racial Issue*
   A. *Barbie illustrates the assimilation of minorities; they lose part of their culture, because Americans are supposed to belong to the "same mold."*
   B. *In the '90s we say that we aren't prejudiced and that everyone should be accepted for who they are, but since the dominant culture is white, white men and women unconsciously (or in some cases consciously, I'm afraid) assume that others must take on white norms.*

V. *Conclusion*
   A. *Bring it back around to my childhood play time and the necessity for parents to think about the sorts of toys they are giving their children, so that they don't reinforce and perpetuate these old patterns.*

You'll discover that this outline, while detailed, doesn't contain some of the points raised in the final essay's supporting paragraphs and that it includes a good deal of material that was not used in the final essay. The reason for this discrepancy is simple and illustrates a key point for you to remember about the writing process. As this writer began her essay, she discovered new points that she thought relevant to her thesis. At the same time, she realized that some of her outlined points were tangential and digressive rather than helpful in supporting her main point. She therefore cut some of those points, even though she thought they were valid and interesting ideas. That's one of the most painful but absolutely necessary tasks of the writer: getting rid of material that took some work to create and seems interesting and well written. If cutting some of your previously written material makes the final result better, then it's worth the sacrifice!

Drafting

Having generated a good amount of prewritten material and perhaps developed it into a detailed outline, your next task is to transform that material into an actual essay. Before proceeding with the drafting of your essay, however, it's a good idea first to consider your audience—your instructor only? Your instructor *and* your classmates? An imaginary editor or publisher? A third-grade student? Consider, too, the point you want to make about your topic to that audience. Unlike freewriting, which is by its nature often rambling and disjointed, essays succeed to the degree that they focus on a specific point and develop that point with illustrations and examples.

Thesis and Thesis Statement The main point, the central assertion of your essay, is called a *thesis.* It helps to have a clear sense of your thesis before writing a paper. However, keep in mind that this isn't always necessary: some people use writing as a discovery process and don't arrive at their thesis until they've completed a first draft. Generally, however, the process is easier if you have a thesis in mind—even one that's not yet fully formed or that's likely to change—before you begin drafting.

While the form of thesis statements may vary considerably, there are some qualities that separate effective thesis statements from vague or weak ones. First, your thesis statement should be inclusive but focused; that is, it should be broad enough to encompass your paper's main supporting ideas, but narrow enough to represent a concise explanation of your paper's main point that won't require you to write fifty pages to cover the topic adequately. Furthermore, you want your thesis statement to be a forceful assertion rather than a question or an ambiguous statement of purpose such as, "In this paper I am going to talk about Barbie dolls and their effect on society."

Much more effective, as you will see in the sample student paper that concludes this chapter, is a statement that takes a stand:

> This is certainly one of the more dangerous consequences of Barbie's popularity in our society: a seemingly innocent toy

defines for young girls the sorts of career choices, clothing, and relationships that will be "proper" for them as grown-up women.

Notice how this statement gives an excellent sense of the thematic direction the paper will take: clearly, it will examine the relationship between Barbie dolls and gender-role identification in contemporary America.

Opening Paragraphs In most academic writing, you want to arrive at your thesis statement as quickly as possible so that your reader will have a clear sense of your essay's purpose from the start. Many readers expect to find a thesis statement at the end of the introduction—generally, the final sentence of the first or second paragraph. Effective introductions are often structured so as to lead up to the thesis statement: they draw the reader in by opening with an interesting specific point or question, a quotation, a brief anecdote, a controversial assertion—which serves to introduce the topic generally; a general overview then leads up to the specific statement of the thesis in the last sentence.

In the student essay on pages 43–45, for example, observe how the writer begins with a personal reflection about Barbie. Her anecdote may strike a familiar chord with readers and therefore draw them into the topic. Having made the attempt to arouse her readers' interest in her opening paragraph, the writer moves more pointedly into the general topic, discussing briefly the possible social and psychological implications of her parents' gift choices. This discussion leads into her thesis statement, a focused assertion that concludes her second paragraph.

Keep in mind that many writers wait until they have written a first draft before they worry about an introduction. They simply lead off with a tentative thesis statement, then go back later to look for effective ways to lead up to that statement.

Supporting Paragraphs As you draft the body of your paper, keep two main goals in mind. First, try to make sure that all your supporting paragraphs are aimed at developing your thesis so that you maintain your focus and don't ramble off the topic. Second, work toward presenting your supporting ideas in logical order and try to provide smooth transitions between points.

The order in which you choose to present your ideas depends, in large part, on your topic and purpose. When you are arguing for a particular position, you might begin with less important ideas and work toward a final, crucial point. In this way you can build a case that you "clinch" with your strongest piece of evidence. Other kinds of essays call for different structures. For example, an essay tracing the history of the Barbie doll and its effect on American culture would probably be structured chronologically, from the introduction of the toy to its present-day incarnations, since that would be the most natural way to develop the discussion.

The student essay at the end of this chapter moves from a personal reflection on the topic of Barbie (paragraph 1); to a thesis statement that asserts the point of the paper (2); to a transitional paragraph moving from the writer's childhood experiences and a more general discussion of Barbie's role in reinforcing gender-role stereotypes in other young girls (3); to an overview of how sociologists and historians critique the Barbie phenomenon (4); to an examination of whether Barbie has changed in response to evolving attitudes regarding women in society (5–7), the heart of the writer's argument; to a conclusion that frames the essay by returning to the original, personal example (8). Each new discussion seems to flow naturally into the next because the writer uses a transitional phrase or parallel language to link the first sentence in each paragraph to the end of the preceding paragraph.

Evidence Using evidence effectively is the critical task in composing body paragraphs, because your essay will be convincing only to the degree that you make your arguments credible. Evidence can take many forms, from facts and figures you collect from library research to experiences you learn about in conversations with friends. While library research isn't necessary for every paper, it helps to include at least some "hard" facts and figures gathered from outside sources—journals, newspapers, textbooks—even if you're not writing a full-blown research paper. Frequently, gathering your evidence doesn't require scrolling through computer screens in your school's library; it could be accomplished by watching the six o'clock newscast or while reading the paper over breakfast.

Quotations from secondary sources are another common way of developing and supporting a point in a paragraph. Using another person's spoken or written words will lend your arguments a note of authenticity, especially when your source is a recognized authority in the field about which you're writing. A few points to remember when using quotations:

1. Generally, don't begin or end a supporting paragraph with a quotation. Articulate your point *in your own words* in the first sentence or two of the paragraph; *then* provide the quotation as a way of supporting your point. After the quotation, you might include another focusing sentence or two that analyzes the quotation and suggests how it relates to your point.
2. Keep your quotations brief. Overly lengthy quotations can make a paper difficult to read. You've probably read texts that nearly

put you to sleep because of their overuse of quotations. As a general rule, quote source material only when the precise phrasing is necessary to support your abstract points. Be careful not to allow cited passages to overpower your own assertions.
3. Remember that all of your secondary material—whether quoted or paraphrased—needs to be accurately attributed. Make sure to mention the source's name and include other information (such as the publication date or page number) as required by your instructor.

While quotations, facts, and figures are the most common ways of developing your supporting paragraphs with evidence, you can also use your imagination to come up with other means of substantiating your points. Design a questionnaire, hand it out to your friends, and compile the resulting data as evidence. Interview a local authority on your topic, make notes about the conversation, and draw upon these as evidence. Finally, be your own authority: use your own powers of reasoning to come up with logical arguments that convince your readers of the validity of your assertions.

This body paragraph from the student essay on Barbie provides a good example of a writer using evidence to support her points:

> As Motz observes later in her article, Barbie has changed to adjust to the transforming attitudes of society over time. Both her facial expressions and wardrobe have undergone subtle alterations: "The newer Barbie has a more friendly, open expression, with a hint of a smile, and her lip and eye make-up is muted" (226), and in recent years Barbie's wardrobe has expanded to include some career clothing in addition to her massive volume of recreational attire. This transition appears to represent a conscious effort on the part of Barbie's manufacturers to integrate the concept of women as important members of the work force, with traditional ideals already depicted by Barbie.

The paragraph begins with an assertion of the general point that Barbie has changed in some ways over the years to reflect changes in societal attitudes toward women. This point is then supported with a quotation from an expert, and the page number of the original source is noted parenthetically. (Note that page references in this student essay are from the complete original essay by Motz, published in *The Popular Culture Reader,* not from the excerpt of the Motz essay earlier in this chapter.) The point is further developed with evidence presented in the writer's own words. The paragraph concludes with a final sentence that summarizes the main point of the evidence presented in the previous sentences, keeps the paragraph focused on the essay's thesis that Barbie perpetuates gender stereotypes, and sets the reader up for a transition into the next subtopic.

Obviously, all supporting paragraphs won't take this exact form; essays would be deadly boring if every paragraph looked the same. You'll encounter body paragraphs in professional essays that begin with quotations or end with quotations, for example. Just keep in mind that you want to *support* whatever general point you're making, so each paragraph should include a measure of specific, concrete evidence. The more you practice writing, the more ways you'll discover to develop body paragraphs with illustrations, examples, and evidence.

Conclusions You may have learned in high school English courses that an essay's conclusion should restate the main points made in the paper so that the reader is left with a concise summary that leaves no doubt as to the paper's intention. This was an excellent suggestion for high school students as it reinforced the notion of focusing an essay on a specific, concrete point. In college, however, you'll want to start developing a more sophisticated academic style. Conclusions to college-level essays should do more than merely repeat the paper's main points; they should leave the reader with something to think about.

Of course, what that *something* is depends on your topic, your audiences, and your purpose in writing. Sometimes it may be appropriate to move from an objective discussion of a topic to a more subjective reflection on it. For instance, in analyzing the social effects of Barbie dolls, you might end by reflecting on the doll's significance in your own life or by commenting ironically on feminist critics who in your view make too much of Barbie's influence. Other ways to conclude are providing a provocative quotation, offering a challenge for the future, asserting a forceful opinion, creating a striking image or memorable turn of phrase, or referring back to an image or idea in your introduction.

What you want to avoid is a bland and overly general conclusion along the lines of, "Thus, in conclusion, it would seem to this author that Barbie has had a great and wide-reaching impact on today's contemporary society." Note how the writer of the Barbie essay created a strong conclusion by first returning to the subject of her opening paragraph—her own childhood toys—and then leaving the reader with a relatively memorable final sentence offering a challenge for the future:

> Looking back at my childhood, I see my parents engaged in this same struggle. By surrounding me with toys that perpetuated both feminine and masculine roles, they achieved a kind of balance among the conflicting images in society. However, they also seemed to succumb to traditional social pressures by giving me that Barbie

> Corvette, when all I wanted was a radio-controlled formula-one racer, like the one Emerson Fittipaldi drives. In a time when most parents agree that young girls should be encouraged to pursue their goals regardless of gender boundaries, their actions do not always reflect these ideals. Only when we demand that toys like Barbie no longer perpetuate stereotypes will this reform be complete.

Distancing

Distancing is the easiest part of the writing process because it involves doing nothing more than putting your first draft aside and giving yourself some emotional and intellectual distance from it. Pursue your daily activities, go to work or complete assignments for other classes, take a hike, throw a Frisbee, polish your shoes, do anything but read over your draft . . . ideally for a day or two.

The reason to take the time to distance yourself is simple: you've been working hard on your essay and therefore have a strong personal investment in it. To revise effectively, you need to be able to see your essay dispassionately, almost as though someone else had written it. Stepping away from it for a day or two gives you the opportunity to approach your essay as an editor who has no compunction about changing, reordering, or completely cutting passages that don't work.

Also, the process of distancing allows your mind to work on the essay subconsciously even while you're going about your other non-writing activities. Frequently, during this distancing period, you'll find yourself coming up with new ideas that you can use to supplement your thesis as you revise.

Finally, factoring the process of distancing into the writing process will help you avoid the dread disease of all students: procrastination. Since you have to allot yourself enough time to write a draft *and* let it sit for a couple of days, you'll avoid a last-minute scramble for ideas and supporting material, and you'll have time to do a thorough revision.

One note of warning: Don't get so distanced from your draft that you forget to come back to it. If you do forget, all your prewriting and drafting will have gone to waste.

Revising

Many professional writers believe that revision is the most important stage in the writing process. Writers view the revision stage as an opportunity to clarify their ideas, to rearrange text so that the logical flow of their work is enhanced, to add new phrases or delete ones that don't work, to modify their thesis and change editorial direction . . . or, in some extreme cases, to throw the whole thing out and start over!

Just as with prewriting and drafting, many students dread revision because all the different issues that need to be considered make it appear to be a forbidding task. Most find it helpful to have a clear set of criteria with which to approach their first drafts. Following is such a checklist of questions, addressing specific issues of content, organization, and stylistics/mechanics. If you find that your answer is "no" to any one of these questions, then you need to rework your essay for improvement in that specific area.

Revision Checklist

Introduction

✔ Does the paper begin in a way that draws the reader into the paper while introducing the topic?

✔ Does the introduction provide some general overview that leads up to the thesis?

✔ Does the introduction end with a focused, assertive thesis in the form of a statement (not a question)?

Supporting Paragraphs and Conclusion

✔ Do your supporting paragraphs relate back to your thesis, so that the paper has a clear focus?

✔ Do your body paragraphs connect logically, with smooth transitions between them?

✔ Do your supporting paragraphs have a good balance between general points and specific, concrete evidence?

✔ If you've used secondary sources for your evidence, do you attribute them adequately to avoid any suspicion of plagiarism?

✔ If you've used quotations extensively, have you made sure your quoted material doesn't overpower your own writing?

✔ Does your last paragraph give your readers something to think about rather than merely restate what you've already said elsewhere in the essay?

Style and Mechanics

✔ Have you chosen your words aptly and sometimes inventively, avoiding clichés and overused phrases?

✔ Have you varied your sentence lengths effectively, thus helping create a pleasing prose rhythm?

✔ Have you proofread carefully, to catch any grammatical problems or spelling errors?

Make the minor changes or major overhauls required in your first draft. Then type or print out a second draft, and read it *out loud* to yourself to catch any awkward or unnatural sounding passages, wordy sentences, grammatical glitches, and so on. Reading your prose out loud may seem weird—especially to your roommates who can't help overhearing—but doing so helps you gain some new perspective on the piece of writing you have been so close to, and frequently highlights minor, sentence-level problems that you might otherwise overlook.

Writing Research on Popular Culture

A research essay focusing on popular culture follows the same steps as those presented in the previous discussion of essay writing in general—with a significant addition: the research essay focuses on a central hypothesis or research question, and it includes outside sources. For that reason, you might envision a slightly different sequence of activities for your writing process, one that moves according to the following stages:

- *Topic Selection:* Spend some time thinking about an issue that you actually are interested in or want to know more about. Your teachers will sometimes give you relatively open-ended essay prompts, allowing you to select a research area with which you are familiar and/or interested. Even in those cases in which the teacher narrows the topic significantly—perhaps assigning an essay on the relationship between Barbie dolls and gender stereotyping, or between music lyrics and violence, for example—you still have a great deal of leeway in focusing the topic on elements of interest to you. In the music/violence example, you still have the freedom to select bands and lyrics you know well, and this will make your research much more well informed, while keeping the topic fresh and interesting to you.
- *Focus:* Narrow the topic as much as you can to ensure that your work will be thorough, focused, and well supported with evidence. In the Barbie example at the end of this chapter, the author focused on childhood psychological development as it is affected by stereotype-perpetuating toys such as Barbie. Likewise, in the music/violence example, you might narrow the focus by restricting your research to certain types of popular music, such as punk or hip-hop, or to music by artists of a certain gender or ethnic population. The less global you make your topic, the less you will

find yourself awash in volumes of disparate material as you develop your essay drafts.

- *Working Thesis:* Develop a preliminary research question or hypothesis related to your topic. This working thesis will undoubtedly go through several refinements as you begin researching your topic, but it helps greatly to organize your research material if you begin with a concrete point of view, even if you change it later on, as you find more information on the topic. In the student essay that follows, a research question might have been: do certain toys reinforce gender stereotyping in children? The working hypothesis would probably have supported the affirmative position. In the music/violence topic, a working thesis might be something such as: while many observers believe that lyrics in hip-hop music incite young people to violence, research demonstrates that there is no causal connection between listening to certain types of music and violent behavior. You would then proceed to the next step, to find material that supports (or disproves) this initial hypothesis.
- *Secondary Sources:* Find the most valuable materials written by other people on your chosen topic. As much as possible, include examples from a wide range of sources, including scholarly journals, books, popular literature (such as magazine and newspaper articles), and World Wide Web sites. Don't be daunted if you don't find materials from each of these source categories; in some cases, for example, a topic will be so new and fresh that there haven't been books written about it, and you may have to rely more on newspaper articles and Web sites.
- *Primary Sources:* If possible and applicable to your assignment, include some research that you have conducted, such as interviews with professors who are experts on the topic you are examining, or even with friends and peers who can provide a "person-on-the-street" perspective to balance some of the more academic or journalistic perspectives found in your secondary sources.
- *Critical Reading:* To avoid becoming a passive receptor of someone else's obvious or popular conclusions, analyze your assembled source information to find its literal and implied meanings and to weigh the validity of the information it presents. At the same time, check the validity of your own previously held assumptions and beliefs; as much as possible, try to have an open mind about your topic, even if you have a working hypothesis you are developing. In the above-described working thesis on the

relationship between music and violence, you may find material that disproves your original hypothesis, suggesting that there is in fact a relationship between listening to music and acting violently. You may then want to revise your thesis to reflect the material you have found, if you think that information is valid. Feel free to use or reject discovered information based on your critical analysis of it.

- *Documentation:* Finally, keep careful record of your sources so that you can attribute them accurately, using a bibliographic format appropriate to your research topic and approach. Keep in mind that any time you use source material to support your arguments in academic papers, it is necessary that you document that material. You accomplish this by using footnotes and/or parenthetical in-text citations in the body of your essay, along with bibliographies and/or Works Cited pages at the end of your essay. This academic convention accomplishes two purposes: first, it serves to acknowledge your having relied on ideas and/or actual phrases from outside source material; and second, it allows readers to explore a paper's topic further, should they find the issues raised thought-provoking and worthy of pursuit.

In academic settings, the major systems of documentation—namely, APA, MLA, and CSE—share certain key characteristics; that is, they all furnish readers with uniform information about quoted or paraphrased material from books, journals, newspapers, Web sites, and so forth. While it may seem strange for such a multiplicity of documenting styles to exist, there actually is a good reason why there is not one single documentation format for all academic disciplines: the different documentation styles support the unique needs and preferences of certain academic communities. Social scientists cite their sources by author and date because in the social sciences, broad articulations of concepts, refined through time, are paramount; APA format reflects this. By contrast, researchers working in humanities-related fields rely frequently on direct quotations; the MLA format therefore furnishes page numbers rather than dates.

If you have already selected a major, you will probably be writing most, if not all, of your essays for a certain discipline, such as English literature or psychology. While you will probably want to acquaint yourself to some degree with the basics of all the major citation formats, you will certainly want to learn, memorize, and practice with special diligence the documentation requirements of the area in which you will be majoring. All three of the above-mentioned professional organizations periodically issue revised guidelines for documentation, and if you want to be sure about the specific rules in your area of specialization, you might want to buy one of the following:

MLA Handbook for Writers of Research Papers (7th edition, 2009)
Publication Manual of the American Psychological Association (6th edition, 2009)
The CSE Manual for Authors, Editors, and Publishers (7th edition, 2006)
The Chicago Manual of Style (16th edition, 2010)

Furthermore, there are numerous handbooks available, such as the *Prentice Hall Guide to Research: Documentation*, 6th edition, 2004, which provide detailed information on documentation in all of the disciplines. In the absence of such books, the following section gives features of the two most popular documentation styles, the MLA and the APA.

Modern Language Association Documentation Format

- Within the body of the text, all sources are cited within parentheses (known in the academic world as "in-text parenthetical citations"), using the author's name and the number of the page from which the source was derived. You should include an in-text citation any time you use another writer's ideas or phrasings within the text of your own paper, either by direct quotation or by paraphrase.
- At the end of the paper, sources are listed alphabetically, on a page or pages with the heading "Works Cited." In the "Works Cited" section, list book-derived citations using the following information, in this order: the author's name exactly as it appears on the book's title page, last name first; the title of the book, in italics; the place of publication followed by a colon; the publisher, followed by a comma; and the date of publication. A typical MLA-formatted book listing will look like this:

Berger, Arthur Asa. *Television as an Instrument of Terror: Essays on Media, Popular Culture, and Everyday Life*. New Brunswick, N.J.: Transaction Books, 1980.

A typical MLA journal or magazine citation will contain six pieces of information: the author, listed last name first; the article's title in quotation marks; the journal's title in italics; the volume number followed by the issue number; the date of publication; and the article's page numbers. A typical MLA-formatted journal listing will appear in this way:

Auerbach, Jeffrey. "Art, advertising, and the legacy of empire." *Journal of Popular Culture* 35.4 (2002): 1–23.

For files acquired from the World Wide Web, give the author's name (if known), the full title of the work in quotation marks, the title of the complete work (if applicable) in italics, and the full HTTP address. For example:

Brooke, Collin. "Perspective: Notes Toward the Remediation of Style." *Enculturation: Special Multi-journal Issue on Electronic Publication* 4.1 (Spring 2002).

American Psychological Association Documentation Format

- Within the body of the text, all sources are cited within parentheses, using the author's name, along with the year of publication. That latter bit of information—the publication date—is the important difference in parenthetical in-text citation format between the APA and MLA documentation styles. When directly quoting from a source, include the number of the page from which the quotation is taken.
- At the end of the paper, sources are listed alphabetically on a page or pages of reference materials. List book-derived citations using the following information, in order: the author's last name and initials for first name (and middle name if given), last name first; the year of publication in parentheses; the title of the book in italics with only the first word of the title capitalized; the place of publication followed by a colon; and the publisher, followed by a period. A typical APA-formatted book listing will look like this:

Charyn, J. (1989). *Movieland: Hollywood and the great American dream culture.* New York: Putnam.

An APA-formatted journal or magazine citation will contain six pieces of information: the author's name; the date of publication; the article's title; the journal's title, italicized along with the volume number; and the article's page numbers. A typical APA-formatted journal listing will look like this:

Banks, J. (1997). MTV and the globalization of popular culture. *Gazette, 59*(1), 43–44.

For electronic citations, give the author's name (if known), the date of publication or of the latest update, the full title of the work, and the title of the online journal in which the work appears (if applicable).

Then start a sentence with the word "Retrieved," followed by the date on which the source was accessed and the source's URL or HTTP address. For example,

> Cole, S. K. (1999). I am the eye, you are my victim: The pornographic ideology of music video. *Enculturation Magazine.* Retrieved March 4, 2006, from http://enculturation.gmu.edu/2_2/cole/

Of course, there are many other sources—newspapers, interviews, videos, email conversations, just to name a few—that are omitted here for the sake of brevity, but that carry specific formatting requirements within the major documentation styles. You will undoubtedly want to refer to a handbook or a style sheet published by one of the national associations should you be asked to write a more extensive research paper that includes the full range of source materials.

Sample Student Essay

The following essay demonstrates one way of approaching the assignment we presented earlier. As you read, note the essay's introductory paragraphs and thesis statement, the way body paragraphs are developed with illustrations and examples, the way it concludes without simply restating the writer's points, the writer's effective use of words and sentence structure, the ways in which it incorporates source material into the developing arguments, and the correct MLA documentation format. While this is not, strictly speaking, a research essay as described above, it does incorporate source material in the ways discussed above.

Role-Model Barbie: Now and Forever?
CAROLYN MUHLSTEIN

During my early childhood, my parents avoided placing gender boundaries on my play time. My brother and I both had Tonka trucks, and these were driven by Barbie, Strawberry Shortcake, and GI Joe to my doll house, or to condos built with my brother's Erector Set. However, as I got older, the boundaries became more defined, and certain forms of play became "inappropriate." For example, I remember asking for a remote-controlled car one Christmas, anticipating a powerful race car like the ones driven at De Anza Days, the local community fair. Christmas morning waiting for me under the tree was a bright yellow Barbie Corvette. It seemed as though my parents had decided that if I had to have a remote-controlled car, at least it could be a feminine Barbie one! 1

Although I was too young to realize it at the time, this gift represented a subtle shift in my parents' attitudes toward my gender-role choices. Where before my folks seemed content to let me assume either 2 traditional "boy" or traditional "girl" roles in play, now they appeared to be subtly directing me toward traditional female role-playing. This is certainly one of the more dangerous consequences of Barbie's popularity in our society: a seemingly innocent toy defines for young girls the sorts of career choices, clothing, and relationships that will be "proper" for them as grown-up women.

Perhaps the Barbie Corvette was my parents' attempt to steer me 3 back toward more traditional feminine pursuits. Since her birth thirty-five years ago, Barbie has been used by many parents to illustrate the "appropriate" role of a woman in society. During earlier decades, when women were expected to remain at home, Barbie's lifestyle was extremely fitting. Marilyn Ferris Motz writes that Barbie "represents so well the widespread values of modern American society, devoting herself to the pursuit of happiness through leisure and material goods . . . teaching them [female children] the skills by which their future success will be measured" (212). Barbie, then, serves as a symbol of the woman's traditional role in our society, and she serves to reinforce those stereotypes in young girls.

Motz's opinion isn't an isolated one. In fact, the consensus among 4 sociologists, historians, and consumers is that Barbie represents a life of lazy leisure and wealth. Her "forever arched feet" and face "always smiling, eyes wide with admiration" (Tham 180) allow for little more than evenings on the town and strolls in the park. In addition, the accessories Barbie is equipped with are almost all related to pursuits of mere pleasure. According to a Barbie sticker album created by Mattel:

> Barbie is seen as a typical young lady of the twentieth century, who knows how to appreciate beautiful things and, at the same time, live life to the fullest . . . with her fashionable wardrobe and constant journeys to exciting places all over the world, the adventures of Barbie offer a glimpse of what they [girls] might achieve one day. (qtd. in Motz 218)

In this packaging "literature"—and in the countless other adver- 5 tisements and packaging materials that have emerged since Barbie's invention some thirty years ago—the manufacturers exalt Barbie's materialism: her appreciation of "beautiful things," fine clothing, and expensive trips as positive personality traits: qualities which all normal, healthy girls in this society should try to emulate, according to the traditional view.

As Motz observes later in her article, Barbie has changed to ad- 6 just to the transforming attitudes of society over time. Both her facial expressions and wardrobe have undergone subtle alterations: "The newer Barbie has a more friendly, open expression, with a hint of a smile, and her lip and eye make-up is muted" (226), and in recent years Barbie's wardrobe has expanded to include some career clothing in addition to her massive volume of recreational attire. This transition appears to represent a conscious effort on the part of Barbie's manufacturers to integrate the concept of women as important members of the work force, with traditional ideals already depicted by Barbie.

Unfortunately, a critical examination of today's Barbie doll reveals that this so-called integration is actually a cynical, halfhearted attempt to satisfy the concerns of some people—especially those concerned with feminist issues. Sure, Barbie now has office attire, a doctor outfit, a nurse outfit, and a few other pieces of "career" clothing, but her image continues to center on leisure. As Motz observes, "Barbie may try her hand at high-status occupations, but her appearance does not suggest competence and professionalism" (230). Quite the opposite, in fact: there are few, and in some cases, no accessories with which a young girl might imagine a world of professional competence for Barbie. There are no Barbie hospitals and no Barbie doctor offices; instead, she has only mansions, boats, and fast cars. Furthermore, Barbie's arched feet make it impossible for her to stand in anything but heels, so a career as a doctor, an astronaut—or anything else that requires standing up for more than twenty minutes on a fashion runway—would be nearly impossible! 7

From these examples, it's clear that Barbie's manufacturers have failed to reconcile the traditional image of women as sexual, leisure-seeking consumers with the view that women are assertive, career-oriented individuals, because their "revision" of the Barbie image is at best a token one. This failure to reconcile two opposing roles for Barbie parallels the same contradiction in contemporary society. By choice and necessity, women are in the work force in large numbers, seeking equal pay and equal opportunities with men; yet the more traditional voices in our culture continue to perpetuate stereotyped images of women. If we believe that we are at a transitional point in the evolution toward real equality for women, then Barbie exemplifies this transitional stage perfectly. 8

Looking back at my childhood, I see my parents engaged in this same struggle. By surrounding me with toys that perpetuated both feminine and masculine roles, they achieved a kind of balance among the conflicting images in society. However, they also seemed to succumb to traditional social pressures by giving me that Barbie Corvette, when all I wanted was a radio-controlled formula-one racer, like the one Emerson Fittipaldi drives. In a time when most parents agree that young girls should be encouraged to pursue their goals regardless of gender boundaries, their actions do not always reflect these ideals. Only when we demand that toys like Barbie no longer perpetuate stereotypes will this reform be complete. 9

Works Cited

Motz, Marilyn Ferris. "Through Rose-Tinted Glasses." *Popular Culture: An Introductory Text*. Ed. Jack Trachbar and Kevin Lause. Bowling Green, OH: Bowling Green University Press, 1992.

Tham, Hilary. "Barbie's Shoes." *Mondo Barbie*. Ed. Lucinda Ebersole and Richard Peabody. New York: St. Martin's Press, 1993.

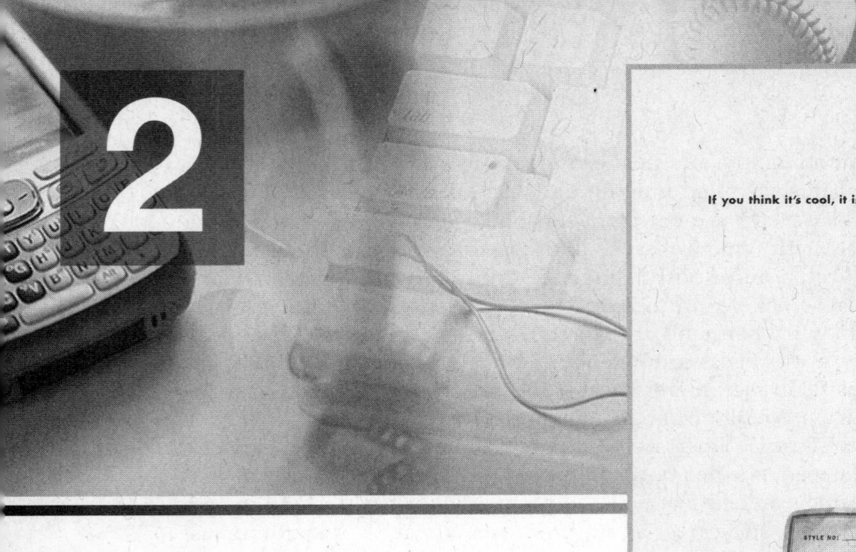

2 Advertising

What you see above is a very simple advertisement for a Timex watch. A picture of the watch, a short statement, a tag with information about the watch and the familiar Timex slogan, some small print at the bottom: there doesn't seem to be much more to it than that. But appearances can be deceiving—and indeed, they often are in advertisements.

Let's take a closer look. The ad is centered on a simple statement: "If you think it's cool, it is." The longest word in the sentence is only five letters, reminding us of other familiar advertising slogans such as "Just do it" and "Coke is it." In addition to their quite basic vocabulary, these slogans share a certain quality of vagueness: the "it" in "Just do it," like the "it" in "Coke is it," are what semioticians might call "floating signifiers": their meaning is open and flexible, determined substantially by the reader of the ad. The same can be said for the "it" in this Timex ad: does "it" refer only to the watch? If so, why doesn't the statement say, "If you think *this watch* is cool, it is"? Clearly, an all-encompassing word like "it" allows the statement to be about more than just the watch.

Even more interesting in this ad is the word "cool": what exactly is "cool"? It's a word that we all define differently, and Timex invites us here to take our own definition of "cool" and associate it with the watch. Whatever each of us thinks of as "cool," that's what this watch is.

While vagueness usually leads to poor communication, you can see how it's used effectively here by the advertiser: "cool" tells us virtually nothing about the watch, but makes us feel good about it nonetheless. And of course, "cool" appeals to a certain audience: precisely the young, upscale, Generation X types who might be reading *Icon,* the glossy and expensive "thoughtstyle" magazine in which we found the ad. So, targeting a smaller audience, Timex can afford to be more specific than Coke can be when it claims to be "it." Still, the watch is "cool" rather than "groovy" (too old) or "rad" (too California-surfer). In that one word alone and in the way it's used, we can see the ad hard at work trying to make its product appealing to potential customers.

When we look at the entire sentence, we can also see a degree of complexity behind its seeming simplicity. Even if we accept that the word "it" refers only to the watch, the sentence invites two different interpretations:

1. "If you think this watch is cool, well, you're right, because it is."
2. "If you think this watch is cool, then it is (because you say it is)."

This is a fine difference, but an important one. The first way of reading the sentence suggests that the watch is naturally, essentially cool, and so the reader is to be congratulated on being perceptive enough to see coolness when he or she comes across it. In the second reading, the watch isn't naturally cool at all; it's the reader who decides that the watch is cool. Either way, the reader of the ad gets a compliment and perhaps an ego-boost: either he or she is cool enough to recognize a cool watch, or he or she has the power to determine coolness. The first option might appeal to a more insecure sort of reader, someone who fears that he or she can't distinguish cool from uncool. The second reading confirms the confidence of a more secure reader, someone who knows perfectly well what's cool and what isn't. In other words, the statement appeals simultaneously to both the "wanna-be cools" and the "already cools" who might be reading *Icon*.

Now you may think that we're reading too much into so simple an advertisement, especially considering the fact that we haven't gotten past the statement yet to consider other elements in the ad: all that white space, the strange information presented on the label (why do we need to know the date of the original design?), the Timex slogan at the bottom of the label. It's true that we're spending far more time interpreting this ad than most readers spend on it as they thumb through *Icon* looking for an interesting article to read. But we're not spending nearly as much time on the ad as its designers did. The fact is that nothing in this ad—or in any ad—is there by mistake; every detail is carefully chosen, every word carefully selected, every photograph carefully arranged. Advertisers know that readers usually spend only a few seconds glancing at ads as they page through a magazine; we drive quickly past billboards and use TV commercial minutes to grab food from the fridge. In those seconds that the advertisers have our attention, they need to make as strong a pitch as possible. All that we're doing with the Timex ad is speculating about each of the choices that the designers of the ad made in creating their pitch. In several writing and discussion assignments in this chapter, you'll be asked to do the same kind of analysis with ads that you select, and in readings in this chapter you'll see more detailed and complete analyses of ads that can serve, along with this mini-analysis of the Timex ad, as models for your own interpretations.

Keep in mind, too, that advertising agencies spend a great deal of time and money trying to understand the complex psychodynamics of their target audiences and then tailoring ads to appeal to those audiences. Even their simplest and most seemingly direct advertisements still carry subtly powerful messages—about "coolness" as well as about appropriate modes of behavior, standards of beauty and success, gender roles, and a variety of other markers for normalcy and status. In tailoring ads to appeal both to basic human impulses and to more culturally conditioned attitudes, they also ultimately reinforce and even engender such impulses and attitudes. So although advertisements like the one above seem to be thoroughly innocuous and unimportant, the argument of many pop culture critics is that they have quite an influence—perhaps all the more so because we think they're so bland and harmless.

Several readings in this chapter explain in further detail the ways in which we can be manipulated by advertising. Jib Fowles, for example, points out a variety of strategies advertisements use to appeal to our emotions even though we may think we are making product choices using our intellect. The readings in the second section of the chapter look at the future(s) of advertising and try to speculate on what's in store in the ongoing "dance" of consumers and advertisers. As the appeals and strategies of advertisers become more familiar to us, they may become less effective, and so advertisers are constantly on the lookout for new techniques and new venues for delivering their messages. As Alice Park reports in the final article, through research in the new field of "neuromarketing," advertisers may even be trying to look directly into our brains to see how to move us and make their products more appealing.

Whatever your view of advertising, keep in mind as you read the following sections that everything in advertisements—from sexy models to simple black-and-white pictures of watches—exist solely for three well-calculated reasons: to sell, sell, and sell.

Approaches to Advertising

The Cult You're In

KALLE LASN

We begin this chapter on advertising with an intriguing, lyrical, but quite bleak piece by one of advertising's most interesting critics, Kalle Lasn. Lasn is one of the founders of Adbusters Media Foundation, which publishes Adbusters *magazine and coordinates such "culture jamming" campaigns as "TV Turn-Off Week," "Buy Nothing Day," and "Car Free Day" (http://www.adbusters.org). The selection reprinted here comes from Lasn's book* Culture Jam: The Uncooling of America.

Through his book, magazine, Web site, and "culture jamming" campaigns, Lasn delivers a critique of contemporary consumer culture, focused in particular on advertising, the influence of mass media, and the power of large corporations. In Lasn's words, his movement is "about reclaiming democracy, returning this country to its citizens as citizens, not marketing targets or demographics. It's about being a skeptic and not letting advertising tell you what to think."

In the following article, Lasn describes a scenario in which advertising does tell us what to think, and even what to dream, exerting a profound and complete power over our lives as citizen-consumers. Whether this scenario is an accurate description of the present or a disturbing possibility for the future is for you to decide. ***Before you read****, consider the title of this article: "The Cult You're In." What effect does it have to be told in this title that you're in a cult? What do you already know about cults that might influence your reaction to the title?*

A beeping truck, backing up in the alley, jolts you out of a scary dream—a mad midnight chase through a supermarket, ending with a savage beating at the hands of the Keebler elves. You sit up in a cold sweat, heart slamming in your chest. It was only a nightmare. Slowly, you reintegrate, remembering who and where you are. In your bed, in your little apartment, in the very town you grew up in. 1

It's a "This Is Your Life" moment—a time for mulling and stock-taking. You are still here. Just a few miles from the place you had your first kiss, got your first job (drive-through window at Wendy's), bought your first car ('73 Ford Torino), went nuts with the Wild Turkey on prom night and pulled that all-nighter at Kinko's, photocopying transcripts to send to the big schools back East. 2

Those big dreams of youth didn't quite pan out. You didn't get into Harvard, didn't get courted by the Bulls, didn't land a recording contract with EMI (or anyone else), didn't make a million by age twenty-five. And so you scaled down your hopes of embarrassing riches to reasonable expectations of adequate comfort—the modest condo downtown, the Visa card, the Braun shaver, the one good Armani suit. 3

Even this more modest star proved out of reach. The state college you graduated from left you with a $35,000 debt. The work you found hardly dented it: dreadful eight-to-six days in the circulation department of a bad lifestyle magazine. You learned to swallow hard and just do the job—until the cuts came and the junior people were cleared out with a week's severance pay and sober no-look nods from middle management. You began paying the rent with Visa advances. You got call-display to avoid the collection agency. 4

There remains only one thing no one has taken away, your only real equity. And you intend to enjoy fully that Fiat rustmaster this weekend. You can't run from your problems, but you may as well drive. Road Trip. Three days to forget it all. Three days of living like an animal (in the best possible sense), alert to sights and sounds and smells: Howard Stern on the morning radio, Slumber Lodge pools along the I-14. "You may find yourself behind the wheel of a large automobile," sings David Byrne from a tape labeled "Road Tunes One." The Fiat is, of course, only large at heart. "You know what FIAT stands for?" Liv said when she first saw it. "Fix It Again, Tony." You knew then that this was a girl you could travel to the ends of the Earth with. Or at least to New York City. 5

The itinerary is set. You will order clam chowder from the Soup Nazi, line up for standby Letterman tickets and wander around Times Square (Now cleaner! Safer!) with one eye on the Jumbotron. It's a place you've never been, though you live there in your mind. You will jog in Battery Park and sip Guinness at Michael's Pub on Monday night (Woody Allen's night), and you will dance with Liv in the Rainbow Room on her birthday. Ah Liv, who when you first saw her spraying Opium on her wrist at the cosmetics counter reminded you so much of Cindy Crawford—though of late she's put on a few pounds and now looks better when you close your eyes and imagine. 6

And so you'll drive. You'll fuel up with Ho Ho's and Pez and Evian and magazines and batteries for your Discman, and then you'll bury the pedal under your Converse All-Stars—like the ones Kurt Cobain died in. Wayfarers on, needle climbing and the unspoken understanding that you and Liv will conduct the conversation entirely in movie catchphrases. 7

"Mrs. Nixon would like you to pass the Doritos." 8

"You just keep thinking, Butch. That's what you're good at." 9

"It's over, Rock. Nothing on Earth's gonna save you now." 10

It occurs to you that you can't remember the last time Liv was just Liv and you were just you. You light up a Metro, a designer cigarette so obviously targeted at your demographic . . . which is why you steered clear of them until one day you smoked one to be ironic, and now you can't stop. 11

You'll come back home in a week. Or maybe you won't. Why should you? What's there to come back *for*? On the other hand, why should you stay? 12

A long time ago, without even realizing it, just about all of us were recruited into a cult. At some indeterminate moment, maybe when we were feeling particularly adrift or vulnerable, a cult member showed up and made a beautiful presentation. "I believe I have something to ease your pain." She made us feel welcome. We understood she was offering us something to give life meaning. She was wearing Nike sneakers and a Planet Hollywood cap. 13

Do you *feel* as if you're in a cult? Probably not. The atmosphere is quite un-Moonielike. We're free to roam and recreate. No one seems to be forcing us to do anything we don't want to do. In fact, we feel privileged to be here. The rules don't seem oppressive. But make no mistake: There are rules. 14

By consensus, cult members speak a kind of corporate Esperanto: words and ideas sucked up from TV and advertising. We wear uniforms—not white robes but, let's say, Tommy Hilfiger jackets or Airwalk sneakers (it depends on our particular subsect). We have been recruited into roles and behavior patterns *we did not consciously choose.* 15

Quite a few members ended up in the slacker camp. They're bunked in spartan huts on the periphery, well away from the others. There's no mistaking cult slackers for "downshifters"—those folks who have *voluntarily* cashed out of their high-paying jobs and simplified their lives. Slackers are downshifters by necessity. They live frugally because they are poor. (Underemployed and often overeducated, they may never get out of the rent-and-loan-repayment cycle.) 16

There's really not much for the slackers to *do* from day to day. They hang out, never asking, never telling, just offering intermittent wry observations. They are postpolitical, postreligious. They don't define themselves by who they vote for or pray to (these things are pretty much prescribed in the cult anyway). They set themselves apart in the only way cult members can: by what they choose to wear and drive and listen to. The only things to which they confidently ascribe value are things other people have already scouted, deemed worthy and embraced. 17

Cult members aren't really citizens. The notions of citizenship and nationhood make little sense in this world. We're not fathers and mothers and brothers: We're consumers. We care about sneakers, music and Jeeps. The only *Life, Freedom, Wonder* and *Joy* in our lives are the brands on our supermarket shelves. 18

Are we happy? Not really. Cults promise a kind of boundless contentment—punctuated by moments of bliss—but never quite deliver on that promise. They fill the void, but only with a different kind of void. Disillusionment eventually sets in—or it would if we were allowed to think much about it. Hence the first commandment of a cult: *Thou shalt not think.* Free thinking will break the trance and introduce competing perspectives. Which leads to doubt. Which leads to contemplation of the nearest exit. 19

How did all this happen in the first place? Why have we no memory of it? When were we recruited? 20

The first solicitations began when we were very young. If you close your eyes and think back, you may remember some of them. 21

You are four years old, tugging on your mother's sleeve in the supermarket. There are products down here at eye level that she cannot see. Cool products with cartoon faces on them. Toys familiar from Saturday morning television. You want them. She keeps pushing her cart. You cry. She doesn't understand. 22

You are eight. You have allowance money. You savor the buying experience. A Coke here, a Snickers bar there. Each little fix means not just getting what you want, but *power.* For a few moments *you* are the center of attention. *You* call the shots. People smile and scurry around serving you. 23

Michael Jordan goes up on your bedroom door. He is your first hero, throwing a glow around the first brand in your life—Nike. You wanna be like Mike. 24

Other heroes follow. Sometimes they contradict each other. Michael Jackson drinks Pepsi but Michael Jordan drinks Coke. Who is the false prophet? Your friends reinforce the brandhunting. Wearing the same stuff and hearing the same music makes you a fraternity, united in soul and form. 25

You watch TV. It's your sanctuary. You feel neither loneliness nor solitude here. 26

You enter the rebel years. You strut the malls, brandishing a Dr. Pepper can full of Scotch, which you drink right under the noses of the surveillance guards. One day you act drunk and trick them into "arresting" you—only this time it actually *is* soda in the can. You are immensely pleased with yourself. 27

You go to college, invest in a Powerbook, ride a Vespa scooter, don Doc Martens. In your town, a new sports complex and performing arts center name themselves after a car manufacturer and a software company. You have moved so far into the consumer maze that you can smell the cheese. 28

After graduating you begin to make a little money, and it's quite seductive. The more you have, the more you think about it. 29

30 You buy a house with three bathrooms. You park your BMW outside the double garage. When you grow depressed, you go shopping.

31 The cult rituals spread themselves evenly over the calendar: Christmas, Super Bowl, Easter, pay-per-view boxing match, summer Olympics, Mother's Day, Father's Day, Thanksgiving, Halloween. Each has its own imperatives—stuff you have to buy, things you have to do.

32 You're a lifer now. You're locked and loaded. On the go, trying to generate more income to buy more things and then, feeling dissatisfied but not quite sure why, setting your sights on even greater income and more acquisitions. When "consumer confidence is down," spending is "stagnant," the "retail sector" is "hurting" and "stingy consumers are giving stores the blues," you do your bit for the economy. You are a star.

33 Always, always you have been free to dream. The motivational speakers you watched on late-night TV preached that even the most sorry schleppers can achieve their goals if they visualize daily and stay committed. *Think and grow rich.*

34 Dreams, by definition, are supposed to be unique and imaginative. Yet the bulk of the population is dreaming the same dream. It's a dream of wealth, power, fame, plenty of sex and exciting recreational opportunities.

35 What does it mean when a whole culture dreams the same dream?

Examining the Text

1. What is the function of the story that opens this reading? What feelings does the story evoke in you?

2. What is the effect of all of the products and brand names that Lasn includes in this article?

3. How does Lasn define the term "cult"? How is his definition different from (and similar to) the common usage of this word?

4. *Thinking rhetorically*: In this article, Lasn uses the rhetorical strategy of direct address—that is, he uses the pronoun "you" and directly addresses readers of the article. Why do you think Lasn uses this strategy? What effect does it have on you as a reader? How does the strategy of direct address contribute to (or detract from) Lasn's argument?

For Group Discussion

Discuss the characteristics of the cult that Lasn describes. Who are its members (and nonmembers)? What are its rules? How are we initiated into this cult? What are the cult's beliefs and rituals? How do we get ourselves out of this cult? After discussing these questions, decide on the extent to which you're persuaded by Lasn's argument that contemporary consumer culture is a kind of cult.

BUY NOTHING DAY
NOVEMBER 29, 2002 WWW.ADBUSTERS.ORG

Writing Suggestion

Lasn ends his essay by asking, "What does it mean when a whole culture dreams the same dream?" Try writing a response to this question. What are the characteristics of this dream that Lasn claims are shared by the entire culture? Why is it a problem if everyone dreams the same dream? Alternately, you can take issue with the question itself, either by arguing that what it implies isn't true (in other words, that we each dream different dreams), or by arguing that it's perfectly acceptable if we all dream the same dream. Be sure to support any claims in your essay with specific evidence drawn from Lasn's argument as well as from your own experiences and observations.

You might consider using the black-and-white image above as one of the examples in your essay. This image, a poster for Adbuster's "Buy Nothing Day," graphically presents the problem Lasn discusses in "The Cult You're In," and it also points to a solution, of sorts. How might the image be used to bolster an argument either for or against Lasn's assertions?

Advertising's Fifteen Basic Appeals

JIB FOWLES

In the following essay, Jib Fowles looks at how advertisements work by examining the emotional, subrational appeals that they employ. We are confronted daily by hundreds of ads, only a few of which actually attract our attention. These few do so, according to Fowles, through "something primary and primitive, an emotional appeal, that in effect is the thin edge of the wedge, trying to find its way into a mind." Drawing on research done by the psychologist Henry A. Murray, Fowles describes fifteen emotional appeals or wedges that advertisements exploit.

Underlying Fowles's psychological analysis of advertising is the assumption that advertisers try to circumvent the logical, cautious, skeptical powers we develop as consumers, to reach, instead, the "unfulfilled urges and motives swirling in the bottom half of [our] minds." In Fowles's view, consumers are well advised to pay attention to these underlying appeals in order to avoid responding unthinkingly.

As you read, *note which of Fowles's fifteen appeals seem most familiar to you. Do you recognize these appeals in ads you can recall? How have you responded?*

EMOTIONAL APPEALS

The nature of effective advertisements was recognized full well by the late media philosopher Marshall McLuhan. In his *Understanding Media,* the first sentence of the section on advertising reads, "The continuous pressure is to create ads more and more in the image of audience motives and desires." 1

By giving form to people's deep-lying desires, and picturing states of being that individuals privately yearn for, advertisers have the best chance of arresting attention and affecting communication. And that is the immediate goal of advertising: to tug at our psychological shirt sleeves and slow us down long enough for a word or two about whatever is being sold. We glance at a picture of a solitary rancher at work, and "Marlboro" slips into our minds. 2

Advertisers (I'm using the term as a shorthand for both the products' manufacturers, who bring the ambition and money to the process, and the advertising agencies, who supply the know-how) are ever more compelled to invoke consumers' drives and longings; this is the "continuous pressure" McLuhan refers to. Over the past century, the American marketplace has grown increasingly congested as more and more products have entered into the frenzied competition after the public's dollars. The economies of other nations are quieter than ours since the volume of goods being hawked does not so greatly exceed demand. In some economies, consumer wares are scarce enough that no advertising at all is necessary. But in the United States, we go to the other extreme. In order to stay in business, an advertiser must strive to cut through the considerable commercial hub-bub by any means available—including the emotional appeals that some observers have held to be abhorrent and underhanded. 3

The use of subconscious appeals is a comment not only on conditions among sellers. As time has gone by, buyers have become stoutly resistant to advertisements. We live in a blizzard of these messages and have learned to turn up our collars and ward off most of them. A study done a few years ago at Harvard University's Graduate School of Business Administration ventured that the average American is exposed to some 500 ads daily from television, newspapers, magazines, radio, billboards, direct mail, and so on. If for no other reason than to preserve one's sanity, a filter must be developed in every mind to lower the number of ads a person is actually aware of—a number this particular study estimated at about seventy-five ads per day. (Of these, only twelve typically produced a reaction—nine positive and three negative, on the average.) To be among the few messages that do manage to gain access to minds, advertisers must be strategic, perhaps even a little underhanded at times. 4

There are assumptions about personality underlying advertisers' efforts to communicate via emotional appeals, and while these assumptions have stood the test of time, they still deserve to be aired. Human beings, it is presumed, walk around with a variety of unfulfilled urges and motives swirling in the bottom half of their minds. Lusts, ambitions, tendernesses, vulnerabilities—they are constantly bubbling up, seeking resolution. These mental forces energize people, but they are too crude and irregular to be given excessive play in the real world. They must be capped with the competent, sensible behavior that permits individuals to get along well in society. However, this upper layer of mental activity, shot through with caution and rationality, is not receptive to advertising's pitches. Advertisers want to circumvent this shell of consciousness if they can, and latch on to one of the lurching, subconscious drives. 5

In effect, advertisers over the years have blindly felt their way around the underside of the American psyche, and by trial and error have discovered the softest points of entree, the places where their messages have the greatest likelihood of getting by consumers' defenses. As McLuhan says elsewhere, "Gouging away at the surface of public sales resistance, the ad men are constantly breaking through into the *Alice in Wonderland* territory behind the looking glass, which is the world of subrational impulses and appetites." 6

An advertisement communicates by making use of a specially selected image (of a supine female, say, or a curly-haired child, or a celebrity) which is designed to stimulate "subrational impulses and desires" even when they are at ebb, even if they are unacknowledged by their possessor. Some few ads have their emotional appeal in the text, but for the greater number by far the appeal is contained in the artwork. This makes sense, since visual communication better suits more primal 7 levels of the brain. If the viewer of an advertisement actually has the importuned motive, and if the appeal is sufficiently well fashioned to call it up, then the person can be hooked. The product in the ad may then appear to take on the semblance of gratification for the summoned motive. Many ads seem to be saying, "If you have this need, then this product will help satisfy it." It is a primitive equation, but not an ineffective one for selling.

Thus, most advertisements appearing in national media can be understood as having two orders of content. The first is the appeal to deep-running drives in the minds of consumers. The second is information regarding the good[s] or service being sold: its name, its manufacturer, its picture, its packaging, its objective attributes, its functions. For example, the reader of a brassiere advertisement sees a partially undraped but blandly unperturbed woman standing in an otherwise commonplace public setting, and may experience certain sensations; the reader also sees the name "Maidenform," a particular brassiere style, and, in tiny print, words about the material, colors, price. Or, the viewer of a television commercial sees a demonstration with four small boxes labeled 650, 650, 650, and 800; something in the viewer's mind catches hold of this, as trivial as thoughtful consideration might reveal it to be. The viewer is also exposed to the name "Anacin," its bottle, and its purpose. 8

Sometimes there is an apparently logical link between an ad's emotional appeal and its product information. It does not violate common sense that Cadillac automobiles be photographed at country clubs, or that Japan Air Lines be associated with Orientalia. But there is no real need for the linkage to have a bit of reason behind it. Is there anything inherent to the connection between Salem cigarettes and mountains, Coke and a smile, Miller Beer and comradeship? The link being forged in minds between product and appeal is a pre-logical one. 9

People involved in the advertising industry do not necessarily talk in the terms being used here. They are stationed at the sending end of this communications channel, and may think they are up to any number of things—Unique Selling Propositions, explosive copywriting, the optimal use of demographics or psychographics, ideal media buys, high recall ratings, or whatever. But when attention shifts to the receiving end of the channel, and focuses on the instant of reception, then commentary becomes much more elemental: an advertising message contains something primary and primitive, an emotional appeal, that in effect is the thin end of the wedge, trying to find its way into a mind. Should this occur, the product information comes along behind. 10

When enough advertisements are examined in this light, it becomes clear that the emotional appeals fall into several distinguishable 11 categories, and that every ad is a variation on one of a limited number of basic appeals. While there may be several ways of classifying these appeals, one particular list of fifteen has proven to be especially valuable.

Advertisements can appeal to:

1. The need for sex
2. The need for affiliation
3. The need to nurture
4. The need for guidance
5. The need to aggress
6. The need to achieve
7. The need to dominate
8. The need for prominence
9. The need for attention
10. The need for autonomy
11. The need to escape
12. The need to feel safe
13. The need for aesthetic sensations
14. The need to satisfy curiosity
15. Physiological needs: food, drink, sleep, etc.

MURRAY'S LIST

Where does this list of advertising's fifteen basic appeals come from? 12
Several years ago, I was involved in a research project which was to have as one segment an objective analysis of the changing appeals made in post–World War II American advertising. A sample of magazine ads would have their appeals coded into the categories of psychological needs they seemed aimed at. For this content analysis to happen, a complete roster of human motives would have to be found.

The first thing that came to mind was Abraham Maslow's famous 13
four-part hierarchy of needs. But the briefest look at the range of appeals made in advertising was enough to reveal that they are more varied, and more profane, than Maslow had cared to account for. The search led on to the work of psychologist Henry A. Murray, who together with his colleagues at the Harvard Psychological Clinic has constructed a full taxonomy of needs. As described in *Explorations in Personality,* Murray's team had conducted a lengthy series of in-depth interviews with a number of subjects in order to derive from scratch what they felt to be the essential variables of personality. Forty-four

variables were distinguished by the Harvard group, of which twenty were motives. The need for achievement ("to overcome obstacles and obtain a high standard") was one, for instance; the need to defer was another; the need to aggress was a third; and so forth.

Murray's list had served as the groundwork for a number of subsequent projects. Perhaps the best-known of these was David C. McClelland's extensive study of the need for achievement, reported in his *The Achieving Society.* In the process of demonstrating that a people's high need for achievement is predictive of later economic growth, McClelland coded achievement imagery and references out of a nation's folklore, songs, legends, and children's tales. 14

Following McClelland, I too wanted to cull the motivational appeals from a culture's imaginative product—in this case, advertising. To develop categories expressly for this purpose, I took Murray's twenty motives and added to them others he had mentioned in passing in *Explorations in Personality* but not included on the final list. The extended list was tried out on a sample of advertisements, and motives which never seemed to be invoked were dropped. I ended up with eighteen of Murray's motives, into which 770 print ads were coded. The resulting distribution is included in the 1976 book *Mass Advertising as Social Forecast.* 15

Since that time, the list of appeals has undergone refinements as a result of using it to analyze television commercials. A few more adjustments stemmed from the efforts of students in my advertising classes to decode appeals; tens of term papers surveying thousands of advertisements have caused some inconsistencies in the list to be hammered out. Fundamentally, though, the list remains the creation of Henry Murray. In developing a comprehensive, parsimonious inventory of human motives, he pinpointed the subsurface mental forces that are the least quiescent and most susceptible to advertising's entreaties. 16

FIFTEEN APPEALS

1. *Need for sex.* Let's start with sex, because this is the appeal which seems to pop up first whenever the topic of advertising is raised. Whole books have been written about this one alone, to find a large audience of mildly titillated readers. Lately, due to campaigns to sell blue jeans, concern with sex in ads has redoubled. 17

The fascinating thing is not how much sex there is in advertising, but how little. Contrary to impressions, unambiguous sex is rare in these messages. Some of this surprising observation may be a matter of definition: the Jordache ads with the lithe, blouse-less female astride a similarly clad male is clearly an appeal to the audience's sexual drives, 18 but the same cannot be said about Brooke Shields in the Calvin Klein commercials. Directed at young women and their credit-card carrying mothers, the image of Miss Shields instead invokes the need to be looked at. Buy Calvins and you'll be the center of much attention, just as Brooke is, the ads imply; they do not primarily inveigle their target audience's need for sexual intercourse.

In the content analysis reported in *Mass Advertising as Social Forecast,* only two percent of ads were found to pander to this motive. Even *Playboy* ads shy away from sexual appeals: a recent issue contained eighty-three full-page ads, and just four of them (or less than five percent) could be said to have sex on their minds. 19

The reason this appeal is so little used is that it is too blaring and tends to obliterate the product information. Nudity in advertising has the effect of reducing brand recall. The people who do remember the product may do so because they have been made indignant by the ad; this is not the response most advertisers seek. 20

To the extent that sexual imagery is used, it conventionally works better on men than women; typically a female figure is offered up to the male reader. A Black Velvet liquor advertisement displays an attractive woman wearing a tight black outfit, recumbent under the legend, "Feel the Velvet." The figure does not have to be horizontal, however, for the appeal to be present as National Airlines revealed in its "Fly me" campaign. Indeed, there does not even have to be a female in the ad; "Flick my Bic" was sufficient to convey the idea to many. 21

As a rule, though, advertisers have found sex to be a tricky appeal, to be used sparingly. Less controversial and equally fetching are the appeals to our need for affectionate human contact. 22

2. *Need for affiliation.* American mythology upholds autonomous individuals, and social statistics suggest that people are ever more going it alone in their lives, yet the high frequency of affiliative appeals in ads belies this. Or maybe it does not: maybe all the images of companionship are compensation for what Americans privately lack. In any case, the need to associate with others is widely invoked in advertising and is probably the most prevalent appeal. All sorts of goods and services are sold by linking them to our unfulfilled desires to be in good company. 23

According to Henry Murray, the need for affiliation consists of desires "to draw near and enjoyably cooperate or reciprocate with another; to please and win affection of another; to adhere and remain loyal to a friend." The manifestations of this motive can be segmented into several different types of affiliation, beginning with romance. 24

Courtship may be swifter nowadays, but the desire for pair-bonding is far from satiated. Ads reaching for this need commonly depict a youngish male and female engrossed in each other. The head of the male is usually higher than the female's, even at this late date; she 25 may be sitting or leaning while he is standing. They are not touching in the Smirnoff vodka ads, but obviously there is an intimacy, sometimes frolicsome, between them. The couple does touch for Martell Cognac when "The moment was Martell." For Wind Song perfume they have touched, and "Your Wind Song stays on his mind."

Depending on the audience, the pair does not absolutely have to be young—just together. He gives her a DeBeers diamond, and there is a tear in her laugh lines. She takes Geritol and preserves herself for him. And numbers of consumers, wanting affection too, follow suit. 26

Warm family feelings are fanned in ads when another generation is added to the pair. Hallmark Cards brings grandparents into the picture, and Johnson and Johnson Baby Powder has Dad, Mom, and baby, all fresh from the bath, encircled in arms and emblazoned with "Share the Feeling." A talc has been fused to familial love. 27

Friendship is yet another form of affiliation pursued by advertisers. Two women confide and drink Maxwell House coffee together; two men walk through the woods smoking Salem cigarettes. Miller Beer promises that afternoon "Miller Time" will be staffed with three or four good buddies. Drink Dr. Pepper, as Mickey Rooney is coaxed to do, and join in with all the other Peppers. Coca-Cola does not even need to portray the friendliness; it has reduced this appeal to "a Coke and a smile." 28

The warmth can be toned down and disguised, but it is the same affiliative need that is being fished for. The blonde has a direct gaze and her friends are firm businessmen in appearance, but with a glass of Old Bushmills you can sit down and fit right in. Or, for something more upbeat, sing along with the Pontiac choirboys. 29

As well as presenting positive images, advertisers can play to the need for affiliation in negative ways, by invoking the fear of rejection. If we don't use Scope, we'll have the "Ugh! Morning Breath" that causes the male and female models to avert their faces. Unless we apply Ultra Brite or Close-Up to our teeth, it's good-bye romance. Our family will be cursed with "House-a-tosis" if we don't take care. Without Dr. Scholl's antiperspirant foot spray, the bowling team will keel over. There go all the guests when the supply of Dorito's nacho cheese chips is exhausted. Still more rejection if our shirts have ring-around-the-collar, if our car needs to be Midasized. But make a few purchases, and we are back in the bosom of human contact. 30

As self-directed as Americans pretend to be, in the last analysis we remain social animals, hungering for the positive, endorsing feelings that only those around us can supply. Advertisers respond, urging us to "Reach out and touch someone," in the hopes our monthly bills will rise. 31

3. *Need to nurture.* Akin to affiliative needs is the need to take care of small, defenseless creatures—children and pets, largely. Reciprocity is of less consequence here, though; it is the giving that counts. Murray 32

uses synonyms like "to feed, help, support, console, protect, comfort, nurse, heal." A strong need it is, woven deep into our genetic fabric, for if it did not exist we could not successfully raise up our replacements. When advertisers put forth the image of something diminutive and furry, something that elicits the word "cute" or "precious," then they are trying to trigger this motive. We listen to the childish voice singing the Oscar Mayer wiener song, and our next hotdog purchase is prescribed. Aren't those darling kittens something, and how did this Meow Mix get into our shopping cart?

This pitch is often directed at women, as Mother Nature's chief nurturers. "Make me some Kraft macaroni and cheese, please," says the elfin preschooler just in from the snowstorm, and mothers' hearts go out, and Kraft's sales go up. "We're cold, wet, and hungry," whine the husband and kids, and the little woman gets the Manwiches ready. A facsimile of this need can be hit without children or pets: the husband is ill and sleepless in the television commercial, and the wife grudgingly fetches the NyQuil. 33

But it is not women alone who can be touched by this appeal. The father nurses his son Eddie through adolescence while the John Deere lawn tractor survives the years. Another father counts pennies with his young son as the subject of New York Life Insurance comes up. And all over America are businessmen who don't know why they dial Qantas Airlines when they have to take a trans-Pacific trip; the koala bear knows. 34

4. *Need for guidance.* The opposite of the need to nurture is the need to be nurtured: to be protected, shielded, guided. We may be loath to admit it, but the child lingers on inside every adult—and a good thing it does, or we would not be instructable in our advancing years. Who wants a nation of nothing but flinty personalities? 35

Parent-like figures can successfully call up this need. Robert Young recommends Sanka coffee, and since we have experienced him for twenty-five years as television father and doctor, we take his word for it. Florence Henderson as the expert mom knows a lot about the advantages of Wesson oil. 36

The parent-ness of the spokesperson need not be so salient; sometimes pure authoritativeness is better. When Orson Welles scowls and intones, "Paul Masson will sell no wine before its time," we may not know exactly what he means, but we still take direction from him. There is little maternal about Brenda Vaccaro when she speaks up for Tampax, but there is a certainty to her that many accept. 37

A celebrity is not a necessity in making a pitch to the need for guidance, since a fantasy figure can serve just as well. People accede to the Green Giant, or Betty Crocker, or Mr. Goodwrench. Some advertisers can get by with no figure at all: "When E.F. Hutton talks, people listen." 38

Often it is tradition or custom that advertisers point to and consumers take guidance from. Bits and pieces of American history are used to sell whiskeys like Old Crow, Southern Comfort, Jack Daniel's. We conform to traditional male/female roles and age-old social norms when we purchase Barclay cigarettes, which informs us *"The pleasure is back."* 39

The product itself, if it has been around for a long time, can constitute a tradition. All those old labels in the ad for Morton salt convince us that we should continue to buy it. Kool-Aid says "You loved it as a kid. You trust it as a mother," hoping to get yet more consumers to go along. 40

Even when the product has no history at all, our need to conform to tradition and to be guided are strong enough that they can be invoked through bogus nostalgia and older actors. Country-Time lemonade sells because consumers want to believe it has a past they can defer to. 41

So far the needs and the ways they can be invoked which have been looked at are largely warm and affiliative; they stand in contrast to the next set of needs, which are much more egoistic and assertive. 42

5. *Need to aggress.* The pressures of the real world create strong retaliatory feelings in every functioning human being. Since these impulses can come forth as bursts of anger and violence, their display is normally tabooed. Existing as harbored energy, aggressive drives present a large, tempting target for advertisers. It is not a target to be aimed at thoughtlessly, though, for few manufacturers want their products associated with destructive motives. There is always the danger that, as in the case of sex, if the appeal is too blatant, public opinion will turn against what is being sold. 43

Jack-in-the-Box sought to abruptly alter its marketing by going after older customers and forgetting the younger ones. Their television commercials had a seventy-ish lady command, "Waste him," and the Jack-in-the-Box clown exploded before our eyes. So did public reaction until the commercials were toned down. Print ads for Club cocktails carried the faces of octogenarians under the headline, "Hit me with a Club"; response was contrary enough to bring the campaign to a stop. 44

Better disguised aggressive appeals are less likely to backfire: Triumph cigarettes has models making a lewd gesture with their uplifted cigarettes, but the individuals are often laughing and usually in close company of others. When Exxon said, "There's a Tiger in your tank," the implausibility of it concealed the invocation of aggressive feelings. 45

Depicted arguments are a common way for advertisers to tap the audience's needs to aggress. Don Rickles and Lynda Carter trade gibes, and consumers take sides as the name of Seven-Up is stitched on 46 minds. The Parkay tub has a difference of opinion with the user; who can forget it, or who (or what) got the last word in?

6. *Need to achieve.* This is the drive that energizes people, causing them to strive in their lives and careers. According to Murray, the need for achievement is signalled by the desires "to accomplish something difficult. To overcome obstacles and attain a high standard. To excel one's self. To rival and surpass others." A prominent American trait, it is one that advertisers like to hook on to because it identifies their product with winning and success. 47

The Cutty Sark ad does not disclose that Ted Turner failed at his latest attempt at yachting's America Cup; here he is represented as a champion on the water as well as off in his television enterprises. If we drink this whiskey, we will be victorious alongside Turner. We can also succeed with O.J. Simpson by renting Hertz cars, or with Reggie Jackson by bringing home some Panasonic equipment. Cathy Rigby and Stayfree Maxipads will put people out front. 48

Sports heroes are the most convenient means to snare consumers' needs to achieve, but they are not the only one. Role models can be established, ones which invite emulation, as with the profiles put forth by Dewar's scotch. Successful, tweedy individuals relate they have "graduated to the flavor of Myer's rum." Or the advertiser can establish a prize: two neighbors play one-on-one basketball for a Michelob beer in a television commercial, while in a print ad a bottle of Johnnie Walker Black Label has been gilded like a trophy. 49

Any product that advertises itself in superlatives—the best, the first, the finest—is trying to make contact with our needs to succeed. For many consumers, sales and bargains belong in this category of appeals, too; the person who manages to buy something at fifty percent off is seizing an opportunity and coming out ahead of others. 50

7. *Need to dominate.* This fundamental need is the craving to be powerful—perhaps omnipotent, as in the Xerox ad where Brother Dominic exhibits heavenly powers and creates miraculous copies. Most of us will settle for being just a regular potentate, though. We drink Budweiser because it is the King of Beers, and here comes the powerful Clydesdales to prove it. A taste of Wolfschmidt vodka and "The spirit of the Czar lives on." 51

The need to dominate and control one's environment is often thought of as being masculine, but as close students of human nature advertisers know, it is not so circumscribed. Women's aspirations for control are suggested in the campaign theme, "I like my men in English Leather, or nothing at all." The females in the Chanel No. 19 ads are "outspoken" and wrestle their men around. 52

Male and female, what we long for is clout; what we get in its place is Mastercard. 53

8. *Need for prominence.* Here comes the need to be admired and respected, to enjoy prestige and high social status. These times, it appears, are not so egalitarian after all. Many ads picture the trappings of high position; the Oldsmobile stands before a manorial doorway, the Volvo is parked beside a steeplechase. A book-lined study is the setting for Dewar's 12, and Lenox China is displayed in a dining room chock full of antiques. 54

Beefeater gin represents itself as "The Crown Jewel of England" and uses no illustrations of jewels or things British, for the words are sufficient indicators of distinction. Buy that gin and you will rise up the prestige hierarchy, or achieve the same effect on yourself with Seagram's 7 Crown, which ambiguously describes itself as "classy." 55

Being respected does not have to entail the usual accoutrements of wealth: "Do you know who I am?" the commercials ask, and we learn that the prominent person is not so prominent without his American Express card. 56

9. *Need for attention.* The previous need involved being *looked up to,* while this is the need to be *looked at.* The desire to exhibit ourselves in such a way as to make others look at us is a primitive, insuppressible instinct. The clothing and cosmetic industries exist just to serve this need, and this is the way they pitch their wares. Some of this effort is aimed at males, as the ads for Hathaway shirts and Jockey underclothes. But the greater bulk of such appeals is targeted singlemindedly at women. 57

To come back to Brooke Shields: this is where she fits into American marketing. If I buy Calvin Klein jeans, consumers infer, I'll be the object of fascination. The desire for exhibition has been most strikingly played to in a print campaign of many years' duration, that of Maidenform lingerie. The woman exposes herself, and sales surge. "Gentlemen prefer Hanes" the ads dissemble, and women who want eyes upon them know what they should do. Peggy Fleming flutters her legs for L'eggs, encouraging females who want to be the star in their own lives to purchase this product. 58

The same appeal works for cosmetics and lotions. For years, the little girl with the exposed backside sold gobs of Coppertone, but now the company has picked up the pace a little: as a female, you are supposed to "Flash 'em a Coppertone tan." Food can be sold the same way, especially to the diet-conscious; Angie Dickinson poses for California avocados and says, "Would this body lie to you?" Our eyes are too fixed on her for us to think to ask if she got that way by eating mounds of guacamole. 59

10. *Need for autonomy.* There are several ways to sell credit card services, as has been noted: Mastercard appeals to the need to dominate, and American Express to the need for prominence. When Visa 60

claims, "You can have it the way you want it," yet another primary motive is being beckoned forward—the need to endorse the self. The focus here is upon the independence and integrity of the individual; this need is the antithesis of the need for guidance and is unlike any of the social needs. "If running with the herd isn't your style, try ours," says Rotan-Mosle, and many Americans feel they have finally found the right brokerage firm.

The photo is of a red-coated Mountie on his horse, posed on 61
a snow-covered ledge; the copy reads, "Windsor—One Canadian stands alone." This epitome of the solitary and proud individual may work best with male customers, as may Winston's man in the red cap. But one-figure advertisements also strike the strong need for autonomy among American women. As Shelly Hack strides for Charlie perfume, females respond to her obvious pride and flair; she is her own person. The Virginia Slims tale is of people who have come a long way from subservience to independence. Cachet perfume feels it does not need a solo figure to work this appeal, and uses three different faces in its ads; it insists, though, "It's different on every woman who wears it."

Like many psychological needs, this one can also be appealed 62
to in a negative fashion, by invoking the loss of independence or self-regard. Guilt and regrets can be stimulated: "Gee, I could have had a V-8." Next time, get one and be good to yourself.

11. *Need to escape.* An appeal to the need for autonomy often co- 63
occurs with one for the need to escape, since the desire to duck out of our social obligations, to seek rest or adventure, frequently takes the form of one-person flight. The dashing image of a pilot, in fact, is a standard way of quickening this need to get away from it all.

Freedom is the pitch here, the freedom that every individual 64
yearns for whenever life becomes too oppressive. Many advertisers like appealing to the need for escape because the sensation of pleasure often accompanies escape, and what nicer emotional nimbus could there be for a product? "You deserve a break today," says McDonald's, and Stouffer's frozen foods chime in, "Set yourself free."

For decades men have imaginatively bonded themselves to 65
the Marlboro cowboy who dwells untarnished and unencumbered in Marlboro Country some distance from modern life; smokers' aching needs for autonomy and escape are personified by that cowpoke. Many women can identify with the lady ambling through the woods behind the words, "Benson and Hedges and mornings and me."

But escape does not have to be solitary. Other Benson and 66
Hedges ads, part of the same campaign, contain two strolling figures. In Salem cigarette advertisements, it can be several people who escape together into the mountaintops. A commercial for Levi's

pictured a cloudbank above a city through which ran a whole chain of young people.

There are varieties of escape, some wistful like the Boeing "Someday" campaign of dream vacations, some kinetic like the play and parties in soft drink ads. But in every instance, the consumer exposed to the advertisement is invited to momentarily depart his everyday life for a more carefree experience, preferably with the product in hand. 67

12. *Need to feel safe.* Nobody in their right mind wants to be intimidated, menaced, battered, poisoned. We naturally want to do whatever it takes to stave off threats to our well-being, and to our families'. It is the instinct of self-preservation that makes us responsive to the ad of the St. Bernard with the keg of Chivas Regal. We pay attention to the stern talk of Karl Malden and the plight of the vacationing couples who have lost all their funds in the American Express travelers cheques commercials. We want the omnipresent stag from Hartford Insurance to watch over us too. 68

In the interest of keeping failure and calamity from our lives, we like to see the durability of products demonstrated. Can we ever forget that Timex takes a licking and keeps on ticking? When the American Tourister suitcase bounces all over the highway and the egg inside doesn't break, the need to feel safe has been adroitly plucked. 69

We take precautions to diminish future threats. We buy Volkswagen Rabbits for the extraordinary mileage, and MONY insurance policies to avoid the tragedies depicted in their black-and-white ads of widows and orphans. 70

We are careful about our health. We consume Mazola margarine because it has "corn goodness" backed by the natural food traditions of the American Indians. In the medicine cabinet is Alka-Seltzer, the "home remedy"; having it, we are snug in our little cottage. 71

We want to be safe and secure; buy these products, advertisers are saying, and you'll be safer than you are without them. 72

13. *Need for aesthetic sensations.* There is an undeniable aesthetic component to virtually every ad run in the national media: the photography or filming or drawing is near-perfect, the type style is well chosen, the layout could scarcely be improved upon. Advertisers know there is little chance of good communication occurring if an ad is not visually pleasing. Consumers may not be aware of the extent of their own sensitivity to artwork, but it is undeniably large. 73

Sometimes the aesthetic element is expanded and made into an ad's primary appeal. Charles Jordan shoes may or may not appear in the accompanying avant-grade photographs; Kohler plumbing fixtures catch attention through the high style of their desert settings. Beneath the slightly out of focus photograph, languid and sensuous in tone, 74

General Electric feels called upon to explain, "This is an ad for the hair dryer."

This appeal is not limited to female consumers: J&B scotch says 75
"It whispers" and shows a bucolic scene of lake and castle.

14. *Need to satisfy curiosity.* It may seem odd to list a need for 76
information among basic motives, but this need can be as primal and compelling as any of the others. Human beings are curious by nature, interested in the world around them, and intrigued by tidbits of knowledge and new developments. Trivia, percentages, observations counter to conventional wisdom—these items all help sell products. Any advertisement in a question-and-answer format is strumming this need.

A dog groomer has a question about long distance rates, and Bell 77
Telephone has a chart with all the figures. An ad for Porsche 911 is replete with diagrams and schematics, numbers and arrows. Lo and behold, Anacin pills have 150 more milligrams than its competitors; should we wonder if this is better or worse for us?

15. *Physiological needs.* To the extent that sex is solely a biological 78
need, we are now coming around full circle, back toward the start of the list. In this final category are clustered appeals to sleeping, eating, drinking. The art of photographing food and drink is so advanced, sometimes these temptations are wondrously caught in the camera's lens: the crab meat in the Red Lobster restaurant ads can start us salivating, the Quarterpounder can almost be smelled, the liquor in the glass glows invitingly. Imbibe, these ads scream.

STYLES

Some common ingredients of advertisements were not singled out 79
for separate mention in the list of fifteen because they are not appeals in and of themselves. They are stylistic features, influencing the way a basic appeal is presented. The use of humor is one, and the use of celebrities is another. A third is time imagery, past and future, which goes to several purposes.

For all of its employment in advertising, humor can be treacher- 80
ous, because it can get out of hand and smother the product information. Supposedly, this is what Alka-Seltzer discovered with its comic commercials of the late sixties; "I can't believe I ate the whole thing," the sad-faced husband lamented, and the audience cackled so much it forgot the antacid. Or, did not take it seriously.

But used carefully, humor can punctuate some of the softer ap- 81
peals and soften some of the harsher ones. When Emma says to the Fruit-of-the-Loom fruits, "Hi, cuties. Whatcha doing in my laundry

basket?" we smile as our curiosity is assuaged along with hers. Bill Cosby gets consumers tickled about the children in his Jell-O commercials, and strokes the need to nurture.

An insurance company wants to invoke the need to feel safe, but does not want to leave readers with an unpleasant aftertaste; cartoonist Rowland Wilson creates an avalanche about to crush a gentleman who is saying to another, "My insurance company? New England Life, of course. Why?" The same tactic of humor undercutting threat is used in the cartoon commercials for Safeco when the Pink Panther wanders from one disaster to another. Often humor masks aggression: comedian Bob Hope in the outfit of a boxer promises to knock out the knock-knocks with Texaco; Rodney Dangerfield, who "can't get no respect," invites aggression as the comic relief in Miller Lite commercials. 82

Roughly fifteen percent of all advertisements incorporate a celebrity, almost always from the fields of entertainment or sports. The approach can also prove troublesome for advertisers, for celebrities are human beings too, and fully capable of the most remarkable behavior. If anything distasteful about them emerges, it is likely to reflect on the product. The advertisers making use of Anita Bryant and Billy Jean King suffered several anxious moments. An untimely death can also react poorly on a product. But advertisers are willing to take risks because celebrities can be such a good link between producers and consumers, performing the social role of introducer. 83

There are several psychological needs these middlemen can play upon. Let's take the product class of cameras and see how different celebrities can hit different needs. The need for guidance can be invoked by Michael Landon, who plays such a wonderful dad on "Little House on the Prairie"; when he says to buy Kodak equipment, many people listen. James Garner for Polaroid cameras is put in a similar authoritative role, so defined by a mocking spouse. The need to achieve is summoned up by Tracy Austin and other tennis stars for Canon AE-1; the advertiser first makes sure we see these athletes playing to win. When Cheryl Tiegs speaks up for Olympus cameras, it is the need for attention that is being targeted. 84

The past and future, being outside our grasp, are exploited by advertisers as locales for the projection of needs. History can offer up heroes (and call up the need to achieve) or traditions (need for guidance) as well as art objects (need for aesthetic sensations). Nostalgia is a kindly version of personal history and is deployed by advertisers to rouse needs for affiliation and for guidance; the need to escape can come in here, too. The same need to escape is sometimes the point of futuristic appeals but picturing the avant-garde can also be a way to get at the need to achieve. 85

ANALYZING ADVERTISEMENTS

When analyzing ads yourself for their emotional appeals, it takes a bit of practice to learn to ignore the product information (as well as one's own experience and feelings about the product). But that skill comes soon enough, as does the ability to quickly sort out from all the non-product aspects of an ad the chief element which is the most striking, the most likely to snag attention first and penetrate brains farthest. The key to the appeal, this element usually presents itself centrally and forwardly to the reader or viewer. 86

Another clue: the viewing angle which the audience has on the ad's subjects is informative. If the subjects are photographed or filmed from below and thus are looking down at you much as the Green Giant does, then the need to be guided is a good candidate for the ad's emotional appeal. If, on the other hand, the subjects are shot from above and appear deferential, as is often the case with children or female models, then other needs are being appealed to. 87

To figure out an ad's emotional appeal, it is wise to know (or have a good hunch about) who the targeted consumers are; this can often be inferred from the magazine or television show it appears in. This piece of information is a great help in determining the appeal and in deciding between two different interpretations. For example, if an ad features a partially undressed female, this would typically signal one appeal for readers of *Penthouse* (need for sex) and another for readers of *Cosmopolitan* (need for attention). 88

It would be convenient if every ad made just one appeal, were aimed at just one need. Unfortunately, things are often not that simple. A cigarette ad with a couple at the edge of a polo field is trying to hit both the need for affiliation and the need for prominence; depending on the attitude of the male, dominance could also be an ingredient in this. An ad for Chimere perfume incorporates two photos: in the top one the lady is being commanding at a business luncheon (need to dominate), but in the lower one she is being bussed (need for affiliation). Better ads, however, seem to avoid being too diffused; in the study of post–World War II advertising described earlier, appeals grew more focused as the decades passed. As a rule of thumb, about sixty percent have two conspicuous appeals; the last twenty percent have three or more. Rather than looking for the greatest number of appeals, decoding ads is most productive when the loudest one or two appeals are discerned, since those are the appeals with the best chance of grabbing people's attention. 89

Finally, analyzing ads does not have to be a solo activity and probably should not be. The greater number of people there are involved, the better chance there is of transcending individual biases and discerning the essential emotional lure built into an advertisement. 90

DO THEY OR DON'T THEY?

Do the emotional appeals made in advertisements add up to the sinister manipulation of consumers?

It is clear that these ads work. Attention is caught, communication occurs between producers and consumers, and sales result. It turns out to be difficult to detail the exact relationship between a specific ad and a specific purchase, or even between a campaign and subsequent sales figures, because advertising is only one of a host of influences upon consumption. Yet no one is fooled by this lack of perfect proof; everyone knows that advertising sells. If this were not the case, then tight-fisted American businesses would not spend a total of fifty billion dollars annually on these messages. 91

But before anyone despairs that advertisers have our number to the extent that they can marshal us at will and march us like automatons to the check-out counters, we should recall the resiliency and obduracy of the American consumer. Advertisers may have uncovered the softest spots in minds, but that does not mean they have found truly gaping apertures. There is no evidence that advertising can get people to do things contrary to their self-interests. Despite all the finesse of advertisements, and all the subtle emotional tugs, the public resists the vast majority of the petitions. According to the marketing division of the A.C. Nielsen Company, a whopping seventy-five percent of all new products die within a year in the marketplace, the victims of consumer disinterest which no amount of advertising could overcome. The appeals in advertising may be the most captivating there are to be had, but they are not enough to entrap the wiley consumer. 92

The key to understanding the discrepancy between, on the one hand, the fact that advertising truly works, and, on the other, the fact that it hardly works, is to take into account the enormous numbers of people exposed to an ad. Modern-day communications permit an ad to be displayed to millions upon millions of individuals; if the smallest fraction of that audience can be moved to buy the product, then the ad has been successful. When one percent of the people exposed to a television advertising campaign reach for their wallets, that could be one million sales, which may be enough to keep the product in production and the advertisements coming. 93

In arriving at an evenhanded judgment about advertisements and their emotional appeals, it is good to keep in mind that many of the purchases which might be credited to these ads are experienced as genuinely gratifying to the consumer. We sincerely like the goods or service we have bought, and we may even like some of the emotional drapery that an ad suggests comes with it. It has sometimes been noted that the most avid students of advertisements are the people who have just 94 bought the product; they want to steep themselves in the associated imagery. This may be the reason that Americans, when polled, are not negative about advertising and do not disclose any sense of being misused. The volume of advertising may be an irritant, but the product information as well as the imaginative material in ads are partial compensation.

A productive understanding is that advertising messages in- 95
volve costs and benefits at both ends of the communications channel. For those few ads which do make contact, the consumer surrenders a moment of time, has the lower brain curried, and receives notice of a product; the advertiser has given up money and has increased the chance of sales. In this sort of communications activity, neither party can be said to be the loser.

Examining the Text

1. Fowles's claim in this essay is that advertisers try to tap into basic human needs and emotions, rather than consumers' intellect. How does he go about proving this claim? What examples or other proof strike you as particularly persuasive? Where do you see weaknesses in Fowles's argument?

2. What do advertisers assume about the personality of the consumer, according to Fowles? How do these assumptions contribute to the way they sell products? Do you think that these assumptions about personality are correct? Why or why not?

3. Fowles's list of advertising's fifteen basic appeals is, as he explains, derived from Henry Murray's inventory of human motives. Which of these motives strike you as the most significant or powerful? What other motives would you add to the list?

4. *Thinking rhetorically*: What do you think is Fowles's ultimate purpose in writing this article? Who is he targeting as the audience for his arguments, and what do you think he intends this audience to do or to think after reading the article? What, if any, real-world effects do you imagine Fowles wants to achieve by writing this article?

For Group Discussion

In his discussion of the way advertising uses "the need for sex" and "the need to aggress," Fowles debunks the persistent complaints about the use of sex and violence in the mass media. What current examples support Fowles's point? Discuss your responses to his explanations.

Writing Suggestion

Working with Fowles's list of the fifteen appeals of advertising, survey a recent magazine, looking at all the ads and categorizing them based on their predominant appeal. In an essay, describe what your results tell you about the magazine and its readership. Based on your survey, would you amend Fowles's list? What additions or deletions would you make?

How Advertising Informs to Our Benefit

JOHN E. CALFEE

This article, adapted from John E. Calfee's book Fear of Persuasion: A New Perspective on Advertising and Regulation, *provides a different view of the effect of advertising on our society. Calfee, a former Federal Trade Commission economist and a resident scholar at the American Enterprise Institute, argues that advertising actually provides many benefits to consumers. Calfee relates several specific cases in which advertisements spread important health information to people who might not have learned about it otherwise. Because advertisers have huge budgets and can reach into virtually every home through television, newspapers, billboards, and radio campaigns, advertisements have the potential to spread information in a way that government-sponsored public service initiatives cannot.*

Calfee also diverges from previous articles in this chapter by suggesting that regulations on advertising are unnecessary and counterproductive. Indeed, Calfee argues that advertising is, to a large extent, self-regulating. Free-market competition compels companies to be truthful, or else competitors will challenge their claims, resulting in negative publicity.

***As you read this article,** consider your own feelings about advertising: do you think it's a destructive force in our society or a valuable tool for disseminating information? Given the power and reach of advertising, how can it be used as a positive information resource?*

A great truth about advertising is that it is a tool for communicating information and shaping markets. It is one of the forces that compel sellers to cater to the desires of consumers. Almost everyone knows this because consumers use advertising every day, and they miss advertising when they cannot get it. This fact does not keep politicians and opinion leaders from routinely dismissing the value of advertising. But the truth is that people find advertising very useful indeed. 1

Of course, advertising primarily seeks to persuade and everyone knows this, too. The typical ad tries to induce a consumer to do one particular thing—usually, buy a product—instead of a thousand other things. There is nothing obscure about this purpose or what it means for buyers. Decades of data and centuries of intuition reveal that all consumers everywhere are deeply suspicious of what advertisers say and why they say it. This skepticism is in fact the driving force that makes advertising so effective. The persuasive purpose of advertising 2 and the skepticism with which it is met are two sides of a single process. Persuasion and skepticism work in tandem so advertising can do its job in competitive markets. Hence, ads represent the seller's self interest, consumers know this, and sellers know that consumers know it.

By understanding this process more fully, we can sort out much 3 of the popular confusion surrounding advertising and how it benefits consumers.

HOW USEFUL IS ADVERTISING?

Just how useful is the connection between advertising and informa- 4 tion? At first blush, the process sounds rather limited. Volvo ads tell consumers that Volvos have side-impact air bags, people learn a little about the importance of air bags, and Volvo sells a few more cars. This seems to help hardly anyone except Volvo and its customers.

But advertising does much more. It routinely provides immense 5 amounts of information that benefits primarily parties other than the advertiser. This may sound odd, but it is a logical result of market forces and the nature of information itself.

The ability to use information to sell products is an incentive to 6 create new information through research. Whether the topic is nutrition, safety, or more mundane matters like how to measure amplifier power, the necessity of achieving credibility with consumers and critics requires much of this research to be placed in the public domain, and that it rest upon some academic credentials. That kind of research typically produces results that apply to more than just the brands sold by the firm sponsoring the research. The lack of property rights to such "pure" information ensures that this extra information is available at no charge. Both consumers and competitors may borrow the new information for their own purposes.

Advertising also elicits additional information from other 7 sources. Claims that are striking, original, forceful or even merely obnoxious will generate news stories about the claims, the controversies they cause, the reactions of competitors (A price war? A splurge of comparison ads?), the reactions of consumers and the remarks of governments and independent authorities.

Probably the most concrete, pervasive, and persistent example 8 of competitive advertising that works for the public good is price advertising. Its effect is invariably to heighten competition and reduce prices, even the prices of firms that assiduously avoid mentioning prices in their own advertising.

There is another area where the public benefits of advertising 9 are less obvious but equally important. The unremitting nature of consumer interest in health, and the eagerness of sellers to cater to consumer desires, guarantee that advertising related to health will provide a storehouse of telling observations on the ways in which the benefits of advertising extend beyond the interests of advertisers to include the interests of the public at large.

A CASCADE OF INFORMATION

10 Here is probably the best documented example of why advertising is necessary for consumer welfare. In the 1970s, public health experts described compelling evidence that people who eat more fiber are less likely to get cancer, especially cancer of the colon, which happens to be the second leading cause of deaths from cancer in the United States. By 1979, the U.S. Surgeon General was recommending that people eat more fiber in order to prevent cancer.

11 Consumers appeared to take little notice of these recommendations, however. The National Cancer Institute decided that more action was needed. NCI's cancer prevention division undertook to communicate the new information about fiber and cancer to the general public. Their goal was to change consumer diets and reduce the risk of cancer, but they had little hope of success given the tiny advertising budgets of federal agencies like NCI.

12 Their prospects unexpectedly brightened in 1984. NCI received a call from the Kellogg Corporation, whose All-Bran cereal held a commanding market share of the high-fiber segment. Kellogg proposed to use All-Bran advertising as a vehicle for NCI's public service messages. NCI thought that was an excellent idea. Soon, an agreement was reached in which NCI would review Kellogg's ads and labels for accuracy and value before Kellogg began running their fiber–cancer ads.

13 The new Kellogg All-Bran campaign opened in October 1984. A typical ad began with the headline, "At last some news about cancer you can live with." The ad continued: "The National Cancer Institute believes a high-fiber, low-fat diet may reduce your risk of some kinds of cancer. . . . That's why one of their strongest recommendations is to eat high-fiber foods. If you compare, you'll find Kellogg's All-Bran has nine grams of fiber per serving. No other cereal has more. So start your day with a bowl of Kellogg's All-Bran or mix it with your regular cereal."

14 The campaign quickly achieved two things. One was to create a regulatory crisis between two agencies. The Food and Drug Administration thought that if a food was advertised as a way to prevent cancer, it was being marketed as a drug. Then the FDA's regulations for drug labeling would kick in. The food would be reclassified as a drug and would be removed from the market until the seller either stopped

making the health claims or put the product through the clinical testing necessary to obtain formal approval as a drug.

But food advertising is regulated by the Federal Trade Commis- 15
sion, not the FDA. The FTC thought Kellogg's ads were nondeceptive and were therefore perfectly legal. In fact, it thought the ads should be encouraged. The Director of the FTC's Bureau of Consumer Protection declared that "the [Kellogg] ad has presented important public health recommendations in an accurate, useful, and substantiated way. It informs the members of the public that there is a body of data suggesting certain relationships between cancer and diet that they may find important." The FTC won this political battle, and the ads continued.

The second instant effect of the All-Bran campaign was to un- 16
leash a flood of health claims. Vegetable oil manufacturers advertised that cholesterol was associated with coronary heart disease, and that vegetable oil does not contain cholesterol. Margarine ads did the same, and added that vitamin A is essential for good vision. Ads for calcium products (such as certain antacids) provided vivid demonstrations of the effects of osteoporosis (which weakens bones in old age), and recounted the advice of experts to increase dietary calcium as a way to prevent osteoporosis. Kellogg's competitors joined in citing the National Cancer Institute dietary recommendations.

Nor did things stop there. In the face of consumer demand for bet- 17
ter and fuller information, health claims quickly evolved from a blunt tool to a surprisingly refined mechanism. Cereals were advertised as high in fiber and low in sugar or fat or sodium. Ads for an upscale brand of bread noted: "Well, most high-fiber bran cereals may be high in fiber, but often only one kind: insoluble. It's this kind of fiber that helps promote regularity. But there's also a kind of fiber known as soluble, which most high-fiber bran cereals have in very small amounts, if at all. Yet diets high in this kind of fiber may actually lower your serum cholesterol, a risk factor for some heart diseases." Cereal boxes became convenient sources for a summary of what made for a good diet.

INCREASED INDEPENDENT INFORMATION

The ads also brought powerful secondary effects. These may have been 18
even more useful than the information that actually appeared in the ads themselves.

One effect was an increase in media coverage of diet and health. 19
Consumer Reports, a venerable and hugely influential magazine that carries no advertising, revamped its reports on cereals to emphasize fiber and other ingredients (rather than testing the foods to see how well they did at providing a complete diet for laboratory rats).

The health-claims phenomenon generated its own press coverage, with articles like "What Has All-Bran Wrought?" and "The Fiber Furor." These stories recounted the ads and the scientific information that prompted the ads; and articles on food and health proliferated. Anyone who lived through these years in the United States can probably remember the unending media attention to health claims and to diet and health generally.

Much of the information on diet and health was new. This was no 20
coincidence. Firms were sponsoring research on their products in the hope of finding results that could provide a basis for persuasive advertising claims. Oat bran manufacturers, for example, funded research on the impact of soluble fiber on blood cholesterol. When the results came out "wrong," as they did in a 1990 study published with great fanfare in *The New England Journal of Medicine,* the headline in *Advertising Age* was "Oat Bran Popularity Hitting the Skids," and it did indeed tumble. The manufacturers kept at the research, however, and eventually the best research supported the efficacy of oat bran in reducing cholesterol (even to the satisfaction of the FDA). Thus did pure advertising claims spill over to benefit the information environment at large.

The shift to higher fiber cereals encompassed brands that had 21
never undertaken the effort necessary to construct believable ads about fiber and disease. Two consumer researchers at the FDA reviewed these data and concluded they were "consistent with the successful educational impact of the Kellogg diet and health campaign: consumers seemed to be making an apparently thoughtful discrimination between high- and low-fiber cereals," and that the increased market shares for high-fiber non-advertised products represented "the clearest evidence of a successful consumer education campaign."

Perhaps most dramatic were the changes in consumer awareness 22
of diet and health. An FTC analysis of government surveys showed that when consumers were asked about how they could prevent cancer through their diet, the percentage who mentioned fiber increased from 4% before the 1979 Surgeon General's report to 8.5% in 1984 (after the report but before the All-Bran campaign) to 32% in 1986 after a year and a half or so of health claims (the figure in 1988 was 28%). By far the greatest increases in awareness were among women (who do most of the grocery shopping) and the less educated: up from 0% for women without a high school education in 1984 to 31% for the same group in 1986. For women with incomes of less than $15,000, the increase was from 6% to 28%.

The health-claims advertising phenomenon achieved what years 23
of effort by government agencies had failed to achieve. With its mastery of the art of brevity, its ability to command attention, and its use of television, brand advertising touched precisely the people the public

health community was most desperate to reach. The health claims expanded consumer information along a broad front. The benefits clearly extended far beyond the interests of the relatively few manufacturers who made vigorous use of health claims in advertising.

A PERVASIVE PHENOMENON

Health claims for foods are only one example, however, of a pervasive phenomenon—the use of advertising to provide essential health information with benefits extending beyond the interests of the advertisers themselves. 24

Advertising for soap and detergents, for example, once improved private hygiene and therefore, public health (hygiene being one of the underappreciated triumphs in twentieth century public health). Toothpaste advertising helped to do the same for teeth. When mass advertising for toothpaste and tooth powder began early in this century, tooth brushing was rare. It was common by the 1930s, after which toothpaste sales leveled off even though the advertising, of course, continued. When fluoride toothpastes became available, advertising generated interest in better teeth and professional dental care. Later, a "plaque reduction war" (which first involved mouthwashes, and later toothpastes) brought a new awareness of gum disease and how to prevent it. The financial gains to the toothpaste industry were surely dwarfed by the benefits to consumers in the form of fewer cavities and fewer lost teeth. 25

Health claims induced changes in foods, in nonfoods such as toothpaste, in publications ranging from university health letters to mainstream newspapers and magazines, and of course, consumer knowledge of diet and health. 26

These rippling effects from health claims in ads demonstrated the most basic propositions in the economics of information. Useful information initially failed to reach people who needed it because information producers could not charge a price to cover the costs of creating and disseminating pure information. And this problem was alleviated by advertising, sometimes in a most vivid manner. 27

Other examples of spillover benefits from advertising are far more common than most people realize. Even the much-maligned promotion of expensive new drugs can bring profound health benefits to patients and families, far exceeding what is actually charged for the products themselves. 28

The market processes that produce these benefits bear all the classic features of competitive advertising. We are not analyzing public service announcements here, but old-fashioned profit-seeking brand advertising. Sellers focused on the information that favored their own 29 products. They advertised it in ways that provided a close link with their own brand. It was a purely competitive enterprise, and the benefits to consumers arose from the imperatives of the competitive process.

One might see all this as simply an extended example of the eco- 30
nomics of information and greed. And indeed it is, if by greed one means the effort to earn a profit by providing what people are willing to pay for, even if what they want most is information rather than a tangible product. The point is that there is overwhelming evidence that unregulated economic forces dictate that much useful information will be provided by brand advertising, and only by brand advertising.

Of course, there is much more to the story. There is the question of 31
how competition does the good I have described without doing even more harm elsewhere. After all, firms want to tell people only what is good about their brands, and people often want to know what is wrong with the brands. It turns out that competition takes care of this problem, too.

ADVERTISING AND CONTEXT

It is often said that most advertising does not contain very much infor- 32
mation. In a way, this is true. Research on the contents of advertising typically finds just a few pieces of concrete information per ad. That's an average, of course. Some ads obviously contain a great deal of information. Still, a lot of ads are mainly images and pleasant talk, with little in the way of what most people would consider hard information. On the whole, information in advertising comes in tiny bits and pieces.

Cost is only one reason. To be sure, cramming more information 33
into ads is expensive. But more to the point is the fact that advertising plays off the information available from outside sources. Hardly anything about advertising is more important than the interplay between what the ad contains and what surrounds it. Sometimes this interplay is a burden for the advertiser because it is beyond his control. But the interchange between advertising and environment is also an invaluable tool for sellers. Ads that work in collaboration with outside information can communicate far more than they ever could on their own.

The upshot is advertising's astonishing ability to communicate a 34
great deal of information in a few words. Economy and vividness of expression almost always rely upon what is in the information environment. The famously concise "Think Small" and "Lemon" ads for the VW "Beetle" in the 1960s and 1970s were highly effective with buyers concerned about fuel economy, repair costs, and extravagant styling in American cars. This was a case where the less said, the better. The ads were more powerful when consumers were free to bring their own ideas about the issues to bear.

The same process is repeated over again for all sorts of products. Ads for computer modems once explained what they could be used for. Now a simple reference to the Internet is sufficient to conjure an elaborate mix of equipment and applications. These matters are better left vague so each potential customer can bring to the ad his own idea of what the Internet is really for. 35

Leaning on information from other sources is also a way to enhance credibility, without which advertising must fail. Much of the most important information in advertising—think of cholesterol and heart disease, antilock brakes and automobile safety—acquires its force from highly credible sources other than the advertiser. To build up this kind of credibility through material actually contained in ads would be cumbersome and inefficient. Far more effective, and far more economical, is the technique of making challenges, raising questions and otherwise making it perfectly clear to the audience that the seller invites comparisons and welcomes the tough questions. Hence the classic slogan, "If you can find a better whiskey, buy it." 36

Finally, there is the most important point of all. Informational sparseness facilitates competition. It is easier to challenge a competitor through pungent slogans—"Where's the beef?," "Where's the big saving?"—than through a step-by-step recapitulation of what has gone on before. The bits-and-pieces approach makes for quick, unerring attacks and equally quick responses, all under the watchful eye of the consumer over whom the battle is being fought. This is an ideal recipe for competition. 37

It also brings the competitive market's fabled self-correcting forces into play. Sellers are less likely to stretch the truth, whether it involves prices or subtleties about safety and performance, when they know they may arouse a merciless response from injured competitors. That is one reason the FTC once worked to get comparative ads on television, and has sought for decades to dismantle government or voluntary bans on comparative ads. 38

"LESS-BAD" ADVERTISING

There is a troubling possibility, however. Is it not possible that in their selective and carefully calculated use of outside information, advertisers have the power to focus consumer attention exclusively on the positive, i.e., on what is good about the brand or even the entire product class? Won't automobile ads talk up style, comfort, and extra safety, while food ads do taste and convenience, cigarette ads do flavor and lifestyle, and airlines do comfort and frequency of departure, all the while leaving consumers to search through other sources to find all the things that are wrong with products? 39

In fact, this is not at all what happens. Here is why: Everything 40
for sale has something wrong with it, if only the fact that you have to pay for it. Some products, of course, are notable for their faults. The most obvious examples involve tobacco and health, but there are also food and heart disease, drugs and side effects, vacations and bad weather, automobiles and accidents, airlines and delay, among others.

Products and their problems bring into play one of the most im- 41
portant ways in which the competitive market induces sellers to serve the interests of buyers. No matter what the product, there are usually a few brands that are "less bad" than the others. The natural impulse is to advertise that advantage—"less cholesterol," "less fat," "less dangerous," and so on. Such provocative claims tend to have an immediate impact. The targets often retaliate; maybe their brands are less bad in a different respect (less salt?). The ensuing struggle brings better information, more informed choices, and improved products.

Perhaps the most riveting episode of "less-bad" advertising ever 42
seen occurred, amazingly enough, in the industry that most people assume is the master of avoiding saying anything bad about its product.

Less-Bad Cigarette Ads

Cigarette advertising was once very different from what it is today. 43
Cigarettes first became popular around the time of World War I, and they came to dominate the tobacco market in the 1920s. Steady and often dramatic sales increases continued into the 1950s, always with vigorous support from advertising. Tobacco advertising was duly celebrated as an outstanding example of the power and creativity of advertising. Yet amazingly, much of the advertising focused on what was wrong with smoking, rather than what people liked about smoking.

The very first ad for the very first mass-marketed American ciga- 44
rette brand (Camel, the same brand recently under attack for its use of a cartoon character) said, "Camel Cigarettes will not sting the tongue and will not parch the throat." When Old Gold broke into the market in the mid-1920s, it did so with an ad campaign about coughs and throats and harsh cigarette smoke. It settled on the slogan, "Not a cough in a carload."

Competitors responded in kind. Soon, advertising left no doubt 45
about what was wrong with smoking. Lucky Strike ads said, "No Throat Irritation—No Cough . . . we . . . removed . . . harmful corrosive acids," and later on, "Do you inhale? What's there to be afraid of? . . . famous purifying process removes certain impurities." Camel's famous tag line, "more doctors smoke Camels than any other brand," carried a punch precisely because many authorities thought smoking was unhealthy (cigarettes were called "coffin nails" back then), and smokers were eager for reassurance in the form of smoking by doctors

themselves. This particular ad, which was based on surveys of physicians, ran in one form or another from 1933 to 1955. It achieved prominence partly because physicians practically never endorsed nontherapeutic products.[1]

Things really got interesting in the early 1950s, when the first persuasive medical reports on smoking and lung cancer reached the public. These reports created a phenomenal stir among smokers and the public generally. People who do not understand how advertising works would probably assume that cigarette manufacturers used advertising to divert attention away from the cancer reports. In fact, they did the opposite. 46

Small brands could not resist the temptation to use advertising to scare smokers into switching brands. They inaugurated several spectacular years of "fear advertising" that sought to gain competitive advantage by exploiting smokers' new fear of cancer. Lorillard, the beleaguered seller of Old Gold, introduced Kent, a new filter brand supported by ad claims like these: "Sensitive smokers get real health protection with new Kent," "Do you love a good smoke but not what the smoke does to you?" and "Takes out more nicotine and tars than any other leading cigarette—the difference in protection is priceless," illustrated by television ads showing the black tar trapped by Kent's filters. 47

Other manufacturers came out with their own filter brands, and raised the stakes with claims like, "Nose, throat, and accessory organs not adversely affected by smoking Chesterfields. First such report ever published about any cigarette," "Takes the fear out of smoking," and "Stop worrying . . . Philip Morris and only Philip Morris is entirely free of irritation used [sic] in all other leading cigarettes." 48

These ads threatened to demolish the industry. Cigarette sales plummeted by 3% in 1953 and a remarkable 6% in 1954. Never again, not even in the face of the most impassioned anti-smoking publicity by the Surgeon General or the FDA, would cigarette consumption decline as rapidly as it did during these years of entirely market-driven anti-smoking ad claims by the cigarette industry itself. 49

Thus advertising traveled full circle. Devised to bolster brands, it denigrated the product so much that overall market demand actually declined. Everyone understood what was happening, but the fear ads continued because they helped the brands that used them. The new filter brands (all from smaller manufacturers) gained a foothold even as their ads amplified the medical reports on the dangers of smoking. 50

[1]The ad ran in many outlets, including *The Journal of the American Medical Association*, which regularly carried cigarette advertisements until the early 1950s. Incidentally, Camel was by no means the only brand that cited medical authorities in an effort to reassure smokers.

It was only after the FTC stopped the fear ads in 1955 (on the grounds that the implied health claims had no proof) that sales resumed their customary annual increases.

Fear advertising has never quite left the tobacco market despite the regulatory straight jacket that governs cigarette advertising. In 1957, when leading cancer experts advised smokers to ingest less tar, the industry responded by cutting tar and citing tar content figures compiled by independent sources. A stunning "tar derby" reduced the tar and nicotine content of cigarettes by 40% in four years, a far more rapid decline than would be achieved by years of government urging in later decades. This episode, too, was halted by the FTC. In February 1960 the FTC engineered a "voluntary" ban on tar and nicotine claims. 51

Further episodes continue to this day. In 1993, for example, Liggett planned an advertising campaign to emphasize that its Chesterfield brand did not use the stems and other less desirable parts of the tobacco plant. This continuing saga, extending through eight decades, is perhaps the best documented case of how "less-bad" advertising completely offsets any desires by sellers to accentuate the positive while ignoring the negative. *Consumer Reports* magazine's 1955 assessment of the new fear of smoking still rings true: 52

> . . . companies themselves are largely to blame. Long before the current medical attacks, the companies were building up suspicion in the consumer by the discredited "health claims" in their ads. . . . Such medicine-show claims may have given the smoker temporary confidence in one brand, but they also implied that cigarettes in general were distasteful, probably harmful, and certainly a "problem." When the scientists came along with their charges against cigarettes, the smoker was ready to accept them.

And that is how information works in competitive advertising. 53

Less-bad can be found wherever competitive advertising is allowed. I already described the health-claims-for-foods saga, which featured fat and cholesterol and the dangers of cancer and heart disease. Price advertising is another example. Prices are the most stubbornly negative product feature of all, because they represent the simple fact that the buyer must give up something else. There is no riper target for comparative advertising. When sellers advertise lower prices, competitors reduce their prices and advertise that, and soon a price war is in the works. This process so strongly favors consumers over the industry that one of the first things competitors do when they form a trade group is to propose an agreement to restrict or ban price advertising (if not ban all advertising). When that fails, they try to get advertising regulators to stop price ads, an attempt that unfortunately often succeeds. 54

Someone is always trying to scare customers into switching 55
brands out of fear of the product itself. The usual effect is to impress upon consumers what they do not like about the product. In 1991, when Americans were worried about insurance companies going broke, a few insurance firms advertised that they were more solvent than their competitors. In May 1997, United Airlines began a new ad campaign that started out by reminding fliers of all the inconveniences that seem to crop up during air travel.

Health information is a fixture in "less-bad" advertising. Ads for 56
sleeping aids sometimes focus on the issue of whether they are habit-forming. In March 1996, a medical journal reported that the pain reliever acetaminophen, the active ingredient in Tylenol, can cause liver damage in heavy drinkers. This fact immediately became the focus of ads for Advil, a competing product. A public debate ensued, conducted through advertising, talk shows, news reports and pronouncements from medical authorities. The result: consumers learned a lot more than they had known before about the fact that all drugs have side effects. The press noted that this dispute may have helped consumers, but it hurt the pain reliever industry. Similar examples abound.

We have, then, a general rule: sellers will use comparative ad- 57
vertising when permitted to do so, even if it means spreading bad information about a product instead of favorable information. The mechanism usually takes the form of less-bad claims. One can hardly imagine a strategy more likely to give consumers the upper hand in the give and take of the marketplace. Less-bad claims are a primary means by which advertising serves markets and consumers rather than sellers. They completely refute the naive idea that competitive advertising will emphasize only the sellers' virtues while obscuring their problems.

Examining the Text

1. What points does Calfee make with his example of advertising for Kellogg's All-Bran cereal? According to Calfee, what are the advantages and disadvantages of using ads to inform consumers about health issues?

2. According to Calfee, what are the "spillover benefits" of advertising?

3. What are some of the ways that free-market competition in advertising benefits consumers? Does Calfee see any reason for government or industry regulation of advertising?

4. *Thinking rhetorically*: How would you describe the tone of this article? Considering the fact that Calfee is arguing an unusual position—that advertising is good for us—how does the tone of the article help him convey his arguments effectively? What other rhetorical strategies does Calfee use to make his position persuasive?

For Group Discussion

This activity requires that each member of the group bring four or five ads to class—either from a magazine, newspaper, or brochure—in order to test Calfee's proposition that ads provide consumers with useful information. In your group, make a list of the useful information that each ad presents. That is, what helpful facts do you learn from the ad? Then discuss the other kinds of information or content presented in each ad. (You might reread Jib Fowles's "Advertising's Fifteen Basic Appeals" to get some ideas.) What conclusions can you draw from this comparison? Do your conclusions coincide with Calfee's claims? Are certain kinds of ads—or ads for certain products—more likely to contain helpful information?

Writing Suggestion

Calfee discusses the history of cigarette advertising, noting the predominance of "less-bad" claims and "fear advertising" in mid-twentieth-century cigarette ad campaigns. Find five or six recent cigarette advertisements in magazines or newspapers and analyze the information these ads present and the strategies they use to sell their product. Then write an essay in which you first summarize Calfee's discussion of the history of cigarette advertising; use quotations and paraphrases from the article to develop your summary. In the remainder of your essay, discuss what you see as the current state of cigarette advertising based on your analysis of recent ads.

Jesus Is a Brand of Jeans

JEAN KILBOURNE

We realize that the title of this article may seem blasphemous to some readers, but it's a fact: there is an Italian company called Jesus Jeans (http://www.jesusjeans.com/uk/index.asp) that has been producing clothing since 1971. Of course, Jean Kilbourne isn't using the significant space of her title just to report a fact; she undoubtedly knows that her title will cause shock and discomfort to some readers, and we suspect that this is precisely the reaction she wants. The point of Kilbourne's article, after all, is to show that nothing is sacred in the world of advertising, that ads exploit all aspects of our culture and our lives—even our deeply held religious beliefs—in order to succeed at getting us to buy products. Kilbourne argues that we are inundated with ads telling us that products can meet our deepest needs, that we can be happier, more popular, more successful—more anything, it seems—simply by buying the right things.

Kilbourne is well known for her research into the individual and cultural impact of advertising, and she is the author of several books on the subject, including Can't Buy My Love: How Advertising Changes the Way We Think and Feel. *She is also the creator of award-winning documentaries such as* Killing Us Softly, Pack of Lies, *and* Slim Hopes, *and a popular speaker on college campuses and in communities, where her message is that we should pay attention to the messages that advertising conveys, especially messages that are harmful to girls and women.*

In the article that follows, Kilbourne makes several broad and direct statements about what she sees as the powerful impact of advertising. As you read, be sure to underline the strong central claims that Kilbourne makes in order to get at the essence of her argument. Pay attention as well to the ways that she supports her claims with specific evidence and analysis.

A recent ad for Thule car-rack systems features a child in the backseat of a car, seatbelt on. Next to the child, assorted sporting gear is carefully strapped into a child's carseat. The headline says: "We Know What Matters to You." In case one misses the point, further copy adds: "Your gear is a priority." 1

Another ad features an attractive young couple in bed. The man is on top of the woman, presumably making love to her. However, her 2 face is completely covered by a magazine, open to a double-page photo of a car. The man is gazing passionately at the car. The copy reads, "The ultimate attraction."

These ads are meant to be funny. Taken individually, I suppose they might seem amusing or, at worst, tasteless. As someone who has studied ads for a long time, however, I see them as part of a pattern: just two of many ads that state or imply that products are more important than people. Ads have long promised us a better relationship via a product: *buy this and you will be loved*. But more recently they have gone beyond that proposition to promise us a relationship with the product itself: *buy this and it will love you*. The product is not so much the means to an end, as the end itself. 3

After all, it is easier to love a product than a person. Relationships with human beings are messy, unpredictable, sometimes dangerous. "When was the last time you felt this comfortable in a relationship?" asks an ad for shoes. Our shoes never ask us to wash the dishes or tell us we're getting fat. Even more important, products don't betray us. "You can love it without getting your heart broken," proclaims a car ad. One certainly can't say that about loving a human being, as love without vulnerability is impossible. 4

We are surrounded by hundreds, thousands of messages every day that link our deepest emotions to products, that objectify people and trivialize our most heartfelt moments and relationships. Every emotion is used to sell us something. Our wish to protect our children is leveraged to make us buy an expensive car. A long marriage simply provides the occasion for a diamond necklace. A painful reunion between a father and his estranged daughter is dramatized to sell us a phone system. Everything in the world—nature, animals, people—is just so much stuff to be consumed or to be used to sell us something. 5

The problem with advertising isn't that it creates artificial needs, but that it exploits our very real and human desires. Advertising promotes a bankrupt concept of *relationship*. Most of us yearn for committed relationships that will last. We are not stupid: we know that buying a certain brand of cereal won't bring us one inch closer to that goal. But we are surrounded by advertising that yokes our needs with products and promises us that *things* will deliver what in fact they never can. In the world of advertising, lovers are things and things are lovers. 6

It may be that there is no other way to depict relationships when the ultimate goal is to sell products. But this apparently bottomless consumerism not only depletes the world's resources, it also depletes our inner resources. It leads inevitably to narcissism and solipsism. It becomes difficult to imagine a way of relating that isn't objectifying and exploitative. 7

Tuned in

Most people feel that advertising is not something to take seriously. Other aspects of the media are serious—the violent films, the trashy talk shows, the bowdlerization of the news. But not advertising! Although much more attention has been paid to the cultural impact of advertising in recent years than ever before, just about everyone still feels personally exempt from its influence. What I hear more than anything else at my lectures is: "I don't pay attention to ads . . . I just tune them out . . . they have no effect on me." I hear this most from people wearing clothes emblazoned with logos. In truth, we are all influenced. There is no way to tune out this much information, especially when it is designed to break through the "tuning out" process. As advertising critic Sut Jhally put it: "To not be influenced by advertising would be to live outside of culture. No human being lives outside of culture." 8

Much of advertising's power comes from this belief that it does not affect us. As Joseph Goebbels said: "This is the secret of propaganda: those who are to be persuaded by it should be completely immersed in the ideas of the propaganda, without ever noticing that they are being immersed in it." Because we think advertising is trivial, we are less on guard, less critical, than we might otherwise be. While we're laughing, sometimes sneering, the commercial does its work. 9

Taken individually, ads are silly, sometimes funny, certainly nothing to worry about. But cumulatively they create a climate of cynicism that is poisonous to relationships. Ad after ad portrays our real lives as dull and ordinary, commitment to human beings as something to be avoided. Because of the pervasiveness of this kind of message, we learn from childhood that it is far safer to make a commitment to a product than to a person, far easier to be loyal to a brand. Many end up feeling romantic about material objects yet deeply cynical about other human beings. 10

Unnatural Passions

We know by now that advertising often turns people into objects. Women's bodies—and men's bodies too these days—are dismembered, packaged and used to sell everything from chainsaws to chewing gum, champagne to shampoo. Self-image is deeply affected. The self-esteem of girls plummets as they reach adolescence partly because they cannot possibly escape the message that their bodies are objects, and imperfect objects at that. Boys learn that masculinity requires a kind of ruthlessness, even brutality. 11

Advertising encourages us not only to objectify each other but to feel passion for products rather than our partners. This is especially 12 dangerous when the products are potentially addictive, because addicts do feel they are in a relationship with their substances. I once heard an alcoholic joke that Jack Daniels was her most constant lover. When I was a smoker, I felt that my cigarettes were my friends. Advertising reinforces these beliefs, so we are twice seduced—by the ads and by the substances themselves.

The addict is the ideal consumer. Ten percent of drinkers consume over sixty percent of all the alcohol sold. Most of them are alcoholics or people in desperate trouble—but they are also the alcohol industry's very best customers. Advertisers spend enormous amounts of money on psychological research and understand addiction well. They use this knowledge to target children (because if you hook them early they are yours for life), to encourage all people to consume more, in spite of often dangerous consequences for all of us, and to create a climate of denial in which all kinds of addictions flourish. This they do with full intent, as we see so clearly in the "secret documents" of the tobacco industry that have been made public in recent years. 13

The consumer culture encourages us not only to buy more but to seek our identity and fulfillment through what we buy, to express our individuality through our "choices" of products. Advertising corrupts relationships and then offers us products, both as solace and as substitutes for the intimate human connection we all long for and need. 14

In the world of advertising, lovers grow cold, spouses grow old, children grow up and away—but possessions stay with us and never change. Seeking the outcomes of a healthy relationship through products cannot work. Sometimes it leads us into addiction. But at best the possessions can never deliver the promised goods. They can't make us happy or loved or less alone or safe. If we believe they can, we are doomed to disappointment. No matter how much we love them, they will never love us back. 15

Some argue that advertising simply reflects societal values rather than affecting them. Far from being a passive mirror of society, however, advertising is a pervasive medium of influence and persuasion. Its influence is cumulative, often subtle and primarily unconscious. A former editor-in-chief of *Advertising Age,* the leading advertising publication in North America, once claimed: "Only eight percent of an ad's message is received by the conscious mind. The rest is worked and re-worked deep within, in the recesses of the brain." 16

Advertising performs much the same function in industrial society as myth did in ancient societies. It is both a creator and perpetuator of the dominant values of the culture, the social norms by which most people govern their behaviour. At the very least, advertising helps to create a climate in which certain values flourish and others are not reflected at all. 17

Advertising is not only our physical environment, it is increasingly our spiritual environment as well. By definition, however, it is only interested in materialistic values. When spiritual values show up in ads, it is only in order to sell us something. Eternity is a perfume by Calvin Klein. Infiniti is an automobile, and Hydra Zen a moisturizer. Jesus is a brand of jeans. 18

Sometimes the allusion is more subtle, as in the countless alcohol ads featuring the bottle surrounded by a halo of light. Indeed products such as jewellery shining in a store window are often displayed as if they were sacred objects. Advertising co-opts our sacred symbols in order to evoke an immediate emotional response. Media critic Neil Postman referred to this as "cultural rape." 19

It is commonplace to observe that consumerism has become the religion of our time (with advertising its holy text), but the criticism usually stops short of what is at the heart of the comparison. Both advertising and religion share a belief in transformation, but most religions believe that this requires sacrifice. In the world of advertising, enlightenment is achieved instantly by purchasing material goods. An ad for a watch says, "It's not your handbag. It's not your neighbourhood. It's not your boyfriend. It's your watch that tells most about who you are." Of course, this cheapens authentic spirituality and transcendence. This junk food for the soul leaves us hungry, empty, malnourished. 20

Substitute Stories

Human beings used to be influenced primarily by the stories of our particular tribe or community, not by stories that are mass-produced and market-driven. As George Gerbner, one of the world's most respected researchers on the influence of the media, said: "For the first time in human history, most of the stories about people, life and values are told not by parents, schools, churches, or others in the community who have something to tell, but by a group of distant conglomerates that have something to sell." 21

Although it is virtually impossible to measure the influence of advertising on a culture, we can learn something by looking at cultures only recently exposed to it. In 1980 the Gwich'in tribe of Alaska got television, and therefore massive advertising, for the first time. Satellite dishes, video games and VCRs were not far behind. Before this, the Gwich'in lived much the way their ancestors had for generations. Within 10 years, the young members of the tribe were so drawn by television they no longer had time to learn ancient hunting methods, their parents' language or their oral history. Legends told around campfires could not compete with Beverly Hills 90210. Beaded moccasins gave way to Nike sneakers, and "tundra tea" to Folger's instant coffee. 22

As multinational chains replace local character, we end up in a world in which everyone is Gapped and Starbucked. Shopping malls kill vibrant downtown centres locally and create a universe of uniformity internationally. We end up in a world ruled by, in John Maynard Keynes's phrase, the values of the casino. On this deeper level, rampant commercialism undermines our physical and psychological health, our environment and our civic life, and creates a toxic society. 23

Advertising creates a world view that is based upon cynicism, dissatisfaction and craving. Advertisers aren't evil. They are just doing their job, which is to sell a product; but the consequences, usually unintended, are often destructive. In the history of the world there has never been a propaganda effort to match that of advertising in the past 50 years. More thought, more effort, more money goes into advertising than has gone into any other campaign to change social consciousness. The story that advertising tells is that the way to be happy, to find satisfaction—and the path to political freedom, as well—is through the consumption of material objects. And the major motivating force for social change throughout the world today is this belief that happiness comes from the market. 24

Examining the Text

1. How does Kilbourne answer the common criticism that advertising is trivial and has little power over us? Do you find Kilbourne's response persuasive? Why or why not?

2. In what ways does Kilbourne think advertising affects our relationships with other people? What specific examples does she give to support these claims? Have you seen evidence of this destructive impact of advertising in your own life or in your observations of others?

3. According to Kilbourne, in what ways is advertising related to myth in ancient societies? In what ways does it serve some of the same functions as religion does today? What do you think of these comparisons that Kilbourne makes?

4. The image on page 92, "Your Gaze Hits the Side of My Face," was created by artist Barbara Kruger. Which of the themes discussed by Kilbourne do you see reflected in this image?

5. *Thinking rhetorically*: Having read the entire article and understood Kilbourne's key points, do you think she made the right decision to give it such a potentially controversial title? What rhetorical impact does Kilbourne want to achieve with the title? Do you think she succeeds?

For Group Discussion

Many elements of Kilbourne's argument echo points made by Jib Fowles in his article about the basic appeals of advertising. Take a look back through Fowles's article and any notes or summary you wrote of it. Then work with your peers to compare the Kilbourne's argument with Fowles's list of appeals. Which of the fifteen appeals occupy most of Kilbourne's attention? Which appeals does she disregard? Do you think Kilbourne's analysis confirms Fowles's explanation of how advertising works? What does Kilbourne's analysis add to the mix? Finally, be prepared to report your group's conclusions to the rest of the class.

Writing Suggestion

As she develops her analysis, Kilbourne makes brief references to a number of advertisements that help to prove her points. For this assignment, look through magazines and newspapers for a single advertisement that you think either supports or contradicts one or more of Kilbourne's claims about advertising. Begin your essay by providing a brief summary of Kilbourne's ideas. Then analyze the advertisement you've chosen. (You may want to review the "Reading Images" section in Chapter 1.) Be sure to connect your analysis of specific features of the ad to specific points that Kilbourne is making, either by providing quotations from the article or by summarizing Kilbourne's points in your own words.

"Your Gaze Hits the Side of My Face," by Barbara Kruger. *(Courtesy of the Mary Boone Gallery, New York)*

Interview with Mark Crispin Miller

PBS FRONTLINE

A colleague who shall remain nameless once suggested an intriguing way for teachers to supplement their generally meager salaries: we could have our classes sponsored. We live in an age where double plays in baseball are sponsored by Jiffy Lube, where pro football games include the "Taco Bell Half-time Report," and where our shirts, shorts, shoes, and even underwear are imprinted with product names and logos. Why shouldn't teachers take advantage of a little corporate sponsorship? After all, we've got a captive audience of a very desirable demographic group (that's you). For a few extra dollars, we could easily play an advertising jingle softly in the background before class starts; we could say "This class is brought to you by Snapple!" at the beginning of class, and distribute free samples as students leave at the end of class.

While we hope this scenario seems strange to you, it may in fact become more plausible after you read the following interview with Mark Crispin Miller, a well-known media critic and commentator who is also a professor of Culture and Communication at NYU. As Miller puts it, "Advertising wants to become the air we breathe," and so we're finding it in more and more places—perhaps even eventually the classroom. The interview with Miller was part of PBS's The Persuaders, *a 2004 in-depth report on advertising, marketing, brands, and the state of American business and culture. The program included interviews with other prominent people in the field (including Bob Garfield, author of our next article); the interviews are available online at http://www.pbs.org/wgbh/pages/frontline/shows/persuaders/.*

***Before you read,** browse this Web site to get a sense of the context in which Miller's interview is situated. You can watch the full televised program online, read interviews and commentary, and even add a comment yourself in the Discussion section of the site.*

To start, we're hoping you could just give us kind of an overview of the messaging landscape, particularly all the clutter in media today and what that means for us. 1

Various experts have recently tried to quantify the amount of advertising that suffuses the culture. We hear that each one of us encounters in an average day 2,000 messages or a million solicitations. I don't know how anybody can come up with a figure like that. I think it's probably more poignant than accurate to note that there is so much clutter in the landscape. It's really more accurate to say that the landscape is clutter. There is nothing other than clutter. 2

It's not as if we have some preexistent blank space that's clean and tidy, and there happen to be a lot of ants floating around in it. It's extremely difficult to cut through that clutter to find a space that's not in some sense advertising already. All the old safe havens—schools, churches, urinals—one by one, they've all basically been appropriated by the advertising/public relations force so that it's actually accurate to say that we live in a universe of propaganda. 3

Then what's the messenger to do now? 4

Well, this is a problem for all of us. It's a special problem for the advertisers themselves. They are the ones who make clutter. They are, therefore, also the ones who are always trying desperately to break through the clutter. That's the line you always hear in ad agencies: "We can break through the clutter with this." Well, every effort to break through the clutter is just more clutter. 5

Ultimately, if you don't have clean, plain borders and backdrops for your ads, if you don't have that blank space, that commons, that virgin territory, you have a very hard time making yourself heard. The most obvious metaphor is a room full of people, all screaming to be heard. 6

What this really means, finally, is that advertising is asphyxiating itself and really has been doing so for a couple of decades now. Some years ago, one advertising professor suggested in *Advertising Age*, in all seriousness, that advertisers generally would probably make more money by ceasing to advertise on TV entirely. TV had become so crowded, it had become so hard to break through the clutter of TV—with more clutter—that it was not even worth the investment, he argued. This was an argument that people in advertising took very seriously. Of course, many of them passionately resented it, but he did have a point, and the point only becomes more and more relevant as time goes on. 7

Should advertisers stop advertising? 8

Well, some advertisers actually have, in a sense, begun to stop advertising per se. When we talk about advertising, you usually mean "white propaganda"; that is to say, ads that are obviously ads. They announce themselves as ads. Beyond that, you get into a much subtler realm of propagandizing where people aren't quite aware, or aware at all, that they're being solicited, where the world you move through is an ad. 9

As advertising per se has come to encounter more and more sales resistance—which is understandable, as people become more and more distrustful of these messages and harder and harder to stimulate, more and more blasé—the advertisers have tried ever stealthier means to implant in your mind, in your soul, the urge to drink this or eat that or whatever it is. So you've got all kinds of methods that border on what people [in] 10 spycraft call "black propaganda"; for example, folks who are paid to go to bars and chat up a new cigarette brand or brand of beer as if they were real people spontaneously celebrating this thing. You've got TV shows that are ostensibly ad-free, but they have logos and buildings and so on worked into the story so that the whole thing is really a commercial.

So we're moving away from advertising per se towards a more fundamental kind of pitch, which is what propaganda, generally speaking, always wants to do anyway. Advertising is just a commercial form of propaganda. What propaganda has always wanted to do is not simply to suffuse the atmosphere, but to become the atmosphere. It wants to become the air we breathe. It wants us not to be able to find a way outside of the world that it creates for us. 11

There is this company in [Scott Donaton's book] Madison & Vine *that talks about how [the movie]* Cast Away *is this great advertisement for FedEx because it's not an advertisement for FedEx, but it advertises it perfectly, and that basically there are people spending a lot of money and research figuring out how to blur the line between what was content and what was advertising. Not that we should worry too much, but is our culture at risk of becoming pure advertising now?* 12

The worry is not so much that the actual ads themselves will become ubiquitous. Rather, it's that advertising—all propaganda—desires for itself a background that will not contradict it. It desires for itself a neighborhood that it feels safe in. In fact, people in advertising use the expression "good environment." Certain shows are a "good environment" for their messages. Now, when, for example, we were waiting for the 1991 Gulf War to begin, everybody knew roughly when the war was going to start, because the date had been announced, and there was tremendous suspense and fear and so on. As the zero hour approached, which was January 15, 1991, more and more mainstream advertisers suddenly bailed on their advertising contracts. They were under the misimpression that our media might bring extremely graphic images of warfare into our homes, so you wouldn't want to put your Oil of Olay commercial on and then see somebody burned to a crisp inside a tank, right? That would be to put the ad in a bad neighborhood, in a bad environment. 13

So for the first few nights of the war, there were no major advertisers [on television]. It was all curious little independent advertisers. It was a strange thing. After a few days, it became obvious that the whole spectacle was itself an ad, that [it] was advertising the precision and might of the American armed forces. The whole spectacle was managed by the Pentagon. So AT&T, McDonald's, the whole bunch of them went back on the air, and it didn't take them long to start to use war-related motifs in their commercials to make the thing even more unified. 14

But at that point, they actually still had 30- and 60-second advertisements. Now it seems we're moving into a programming universe where the advertisement is part of the show. 15

That's exactly right. If you don't look very carefully, if you kind of half-close your eyes, you might think that advertising is disappearing, because the fact is that traditional forms of advertising—the minute-long spot; the 30-second spot; the split 30s, [which are] two 15-second ads, and so on; the magazine ad; the newspaper ad; the billboard—it might seem that many of them are being phased out. 16

But they're not being phased out in favor of plain old civic space. They're being phased out in favor of a kind of advertising, a kind of propaganda, that's far more profound. It's far more deeply rooted. The aim here is not so much to find a show that people like and then get your ads on it. The aim here is for the advertisers to create a show that is itself an extended ad. In a curious way, we're moving back in time to the days when advertisers actually presented radio shows and TV shows. But this is far more sophisticated than that. 17

Formerly, when an advertiser would produce, say, a musical show, the music had to be paramount. The music had to be good; it had to be popular. That would then, presumably, make a difference to the advertisers. Commercials would benefit from the association with that nice music. Nowadays, when an advertiser envisions a show that's just right for his product, you don't really have content that's very easy to tell apart from a commercial for the product itself. 18

It's hard for many of us to remember, and impossible for the younger of us to know, that advertising was for decades always regarded as a bit of an intrusion, a nuisance, an interruption: "Don't go away; we'll be right back." And then they'd pitch something—you know, Bufferin or Chevys or whatever. The same with ads in print media: You're going to have to skip over the pages of ads to get to the text. 19

Well, as long as ads struck people as interruptive, as long as they struck them as a kind of momentary detour away from the road you wanted to be taking, the story you wanted to be following, they were also strangely candid about what they were. They were commercials. That came with the territory. You had to listen to a commercial in order to hear the music on the radio. You had to sit through two or three commercials in order to keep watching the episode of *The Fugitive* you were watching or whatever it was, you see? Now that paradigm of the ad as an explicit interruption, as a departure from the thing you're watching, that whole paradigm is giving way to a kind of programming that's already like an ad itself. There's no need to interrupt it, because it's selling things all the time anyway. 20

I have a very good example. In the '50s, Philip Morris was the sponsor of the top-rated TV show in the United States, *I Love Lucy*. Everybody loved *I Love Lucy*. Everybody watched it. Philip Morris advertised on it and was the sponsor. All of a sudden—I believe it was in 1955—Philip Morris dropped the show. Now, why on Earth would they do that? Well, they discovered that the show was often so funny, or at least struck its audience as so funny, that people were still wiping the tears from their eyes and squeezing out the last few chuckles while the commercials were running. [The] experience was too intense, you see? 21

What we've done is we have moved from *I Love Lucy,* which was over-the-top farcical, but at its best hilariously funny, funny just for the sake of being funny, we've moved from that to the paradigm of shows like *Friends,* which can be clever, which is often very witty. I don't mean to take away from *Friends*, but *Friends* is a much more subdued experience than *I Love Lucy*. We also don't tend to see the same kinds of shows about the uncanny that used to be quite popular on TV in the '60s, say, like *The Twilight Zone* and *Thriller,* because these shows were really frightening, really suspenseful. They had an intensity that today's advertisers would really prefer not to compete with their own messages. 22

But then we move even from advertising-friendly shows like Friends *to shows as advertisements, like, say,* The Restaurant, *which is basically an American Express Small Business Card advertisement masquerading as a program; or* Sex and the City, *with an entire plot line sponsored by Absolut Vodka. So isn't that an intrusion on a somewhat sacred space?* 23

Well, what's most worrisome about this is that advertising, being a form of propaganda, wants no contradiction. So that means we have to ask ourselves, what is the kind of content that makes advertisers feel better? What is the kind of content that makes an ad not seem jarring? 24

A certain kind of intense experience, an intense dramatic or aesthetic experience, tends to make advertising look like what it is, which is trivial; which is just a pitch, just trying to sell you something. What advertising is doing is trying to addict us to products, trying to get us to see consumption as the only way to live and ourselves as consumers as the only way to be. So the problem with an advertising-friendly cultural environment is that anything that's intense in any way is at risk of being erased, so that the usual smiley face of advertising, with all of its special effects, can dominate your consciousness. 25

Is there a problem with the fact that the plots and characters of our dramas are now built around the products within them? 26

Advertising has become the point. The TV shows are made not just to make ads look good but to function as enhancements or repetitions of the ad. The TV shows themselves are ads. The radio playlists now are themselves ads. More and more you've got newspaper sections that are nothing but articles about new kinds of products or new kinds of vacations and so on. 27

The same thing has happened in the world of news. Decades back, the TV networks would themselves, at times, produce extremely powerful documentaries. CBS, in its heyday, did this great documentary about migrant farm workers called *Harvest of Shame.* In the early '70s, they did this very powerful documentary about the military-industrial complex called *The Selling of the Pentagon.* Well, no advertiser wants to have his ad come up in the middle of or after a show like that. 28

It's too sobering; it's too much about reality; it's too troubling; it's too much of a bummer. So the news, too, becomes increasingly magazine-like. The stories are more and more tacitly censored—not necessarily explicitly censored, but they just don't seem to play properly—so that the news has to become an adjunct to advertising as well. This is no way to have a functioning culture in a democratic society. It's a way that turns all the content of all the culture industries into [a] mere continuation of advertising. 29

Some of the people we've talked to have argued that the level of choice offered to consumers today is basically a form of democracy. In other words, consumption is democracy because we're giving consumers choice and giving consumers information. What's wrong with that? What's wrong with people achieving their meaning by relating to brands? 30

Well, the fact is that this is an old argument, the argument that we're giving the people what they want. They're voting with their dollars—what could be more democratic than that? It's an old argument. It goes back to the '30s at least. 31

Well, it's profoundly skewed. This argument is deeply wrong in a way that some of the greatest founders of this republic would have understood immediately. The political realm and the realm of consumption are two very different things. Take a look at advertisements. What is their ideology? What is their message? What do they value? What do they ask of us? Commercials say to us endlessly: "You come first, and you can only be empowered if you use this, you buy this. You come first." 32

Now, what republican democracy requires is what some have called civic virtue; that is to say, a willingness to sacrifice anything, any advantage, any pleasure, even life itself, for the greater good. This is an old, old ideal that comes from the Roman republic. There is a contradiction between that notion of service to the greater good, that kind of patriotism, that kind of self-effacement, that kind of 33 self-sacrifice and the sort of sociopathic self-gourmandizing, the constant feeding, constant acquisition. The fact is, there's an antisocial dimension to aggressive consumption.

And that, I think, points to the key flaw in that claim by the champions of advertising that this is a form of democracy. It's not. It only has to do with a very narrow realm of daily life. I don't mean to say that material life is unimportant, but which product you buy is a fairly trivial question. In the political realm, democracy involves a lot more than going shopping. It involves participation; it involves dissent; it involves trying to improve the world you live in; it involves taking your civic responsibility seriously. So you can't really say that there's anything truly democratic about advertising. 34

Moreover, there's a flaw in the argument in that advertising can't be democratic, because it can only appeal to the people who can afford to buy the things that they're selling. So it's already addressing only that sector of the population that has a certain amount of disposable income. All those people who can't afford to buy personal computers, long-distance phone service, cable TV, you name it, what, they're not a part of the democracy? Well, according to the advertisers they're not, because the democracy is a big shopping excursion where we all get to buy whatever we want. 35

That said, what happens as the techniques of marketing and advertising spill over into politics? 36

Advertising, like all propaganda, tends to work despite your will and reason. It wants to work around your reason. It's not persuasion. Sometimes people in advertising like to say they're in the business of persuasion. It's not persuasion. They want it to work on a much more visceral level than the persuasive level. They're not arguing with us. They're trying to push our buttons. They're trying to bring a tear to the eye, trying to give you a hunger pang, trying to make you mad. 37

Now, these same tricks are used routinely by political handlers and by political parties. The Republican Party, for example, seems to trade in almost nothing but resentment and anger. That's what it's about. There's nothing coherent or logical about it. How can you have a democracy, a, when all the stuff you're taking in about the outside world actually is kind of subjugated to the purpose of selling products? You're going to get a very poor picture of reality that way. And b, what kind of a democracy can you have when those who should be rational citizens acting in their own best interests and acting for the good of all [are] constantly being bombarded by stimuli that are intended to get around [their] reason? They want couch potatoes that will simply emote in response to the stimulus. You can't have a democracy that way. 38

Examining the Text

1. What does Miller mean when he describes our social and cultural environment as "a universe of propaganda"? According to Miller, how is advertising different from propaganda? What is the difference between "white propaganda" and "black propaganda"?
2. Miller comments that advertising wants a "good environment" and "no contradiction." What does he mean by this? Why is this a problem, according to Miller?
3. How does Miller respond to the argument that advertising gives us information and choice and therefore aids democracy? What do you think of Miller's response?
4. *Thinking rhetorically*: What effect did the interview format of the article have on you as a reader? In general, what are some of the strengths and weaknesses of directly recording the answers of an interviewee rather than paraphrasing and commenting on them? In other words, what's gained and what's lost when we don't have an author commenting on Miller's answers?

For Group Discussion

The interview took place in 2006, and some of the trends Miller discerned then may have either withered or developed more fully in the intervening years. For instance, Miller mentions TV shows that are wholly or partially extended advertisements; one sees this quite often in shows like *American Idol* and *Biggest Loser*, which have CDs, spinoff books, and other merchandise. Working in a group, create a list of Miller's observations about the current (then) and future state of advertising and marketing. What advertising strategies have become common now? What other kinds of "black propaganda" do you see around you? Are there any new locations or strategies for advertising that Miller hadn't anticipated?

Writing Suggestion

Visit the Interviews page at the PBS Frontline Web site for The Producers: *http://www.pbs.org/wgbh/pages/frontline/shows/persuaders/interviews/*. After reading through the brief descriptions there of the other seven interviews, choose the one that interests you most and read that interview in full. Write an outline and a brief summary of the interview, paying particular attention to those areas of the interview that engage some of the same concerns as Miller does. Then, compose a comparison essay in which you discuss the similarities and differences in the two interviews. What aspects of advertising and marketing does each interviewee see as crucial? How does each interviewee envision the current state of advertising and its future directions? What examples and other evidence does each interviewee offer to support his or her points? Consider concluding your essay with a paragraph that explains which interview yielded more insight for you into the current and future influence of advertising on our culture.

The Post Advertising Age

BOB GARFIELD

Bob Garfield is a regular columnist for Advertising Age, *a frequent TV and radio commentator on advertising and media, and the author of* The Chaos Scenario, *a book about seismic shifts in the world of media, marketing, advertising, and business. The article that follows is an excerpt from one of his* Ad Age *columns and part of a series called "Chronicles of the Media Revolution." Garfield offers an insider's view of the current and future state of advertising, and so we can eavesdrop, as it were, on the advice he gives here primarily to people working in the ad industry. For Garfield, the eventual shift to a new business model of advertising, one with a significant online presence, is a given; he describes "five reasons the online world will not only transform traditional modes of advertising, it will largely displace them altogether." For now, though (and this article was written in 2007), the landscape is "chaotic," with old marketing strategies in decline and new online venues not yet fully formed.* ***As you read****, keep in mind the date this article was published. To what extent have Garfield's predictions already been realized? Which ones seem to have fallen by the wayside?*

Maybe you'd better lean forward. Presently you will be given five reasons to consider something barely imaginable: a post-apocalyptic media world substantially devoid of brand advertising as we have long known it. 1

It's a world in which Canadian trees are left standing and broadcast towers aren't. It's a world in which consumer engagement occurs without consumer interruption, in which listening trumps dictating, in which the Internet is a dollar store for movies and series, in which ad agencies are marginalized and Cannes is deserted in the third week of June. It is a world, to be specific, in which marketing—and even branding—are conducted without much reliance on the 30-second spot or glossy spread. 2

Because nobody is much interested in seeing them, and because soon they will be largely unnecessary. 3

Perhaps you are already rolling your eyes. Perhaps you believe that vast structures on which vast societies and vast economies depend do not easily lose their primacy. Perhaps you believe that the TV commercial and magazine spread—and radio spot and newspaper classified—are forever and immutable, like the planets orbiting the sun. Good for you. 4

Now, say hello to Pluto—the suddenly former planet. Forever and immutable, it turns out, are subject to demotion. This could be grim news for the agency business, which continues its erratic Pluto-like orbit around marketing budgets as if unaware that it has lost its stature—and its relevance is next to go. In due course, you shall see how circumstances have conspired to threaten its place on the cosmic map altogether. 5

VIDEO KILLED WHOM?

To support the analogy of planetary delisting, we needn't go back 5 billion years to the origin of the solar system. Instead, just think back to approximately the day before yesterday. Remember how they used to talk about "the MTV generation"? 6

It was shorthand for the post–baby boomers who couldn't be stimulated unless you basically jammed kaleidoscopes in their eyeballs. They had cut their teeth on the rapid-fire editing and visual noise of music video, so all media were obliged to pick up the pace or lose the attention of an entire generation. And just in case the symbolism escaped you, don't forget the first song that ever played on MTV: 7

"Video Killed the Radio Star," by the Buggles. 8

Ironic, eh? But not as ironic as this: The latest thing the MTV generation has begun losing interest in is MTV, where ratings fell sharply last year. Short Attention Span Theater has changed venues and is now housed on YouTube. Online video is killing the video star. [. . .] 9

Mass media, of course, do not exist in a vacuum. They have a perfect symbiotic relationship with mass marketing. Advertising underwrites the content. The content delivers audience. Audiences receive the marketing messages and patronize the advertisers, and so on in what for centuries was an efficient cycle of economic life. The first element of Chaos presumes the fragmentation of mass media creates a different sort of cycle: an inexorable death spiral, in which audience fragmentation and ad-avoidance hardware lead to an exodus of advertisers, leading in turn to an exodus of capital, leading to a decline in the quality of content, leading to further audience defection, leading to further advertiser defection and so on to oblivion. The refugees—audience and marketers alike—flee to the Internet. There they encounter the second, and more ominous, Chaos component: the Internet's awkward infancy. 10

The online space isn't remotely developed enough—nor will it be anytime soon—to absorb the advertising budgets of the top 100 marketers, to match the reach of traditional media or to fulfill the content desires of the audience. (Maybe viewers no longer demand their MTV, 11 but what remains of the mass audience is in no hurry to surrender its *Los Angeles Times* and "Lost.") A collapsing old model. An unconstructed new model. Paralyzed marketers. Disenchanted consumers. It's all so . . . chaotic.

THE ECONOMICS OF ABUNDANCE

How long it will be before order is restored is anybody's guess. What is certain is that the Brave New World, when it emerges, will be far better for marketers than the old one. What is nearly as certain is that many existing ad agencies and some media agencies will be left behind. And the reason they will be left behind is their stubborn notion that they can somehow smoothly transition to a digital landscape. 12

[. . .] We are not witnessing the beginning of the end of old media. We are witnessing the middle of the end of old media. Both print and broadcast—burdened with unwieldy, archaic and crushingly expensive means of distribution—are experiencing the disintegration of the audience critical mass they require to operate profitably. Moreover, they are losing that audience to the infinitely fragmented digital media, which have near-zero distribution costs and are overwhelmingly free to the user. 13

Free is a tough price to compete with. As documented by Woodward and Bernstein, Deep Throat's advice to unraveling Watergate was to "Follow the money." In imagining Chaos 2.0, you must follow the no-money. And when you do, you'll have taken the Chaos Scenario one step further: to a digital landscape in which marketing achieves hitherto unimaginable effectiveness, but in which display advertising's main role will be to quickly, straightforwardly, informatively draw you into a broader brand experience. 14

"I always found Marshall McLuhan annoying," says Bruce M. Owen, senior fellow at Stanford University and author of the seminal "Television Economics," "but the medium conditions the message. It's already happening." 15

The promised details to follow momentarily, but consider for a moment Nike Plus, the joint project of Nike and Apple in which the iPod becomes a tool for monitoring running pace and style. The website combines utility, community, information and, of course, online sales. It is the marketing program, the CRM engine and the store. The sole function of the TV commercial—which is an elaborate demo minus celebrities and narrative and jokes—is to drive traffic to the site. 16

Now, multiply that formula by the Leading National Advertisers plus the entire Long Tail. Furthermore, thanks to emerging digital tools, there are endless permutations of the formula. Herewith, at 17 last, five reasons the online world will not only transform traditional modes of advertising, it will largely displace them altogether.

1. People don't like ads

Sure, when your ad characters draw a parade crowd on Madison Avenue or you strut up to the awards stage in Cannes with ratty sneakers and fake indifference, of course you feel loved. Alas, you aren't, especially. In fact, you are mainly resented. A 2006 Forrester Research survey found that 63% of respondents believe there are too many ads, and 47% say ads spoil their reading or viewing enjoyment. This isn't just talk. Depending on whose numbers you believe, between 50% and 70% of DVR users skip ads. The historical quid pro quo—acquiescence to advertising in exchange for free or subsidized content—is yet another casualty of the revolution. 18

"The more access people have to technology," says Forrester senior analyst Peter Kim, "the more they will use it to skip advertising. When you as a consumer want content, you just want content. You don't want to be interrupted." 19

Nor is there any reason to think interruption is better-tolerated online. Forrester reports that only 2% of consumers trust banner ads and 81% of broadband users deploy spam filters and pop-up blockers. 20

Though it is a $1.65 billion acquisition in search of a business model, YouTube won't even consider appending ads to its videos, because it knows it would alienate its audience. And though much has been made of ads posted on sites and going viral, only a handful—notably "Ronaldinho" for Nike and "Evolution" for Dove—have ever broken through. The sequel to "Evolution," for Dove Pro-Age, has languished, barely noticed, on YouTube in spite of a ginned-up controversy about nude, older models. 21

2. But they crave information

Consumers may not much care for commercials, but they like goods and services just fine and are in constant search of information about them. Oddly, in its obsession with not repelling audiences, advertising over the past two decades has provided more and more production spectacle, more and more belly laughs, but less and less information. Very quickly, because information is at its very core, the online world will fill the vacuum. 22

But why would display ads be the principal means of doing so? In 2007, according to ZenithOptimedia, $10.5 billion will be spent on display, including video, but $14 billion will be spent on search. Why? Because search is contextual, measurable and information-rich. The double-edged sword of search, of course, is that it captures shoppers in the process of shopping but does little to build brand awareness for 23 the general population. On the other hand, building brand awareness for the general population is also wildly inefficient. As online display advertising itself becomes more targeted and measurable, it will be best deployed as a sort of street signage—posted on extremely vertical social networks or served based on user profiles—directing the audience to where the real information is: brand or third-party websites, or embedded in highly utilitarian content.

Hence, a new breed of aggregators—not of content, like Yahoo or Digg—but of vertical channels. Magnify.net hosts thousands of video-sharing communities and Ning.com thousands of equally vertical social networks—from "American Idol Fans" to "Asthma Parents" to "Draft Gore." Marc Andreessen, founder of Netscape, is co-founder of Ning.com. 24

"People are interested in what they are interested in," he says. "The magical part of social networking is the people [specific category] advertisers are interested in are magically coming together." And they're trackable all the way down to the individual user, so why waste anyone's time with what co-founder Gina Bianchini calls "undifferentiated aspirational messages"? 25

As for how you serve the information once you've gotten the audience's attention, the digital tools for doing so get ever more impressive. 26

One particular eye-opener, from Vancouver, Canada, is VideoClix, a hypervideo application that lets the user roll over any part of the image—a car in the background, for instance—and click for information about make, model and so on. A second click directs the user to the manufacturer, retailer or whatever. It's like VH1's old "Pop-Up Video" show, only the user alone controls what to pop up. Thus, it exploits the online third dimension, beyond audio and video: info-depth. 27

"It's a layer of information," says founder Babak Maghfourian, "that people will demand." 28

Apart from its potentially staggering utility, particularly in the product-placement sphere, VideoClix and other tools threaten the very nature of brand advertising. As *Wired* editor in chief and Long Tail proponent Chris Anderson likes to observe, "Brands are a proxy for information." In other words, brandedness itself conveys to consumers a minimum assurance of quality, reliability and distribution. Obviously, brands convey other things as well—including values, status and personality—but their most basic function will be usurped by the information readily available at a mouse click or an instant PDA scan at retail. 29

3. The consumer is in control. No, really

"I guess the most important thing that I would be asking myself," says media economist Bruce Owen, "is: How can I make advertising something that people are not only willing to put up with but actually have positive willingness to take?" 30

Considering the statistics you've just been reading, that sounds 31
almost preposterously naive—like asking commuters to vote for traffic. But not only is there an answer to his musing, that answer presages a Golden Age of marketing. The fact is, people care deeply—sometimes perversely—about consumer goods, from Tag Heuer to North Face to Tab. What they don't like is being told what they should care about or when they should be caring. Forrester's research reveals that 48% of consumers believe it is their right to decide whether or not to receive ad messages. Opt-in e-mails were deemed twice as trustworthy as TV commercials and 10 times more trustworthy than banner ads precisely because the consumer chooses whether to engage.

This may be culturally difficult for advertisers to accept, having 32
spent two centuries trying to browbeat/seduce captive audiences. But take heart. Once the consumer is in the driver's seat, he or she will often cheerfully drive right in your direction.

"I'm amazed that anyone would go online to the American Ex- 33
press site to learn about credit cards," says Ted Shergalis, founder and chief product officer of [x+1], a web-optimization firm, "but they do. By the millions every day." Yet the same consumers may TiVo right past Ellen DeGeneres in an AmEx TV spot, because "they want the information on their terms."

4. Diversion of ad budgets

In order to exploit the Internet's phenomenal capacity for targeting 34
and optimizing messages in ads and on websites, advertisers will have to invest vast resources in information-technology infrastructure—hardware, software and flesh-and-bloodware—to crunch the vast amount of data that will be pouring in every second of every day. In the aggregate, this will amount to many billions of dollars. Much, if not most, of the money will come from existing ad budgets.

This will accelerate the destruction of mass media/mass advertising 35
symbiosis (see "death spiral" above) and unlock the very power of aggregation, information, optimization and customer-relationship management that will render most image advertising impotent and superficial.

5. Pay-per-view

Let us not forget what the advertising yin is the yang of: free media. But 36
what if, in the near future, most content is paid for by the user, either via subscription, like HBO, or a la carte, like pay-per-view or iTunes? This would eliminate advertising from the equation. If micropayments ever become practical, pay as you go would allow users to seamlessly buy, for instance, newspaper content on an edition-by-edition or even article-by-article basis. As Bruce Owen puts it, "The willingness to pay by consumers is far greater per eyeball than the willingness of advertisers."

In February, citing the pioneering efforts of Wal-Mart, Amazon and iTunes, Adams Media Research projected that paid streams and downloads will quickly overtake advertising as the revenue model for video content. "By 2011," according to the report, "advertiser spending on Internet video streams to PCs and TVs will approach $1.7 billion, but movie and TV downloads will generate consumer spending of $4.1 billion." Likewise, in a January report titled "The Digital Consumer: Examining Trends in Digital Media," the investment firm Oppenheimer & Co. concludes the same: Content "is not likely to be ad-supported." 37

In other words, Madison Avenue has problems out the yin-yang. 38

[. . .] Then there was that other fellow. 39

Advertising Age: "Do you buy the Chaos Scenario?"

Bill Gates: "No. . . . You'll see a little bit more turmoil, in terms of who succeeds and who doesn't, but it's not some overnight cataclysm."

Ad Age: "Is it fair to assume that the advertising people are exposed to, that they actually permit into their lives, will be more informational and less, let's just say, entertaining and creative and whimsical than advertising we've seen in the past?"

Mr. Gates: "I wouldn't say that."

On the other hand, of the $500 million Microsoft allocated to the introduction of its Vista operating system, 30% went online. If every national advertiser did the same tomorrow, Madison Avenue and Hollywood wouldn't be chaotic. They would be Pluto, relegated to some barren, subordinate outer orbit of the economy. And a lot of people would be singing a different tune. 40

And now we meet in an abandoned studio
We hear the playback and it seems so long ago
And you remember the jingles used to go
Video killed the radio star
Video killed the radio star
In my mind and in my car
We can't rewind; we've gone too far

—The Buggles, 1979

Examining the Text

1. What reasons does Garfield give for describing the current state of advertising and marketing as "chaotic"? What does he mean when he says "In imagining Chaos 2.0, you must follow the no-money"?

2. In paragraph 16, Garfield briefly mentions Nike Plus as an example of effective, Chaos 2.0 marketing. How was this advertising campaign structured and why was it so effective, according to Garfield?
3. What are some of the reasons why Garfield thinks people will accept and even embrace online advertising in the future? Do you agree with Garfield? Why or why not?
4. Why do you think Garfield includes the skeptical quote from Bill Gates toward the end of his article? How does Garfield contextualize this quote in order to help him prove his (that is, Garfield's) point?
5. *Thinking rhetorically:* Garfield begins his article with a direct address to the reader ("you"), a hypothetical scenario, sentence fragments, and a reference to Pluto, "the suddenly former planet." What effect did these opening paragraphs have on you as a reader? Do you think there are elements of the opening that are too informal?

For Group Discussion

As a group, choose one of the five principles that Garfield discusses in this article. First, reread that section and briefly discuss its key points, making sure that everyone in the group agrees on your general summary. Next, make a list of examples from the current advertising and marketing world that either illustrate or disprove the principle, keeping in mind that Garfield wrote this article in 2007. Think of advertising that you see in typical venues—TV, magazines, billboards—as well as ads online and in other, less traditional places (e.g., gas station pumps). Finally, decide as a group on whether the principle you discussed still holds true today. Would you offer any modifications of the principle to update it for the contemporary context?

Writing Suggestion

Throughout the article, but especially in the five principles discussed at the end, Garfield envisions a future world in which online advertising plays an increasingly significant role. For this assignment, you'll have a chance to collect data on the current state of online advertising and speculate on Garfield's predictions.

First, spend 30 minutes browsing the Web; visit the sites you typically visit, but as you do, make note of all of the ads you encounter. Try to record as many details as you can about these ads: What products are being advertised? How large are the ads? Are they interactive? Do they include sound or video? Are they banner ads or pop-ups? Where on the Web page do they occur? How many ads are on each page? How much information do the ads offer?

After recording your data, represent it in a table—either using a spreadsheet program or in a hand-drawn table. Note any repetitions or patterns that occur—for instance, if a certain site has many ads (or no ads), if many of the ads are for similar products, and so on. Based on what you discover, write an essay in which you describe your online advertising experience and draw any relevant conclusions about Garfield's principles.

*The Brain: Marketing to Your Mind**

ALICE PARK

We conclude this chapter with an article that reports on a potentially powerful new tool at the disposal of advertisers and marketers—a tool that could help them look directly into the brains of consumers in order to find out how to persuade us most smoothly and effectively to make a specific purchase. As Alice Park explains in this Time *magazine article, "Now researchers can go straight to the decider in chief—the brain itself, opening the door to a controversial new field dubbed neuromarketing." The traditional (and crude) marketing tools of surveys and focus groups could give way to high-tech fMRI scanners and EEG tests in which our brains are hooked up to various instruments as we look at products and contemplate making purchases. You can see why advertising agencies would be eager to develop this technology and use its findings to help them craft more effective ads. The benefits of this technology for consumers strikes us as far more debatable. After all, if our brains can be more easily manipulated we would seem to have far less control over our purchasing (and other) decisions.* ***As you read,*** *think about your own opinion of neuromarketing. Are you positive, negative, or neutral about this development in advertising research?*

Are you a Coke or Pepsi drinker? Do you pull into McDonald's golden arches or prefer to "have it your way" at Burger King? When it comes to toothpaste, which flavor gets you brushing, Colgate or Crest? If you think it's just your taste buds that guide these preferences, you may be surprised by what neuroscientists are discovering when they peer inside the brain as it makes everyday choices like these. 1

Don't worry—no one's scanning your head as you stand in front of the beverage aisle or sit in line at the drive-through. Instead, brain scientists are asking volunteers to ponder purchasing choices while lying inside high-tech brain scanners. The resulting real-time images indicate where and how the brain analyzes options, weighs risks and rewards, factors in experiences and emotions and ultimately sets a preference. "We can use brain imaging to gain insight into the mechanisms behind people's decisions in a way that is often difficult to get at simply by asking a person or watching their behavior," says Dr. Gregory Berns, a psychiatrist at Emory University. 2

*Alice Park, "The Brain: Marketing to Your Mind" in Time, January 19, 2007.

To scientists, it's all part of the larger question of how the human brain makes decisions. But the answers may be invaluable to Big Business, which plowed an estimated $8 billion in 2006 into market research in an effort to predict—and sway—how we would spend our money. In the past, marketers relied on relatively crude measures of what got us buying: focus-group questionnaires and measurements of eye movements and perspiration patterns (the more excited you get about something, the more you tend to sweat). Now researchers can go straight to the decider in chief—the brain itself, opening the door to a controversial new field dubbed neuromarketing. 3

For now, most of the research is purely academic, although even brain experts anticipate that it's just a matter of time before their findings become a routine part of any smart corporation's marketing plans. Some lessons, particularly about how the brain interprets brand names, are already enticing advertisers. Take, for example, the classic taste test. P. Read Montague of Baylor College of Medicine performed his version of the Pepsi Challenge inside a functional magnetic resonance imaging (fMRI) machine in 2004. Montague gave 67 people a blind taste test of both Coke and Pepsi, then placed his subjects in the scanner, whose magnetic field measures how active cells are by recording how much oxygen they consume for energy. After tasting each drink, all the volunteers showed strong activation of the reward areas of the brain—which are associated with pleasure and satisfaction—and they were almost evenly split in their preferences for the two brands. But when Montague repeated the test and told them what they were drinking, three out of four people said they preferred Coke, and their brains showed why: not only were the reward systems active, but memory regions in the medial prefrontal cortex and hippocampus also lit up. "This showed that the brand alone has value in the brain system above and beyond the desire for the content of the can," says Montague. In other words, all those happy, energetic and glamorous people drinking Coke in commercials did exactly what they were supposed to do: seeped into the brain and left associations so powerful they could even override a preference for the taste of Pepsi. 4

Stanford neuroscientist Brian Knutson has zeroed in on a more primitive aspect of making choices. "We come equipped to assess potentially good things and potentially bad things," he says. "There should be stuff in your brain that promotes your survival, whether you have learned those things or not—such as being scared of the dark or the unknown." Knutson calls these anticipatory emotions, and he believes that even before the cognitive areas of the brain are brought in to assess options, these more intuitive and emotional regions are already priming the decision-making process and can foreshadow the outcome. Such primitive triggers almost certainly afforded survival advantages to our ancestors when they decided which plants to pick or which caves to enter, but Knutson surmises that vestiges of this system 5 are at work as we make more mundane choices at the mall. There, it's the match between the value of a product and its price that triggers an anticipation of pleasure or pain.

To test his theory, Knutson and his team devised a way to mimic these same intuitive reactions in the lab. He gave subjects $20 each and, while they were in the fMRI machine, presented them with pictures of 80 products, each followed by a price. Subjects then had the option of purchasing each item on display. As they viewed products they preferred, Knutson saw activity in the nucleus accumbens, a region of the brain involved in anticipating pleasant outcomes. If, on the other hand, the subjects thought the price of these items was too high, there was increased activity in the insula—an area involved in anticipating pain. "The idea is that if you can look into people's brains right before they make certain decisions, you can get a handle on these two feelings and do a better job of predicting what they are about to do," Knutson says. "I believe anticipatory emotions not only bias but drive decision making." 6

All of this, of course, is whirring along at the brain's split-second pace, and as imaging technology improves, Knutson is hopeful that he and others will be able to see in even more detail the circuits in the brain activated during a decision. Already, according to Montague, these images have revealed surprising things about how the brain pares down the decision-making process by setting up shortcuts to make its analysis more efficient. To save time, the brain doesn't run through the laundry list of risks, benefits and value judgments each time. Whenever it can, it relies on a type of "quick key" that takes advantage of experiences and stored information. That's where things like brands, familiarity and trust come in—they're a shortcut for knowing what to expect. "You run from the devil you know," says Montague. "And you run to the brand that you know, because to sit there and deliberate chews up time, and that makes you less efficient than the next guy." 7

That's certainly music to advertisers' ears, but, warn neuroscientists, it's unlikely that our purchasing behavior follows a single pathway. Montague, for one, is investigating how factors like trust, altruism and the feeling of obligation when someone does you a favor can divert and modify steps in the decision-making tree. "The capacity to use brain responses and relate them to behavior has accelerated at a breathtaking pace over the past four years and yielded an incredible amount of information," he says. How marketers use that data to hone their messages remains to be seen. 8

Examining the Text

1. According to Montague's study, how and why do brand names affect our choices to buy certain products?

2. What are "anticipatory emotions" and what role do they play, according to Brian Knutson, in the way our brains work to process information?

3. *Thinking rhetorically:* How would you describe the tone of Park's article? Can you determine her opinion of neuromarketing? How does the tone of this author differ from the tone of the previous two articles?

For Group Discussion

In a group, discuss whether you would be willing to participate in a study like the ones described here. That is, would you volunteer to be put in an fMRI machine and sample a product or answer some questions so that researchers can determine how your brain works when you're making purchasing decisions? There's no right or wrong answer to this question, but it might be interesting for you to decide for yourself and also hear about what decision your peers would make, and why.

Writing Suggestion

Park's article was written in 2007 and reports on studies done several years earlier. To find out about the current status of neuromarketing, do some research using the Internet and other online databases. Have Montague's and Knutson's studies been discussed or reproduced? Are there other scientists studying the ways our brains respond to ads and other marketing stimuli? Have marketing agencies and advertisers taken up neuromarketing in any significant way? Once you've looked into current research in these areas, write a report in which you update Park's study and explain current findings in the field of neuromarketing.

ADDITIONAL SUGGESTIONS FOR WRITING ABOUT ADVERTISING

1. Choose a magazine, television, or radio advertisement that you find particularly interesting, appealing, or puzzling, and write a narrative essay describing your response to the ad.

Begin by recording your initial impressions of the ad. What do you notice first, and why are you drawn to that element of the ad? What emotions or thoughts strike you as you first look at the ad? Then describe your step-by-step progress through the ad. Where does your eye go next? How do your thoughts or emotions change as you notice more of the ad? Finally, record your impressions after you've taken in all of the ad. How does this final impression differ from your first impression?

You might conclude your narrative by commenting on whether, based on your response, the ad achieves its objective of selling the product. In other words, do you think you responded as the designers of the ad intended?

2. Devise your own ad campaign for a product with which you're familiar, including several different ads, each appealing to a different audience.

After deciding on the product, briefly describe each audience group. Choose the form in which you want your advertisements to appear (magazine ads, TV commercials, audio presentations, billboards, or other forms and venues) and then decide on the persuasive methods that you want to use. Do you want to appeal to emotion or intellect or both? What motives will you try to reach? You might refer to Fowles's list of advertising's basic appeals.

Finally, design the ads and briefly explain the reasoning behind each design.

3. Choose recent issues of a women's magazine and a men's magazine, and compare and contrast the ads in each.

How many advertisements are there? What products are being advertised? What techniques are used in the ads and how do these techniques differ significantly between men's and women's magazines? What are the differences in the appeals the ads make? What are the differences in the images of men and women?

From your findings, draw conclusions about how advertisers envision and represent differences in gender. What (if any) stereotypes of men and women do the ads present?

4. Imagine that you are a member of a citizens' group working to improve the quality of advertising. What specific recommendations would you make and what standards would you want to see enforced? Illustrate your ideas with ads you can find that either meet or fall below these standards.

Internet Activities

1. On the Web, you'll find sites representing the products and services of almost all major U.S. corporations and of many smaller businesses as well. These corporate Web sites can be seen as extensive advertisements. Though they differ in style and strategy from television and magazine advertisements, they share the goal of informing consumers about a product or service and persuading consumers in their purchasing decisions.

At the *Common Culture* Web site, you'll find links to the sites of companies selling a variety of products. Choose one of those product categories and investigate the links. As you browse through the companies' Web sites, make a list of the kind of information that's offered there, the organization of the site, the graphics and other interactive elements that are used, the style and tone of the writing, and the mood created at the site. Then write an essay in which you describe the similarities and differences of two or more sites. What strategies do these sites use to promote the company's products and services? Which strategies do you find effective, and why? You might conclude your essay by commenting on the distinctive features of Web sites as advertisements. How are they different from magazine and television ads?

2. You've probably noticed that many Web sites contain a wide range of advertisements—banner ads, pop-up ads, paid sponsor links, and so on—for other sites or for products and services offered by specific companies. At the *Common Culture* Web site, you'll find links to examples and additional information about Web advertising. Visit these links and take some time to browse the Web and familiarize yourself with the advertising strategies there. Then, write an essay in which you first describe the characteristics of advertising on the Web, and then compare and contrast Web advertising to television commercials and to print ads. What common features are shared by ads in these different media? How do the differences in media shape the content and style of advertisements? Be sure to draw on the ideas discussed by Bob Garfield in "The Post-Advertising Age" as you write your essay.

Reading Images

The image entitled "Absolute End" on page CI-2 is taken from Adbusters (*http://www.adbusters.org*); it's one of their "spoof ads" that draws on familiar themes and motifs in advertising in order to undermine the messages that the ads themselves convey. Adbusters has spoofed such popular ad campaigns as Obsession perfume and the "Joe Camel" cigarette ads. The idea is to turn ads against themselves, to use the very style of the manufacturers' advertisements in exposing the harm that these ads and products can cause.

"Absolute End" is one of several spoofs of the Absolut vodka ads in which the shape of the vodka bottle is superimposed over some geographic location (for instance, New York's Central Park). Here, the familiar bottle shape (made familiar in part by the Absolut vodka ads themselves) is used as a chalk drawing on a pavement, calling to mind the chalk drawings that trace the shape of a murder victim's body.

Clearly, "Absolute End" is not an advertisement for Absolut vodka. However, it's not an ad directly against Absolut vodka, either. It seems, rather, to be an ad against alcohol advertising in general. The text in the image makes the message explicit:

> Nearly 50% of automobile fatalities are linked to alcohol. 10% of North Americans are alcoholics. A teenager sees 100,000 alcohol ads before reaching the legal drinking age.

In an essay, analyze the techniques used in this image to convey its message. For instance, consider how the perspective of the photograph influences your reaction to it: why is the viewer positioned above the scene that the photograph depicts? Consider also what's left out of the photograph: why is there no victim's body in this scene? Who is included in the scene, and why? Consider also the color scheme and other visual components of the image. Finally, be sure to discuss the text that's included: the "title" of the image and the three sentences that state its message.

Conclude your analysis by discussing whether or not you think a "spoof ad" like this one is an effective way to convey a message. What are the advantages and disadvantages of using a visual statement like this rather than a purely textual one (for instance, a newspaper article about alcohol, drunk driving, and advertising)?

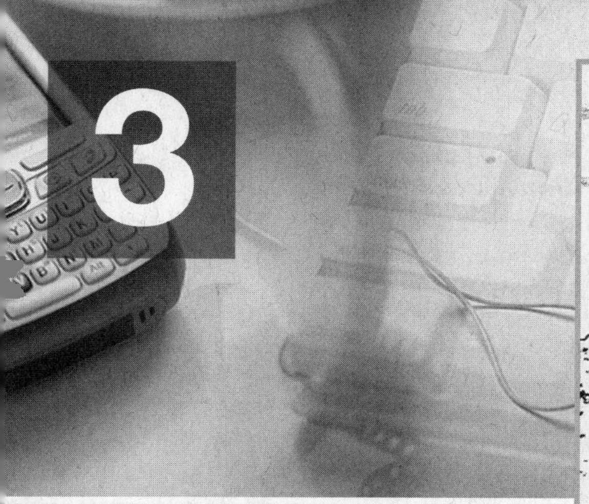

3

Television

BOYS ALWAYS FOUND SUNSET ON THE PRAIRIE A PARTICULARLY MOVING EXPERIENCE

Drawing by Glen Baxter; © 1991 The New Yorker Magazine, Inc.

We may laugh at these "boys" who stand in the middle of the barren Southwest desert watching a sunset on TV as the real sun sets behind them. Yet the joke is also on us because—like the cowboys—we might often find ourselves more engaged, more entertained, and even more emotionally touched by what we watch on television than by our own experiences in real life.

Some critics even suggest that people regard what they see on television as more real than what goes on around them and thus virtually narrow their world to what comes to them on "the tube." Paradoxically, television's greatest benefit is its potential to broaden our experience, to bring us to places we could never visit, to people we could never meet, and to a range of ideas otherwise unavailable to many people.

This complex relationship between television, individual viewers, and society as a whole leads thoughtful people to examine closely the way television diverts our attention from what could be our own rich, nonmediated experiences; the way it entertains and informs us through otherwise inaccessible experiences; the way it shapes our perceptions of the world around us.

The readings in the first part of this chapter address some of the important questions raised in regard to this ubiquitous medium. How accurately does television represent reality? How strongly do its distortions of reality affect our ideas and behavior? Why do Americans spend so much time watching television? What essential needs and desires does television satisfy? To what extent does television intervene in our everyday lives, influencing families and communities, domestic space, and leisure time? Can watching TV actually make us smarter? Will new technological developments change how we watch television in the future?

The readings in the second part of the chapter address some of these questions by focusing on a particular type of television show: the comedy news or "infotainment" show. The three articles in this casebook are written in response to a shift in how Americans find out about what's going on in the world. Newspapers, radio, and nightly news shows on TV used to be the standard sources of information. With the advent of the Internet, people increasingly get their news from such Web sites as cnn.com and aol.com. More recently, people—and particularly young people—are turning to cable TV comedy shows such as *The Daily Show* and *The Colbert Report* to learn about current events, politics, the economy, and domestic and international news. To understand why these shows are so popular and what impact they're having on American culture, the authors draw comparisons to other, related artifacts: Russell Peterson's article compares *The Daily Show* and *The Colbert Report* to late-night mainstream comedy shows; Gerald Erion discusses their similarities and differences from conventional television news shows; and Jeffrey Jones discusses these shows in relation to mainstream journalism. We hope this casebook demonstrates that focusing on a particular type of TV show can yield diverse interpretations and complex insights.

As you read these articles, remember the television-entranced cowboys at the opening of the chapter. As you hone your own critical abilities, you will go beyond being a passive observer to become an active, critically engaged viewer.

The Cultural Influences of Television

Society's Storyteller: How TV Creates the Myths by Which We Live

GEORGE GERBNER

We begin this selection of readings with a thoughtful piece by one of television's most prominent scholars, George Gerbner. Gerbner is best known for research on the "mean world syndrome"; through extensive studies, Gerbner and his staff found that people who were heavy viewers of TV were more likely to view their social surroundings as hostile and threatening, and that TV therefore promoted a distorted view of reality. In the article that follows, Gerbner takes a broader view, connecting television to the fundamental human need to tell and hear stories. He argues that television today provides many of the same functions as myth did in ancient cultures. Because of its great appeal, and also because of the distorted view of reality that it presents, Gerbner sees the need for media literacy and for critical engagement with television watching and programming.

This article was written in 1993—before the widespread use of the Internet and mobile technology. ***As you read,*** *test Gerbner's statements about television with your own experience—not just now but throughout your life. Have other technologies diminished the influence of television for you? for your friends and family? for society as a whole?*

Storytelling is the great process that makes us recognizably human. A story is an attempt to make the invisible visible—it has to do with relationships, with intellectual connections. We have to have some device to make the visible, dramatic, revealing and embodied in human beings whose characteristics we know and whose actions we can understand. We live our lives in terms of the stories we tell. 1

What are these stories? How do we weave them into the very complicated uniquely human structure called culture? Basically there are three kinds of stories: 2

- **There are stories essentially about *how things work.*** Stories that make the inner dynamics of life visible are typically called fiction and drama, sometimes mythology. There is no other way to tell the truth about how things work except to construct the facts of the case so as to lead to the natural development of the underlying message and significance of how things really work.

- **Into that context will fit the second kind of story—a story about *what things are.*** It is a kind of factual story: the legend of yesterday or the news of today. It has no meaning by itself, it only has meaning when we fit it into an immensely complex structure about the meaning of it all.
- **A third kind of story is a *story of action.*** It's really a story of value and choice, the prerequisites for action. If this is how things work and this is what things are, we then contemplate a complex of choices, and *do something*. A story like this presents a desirable goal within a lifestyle. It can be an instruction or a sermon, but mostly it is a commercial—a story of value and choice with which we are surrounded all the time. We happen to live in a culture which offers many, many things to obtain, presumably desirable goals. This is what you ought to do, ought to buy, ought to vote for, ought to consider.

The three kinds of stories have always been woven together in many intricate combinations in a seamless fabric of culture, in different ways at different times. Humankind has woven together the stories that we tell, as we humanize our children and ourselves, in three different ways: the Pre-Print Era (30–50,000 years long), the Print Era (300 years long) and now the Age of Telecommunications. 3

Basically the age of telecommunications is the age of television. And television is the central cultural instrument, the historical predecessor of which is not print or even radio, but pre-print religion. Television is that ritual mythbuilder—totally involving, compelling, and institutionalizing as the mainstream of the socializing process. 4

Five Functions of Television as Myth

As in pre-print cultures, television (or storytelling) provides five functions for society. 5

First of all, television is *ritual*. It is very different from print and film because it is less selectively used. Most people don't watch television by the program, but by the clock. In the average home, the television is on more than seven hours per day. It has its own rhythm, often governing the rhythm of the home. 6

Secondly, television is highly *institutionalized*. There are basically only a few major sources of television program production. A group of about 100 people in Hollywood produce more than 95 percent of all the programs and essentially determine what most Americans will see. 7

Furthermore, television is an institution that is in the business of assembling people and selling them to advertisers at a price. There's an overall concept of programming (storytelling)—whether it is news, 8 drama, talk shows, audience participation, daytime serials, whatever—predicated on the formula of "cost per thousand." The basic formula that determines any programming is "how cheap can we provide this without offending too many of the people who will tune in anyway?"

Television is also *total* in its grasp of an otherwise heterogeneous 9 mass audience. Only about seven percent of children's viewing time goes into "children's programming" so most children watch what adults watch. Of course there is very little regional, ethnic, religious or other separate programming. So there is a totality of audience and a uniformity of programming concept and program structure.

Needless to say, television is *entertaining* (compelling) because it 10 is predicated upon giving some kind of apparent reward all the time. We can argue about the quality of the reward; we cannot argue that no one is driven to watch television, yet people watch it a great deal. Why? Because it brings, I believe, some sense of instant satisfaction. It is the first instrument of humankind to bring the millions of people who have always been "out of it" into the mainstream of cultural life. It has brought the famous, the powerful, the beautiful into the lowliest homes.

People watch television because no one is going to take it away 11 from them. And they will watch it until and unless something more attractive can be provided in their everyday lives. Television is a great bond among otherwise very heterogeneous and diversified groups.

Finally, television is the overall *socializing process* superimposed 12 on all the other processes. By the time children can speak (let alone go to school and perhaps learn to read), they will have absorbed thousands of hours of living in a highly compelling world. They see everything represented: all the social types, situations, art and science. Our children learn—and we ourselves learn and maintain—certain assumptions about life that bear the impact and the imprint of this most early and continued daily ritual. In our age, it is television mythology we grow up in and grow up with.

Our studies for over 14 years show that television basically keeps 13 those who are already in the mainstream more embedded in it by helping them hold its tenets more rigidly. Then, television brings members of those groups that have less, or more, than television offers into the mainstream, too.

What is the mainstream like? Let me pick out some of the more 14 salient features on the basis of some 4,000 programs and 15,000 characters that we have analyzed.

First of all, TV is a world in which men outnumber women at least 15 three to one. This male cast makes the world revolve mostly around questions of power. That is why television is so violent: the best, quickest demonstration of power is a show-down that resolves the issue of who can get away with what against whom. On television, there is an incident of (this kind of) violence on the average of five times an hour.

It is also a world in which a few professions (doctors, lawyers. entertainers, law enforcers and lawbreakers) far outnumber all other working people put together. It is a mean and dangerous world, and we find that those who watch more television are more insecure and apprehensive. They demand more protection. They are more likely to even approve of, if not welcome, repression, if it comes in the name of security. This is a dangerous syndrome we call the "mean world syndrome." It is potentially highly volatile, both politically and morally. 16

The Need for Media Literacy

There seems to be no doubt that television's appeal is based on its intimate connection with viewers' needs and aspirations. Although we may improve its content, we certainly will not break that link, and we definitely will not abolish television altogether. At best, we can only teach people how it works and how to use it in ways that are healthy for themselves and for the society. 17

Our sense of powerlessness about television is devastating and mystifying. To accept it is to accept disenfranchisement. Television is a hidden curriculum for all people, financed by a hidden taxation without representation, paid by everyone regardless of whether they use the service or not. You pay when you wash, not when you watch. Every time you buy a bar of soap a fraction of that price is a tax levy for TV advertising. The total tax amounts to between $55–65 per household a year depending upon the market in which you live. 18

What then should be the terms of our engagement? That *there is* an engagement is clear. It has to do with very basic conceptions of life and the dynamics of our society. The more explicit we can make the engagement, the better we can address it. 19

Bringing these terms of engagement to consciousness is the number one task of education today, which is no longer in the business of *dispensing* knowledge, but rather instilling good habits for *managing* knowledge. Pupils today learn most of their information from television before the teacher can teach it, and they bring it with them to school. This is a greatest challenge for education today. 20

It is also very important, I believe, for traditional religions to address explicitly and specifically the issue of television as a cultural mechanism. Taking a position, or some combination of positions, already is an important step toward being in control of our own world, of our own perspective. Whether or not your awareness activity is formal media literacy training, any steps toward critical interaction with the television you see represent huge steps forward. 21

Above all, turning off the set is not liberation, but an illusion. *You* can turn off the set, but you still live in a world in which vast numbers of people don't. If you don't get information and ideas through 22 the "box," yourself, you get them through the cultural "environment" created by the millions of people who *are* watching.

Examining the Text

1. Why do you think Gerbner begins by dividing stories into three categories? How do these different categories of stories relate to television and television programming?

2. In what ways, according to Gerbner, does television serve the same function as myth did in ancient cultures? Do all of these functions still apply to the role of television in the twenty-first century? Which ones, if any, seem to be diminishing or increasing?

3. According to Gerbner, what are the key elements of media literacy?

4. *Thinking rhetorically*: Gerbner uses an interesting technique of italicizing key words. What kinds of words did he choose to italicize? What do you think of this technique? Did it help give you a better understanding of Gerbner's article? Why or why not?

For Group Discussion

Gerbner doesn't mention any specific television shows in this article. In a group, come up with a list of the top 10 or 20 TV shows that you watch most often. Use Gerbner's categories to classify these shows according to the type of stories they tell (about how things work, what things are, or stories of action); if they tell more than one type of story, choose the predominant mode. Is one type of story more popular than the others? If so, speculate on why this might be so. Then test your list and your own TV viewing practices against the five functions of TV that Gerbner discusses. Be prepared to share the insights of your group with the rest of the class.

Writing Suggestion

The television schedule is a fine example of nonacademic but very common reading material in our culture. Millions of people read TV schedules every day and think nothing of it. This writing assignment asks you to reflect on *how* you read TV schedules and to interpret what meanings can be found in these common documents.

On page 122 is a reproduction of a page from the TV listings in the *Los Angeles Times* newspaper, listing the televised offerings of many channels on Tuesday, March 8, 2011. Begin writing about this document by describing it: What are its distinguishing features? How is the information organized? How does its appearance differ from the pages of this textbook? Next, take notes describing the strategies you use in reading this document: Where do you begin? Where does your eye go next? What factors influence your choices? Are there parts of the document that you ignore completely? Why? Finally, write down your thoughts about the content of this schedule: To what extent do the TV programs scheduled for this evening confirm or contradict Gerbner's claims in "Society's Storyteller"? As you bring these observations together in an essay, highlight what you see as the two or three most important features of TV schedules in general, based on your observations of this specific example.

Monday 6/20 PRIME TIME

Tonight's Highlights

Pacific	8:00pm	8:30pm	9:00pm	9:30pm	10:00pm	10:30pm
SPONSORED SPOTLIGHT						
TNT	**Law & Order:** A suspicious suicide is investigated by Fontana and Green, who believe foul play is involved. HD		**Law & Order:** DA Arthur Branch's influential acquaintance (Stevie Ray Dallimore) becomes a murder suspect. Branch: Fred Dalton Thompson. Housman: Brennan Brown. HD L		**The Closer:** The team scrambles to locate a missing young woman in the Season 6 finale. The case also swirls around a crack addict and a potentially shady rehab facility. HD LV	
BROADCAST						
ABC	**The Bachelorette:** Ashley and 11 suitors visit Chiang Mai, Thailand, where three are eliminated. But first, one accompanies her to an ancient temple and eight others engage in Muay Thai boxing (and must fight each other). There's also a two-on-one river-rafting expedition. HD NEW				(10:01) **Extreme Makeover: Weight Loss Edition:** A 25-year-old ex-football player who weighs 651 lbs. HD L NEW	
CBS	**How I Met Your Mother:** Marshall go green. HD DL	**How I Met Your Mother:** The gang has a race. HD DL	**Two and a Half Men:** Lyndsey moves into Charlie's. HD DL	(9:31) **Mike & Molly:** The first Valentine's Day. HD DL	**Hawaii Five-0:** Danny's brother Matt visits, but Danny soon learns that Matt is the target of an FBI investigation. HD LV	
The CW	**90210:** Jen learns of Naomi's rape and decides to avenge her sister. HD L		**Gossip Girl:** Blair takes a business class and tries to become the instructor's assistant. HD D		**Local Programming**	
Fox	**MasterChef:** The Top 18 are selected after all the hopefuls are tested on basic kitchen techniques, including chopping apples. HD L		**MasterChef:** Two hopefuls are eliminated and the remaining 16 advance to the next round of the competition. HD DL		**Local Programming**	
ION	**Without a Trace:** A violin prodigy vanishes from a concert hall. Elizabeth Rice. L		**Criminal Minds:** A serial killer targets prostitutes in Washington, D.C. DLV		**Criminal Minds:** Morgan is arrested as a serial killer by a detective. L	
MyNetworkTV	**Law & Order: CI:** A computer techie's murder.		**Law & Order: CI:** A businessman's murder. L		**Local Programming**	
NBC	**America's Got Talent:** Seattle is the setting for continuing auditions. HD L		**Law & Order: Criminal Intent:** A Wall Street big shot is killed, and several parties may have benefited from his death. HD LV		**Law & Order: Los Angeles:** A tragic birthday party kicks off a probe which leads detectives to a party-goer. HD DLV NEW	
PBS	**Antiques Roadshow:** Part 2 of 3. In Wichita, a company known for its lanterns. HD		**Antiques Roadshow:** Conclusion. In Wichita, items include a 1920s toy truck. HD		**Abraham and Mary Lincoln: A House Divided:** Part 1 of 6.	
Univision	**Teresa** HD				**Triunfo del Amor** HD	
CABLE						
A&E	**Hoarders:** A home with over 2000 rats that are the owner's pets.		**Hoarders:** A woman collects dolls; and a woman has no water or heat in her home. NEW		**Intervention:** A woman battles heroin addiction. L NEW	
ABC Family	**Secret Life of the American Teenager:** Ashley forges ahead with her trip. HD D NEW		**Switched at Birth:** Kathryn assists Regina with her job search. HD DL NEW		**Secret Life of the American Teenager:** Ashley forges ahead with her trip. HD D	
AMC	MOVIE ★★ **The Perfect Storm** (2000): Fact-based adventure about a boat skipper (George Clooney) and his crew in the path of a confluence of massive storms. Mind-blowing effects, but the characters are one-dimensional. Mark Wahlberg. Adapted from the Sebastian Junger bestseller. LV					
Animal Planet	**Whale Wars:** The Shepherds think they've located the Nisshin Maru on the radar. LV		**AP Investigate/Captive Hunting:** An investigation into canned-hunting operations. LV NEW		**River Monsters Goes Tribal:** Jeremy joins tribal fishermen in the South Pacific.	
BBC Amer.	**Top Gear:** The hosts head to America. HD		**Top Gear:** The hosts race up America's East Coast. HD			(10:20) **May's Road Trip**
BET	MOVIE (7:30) ★★ **Harlem Nights** (1989): Eddie Murphy wrote, directed and teams up with Richard Pryor as 1930s nightclub owners fending off the mob. Bennie: Redd Foxx. Phil: Danny Aiello.				MOVIE **I Do...I Did!** (2009): A man is married to two women.	
BIO	**Growing Up Twisted**	**Growing Up Twisted**	**Biography:** A profile of guitar legend Jimi Hendrix draws from Hendrix's own words. HD			
Bravo	**Real Housewives of New Jersey:** Jacqueline plays referee for Teresa and Melissa. HD		**Real Housewives of Orange County:** Previously unseen footage. NEW		**Platinum Hit:** The aspiring hit-makers display their rapping abilities. NEW	
Cartoon	**Adventure Time** HD	**MAD** HD NEW	**King/Hill** HD L	**King of the Hill** HD	**American Dad!** DL	**American Dad!** DL
Cinemax	MOVIE **Up in the Air** (2009): Loner Ryan Bingham (George Clooney) is forced to take a colleague on a business trip when she proposes changes to their company, which specializes in firing people. HD PG				MOVIE **Date Night** (2010): Couple run for their lives after a case of mistaken identity. HD PG-13	
CMT	MOVIE ★★★ **Tombstone** (1993): Retelling of the O.K. Corral shootout. Kurt Russell, Val Kilmer, Michael Biehn, Powers Boothe. LV					
CNBC	**Mad Money**		**Business/Welch**	**Business/Welch**	**To Be Announced**	
CNN	**Anderson Cooper 360** HD		**Piers Morgan Tonight** HD		**Anderson Cooper 360** HD	
Comedy Cen.	MOVIE (6:41) **40-Year-Old Virgin:** Steve Carell.		**Always Sunny** LV	**Always Sunny** LV	**Always Sunny** L	**Always Sunny** L
Cooking Ch.	**Iron Chef:** A corn cook-off. HD		**All-Star Grill:** Grilling recipes are shared. HD		**Originals** HD	**Eat Street** HD
Discovery	**Desert Car Kings:** A 1955 Ford F100 restoration becomes complicated. L		**Desert Car Kings:** An accident hampers a Barracuda restoration. L		**Desert Car Kings:** A 1966 Chevrolet Chevelle turns out to be a rare SS model. L	
Discovery Fit	**Strange Addict.**	**Strange Addict.**	**Strange Addict.**	**Strange Addict.**	**World's Worst Teens:** A promiscuous girl. DL	
Disney	**Good Luck Charlie:** Amy and Charlie perform.	**Shake It Up:** Rocky tries an image change.	MOVIE **College Road Trip** (2008): Family-friendly comedy in which a dad and his daughter drive across country to visit the college of her dreams.			**Good Luck Charlie:** Amy and Charlie perform.
Disney XD	**Pair of Kings** NEW	**Kickin' It** NEW	**I'm in the Band** NEW	**Phineas & Ferb** HD	**Phineas & Ferb** HD	**Zeke and Luther**
E!	**Sex and the City** DLS	**Sex and the City:** Sam dates a rich man. DLS	**Keeping Up With the Kardashians** DL	**Ice Loves Coco:** Coco's pregnant sister visits.	**True Hollywood Story:** Holly Madison is the focus. LS	
Encore	MOVIE **The Proposal** (2009): A businesswoman (Sandra Bullock) rushes into a marriage of convenience with her young assistant (Ryan Reynolds) in order to prevent being deported. HD PG-13				MOVIE (9:50) ★★ **Predator 2** (1990): Gory sequel. HD	
ESPN	**SportsCenter** HD NEW		**Baseball Tonight** HD	**NFL Live** HD	**SportsCenter** HD NEW	
ESPN2	**NBA Tonight Draft Preview** HD NEW		**SportsNation** HD	**SportsNation** HD	**NBA Tonight:** Team needs and top prospects. HD	
Flix	MOVIE ★★ **Hannibal** (2001): In Italy, Dr. Hannibal Lecter (Anthony Hopkins) becomes the target of a revenge plot, attracting the attention of the FBI's Clarice Starling (Julianne Moore). Far-fetched and gory but handsomely mounted. Ray Liotta. R					MOVIE (10:15) ★ **Domestic Dist.** PG-13
Food	**Unwrapped:** A look at comfort foods.	**Kid in a Candy Store**	**Diners, Drive-Ins and Dives**	**Diners, Drive-Ins and Dives**	**Meat & Potatoes** NEW	**The Best Thing I Ever Ate** NEW
Fox Movie Channel	MOVIE (7:30) ★★★ **An Unmarried Woman** (1978): Jill Clayburgh as a vulnerable woman trying to readjust to being single. Alan Bates, Michael Murphy, Cliff Gorman. Patti: Lisa Lucas. LS				**Life After Film School**	MOVIE **Soul Food:** Vanessa L. Williams.
Fox News	**O'Reilly Factor** HD		**Hannity** HD		**On the Record With Greta Van Susteren** HD	
FX	MOVIE **You Don't Mess With the Zohan** (2008): A highly skilled Israeli commando (Adam Sandler) fakes his own death to fulfill a secret dream: to work as a hairdresser in New York City. Emmanuelle Chriqui, John Turturro, Emmanuelle Chriqui. HD DLSV					

Content Ratings: Appropriate for all children | For children age 7 and older | General audience | Parental guidance suggested | May be unsuitable for children under 14 | Mature audience only

Television Addiction Is No Mere Metaphor

ROBERT KUBEY AND MIHALY CSIKSZENTMIHALYI

We all know that certain substances are addictive; indeed, we know that cigarettes, alcohol, and drugs are dangerous in large part because we can become addicted to them and end up using them to our own physical and psychological detriment. Certain activities, such as gambling, are also recognized as addictive. But can the activity of watching television be considered addictive? Are heavy television viewers "addicts" in the same way that alcoholics and long-term smokers are?

Robert Kubey and Mihaly Csikszentmihalyi address these questions in the following article, which was originally published in Scientific American. *Kubey and Csikszentmihalyi are both college professors: Kubey is the director of the Center for Media Studies at Rutgers University, and Csikszentmihalyi is the C. S. and D. J. Davidson Professor of Psychology at Claremont Graduate University. In this article, they combine their expertise in media studies and psychology in order to examine the phenomenon of "TV addiction."*

Although some social commentators see humor in the idea of couch potatoes "spudding out" in front of the television, Kubey and Csikszentmihalyi bring sociological and biological evidence to bear on their explanation of the addictive power television has over us. ***Before you read,*** *think about what the term* addiction *means to you. Do you know anyone who you think is "addicted" to television? What do you think are the causes and consequences of this addiction?*

Perhaps the most ironic aspect of the struggle for survival is how easily organisms can be harmed by that which they desire. The trout is caught by the fisherman's lure, the mouse by cheese. But at least those creatures have the excuse that bait and cheese look like sustenance. Humans seldom have that consolation. The temptations that can disrupt their lives are often pure indulgences. No one has to drink alcohol, for example. Realizing when a diversion has gotten out of control is one of the great challenges of life. 1

Excessive cravings do not necessarily involve physical substances. Gambling can become compulsive; sex can become obsessive. One activity, however, stands out for its prominence and ubiquity—the world's most popular leisure pastime, television. Most people admit 2 to having a love–hate relationship with it. They complain about the "boob tube" and "couch potatoes," then they settle into their sofas and grab the remote control. Parents commonly fret about their children's viewing (if not their own). Even researchers who study TV for a living marvel at the medium's hold on them personally. Percy Tannenbaum of the University of California at Berkeley has written: "Among life's more embarrassing moments have been countless occasions when I am engaged in conversation in a room while a TV set is on, and I cannot for the life of me stop from periodically glancing over to the screen. This occurs not only during dull conversations but during reasonably interesting ones just as well."

Scientists have been studying the effects of television for 3 decades, generally focusing on whether watching violence on TV correlates with being violent in real life (see "The Effects of Observing Violence," by Leonard Berkowitz; *Scientific American,* February 1964; and "Communication and Social Environment," by George Gerbner, September 1972). Less attention has been paid to the basic allure of the small screen—the medium, as opposed to the message.

The term "TV addiction" is imprecise and laden with value judg- 4 ments, but it captures the essence of a very real phenomenon. Psychologists and psychiatrists formally define substance dependence as a disorder characterized by criteria that include spending a great deal of time using the substance; using it more often than one intends; thinking about reducing use or making repeated unsuccessful efforts to reduce use; giving up important social, family, or occupational activities to use it; and reporting withdrawal symptoms when one stops using it.

All these criteria can apply to people who watch a lot of televi- 5 sion. That does not mean that watching television, per se, is problematic. Television can teach and amuse; it can reach aesthetic heights; it can provide much needed distraction and escape. The difficulty arises when people strongly sense that they ought not to watch as much as they do and yet find themselves strangely unable to reduce their viewing. Some knowledge of how the medium exerts its pull may help heavy viewers gain better control over their lives.

A BODY AT REST TENDS TO STAY AT REST

The amount of time people spend watching television is astonishing. 6 On average, individuals in the industrialized world devote three hours a day to the pursuit—fully half of their leisure time, and more than on any single activity save work and sleep. At this rate, someone who lives to seventy-five would spend nine years in front of the tube. To some commentators, this devotion means simply that people enjoy

TV and make a conscious decision to watch it. But if that is the whole story, why do so many people experience misgivings about how much they view? In Gallup polls in 1992 and 1999, two out of five adult respondents and seven out of ten teenagers said they spent too much time watching TV. Other surveys have consistently shown that roughly 10 percent of adults call themselves TV addicts.

To study people's reactions to TV, researchers have undertaken labo- 7
ratory experiments in which they have monitored the brain waves (using an electroencephalograph, or EEG), skin resistance or heart rate of people watching television. To track behavior and emotion in the normal course of life, as opposed to the artificial conditions of the lab, we have used the Experience Sampling Method (ESM). Participants carried a beeper, and we signaled them six to eight times a day, at random, over the period of a week; whenever they heard the beep, they wrote down what they were doing and how they were feeling using a standardized scorecard.

As one might expect, people who were watching TV when we 8
beeped them reported feeling relaxed and passive. The EEG studies similarly show less mental stimulation, as measured by alpha brain-wave production, during viewing than during reading.

What is more surprising is that the sense of relaxation ends when 9
the set is turned off, but the feelings of passivity and lowered alertness continue. Survey participants commonly reflect that television has somehow absorbed or sucked out their energy, leaving them depleted. They say they have more difficulty concentrating after viewing than before. In contrast, they rarely indicate such difficulty after reading. After playing sports or engaging in hobbies, people report improvements in mood. After watching TV, people's moods are about the same or worse than before.

Within moments of sitting or lying down and pushing the 10
"power" button, viewers report feeling more relaxed. Because the relaxation occurs quickly, people are conditioned to associate viewing with rest and lack of tension. The association is positively reinforced because viewers remain relaxed throughout viewing, and it is negatively reinforced via the stress and dysphoric rumination that occurs once the screen goes blank again.

Habit-forming drugs work in similar ways. A tranquilizer that 11
leaves the body rapidly is much more likely to cause dependence than one that leaves the body slowly, precisely because the user is more aware that the drug's effects are wearing off. Similarly, viewers' vague learned sense that they will feel less relaxed if they stop viewing may be a significant factor in not turning the set off. Viewing begets more viewing.

Thus, the irony of TV: people watch a great deal longer than they 12
plan to, even though prolonged viewing is less rewarding. In our ESM studies the longer people sat in front of the set, the less satisfaction

they said they derived from it. When signaled, heavy viewers (those who consistently watch more than four hours a day) tended to report on their ESM sheets that they enjoy TV less than light viewers did (less than two hours a day). For some, a twinge of unease or guilt that they aren't doing something more productive may also accompany and depreciate the enjoyment of prolonged viewing. Researchers in Japan, the U.K. and the U.S. have found that this guilt occurs much more among middle-class viewers than among less affluent ones.

GRABBING YOUR ATTENTION

What is it about TV that has such a hold on us? In part, the attraction 13 seems to spring from our biological "orienting response." First described by Ivan Pavlov in 1927, the orienting response is our instinctive visual or auditory reaction to any sudden or novel stimulus. It is part of our evolutionary heritage, a built-in sensitivity to movement and potential predatory threats. Typical orienting reactions include dilation of the blood vessels to the brain, slowing of the heart, and constriction of blood vessels to major muscle groups. Alpha waves are blocked for a few seconds before returning to their baseline level, which is determined by the general level of mental arousal. The brain focuses its attention on gathering more information while the rest of the body quiets.

In 1986, Byron Reeves of Stanford University, Esther Thorson 14 of the University of Missouri and their colleagues began to study whether the simple formal features of television—cuts, edits, zooms, pans, sudden noises—activate the orienting response, thereby keeping attention on the screen. By watching how brain waves were affected by formal features, the researchers concluded that these stylistic tricks can indeed trigger involuntary responses and "derive their attentional value through the evolutionary significance of detecting movement. . . . It is the form, not the content, of television that is unique."

The orienting response may partly explain common viewer re- 15 marks such as: "If a television is on, I just can't keep my eyes off it," "I don't want to watch as much as I do, but I can't help it," and "I feel hypnotized when I watch television." In the years since Reeves and Thorson published their pioneering work, researchers have delved deeper. Annie Lang's research team at Indiana University has shown that heart rate decreases for four to six seconds after an orienting stimulus. In ads, action sequences, and music videos, formal features frequently come at a rate of one per second, thus activating the orienting response continuously.

Lang and her colleagues have also investigated whether formal 16 features affect people's memory of what they have seen. In one of their studies, participants watched a program and then filled out a score sheet. Increasing the frequency of edits—defined here as a change from one camera angle to another in the same visual scene—improved memory recognition, presumably because it focused attention on the screen. Increasing the frequency of cuts—changes to a new visual scene—had a similar effect but only up to a point. If the number of cuts exceeded ten in two minutes, recognition dropped off sharply.

Producers of educational television for children have found that formal features can help learning. But increasing the rate of cuts and edits eventually overloads the brain. Music videos and commercials that use rapid intercutting of unrelated scenes are designed to hold attention more than they are to convey information. People may remember the name of the product or band, but the details of the ad itself float in one ear and out the other. The orienting response is overworked. Viewers still attend to the screen, but they feel tired and worn out, with little compensating psychological reward. Our ESM findings show much the same thing. 17

Sometimes the memory of the product is very subtle. Many ads today are deliberately oblique: they have an engaging story line, but it is hard to tell what they are trying to sell. Afterward you may not remember the product consciously. Yet advertisers believe that if they have gotten your attention, when you later go to the store you will feel better or more comfortable with a given product because you have a vague recollection of having heard of it. 18

The natural attraction to television's sound and light starts very early in life. Dafna Lemish of Tel Aviv University has described babies at six to eight weeks attending to television. We have observed slightly older infants who, when lying on their backs on the floor, crane their necks around 180 degrees to catch what light through yonder window breaks. This inclination suggests how deeply rooted the orienting response is. 19

"TV IS PART OF THEM"

That said, we need to be careful about overreacting. Little evidence suggests that adults or children should stop watching TV altogether. The problems come from heavy or prolonged viewing. 20

The Experience Sampling Method permitted us to look closely at most every domain of everyday life: working, eating, reading, talking to friends, playing a sport, and so on. We wondered whether heavy viewers might experience life differently than light viewers do. Do they dislike being with people more? Are they more alienated from work? What we found nearly leaped off the page at us. Heavy viewers report 21 feeling significantly more anxious and less happy than light viewers do in unstructured situations, such as doing nothing, daydreaming, or waiting in line. The difference widens when the viewer is alone.

Subsequently, Robert D. McIlwraith of the University of Manitoba extensively studied those who called themselves TV addicts on surveys. On a measure called the Short Imaginal Processes Inventory (SIPI), he found that the self-described addicts are more easily bored and distracted and have poorer attentional control than the nonaddicts. The addicts said they used TV to distract themselves from unpleasant thoughts and to fill time. Other studies over the years have shown that heavy viewers are less likely to participate in community activities and sports and are more likely to be obese than moderate viewers or nonviewers. 22

The question that naturally arises is: In which direction does the correlation go? Do people turn to TV because of boredom and loneliness, or does TV viewing make people more susceptible to boredom and loneliness? We and most other researchers argue that the former is generally the case, but it is not a simple case of either/or. Jerome L. and Dorothy Singer of Yale University, among others, have suggested that more viewing may contribute to a shorter attention span, diminished self-restraint, and less patience with the normal delays of daily life. More than twenty-five years ago, psychologist Tannis M. MacBeth Williams of the University of British Columbia studied a mountain community that had no television until cable finally arrived. Over time, both adults and children in the town became less creative in problem solving, less able to persevere at tasks, and less tolerant of unstructured time. 23

To some researchers, the most convincing parallel between TV and addictive drugs is that people experience withdrawal symptoms when they cut back on viewing. Nearly forty years ago, Gary A. Steiner of the University of Chicago collected fascinating individual accounts of families whose set had broken—this back in the days when households generally had only one set: "The family walked around like a chicken without a head." "It was terrible. We did nothing—my husband and I talked." "Screamed constantly. Children bothered me, and my nerves were on edge. Tried to interest them in games, but impossible. TV is part of them." 24

In experiments, families have volunteered or been paid to stop viewing, typically for a week or a month. Many could not complete the period of abstinence. Some fought, verbally and physically. Anecdotal reports from some families that have tried the annual "TV turn-off" week in the U.S. tell a similar story. 25

If a family has been spending the lion's share of its free time watching television, reconfiguring itself around a new set of activities is no easy task. Of course, that does not mean it cannot be done or that all families implode when deprived of their set. In a review of these cold-turkey studies, Charles Winick of the City University of 26

New York concluded: "The first three or four days for most persons were the worst, even in many homes where viewing was minimal and where there were other ongoing activities. In over half of all the households, during these first few days of loss, the regular routines were disrupted, family members had difficulties in dealing with the newly available time, anxiety and aggressions were expressed. . . . People living alone tended to be bored and irritated. . . . By the second week, a move toward adaptation to the situation was common." Unfortunately, researchers have yet to flesh out these anecdotes; no one has systematically gathered statistics on the prevalence of these withdrawal symptoms.

Even though TV does seem to meet the criteria for substance 27 dependence, not all researchers would go so far as to call TV addictive. McIlwraith said in 1998 that "displacement of other activities by television may be socially significant but still fall short of the clinical requirement of significant impairment." He argued that a new category of "TV addiction" may not be necessary if heavy viewing stems from conditions such as depression and social phobia. Nevertheless, whether or not we formally diagnose someone as TV-dependent, millions of people sense that they cannot readily control the amount of television they watch.

SLAVE TO THE COMPUTER SCREEN

Although much less research has been done on video games and com- 28 puter use, the same principles often apply. The games offer escape and distraction; players quickly learn that they feel better when playing; and so a kind of reinforcement loop develops. The obvious difference from television, however, is the interactivity. Many video and computer games minutely increase in difficulty along with the increasing ability of the player. One can search for months to find another tennis or chess player of comparable ability, but programmed games can immediately provide a near-perfect match of challenge to skill. They offer the psychic pleasure—what one of us (Csikszentmihalyi) has called "flow"—that accompanies increased mastery of most any human endeavor. On the other hand, prolonged activation of the orienting response can wear players out. Kids report feeling tired, dizzy and nauseated after long sessions.

In 1997, in the most extreme medium-effects case on record, 700 29 Japanese children were rushed to the hospital, many suffering from "optically stimulated epileptic seizures" caused by viewing bright flashing lights in a Pokémon video game broadcast on Japanese TV. Seizures and other untoward effects of video games are significant enough that software companies and platform manufacturers now routinely include warnings in their instruction booklets. Parents have reported to us that rapid movement on the screen has caused motion sickness in their young children after just fifteen minutes of play. Many youngsters, lacking self-control and experience (and often supervision), continue to play despite these symptoms.

Lang and Shyam Sundar of Pennsylvania State University have been studying how people respond to Web sites. Sundar has shown people multiple versions of the same Web page, identical except for the number of links. Users reported that more links conferred a greater sense of control and engagement. At some point, however, the number of links reached saturation, and adding more of them simply turned people off. As with video games, the ability of Web sites to hold the user's attention seems to depend less on formal features than on interactivity. 30

For growing numbers of people, the life they lead online may often seem more important, more immediate, and more intense than the life they lead face-to-face. Maintaining control over one's media habits is more of a challenge today than it has ever been. TV sets and computers are everywhere. But the small screen and the Internet need not interfere with the quality of the rest of one's life. In its easy provision of relaxation and escape, television can be beneficial in limited doses. Yet when the habit interferes with the ability to grow, to learn new things, to lead an active life, then it does constitute a kind of dependence and should be taken seriously. 31

Examining the Text

1. According to Kubey and Csikszentmihalyi, what factors distinguish TV addiction from simple TV viewing?

2. What biological evidence do Kubey and Csikszentmihalyi summon to support their claims of TV's addictive capabilities? What is the "orienting response," and how does it function in the context of TV viewing?

3. What do Kubey and Csikszentmihalyi mean when they ask, "In which direction does the correlation go?" How do they address the problem of correlation and causation in TV addiction?

4. According to Kubey and Csikszentmihalyi, in what ways are video games and computer use similar to and different from TV viewing? How do these similarities and differences affect the question of addiction that Kubey and Csikszentmihalyi discuss?

5. *Thinking rhetorically:* The title of Kubey and Csikszentmihalyi's article draws attention to the fact that many people use the term addiction as a metaphor. For instance, you might hear people saying that they're addicted" to watching "Survivor" or that they're "addicted" to Brown Sugar Cinnamon Frosted Pop-Tarts. What are some of the differences between using "addiction" as a metaphor and using it as a clinical term, as Kubey and Csikszentmihalyi do? Can you think of other terms that function as common metaphors in our culture, like "addiction" does?

For Group Discussion

In a group with several other students, choose an addiction about which you have some knowledge (for instance, gambling, smoking, or drinking alcohol). Make a list of all that you know about this addiction: who suffers from it, what problems it causes, why it occurs, how society has responded, what laws exist that address the addiction, what economic consequences it has, how it can be "cured," and so on. Then compare the list you've compiled to the facts about television addiction that Kubey and Csikszentmihalyi discuss in the reading. Based on this comparison, do you think that excessive television viewing can genuinely be considered an "addiction"? Why or why not?

Writing Suggestion

For this assignment you'll need access to the Internet to research "Digital Detox Week," formerly known as "TV Turn-Off Week" and described briefly by Kubey and Csikszentmihalyi in their article. The original "TV Turn-Off Week" campaign was promoted by Adbusters and is now sponsored by Campaign for a Commercial-Free Childhood. In 2008, it evolved to include the computer screen as well as the TV screen in recognition of the new modes of distribution of TV and video content as well as the increasingly addictive powers of other screens into which we often stare.

At *http://www.adbusters.org/campaigns/digitaldetox/* you can read more about this event, including personal accounts of people who participated. You can also look at posters and videos that people created to publicize the event, and read related articles. After reading through all this information, write an essay in which you argue either for or against the merits of "Digital Detox Week." Be sure to use quotations and/or statistics from the article by Kubey and Csikszentmihalyi in your argument. Feel free to include anecdotes or observations from your own experiences as a viewer of TV screens and other screens to help bolster your position.

Watching TV Makes You Smarter

STEVEN JOHNSON

If your parents have ever complained that you watch too much TV, just tell them, "But Mom, Dad, watching TV is mentally stimulating and can actually make me smarter!" When they look at you in disbelief, refer them to the following article in which Steven Johnson makes precisely that argument: that watching TV—or at least, watching some of the shows currently on TV—gives you a good cognitive workout. The article, adapted from Johnson's best seller, Everything Bad Is Good for You: How Today's Popular Culture Is Actually Making Us Smarter, *compares past and present TV shows and conclude that viewers today are required to exercise their mental faculties in order to make sense of complex, multilayered plots and characters.*

Although Johnson refers to many past and present shows in this article, his primary examples of intellectually challenging shows are 24, The West Wing, The Sopranos, *and* ER. *He argues that these shows combine the complicated plot threads of soap opera with the realistic characters and important social issues of nighttime drama. As a result, in any given episode of a show, viewers have to follow intersecting narrative threads that include many distinct characters, each with their own continuing story line. These shows often have fast-paced, specialized dialogue that's purposely difficult for viewers to follow. Watching the shows engages viewers in the pleasures of solving puzzles and unlocking mysteries, and so these shows provide a mentally stimulating hour of TV viewing—punctuated, of course, by commercial breaks.*

It certainly goes against common perceptions of TV to suggest that watching shows is mentally stimulating; you're far more likely to find arguments that TV viewing can give you a skewed perception of reality. Because Johnson makes such an unusual argument, it's interesting to pay attention to the strategies he uses to try to convince readers that he's correct. ***As you read,*** *notice the different kinds of evidence that Johnson uses to prove his point. What evidence do you find most convincing? What evidence do you find questionable?*

THE SLEEPER CURVE

Scientist A: Has he asked for anything special?
Scientist B: Yes, this morning for breakfast . . . he requested something called "wheat germ, organic honey and tiger's milk."
Scientist A: Oh, yes. Those were the charmed substances that some years ago were felt to contain life-preserving properties.
Scientist B: You mean there was no deep fat? No steak or cream pies or . . . hot fudge?
Scientist A: Those were thought to be unhealthy.

From Woody Allen's *Sleeper*

On Jan. 24, the Fox network showed an episode of its hit drama *24*, the real-time thriller known for its cliffhanger tension and often-gruesome violence. Over the preceding weeks, a number of public controversies had erupted around *24*, mostly focused on its portrait of Muslim terrorists and its penchant for torture scenes. The episode that was shown on the 24th only fanned the flames higher: in one scene, a terrorist enlists a hit man to kill his child for not fully supporting the jihadist 1 cause; in another scene, the secretary of defense authorizes the torture of his son to uncover evidence of a terrorist plot.

But the explicit violence and the post-9/11 terrorist anxiety are not 2 the only elements of *24* that would have been unthinkable on prime-time network television twenty years ago. Alongside the notable change in content lies an equally notable change in form. During its forty four minutes—a real-time hour, minus sixteen minutes for commercials—the episode connects the lives of twenty one distinct characters, each with a clearly defined "story arc," as the Hollywood jargon has it: a defined personality with motivations and obstacles and specific relationships with other characters. Nine primary narrative threads wind their way through those forty four minutes, each drawing extensively upon events and information revealed in earlier episodes. Draw a map of all those intersecting plots and personalities, and you get structure that—where formal complexity is concerned—more closely resembles *Middlemarch* than a hit TV drama of years past like *Bonanza*.

For decades, we've worked under the assumption that mass culture 3 follows a path declining steadily toward lowest-common-denominator standards, presumably because the "masses" want dumb, simple pleasures and big media companies try to give the masses what they want. But as that *24* episode suggests, the exact opposite is happening: the culture is getting more cognitively demanding, not less. To make sense of an episode of *24*, you have to integrate far more information than you would have a few decades ago watching a comparable show. Beneath the violence and the ethnic stereotypes, another trend appears: to keep up with entertainment like *24*, you have to pay attention, make inferences, track shifting social relationships. This is what I call the Sleeper Curve: the most debased forms of mass diversion—video games and violent television dramas and juvenile sitcoms—turn out to be nutritional after all.

I believe that the Sleeper Curve is the single most important 4 new force altering the mental development of young people today, and I believe it is largely a force for good: enhancing our cognitive faculties, not dumbing them down. And yet you almost never hear this story in popular accounts of today's media. Instead, you hear dire tales of addiction, violence, mindless escapism. It's assumed that shows that promote smoking or gratuitous violence are bad for us, while those that thunder against teen pregnancy or intolerance have a positive role in society. Judged by that morality-play standard, the story of popular culture over the past fifty years—if not 500—is a story of decline: the morals of the stories have grown darker and more ambiguous, and the antiheroes have multiplied.

The usual counterargument here is that what media have lost in 5 moral clarity, they have gained in realism. The real world doesn't come in nicely packaged public-service announcements, and we're better off with entertainment like *The Sopranos* that reflects our fallen state with all its ethical ambiguity. I happen to be sympathetic to that argument, but it's not the one I want to make here. I think there is another way to assess the social virtue of pop culture, one that looks at media as a kind of cognitive workout, not as a series of life lessons. There may indeed be more "negative messages" in the mediasphere today. But that's not the only way to evaluate whether our television shows or video games are having a positive impact. Just as important—if not more important—is the kind of thinking you have to do to make sense of a cultural experience. That is where the Sleeper Curve becomes visible.

TELEVISED INTELLIGENCE

6 Consider the cognitive demands that televised narratives place on their viewers. With many shows that we associate with "quality" entertainment—*The Mary Tyler Moore Show, Murphy Brown, Frasier*—the intelligence arrives fully formed in the words and actions of the characters on-screen. They say witty things to one another and avoid lapsing into tired sitcom clichés, and we smile along in our living rooms, enjoying the company of these smart people. But assuming we're bright enough to understand the sentences they're saying, there's no intellectual labor involved in enjoying the show as a viewer. You no more challenge your mind by watching these intelligent shows than you challenge your body watching *Monday Night Football*. The intellectual work is happening on-screen, not off.

7 But another kind of televised intelligence is on the rise. Think of the cognitive benefits conventionally ascribed to reading: attention, patience, retention, the parsing of narrative threads. Over the last half-century, programming on TV has increased the demands it places on precisely these mental faculties. This growing complexity involves three primary elements: multiple threading, flashing arrows and social networks.

8 According to television lore, the age of multiple threads began with the arrival in 1981 of *Hill Street Blues*, the Steven Bochco police drama invariably praised for its "gritty realism." Watch an episode of *Hill Street Blues* side by side with any major drama from the preceding decades—*Starsky and Hutch*, for instance, or *Dragnet*—and the structural transformation will jump out at you. The earlier shows follow one or two lead characters, adhere to a single dominant plot and reach a decisive conclusion at the end of the episode. Draw an outline of the narrative threads in almost every *Dragnet* episode, and it will be a single line: from the initial crime scene, through the investigation, to the eventual cracking of the case. A typical *Starsky and Hutch* episode offers only the slightest variation on this linear formula: the introduction of a

comic subplot that usually appears only at the tail ends of the episode, creating a structure that looks like this graph. The vertical axis represents the number of individual threads, and the horizontal axis is time.

"STARSKY AND HUTCH" (ANY EPISODE)

A *Hill Street Blues* episode complicates the picture in a number of profound ways. The narrative weaves together a collection of distinct strands—sometimes as many as ten, though at least half of the threads involve only a few quick scenes scattered through the episode. The number of primary characters—and not just bit parts—swells significantly. And the episode has fuzzy borders: picking up one or two threads from previous episodes at the outset and leaving one or two threads open at the end. Charted graphically, an average episode looks like this: 9

HILL STREET BLUES (EPISODE 85)

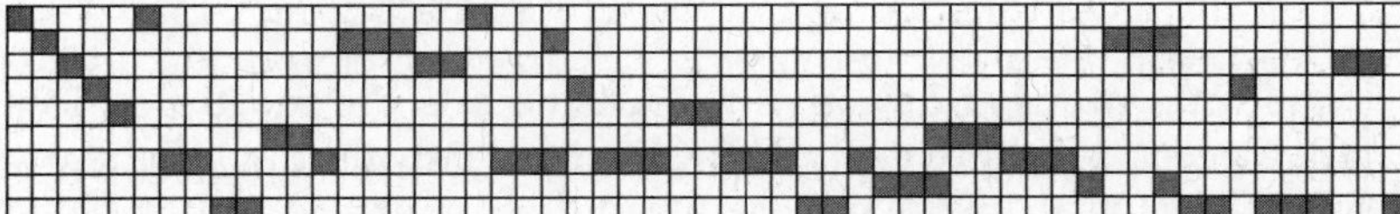

Critics generally cite *Hill Street Blues* as the beginning of "serious drama" native in the television medium—differentiating the series from the single-episode dramatic programs from the '50s, which were Broadway plays performed in front of a camera. But the *Hill Street* innovations weren't all that original; they'd long played a defining role in popular television, just not during the evening hours. The structure of a *Hill Street* episode—and indeed of all the critically acclaimed dramas that followed, from *thirtysomething* to *Six Feet Under*—is the structure of a soap opera. *Hill Street Blues* might have sparked a new golden age of television drama during its seven-year run, but it did so by using a few crucial tricks that *Guiding Light* and *General Hospital* mastered long before. 10

Bochco's genius with *Hill Street* was to marry complex narrative structure with complex subject matter. *Dallas* had already shown that the extended, interwoven threads of the soap-opera genre could survive the weeklong interruptions of a prime-time show, but the actual content of *Dallas* was fluff. (The most probing issue it addressed was the question, now folkloric, of who shot J.R.) *All in the Family* and *Rhoda* showed that you could tackle complex social issues, but they did their tackling in the comfort of the sitcom living room. *Hill Street* had richly drawn characters confronting difficult social issues and a narrative structure to match. 11

Since *Hill Street* appeared, the multi-threaded drama has become 12
the most widespread fictional genre on prime time: *St. Elsewhere*, *L.A. Law*, *thirtysomething*, *Twin Peaks*, *N.Y.P.D. Blue*, *ER*, *The West Wing*, *Alias*, *Lost*. (The only prominent holdouts in drama are shows like *Law and Order* that have essentially updated the venerable *Dragnet* format and thus remained anchored to a single narrative line.) Since the early '80s, however, there has been a noticeable increase in narrative complexity in these dramas. The most ambitious show on TV to date, *The Sopranos*, routinely follows up to a dozen distinct threads over the course of an episode, with more than twenty recurring characters. An episode from late in the first season looks like this:

THE SOPRANOS (EPISODE 8)

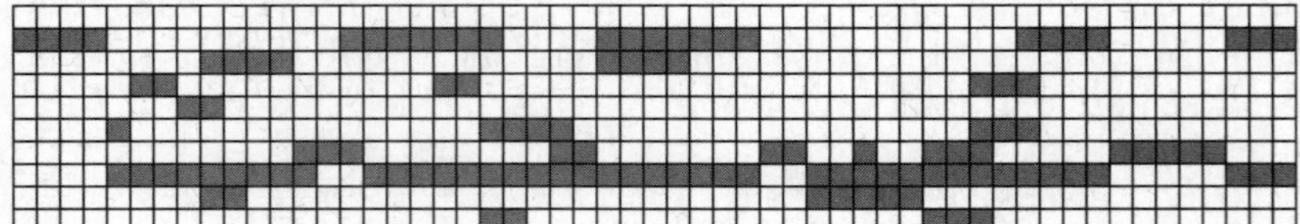

The total number of active threads equals the multiple plots 13
of "Hill Street," but here each thread is more substantial. The show doesn't offer a clear distinction between dominant and minor plots; each story line carries its weight in the mix. The episode also displays a chordal mode of storytelling entirely absent from "Hill Street": a single scene in *The Sopranos* will often connect to three different threads at the same time, layering one plot atop another. And every single thread in this "Sopranos" episode builds on events from previous episodes and continues on through the rest of the season and beyond.

Put those charts together, and you have a portrait of the Sleeper 14
Curve rising over the past thirty years of popular television. In a sense, this is as much a map of cognitive changes in the popular mind as it is a map of on-screen developments, as if the media titans decided to condition our brains to follow ever-larger numbers of simultaneous threads. Before "Hill Street," the conventional wisdom among television execs was that audiences wouldn't be comfortable following more than three plots in a single episode, and indeed, the "Hill Street" pilot, which was shown in January 1981, brought complaints from viewers that the show was too complicated. Fast-forward two decades, and shows like *The Sopranos* engage their audiences with narratives that make *Hill Street* look like *Three's Company*. Audiences happily embrace that complexity because they've been trained by two decades of multi-threaded dramas.

Multi-threading is the most celebrated structural feature of the mod- 15
ern television drama, and it certainly deserves some of the honor that has been doled out to it. And yet multi-threading is only part of the story.

THE CASE FOR CONFUSION

Shortly after the arrival of the first-generation slasher movies—*Halloween*, *Friday the 13th*—Paramount released a mock-slasher flick called *Student Bodies*, parodying the genre just as the "Scream" series would do fifteen years later. In one scene, the obligatory nubile teenage baby sitter hears a noise outside a suburban house; she opens the door to investigate, finds nothing and then goes back inside. As the door shuts behind her, the camera swoops in on the doorknob, and we see that she has left the door unlocked. The camera pulls back and then swoops down again for emphasis. And then a flashing arrow appears on the screen, with text that helpfully explains: "Unlocked!" 16

That flashing arrow is parody, of course, but it's merely an exaggerated version of a device popular stories use all the time. When a sci-fi script inserts into some advanced lab a nonscientist who keeps asking the science geeks to explain what they're doing with that particle accelerator, that's a flashing arrow that gives the audience precisely the information it needs in order to make sense of the ensuing plot. ("Whatever you do, don't spill water on it, or you'll set off a massive explosion!") These hints serve as a kind of narrative handholding. Implicitly, they say to the audience, "We realize you have no idea what a particle accelerator is, but here's the deal: all you need to know is that it's a big fancy thing that explodes when wet." They focus the mind on relevant details: "Don't worry about whether the baby sitter is going to break up with her boyfriend. Worry about that guy lurking in the bushes." They reduce the amount of analytic work you need to do to make sense of a story. All you have to do is follow the arrows. 17

By this standard, popular television has never been harder to follow. If narrative threads have experienced a population explosion over the past twenty years, flashing arrows have grown correspondingly scarce. Watching our pinnacle of early '80s TV drama, *Hill Street Blues*, we find there's an informational wholeness to each scene that differs markedly from what you see on shows like *The West Wing* or *The Sopranos* or *Alias* or *ER*. 18

"Hill Street" has ambiguities about future events: will a convicted killer be executed? Will Furillo marry Joyce Davenport? Will Renko find it in himself to bust a favorite singer for cocaine possession? But the present-tense of each scene explains itself to the viewer with little ambiguity. There's an open question or a mystery driving each of these stories—how will it all turn out?—but there's no mystery about the immediate activity on the screen. A contemporary drama like *The West Wing*, on the other hand, constantly embeds mysteries into 19 the present-tense events: you see characters performing actions or discussing events about which crucial information has been deliberately withheld. Anyone who has watched more than a handful of *The West Wing* episodes closely will know the feeling: scene after scene refers to some clearly crucial but unexplained piece of information, and after the sixth reference, you'll find yourself wishing you could rewind the tape to figure out what they're talking about, assuming you've missed something. And then you realize that you're supposed to be confused. The open question posed by these sequences is not, "How will this turn out in the end?" The question is, "What's happening right now?"

The deliberate lack of hand-holding extends down to the micro- 20
level of dialogue as well. Popular entertainment that addresses technical issues—whether they are the intricacies of passing legislation, or of performing a heart bypass, or of operating a particle accelerator—conventionally switches between two modes of information in dialogue: texture and substance. Texture is all the arcane verbiage provided to convince the viewer that they're watching Actual Doctors at Work; substance is the material planted amid the background texture that the viewer needs make sense of the plot.

Conventionally, narratives demarcate the line between texture 21
and substance by inserting cues that flag or translate the important data. There's an unintentionally comical moment in the 2004 blockbuster *The Day After Tomorrow* in which the beleaguered climatologist (played by Dennis Quaid) announces his theory about the imminent arrival of a new ice age to a gathering of government officials. In his speech, he warns that "we have hit a critical desalinization point!" At this moment, the writer-director Roland Emmerich—a master of brazen arrow-flashing—has an official follow with the obliging remark: "It would explain what's driving this extreme weather." They might as well have had a flashing "Unlocked!" arrow on the screen.

The dialogue on shows like *The West Wing* and *ER*, on the other 22
hand, doesn't talk down to its audiences. It rushes by, the words accelerating in sync with the high-speed tracking shots that glide through the corridors and operating rooms. The characters talk faster in these shows, but the truly remarkable thing about the dialogue is not purely a matter of speed; it's the willingness to immerse the audience in information that most viewers won't understand. Here's a typical scene from *ER*.:

[Weaver and Wright push a gurney carrying a 16-year-old girl. Her 23
parents, Janna and Frank Mikami, follow close behind. Carter and Lucy fall in.]

Weaver: 16-year-old, unconscious, history of biliary atresia.
Carter: Hepatic coma?

Weaver: Looks like it.
Mr. Mikami: She was doing fine until six months ago.
Carter: What medication is she on?
Mrs. Mikami: Ampicillin, tobramycin, vitamins a, d and k.
Lucy: Skin's jaundiced.
Weaver: Same with the sclera. Breath smells sweet.
Carter: Fetor hepaticus?
Weaver: Yep.
Lucy: What's that?
Weaver: Her liver's shut down. Let's dip a urine. [To Carter] Guys, it's getting a little crowded in here, why don't you deal with the parents? Start lactulose, 30 cc's per NG.
Carter: We're giving medicine to clean her blood.
Weaver: Blood in the urine, two-plus.
Carter: The liver failure is causing her blood not to clot.
Mrs. Mikami: Oh, God. . . .
Carter: Is she on the transplant list?
Mr. Mikami: She's been Status 2a for six months, but they haven't been able to find her a match.
Carter: Why? What's her blood type?
Mr. Mikami: AB.
[This hits Carter like a lightning bolt. Lucy gets it, too. They share a look.]

There are flashing arrows here, of course—"The liver failure is causing her blood not to clot"—but the ratio of medical jargon to layperson translation is remarkably high. From a purely narrative point of view, the decisive line arrives at the very end: "AB." The 16-year-old's blood type connects her to an earlier plot line, involving a cerebral-hemorrhage victim who—after being dramatically revived in one of the opening scenes—ends up brain-dead. Far earlier, before the liver-failure scene above, Carter briefly discusses harvesting the hemorrhage victim's organs for transplants, and another doctor makes a passing reference to his blood type being the rare AB (thus making him an unlikely donor). The twist here revolves around a statistically unlikely event happening at the E.R.—an otherwise perfect liver donor showing up just in time to donate his liver to a recipient with the same rare blood type. But the show reveals this twist with remarkable subtlety. To make sense of that last "AB" line—and the look of disbelief on Carter's and Lucy's faces—you have to recall a passing remark uttered earlier regarding a character who belongs to a completely different thread. Shows like *ER* may have more blood and guts than popular TV had a generation ago, but when it comes to storytelling, they possess a quality that can only be described as subtlety and discretion. 24

EVEN BAD TV IS BETTER

Skeptics might argue that I have stacked the deck here by focusing on relatively highbrow titles like *The Sopranos* or *The West Wing*, when in fact the most significant change in the last five years of narrative entertainment involves reality TV. Does the contemporary pop cultural landscape look quite as promising if the representative show is *Joe Millionaire* instead of *The West Wing*? 25

I think it does, but to answer that question properly, you have to avoid the tendency to sentimentalize the past. When people talk about the golden age of television in the early '70s—invoking shows like *The Mary Tyler Moore Show* and *All in the Family*—they forget to mention how awful most television programming was during much of that decade. If you're going to look at pop-culture trends, you have to compare apples to apples, or in this case, lemons to lemons. The relevant comparison is not between *Joe Millionaire* and *M*A*S*H*; it's between *Joe Millionaire* and *The Newlywed Game*, or between *Survivor* and *The Love Boat*. 26

What you see when you make these head-to-head comparisons is that a rising tide of complexity has been lifting programming at the bottom of the quality spectrum and at the top. *The Sopranos* is several times more demanding of its audiences than "Hill Street" was, and *Joe Millionaire* has made comparable advances over *Battle of the Network Stars*. This is the ultimate test of the Sleeper Curve theory: Even the junk has improved. 27

If early television took its cues from the stage, today's reality programming is reliably structured like a video game: a series of competitive tests, growing more challenging over time. Many reality shows borrow a subtler device from gaming culture as well: the rules aren't fully established at the outset. You learn as you play. 28

On a show like *Survivor* or *The Apprentice*, the participants—and the audience—know the general objective of the series, but each episode involves new challenges that haven't been ordained in advance. The final round of the first season of *The Apprentice*, for instance, threw a monkey wrench into the strategy that governed the play up to that point, when Trump announced that the two remaining apprentices would have to assemble and manage a team of subordinates who had already been fired in earlier episodes of the show. All of a sudden, the overarching objective of the game—do anything to avoid being fired—presented a potential conflict to the remaining two contenders: the structure of the final round favored the survivor who had maintained the best relationships with his comrades. Suddenly, it wasn't enough just to have clawed your way to the top; you had to have made friends while clawing. The original *Joe Millionaire* went so far as to undermine 29 the most fundamental convention of all—that the show's creators don't openly lie to the contestants about the prizes—by inducing a construction worker to pose as man of means while twenty women competed for his attention.

Reality programming borrowed another key ingredient from games: the intellectual labor of probing the system's rules for weak spots and opportunities. As each show discloses its conventions, and each participant reveals his or her personality traits and background, the intrigue in watching comes from figuring out how the participants should best navigate the environment that has been created for them. The pleasure in these shows comes not from watching other people being humiliated on national television; it comes from depositing other people in a complex, high-pressure environment where no established strategies exist and watching them find their bearings. That's why the water-cooler conversation about these shows invariably tracks in on the strategy displayed on the previous night's episode: why did Kwame pick Omarosa in that final round? What devious strategy is Richard Hatch concocting now? 30

When we watch these shows, the part of our brain that monitors the emotional lives of the people around us—the part that tracks subtle shifts in intonation and gesture and facial expression—scrutinizes the action on the screen, looking for clues. We trust certain characters implicitly and vote others off the island in a heartbeat. Traditional narrative shows also trigger emotional connections to the characters, but those connections don't have the same participatory effect, because traditional narratives aren't explicitly about strategy. The phrase "Monday-morning quarterbacking" describes the engaged feeling that spectators have in relation to games as opposed to stories. We absorb stories, but we second-guess games. Reality programming has brought that second-guessing to prime time, only the game in question revolves around social dexterity rather than the physical kind. 31

THE REWARDS OF SMART CULTURE

The quickest way to appreciate the Sleeper Curve's cognitive training is to sit down and watch a few hours of hit programming from the late '70s on Nick at Nite or the SOAPnet channel or on DVD. The modern viewer who watches a show like "Dallas" today will be bored by the content—not just because the show is less salacious than today's soap operas (which it is by a small margin) but also because the show contains far less information in each scene, despite the fact that its soap-opera structure made it one of the most complicated narratives on 32 television in its prime. With *Dallas*, the modern viewer doesn't have to think to make sense of what's going on, and not having to think is boring. Many recent hit shows—*24*, *Survivor*, *The Sopranos*, *Alias*, *Lost*, *The Simpsons*, *ER*—take the opposite approach, layering each scene with a thick network of affiliations. You have to focus to follow the plot, and in focusing you're exercising the parts of your brain that map social networks, that fill in missing information, that connect multiple narrative threads.

33 Of course, the entertainment industry isn't increasing the cognitive complexity of its products for charitable reasons. The Sleeper Curve exists because there's money to be made by making culture smarter. The economics of television syndication and DVD sales mean that there's a tremendous financial pressure to make programs that can be watched multiple times, revealing new nuances and shadings on the third viewing. Meanwhile, the Web has created a forum for annotation and commentary that allows more complicated shows to prosper, thanks to the fan sites where each episode of shows like *Lost* or *Alias* is dissected with an intensity usually reserved for Talmud scholars. Finally, interactive games have trained a new generation of media consumers to probe complex environments and to think on their feet, and that gamer audience has now come to expect the same challenges from their television shows. In the end, the Sleeper Curve tells us something about the human mind. It may be drawn toward the sensational where content is concerned—sex does sell, after all. But the mind also likes to be challenged; there's real pleasure to be found in solving puzzles, detecting patterns, or unpacking a complex narrative system.

34 In pointing out some of the ways that popular culture has improved our minds, I am not arguing that parents should stop paying attention to the way their children amuse themselves. What I am arguing for is a change in the criteria we use to determine what really is cognitive junk food and what is genuinely nourishing. Instead of a show's violent or tawdry content, instead of wardrobe malfunctions or the F-word, the true test should be whether a given show engages or sedates the mind. Is it a single thread strung together with predictable punch lines every thirty seconds? Or does it map a complex social network? Is your onscreen character running around shooting everything in sight, or is she trying to solve problems and manage resources? If your kids want to watch reality TV, encourage them to watch *Survivor* over *Fear Factor*. If they want to watch a mystery show, encourage *24* over *Law and Order*. If they want to play a violent game, encourage Grand Theft Auto over Quake. Indeed, it might be just as helpful to have a rating system that used mental labor and not obscenity and violence as its classification scheme for the world of mass culture.

Kids and grown-ups each can learn from their increasingly shared 35 obsessions. Too often we imagine the blurring of kid and grown-up cultures as a series of violations: the nine-year-olds who have to have nipple broaches explained to them thanks to Janet Jackson; the middle-aged guy who can't wait to get home to his Xbox. But this demographic blur has a commendable side that we don't acknowledge enough. The kids are forced to think like grown-ups: analyzing complex social networks, managing resources, tracking subtle narrative intertwinings, recognizing long-term patterns. The grown-ups, in turn, get to learn from the kids: decoding each new technological wave, parsing the interfaces, and discovering the intellectual rewards of play. Parents should see this as an opportunity, not a crisis. Smart culture is no longer something you force your kids to ingest, like green vegetables. It's something you share.

Examining the Text

1. What does Johnson mean by the term the *Sleeper Curve?* How is this term related to the opening quotation from Woody Allen's movie, *Sleeper?*

2. In paragraph 5, Johnson makes a distinction between seeing the media "as a kind of cognitive workout, not as a series of life lessons." Explain this distinction in your own words. What TV shows might fall into the category of "cognitive workout"? What shows would be more likely to offer "life lessons"?

3. What does Johnson mean by "flashing arrows" in TV shows? What function do flashing arrows serve? How have they changed over the years?

4. According to Johnson, what kind of intellectual and social complexity does reality TV provide its viewers? Do you think Johnson's argument about reality TV is persuasive? Why or why not?

5. *Thinking rhetorically:* Following up on the "as you read" suggestion in the introduction to this article, think about the evidence that Johnson uses to support his claim that current TV shows are cognitively stimulating. Select one specific piece of evidence from the article that you find very convincing and one that you find unconvincing. Based on a comparison of these two pieces of evidence, what general conclusions can you draw about the characteristics of good and weak evidence?

For Group Discussion

In a small group, have one of the group members read aloud the last paragraph of the article, in which Johnson discusses how parents and children can benefit from "smart culture" on TV. Make a list of the benefits for kids and the benefits for parents. Then discuss whether you think each of the benefits can be realistically achieved by watching "smart TV." Draw on your own experiences and your own knowledge of TV programs in order to decide whether Johnson's argument is reasonable or whether he's overstating the positives of watching TV.

Writing Suggestion

Johnson provides some visual evidence to support his assertion that TV shows have become increasingly complex. The three graphs included in the article show the number of plot threads in single episodes of *Starsky and Hutch, Hill Street Blues,* and *The Sopranos.* A quick visual comparison of these graphs does indeed suggest that *The Sopranos* has more plot threads and more interweaving of these threads than the two earlier shows. Your assignment is to create a similar chart for a current TV show of your choice. Choose a show to watch, and as you're watching keep note of each time a new plot thread occurs or there's a reference to another thread. After the show is over, plot these elements on a simple chart in which the vertical axis represents each plot thread and the horizontal axis represents time. To make the task easier, label each plot thread on the vertical axis (something Johnson doesn't do). After you've finished the chart, write a paragraph in which you draw conclusions about the relative complexity of the show as compared to the three examples Johnson offers.

Gin, Television, and Social Surplus

CLAY SHIRKY

We conclude this selection of general readings about television with an article that points to both its past and its future. Clay Shirky draws an explicit contrast between Gilligan's Island *and Wikipedia—that is, between TV sit-coms and the participatory projects like Wikipedia, which are currently underway on the Internet. One of Shirky's key ideas is that television takes care of something that we have in surplus—time—by defusing it, whereas projects on the Internet draw on our free time more productively, engaging us in creative, collaborative activities.*

This article has an interesting history: it is adapted from a talk that Shirky gave at a 2008 Web 2.0 conference and can be found online at a blog that Shirky developed to promote his latest book, Here Comes Everybody: The Power of Organizing Without Organizations. *The ideas here have been what we might describe as multiply mediated: oral presentation, online blog, print article. Shirky himself is equally multiple, so to speak. Here's how he describes his career on his home page: "I have been a producer, programmer, professor, designer, author, consultant, sometimes working with people who wanted to create a purely intellectual or aesthetic experience online, sometimes working with people who wanted to use the Internet to sell books or batteries or banking."* ***Before you read the article,*** *take a look at Shirky's home page (http://www.shirky.com) and the blog he maintains (http://www.shirky.com/weblog/) to read about some of his other projects, articles, and ideas.*

I was recently reminded of some reading I did in college, way back in the last century, by a British historian arguing that the critical technology, for the early phase of the industrial revolution, was gin. 1

The transformation from rural to urban life was so sudden, and so wrenching, that the only thing society could do to manage was to drink itself into a stupor for a generation. The stories from that era are amazing—there were gin pushcarts working their way through the streets of London. 2

And it wasn't until society woke up from that collective bender that we actually started to get the institutional structures that we associate with the industrial revolution today. Things like public libraries and museums, increasingly broad education for children, elected leaders—a lot of things we like—didn't happen until having all of those people together stopped seeming like a crisis and started seeming like an asset. 3

It wasn't until people started thinking of this as a vast civic surplus, one they could design for rather than just dissipate, that we started to get what we think of now as an industrial society. 4

If I had to pick the critical technology for the twentieth century, the bit of social lubricant without which the wheels would've come off the whole enterprise, I'd say it was the sitcom. Starting with the Second World War, a whole series of things happened—rising GDP per capita, rising educational attainment, rising life expectancy and, critically, a rising number of people who were working five-day work weeks. For the first time, society forced onto an enormous number of its citizens the requirement to manage something they had never had to manage before—free time. 5

And what did we do with that free time? Well, mostly we spent it watching TV. 6

We did that for decades. We watched *I Love Lucy*. We watched *Gilligan's Island*. We watch *Malcolm in the Middle*. We watch *Desperate Housewives*. *Desperate Housewives* essentially functioned as a kind of cognitive heat sink, dissipating thinking that might otherwise have built up and caused society to overheat. 7

And it's only now, as we're waking up from that collective bender, that we're starting to see the cognitive surplus as an asset rather than as a crisis. We're seeing things being designed to take advantage of that surplus, to deploy it in ways more engaging than just having a TV in everybody's basement. 8

This hit me in a conversation I had about two months ago. As Jen said in the introduction, I've finished a book called *Here Comes Everybody*, which has recently come out, and this recognition came out of a conversation I had about the book. I was being interviewed by a TV producer to see whether I should be on her show, and she asked me, "What are you seeing out there that's interesting?" 9

I started telling her about the *Wikipedia* article on Pluto. You may 10
remember that Pluto got kicked out of the planet club a couple of years ago, so all of a sudden there was all of this activity on *Wikipedia*. The talk pages light up, people are editing the article like mad, and the whole community is in a ruckus—"How should we characterize this change in Pluto's status?" And a little bit at a time they move the article—fighting offstage all the while—from, "Pluto is the ninth planet," to "Pluto is an odd-shaped rock with an odd-shaped orbit at the edge of the solar system."

So I tell her all this stuff, and I think, "Okay, we're going to have a 11
conversation about authority or social construction or whatever." That wasn't her question. She heard this story, and she shook her head and said, "Where do people find the time?" That was her question. And I just kind of snapped. And I said, "No one who works in TV gets to ask that question. You know where the time comes from. It comes from the cognitive surplus you've been masking for fifty years."

So how big is that surplus? So if you take *Wikipedia* as a kind of 12
unit, all of *Wikipedia*, the whole project—every page, every edit, every talk page, every line of code, in every language that *Wikipedia* exists in—that represents something like the cumulation of 100 million hours of human thought. I worked this out with Martin Wattenberg at IBM; it's a back-of-the-envelope calculation, but it's the right order of magnitude, about 100 million hours of thought.

And television watching? Two hundred billion hours, in the U.S. 13
alone, every year. Put another way, now that we have a unit, that's 2,000 *Wikipedia* projects a year spent watching television. Or put still another way, in the U.S., we spend 100 million hours every weekend, just watching the ads. This is a pretty big surplus. People asking, "Where do they find the time?" when they're looking at things like *Wikipedia* don't understand how tiny that entire project is, as a carve-out of this asset that's finally being dragged into what Tim calls an architecture of participation.

Now, the interesting thing about a surplus like that is that soci- 14
ety doesn't know what to do with it at first—hence the gin, hence the sitcoms. Because if people knew what to do with a surplus with reference to the existing social institutions, then it wouldn't be a surplus, would it? It's precisely when no one has any idea how to deploy something that people have to start experimenting with it, in order for the surplus to get integrated, and the course of that integration can transform society.

The early phase for taking advantage of this cognitive surplus, the 15
phase I think we're still in, is all special cases. The physics of participation is much more like the physics of weather than it is like the physics of gravity. We know all the forces that combine to make these kinds of things work: there's an interesting community over here, there's an interesting sharing model over there, those people are collaborating on

open source software. But despite knowing the inputs, we can't predict the outputs yet because there's so much complexity.

The way you explore complex ecosystems is you just try lots and lots and lots of things, and you hope that everybody who fails fails informatively so that you can at least find a skull on a pikestaff near where you're going. That's the phase we're in now. 16

Just to pick one example, one I'm in love with, but it's tiny. A couple of weeks ago one of my students at ITP forwarded me a project started by a professor in Brazil, in Fortaleza, named Vasco Furtado. It's a Wiki Map for crime in Brazil. If there's an assault, if there's a burglary, if there's a mugging, a robbery, a rape, a murder, you can go and put a push-pin on a Google Map, and you can characterize the assault, and you start to see a map of where these crimes are occurring. 17

Now, this already exists as tacit information. Anybody who knows a town has some sense of, "Don't go there. That street corner is dangerous. Don't go in this neighborhood. Be careful there after dark." But it's something society knows without society really knowing it, which is to say there's no public source where you can take advantage of it. And the cops, if they have that information, they're certainly not sharing. In fact, one of the things Furtado says in starting the Wiki crime map was, "This information may or may not exist some place in society, but it's actually easier for me to try to rebuild it from scratch than to try and get it from the authorities who might have it now." 18

Maybe this will succeed or maybe it will fail. The normal case of social software is still failure; most of these experiments don't pan out. But the ones that do are quite incredible, and I hope that this one succeeds, obviously. But even if it doesn't, it's illustrated the point already, which is that someone working alone, with really cheap tools, has a reasonable hope of carving out enough of the cognitive surplus, enough of the desire to participate, enough of the collective goodwill of the citizens, to create a resource you couldn't have imagined existing even five years ago. 19

So that's the answer to the question, "Where do they find the time?" Or, rather, that's the numerical answer. But beneath that question was another thought, this one not a question but an observation. In this same conversation with the TV producer, I was talking about *World of Warcraft* guilds, and as I was talking, I could sort of see what she was thinking: "Losers. Grown men sitting in their basement pretending to be elves." 20

At least they're doing something. 21

Did you ever see that episode of *Gilligan's Island* where they almost get off the island and then Gilligan messes up and then they don't? I saw that one. I saw that one a lot when I was growing up. And every half-hour that I watched that was a half an hour I wasn't posting at my blog or editing *Wikipedia* or contributing to a mailing list. Now, 22

I had an ironclad excuse for not doing those things, which is none of those things existed then. I was forced into the channel of media the way it was because it was the only option. Now it's not, and that's the big surprise. However lousy it is to sit in your basement and pretend to be an elf, I can tell you from personal experience it's worse to sit in your basement and try to figure if Ginger or Mary Ann is cuter.

And I'm willing to raise that to a general principle. It's better to do something than to do nothing. Even lolcats, even cute pictures of kittens made even cuter with the addition of cute captions, hold out an invitation to participation. When you see a lolcat, one of the things it says to the viewer is, "If you have some sans-serif fonts on your computer, you can play this game, too." And that message—I can do that, too—is a big change. 23

This is something that people in the media world don't understand. Media in the twentieth century was run as a single race—consumption. How much can we produce? How much can you consume? Can we produce more and you'll consume more? And the answer to that question has generally been yes. But media is actually a triathlon, it's three different events. People like to consume, but they also like to produce, and they like to share. 24

And what's astonished people who were committed to the structure of the previous society, prior to trying to take this surplus and do something interesting, is that they're discovering that when you offer people the opportunity to produce and to share, they'll take you up on that offer. It doesn't mean that we'll never sit around mindlessly watching *Scrubs* on the couch. It just means we'll do it less. 25

And this is the other thing about the size of the cognitive surplus we're talking about. It's so large that even a small change could have huge ramifications. Let's say that everything stays 99 percent the same, that people watch 99 percent as much television as they used to, but 1 percent of that is carved out for producing and for sharing. The Internet-connected population watches roughly a trillion hours of TV a year. That's about five times the size of the annual U.S. consumption. One per cent of that is 100 *Wikipedia* projects per year worth of participation. 26

I think that's going to be a big deal. Don't you? 27

Well, the TV producer did not think this was going to be a big deal; she was not digging this line of thought. And her final question to me was essentially, "Isn't this all just a fad?" You know, sort of the flagpole-sitting of the early twenty-first century? It's fun to go out and produce and share a little bit, but then people are going to eventually realize, "This isn't as good as doing what I was doing before," and settle down. And I made a spirited argument that no, this wasn't the case, that this was in fact a big one-time shift, more analogous to the industrial revolution than to flagpole-sitting. 28

I was arguing that this isn't the sort of thing society grows out of. It's the sort of thing that society grows into. But I'm not sure she believed me, in part because she didn't want to believe me, but also in part because I didn't have the right story yet. And now I do. 29

I was having dinner with a group of friends about a month ago, and one of them was talking about sitting with his four-year-old daughter watching a DVD. And in the middle of the movie, apropos of nothing, she jumps up off the couch and runs around behind the screen. That seems like a cute moment. Maybe she's going back there to see if Dora is really back there or whatever. But that wasn't what she was doing. She started rooting around in the cables. And her dad said, "What you doing?" And she stuck her head out from behind the screen and said, "Looking for the mouse." 30

Here's something four-year-olds know: A screen that ships without a mouse ships broken. Here's something four-year-olds know: Media that's targeted at you but doesn't include you may not be worth sitting still for. Those are things that make me believe that this is a one-way change. Because four-year-olds, the people who are soaking most deeply in the current environment, who won't have to go through the trauma that I have to go through of trying to unlearn a childhood spent watching *Gilligan's Island*, they just assume that media includes consuming, producing, and sharing. 31

It's also become my motto, when people ask me what we're doing—and when I say "we," I mean the larger society trying to figure out how to deploy this cognitive surplus, but I also mean we, especially, the people in this room, the people who are working hammer and tongs at figuring out the next good idea. From now on, that's what I'm going to tell them: We're looking for the mouse. We're going to look at every place that a reader or a listener or a viewer or a user has been locked out, has been served up passive or a fixed or a canned experience, and ask ourselves, "If we carve out a little bit of the cognitive surplus and deploy it here, could we make a good thing happen?" And I'm betting the answer is yes. 32

Examining the Text

1. According to Shirky, what similar functions did gin and television sitcoms serve when they were first introduced? Why do you think Shirky begins his article with this analogy? Do you think that the analogy is effective despite the significant differences between gin and television?

2. What does Shirky mean by a social or cognitive surplus? Do you agree that time is currently a surplus?

3. In paragraph 15, Shirky writes, "The physics of participation is much more like the physics of weather than it is like the physics of gravity." Take a look at the sentences that follow and try to explain in your own words what Shirky means. How does this statement contribute to his overall argument?

4. In paragraphs 12 and 13, Shirky presents a "back-of-the-envelope calculation" related to the number of hours people spend watching TV and the number of hours invested in a project like *Wikipedia*. Later in the article, he offers a similar estimation. What effect do the numbers and statistics that Shirky provides have on your opinion of his argument? Does the fact that these numbers are "guesstimates" rather than hard data have any impact on their relevance for you?
5. What is the point that Shirky makes in his story of the four-year-old who looks for the mouse for her television set? Why do you think Shirky leaves this story until the end of his article? As a slogan, what does "we're looking for the mouse" imply?
6. *Thinking rhetorically:* As we noted in the introduction, this article was initially a talk that Shirky presented at a conference. What signs of its beginnings as an oral presentation do you still see in the article? Do you think that these stylistic features help to advance or detract from Shirky's argument when it's presented in writing?

For Group Discussion

Toward the end of the article, Shirky returns several times to the idea that the Internet offers opportunities to participate and produce, whereas television offers only opportunities to consume. In a small group, list all the ways in which each of you has become more of a participant in broader social and cultural activities because of the Internet, whether it's creating a MySpace profile, posting videos on YouTube, or playing online games, for example. What benefits do you think you get from interacting on the Internet, and how are these different from the benefits you derive from watching TV? Based on your own experiences as participants and producers, do Shirky's predictions about the future seem persuasive to you?

Writing Suggestion

Shirky's basic premise about television—that it renders us passive consumers of media produced by others—may be undermined by new developments in the television industry that are aimed at engaging viewers and giving them more opportunities to interact with programs. In addition to shows that solicit our votes to affect or determine final outcomes (e.g., *Big Brother, American Idol*), many TV programs have Web sites where fans can contribute to discussions and find additional information about contestants and episodes (e.g., *Biggest Loser, Survivor*). ABC's *Lost* is well-known for the active participation of its fans in alternative forums, including Web sites, novels, podcasts, and other venues.

As a prewriting exercise for this assignment, make a list of the ways in which television programs use the Internet and other technologies to offer viewers more opportunities to interact and produce. Select what you see as the two or three most significant developments from this list and draft an essay in which you use these developments to argue against Shirky's claims about television. In your essay, discuss specific examples of interactive television programming—perhaps drawing on your own experience with these programs, as well.

Infotainment

Losing Our Religion

RUSSELL PETERSON

The first article in our case study on "infotainment TV" is adapted from the first chapter of Russell Peterson's 2008 Strange Bedfellows: How Late-Night Comedy Turns Democracy into a Joke. *As you can tell from the title and subtitle of the book, Peterson sees a clear mismatch between politics and comedy—or at least certain kinds of comedy. Jay Leno, David Letterman, and other mainstream late-night comedy hosts incur Peterson's criticism, whereas cable hosts Jon Stewart and Steven Colbert merit praise.*

Peterson draws a crucial distinction between cynicism and satire. As he puts it, "Unlike satire, which scolds and shames, [cynicism] merely shrugs" (paragraph 15). In other words, the satire of Stewart and Colbert are a kind of call to action, delivering a serious criticism of the political system, whereas the cynical and derisive political jokes of late-night comedy present a bleak and ultimately unproductive view of American democracy. Peterson knows something of the combination of politics and comedy: he's a former stand-up comedian and political cartoonist who currently teaches in the American Studies Department at the University of Iowa.

In drawing comparisons between late-night comedy and the comedy found on cable TV news shows, Peterson asks us to consider what we find funny. Toward the end of the article, he discusses two theorists—Sigmund Freud and Henri Bergson—who try to define the purpose of jokes and the function of laughter. **Before you read** *this article, think about the kinds of comedy and the individual comedians that you find funny. In particular, consider the late-night TV hosts and cable figures who Peterson discusses: Leno, Letterman, O'Brien, Stewart, and Colbert. Why do you appreciate the humor of some comedians but not of others?*

On the second Saturday after Easter, the city of Washington, D.C. witnessed a miracle of sorts. The president of the United States appeared before the assembled members of the White House Correspondents Association accompanied by an uncanny doppelganger. This apparent clone, who stood stage right of the commander in chief at a matching podium, not only looked and sounded like George W. Bush, he seemed to give voice to the president's subconscious thoughts: "Here I am at another one of these dang press dinners: Could be 1

.ome asleep, little Barney curled up at my feet. Nooo. I gotta pretend I like being here. Being here really ticks me off. The way they try to embarrass me by not editing what I say. Well, let's get things going so I can get to bed?"[1]

2 The president's double, actor Steve Bridges, did a heckuva job reproducing his voice and gestures, and the crowd loved it. The members of the media elite erupted in laughter when George W. Bush's "inner voice" pronounced the first lady *"muy caliente."* It was the funniest and most elaborate presidential comedy routine since Bill Clinton's "Final Days" video, back in 2000.

3 But this wasn't the miracle, just a clever bit of stagecraft. The miracle came after the Dueling Bushes routine, when Comedy Central's faux pundit Stephen Colbert stepped up to the lectern. What he said was not in itself so remarkable; the content of his routine was very much of a piece with the tongue-in-cheek right-wing pontificating seen four nights a week on *The Colbert Report*—a few of the jokes were even recycled from the show. What made his monologue startling—even awe-inspiring—was the fact that although the primary target of Colbert's ironic attack, the president of the United States, was sitting not six feet away from him, he pulled nary a punch. "The greatest thing about this man is, he's steady," proclaimed the comedian, with his impenetrable mock-sincerity. "You know where he stands. He believes the same thing Wednesday that he believed on Monday, no matter what happened Tuesday. Events can change; this man's beliefs never will." The president squirmed, his mottled face betraying the effort behind a strained smile. The audience, who had greeted the Bush/Bridges act with full-throated laughter, now sounded subdued, lapsing at times into uncomfortable silence. Colbert appeared undaunted. It was a brave and bracing performance, demonstrating what the comedian would call (in character) *muchos huevos grandes.*

4 That we live in a country where one can publicly criticize the head of state is of course a kind of miracle in itself, one we perhaps too often take for granted. But to see *this* president—whose administration has specialized in intimidating critics and marginalizing dissent—mocked so mercilessly, to his face, in front of a cozy gathering of Washington insiders (who would suffer their own share of Colbert's satirical punishment that night), was like witnessing Moses calling down a plague of frogs on Pharaoh and his courtiers. That is, if Moses had been funny.

5 Yet the mainstream media, whose shindig this was, appeared to leave all memory of Colbert's astonishing performance in the banquet hall, along with the parsley on their plates. Monday morning's *New York Times* ran a bubbly account of the president's "double" routine

without so much as mentioning Colbert's name. Television news, both network and cable, followed suit, fawning over the video of the Bush "twins" as if it were the latest baby panda footage but avoiding any reference to the evening's controversial headliner.[2]

While the diners and the media corporations they represented seemed to be experiencing selective amnesia, though, the Internet was going Colbert-crazy. Liberal blogs sang his praises, while conservative commentators condemned him for disrespecting the nation's chief executive (something most of them had little problem countenancing when that office was held by Bill Clinton). Someone launched a "Thank You, Stephen Colbert" Web page, which in no time had registered the gratitude of thousands of netizens who felt that President Bush had for too long been treated far too gently by the mainstream press.[3] 6

When this cyber-rumbling began to grow too loud to ignore, a few members of the diners' club decided they had better say something. But they succeeded only in proving their critics right: the mainstream media's belated response to Colbert was characterized by groupthink and a preoccupation with style over substance. (Sure, his jokes pointed out some unpleasant truths, but did he have to be so blunt about it?) "The only thing worse than the mainstream media's ignoring Stephen Colbert's astonishing sendup of the Bush administration and its media courtiers," wrote *Salon's* Joan Walsh, "is what happened when they started to pay attention to it." Indeed, from *Hardball's* human airhorn Chris Matthews—who began his Siskel-and-Ebert bit with fellow irony-challenged critic Mike Allen of *Time* magazine by asking, "Why was he [Colbert] so bad?"—to Lloyd Grove of the *Daily News* to the *New York Observer's* Christopher Lehman to alternative-media-emeritus Ana Marie Cox (formerly of the Wonkette blog, now safely ensconced in the media mainstream as a Time-Warner columnist, cable news bloviator, and, incidentally, Mrs. Christopher Lehman), the pundit establishment seemed to be on the same page. "The dreary consensus," noted Walsh, was that "Colbert just wasn't funny."[4] 7

What is and isn't funny is of course a subjective judgment, but there may have been more to this near-unanimity among the top tier of television and print journalists—who happen to comprise most of the guest list at events like the White House Correspondents Dinner—than the fact that they all share remarkably similar tastes. "Why so defensive?" asked the *Washington Post*'s media critic, Dan Froomkin.[5] Perhaps it was because a mere comedian had not only embarrassed the press corps's guest of honor but had also shown up his hosts by beating them at what was supposed to be their own game: speaking truth to power. The Fourth Estate is called that because it is meant to act as 8 an extragovernmental check on the judicial, legislative, and executive branches. But the news media's compliant behavior in the wake of 9/11 and the run-up to the invasion of Iraq, their failure to aggressively pursue a raft of administration scandals, and even the cozy ritual of the Correspondents Dinner itself belie that adversarial ideal. Colbert used the occasion to backhandedly chide the press for their lazy complicity: "Here's how it works: the president makes decisions. He's the decider. The press secretary announces those decisions, and you people of the press type those decisions down. Make, announce, type. Just put 'em through a spell check and go home. . . . Write that novel you got kicking around in your head. You know, the one about the intrepid Washington reporter with the courage to stand up to the administration. You know—fiction!"

It's hard to imagine a sharper critique of the press's failure to act as a watchdog, short of hitting Wolf Blitzer in the schnozz with a rolled-up newspaper. Colbert's real achievement, however, lies not in policing the standards of another profession but in asserting those of his own: for if "speaking truth to power" is part of the journalist's job, it is the satirist's primary mission—a higher calling, in fact, than merely being funny. 9

But if Colbert was just doing his job, why did it make the audience so uncomfortable? If this was just a case of satire fulfilling its function, why call it a miracle? Because, in spite of the fact that comedy *about* politics is now as common as crabgrass, political comedy—that is, genuine satire, which uses comedic means to advance a serious critique—is so rare we might be tempted to conclude it is extinct. Seeing it right there in front of God, the president, and the press corps was an astonishing moment, which stood out from the mundane rituals of politics and the press commonly seen on C-SPAN, *Meet the Press*, and the nightly news. It was like seeing an ivory-billed woodpecker alight on your satellite dish. 10

So "miracle" is indeed the word. Though some branded Colbert a heretic (the *Washington Post's* nominally liberal columnist Richard Cohen called him a "bully" for picking on the poor president), others saw him as a satirical evangelist, a Jonathan Edwards who took his text from the First Book of Jonathan Swift.[6] If the president and the press didn't laugh very much during the course of this sermon, it was because they recognized themselves as the sinners in the hands of an angry comedian. 11

Of course, it is possible that Colbert approached the dais with no mission in mind beyond making 'em laugh—though one suspects he and his writers are smart enough to know what they were getting into. Even if most of its practitioners would be loath to admit it, satire is a moral art. It calls on people and institutions to do their duty, as when 12

Colbert scolded the press for their recent toothlessness: "Over the last five years you people were so good—over tax cuts, WMD intelligence, the effect of global warming," he said, wistfully. "We Americans didn't want to know, and you had the courtesy not to try to find out.. Those were good times, as far as we knew."

This is the satirist as revivalist preacher, calling his congregation 13 back to the True Faith. And in America—which, despite the efforts of the Christian Right, remains a secular nation—the name of that Faith is Democracy. Its holy book is the Constitution, its clergy the Supreme Court and our elected representatives, its congregants We the People, its rituals voting and vigilance. Like other faiths—but unlike other governmental systems, which are held in place primarily through the threat of force—democracy depends on the devotion of its followers to sustain it. Some of the people, some of the time, must keep on believing that our electoral choices matter, that if we speak out our voices will be heard, that our representatives truly represent our interests. It's a tall order, but if we were to abandon all hope that democracy could endure—if democratic apathy reached the point of democratic atheism—our national faith would go the way of the cults of Baal, Zeus, Quetzalcoatl, and other unemployed divinities.

Thankfully, our civic religion has not yet reached its moment of 14 Nietzschean doom. But its tenets—equal justice for all; government of, by, and for the people—have been subjected to a subtle yet constant and corrosive barrage of blasphemous derision. It echoes from the office water cooler to the corner bar to the corridors of government itself. Most seductively, it rings out amidst the pealing laughter that emanates from millions of Americans' televisions each night.

THE LESSER OF TWO WEASELS: ANTI-POLITICAL COMEDY

While genuine satire arises from a sense of outrage, the topi- 15 cal jokes heard in mainstream late-night monologues are rooted in mere cynicism. Unlike satire, which scolds and shames, this kind of comedy merely shrugs. Unlike Colbert, whose appearance at the Correspondents Dinner evoked a democratic revivalist, Jay Leno, David Letterman, and Conan O'Brien are evangelists of apathy.

The difference is easier to discern if we go back to a presidential 16 election year. So pick up that remote, hit rewind, and keep going, all the way back to 2004:

Political pundits are saying President George W. Bush has made gains in two key states: dazed and confused. (Letterman)

You see the pictures in the paper today of John Kerry windsurfing? . . . Even his hobby depends on which way the wind blows. (Leno)
Earlier today, President Bush said Kerry will be a tough and hard-charging opponent. That explains why Bush's nickname for Kerry is "Math." (O'Brien)
Kerry was here in Los Angeles. He was courting the Spanish vote by speaking Spanish. And he showed people he could be boring in two languages. (Leno)[7]

A larger sampling would prove, as this selection suggests, that the political jokes told by network late-night hosts aim, cumulatively, for a bipartisan symmetry. Although election season "joke counts" maintained by the Center for Media and Public Affairs do not show a perfect one-to-one balance of jokes aimed at Democratic and Republican nominees, as the election got closer, a rough equity emerged, suggesting that George W. Bush was no more or less dumb than John Kerry was boring.[8] So it is in every presidential election year. Even in between, care is taken to target the abuse at "both sides," even if, during the Bush years, it has often meant resorting to time-worn Monica Lewinsky jokes. Maintaining this equilibrium is understood as one of the ground rules of the genre—a tenet so well established that an industry-specific cliché has arisen to describe those who embrace it: "equal-opportunity offenders." 17

The phrase, or the ideal it expresses, is typically brandished by late-night comics as a shield against charges of bias. But it is a paradigm embraced even more fervently by journalists who write about comedy. Bill Maher, Robin Williams, and Carlos Mencia—even an Israeli/Lebanese comedy team who bill their show as "The Arab-Israeli Comedy Hour"—have been celebrated in press accounts as equal-opportunity offenders. Being branded an EOO by the journalistic establishment is something like getting the Good Housekeeping Seal of Approval, though the honor is bestowed with some subjectivity. Sarah Silverman is praised by the *Milwaukee Journal Sentinel* for being one, and criticized by the *Houston Chronicle* for not being enough of one.[9] 18

To offend unequally, on the other hand, is offensive indeed. Page one of the August 22, 2004, *New York Times* Arts and Leisure section features a telling juxtaposition of two articles concerning topical comedy. At the top of the page, the *Times* frets that a few of those making jokes about President Bush have transgressed the boundaries of "just kidding" and crossed the line into genuine (gasp!) satire. Though Jon Stewart, for example, "has repeatedly insisted that he's nonpartisan," his jokes about the incumbent "have started to seem like a sustained argument with the president." A comedian using humor to express an opinion? *J'accuse!* Yet below the fold, the *Times* toasts *South Park* 19 creators Matt Stone and Trey Parker's upcoming film, *Team America,* which promises to "take aim at sanctimonious right-wing nutjobs and smug Hollywood liberals alike." Parker takes the opportunity to assert his EOO bona fides: "People who go [to the film] will be really confused about whose side we're on. That's because we're really confused." Ah, that's what we like to see—fair and balanced comedy.[10]

Journalists' peculiar devotion to the equal-opportunity offender 20
ideal results from a tendency to project their own profession's standards of objectivity onto comedians. Expecting Jay Leno to play by the same rules as Anderson Cooper is a bit like squeezing apples to get orange juice, but conventional wisdom seems to take this conflation of journalistic and comedic ethics for granted—the Pew poll, after all, asks its respondents to consider *The Tonight Show* and CNN side by side. Comedians' own reasons for maintaining balance, however, have little to do with abstract notions of fairness; it's more a matter of pragmatism than idealism. As Jay Leno put it, once a comedian takes a political side, "you've lost half the crowd already."[11] These guys are in show *business,* after all, and it doesn't pay to alienate 50 percent of your potential viewers. Such bottom-line considerations, incidentally, help explain why *The Colbert Report* and *The Daily Show* can afford to be more politically "risky" than Leno's: a little over a million viewers—a narrowly interested but loyal core—amounts to a pretty respectable audience for a cable show like the *Report,* but for *The Tonight Show,* which averages six million viewers nightly, it would be a disaster.[12]

The bigger difference between the network and cable shows' hu- 21
mor has to do with what the jokes say, not how many of them are aimed at Democrats versus Republicans. On closer examination, the only political thing about the mainstream jokes quoted above is that they happen to be about politicians. They are personality jokes, not that different from the ones those same comedians tell about Paris Hilton or Ozzy Osbourne—just replace "dumb" and "boring" with "slutty" and "drug-addled." And unlike Colbert's jokes about Bush's inflexibility or his tendency to think with his "gut," the jokes told on the network shows rarely transcend the level of pure *ad hominem* mockery to consider how such personal traits might manifest themselves in terms of policy.

The bottom line of all the jokes about Bush's dumbness, Kerry's 22
dullness, Al Gore's stiffness, Bob Dole's "hey-you-kids-get-outta-my-yard" crankiness, and so on is that all politicians are created equal—equally unworthy, that is—and that no matter who wins the election, the American people lose. Thus, despite their efforts to play it safe by offending equally (and superficially), the mainstream late-night comics actually present an extremely bleak and cynical view of American democracy.

What, then, is the secret of their appeal? Why do millions of us tune in, night after night, to be told—not overtly, but insinuatingly and consistently—that our cherished system of self-government is a joke? Perhaps because this confirms what we have always suspected: democracy is a nice idea but not, ultimately, a practical one. And if Americans doubt democracy, we hate politics. Politics is treated like an infection, or a tumor. It is to be avoided if possible, and when found lurking—in a sitcom writers' room, in an Oscar acceptance speech, in the funnies (*Doonesbury* has been exiled to the editorial pages of many of the papers that carry it)—it must be excised before it can infect the nation's body non-politic. Politics is *icky*. 23

Even our politicians disdain politics. A candidate can't go wrong by running against Washington, D.C., and all that it supposedly stands for. George W. "I'm from Texas" Bush successfully campaigned as an anti-establishment "outsider"—and his dad was the president! Ronald Reagan got applause when he proclaimed that government was not the solution, but the problem—though he himself had just campaigned for, and achieved, the government's top job.[13] 24

Most Americans see nothing strange in this; for as much as we like to wave the flag and pledge our allegiance to the republic for which it stands, as a people we regard our government, its institutions, and its representatives (save those who take care to inoculate themselves with anti-political rhetoric) with contempt. This feeling is reflected not only in our appallingly low voter turnout rates but also in our culture—particularly in our humor. 25

Which is why most of this country's "political" humor—from Artemus Ward to Will Rogers, from Johnny Carson to Jay Leno, from Andy Borowitz to JibJab.com—has in fact been *anti*-political. "All politics is applesauce," Rogers once said, by which he did not mean that it was a tasty side dish with pork chops.[14] He meant that progress was the opposite of Congress, that the Democrats were worse than any other party except for the Republicans and vice versa, that six of one was half a dozen of the other. Will Rogers was an equal-opportunity offender. 26

Rogers's observation that "both parties have their good and bad times . . . they are each good when they are out, and . . . bad when they are in" reappears almost seventy years later as Jay Leno's characterization of the 2000 election as a choice between "the lesser of two weasels." It appears again, in an "edgier" guise, when the *South Park* kids are given the opportunity to learn about democracy by nominating and voting for a new school mascot: "We're supposed to vote between a giant douche and a turd sandwich," Stan tells his parents, "I just don't see the point." His parents react with shocked sanctimony: "Stanley," scolds his mother, "do you know how many 27 people died so you could have the right to vote?" Mom just doesn't get it.[15]

Whether the metaphor describes electoral choice as a contest be- 28
tween a pair of rodents or between a feminine hygiene product and a piece of excrement, it's the same old joke. Anti-political humor is everywhere; clean or dirty, hip or square, as told by professionals over the airwaves and amateurs over the cubicle divider. In fact, what I think of as the quintessential anti-political joke is one I heard not from any television show but from my dad—and although this version dates from 1980, all that is necessary to make it work in any other presidential election year is to change the names:

Q: If Jimmy Carter, Ronald Reagan, and John Anderson [that year's third-party threat] were all in a rowboat in the middle of the ocean, and the boat flipped over, who would be saved?
A: The United States.

WHAT IS GOVERNMENT FOR? WHAT ARE JOKES FOR?

The implications of the rowboat riddle are fairly grim: no choice would 29
be better than the choice we have, and anyone who would presume to be worthy of the people's vote deserves to drown like a rat. Yet this nihilistic punch line is no more than a crystallization of the message repeated night after night, joke after joke, by Jay, Dave, and Conan. Late-night's anti-political jokes are implicitly anti-democratic. They don't criticize policies for their substance, or leaders for their official actions (as opposed to their personal quirks, which have little to do with politics per se); taken as a whole, they declare the entire system—from voting to legislating to governing—an irredeemable sham.

To understand the appeal of such anti-democratic heresy, it is help- 30
ful to start with a couple of fundamental questions. First, what is government for? The answer, according to the framers of the Constitution, is to provide for the common defense, to promote the general welfare, and so on. Or as Abraham Lincoln more succinctly put it, our government is for the people—as well as by and of them. We, the people, choose our government and therefore—indirectly, at least—are the government. The U.S. is "us." Most of us learned this in elementary school.

When we grow up, however, this naïve faith in representative de- 31
mocracy joins Santa Claus and the Easter Bunny on the scrap heap of our childish beliefs. Even if we continue to believe, we tend to be a little bit embarrassed about it. The majority of voters, in most election years, would probably tell anyone who asked that they were holding their

noses as they entered the voting booth. We participate in the political process in only the most minimal ways: we ignore local elections, few of us attend caucuses or work as campaign volunteers, and between the first Wednesday of November and the kickoff of the next season of attack ads, we pay little attention to what our representatives do (unless there's a sex scandal, of course). We treat democracy, our civic religion, only about as seriously as what so-called C-and-E Christians (for Christmas and Easter—the only occasions they bother to show up in church) treat theirs. And of course the majority of those eligible to vote don't even bother.

Even lapsed voters may still profess faith in the democratic ideal, but are likely to consider it lost to some more perfect past—before Watergate, Irangate, or Monicagate; before PACs and lobbyists; back in the days when politicians were statesmen, not these clowns you see running for office nowadays. In just a century and a half, this version of the anti-political argument goes, we've gone from Lincoln versus Douglas to a douche versus a turd. 32

Of course, this is nostalgic nonsense; American leaders have been failing to live up to their predecessors since Adams succeeded Washington. The problem with the democratic ideal—with any ideal—is that reality will always fall short. Our candidates can never measure up to the Founding Fathers' patriarchal nobility, nor can our day-to-day experience of liberty, equality, and justice live up to the ringing words of the Declaration of Independence. Some years ago, Professor Louis Rubin dubbed the gap between the City on a Hill of our star-spangled dreams and the somewhat less utopian actualities of the nation we actually inhabit "the Great American Joke": "On the one hand there are the ideals of freedom, equality, self-government, the conviction that ordinary people can evince the wisdom to vote wisely, and demonstrate the capacity for understanding and cherishing the highest human values through embodying them in their political and social institutions. On the other hand there is the *Congressional Record*."[16] When you live in a country founded upon ideals—rather than the mere commonalities of tradition, language, and culture that formed the basis of older nations—you are doomed to perpetual disappointment. 33

But before further considering America's strained relation with its founding principles, let us turn to the second question: what are jokes for? This seemingly trivial query has in fact tested the cognitive powers of some pretty heavy-duty thinkers, from Aristotle to Immanuel Kant to Thomas Hobbes. Sigmund Freud provided one of the most useful contributions to this body of inquiry a century ago, in a book entitled *Jokes and Their Relation to the Unconscious*.[17] The purpose of joking, he theorized, is to help individuals cope with societal repression. At the core of all of Freud's work lies the assumption that even the most well-adjusted of us are carrying a heavy burden of hostility and sexual aggression. 34

Bottling all that up can make us crazy, but if we allowed ourselves to express these impulses in an open and straightforward way, civilized society would be impossible—day-to-day life would resemble some unholy double feature of *Mad Max* and *Animal House*. So how do we get through the day? Freud identified a number of ways—many of which don't cost a hundred dollars an hour—including telling, and laughing at, jokes. Laughter is a safety valve for our anti-social drives. The rules of polite society (and the need to keep your job) prevent you from acting on your intensely felt desire to punch your boss in the teeth, but you can safely express that hostile impulse by imitating his stupid, jackass laugh for your coworkers during happy hour at the local bar.

Thus, laughter helps the individual cope with society. But might 35
it also help society cope with the individual? According to Freud's contemporary, the philosopher Henri Bergson, the principal function of laughter is not so much to keep people sane as to keep them in line. "By laughter," he wrote, "society avenges itself for the liberties taken with it."[18] Whenever we laugh at someone whose comportment or behavior is somehow "wrong"—whether he or she is a nerd, a klutz, a pervert, a ninny, or a fanatic—we reinforce what we consider to be "normal," non-laughable behavior. Laughter enforces conformity; it's the border collie that helps maintain the herd mentality.

How do these turn-of-the-twentieth-century Continental theories 36
apply to contemporary American political comedy? First, and most obvious, laughing at political big shots is satisfying in the same way as laughing at your boss (because you can't punch the president, either). In fact, says Freud, if the target is big and important enough, the joke doesn't even have to be that good, "since we count any rebellion against authority as a merit" (a loophole *Saturday Night Live* has been exploiting for years).[19] Add to this basic truth the fact that America was born in rebellion and celebrates anti-authoritarianism in any form, from the Boston patriots' dumping tea in the harbor to Elvis's hip-swiveling impudence, and it's not hard to see how this point resonates with particular force in our culture.

Bergson's argument about laughter and social conformity speaks 37
to one of the main sources of our democratic skepticism. If we take the idea that "all men are created equal" to be a fundamental American "norm" (and there is no principle we claim to hold dearer), then grasping at political power—seeking, that is, to escape the very equality that allows any one of us to run for office in the first place—is a violation of that norm. A fella (or even a gal) would have to think he's pretty hot stuff to sit in the House or Senate—to say nothing of the White House—and round these parts we don't cotton to folks what's too big for their britches. This is the central paradox of American representative democracy: the egalitarian idea that anyone can grow up to be president is

inseparable from the notion that none of us deserves such an honor. This is why potential leaders of the free world go to such absurd lengths to look like someone you'd like to have a beer with: *I guess it's okay he wants to be president, as long as he doesn't think he's any better than us.*

Oddly enough, our devotion to the principles on which our government is founded—liberty (no one can tell me what I can and cannot do) and egalitarianism (none of us is any better than anyone else)—makes it impossible for us to believe in government itself. Government makes all kinds of demands on our liberty—we must pay our taxes, obey the laws, serve on juries, or even, at various points in our history, serve in the military. Moreover, it derives its authority to do all of this based on the unacceptably contradictory principle that our elected representatives, who supposedly serve at our pleasure, are also somehow the boss of us. 38

We carry this paradox, and the resentment that goes along with it, in the backs of our minds even as we cast our ballots, salute the flag, or send our children off to war. It is the shadow side of our patriotism; the doubt at the heart of our devotion; our secular, civic version of original sin. It's the small, insistent voice that grumbles, even as we recite the Pledge of Allegiance or sing "The Star-Spangled Banner." *Yeah, right*. It is the voice of anti-political, anti-democratic heresy, echoing down the centuries, and from all across the political spectrum. It is the common complaint of left-wing anarchists like Abbie Hoffman (author of *Revolution for the Hell of It*), right-wing libertarians like anti-tax crusader Grover Norquist, civilly disobedient dropouts like Henry David Thoreau—even anti-state vigilantes like Timothy McVeigh.[20] In their own lighthearted way, late-night comics are torchbearers in this same anti-political parade. Unlike McVeigh, the damage they do is merely insidious, and largely invisible; but unlike Hoffman, Norquist, and Thoreau, they reach tens of millions of Americans each night. 39

DEFENDING THE FAITH: A PLACE FOR SATIRE?

In spite of its anti-democratic implications, anti-politics (and anti-political humor) is itself a bedrock American tradition: a contrarian habit as old as the republic itself. Atop this foundation of anti-political disdain, we have in recent decades been building a towering Fortress of Irony, reaching, by the turn of the twenty-first century, a point where it seems as if every communication is enclosed in air quotes. In contemporary America, sincerity is suspect, commitment is lame, and believing in stuff is for suckers. 40

Late-night comics did not invent the air-quote culture, anymore than they invented our anti-political sentiments, but they have played a leading role in proselytizing this cynical message. Election after 41 election, night after night, joke after joke, they have reinforced the notion that political participation is pointless, parties and candidates are interchangeable, and democracy is futile.

This is not to suggest that comedy that takes politics as its subject 42
matter is inherently destructive. Mocking our elected representatives and our institutions is an American birthright, and exercising that right is worthwhile, if only to maintain it. The problem is not the presence, or even the proliferation, of political comedy per se. The problem is that too little of it is actually "political" in any meaningful way. Genuine political satire, like good investigative journalism, can function as democracy's feedback loop. It can illuminate injustices, point out hypocrisy, and tell us when our government is not living up to its ideals, thereby raising the awareness that is the first step toward alleviating any of these problems. Real satire—such as Colbert's excoriation of the press and the president—sounds the alarm: something is wrong, people must be held to account, things must be made right. Anti-political humor—the far more common kind, practiced by Leno, Letterman, and O'Brien, among others—merely says, resignedly, "Eh, what are you gonna do?"

Yet the public, and especially the press, are so blinded by anti- 43
political disdain and unblinking devotion to the equal-opportunity offender idea, that we have difficulty distinguishing genuine satire from the ersatz kind, even when we see it. In a feature on *The Colbert Report* (published several months before the Correspondents Dinner), *Newsweek* stubbornly hangs on to the news media's beloved apolitical paradigm: "[Though his] character is clearly a parody of God-fearing, pro-business, Bush-loving Republicans . . . Colbert guards his personal views closely, and if you watch the show carefully you'll see subtle digs at everyone on the political-media map." With what seems like willful naiveté, the magazine seizes on the host's rote disclaimer that his show is strictly for laughs: "Despite the fact that politics is a primary inspiration and target, Colbert isn't interested in being political."[21]

Whether he's interested or not, though, Colbert's show *is* po- 44
litical, in a way that the more traditional late-night programs—and, even for all their enthusiastic offensiveness, the works of Stone and Parker—are not. *The Colbert Report* is not an equal-opportunity offender. Neither is *The Daily Show.* Nor, for that matter, is Bill Maher, who has definitely met a man (or two) he didn't like. This is not to say that the *Report* is liberal propaganda, nor to deny that Colbert, Stewart, and Maher take satirical shots at "both sides"—though perhaps it is worth considering what would be so terrible about comedy that expresses a consistent point of view. But the important difference between the smallish vanguard of cable comics and the late-night mainstream is not so much a matter of taking political sides as of taking politics seriously. It is the difference between engaging with the

subject and merely dismissing it. Satire, at its best, is not just a drive-by dissing but exactly what the *Times* accuses Jon Stewart of presenting: "a sustained argument."[22] Consider the way Colbert deconstructs Bush's fetish for "resolve." Watch how *The Daily Show* analyzes official rhetoric, as when Stewart goes sound bite for sound bite with a videotaped politician, calling attention to every outrage and evasion. Left or right, right or wrong, fair or unfair, this is comedy that engages us in politics instead of offering us an easy out. It is a form of debate, not just entertainment; and as such, it should be welcomed, not treated as "rude," or inappropriate.

Undoubtedly, many of the guests at the Correspondents Dinner— 45
including the president—would have had a more pleasant evening listening to the inoffensive humor of, say, Jay Leno. There's nothing wrong with innocent laughter, of course. But insofar as our appetite for the dismissive, plague-on-both-their-houses, progress versus Congress, Tweedledum versus Tweedledee, pot-calling-the-kettle-black variety of "political" humor reflects our fundamental doubts about the value of political participation, and the viability of democracy, it is no laughing matter.

NOTES

[1]The 2006 White House Correspondents Association Dinner was first broadcast on C-SPAN, April 29, 2006.

[2]Elisabeth Bumiller, "A New Set of Bush Twins Appear at Annual Correspondents' Dinner," *New York Times,* May 1, 2006, Lexis-Nexis, via Infohawk, http://web.lexisnexis.com.proxy.lib.uiowa.edu. On "followed suit," see Dan Froomkin, "The Colbert Blackout," *Washington Post,* May 2, 2006, http://www.washingtonpost.com/wpdyn/content/blog/2006/05/02/ BL2006050200755.html (accessed March 14, 2007). See also Josh Kalven and Simon Maloy, "Media Touted Bush's Routine at Correspondents' Dinner, Ignored Colbert's Skewering," *Media Matters,* May 1, 2006; Julie Millican, "For Third Day in a Row, Good Morning America Touted Bush's White House Correspondents Dinner Skit While Ignoring Colbert's Routine," *Media Matters,* May 3, 2006, both available at http://mediamatters.org.

[3]Froomkin, "The Colbert Blackout"; "Thank You, Stephen Colbert" Web site, http://thankyoustephencolbert.org.

[4]Joan Walsh, "Making Colbert Go Away," *Salon,* May 3, 2006, http://www.salon.com/opinion/feature/2006/05/03/correspondents/index_np.html (accessed June 1, 2006), including Grove, Lehman, and Cox quotes; Mike Allen and Chris Matthews, *Hardball with Chris Matthews,* MSNBC, May 1, 2006.

[5]Dan Froomkin, "Why So Defensive?" *Washington Post,* May 4, 2006, http://www.washingtonpost.com/wp-dyn/content/blog/2006/05/04/BL2006050400967.html (accessed June 1, 2006).

[6]Richard Cohen, "So Not Funny," *Washington Post*, May 4, 2006, http://www.washingtonpost.com/wp-dyn/content/article/2006/ 05/03/AR2006050302202 html (accessed June 1, 2006).

[7]Letterman, retrieved from About.com Political Humor, "Late-Night Jokes about President Bush from 2004," comp. Daniel Kurtzman, http://politicalhumor.about.com/library/blbush2004jokes.htm (accessed June 1, 2006); Leno and O'Brien, retrieved from About.com Political Humor, "Late-Night Jokes about John Kerry," comp. Daniel Kurtzman, http://politicalhumor.about.com/library/bljohnkerryjokes.htm (accessed June 1, 2006).

[8]Center for Media and Public Affairs (CMPA), "Joke Archive, through August 24, 2004," http://www.cmpa.com/politicalHumor/archiveapri116th.htm (accessed March 14, 2007). President Bush held a commanding lead over Kerry for the year to date, but when Kerry became the presumptive and then official nominee, the numbers started to even out. Unfortunately, data for the months leading up to the election are unavailable, but in examining this and the other years' joke counts, the trend is clear.

[9]Alex Strachan, "Maher Targets Left and Right in Comedy Special," *Montreal Gazette*, Nov. 1, 2003; Doug Moore, "Williams' Act Has St. Louis Laughing at Itself," *St. Louis Post-Dispatch Everyday Magazine*, March 21, 2002; Gary Budzak, "Outspoken Honduras Native an Equal-Opportunity Offender," *Columbus Dispatch*, Jan. 6, 2005; Debra Pickett, "Middle East Duo Bets That Misery Loves Comedy," *Chicago Sun-Times*, June 6, 2003; Duane Dudek, "Blinded by the Bite; Silverman Skewers All with a Smile in 'Jesus,' " *Milwaukee Journal Sentinel*, Dec. 16, 2005; Bruce Westbrook, "Provocative Comedy: No Magic in Silverman's 'Jesus,' " *Houston Chronicle*, Dec. 9, 2005, Lexis-Nexis, via Infohawk, http://web.lexis-nexis.com.proxy.lib.uiowa.edu.

[10]Jason Zengerle, "The State of the George W. Bush Joke," and Sharon Waxman, "The Boys from 'South Park' Go to War," *New York Times*, Aug. 22, 2004, national ed., Arts and Leisure, 1.

[11]Marshall Sella, "The Stiff Guy vs. the Dumb Guy," *New York Times Magazine*, Sept. 24, 2000, 74.

[12]*Tonight Show* viewership 6.4 million viewers, per Toni Fitzgerald, "Sunrise Surprise: The CBS Early Show," *Media Life*, March 1, 2007, http://www.medialifemagazine.com/artman/publish/article_10482.asp (accessed March 15, 2007); *Colbert Report* viewership approximately 1.2 million, *Daily Show's* 1.6 million, per Julie Bosman, "Serious Book to Peddle? Don't Laugh, Try a Comedy Show," *New York Times*, Feb. 25, 2007, Lexis-Nexis, via Infohawk, http://web.lexis-nexis.com.proxy.lib.uiowa.edu.

[13]In his first debate with Al Gore in 2000, Bush said, "I fully recognize I'm not of Washington. I'm from Texas." See Richard L. Berke, "Bush and Gore Stake Out Differences in First Debate," *New York Times*, Oct. 4, 2000. Reagan's "government is the problem" remark is from his First Inaugural speech, as printed under the headline "Let Us Begin an Era of National Renewal," *New York Times*, Jan. 21, 1981, Lexis-Nexis, via Infohawk, http://web.lexis-nexis.com.proxy.lib.uiowa.edu.

[14]Will Rogers, quoted in *Bartlett's Familiar Quotations*, 15th ed., ed. Emily Morrison Beck (Boston: Little, Brown, 1980), 765.

[15]Will Rogers, *The Best of Will Rogers,* ed. Bryan B. Sterling (New York: Crown Publishers, 1979), 55; Leno, *Tonight,* Nov. 6, 2000; *South Park,* episode 808, "Douche and Turd," first aired Oct. 27, 2004.

[16]Louis D. Rubin, "The Great American Joke," in *What's So Funny? Humor in American Culture,* ed. Nancy A. Walker (Wilmington, DE: Scholarly Resources, 1998), 109–110.

[17]Sigmund Freud, *Jokes and Their Relation to the Unconscious,* trans. James Strachey (New York: W. W. Norton, 1963).

[18]Henri Bergson, *Laughter: An Essay on the Meaning of the Comic,* trans. Cloudesley Brereton and Fred Rothwell (Los Angeles: Green Integer Books, 1999), 176.

[19]Freud, *Jokes,* 105.

[20]Abbie Hoffman (a.k.a. "Free"), *Revolution for the Hell of It* (New York: Dial Books, 1968). For a useful overview of the history of American anti-political sentiment, see Garry Wills, *A Necessary Evil: A History of American Distrust of Government* (New York: Simon & Schuster, 1999).

[21]Marc Peyser, "The Truthiness Teller," *Newsweek,* Feb. 13, 2006, Lexis-Nexis via Infohawk, http://web.lexis-nexis.com.proxy.lib.uiowa.edu.

[22]Zengerle, "The State of the George W. Bush Joke," 1.

Examining the Text

1. Peterson opens this article with an anecdote about Stephen Colbert's talk at the White House Correspondents Association dinner in 2006. Why does Peterson refer to the Colbert episode as a "miracle"? What significance does Peterson draw from the media's reactions to Colbert's jokes?

2. Peterson refers to the satirist as a kind of "revivalist preacher" (paragraph 13); what does he mean by this? What sort of revival does Peterson think Colbert and Stewart deliver? How is this understanding of satire related to the title of the article: "Losing Our Religion"?

3. According to Peterson, what are the key differences between the genuine satire of cable TV hosts like Colbert and the mere cynicism of mainstream late-night comedy? Why does Peterson consider it cynical to be an "equal-opportunity offender" like Leno, Letterman, and O'Brien are?

4. Peterson claims that "Late-night's anti-political jokes are implicitly anti-democratic." What examples does he provide to support this claim? Do you find the examples—and the claim itself—persuasive? Do you agree with Peterson's assessment of the anti-democratic sentiment that is "the shadow side of our patriotism" (paragraph 39)?

5. *Thinking rhetorically:* Peterson is clearly no fan of the George W. Bush administration; for instance, he states early in the article that this administration "has specialized in intimidating critics and marginalizing dissent" (paragraph 4). What effect does Peterson's clear political affiliation have on your response to the article? If you agree with Peterson's political stance, does it make you more likely to accept his analysis? If you disagree with his political stance, do you find yourself looking for reasons to disagree with his analysis as well?

For Group Discussion

According to Peterson, cable TV news shows like *The Daily Show* and *The Colbert Report* offer the possibility of "genuine political satire" (paragraph 42); it is "comedy that engages us in politics, instead of offering us an easy way out" (paragraph 44). In a small group, discuss the extent to which you agree with Peterson's argument. If you watch these shows, do you think that they've influenced your attitude toward politics? In your experience, do these shows present a substantively different view of politics than you see in late-night comedy or elsewhere on TV?

Writing Suggestion

Peterson makes a number of claims about the typical American attitude toward politics:

- "Politics is treated like an infection, or a tumor. It is to be avoided if possible . . ." (paragraph 23).
- "Even our politicians disdain politics. A candidate can't go wrong by running against Washington, D.C., and all that it supposedly stands for" (paragraph 24).
- "The majority of voters, in most election years, would probably tell anyone who asked that they were holding their noses as they entered the voting booth. We participate in the political process in only the most minimal ways" (paragraph 31).

To test these claims, interview several fellow students about their political attitudes, and write an essay in which you report on what you discovered from these interviews.

As a first step, draft a series of questions to ask; you might consider asking questions about actual political participation ("Have you ever volunteered for a campaign?"), about knowledge of politics ("Can you name the U.S. Representative for your home district?"), and about attitudes toward politics and politicians ("Do you think most politicians are honest?"). Remember that if you ask specific questions you're more likely to get interesting responses; for this reason, you should avoid simply asking "What's your attitude toward politics?"

After you've drafted your list of questions and selected your interviewees, conduct the interviews. If you interview people face-to-face or over the phone, be sure to take notes that you can use later as you write your essay; you might also choose to interview people via email, but keep in mind that their responses might not be as detailed as if they were speaking, and that you won't have the opportunity to ask follow-up questions.

After conducting the interviews, identify four or five key ideas that emerged and focus your essay on explaining those ideas. In other words, don't simply present the transcripts of the interviews, but rather use selected quotations from the interviews to support specific points you discovered.

Amusing Ourselves to Death with Television News: Jon Stewart, Neil Postman, and the Huxleyan Warning

GERALD J. ERION

While most people would agree that they watch television primarily to be entertained, the term "infotainment"—along with the range of news and educational shows on TV—implies that we can be simultaneously informed and entertained. In the article that follows, though, Gerald Erion argues that TV does a very poor job of informing us, particularly about important issues and events. Erion draws on the work of Neil Postman to argue that the medium of television simply can't represent serious public discourse: "Just as ventriloquism and mime don't play well on radio, 'thinking does not play well on television'" (p. 90). Erion here is quoting from Postman's book Amusing Ourselves to Death; *you can tell from the title of this book that Postman, and Erion, think we're making a critical mistake if we expect television to inform us about serious issues.*

However, Erion sees value in The Daily Show *precisely because it also critiques television. He argues that several features of the show offer a Postman-esque condemnation of television news, and he also draws on Stewart's controversial 2004 appearance on* Crossfire *to support his thesis that Stewart is quite critical of mainstream television.*

Erion teaches courses in philosophy and general education at Medaille College in Buffalo, New York. The article that follows first appeared in a collection of essays entitled The Daily Show and Philosophy, *in which authors applied various philosophical principles and approaches to study* The Daily Show. ***As you read*** *this article, pay attention to the connections that Erion draws between Neil Postman, Marshall McLuhan, Aldous Huxley, and finally Jon Stewart. How do the lines of influence operate?*

---

1 While *The Daily Show* is undoubtedly funny, it also provides an intriguing study of our contemporary media environment. Indeed, hidden within many of Jon Stewart's funniest jokes are implicit critiques of the way television tends to report its news and host its public discussions of important issues. For instance, Stewart's opening rundown of the news as television covers it doesn't merely ridicule the day's major players and events, but also makes fun of the way television gathers and presents the news. In this way, over-the-top graphics and music packages, attractive

but superficial "Senior Correspondents," and all the other trappings of television newscasts become fodder for *The Daily Show's* writing staff. More than just a "fake news" program, *The Daily Show* offers a rare brand of humor that requires its audience to recognize a deeper, more philosophical criticism of contemporary television news.

From time to time, Stewart takes these implicit critiques of contemporary media and makes them explicit. Such was the case during his October 2004 appearance on CNN's since-cancelled *Crossfire,* when Stewart begged his hosts to "stop hurting America" with their substitution of entertaining pseudo-journalism for serious reporting and debate. Through this bold, format-breaking effort, Stewart highlighted the difference between thoughtful discussion and the theater of today's vapid television punditry. As we will see, Stewart's analysis of the present state of mass communication echoes that of the celebrated New York University media theorist Neil Postman, whose discerning insights ground some of Stewart's sharpest comic bits. 2

AMUSING OURSELVES TO DEATH

Neil Postman's *Amusing Ourselves to Death* is a book about the many forms of human communication and how those forms influence the messages that we communicate to one another. Postman acknowledges a significant intellectual debt here to Marshall McLuhan, and sees his own thesis as something of a revised version of McLuhan's famous pronouncement that "the medium is the message."[1] However, Postman extends McLuhan's ideas in ways that are both distinctive and significant. 3

For example, consider Postman's discussion of smoke signals. While the medium of smoke might be an effective way to communicate relatively simple messages over intermediate distances, many other types of messages can't be transmitted this way. Philosophical arguments, for instance, would be especially difficult to conduct with smoke signals because, as Postman puts it: "Puffs of smoke are insufficiently complex to express ideas on the nature of existence [or other philosophical concepts], and even if they were not, a Cherokee philosopher would run short of either wood or blankets long before he reached his second axiom. You cannot use smoke to do philosophy. Its form excludes the content."[2] So, the medium of smoke has a significant influence on the kind of content it can be used to communicate. At a minimum, smoke signaling restricts both the complexity and the duration of the messages it carries. Likewise, we shall see that *The Daily Show's* comedy often reflects the restrictions placed by our contemporary electronic media (including television) upon their content. 4

THE HUXLEYAN WARNING

5 Now, as Postman sees it, *all* media influence their content, and in a multitude of different ways. He writes: "[Mine] is an argument that fixes its attention on the forms of human conversation, and postulates that how we are obliged to conduct such conversations will have the strongest possible influence on what ideas we can conveniently express" (p. 6). This goes not only for smoke signals, but also for speech and written language, and even for the electronic media that are so important in our contemporary lives.

6 Of particular interest here is the ubiquitous medium of television, which Postman sees as a historic extension of such earlier media as the telegraph, photography, radio, and film.[3] How does television influence its content, according to Postman? His theory is complex, but in essence it maintains that television's inherent "bias" implies a tendency to render its content—even its most important news reports, political and religious discussions, and educational lessons—more *entertaining* than they would be otherwise, and consequently less serious, less rational, less relevant, and less coherent as well (pp. 67–80, 85–98).

7 The fact that television provides entertainment isn't, in and of itself, a problem for Postman. He warns, however, that dire consequences can befall a culture in which the most important public discourse, conducted via television, becomes little more than irrational, irrelevant, and incoherent entertainment. Again, we shall see that this is a point often suggested by *The Daily Show's* biting satire. In a healthy democracy, the open discussion of important issues must be serious, rational, and coherent. But such discussion is often time-consuming and unpleasant, and thus incompatible with television's drive to entertain. So, it's hardly surprising to see television serving up important news analyses in sound bites surrounded by irrelevant graphics and video footage, or substituting half-minute ad spots for substantial political debates. On television, thoughtful conversations about serious issues are reserved for only the lowest-rated niche programs. Just as ventriloquism and mime don't play well on radio, "thinking does not play well on television" (p. 90).[4] Instead, television serves as a hospitable home for the sort of "gut"-based discourse celebrated by Stephen Colbert.[5]

8 When we grow comfortable with the substitution of televised entertainment for serious public discourse, we begin the process of (to use Postman's words) "amusing ourselves to death." As Postman explains, this form of cultural corrosion is like that described in Aldous Huxley's classic novel *Brave New World,* in which the citizenry is comfortably and willingly distracted by the pleasures of *soma,* Centrifugal Bumble-puppy, and the feelies (pp. vii–viii, 155–6).

POSTMAN AND TELEVISION NEWS

Postman and the writing staff of *The Daily Show* seem to agree that television's presentation of news tends to degrade its content in significant ways. Consider Postman's explanation of the ironic title of his chapter on television news, "Now . . . this": "There is no murder so brutal, no earthquake so devastating, no political blunder so costly—for that matter no ball score so tantalizing or weather report so threatening—that it cannot be erased from our minds by a newscaster saying 'Now . . . this'" (p. 99). Thus, Postman maintains that the use of "Now . . . this" is a tacit admission of the incoherence of television news, and "a compact metaphor for the discontinuities in so much that passes for public discourse in present-day America" (p. 99). 9

Of course, Postman believes that television does more to the news than disrupt its coherence. Revisiting his general thesis about how television influences its content, Postman also claims that televised news is irrational, irrelevant, and trivial. As he explains, television presents us "not only with fragmented news but news without context, without consequences, without value, and therefore without essential seriousness; that is to say, news as pure entertainment" (p. 100). So, even weighty news subjects can become entertaining under the influence of television, as the typical American newscast showcases a company of attractive reporters skipping from dramatic local stories to dramatic international stories, to celebrity gossip, to weather forecasts, to sports scores, to a closing story about babies or puppies or kittens. Commercials are scattered throughout. Music, graphics, and captivating video footage add touches of theater to the program. Quick transitions from one segment to the next ensure that audience members don't become bored—or troubled—for long.[6] Instead of useful and important information, then, viewers are treated to the impotent but entertaining trivia that Postman calls "disinformation," which isn't necessarily false but *misleading,* creating the *illusion of knowing* and undermining one's motivation to learn more (p. 107). Consequently, Postman writes, "Americans are the best entertained and quite likely the least well-informed people in the Western world" (p. 106). 10

THE DAILY SHOW AND TELEVISION NEWS

Now, as far as I know, the writing staff of *The Daily Show* doesn't publicly acknowledge Postman's influence. It's even possible that they've never heard of Postman. Nonetheless, it's clear that these general ideas about television news, whatever their sources, can help us to see the significance of some of the program's wittiest and most inspired jokes. 11

The Daily Show is often described as a "fake news" program, but in fact, it's more than that. Much of its humor rests on Postman-like insights that highlight the peculiar ways in which the medium of television itself influences the news that it conveys.

For example, most episodes of *The Daily Show* begin with Stewart's rundown of the day's headlines as reported by the major television news programs. A comedy show that only does "fake news" might simply build jokes around the content of these headlines, or perhaps report fictional news stories in a humorous way. On *The Daily Show,* though, the way in which television seems destined to render its news as entertainment often serves as the basis for these opening segments. In recent years, Stewart and company have often joked about the major networks' coverage of natural disasters. In many of these cases, they simply replay absurd clips of television reporters standing outside during hurricanes, sitting in cars with giant thermometers during heat waves, or paddling canoes through inch-deep "flooded" city streets. Other segments mock the way hordes of television reporters cover celebrity weddings, arrests, and criminal trials. Segments like "International Pamphlet" and "The Less You Know" contain their own jokes but also poke fun at the shallowness of typical television news coverage. Exchanges between Stewart and his Senior Correspondents parody their good-looking but sometimes ill-informed network counterparts.[7] Even *The Daily Show's* clever graphics packages ("Mess O' Potamia," "Crises in Israfghyianonanaq," and so on) offer satirical imitations of the logos, diagrams, and pictorial illustrations so essential to today's television newscasts. Moreover, Stewart himself has attacked the way television is compelled to report "breaking news" with what at times seems to be inadequate or uncorroborated information, mere speculation, and no editing whatsoever; shortly after the Washington, DC-area sniper shootings of 2002, he joked with CNN's Howard Kurtz: "By watching the 24-hour news networks, I learned that the sniper was an olive-skinned, white-black male—men—with ties to Son of Sam, Al Qaeda, and was a military kid, playing video games, white, 17, maybe 40."[8] In these kinds of segments, then, *The Daily Show* is clearly doing more than just "fake news." It's also offering deep satire that relies on its audience's appreciation of the substance of Postman's thesis, that television has a significant and sometimes adverse influence on the news content it reports. 12

At this point, one might be tempted to suggest that *The Daily Show* simply reproduces the unfortunate transformation of reporting into entertainment, as if *The Daily Show* were itself a source of news for its audience members. For instance, Bill O'Reilly (host of the Fox News program *The O'Reilly Factor*) once famously dubbed viewers of *The Daily Show* "stoned slackers" who "get their news from Jon Stewart."[9] However, at least one prominent study by the Annenberg 13

Public Policy Center found that viewers of *The Daily Show* were *better* informed about the positions and backgrounds of candidates in the 2004 U.S. Presidential campaign than most others. Indeed, it's difficult to see how the deepest *Daily Show* jokes could be appreciated by an audience unaware of the relevant social, political, and other newsworthy issues. As Annenberg analyst Dannagal Goldthwaite Young put it in a press release announcing the Center's Election Survey results, "*The Daily Show* assumes a fairly high level of political knowledge on the part of its audience."[10]

CONVERSATION AND *CROSSFIRE*

Postman's ideas about television also illuminate Stewart's infamous October 15, 2004, appearance on CNN's *Crossfire.* First aired in 1982, *Crossfire* was a long-running staple of CNN's lineup that featured curt discussion by hosts and guests supposedly representing both left-wing and right-wing positions on controversial political issues. Co-hosting for Stewart's visit were the unsuspecting Paul Begala and Tucker Carlson, neither of whom seemed prepared for what would become an extraordinary exchange. Instead of simply participating in a typical *Crossfire*-style debate (described by more than one observer as a "shoutfest"), Stewart quickly launched into a Postman-like criticism of the vapid and partisan punditry that passes for serious discussion on programs like *Crossfire.* 14

In fact, this theme is one that Stewart had explored before his *Crossfire* appearance. The recurring *Daily Show* segment, "Great Moments in Punditry as Read by Children," draws laughs simply by having children read from transcripts of shows like *Crossfire*. Moreover, during an interview with Bill Moyers, Stewart claimed that both *Crossfire* and its MSNBC counterpart *Hardball* were "equally dispiriting" in the way their formats degrade political discourse.[11] And in his interview with CNN's Howard Kurtz, Stewart foreshadowed his *Crossfire* appearance by chiding the news network for offering entertainers instead of "real journalists" and pleaded, "You're the news. . . . People need you. Help us. Help us."[12] 15

On the *Crossfire* set, though, Stewart offered his most sustained attack against the shallow conversational style of television. Before either Begala or Carlson could catch his balance, Stewart was already begging them to "stop, stop, stop, stop hurting America" with their "partisan hackery," which he claimed serves only politicians and corporations and does nothing to help ordinary citizens make informed decisions.[13] "We need help from the media," Stewart said, "and they're hurting us." Carlson tried to counter Stewart's charges with the allegation that Stewart himself had been too lenient during the *Daily Show* 16 appearance of 2004 Presidential candidate John Kerry. Stewart replied that there was a fundamental difference between journalism and comedy, snapping back, "I didn't realize that . . . the news organizations look to Comedy Central for their cues on integrity." And when Begala tried to defend the *Crossfire* format by claiming that it was a "debate show," Stewart pointed to Carlson's trademark bow tie as evidence that *Crossfire* is "doing theater, when you should be doing debate." Finally, Stewart charged, "You have a responsibility to the public discourse, and you fail miserably." Because of such remarks, Stewart's *Crossfire* appearance produced a rare opportunity for reflecting about the effects of television on public discourse. Indeed, the incident sparked much additional discussion in, for example, the *New York Times*, *Newsweek*, and countless electronic media outlets.

Once again, we can see that these are the sorts of criticisms 17 developed by Postman in *Amusing Ourselves to Death.* His deepest discussion of such issues concerns ABC's controversial 1983 broadcast of the film *The Day After,* which depicts the bleak effects of a nuclear strike on the American Midwest. Given the film's grave subject matter, ABC decided to follow it with a roundtable discussion moderated by Ted Koppel and featuring such notable figures as Henry Kissinger, Elie Wiesel, Carl Sagan, and William F. Buckley.[14] With a serious theme and a guest list of unquestionable distinction, Koppel proceeded to march his cast through a fragmented eighty minutes of "conversation" in which the participants rarely engaged one another on points of substance. Instead, they used their camera time to push whatever points they had decided to make beforehand, without regard to the contributions of their fellow participants. Postman writes:

> Each of the six men was given approximately five minutes to say something about the subject. There was, however, no agreement on exactly what the subject was, and no one felt obliged to respond to anything anyone else had said. In fact, it would have been difficult to do so, since the participants were called upon seriatim, as if they were finalists in a beauty contest. (p. 89)

To put it another way, this wasn't a genuine discussion, but a 18 *pseudo-discussion* warped by television's drive to entertain. "There were no arguments or counterarguments, no scrutiny of assumptions, no explanations, no elaborations, no definitions" (p. 90), and yet each of these elements is essential to genuine and thoughtful dialogue.

So, how did ABC go wrong? According to Postman, the root 19 problem remains that thoughtful conversation just isn't entertaining, and thus plays poorly on television. Televised discussions about even the most serious of subjects tend to be rendered in forms that are more amusing or dramatic than reflective. On this, both Postman and the writing staff of *The Daily Show* agree.[15] Moreover, CNN President Jonathan Klein cited Stewart's critique when he announced the cancellation of *Crossfire* in January 2005. In an interview with the *Washington Post*, Klein said, "I think [Stewart] made a good point about the noise level of these types of shows, which does nothing to illuminate the issues of the day."

A HUXLEYAN MOMENT OF ZEN?

So, it appears that much of *The Daily Show's* sharpest comedy requires its audience to grasp a Postmanesque criticism of television news. In addition, Stewart himself seems to offer a more general critique of today's televised public discourse that is reminiscent of Postman's in several significant ways. This isn't to say, however, that Postman and Stewart are in perfect agreement. For one thing, Postman argues that the transformation of serious discussion into entertainment is all but inevitable when this discussion takes place on television. Stewart, on the other hand, seems to believe that television can do better. As we've seen, he has even appeared on CNN and used the news network's own programs to issue his call for reform. Postman and Stewart might also disagree about the suitability of television as a vehicle for sophisticated media criticism. Postman writes, for example, that any televised critique of television would likely be "co-opted" by the medium, and thus rendered in the typical fashion as mere entertainment (pp. 161–2).[17] In his eyes, television is simply incapable of carrying serious public discourse, including serious public discourse about mass communication itself. That Stewart has appeared on *Crossfire* and other such programs to address this issue suggests that he believes otherwise. No doubt this is a question worth further consideration, and through any medium capable of giving it a thoughtful hearing.

NOTES

[1]Marshall McLuhan, *Understanding Media: The Extensions of Man* (New York: McGraw-Hill, 1964); see especially pp. 7–21.

[2]Neil Postman, *Amusing Ourselves to Death: Public Discourse in the Age of Show Business* (New York: Penguin, 1985), p. 7. Subsequent citations will be made parenthetically in-text.

[3]Postman develops his sweeping history of American media in chapter 5 of *Amusing Ourselves to Death*, "The Peek-a-Boo World" (pp. 64–80).

[4]Postman acknowledges that, in other parts of the world (pp. 85–6) or in non-commercial contexts (pp. 105–6), television may serve different purposes. However, as he sees it, this does nothing to change the way that television most typically functions in contemporary American society.

[5]Colbert explained the importance of one's gut in the search for truth during his April 2006 White House Correspondents' Association Dinner performance: "Every night on my show, *The Colbert Report,* I speak straight from the gut, OK? I give people the truth, unfiltered by rational argument." On this point Colbert also compared himself to President George W. Bush, who sat at the head table just a few feet away from Colbert's podium:

> We're not so different, he and I. We both get it. Guys like us, we're not some brainiacs on the nerd patrol. We're not members of the Factinista. We go straight from the gut; right, sir? That's where the truth lies, right down here in the gut.
>
> Do you know you have more nerve endings in your gut than you have in your head? You can look it up. Now I know some of you are going to say, "I did look it up, and that's not true." That's because you looked it up in a book. Next time, look it up in your gut. I did, My gut tells me that's how our nervous system works.

[6]As Postman writes, "While brevity does not always suggest triviality, in this cast it surely does. It is simply not possible to convey a sense of seriousness about any event if its implications are exhausted in less than one minute's time" (p. 103).

[7]See also "Stephen Colbert's Guide to Dressing and Expressing Like a TV Journalist" in Jon Stewart, Ben Karlin, and David Javerbaum, *America (The Book): A Citizen's Guide to Democracy Inaction* (New York: Warner Books, 2004), pp. 142–3.

[8]*Reliable Sources,* CNN (November 2, 2002).

[9]*The O'Reilly Factor,* Fox News (September 17, 2004).

[10]"National Annenberg Election Survey" (press release), *Annenberg Public Policy Center* (September 21, 2004), p. 2.

[11]*Now,* PBS (July 11, 2003).

[12]*Reliable Sources,* CNN (November 2, 2002).

[13]*Crossfire,* CNN (October 15, 2004). All quotes below are from CNN's rush transcript of this episode.

[14]Postman actually cites Buckley's own legendary program *Firing Line* as a rare example of television as a "carrier of coherent language and thought in process" that "occasionally shows people in the act of thinking but who also happen to have television cameras pointed at them" (p. 91). *Firing Line* never received high ratings, though, and spent most of its 33 years on public television.

[15]Postman's son Andrew sums all of this up nicely in his "Introduction" to the 20th Anniversary Edition of *Amusing Ourselves to Death,* writing: "When Jon Stewart, host of Comedy Central's *The Daily Show,* went on CNN's *Crossfire* to make this very point—that serious news and show business ought to be distinguishable, for the sake of public discourse and the republic—the hosts seemed incapable of even understanding the words coming out of his mouth" (pp. xiii–xiv).

[16]Howard Kurtz, "Carlson & 'Crossfire,' Exit Stage Left & Right," *Washington Post* (January 6, 2005), C1.

[17]In the final chapter of *Amusing Ourselves to Death,* Postman describes a then-hypothetical but subversive anti-television television program that's

eerily similar to *The Daily Show.* According to Postman, this program would serve an important educational purpose by demonstrating how television recreates and degrades news, political debate, religious thought, and so on. He writes: "I imagine such demonstrations would of necessity take the form of parodies, along the lines of 'Saturday Night Live' and 'Monty Python,' the idea being to induce a national horse laugh over television's control of the public discourse" (pp. 161–2). In the end, Postman rejects the idea of such a show as "nonsense," since he thinks that serious and intelligent televised discussion could never attract an audience large enough to make a difference.

Examining the Text

1. According to Erion, what are the key elements of Neil Postman's critique of television? Why does Postman think that television is ineffective at conveying serious content? Do you agree that "thinking does not play well on television" (paragraph 7)?

2. What examples does Erion provide to support his claim that the humor of *The Daily Show* "rests on Postman-like insights" (paragraph 11)? Do you find this evidence convincing?

3. Erion spends several paragraphs describing and commenting on Stewart's 2004 appearance on CNN's *Crossfire.* Why does Erion find this incident particularly revealing? How does the incident support Erion's claims that Stewart has the same view of television as Postman does?

4. *Thinking rhetorically*: Imagine for a moment that Erion is right and that *The Daily Show* does indeed deliver a Postman-infused, McLuhan-esque critique of television. Would that change the way that you watch *The Daily Show* (or the *Colbert Report,* or similar shows)? Do you think that Erion's purpose in writing this article is ultimately to add more legitimacy and philosophical sophistication to these kinds of shows? What other persuasive goals might Erion be trying to accomplish in this article?

For Group Discussion

Erion focuses his analysis on *The Daily Show* and on Jon Stewart's particular critique of television and news. In a small group, discuss the extent to which Erion's ideas apply to other comedy news shows such as *The Colbert Report* as well as to other "serious" television shows such as *Washington Week in Review.* Do these shows also deliver a Postman-like critique of television? What similarities and differences are there between these other shows and *The Daily Show?*

Writing Suggestion

Watch *The Daily Show* and *The Colbert Report* for a few nights (or look at their videos on the Web), and select one of the standard segments of one of these shows: for example, the Senior Correspondent report or "Great Moments in Punditry" on *The Daily Show,* "The Word" on *The Colbert Report,* or celebrity/newsmaker interviews on both shows. Write down all of the details that you can about the segment: what are its key features, who participates, how long does it last, what specific topics does it take on?

After taking notes about a few instances of this segment, write an analysis in which you explore the messages conveyed by the segment. You should first summarize the key features of the segment, and then suggest how the segment works to deliver a satirical or critical view of television, politics, and/or journalism. In your analysis, draw on quotations and ideas from Erion's article as well as from the other two articles in this section of the television chapter.

"Fake" News versus "Real" News as Sources of Political Information: The Daily Show *and Postmodern Political Reality*

JEFFREY P. JONES

The article that follows was initially published in a 2007 collection entitled Politicotainment: Television's Take on the Real; *the book brings together essays that look at how politics is interpreted and represented in various forms of TV entertainment, including reality shows and drama series. A central premise of the book is that what we know about politics, politicians, and our entire political system is mediated through television;* Politicotainment *focuses on how television shapes and filters our view of reality.*

In this article, Jeffrey P. Jones writes about how The Daily Show *shapes our understanding of politics and political events. A professor at Old Dominion University, Jones has written widely about television, politics, and related topics. Here he draws a specific contrast between what we learn about politics through* The Daily Show *and what we learn through mainstream journalism. Toward the end of the article, Jones writes that "unhindered by the self-imposed constraints placed on reporters by the profession (as well as the co-dependent relationship that exists between government and the press),* The Daily Show *uses a fake news platform to offer discussions of news events that are informative* and *critical, factual* and *interpretive, thorough* yet *succinct" (paragraph 38).*

This statement concludes the close reading that occupies much of the article, in which Jones provides a detailed look at a specific episode of The Daily Show *in order to determine how accurate the show is. Surprisingly, he concludes that* The Daily Show *matches and even surpasses CNN's coverage of a particular campaign event. So although Jon Stewart or Stephen*

Colbert would be very unlikely to describe themselves as "journalists," they nevertheless perform some of the functions of mainstream journalists—and perhaps do a more effective job of it.

Before you read *this article, make a list of journalists with whom you're familiar, whether from television, print, radio, or the Internet. How would you describe the work they do? What function does their work serve in our society? What particular skills and attributes do they need to perform effectively?*

A recurrent claim about young Americans is that they get more of their news about politics and current events from late-night television comedians than they do from the news media. This claim began with a statistic that appeared in a 2000 survey of the electorate conducted by the Pew Research Center for the People & the Press, which reported that 47 percent of people under thirty years old were "informed at least occasionally" about the presidential campaign by late-night talk shows.[1] Though there are numerous methodological and interpretive problems raised by this simple yet ultimately flawed statistic, journalists and other critics have nevertheless transformed it into a myth about young people and their news-consumption habits. Regardless of its accuracy, it seemingly explains why young people have increasingly turned away from traditional outlets of political communication, namely newspapers and television news (Mindich 2005). It also addresses journalistic concerns that audiences are attracted more to entertainment than serious public-affairs reporting, and what's worse, that they may not even be able to distinguish between the two. It also seemingly verifies fears of public ignorance of the political process (Delli Carpini and Keeter 1996), youth disengagement from politics (Buckingham 2000), a declining reading culture (Scheuer 1999), couch potato kids, the entertainmentization of politics (West and Orman 2003), and the cynicism that supposedly grips our society (Hart 1994; Chaloupka 1999). 1

This chapter begins, then, by examining and questioning this myth. But as with many myths that circulate in society, the critic's ability to refute the accuracy of the myth is not likely to diminish its popularity or widespread circulation. Instead, it may be more effective to show why the basic premise of the myth itself is incorrect. That is, in this instance, the idea that late-night comedic television does not (or cannot) impart important news or information about public affairs and thus, by definition, only traffics in the trivial, inane, or absurd. In this chapter, therefore, I turn the myth on its head by asking: What if the myth is true and young people *are* "getting their news" from popular late-night comedy programs such as *The Daily Show with Jon Stewart?* What is it they might learn about politics or current events from this 2 show, and how does that compare with what they might learn about politics were they to watch more respected sources of news such as CNN instead? To begin answering this question, I compare a news item "reported" by *The Daily Show,* a fake news show that parodies a "legitimate" television news broadcast, with the same story as covered by CNN. I follow the Pew Center's lead by examining news reports of the 2004 presidential election, yet from broadcasts much later in the campaign when the viewing public is typically more raptly attuned. I analyze the type of information that is offered in the two reports and how the resulting meanings or "truths" compare.

I argue that even though *The Daily Show* is a fake news show, its 3
faux journalistic style allows the show's writers and host to question, dispel, and critique the manipulative language and symbolizations coming from the presidential campaign while simultaneously opening up deeper truths about politics than those offered by the "objective" reporting of mainstream journalism. By actually showing the high levels of spin and rhetoric produced by the candidates and their campaigns, then offering humorous retorts that cut to the heart of the matter, *The Daily Show* offers its viewers particular (and perhaps more useful) "information" about the campaign that is often missing from "real" journalist reports on the news networks, and hence informs its viewers in ways that mainstream journalism rarely does. Given the extraordinary level of outright distortions, lies, and spin that dominated both the Republican and Democratic campaigns in this election, this chapter concludes that perhaps the postmodern notion that the "fake" is more real than the "real" is not such an unsettling notion when it comes to citizens looking for truth in contemporary political communication on television. And, in turn, perhaps young citizens—if they do indeed get their information from political comedians on television—may not be as misinformed as the current myth suggests.

THE MYTH OF YOUNG PEOPLE AND KNOWLEDGE OF PUBLIC AFFAIRS

In February 2000, the Pew Research Center for the People & the Press 4
reported that 47 percent of people under the age of thirty were "informed at least occasionally" about the campaign or candidates by late-night talk shows (13 percent regularly and 34 percent sometimes). The poll was conducted from 4 to 11 January 2000, before any party primaries had taken place. In January 2004, the Pew Center repeated this survey (conducted 19 December 2003 through 4 January 2004), this time asking respondents if they "learned something" from comedy shows. Twenty-one percent of people under the age of thirty reported

learning something from programs such as *Saturday Night Live* and *The Daily Show* (roughly the same number who learned something from the Internet). As the Pew study notes, "For Americans under thirty, these comedy shows are now mentioned almost as frequently as newspapers and evening network news programs as regular sources for election news." Furthermore, the report exclaims, "one out of every two young people (50%) say they at least sometimes learn about the campaign from comedy shows, nearly twice the rate among people age thirty–forty (27%) and four times the rate among people fifty and older."[2]

5 Before taking these statistics at face value, however, we should examine both the questions and the resulting statistics more closely. Certainly political insiders, heavy news readers/watchers, and political junkies are attuned to news so early in the campaign, for no other reason than to be able to handicap the upcoming horse race. As for the rest of the polity, however, the electoral contests in the small yet important states of Iowa and New Hampshire certainly receive much less of their attention because the party nominee is generally a forgone conclusion by the time most Americans have the opportunity to vote in their state primary election. Hence, for a poll to attempt to measure political knowledge and information about an election so early in the campaign is specious.

6 What is worse, though, is the wording of the question itself: "informed at least occasionally." What does it mean to be "informed" about the campaign—knowledge of who is running for office, what their positions are on issues, who is ahead in the race, who has the biggest war chest, what gaffes have occurred to this point, the names of their wives, what type of underwear they prefer? At what level can most any type of nonfiction program—news reports, talk shows, documentaries, stand-up comedy, advertisements—provide *some* of this information? The question doesn't help us understand the underlying normative assumption of whether the respondent should know the differences between Al Gore's and Bill Bradley's positions on Social Security reform, or whether the respondent is simply expected to know their names and that they are running for office. Furthermore, the question asks "at least occasionally." Does that mean every day, once a week, or once a month, or does it suggest a regular and consistent pattern of consumption? Finally, what assumptions of intentionality are included here? Does the question seek to identify whether citizens brush up against news, or whether they intentionally turn to certain forms of programming for "information"? The survey results provide no answers to these questions. In short, the response to this question really only tells us two things—that comedians mine current affairs for humorous content, and that different programming types differ in their popularity among different demographic groups. It certainly does *not*

measure whether the only or primary source of information about current affairs is obtained by watching late-night comedians on television.

Nevertheless, that hasn't prevented journalists from using the statistic to develop a full-blown myth about young people and their news consumption habits. For instance, CNN anchor Judy Woodruff began a question to *The Daily Show* host Jon Stewart by stating, "We hear more and more that your show and shows like your show are the places that young people *are getting their news*" (emphasis added).[3] Ted Koppel, the anchor for ABC's late-night news show *Nightline* (a program that directly competes with these entertainment shows), similarly assailed Stewart by noting to his viewers, "A lot of television viewers, more, quite frankly, than I'm comfortable with, *get their news* from the comedy channel on a program called 'The Daily Show'" (emphasis added).[4] And perhaps most egregiously, *Newsday* reporter Verne Gay wrote, "A recent study from the Pew Center found that 8 percent of respondents *learned most everything they knew* about a candidate from shows like *The Daily Show* and *Saturday Night Live*" (emphasis added; Gay 2004). 7

As these quotes suggest, reporters have taken great liberty in revising and expanding what the statistic actually reveals. Yet the results of campaign knowledge test conducted on over 19,000 citizens in the summer and fall of 2004 by the University of Pennsylvania's National Annenberg Election Survey did little to temper the myth. The survey reported that "viewers of late-night comedy programs, especially *The Daily show* with Jon Stewart on Comedy Central, are more likely to know the issue positions and backgrounds of presidential candidates than people who do not watch late-night comedy," noting that *Daily Show* viewers "have higher campaign knowledge than national news viewers and newspaper readers."[5] The survey concludes, "traditional journalists have been voicing increasing concern that if young people are receiving political information from late-night comedy shows like *The Daily Show,* they may not be adequately informed on the issues of the day. This data suggests that these fears may be unsubstantiated." The survey also points out, however, that "these findings do not show that *The Daily Show* is itself responsible for the higher knowledge among its viewers." 8

In summary, journalists and other critics of entertainment television have propagated a myth based on dubious evidence that late-night comedy television programming is a central location for the delivery of news (and, by inference, misinformation, and ignorance about politics) for young people, a myth that competing quantitative evidence suggests is incorrect. What neither of these surveys reveals, however, is an assessment of the *content* of these shows—whether they offer viewers anything of value or are relatively meaningless, whether the information provided is accurate and truthful or biased and incorrect, or even how this material compares with other sources of information 9 on public affairs. There is no qualitative assessment, only the assumption that what appears in these formats is not equivalent to that which could be obtained from traditional sources of political information. What follows, then, is an attempt to examine these questions directly, looking at how *The Daily Show* "reports" news and information, and its comparative value in light of reporting available on a more culturally acceptable and respected news source, CNN.

NEWS REPORTS BY *THE DAILY SHOW* AND CNN

Every weeknight (except Fridays), Comedy Central airs *The Daily* 10
Show, a mock news program and hybrid talk show that parodies television news for the first half of the program, then segues into a more typical talk-show interview between host Jon Stewart and a guest. The first half—the news segment—mimics the anchor-centered style of television news reporting, where Stewart narrates the day's top stories accompanied by video evidence. The news segment also uses the news convention of the anchor interviewing reporters "on location," in this instance, with Stewart talking to his faux "senior correspondents," who pretend to be reporting live via satellite (in front of a background image of, say, Baghdad or the White House). The primary interest of my investigation is this "news" segment of the show.

I examined one week of the program during the late stages of the 11
presidential campaign—4 to 7 October 2004—one week after the first presidential debate. I selected one program during this period as a representative text (Thursday, 7 October) for a close textual analysis. This limited selection allows for an in-depth analysis of the information and commentary provided, as well as a direct comparison with news reports from CNN. While the limited range of texts can be criticized as overly restricted, such a close reading of *The Daily Show* has not been conducted to date. Instead, existing studies have examined a broader range of texts from the program across numerous episodes and months of programming (see, for instance, Jones 2005a; and Baym 2005). Here, though, the intention is to make a direct comparison of two entire news reports on the same event. The selection of a single news report also limits the generalizability of my argument, yet the episode selected for scrutiny is not extraordinary. Rather, it is fairly representative, by my reading, of a typical *Daily Show* broadcast. Furthermore, the intentional circumscribing allows for the close reading of a text that cultural studies has proven to be of value. The episode selected illustrates the type of information provided in typical news reports by both *The Daily Show* and CNN, allowing us to compare not just the variety but also the quality of the reports and conclusions that can be drawn from them.

The CNN reports come from three programs, all of which appeared on the same day as *The Daily Show* broadcast: *American Morning* (7 A.M.), *CNN Live Today* (10 A.M.), and *News from CNN* (12 P.M.).[6]

CNN began its 7 A.M. broadcast by reporting on Bush's campaign appearances the previous day, as well as the release of the CIA's Iraq Survey Group report investigating the existence of weapons of mass destruction in Iraq. In reporting Bush's campaign stop in Pennsylvania, CNN White House Correspondent Elaine Quijano pointed out that the president made no mention of a new report by the Iraq Survey Group, which found no evidence of stockpiles of weapons of mass destruction in Iraq when the United States invaded in 2003. Still, Mr. Bush is standing by his decision, insisting that after September 11, the country had to assess every potential threat in a new light. 12

> (Video clip of President Bush speaking in Wilkes-Barre, Pennsylvania): Our nation awakened to an even greater danger, the prospect that terrorists who killed thousands with hijacked airplanes would kill many more with weapons of mass murder. We had to take a hard look at every place where terrorists might get those weapons. One regime stood out, the dictatorship of Saddam Hussein.

During the 10 A.M. report, CNN decided not to continue airing the clip of Bush's speech, instead letting Quijano summarize the president's central point in the statement, as well as note the official White House "reading" of the report, attributed here to "administration officials." 13

But the president did not mention that new CIA report, which found no weapons of mass destruction in Iraq when the United States invaded in 2003. Instead Mr. Bush repeated his argument that taking Saddam Hussein out of power has made the world safer. Administration officials say they believe the report shows Saddam Hussein was a threat that the United States needed to take seriously. They also say they believe it shows that he had the intent and capability to develop weapons of mass destruction. 14

By 12 P.M., CNN was simply reporting the release of the report as this: "Bush also defended the war in Iraq, just as the CIA prepares to report that Saddam Hussein did not have weapons of mass destruction or the means to produce them before U.S. troops invaded Iraq." 15

Jon Stewart also began his broadcast by announcing the release of the CIA report and noting its conclusions: 16

> Everything we've been waiting for happened today. The official CIA report, the Duelfer Report, has come out, the one they've been working on for the past two years. It will be the definitive answer on the weapons of mass destruction programs in Iraq, and as it turns out, not so much. Apparently, there were no weapons of mass destruction in Iraq, and their

capabilities have been degraded, and they had pretty much stopped trying anything in '98. And both the president and vice president have come out today in response to the findings and said that they clearly justified the invasion of Iraq. Some people look at a glass as half full, while other people look at a glass and say that it's a dragon.

In this segment, Stewart provides roughly the same amount and type of information provided by CNN, but then goes out of his way to establish that despite clear and convincing evidence to the contrary, Bush and Cheney continue their act as either liars or highly delusional people; they see what they want to see. Here Stewart offers not just the facts, but also draws conclusions from those facts. Journalistic adherence to norms of objectivity generally prevents many reporters and anchors from looking across specific events to explicitly point out repeated patterns of deception or misjudgment by politicians and government officials (unless the reporting occurs in investigative or opinion-editorial pieces). *The Daily Show,* as a fake news program, is not limited by such professional constraints. Viewers are thus invited to focus on the most important aspect of this news event—that this is not just another investigation that proves the official reason for invading Iraq was misguided and wrong. Rather, the import is that the Bush Administration repeatedly refuses to admit its mistake. 17

CNN, on the other hand, simply repeats the administration's position, as is standard journalistic convention, Yet since numerous investigations have produced the same findings (which in the world of science and social science would amount to the establishment of "truth"), why should news media continue to repeat a position that has no basis in fact—just because the government continues to assert the position? Is that "newsworthy," and if not, what news value is being fulfilled? Daniel Boorstin contends that assertions such as this amount to "pseudo-events," a story created by politicians and journalists that has no intrinsic value as a news event *per se,* but is only deemed as such by journalists in the era of "objectivity" (Boorstin 1960). Stewart refuses to play along and, again, ignores the administration's "reading" or justifications because they have no basis in reality (as determined by the numerous other officials, institutions, and nations that have concluded the same thing). 18

Stewart then turns his attention to a Bush campaign stop the day before. "Let's begin tonight on the campaign trail," he says, while talking over a video clip of President Bush in Wilkes-Barre, Pennsylvania. Bush is standing in front of a backdrop/banner with the words "A Safer America, A Stronger Economy" adorned over both of his shoulders. "Yesterday, President Bush's advisors alerted the networks he would be making a major policy speech in Wilkes-Barre, Pennsylvania. 19

The subject . . . [*the graphic highlights the slogan "A Safer America"*]—no, not that. [*The graphic highlights "A Stronger Economy."*] Uh, wrong again. [*The graphic then shows a crossed-out slogan, superimposing the hand–scrawled message, "Recover from unbelievably poor debate performance."*] That's it! That was the subject. Yes, in the week of his, let's call it 'weak' showing against Senator John Kerry on Thursday, the president and his handlers snookered the cable news networks into giving him one hour of free full-on campaign stop pabulum."

CNN also covered this campaign stop in all three of its morning broadcasts. For both the 7 A.M. and 10 A.M. reports, Quijano simply referred to two campaign stops (one of which was in Pennsylvania), noting that Bush had "stepped up his attacks" and had come "out swinging hard against his opponent, "blasting" Kerry and delivering a "blistering assault on Kerry's record." The reporter seeks to summarize the tone and substance of the president's speeches, while characterizing him as on the offensive—exactly what the campaign hopes will be reported. Only the 12 P.M. broadcast noted the campaign's intentions in changing the focus of the speech. Wolf Blitzer introduced the subject by referring to Bush's "attempt to try to reestablish some political momentum," while the correspondent reporting the event pointed out the change in plans: "Well, Wolf, as you know, initially this was a speech that was supposed to focus on medical liability reform. But after President Bush's widely viewed disappointing performance in the first presidential debate, there was a difference in strategy, a change in strategy from the campaign. They changed this to sharp attacks against Senator Kerry and his record on the war on terror, as well as the economy." 20

CNN's reporting of this event is characterized by three tendencies that political scientists argue are typical of news media's reporting in elections: (1) elections are treated as a sports contest between two combatants (typically horse racing or, in this instance, boxing); (2) the press focuses on the campaign's strategies more than the issues themselves; and (3) the press often parrots the message that political campaigns want them to report, circulating the rhetoric and slogans without intensive scrutiny or criticism (see, for instance, Patterson 1993). Stewart also points out the campaign's strategy of deflecting attention from Bush's weak showing in the presidential debates by going on the offensive, but insists on calling attention to the manipulative aspects of the event itself—both the campaign's misleading the press about making a major policy statement (when the presence of the banner itself clearly shows the forethought and planning for this attack speech) and the oral and visual rhetoric that the campaign wants the news media to report and show its viewers. Stewart doesn't accept the contention that the speech is about national security or the economy and focuses instead on the artifice of the event. It is an artifice that the news media help create and facilitate by uncritically continuing to air 21 the Bush speech live, even though the speech does not include the policy material they initially agreed merited free air time as a newsworthy *presidential* statement (as opposed to that of a candidate for office). As Stewart has noted about his show in an earlier interview, "What we try to do is point out the artifice of things, that there's a guy behind the curtain pulling levers" (Hedgpeth 2000). Here he does just that.

Stewart then shows several clips from the Bush speech that CNN chose not to air in any of its three reports. 22

> *Stewart:* [Bush] began by throwing out the first pander.
> *Bush:* It's great to be in Wilkes-Barre, Pennsylvania. It's such an honor to be back here. It's great to be in a part of the world where people work hard, they love their families. . . .
> *Stewart:* [*said out of the side of his mouth*] Yeah, not like New York—family hating jackasses; lazy family haters.

CNN does not show this clip because, given the news values of mainstream journalism, such statements by politicians are not newsworthy; they are typical of political speeches. For reporters assigned to follow the candidate's campaign, in fact, they have heard such statements countless times by this point in the campaign, said to different crowds in different places. For Stewart, however, the clip merits the viewers' attention because it shows that not only is the statement itself ridiculous, but that it is not beneath the president to pander to audiences. This is part of the overall point that Stewart attempts to make throughout the entire news segment—he continually asks the viewer to step outside the staged event to assess what information is available that might shed light on both presidential candidates' fundamental character as people and leaders. 23

Stewart continues covering the event by again showing another clip that CNN chose not to air: 24

> *Stewart:* But then it was rival bashing time. Bush warmed up with a few insults aimed at the Democrats' number two man and his performance in Tuesday night's debate.
> *Bush:* America saw two very different visions of our country and two different hairdos. I didn't pick my vice president for his hairdo. I picked him for his judgment, his experience. . . .
> *Stewart:* [*showing a picture of a bald Dick Cheney*] which, sadly, is as good as his hairdo.

If pandering isn't enough, Stewart shows that it is not beneath Bush to engage in *ad hominem* attacks. Again, CNN chose not to report this part of the president's speech, recognizing that attacks on one's opponents are simply part of electoral politics. Stewart, however, shows 25 the clip not just to provide evidence of Bush's character and campaign style, but also to question the actual point that Bush is attempting to make so unproblematically—the quality of his administration's "judgment and experience" in the conduct of governmental affairs. Both CNN and *The Daily Show* have already provided evidence earlier in their broadcasts that the administration's "experience" of deciding to wage war, based on its "judgment" that there was trustworthy information to do so, was faulty. *The Daily Show,* however, is the only one to make the connection and point it out to viewers.

Like CNN, Stewart then focuses on the major policy statements within Bush's speech. 26

> *Stewart:* Bush then moved onto his economic policy regarding Kerry.
>
> *Bush:* Now the Senator's proposing higher taxes on more than 900,000 small business owners. He says the tax increase is only for the rich. You've heard that kind of rhetoric before. The rich hire lawyers and accountants for a reason—to stick you with the tab.
>
> *Stewart:* Let me get this straight. Don't tax the rich because they'll get out of it? So your policy is, tax the hard-working people because they're dumb-asses and they'll never figure it out? So vote for me, goodnight?

Only during its 12 P.M. broadcast did CNN report this aspect of the president's speech, noting that Bush "also twisted Kerry's plan to roll back the cut taxes for those making more than $200,000, describing it as a tax increase for more than 900,000 small businesses." The CNN report is critical at this juncture by pointing out the Bush campaign's distortion of Kerry's proposal (that is, rolling back Bush's tax cuts does not amount to a proposed tax increase). CNN's focus is on the rhetorical sleight of hand. But that is the extent of their report. Stewart, however, returns the focus to the president's rhetoric by carrying the point to its logical conclusion. He illuminates the contradictory nature of the populist statement by questioning what it is exactly that Bush is trying to articulate, while also reminding viewers of where Bush really stands on taxes and how his policies actually belie the rhetoric employed here. It merits noting that news programs rarely offer direct and damning evidence of contradictory statements or duplicitous comments. The convention they typically rely on is to quote someone else who will point this out (Tuchman 1978). CNN did not even air the actual clip, relying instead on its reporter to summarize Bush's statement. One might argue that CNN has done Bush a favor by *not* airing a statement that is logically somewhat ridiculous and, instead, doing the hard work 27 of actually deciphering for the viewing audience what the president means, thereby making him look more presidential in the process.[7]

The only clip of the president's speech that CNN showed in all 28
three of its broadcasts occurred in the 7 A.M report—his statement concerning the supposed threat posed by "the dictatorship of Saddam Hussein" (quoted above). *The Daily Show* also reported this part of the speech, but with much more scrutiny to what Bush actually said. Stewart here engages in a rhetorical back-and-forth with the video clip of Bush's statement, attempting to come up with the right answer for which nation it is *exactly* that threatens America with weapons of mass destruction:

Stewart: Finally, the president brought the mood down a little, as only he can.

Bush: After September 11, America had to assess every potential threat in a new light. We had to take a hard look at every place where terrorists might get those weapons and one regime stood out.

Stewart: Well, that's true. It would be Saudi Arabia. Fifteen of the nineteen terrorists were actually from there.

Bush: . . . the dictatorship of Saddam Hussein.

Stewart: No, no. I don't think that's it. Um. Oh. It was Iran—proven Al-Qaeda ties, building up the nukes program. I think it was them.

Bush: [*repeating the tape of Bush*] . . . the dictatorship of Saddam Hussein.

Stewart: No, no. I'm sure . . . [pause] . . . Pakistan. Top scientists sold nuclear secrets to . . .

Bush: [*repeating the tape of Bush*] . . . the dictatorship of Saddam Hussein.

Stewart: Could be Yemen. [*a graphic of a clock face with spinning hands is superimposed over a slightly faded image of Stewart, suggesting his thinking for quite some time of the possible countries, all the while Stewart thinks out loud*]. Oh. . . . Kazakhstan is actually a very dangerous. . . . Uzbekistan has always created problems in that region. . . . Turkey—very dangerous. Lebanon has some. . . . Qatar [*the graphic removes the clock face, and the camera focus on Stewart again becomes clear*] . . . Oh, oh, oh, North Korea. They have the bomb. Their leader is crazy. North Korea.

Bush: [*repeating the tape of Bush*] . . . the dictatorship of Saddam Hussein.

Stewart: [holding out his arms in front of him, like a robot, said in a slow monotone voice, with a staccato cadence]: The-dic-ta-tor-ship-of-Sad-dam-Hus-sein. Too-tired-to-fight-it. Must-learn. Re-pe-ti-tion.

Stewart scrutinizes the president's statement on its own terms—"in *every* place where terrorists might get those weapons": Saudi Arabia, Iran, Pakistan, North Korea, and so on. Then, through video repetition, Stewart highlights how the administration continues to repeat assertions over and over until the viewer is turned into an unthinking (or worn out) robot. In the speech itself, of course, Bush does not repeat the line. Yet Stewart recognizes that single speech events such as this do not constitute the reality that news media report and, in turn, help create. Instead, his use of manipulated video emphasizes the repeated pattern of administration efforts to establish something that is untrue, yet which citizens must work to resist because of its repeated assertion. As Stewart is quoted as saying, "We're out to stop that political trend of repeating things again and again until people are forced to believe them" (Armstrong 2003). 29

Stewart finishes the show's coverage of the Bush speech by returning one last time to a Bush pronouncement that was simply too good to pass up for its comedic value, yet also affirms the point about Bush's character that he has attempted to make throughout the telecast: 30

> *Stewart:* But for all that, perhaps the most telling line of the speech came during Bush's seemingly innocuous segue into a story about his wife.
> *Bush:* You're not going to believe this. It's a true story, or kind of true.
> *Stewart:* [*said with sheepish grin*] George W. Bush—I can tell a lie.

Again, CNN doesn't air this clip because there is no news value here—from their perspective, it is a meaningless aside unrelated to either campaign strategy or policy stances. For Stewart, however, it not only ties in nicely with the previous statement about Saddam Hussein and 9/11, but it also neatly demonstrates *exactly* what is at stake in the election of the president. Bush's proclivity to lie, in fact, was something the news media generally ignored in the election campaign, yet was an important criticism of Bush often addressed in numerous venues of popular culture during the campaign—most famously in Michael Moore's documentary film *Fahrenheit 9/11* (Jones 2005b). 31

Stewart concludes the news segment of the show by turning to an event not widely covered by the news media—both John Kerry and Bush soliciting votes by appearing on the afternoon therapy and relationship talk show, *Dr. Phil.* Here he attempts to highlight the deeper truths at work again, this time with the Democratic nominee: 32

> *Stewart:* But like Bush's speech, Kerry's *Dr. Phil* appearance had one moment that most clearly captured the essence of the candidate.

Dr. Phil's Wife: [*Video clip of the Dr. Phil Show, an interview with Senator Kerry conducted with the assistance of Dr. Phil's wife*]: Is one of your daughters more like you than the other?

Kerry: Yes. No. That's . . . gosh . . . I'd like to . . . yes. But I guess . . . yes, the answer is yes.

Dr. Phil's Wife: Which one do you think is more like you?

Kerry: Well . . . um . . . I . . . that's why I hesitated, because I think in some ways my daughter Alexandra is more like me, but in other ways my daughter Vanessa is more like me.

Stewart: [Burying his face into his hands, then moving his hands over his bowed head, gripping his hair, then the back of his neck. Stewart makes no comment, but simply looks at the camera with exasperation and dismay. The audience erupts in laughter.]

When presidential candidates first began appearing on such talk shows with regularity in 1992, the news media covered these appearances as newsworthy events. They did so, in particular, because of the unusual nature of the appearances, but also because the news media disliked the "softball" questions offered up by these "illegitimate" non-reporters (Debenport 1992). Because such appearances rarely feature the candidates' saying much about their position on issues (focusing more instead on personal matters), the news media now generally turn a blind eye to these "campaign stops," treating them as *de rigueur* in the hustle to reach disparate voter groups. *The Daily Show,* however, calls attention to the spectacle performance not just for its groveling and humiliating aspects, but rather to highlight how such performances might actually tell us something important about the candidates. In this instance, Kerry confirmed everything the Bush campaign had said about him: that Kerry is unwilling to be pinned down on anything (despite how insignificant the matter), yet paradoxically will say anything to get elected if he believes that is what the audience wants to hear. That truth comes to light very clearly for viewers when the matter is something as trivial as reflecting upon the relationship with one's daughter. Viewers may not be able to discern whether Kerry is a flip-flopper on foreign-policy issues (say, for instance, his various votes on the Iraq war), but they can certainly recognize mealy-mouthed remarks when it comes to interpersonal relationships. 33

The Daily Show, therefore, has constructed a narrative, weaving together campaign events to give the viewer insight into the candidates and who they might really be. This narrative is formulated from information derived from planned campaign events, yet woven together to tell a story that allows for evaluation of the candidates. Perhaps this is simply an entertainmentized version of a "news analysis" or "op-ed" journalism. But it is a particular brand of "reporting" that might 34 illuminate for viewers the larger issues at stake beyond the isolated events that typically dominate news reporting.

In summary, then, *The Daily Show* has provided viewers information on several major political events that occurred the day before: the CIA report on weapons of mass destruction, Bush's campaign speech, and Kerry's appearance on a popular television program. The audience learns what the CIA report says, learns two of the main points in Bush's speech also reported by news outlets, and learns about Kerry's personal life. *The Daily Show* has not, therefore, short-changed viewers on information they would have seen by watching a "real" newscast. 35

Yet *The Daily Show's* audience also sees more material on these events than that provided by CNN, learning things that CNN didn't report. First, *The Daily Show* highlights political rhetoric itself, showing the false statements, *ad hominem* attacks, pandering, and populist appeals of candidate Bush, not seeing such language as a "given" in politics, but instead as a disturbing quality that exemplifies the character of the politician. Second, and perhaps more important, the program offers viewers information they have heard before, yet are reminded of here as a means of making sense of the events covered in the daily news report: there were no weapons of mass destruction; the administration's actions exemplify its use of bad judgment because it went after the wrong regime; its economic policies are the opposite of what they say they are. Continually, Stewart will not let the viewer lose sight of the greater truths at stake here. He is constantly keeping score, adding it all up, reminding the viewer of what this says about the candidates and the larger terms upon which they should be evaluated. In a single news report, the television news reporters rarely put things together in such a manner. And what the news media ignore may actually provide citizens with the type of meaningful information upon which they can base their electoral decisions. By Stewart's doing so in a typical news-reporting format, he demonstrates the failings of news media in informing viewers, drawing attention to how media serve as conduits for false information and image management, and how it would be easy for citizens to become the unthinking drones and robots that such unquestioned lies and manipulative imagery could lead them to become. 36

One might be tempted to criticize *The Daily Show* for selecting damning video clips that are taken out of context and then used to ridicule or embarrass politicians, all for a laugh. As we have seen, however, the clips used by Stewart are no more out of context than the single clip shown by CNN. Both Stewart and CNN actually highlight the context of the speech—the poor debate performance, as well as the release of the CIA report—yet it is *The Daily Show* that provides even more depth to the speech by showing viewers more of it (six clips compared to one 37 by CNN). Just because CNN and other news organizations make claims of neutrality and objectivity doesn't mean they aren't being selective in what they report and how they report it. Furthermore, Stewart reports the same events and highlights the same "newsworthy" items as CNN, including reaching many of their same conclusions. As journalism critics have pointed out, not only have the length of sound bites drastically decreased over the last twenty years, they are increasingly disappearing altogether from television news reports (despite a very large news hole with twenty-four-hour cable channels). Instead, reporters are simply summarizing what candidates and government officials say, then interpreting those comments in a conversation with the news anchor. Yet as we have also seen, those interpretations offer the viewer little in the way of substantive critical assessments because of the norms and conventions of the profession.

In short, *The Daily Show* has matched CNN's coverage of this 38
particular campaign event, even surpassing it by providing viewers additional information about the candidates beyond policy positions and campaign strategies and maneuvers. Of course, CNN provides a wealth of information about national and world affairs that a comedy program like *The Daily Show* can never cover. Nor would I suggest that citizens could be fully informed by watching a comedy show that provides little more than ten minutes of "reporting." Nevertheless, if we are to assess the quality of information about the presidential campaign provided by a fake news show versus a real one (as the Pew study normatively asserts), then the analysis here suggests that *The Daily Show* can provide quality information that citizens can use in making informed choices about electoral politics.

FAKENESS, REALITY, AND THE POSTMODERN VIEWING PUBLIC

By most accounts, the institution of journalism is in a state of crisis in 39
America (Hachten 2005; Kovach and Rosenstiel 2001). As discussed above, the myth that young people get their news from late-night comedians is partly a desire to explain why young people, in particular, are turning away from broadcast news or print journalism as primary sources of news and information (Mindich 2005). With declining readership and viewership, the institution is economically challenged by dwindling advertising revenues as well as increased costs of production (Roberts et al. 2001; Seelye 2005a). Recent scandals related to professional norms and ethics (from story fabrication by Jason Blair at *The New York Times* and Stephen Glass at *The New Republic* to poor fact-checking on President Bush's Air National Guard records by

Dan Rather at *CBS News*) have contributed to a decline in trust with news media consumers (Johnson 2003; Hachten 2005, 102–112). Concurrently, with new media technologies such as blogs and search-engine portals, citizens are questioning the top-down, gatekeeper role of news media and, instead, increasingly desire a more active role in the determination and construction of what constitutes news and who gets to make it (Gillmor 2004; Seelye 2005b). Furthermore, the press's timidity in questioning and thwarting overt propaganda efforts by the Bush Administration (as both *The New York Times* and *Washington Post* offered *mea culpas* for their lack of serious reporting on assertions and evidence by the Bush Administration in the run-up to the Iraq war) also weakens the news media's claim to serving as effective and trustworthy watchdogs to power (Younge 2004; Seeyle 2005c). Indeed, government propaganda combined with competition between news outlets that offer not just "competing views of the world, but different realities" (such as Fox News, *The New York Times,* and Al-Jazeera) leads to what Kristina Riegert calls the "struggle for credibility" with viewing audiences and voting publics (Riegert 2005).

Hence, what is also in crisis is the belief that news media provide 40

a *realistic* picture of the world. The public is well aware that both television and politics are spectacle performances and, indeed, that the press and government are two mutually reinforcing and constituting institutions.[8] News media are *part of* the political spectacle (Edelman 1988), including journalists-cum-talk-show-pundits (who act more like lapdogs to power than watchdogs of it), cheerleading embedded reporters, and patriotic news anchors who wear their hearts on their sleeves. An increasingly media-savvy public realizes that news programs such as CNN are no more "real" than *The Daily Show* is "fake." Yet mainstream news media continue to believe their claims to truth—and the authenticity of those claims—because of their *authority* to make them in the first place. It is an authority they have asserted (and the public has granted) through their title, special status, institutional-based legitimacy, access to power, and the means of production and distribution. But as Foucault also reminds us, "truth' is a type of discourse that societies accept and *make function as true*" (emphasis added; Foucault 1980, 132). And as postmodernists would have it, the "authentic" exists only in "the imaginings of those who yearn for it" (Webster 1995, 170). Were that to change, or should citizens come to believe that news is inauthentic, untrue, or just another form of constructed spectacle (that is, the credibility gap becomes a chasm), then they might yearn for other means of establishing truth and reality.

The institutional practice of journalism is a modernist means of 41
constructing knowledge of public life that for many years has been widely accepted. Increasingly, though, this means of taking account of

the world is being questioned, if not discredited.[9] In a useful summary of postmodernist thinking, Frank Webster argues that,

> the modernist enthusiasm for genres and styles [of which news is one] is rejected and mocked for its pretensions [by postmodernists]. From this it is but a short step to the postmodern penchant for parody, for tongue-in-cheek reactions to established styles, for a pastiche mode which delights in irony and happily mixes and marches in a 'bricolage' manner. (Webster 1995, 169–170)

And in steps *The Daily Show,* with a tendency for just such post- 42
modern playfulness. But *The Daily Show* is "fake" only in that it refuses to make claims to authenticity (as demonstrated in the analysis above). But being fake does not mean that the information it imparts is untrue. Indeed, as with most social and political satire, its humor offers a means of reestablishing common-sense truths to counter the spectacle, ritual, pageantry, artifice, and verbosity that often cloak the powerful. The rationality of political satire is that it "reminds of common values," and "in its negative response to political excess, it serves to restore equilibrium to politics" (Schutz 1977, 327–28). Citizens know that public artifice exists, which is ultimately why the satire that points it out is funny—they just need someone skillful enough to articulate the critique. The type of fake-yet-real "reporting" performed by *The Daily Show* has led one commentator to claim that *The Daily Show* is "reinventing political journalism" (Baym 2005). Perhaps more to the point, the postmodern audience that comprises its viewership and has made it popular are themselves reinventing what it is they want from political communication.

Though scholars often attack the press for its supposed cynicism 43
(for example, the way in which reporters point out the man behind the curtain), I contend that the press may not do this enough. Shelving journalistic conventions to get at important truths is less cynical than turning a blind eye to the manipulation by either contending that politics will always be this way or assuming that viewers *should* be informed enough or smart enough to connect all the dots themselves. A program like *The Daily Show* refuses to sit idly by while political lies and manipulative rhetoric go unchallenged (or, as Stewart says, "until it becomes true"). Unhindered by the self-imposed constraints placed on reporters by the profession (as well as the co-dependent relationship that exists between government and the press), *The Daily Show* uses a fake news platform to offer discussions of news events that are informative *and* critical, factual *and* interpretive, thorough *yet* succinct. Does that make it biased, unfair, or unbalanced? Not when the program sets its sights on the powerful. As Bryan Keefer, editor of Spinsanity.com, has argued, "the media need to

understand that pointing out the truth isn't the same as taking sides."[10] This, of course, is what a fake news show is licensed to do, and why I contend that it provides such an important voice of political critique on the American political landscape (Jones 2005a).

In an opinion piece in the *Washington Post,* Keefer dares to speak 44
for his generation, justifying its changing relationship to traditional news media and its search for better alternatives. He contends that

> we live in an era when PR pros have figured out how to bend the news cycle to their whims, and much of what's broadcast on the networks bears a striking resemblance to the commercials airing between segments. Like other twenty-somethings, I've been raised in an era when advertising invades every aspect of pop culture, and to me the information provided by mainstream news outlets too often feels like one more product, produced by politicians and publicists. (Keefer 2004)

If the myth of young citizens turning to comedians for news and 45
information about politics ends up proving true, then as this analysis suggests, the fate of the republic doesn't seem in jeopardy if a comedy program like *The Daily Show* is a source for their knowledge of public affairs. As Keefer's comments suggest, at least when people watch a program that blatantly embraces its fakeness, they don't feel like they are being sold a bill of goods. Hence, the postmodern claim that the "fake" is more real than the "real" is perhaps not such an unsettling notion after all.

NOTES

[1]http://people-press.org/reports/display.ph3?Report ID=46.

[2]http://people-press.org/reports/display.php3?Report ID=200.

[3]"Jon Stewart," *Inside Politics,* CNN.com, 3 May 2002.

[4]Transcript of *Nightline,* ABC News, 28 July 2004 (accessed from Lexis-Nexis Academic Universe, 4 August 2004).

[5]http://www.naes04org.

[6]Transcripts of CNN, 7 October 2004 (accessed from Lexis-Nexis Academic Universe, 28 March 2005). I analyze three morning broadcasts of CNN to get some idea of the different ways that a news network reports a story, as well as how these brief reports are modified as the morning progresses.

[7]As one news analyst has noted, "Network newscasts hold to standard conventions, and in so doing, reduce Bush's sloppy, pause-saturated speech to a rightly constructed set of words that suggest clarity of thought and purpose." Such conventions, therefore, make the news media "susceptible to manipulation by the professional speech writers and media handlers who seed public information with pre-scripted soundbites and spin" (Baym 2005, 265).

[8]One only needs to look at popular narratives of either news media or the interactions of media and politics to see this recurrent theme. For examples,

see films such as *Hero, Power, Broadcast News, A Face in the Crowd, Meet John Doe, The Candidate, Wag the Dog, Bulworth, Bob Roberts,* and *Dave.*

[9]Again, witness the movement toward blogging (and even the news media's embrace of it) as a manifestation of this questioning and reformulation. See, for instance, "The State (Columbia, S.C.) Launches Community Blog, Citizen Journalism Push," *Editor & Publisher,* 30 August 2005; and Saul Hansell, "The CBS Evening Blog," *New York Times,* 13 July 2005.

[10]One might be tempted to assert that this is exactly what competing "news" outlets like Fox News claim—that they are simply pointing our alternative truths. The crucial distinction between a program of political satire and a news organization like Fox that claims to be "fair and balanced," however, is their relationships to power. One is committed to critiquing power wherever it lies, while the other has proven its intentional commitment to supporting the powerful through highly orchestrated and sustained efforts by the media corporation's leadership (see Robert Greenwald's documentary *Outfoxed: Rupert Murdoch's War on Journalism).*

REFERENCES

Armstrong, S. 2003. "I Can Scratch the Itch." *The Guardian,* 17 March, p. 8.

Baym, G. 2005. "The Daily Show: Discursive Integration and the Reinvention of Political Journalism." *Political Communication* 22: 259–276.

Boorstin, D. 1960. *The Image: A Guide to Pseudo Events in America.* New York: Atheneum.

Buckingham, D. 2000. *The Making of Citizens: Young People, News and Politics.* London: Routledge.

Chaloupka, W. 1999. *Everybody Knows: Cynicism in America.* Minneapolis: University of Minnesota Press.

Debenport, E. 1992. "Candidates Try To Cut Media Filter." *St. Petersburg Times* (Florida), 11 June, p. 1A.

Delli Carpini, M. X., and Keeter, S. 1996. *What Americans Know About Politics and Why It Matters.* New Haven: Yale University Press.

Edelman, M. 1988. *Constructing the Political Spectacle.* Chicago: University of Chicago Press.

Foucault M. 1980. *Power/Knowledge: Selected Interviews and Other Writings,* 1972–1977. Brighton: Harvester Press.

Gay, V. 2004. "Not Necessarily the News: Meet the Players Who Will Influence Coverage of the 2004 Campaign." *Newsday,* 19 January, p. B6.

Gillmor, D. 2004. *We the People: Grassroots Journalism, by the People, for the People.* Sebastopol, CA: O'Reilly.

Hachten, W.A. 2005. *The Troubles of Journalism.* 3rd ed. Mahwah, NJ: Lawrence Erlbaum Associates.

Hart, R. P. 1994. *Seducing America: How Television Charms the Modern Voter.* New York: Oxford University Press.

Hedgpeth, S. 2000. "Daily Show's Satiric Eye." *Plain Dealer* (Cleveland), 30 July, p. 61.

Johnson, P. 2003. "Trust of Media Keeps on Slipping." *USA Today*, 28 May.

Jones, J. P. 2005a. *Entertaining Polities: New Political Television and Civic Culture.* Lanham, MD: Rowman & Littlefield.

______ 2005b. "The Shadow Campaign in Popular Culture." In *The 2004 Presidential Campaign: A Communication Perspective* (pp. 195–216), edited by R Denton. Lanham, MD: Rowman & Littlefield.

Keefer, B. 2004. "You Call That News? I Don't." *Washington Post*, 12 September, p. B2.

Kovach, B., and Rosenstiel, T. 2001. *The Elements of Journalism: What Newspeople Should Know and the Public Should Expect.* New York: Crown.

Mindich, D. T. Z. 2005. *Tuned Out: Why Americans Under 40 Don't Follow the News.* New York: Oxford University Press.

Patterson, T. E. 1993. *Out of Order.* New York: Random House.

Rich, F. 2003. "Jon Stewart's Perfect Pitch." *New York Times*, 20 April, sec. 2, p. 1.

Riegert, K., with Johansson, A. 2005. "The Struggle for Credibility in the Iraq War." In *The Iraq War: European Perspectives on Polities, Strategy, and Operations.* London: Routledge.

Roberts, G., Kunkle, T., and Layton, C. 2001. *Leaving Readers Behind: The Age of Corporate Newspapering.* Fayetteville: University of Arkansas Press.

Scheuer, J. 1999. *The Sound Bite Society: Television and the American Mind. New York*: Four Walls Eight Windows.

Schutz, C. 1977. *Political Humor: From Aristophanes to Sam Ervin.* New York: Fairleigh Dickinson University Press.

Seelye, K. Q. 2005a. "At Newspapers, Some Clipping." *New York Times*, 10 October, p. C1.

______. 2005b. "Why Newspapers Are Betting on Audience Participation." *New York Times*, 4 July.

______. 2005c. "Survey on News Media Finds Wide Displeasure," *New York Times*, 27 June.

Tuchman, C. 1978. *Making News: A Study in the Construction of Reality.* New York: Free Press.

Webster, F. 1995. *Theories of the Information Society.* London: Routledge.

West, D. M., and Orman, J. 2003. *Celebrity Politics.* Upper Saddle River, NJ: Prentice-Hall.

Younge, G. 2004. "Washington Post Apologizes for Underplaying WMD Skepticism." *The Guardian*, 13 August, p. 2.

Examining the Text

1. As Jones states, in 2000 the Pew Research Center reported that 47 percent of people under the age of thirty were "informed at least occasionally" about the campaign or candidates by late-night talk shows. Why does Jones refer to this statistic as a "myth"? What difference does it make, according to Jones, if this statistic is or isn't accurate?

2. In paragraph 12, Jones states that *The Daily Show* isn't limited by the same professional constraints that apply to mainstream journalism. What are those constraints? How does *The Daily Show's* freedom from these constraints help it deliver more insightful, useful information, according to Jones?

3. Jones notes that *The Daily Show* episode that he observed included a number of video clips that did not appear on CNN and that traditional journalists would not deem "newsworthy" (e.g., Bush's opening remarks in his speech in Wilkes-Barre, Kerry's appearance on Dr. Phil). How does *The Daily Show* make these items relevant? Do you agree that these video clips provide important information about the candidates?

4. What evidence does Jones provide to prove that mainstream journalism is in a state of crisis? What does he mean by "authenticity" in this context?

5. *Thinking rhetorically:* Jones begins the article with a three-paragraph overview of his argument. What do you think of this as an opening strategy? Does it help or hurt your ability to understand the points that Jones makes later in the article? Rereading these opening paragraphs after having read the article, do you think that they provide an accurate summary?

For Group Discussion

Near the end of the article, Jones includes a quotation in which Bryan Keefer reflects on the way that his generation of "twenty-somethings" thinks about the news. Reread this quotation—and the entire last paragraph of the article—and consider the extent to which Keefer's perspective applies to your generation as well. Specifically, do your friends and fellow students see news as a "product, produced by politicians and publicists"? In a discussion with several fellow students, share your response to Keefer's quotation and your overall view of mainstream news.

Writing Suggestion

Replicate Jones's study on a more modest level by watching two different news shows on the same night, taking notes, and comparing their coverage of the events of the day.

Begin the assignment by selecting two news shows that you think will offer interesting similarities and contrasts; you might compare a comedy news show to a "serious" one, as Jones does, or you might choose shows that you think have different political biases.

Next, watch (and if you can, tape) the shows. As you're watching, make note of the order of the stories being discussed, how much time is spent on each story, and what information is conveyed in the story.

Review the summaries you wrote as you watched the shows in order to determine similarities and differences. Do some prewriting in response to the following questions: What conclusions can you draw from the order in which stories were presented and from the time allocated to each? Were there significant differences in the information that the two shows presented on the same stories? What kinds of stories were covered in one show but not in another?

After completing the prewriting activity, formulate a thesis that provides a general statement about the similarities and differences between the two news shows. In the body of your essay, support your thesis, as Jones does, with specific examples drawn from your observations of both shows.

ADDITIONAL SUGGESTIONS FOR WRITING ABOUT TELEVISION

1. This chapter concludes with three essays about the relatively new genre of comedy news shows. Choose another genre (such as reality shows, makeover shows, game shows, situation comedies, detective shows, cartoons, talk shows, soap operas, or live police dramas) and analyze the underlying presuppositions of this genre. What specific beliefs, actions, and relationships do these shows encourage? How and why do these shows appeal to the audience? If everything that you knew were based on your exposure to this genre of show, what kind of world would you expect to encounter, how would you expect people to behave toward each other, and what sort of values would you expect them to have? To support your analysis of the genre, use examples from specific shows, but keep in mind that your essay should address the genre or category of shows in general.

2. According to sociologists and psychologists, human beings are driven by certain basic needs and desires. Some of the articles in this chapter attempt to account for the powerful appeal of television in our culture, suggesting that we rely on television to fulfill needs that aren't met elsewhere. Consider some of the following basic needs and desires that television might satisfy for you or for the broader viewing public:

to be amused
to gain information about the world
to have shared experiences
to find models to imitate
to see authority figures exalted or deflated
to experience, in a controlled and guilt-free situation, extreme emotions
to see order imposed on the world
to reinforce our belief in justice
to experience thrilling or frightening situations
to believe in romantic love
to believe in magic, the marvelous, and the miraculous
to avoid the harsh realities of life
to see others make mistakes

Referring to items on this list, or formulating your own list of needs and desires, compose an essay in which you argue that television succeeds or fails in meeting our basic needs and desires. Use specific television programs that you're familiar with as concrete evidence for your assertions.

3. As the articles on *The Daily Show* and *The Colbert Report* indicate, it's possible for people to interpret the messages of a television show in substantially different ways. Choose a show that you're familiar with and about which you think there can be multiple interpretations. You might think about older shows, such as *Star Trek* or *The Sopranos*, or more recent shows, such as *Family Guy* or *Lost*. You might want to watch a few episodes of the show (all of the ones mentioned above have past episodes available on DVD and through online video streaming) just to remind yourself of the characters, setting, typical plot structure, and other details. Then write an essay in which your thesis states two (or more) possible interpretations of the show. In the body of the essay, explain what details of the show support each of these interpretations. You might conclude the essay by stating which interpretation you find most persuasive.

Internet Activities

1. Game shows have long been a popular television genre, and their popularity of late seems to be on the rise. One reason may be found in their similarity to reality TV shows, in that they allow for a degree of audience interactivity that scripted shows like dramas and comedies lack; after all, viewers can become participants on game shows and gain instant celebrity if they do well. Game shows also seem to appeal to our greed (or our desire to get rich quickly and without too much work) as well as to our competitive nature. In preparation for writing an essay on game shows, recall some of the ones that you've seen on TV, and check the *Common Culture* Web site for links to sites related to game shows. Then, write an essay in which you analyze the reasons why this television genre is appealing to viewers. As part of your essay, you might decide to compare and contrast game shows to reality television shows to determine the relative appeal of these two genres.

2. Although it's difficult to predict developments having to do with the Internet, a possibility discussed by experts is that television and the World Wide Web will, in some way, merge. Perhaps your TV screen will become your computer monitor, or you'll be able to order movies and view television shows through your computer and Internet connection. Already we see some early connections between the two media, for instance in the live Web casts that some TV shows are doing, or in exclusive Web casts (that is, programs or videos that are shown only on the Web and not on TV). In addition, most news and sports shows have companion Web sites that offer viewers additional information, pictures, interviews, etc. Consider some of these developments, discussed in further detail at the links provided at the *Common Culture* Web site. Then, write an essay in which you discuss the ways in which the Web competes with or complements television. Do the two media provide the same kind of information and entertainment, or do they offer fundamentally different viewing experiences?

Reading Images

The photograph on page CI-2 was taken at the October 2010 event staged and promoted by Jon Stewart and Stephen Colbert. Held at the National Mall in Washington, D.C., the event was variously named "The Rally to Restore Sanity" (http://www.rallytorestoresanity.com/), the "March to Keep Fear Alive" (http://www.keepfearalive.com/), and the "Rally to Restore Sanity and/or Fear" (http://www.rallytorestoresanityandorfear.com/). You may have heard about the event or perhaps even participated in it; for a few weeks, it received a lot of news coverage in the mainstream media and, of course, on *The Daily Show* and *The Colbert Report*. The photograph shows Stephen Colbert's entrance onto the stage of the rally, evoking the rescue of the 33 trapped Chilean miners that had occurred several weeks earlier.

Begin your analysis of the photograph by describing it in detail: what actions are taking place, what colors are prevalent, what is the perspective and focal point of the photograph? Next, identify two or three of the most significant components of the photograph (e.g., Stephen Colbert's outfit, the Fenix capsule from which Colbert emerges, the actions of the people on stage, the background, and color scheme). In a few sentences, discuss the meanings that you think each element conveys. Given the fact that this was a highly staged moment, why do you think Colbert and Stewart chose the elements represented in this photograph?

Next, do some research and find out more about the event itself. In addition to the Web sites mentioned above, there are many news articles, blogs, and videos associated with the event that are available online. How does this additional information about the event affect your interpretation of the image?

Next, review the three articles on *The Daily Show* and *The Colbert Report* that are included in this chapter. What concepts discussed in these articles—all of which were written prior to the event—influence your interpretation of the image? Does the image reveal, for instance, the kind of satire that Russell Peterson discusses? How does the event itself complicate the idea of newsworthiness and authenticity raised by Jeffrey Jones?

Finally, combine all of these perspectives—your analysis of the photograph on its own, your knowledge about the event, and your understanding of concepts in the reading—to develop a full discussion of the meaning of this photograph.

4

Popular Music

A spiky-haired dancer, his arms outstretched, stands in stark silhouette against a vibrant green background. Electronic pulses from his graphically contrasting MP3 player reach his brain through earbuds as he stares pointedly at the reader, his rhythmic dance move frozen in time. The listener appears to be transported by the music, in a state of energized trance.

By virtue of its sheer volume, rhythm, and encompassing presentation, music has the capacity to take us to "completely different" psychic spaces. It can lift us from our ordinary sense of reality and profoundly affect our moods, emotions, energy level, and even our level of sexual arousal. Furthermore, the lyrics, when combined with these powerful aural appeals, become all the more potent and suggestive, influencing our feelings of isolation or belonging, our relation to parents and friends, our attitudes toward authority figures, our notions about romance, and our views about gender and race.

The articles in this chapter discuss the ways in which people are "constructed" by what they hear—that is, how their beliefs, values, attitudes, and morals are shaped by the music they listen to. Some observers see this phenomenon as potentially dangerous, since it encourages people—especially young people—to transgress the boundaries imposed by civilized society. However, other critics contend that popular music plays a very positive role in contemporary society, since it allows people to voice feelings and ideas that would otherwise not be widely heard. This is especially the case with rap and hip-hop music, as several writers in the first section of this chapter observe. Originally created by and intended for young, African American inner-city audiences, hip-hop subsequently gained widespread acceptance, to the point that it became a major force in the recording industry, thus giving previously disenfranchised urban youth a more pervasive presence in the popular culture. However, some observers of pop-musical trends have begun to question the sustainability of hip-hop as a mainstream form, so this chapter also addresses the current debate over the question, "Is hip-hop dead," or is it still a vital musical force to be reckoned with? The second portion of this chapter confronts the serious financial problem facing the recording industry, as brick-and-mortar record stores continue to close all over the country and file sharing and other means of free Internet access have drastically reduced the revenues of recording artists, along with their producers and managers.

As you read these essays, perhaps hooked up to your iPod and blasting the latest, Lil Wayne, M.I.A., Rihanna, Annihilation Time, or Tupac posthumous release, you might consider these very practical issues, along with the broader implications of music in your life: the reasons why you listen to certain kinds of music, the messages embodied in their lyrics and rhythm, and the pleasures and possible dangers inherent in letting popular music move you to a completely different frame of mind.

Is Hip-Hop Dead?

5 Things That Killed Hip-Hop

J-ZONE

A recent album by American hip-hop artist Nas appeared with the title, "Hip Hop Is Dead." In a radio interview, Nas commented, "Hip hop is dead because we as artists no longer have the power." He went on to say, ". . . basically America is dead. There is no political voice. Music is dead. Our way of thinking is dead, our commerce is dead. Everything in this society has been done. That's where we are as a country." These comments, along with the album's title itself, sent a shock wave through the hip-hop community, with much argument on both sides flying through the blogosphere. Some argued that hip-hop as a musical subgenre is as vital and vibrant and authentic a voice of the inner city as it ever was, while others pointed to declining sales and changing mainstream tastes to support Nas's claim of rap music's impending demise. We lead off this section on hip-hop music with one such opinion piece: this one written by J-Zone, a hip-hop artist based in Queens, New York, who is intimately familiar with all things hip-hop, having majored in music at the State University of New York, worked as a head engineer, achieved prominence with several albums of his own music, and helped produce numerous releases for other artists.

The article, "5 Things That Killed Hip-Hop," appeared as a posting on a popular rap-centered Web site, where the writing of a number of prominent hip-hop critics and artists frequently appears in blog form. The blog must increasingly be considered as a legitimate literary subgenre. An abridgment of the phrase "Web log," it consists of a series of Internet posts about topics as varied as political opinion; depictions of events, such as breaking news or cultural happenings; diary-like personal history; or other media-based communications, such as video or art. While most blogs are mainly textual, the writing in them differs radically from the kinds of academic discourse you produce, and generally read, for your classes. ***As you read*** *this article, therefore, pay attention to the ways in which J-Zone often purposely breaks grammatical rules and uses decidedly nonacademic language for rhetorical purpose: that is, engages the reader with a friendly, conversational and easy-to-read tone, and to establish "street credibility" for himself as he discusses the current state of hip-hop music in American culture.*

I realize that arguing about music is pointless cause we all got different opinions. A few people wanted my opinion on the "is hip hop dead?" matter and I just put my opinion on my sites. For some reason, it's gotten a lot of unexpected feedback, but what I'm saying isn't really new, nor is there a right or wrong answer to that question. If u agree with me that's cool, if you disagree that's cool too. It's music, not life and death. At the least, to read it is a way to kill some time. 1

Everybody's saying it. Nas titled his album that. People are debating and a few brothers asked me for my humble opinion. So as I watch the Celtics lose their 17th straight on Sportscenter, I'll do a music related blog for once. After all, it affects me right? 5 things I feel are the biggest culprits of rap's downfall. Well actually before I exercise my freedom of speech and somebody gets upset for nothing, let me clarify. 2

A. I am NOT saying that there isn't a batch of stellar records released yearly, or a group of dope producers delivering fly shit or a handful of rappers that still make you wanna listen. I also know music is subjective and it's all opinion. The great music of today may be on par with the great of yesterday, but in the grand scheme of things, the negatives far outweigh the positives. 3

B. There's 3 things you can never argue about . . . Religion, Politics and Hip-Hop. Cause no matter your opinion, somebody will tyrannically oppose and get all fuckin emotional. It's just my humble opinion, relax. Who cares anyway? 4

C. For the record, the politics at major labels, press and radio are not listed here because they've been around since the beginning of time. And we have ourselves to blame for not manning up to take control of those. Yo Flex, drop a bomb on that. OK, where was I? 5

CLANS, POSSES, CREWS & CLIQUES: WHO U WIT?

Safety in numbers. Movements, collaborations, big name guests, teams, crew beef, etc. The days of the solo roller are over. In the prime of rap, you were judged solely on your music. Rakim, Nas & Biggie (early on), LL, Kane . . . they all built their legend on music alone. Hell, Rakim had no guests on his first 4 albums. Sure there was Juice Crew, Native Tongues, Lench Mob crew, etc. But it wasn't mandatory. Then for some reason, in the mid-late 90's, it became totally necessary to have a movement. A crew with 1,000 different artists all on the same team. Touring together, crew t-shirts, beef with other crews, collaborations, etc. Not that that's a bad thing, but it's like people cannot identify with one artist, there has to be a movement or somebody else involved to validate them. Look at today's most successful artists. They all have a movement. Roc-A-Fella, Def Jux, Stonesthrow, Rhymesayers, G-Unit, Dipset, Wu-Tang, Hieroglyphics, Okayplayer, etc. Or if you're not part 6 of a movement, you collaborate with other high profile artists. Doom, Danger Mouse, etc. It's all about cross-pollinating fan bases. You don't? You die. And for some reason, I see Da Youngstas' album, *Da Aftermath*, as the beginning of this from a beat standpoint. That and Run DMC's *Down With the King* (both 1993) were the first albums I can remember to use a lot of different producers with totally different sounds. It worked back then, they were dope albums. But it wound up being a cancer.

Nowadays you need a Timbaland track, a Neptunes track, a Just 7
Blaze track, a Dre track, a Kanye track for people to really care . . . and for the most part it sounds like a collection of songs, not an album. Why not let one of them just do the whole fuckin album? Can't please everybody, why make a futile attempt? Good albums are about a vibe. Wu-Tang was a movement, but it was cohesive and made sense because they all vibed together and RZA was the sonic glue. Sans *Illmatic*, *Ready to Die* and a few others, every single great rap album had a maximum of 3 producers and 3 guests. In this fascination with movements, name association and special guests, we've lost album cohesiveness and the focus on just music. It's no longer about how dope you are, it's who you rollin with and who's cosigning what you do. And usually 92% of the crew isn't up to par with the few star artists in the crew. Quantity rules, not quality. You can have a 5 mic album, but nobody cares unless there's a bunch of other people involved. 10 producers and 7 guests. And now so and so with a platinum album can put his wack ass brother or cousin on and cheapen the game, cause they're part of the movement and it's about who you with. Back in 88, Milk D said he had *"a great big bodyguard"* on *Top Billin*. But that was it. Later on there would be a Great Big Bodyguard solo album.

TOO MUCH MUSIC

Like the crew theory, this is about quantity. People want more, even 8
if it means a dip in quality. Some people can put out music quickly and do it well. Some people just want to bombard the market for the sake of doing it. Rakim did albums every 2 years. EPMD, Scarface and Ice Cube did it every year and that was considered fast. Nowadays, if you don't have 2 albums, 5 mix tapes and 10 guest appearances a year, you're slippin and people forget you. This attempt to keep up with the rush has cheapened the music. Now you have regular mixtapes marketed as albums, just a bunch of thrown together songs for the fuck of it. But to survive these days, you have to do that to stay in the public eye. There's far too many slim line case CD-R mix tapes out, and as important as mix tapes are to rap, the very vehicle that helped it grow is now playing a part in killing it. Now everybody has forgotten how to make cohesive projects, so we cover it up by labeling it as a mix tape.

The value and pride that full length albums used to symbolize are no more. Mixtapes now triple the number official albums in artist's catalog and never has music seemed so cheap and fast food. Not to mention, when the majors went completely awry in the late 90's, the indie rap scene went out of control with too much product.

When I debuted in 1999, there were maybe 25–30 other indie vinyl releases out that mattered. And mine was one of the only full-length albums. So it was only a matter of time before I got a listen, it didn't matter that I had no big names on my record and came outta nowhere. Try that now. To go to a store and see the foot high stack of one sheets for new records, mix CD's and DVD's dropping weekly makes you see you have a snowballs chance to survive in that world. Look at how many releases a week are on Hiphopsite, Sandbox, Fat Beats, UGHH, etc. The high profile artists get some attention, and everybody else gets ordered in ones and twos, if that. So today's new talent making his debut is in for an uphill battle. Great records go unnoticed. Rap is now a disposable art. Mr. Walt of Da Beatminerz once said, "You work 16 months on an album and get a 2 week window of opportunity. After that your record is as good as dead for most people." That sums it up. 9

TOO COOL TO HAVE FUN / NO BALANCE IN RAP

When rap stopped being fun, I knew we were in big trouble. Not too many people are doin music for fun anymore. Ask yourself, "would I still mess with music as a hobby if there wasn't any money in it?" Too many people would say no. We all wanna get paid. Shit, I got bills too, I love money! But too many people just seem like they'd rather be doing other shit. You read in interviews, "I don't care about no rap, I'd rather be hustling. I just do this cause I can." Hey, whatever floats your boat, I can relate, there's been artists like that since the beginning of time, but they were never the majority until now. Having fun is nowhere near as important as your life before you got signed. And there's plenty of battle MC's, political MC's and killer thugs but it seems there's not many funny artists no more. Like on some Biz Mark, Humpty Hump, The Afros shit. Not afraid to go to the extreme and have fun. God forbid you use your imagination or rap about something not involving Hip-Hop, the hood, you bein the shit, the end of the world or what color your car interior is. 10

I live in Queens, less than a mile from 50 Cent's old house. Nobody really knows I make music over here. Some kid from over here saw me in The Source a while back and said "Yo I ain't know you was in it like that, yo why you ain't tryin to pump your shit out here and let 11 people know, you should rep the hood? 50 did it." Why should I? I'm not on the block tryin to push weight, I'm out there walking to Walgreens for my Grandmother, on my way to the park for a game of 21 or to watch a game at the local high school. I'm a grown ass man with a college degree and I like my neighborhood, but I choose to rap about my beat up car, not dancing in clubs, women with bad hygiene and too many kids or ball playin rappers with limited ball skills, cause I ain't a street cat and I'd rather show the lighter side of life. And that was never a problem back in the day.

Okay those ain't completely new topics, but it's like rappin about those things these days gets you marked as novelty rap. Biz rhymed about a lot of this same shit back in the day, but it was still accepted as legit Hip-Hop. 2007? He could never do a song like "The Dragon." Little Shawn & Father MC rapped about the ladies with some R&B beats. De La Soul were labeled as hippies. But all those dudes would beat yo fuckin ass if you got out of line! They were soft by no means, they just wanted to do the music they enjoyed, cause rap is supposed to be a way to have fun and get away from the everyday stress, while not limiting yourself. The thing that made rap so dope in the "golden era" was the balance of styles. You had clown princes like Biz, Humpty Hump, Kwame and ODB later on. You had political brothers like X-Clan, PE, Lakim Shabazz, Poor Righteous Teachers, Kam, etc. You had the explicit shit on Rap-A-Lot and the whole 2 Live movement in Miami. Hip-house like Twin Hype, new jack shit like Wrecks-N-Effect, the whole Native Tongues thing, the hard South Central LA shit, the Oakland funk . . . and they all co-existed, were all dope and they all had fun regardless of their style. King Sun made *On The Club Tip* and then did *Universal Flag*. Lakim Shabazz, Twin Hype and Wrecks-N-Effect had raw battle rap, Geto Boys and Ganksta Nip were hilarious, PE had the yin and yang of Chuck and Flav and ODB was a ferocious battle MC. 12

Even the more serious political rap . . . everybody seemed to be enjoying making music. Gangsta rappers had a fuckin sense of humor back then. Mob Style might have been the hardest group I've ever heard and they lived it. But them dudes also showed other sides and sounded like they enjoyed music, because it was an escape from everyday bullshit. Tim Dog, was hilarious and hard at the same time. Even if it was a joke to some, the shit was good listening. Suga Free is an ice cold pimp for real, but he has a sense of humor and approaches his music doin what he feels. Who says rappin about a girl with no teeth or going to the store with coupons ain't "real"? Everything is "real," people forget that. Everybody is so concerned with being feared and taken seriously, they can't come off those insecurities and do some guilty pleasure shit. Even the producers. If you can't show your other 13 sides and bug out in your music, where can you do it? Stop being scared and break some fuckin rules. Put some 300 pound girls in your video for once! Laugh at yourself, dog, you ain't no killer 24/7. You ain't battling MC's and being a lyrical lyricist mixtape murder 24/7. Havin fun is almost hip-hop faux pas these days. Rap is dead without balance . . . period.

LAW & ORDER: MPC AND SAMPLING

"Boop Boop, it's the sound of the police!" Yup, the legal police. Hip-hop is based in illegality, but not maliciously. Ironically, many people got into it to stay out of legal troubles, but technically this positive move is also seen as a life of crime by the powers that be. Mix tapes, remixes, sampling, parodies (somewhat) . . . the appeal of hip-hop was always rearranging the old to create the new. It's the lifeline of the music. One man's treasure is apparently another man's trash. In the wake of DJ Drama getting busted by the Feds for selling mix tapes that the labels and artists themselves approve and benefit from, it has never been more evident that the RIAA and their legal vendetta have just pulled the IV. We all knew that the late 80's way of taking 8 bar James Brown loops and not clearing was bound to catch up to us. I can live with that. You have a platinum album and loop somebody's whole shit, break'em off some money and publishing, its only right. But then the lawyers and courts got tyrannical. Now 1/8 of a second sample can run you the risk of legal action. Ouch. I remember having a beat placed on a TV show and the music supervisor panicked after the fact because he swore the snare I used sounded like it was sampled. Wow. I understand melodies, but somebody can own a snare sound now? 14

This is pretty lousy, but to this point it only affected some of the major label stuff and big corporate gigs. No more. MySpace is now shutting down pages that post remixes. WHAT!? I find that completely ass backwards. I know a few dudes that were warned, and others shut down without notice for posting remixes of major label songs with COMMERCIALLY AVAILABLE ACAPELLAS! WELL WHAT THE FUCK IS AN ACAPELLA AVAILABLE ON A RECORD FOR?! TO BE REMIXED! DING DING . . . MESSAGE! Now to take that remix and release it on a major label and make 50 grand is one thing. But to have fun with remixes and post them on a MySpace page, where ZERO DOLLARS can be made directly off of it, is completely harmless promotion for all parties involved. Not anymore. 15

Back in the day to be on a Kid Capri, Double R, S&S, Doo Wop, Silver Surfer, etc. mixtape was the best thing to happen to an artist and their label. An unknown producer leaking a dope remix to a popular 16 artist's record was a way to get buzz and a way for the industry to find new talent. Taking pieces of old music and creating something new (like the Bomb Squad) wasn't looked upon with the seriousness of a gunpoint mugging. But in a day where album sales are down, no artists or labels are seeing any money, CD's have foolishly been raised in price, interpolating one line of *Jingle Bells* in your song can get you sued and you can't post a remix for promotional and listening purposes only . . . you can see the music and legal industries have officially declared war on rap as a knee jerk reaction to their own failures. And as idiotic and unjust as things have become, they have the loopholes of law on their side.

THE INTERNET

Talk about a double edged sword. Never has it been so easy to get your music heard. If I make a dope beat, I can put it on my MySpace page and it's up in an hour (depending on the servers, it may be "processing" for about 3 years). No more spending money and wasting time for records and test presses. Now people in Arkansas that only have MTV and the Internet can hear my music. Limited distribution isn't as big a problem as before. Everybody is almost equal, and we all have MySpace pages. But look at the flipside: everybody is almost equal, and we all have MySpace pages. There is so much shit out and the Internet lurks with a million people doing the same thing, it's virtually impossible to stand out. Back in the day, you had to work your way up in the business. Having a record was in most cases a privilege and a reward for your hard work. Catalog meant something. We're in an MP3 world now, and somebody in their bedroom is on an equal plane with somebody that's paid dues and worked hard. That's great for the kid with talent and no vehicle to get heard. That sucks for the no talent hacks on MySpace that post advertisements for their wack music on your comments page. 17

The Internet also killed rap's number one asset. Anticipation. 18
How many can remember buying a mixtape and hearing 3 dope joints from an upcoming album on a mixtape? You couldn't wait to cop the album. And you didn't hear the album 3 months in advance cause there was no way to spread it that fast. And in rare cases where the album leaked, you had to get a tape dub and even when you did, you still bought it. I remember hearing *Lots of Lovin, Straighten It Out, TROY* and *Ghettos of the Mind* from *Mecca and the Soul Brother* 2 months before it came out. But I couldn't find any other songs. That drove the anticipation up and got everybody talking. We were all eager to support. In 2007, the album would leak months in advance, you burn it

and that's it. I'm not complaining cause that won't change things, but that was a large part of what appealed to me and many others about music, especially rap. No more. No artwork & physical CD to read the credits and shoutouts (remember those!?), no anticipation, it's old news by street date, the shit don't sell and here we are. Tower's closing, the legendary Beat Street is closed, Music Factory is a wrap . . . people don't realize that rap as we know it is done. Labels are fuckin suing common civilians for file sharing! A physical copy no longer matters unless you're a collector.

Back in the day, you would never see Internet beef. It's just stupid junior high shit. People leaving threats and talkin shit via MySpace, people getting hurt over e-beef at shows, kids on message boards flexin muscle and actin hard. Great! Now that we have a bunch of killers on wax, we got a bunch of em posting in forums. Cute. You can sit in a bedroom in Mexico and talk about knockin out somebody in Finland and it will never come back to you. Hip-hop bravado and the anonymity of the Web . . . it don't get more junior high. The Internet was the blessing and the curse of rap music. I may catch heat for this, but I think the best thing is to blow up the industry and start over. There is still great music and I will enjoy making this music til I pass on, even if only as a hobby. I will still be diggin for records, makin beats, playing instruments and watching old movies for inspiration. But sometimes things need to fall apart to give birth to greater things. The fall of rap in its current state may give birth to something bigger and better. It's what I'm banking on, cause realistically, how much longer can it go down this road? I'm not saying go back in time. Classic rap artists may have been influenced by Cold Crush and Melle Mel, but they took that influence and added something different on to it to create something new, and until that principle can be followed again, I say fuck fixing an abandoned building. Hit it with a wrecking ball and rebuild! 19

Examining the Text

1. In his reason #5 section, the author cites "clans, posses, crews and cliques" as being at least partially responsible for hip-hop's decline. In what way have the increasing numbers of people involved in a song/album's production contributed to a lessening in musical quality, according to J-Zone? In your experience, is this phenomenon unique to hip-hop, or has it affected all forms of popular music, either positively or negatively, or both?

2. Hip-hop artist Lil Wayne was recently quoted in a *Rolling Stone* magazine article as saying he has recorded "somewhere in the thousands" of songs in recent years. The article concludes, "Wayne makes new songs the way you make lunch, and songs have a way of getting out" on Web sites and in stores. With the advent of inexpensive consumer-level music production, creating and distributing mixes in the form of digital play lists has increased dramatically in the last several years—not just for established artists such as Lil Wayne, but for lesser-known artists as well. How has the proliferation of "mixtapes"—compilations of songs recorded in a specific order, originally onto a compact audio cassette tape, but more recently in compact disk or MP3 format—negatively affected the overall quality of hip-hop, according to J-Zone? Does he suggest a solution to the problem of "too much music," or is the situation out of control and beyond repair, in his opinion . . . and in yours?

3. What does the author mean when he laments that there's "no balance in rap" anymore? What are some examples of a greater sense balance in hip-hop's "golden era," in the opinion of J-Zone? How does J-Zone's personal experience serve as an example of this phenomenon, and how might the situation be remedied, according to this article?

4. MPC devices (the acronym stands for MIDI Production Center or, more recently, Music Production Center) are electronic musical instruments produced by the Japanese company Akai and others, beginning in about 1990. These devices allow contemporary music artists to sample short sequences of previously recorded music and insert those passages into their own tracks. What is this author's opinion about sampling other people's work in hip-hop songs? How has the MPC phenomenon contributed to the impending "death" of hip-hop, in the view of author J-Zone?

5. *Thinking rhetorically:* Blogs are sometimes criticized as being highly charged expressions of opinion, frequently unsupported by evidence, disorganized, and lacking critical distance and balance. In what ways does "5 Things That Killed Hip-Hop" conform to this stereotype about blogs? In what ways does it disprove that criticism, both in its form and content?

For Group Discussion

In his reason #1 section, J-Zone presents a balanced commentary on the role the Internet has played in the current state of hip-hop. In his view, what are the positive effects of the cyberculture on hip-hop music and production, and in what ways has the Web negatively affected hip-hop? In small groups, expand this discussion beyond the boundaries of rap and hip-hop: how has the Internet affected popular music, the music industry, and your lives as consumers of and listeners to music? Make a two-column list of the various positive and negative Web-related factors, and, after re-convening the whole class, have each group report on its list of factors. In the full-class discussion, try to arrive at some consensus about the effect of the Web on popular music generally: on the whole, has it had a positive or negative effect?

Writing Suggestion

Go to one of the many popular blog sites on the Web and create a presence for yourself there. While it's important to remember that the style you use for your blog will differ dramatically from the language, style, and structure you use for your academic essays, one of the goals for any writing course is for you to get practice in a variety of styles, and blogging is increasingly becoming an accepted mode of discourse. For example, in the business community, numerous companies, agencies, and other institutions have begun creating a public relations presence through the use of blogs. Professional journalists, likewise, are becoming increasingly reliant on blogging, as are motion picture and music critics, for example. In this assignment, you will write a music-related blog for the rest of the current school term. Using this format, you will communicate your ideas on the current state of the music industry, discuss your favorite kinds of popular music, review recent albums, and explore the various possibilities for accessing music, such as satellite and Web-based radio, file sharing services (the legal ones, of course!), brick-and-mortar record emporiums, concerts, and so forth. Your instructor will promise not to grade your grammar, syntax, and organization; this will be a platform where those concerns are temporarily suspended, so that your imagination can range freely over whatever topic you find interesting.

WORD: Jay-Z's "Decoded" and the Language of Hip-Hop

KELEFA SANNEH

If pressed to enumerate the greatest figures in modern American poetry, probably very few academics in high school or college English departments would think to include Jay-Z or Eminem in their ranks. However, to an increasing number of critics and literary scholars—not to mention rappers themselves—hip-hop is the source of some of the most provocative and innovative movements in poetry today. Because the media have devoted so much print and televised air time to the supposedly controversial content of rap lyrics, this uproar may have obscured a veritable revolution in poetics. The following article by Kelefa Sanneh, a noted American journalist and contemporary music critic, examines several recently published texts that attempt to reverse this trend, arguing that the beat of a rap song can actually render poetic meter audible, revealing writer/rappers' complex literary craft.

Included in this article is an examination of a recent book by a noted hip-hop artist, Jay-Z, whose Decoded *delivers a personal memoir about his upbringing in a Brooklyn housing project, his teen years dealing drugs in New Jersey, and his subsequent rise to superstardom as a rap artist and eminently successful businessmen. However, and perhaps more importantly,* Decoded, *like some of the works of the academics discussed in this article, provides readers with an understanding of the "encoded" meanings in the most popular rap lyrics of the past decades. In Jay-Z's words, ". . . it always comes back to the rhymes. There's poetry in hip-hop lyrics—not just mine, but in the work of all the great hip-hop artists, from KRS-One and Rakim to Biggie and Pac to a hundred emcees on a hundred corners all over the world that you've never heard of. The magic of rap is in the way it can take the most specific experience, from individual lives in unlikely places, and turn them into art that can be embraced by the whole world."* ***As you read*** *this article, consider the possibility that the hip-hop music you've been hearing all your life is more than a collection of danceable beats or evocations of the gangsta lifestyle . . . that rap music may contain poetry that rivals the most critically acclaimed works in respected literary journals and anthologies.*

Last year, an English professor named Adam Bradley issued a manifesto to his fellow scholars. He urged them to expand the poetic canon, and possibly enlarge poetry's audience, by embracing, or coöpting, the greatest hits of hip-hop. "Thanks to the engines of global commerce, rap is now the most widely disseminated poetry in the history of the world," he wrote. "The best MCs—like Rakim, Jay-Z, Tupac, and many others—deserve consideration alongside the giants of American poetry. We ignore them at our own expense." 1

The manifesto was called "Book of Rhymes: The Poetics of Hip Hop," and it used the terms of poetry criticism to illuminate not the content of hip-hop lyrics but their form. For Bradley, a couplet by Tupac Shakur— 2

Out on bail, fresh outta jail, California dreamin'
Soon as I stepped on the scene, I'm hearin' hoochies screamin'

—was a small marvel of "rhyme (both end and internal), assonance, and alliteration," given extra propulsion by Shakur's exaggerated stress patterns. Bradley also celebrated some lesser-known hip-hop lyrics, including this dense, percussive couplet by Pharoahe Monch, a cult favorite from Queens: 3

The last batter to hit, blast shattered your hip
Smash any splitter or fastball—that'll be it

Picking through this thicket, Bradley paused to appreciate Monch's use of "apocopated" rhyme, as when a one-syllable word is rhymed with the penultimate syllable of a multisyllabic word 4 (last / blast / fastball). Bradley is right to think that hip-hop fans have learned to appreciate all sorts of seemingly obscure poetic devices, even if they can't name them. Though some of his comparisons are strained (John Donne loved punning, and so does Juelz Santana!), his motivation is easy to appreciate: examining and dissecting lyrics is the only way to "give rap the respect it deserves as poetry."

This campaign for respect enters a new phase with the release of "The Anthology of Rap" a nine-hundred-page compendium that is scarcely lighter than an eighties boom box. It was edited by Bradley and Andrew DuBois, another English professor (he teaches at the University of Toronto; Bradley is at the University of Colorado), who together have compiled thirty years of hip-hop lyrics, starting with transcribed recordings of parties thrown in the late nineteen-seventies—Year Zero, more or less. The book, which seems to have been loosely patterned after the various Norton anthologies of literature, is, among other things, a feat of contractual legwork: Bradley and DuBois claim to have secured permission from the relevant copyright holders, and the book ends with some forty pages of credits, as well as a weak disclaimer ("The editors have made every reasonable effort to secure permissions"), which may or may not hold up in court. 5

Even before "The Anthology of Rap" arrived in stores, keen-eyed fans began pointing out the book's many transcription errors, some of which are identical to ones on ohhla.com, a valuable—though by no means infallible—online compendium of hip-hop lyrics. But readers who don't already have these words memorized are more likely to be bothered by the lack of footnotes; where the editors of the Norton anthologies, those onionskin behemoths, love to explain and over-explain obscure terms and references, Bradley and DuBois provide readers with nothing more than brief introductions. Readers are simply warned that when it comes to hip-hop lyrics "obfuscation is often the point, suggesting coded meanings worth puzzling over." In other words, you're on your own. 6

Happily, readers looking for a more carefully annotated collection of hip-hop lyrics can turn to an unlikely source: a rapper. In recent weeks, "The Anthology of Rap" has been upstaged by "Decoded," the long-awaited print début of Jay-Z, who must now be one of the most beloved musicians in the world. The book, which doesn't credit a co-writer, is essentially a collection of lyrics, liberally footnoted and accompanied by biographical anecdotes and observations. "Decoded" has benefitted from an impressive marketing campaign, including a citywide treasure hunt for hidden book pages. So it's a relief to find that "Decoded" is much better than it needs to be; in fact, it's one of a handful of books that just about any hip-hop fan should own. Jay-Z 7 explains not only what his lyrics mean but how they sound, even how they feel:

> When a rapper jumps on a beat, he adds his own rhythm. Sometimes you stay in the pocket of the beat and just let the rhymes land on the square so that the beat and flow become one. But sometimes the flow chops up the beat, breaks the beat into smaller units, forces in multiple syllables and repeated sounds and internal rhymes, or hangs a drunken leg over the last bap and keeps going, sneaks out of that bitch.

Two paragraphs later, he's back to talking about selling crack cocaine in Brooklyn. His description, and his music, makes it easier to imagine a connection—a rhyme, maybe—between these two forms of navigation, beat and street. And, no less than Bradley and DuBois, Jay-Z is eager to win for hip-hop a particular kind of respect. He states his case using almost the same words Bradley did: he wants to show that "hip-hop lyrics—not just my lyrics, but those of every great MC—are poetry if you look at them closely enough." 8

If you start in the recent past and work backward, the history of hip-hop spreads out in every direction: toward the Last Poets and Gil Scott-Heron, who declaimed poems over beats and grooves in the early seventies; toward Jamaica, where U-Roy pioneered the art of chatting and toasting over reggae records; toward the fifties radio d.j.s who used rhyming patter to seal spaces between songs; toward jazz and jive and the talking blues; toward preachers and politicians and street-corner bullshitters. In "Book of Rhymes," Bradley argues convincingly that something changed in the late nineteen-seventies, in the Bronx, when the earliest rappers (some of whom were also d.j.s) discovered the value of rhyming in time. "Words started bending to the beat," as Bradley puts it; by submitting to rhythm, paradoxically, rappers came to sound more authoritative than the free-form poets, toasters, chatters, patterers, and jokers who came before. 9

The earliest lyrics in the anthology establish the rhyme pattern that many casual listeners still associate with hip-hop. Each four-beat line ended with a rhyme, heavily emphasized, and each verse was a series of couplets, not always thematically or sonically related to each other: 10

> I'm Melle Mel and I rock so well
> From the World Trade to the depths of hell.

Those lines were recorded in December, 1978, at a performance by Grandmaster Flash and the Furious Five at the Audubon Ballroom, on Broadway and 165th Street (the same hall where Malcolm X was assassinated, thirteen years earlier). The springy exuberance of Melle 11

Mel's voice matched the elastic funk of the disco records that many early rappers used as their backing tracks.

12 The rise of Run-D.M.C., in the early nineteen-eighties, helped change that: the group's two rappers, Run and D.M.C., performed in jeans and sneakers, and they realized that hip-hop could be entertaining without being cheerful. They delivered even goofy lyrics with staccato aggression, which is one reason that they appealed to the young Jay-Z—they reminded him of guys he knew. In "Decoded," he quotes a couple of lines by Run:

> Cool chief rocker, I don't drink vodka
> But keep a bag of cheeba inside my locker

13 There is aggression in the phrasing: the first line starts sharply, with a stressed syllable, instead of easing into the beat with an unstressed one. "The words themselves don't mean much, but he snaps those clipped syllables out like drumbeats, bap bap bapbap," Jay-Z writes. "If you listened to that joint and came away thinking it was a simple rhyme about holding weed in a gym locker, you'd be reading it wrong: The point of those bars is to bang out a rhythmic idea."

14 The first Run-D.M.C. album arrived in 1984, but within a few years the group's sparse lyrical style came to seem old-fashioned; a generation of rappers had arrived with a trickier sense of swing. Hip-hop historians call this period the Golden Age (Bradley and DuBois date it from 1985 to 1992), and it produced the kinds of lyrical shifts that are easy to spot in print: extended similes and ambitious use of symbolism; an increased attention to character and ideology; unpredictable internal rhyme schemes; enjambment and uneven line lengths. This last innovation may have been designed to delight anthologizers and frustrate them, too, because it makes hip-hop hard to render in print. Bradley and DuBois claim, with ill-advised certainty, to have solved the problem of line breaks: "one musical bar is equal to one line of verse." But, in fact, most of their lines start before the downbeat, somewhere (it's not clear how they decided) between the fourth beat of one bar and the first beat of the next one. Here they are quoting Big Daddy Kane, one of the genre's first great enjambers, in a tightly coiled passage from his 1987 single, "Raw":

> I'll damage ya, I'm not an amateur but a professional
> Unquestionable, without doubt superb
> So full of action, my name should be a verb.

15 These three lines contain three separate rhyming pairs, and a different anthologist might turn this extract into six lines of varying

length. If Bradley and DuBois followed their own rule, they would break mid-word—"professio-/nal"—because the final syllable actually arrives, startlingly, on the next line's downbeat. In "Book of Rhymes," Bradley argued that "every rap song is a poem waiting to be performed," but the anthology's trouble with line breaks (not to mention punctuation) reminds readers that hip-hop is an oral tradition with no well-established written form. By presenting themselves as mere archivists, Bradley and DuBois underestimate their own importance: a book of hip-hop lyrics is necessarily a work of translation.

As the Golden Age ended, hip-hop's formal revolution was giving way to a narrative revolution. So-called gangsta rappers downplayed wordplay (without, of course, forswearing it) so they could immerse listeners in their first-person stories of bad guys and good times. Shakur and the Notorious B.I.G. created two of the genre's most fully realized personae; when they were murdered, in 1996 and 1997, respectively, their deaths became part of their stories. (Both crimes remain unsolved.) As the anthologizers blast through the nineties ("Rap Goes Mainstream") and the aughts ("New Millennium Rap"), their excitement starts to wane. They assert that the increasing popularity of hip-hop presented a risk of "homogenization and stagnation," without pausing to explain why this should be true (doesn't novelty sell?), if indeed it was. There is little overt criticism, but some rappers get fulsome praise—"socially conscious" is one of Bradley and DuBois's highest compliments—while others get passive-aggressive reprimands. ("Disagreement remains over whether Lil' Kim has been good or bad for the image of women in hip-hop.") Perhaps the form of their project dictates its content. They are sympathetic to rappers whose lyrics survive the transition to the printed page; the verbose parables and history lessons of Talib Kweli, for instance, make his name "synonymous with depth and excellence," in their estimation. But they offer a more measured assessment of Lil Wayne, praising his "play of sound" (his froggy, bluesy voice is one of the genre's greatest instruments) while entertaining the unattributed accusation that he may be merely "a gimmick rapper." Any anthology requires judgments of taste, and this one might have been more engaging if it admitted as much. 16

Jay-Z grew up absorbing many of the rhymes that Bradley and DuBois celebrate. He was born in 1969, and raised in the Marcy Houses, in an area of Brooklyn from which Times Square seemed to be "a plane ride away." (Nowadays, some real-estate agents doubtless consider it part of greater Williamsburg.) "It was the seventies," he writes, "and heroin was still heavy in the hood, so we would dare one another to push a leaning nodder off a bench the way kids on farms tip sleeping cows." He was a skinny, watchful boy with a knack for rhyming but no great interest in the music industry, despite some early brushes 17 with fame—he briefly served as Big Daddy Kane's hype man. Besides, Jay-Z had a day job that was both more dangerous and more reliable: he says he spent much of the late eighties and early nineties selling crack in Brooklyn and New Jersey and down the Eastern Seaboard. He was no kingpin, but he says he was a fairly accomplished mid-level dealer, and though he hated standing outside all day, he found that he didn't hate the routine. "It was an adventure," he says. "I got to hang out on the block with my crew, talking, cracking jokes. You know how people in office jobs talk at the watercooler? This job was almost all watercooler." Then, almost as an afterthought, "But when you weren't having fun, it was hell." Early recordings of Jay-Z reveal a nimble but mild-mannered virtuoso, delivering rat-a-tat syllables (he liked to rap in double-time triplets, delivering six syllables per beat) that often amounted to études rather than songs. But by 1996, when he released his début album, "Reasonable Doubt," on a local independent label, he had slowed down and settled into a style—and, more important, settled into character. The album won him underground acclaim and a record deal with the very above-ground hip-hop label Def Jam, which helped him become one of the genre's most dependable hitmakers. He was a cool-blooded hustler, describing a risky life in conversational verses that hid their poetic devices, disparaging the art of rapping even while perfecting it:

> Who wanna bet us that we don't touch lettuce, stack
> cheddars forever, live treacherous, all the et ceteras.
> To the death of us, me and my confidants, we
> shine. You feel the ambiance—y'all niggas just rhyme.

Too often, hip-hop's embrace of crime narratives has been portrayed as a flaw or a mistake, a regrettable detour from the overtly ideological rhymes of groups like Public Enemy. But in Jay-Z's view Public Enemy is an anomaly. "You rarely become Chuck D when you're listening to Public Enemy," he writes. "It's more like watching a really, really lively speech." By contrast, his tales of hustling were generous, because they made it easy for fans to imagine that they were part of the action. "I don't think any listeners think I'm threatening them," he writes. "I think they're singing along with me, threatening someone else. They're thinking, Yeah, I'm coming for you. And they might apply it to anything, to taking their next math test or straightening out that chick talking outta pocket in the next cubicle." 18

Throughout "Decoded," Jay-Z offers readers a large dose of hermeneutics and a small dose of biography, in keeping with his deserved reputation for brilliance and chilliness. His footnotes are full of pleasingly small-scale exultations ("I like the internal rhymes 19 here") and technical explanations ("The shift in slang—from talking about guns as tools to break things to talking about shooting as blazing—matches the shift in tone"); at one point, he pauses to quote a passage from "Book of Rhymes" in which Bradley praises his use of homonyms. Readers curious about his life will learn something about his father, who abandoned the family when Jay-Z was twelve; a little bit about Bono, who is now one of Jay-Z's many A-list friends; and nothing at all about the time when, as a boy, Jay-Z shot his older brother in the shoulder. (Apparently, there was a dispute over an item of jewelry, possibly a ring, although Jay-Z once told Oprah Winfrey that, at the time, his brother was "dealing with a lot of demons.")

"Decoded" is a prestige project—it will be followed, inevitably, by a rash of imitations from rappers who realize that the self-penned coffee-table book has replaced the Lamborghini Murciélago as hip-hop's ultimate status symbol. In his early years, Jay-Z liked to insist that rapping was only a means to an end—like selling crack, only safer. "I was an eager hustler and a reluctant artist," he writes. "But the irony of it is that to make the hustle work, really work, over the long term, you have to be a true artist, too." Certainly this book emphasizes Jay-Z the true artist, ignoring high-spirited tracks like "Ain't No Nigga" to focus on his moodier ruminations on success and regrets. (The lyrics to "Success" and "Regrets" are, in fact, included.) Readers might be able to trace Jay-Z's growing self-consciousness over the years, as his slick vernacular verses give way to language that's more decorous and sometimes less elegant. In "Fallin'," from 2007, he returned to a favorite old topic, with mixed results: 20

> The irony of selling drugs is sort of like I'm using it
> Guess it's two sides to what substance abuse is

Bradley has written about rappers "so insistent on how their rhymes sound that they lose control over what they are actually saying." But with late-period Jay-Z the reverse is sometimes true: the ideas are clear and precise, but the syntax gets convoluted, and he settles for clumsy near-rhymes like "using it"/"abuse is." For all Bradley and DuBois's talk about "conscious" hip-hop, the genre owes much of its energy to the power of what might be called "unconscious" rapping: heedless or reckless lyrics, full of contradictions and exaggerations (to say nothing of insults). If you are going to follow a beat, as rappers must, then it helps not to have too many other firm commitments. 21

One day four years ago, Jay-Z was reading *The Economist* when he came across an article bearing the heading "Bubbles and Bling." 22

The article was about Cristal, the expensive champagne that figured in the rhymes of Jay-Z and other prominent rappers. In the article, Frédéric Rouzaud, the managing director of the winery behind Cristal, was asked whether these unsought endorsements might hurt his brand. "That's a good question, but what can we do? We can't forbid people from buying it," he said, adding, slyly, "I'm sure Dom Pérignon or Krug would be delighted to have their business." Jay-Z was irritated enough that he released a statement vowing never to drink Cristal again, and he started removing references to Cristal from his old lyrics during concerts. (He eventually switched his endorsement to Armand de Brignac.) In Jay-Z's view, Rouzaud had not only insulted hip-hop culture; he had violated an unspoken promotional arrangement. "We used their brand as a signifier of luxury and they got free advertising and credibility every time we mentioned it," he writes. "We were trading cachet." (Actually, the book, not free of typos, says "cache.")

It's hard not to think about Cristal when Jay-Z insists that his lyrics should be heard—read—as poetry, or when Bradley and DuBois produce an anthology designed to win for rappers the status of poets. They are, all of them, trading cachet, and their eagerness to make this trade suggests that they are trading up—that hip-hop, despite its success, still aches for respect and recognition. It stands to reason, then, that as the genre's place in the cultural firmament grows more secure its advocates will grow less envious of poetry's allegedly exalted status. 23

Another great American lyricist has just published a book of his own: "Finishing the Hat" by Stephen Sondheim is curiously similar in form to "Decoded." Sondheim is just as appealing a narrator as Jay-Z, although he's much less polite. (While Jay-Z has almost nothing bad to say about his fellow rappers, Sondheim is quick to disparage his rivals, subject to a "cowardly but simple" precept: "criticize only the dead.") But where Jay-Z wants to help readers see the poetry in hip-hop, Sondheim thinks poeticism can be a problem: in his discussion of "Tonight," from "West Side Story," he half apologizes for the song's "lapses into 'poetry.'" And where Bradley and DuBois are quick to praise rappers for using trick rhymes and big words, Sondheim is ever on guard against "overrhyming" and other instances of unwarranted cleverness. "In theatrical fact," he writes, "it is usually the plainer and flatter lyric that soars poetically when infused with music." Most rappers are no less pragmatic: they use the language that works, which is sometimes ornate, but more often plainspoken, even homely. (One thinks of Webbie, the pride of Baton Rouge, deftly rhyming "drunk as a fuckin' rhino" with "my people gon' get they shine on.") Maybe future anthologies will help show 24 why the most complicated hip-hop lyrics aren't always the most successful.

It's significant that hip-hop, virtually alone among popular- 25
music genres, has never embraced the tradition of lyric booklets. The genius of hip-hop is that it encourages listeners to hear spoken words as music. Few people listen to speeches or books on tape over and over, but hip-hop seems to have just as much replay value as any other popular genre. Reading rap lyrics may be useful, but it's also tiring. The Jay-Z of "Decoded" is engaging; the Jay-Z of his albums is irresistible. The difference has something to do with his odd, perpetually adolescent-sounding voice, and a lot to do with his sophisticated sense of rhythm. Sure, he's a poet—and, while we're at it, a singer and percussionist, too. But why should any of these titles be more impressive than "rapper"?

In the introduction to "Finishing the Hat," Sondheim explains 26
that "all rhymes, even the farthest afield of the near ones (home/dope), draw attention to the rhymed word." But surely rhyming can deëmphasize the meaning of a word by emphasizing its sound. Rhyme, like other phonetic techniques, is a way to turn a spoken phrase into a musical phrase—a "rhythmic argument," as Jay-Z put it. Bap bap bapbap. Rapping is the art of addressing listeners and distracting them at the same time. Bradley argues in "Book of Rhymes" that hip-hop lyrics represent the genre's best chance for immortality: "When all the club bangers have faded, when all the styles and videos are long forgotten, the words will remain." That gets the relationship backward. On the contrary, one suspects that the words will endure—and the books will proliferate—because the music will, too.

Examining the Text

1. The beginning of this article refers to "the poetic canon" mentioned by an English professor named Adam Bradley in a manifesto to his fellow scholars. Bradley exhorted academics to expand the poetic canon, and possibly enlarge poetry's audience, by including some of the "greatest" hip-hop lyrics. Based on your experience and knowledge of hip-hop, what songs might you place in this list of great hip-hop lyrics, and why would you consider these particular wordings to be worthy of inclusion in the poetic canon?

2. This article is part argumentation/analysis, part book report/book review. What specific books are examined in this text? What are the specific strengths and values of the books examined here, according to the author, and what might be some of the drawbacks of the books mentioned? If you've read extensively in this field, can you add any titles to the list, along with brief descriptions of the merits of these additional books?

3. According to this article, what were some common characteristics of lyrics in the so-called "golden age" of hip-hop? In what ways do lyrics in songs subsequent to this golden age—and up to the present day in hip-hop music—contrast with the themes and stylistic underpinnings of the earlier lyrical output?

4. At the end of the article, the author veers sharply away from his consideration of hip-hop lyrics, bringing up the word choices of a different kind of song writer: the popular Broadway musical songster Stephen Sondheim. What is the author's point in bringing up the work of a non-rap-based artist as he brings this article to a close? Does this reference support or undermine Professor Bradley's original assertion that hip-hop lyrics should be considered right alongside the canonized works of Shakespeare, Keats, Walt Whitman, and Allen Ginsberg?

5. *Thinking rhetorically:* Based upon the tone and the format of this article, who would you say its intended audience is: rap fans, academics, literary critics, or general readers? Provide textual evidence to support your contention, whichever group you think the article aims to persuade. Do you believe the author is trying to convince readers to adopt a particular position with regard to hip-hop as legitimate literary craft; or do you think the article is merely a summary of several recent books focusing on the wordplay in hip-hop songs? Find samples in the text that illustrate the article's thematic core belief.

For Group Discussion

It was suggested earlier in this piece that the literary value of hip-hop music has been obscured by mass media attention to messages allegedly conveyed by certain songs: messages such as negative portrayals of women, glorification of violence and drug dealing, and appeals to crass materialism rather than deeper spiritual and psychological values. As a class, engage in a discussion of whether you agree with this argument: has the artistic value of hip-hop been obscured by sensationalistic diatribes and heated rhetoric concerning morals and values, or has hip-hop been considered fairly, reasonably, and objectively, not only as a conveyor of messages and role models, but also as a valid and legitimate art form?

Writing Suggestion

Drawing upon the examples of rhyme, structure, and theme discussed in the above article, imagine you are assigned to write an essay researching students' attitudes about the literary value of rap music. Design fifteen to twenty questions that you think would be key to ask a group of students at your school, and then administer your survey to as many students as is actually feasible. Having conducted this preliminary research, proceed to write the assigned essay. As you develop your arguments and reveal your conclusions, you might begin by explaining the reasoning behind your choice of questions. Also, take care to explain your hypotheses and intended methodology, and then discuss the results of your study. Consider this question as a possible thematic center for your paper: Is your sample student population representative of the youthful American population at large, or is it significantly different?

The Year Hip-Hop Invented Sex

MEGAN CARPENTIER

There are many kinds of scholarly journals in your college library's online database. Most of them tend to be relatively formal, featuring the kind of staid and respectable voice that students and academic researchers are accustomed to reading and in which they are used to writing. Occasionally, however, a reader/researcher will run into a legitimate scholarly journal that purposely bumps the bounds of traditional academic propriety for rhetorical and thematic effect. As suggested immediately by the journal's title, Bitch Magazine *falls into the latter camp, containing articles generally from a contemporary feminist perspective—pieces that are intended to provoke, and perhaps even shock, while still containing rigorous, deeply informed scholarship, highly articulate writing, and credible research. The following piece is by Megan Carpentier, She is the executive editor of Raw Story. She previously served as an Associate Editor at Talking Points Memo; the editor of news and politics at Air America; an editor at Jezebel.com; and the associate editor at Wonkette. Her work has also been published in the* Washington Post, *the Washington Independent,* The Guardian's *"Comment is free," Foreign Policy's "Madame Secretary" blog,* Glamour's *Glamocracy,* Ms. *Magazine, RH Reality Check, the Women's Media Center,* On The Issues, *the* New York Press, Bitch *and Women's eNews. Prior to becoming a journalist, she spent seven years as a lobbyist in Washington, D.C.. She has a Bachelor's degree in German literature and sociology from Boston University and a Masters of Science in Foreign Service from Georgetown University.*

As you read, *then, consider the effect of the article's language upon you: does it shock you, put you off, or make you wish more researchers penned and/or typed up their tomes with such lively diction and graphic frankness? At the same time, consider the validity of Carpentier's arguments: do you agree that bands and rappers such as N.W.A. and Dr. Dre, who used to dismiss women as bitches and hos, have given way to Sir Mix-A-Lot and Ben Folds, who—by introducing female orgasm in mainstream music—have up-leveled the representations of women generally?*

---

1 Listening to popular (and crossover) hip-hop and R&B music has, for much of my life, too often been an exercise in ignoring lyrics to enjoy a song. It's not easy when music you want to dance to refers to you and your friends as "bitches" and "hos," encourages men to get you drunk enough that you don't mind having sex, and privileges one very specific kind of heteronormative nooky designed to show men how desirable you are by pleasing them.

But somehow the winter of 2009 became a kind of sexual contest between male hip-hop and R&B artists. And, for once, it wasn't about who could rack up more conquests, or get more women to strip, or prove that they were the most sexist. Instead, it was about who could satisfy women sexually, period. 2

Whether it was the aftermath of R&B artist Chris Brown's arrest for assaulting then-girlfriend Rihanna (and his album's subsequent poor performance), or the economic environment in which male unemployment in the African-American community skyrocketed even as African-American women were making historic strides in terms of employment and earning power, or just a belated recognition of the purchasing power of female listeners, late 2009 and early 2010 saw a sea change in how male hip-hop artists addressed female sexuality. From Trey Songz to Usher and Snoop Dogg to Jeremih, male hip-hop artists stopped bragging about how many women they could get to fuck them, and started bragging about why—and it wasn't because of the cash, the fame, or the alcohol. It was suddenly all about how hard, how much, and how good they could get women off. 3

And while female listeners might find it amusing to eavesdrop on Trey and Usher competing for the right to claim they "invented" sex simply because they're interested in their partners enjoying it, it does represent a watershed of sorts. Men who have often been more interested strictly in getting women into bed are finally interested in what their partners have to say about it once they've been there. It's quite a ways from where hip-hop's been. 4

THE DARK (AND ORGASM-FREE) AGES

Bitches ain't shit but hos and tricks
Lick on these nuts and suck the dick
Get the fuck out after you're done

In 1992, when gangsta rap ruled, female orgasm was just about the furthest thing from the minds of Dr. Dre and N.W.A. Women were just accessories and receptacles; an interest in their pleasure wasn't exactly part of the deal. And really, when the best hip-hop had to offer women was Sir Mix-A-Lot's "Baby Got Back," you knew we were off to a tough decade. But at least Mix-A-Lot was trying, in a trying environment, to tell women they didn't have to put up with abuse to get laid. ("A word to the thick soul sistas/ I wanna get with ya/I won't cuss or hit ya.") 5

Not that he got very far with his message: Rap and hip-hop for the rest of the decade, and well into the next, put forth an understanding 6 that women who put themselves in front of the camera in a hip-hop video, or even in the sight line of the artist himself, just didn't count. Unlike artists' mothers or sisters, these women were considered "hos," just in it for the transaction, which involved her body and a man's pleasure. And much of the music reflected the belief that violence could be a perfectly acceptable way of dealing with a ho.

THE NEW MILLENNIUM, WHEN LADIES GOT A LITTLE VOCAL

As rap became more mainstream than ever and rock musicians like Ben Folds started "ironically" appropriating the misogynist, violence-tinged lyrics of their hip-hop colleagues, a few female artists started to raise their own voices. From Missy Elliott and Eve to Lil' Kim and Trina, female artists tried to appeal to fans with music similar to that of their male contemporaries. And yet, with the exception of Elliott, they often fell short of any empowerment that involved more than boasting that they were hot enough to fuck men other women were shaking their money-makers to attract. 7

Lil' Kim, in particular, was happy to brag at her skills in bed, at least when it came to pleasing her lovers. Her 2003 album *La Bella Mafia* brimmed with rhymes about her fellatio skills and how good she was at pleasing her lovers. But even in a song in which she sang about her "magic clit," it was all about how good she was at giving it to men: 8

when it come to sex don't test my skills
'Cause my head game have you head over heels

Not that women can't enjoy giving head, but getting men to enjoy performing cunnilingus—and to come back to do it again—might be a more enviable skill. Kim often moved back and forth in her lyrics between positioning herself as almost superhumanly capable of slaking a man's lust ("Let me show you what I'm all about/ How I make a Sprite can disappear in my mouth") and noting that she could get some action of her own ("I know if I get licked once, I get licked twice"), but at least she was trying to get female listeners to imagine a world where sex wasn't just about pleasing a man. And for a woman who was initially known as the pretty young thing on the sizable arm of Biggie Smalls, that was no mean feat. 9

To women and men alike, the mark of a skillful lover in hip-hop was, inevitably, how easily the men could get women into bed, or, for female rappers, how deftly they could get a guy off. Eve talked about 10 how independent she was, but in a 2002 collaboration with Alicia Keys, that independence was all part of a new game to attract a man.

Baby here I am
Ain't ashamed of my frame
And I know you're watchin'
Puttin' on a show for you

Female orgasm remained secondary to a man's, even when women stormed the charts. But "secondary" is far better than "nonexistent." And introducing cunnilingus to mainstream hip-hop was an important step toward starting an ongoing conversation about whether African-American men "really" didn't go down—as had long been a stereotype—or whether "real" men didn't go down, or, simply, whether how well he treated his lover was a better yardstick by which to measure a man. 11

Simply appropriating the braggadocio of male artists wasn't enough for a full-scale change in the male-centric sex talk that characterized much of hip-hop, of course. A handful of women on the charts didn't make up for the thousands more who were treated as trappings of the rap lifestyle. Nas and Jay-Z still beefed over whether Nas's ex-girlfriend was sleeping around, "hos" and "bitches" were still staple characters of rap lyrics, and, in general, the world portrayed by the hottest songs on the radio and BET was still peopled by men, with women there for decoration and casual, disposable use. ("What good is all the fame if you ain't fuckin' the models," asked Nelly's 2002 hit "Hot in Herre"); Ludacris, in his 2001 hit "Rollout (My Business)," lorded his fame—and attendant pussy magnetism—over other men, rapping 12

is that your wife, your girlfriend or just your main bitch?
You take your pick, while I'm rubbin' the hips
Touchin' lips to the top of the dick and then whoooo!

As most women know (and as the movie *American Pie* aptly demonstrated) if a man gets to that "whoooo!" moment as soon as a woman's lips make contact with his genitals, the likelihood is that he considers the act all but over. Outside of a rap song, many guys would be mortified and apologetic; Ludacris moved on to speculate about getting action from a housekeeper. 13

THE DIVA AGE, WHEN NOTHING IMPROVED

By the late aughts, women in hip-hop and R&B were often divas: regal and worthy of worship, with pipes to envy and attitude aplenty. But judging by the music of Beyoncé or Mary J. Blige (if not their personal 14 lives), this didn't stop men from objectifying and cheating on them. The guys they sang about seemed like they were stuck in the pages of a Karinne "Supahead" Steffans novel; it remained all about what women would do to them, not what they could do for women. But at least women (including, eventually, Steffans herself) started to deem themselves worthy of better.

Beyoncé kicked her cheating lover out of the house, claiming that he wasn't irreplaceable and that a new man who could treat her right was on his way over. Mary J. promised she wouldn't let a man hurt her again. And Rihanna, in "Shut Up and Drive," explicitly warned a guy that she wanted an experienced driver to handle her curves, run all the lights, and—most notably—be prepared to go all night to please her. 15

But still, many male hip-hop artists weren't having it. Lil Wayne's 2008 track "Lollipop" exemplifies how even as Beyoncé was telling "Irreplaceable"'s philanderer that she could do better, the primacy of male pleasure held strong. 16

Make her wanna lick the wrapper
So I let her lick the rapper

His dick, you see, is just so much like a lollipop that he's actually doing women a favor by allowing them to perform fellatio. He spends a couple of lines in the song reciprocating—although, naturally, nothing is said about orgasm—but as long as he proves himself better than his lover's boyfriend, it's all okay. 17

Kid Cudi, Common, and Kanye West came together in 2009 for their own anthem celebrating the enjoyment women obviously got from sexually pleasuring them, called "Make Her Say (I Poke Her Face)." Over a sample of Lady Gaga's "Poker Face" and a series of her throaty moans, each rapper in turn talks himself up. First, Kid Cudi says he's perfectly happy to give his lover what she likes—as long as she brings a female friend along. Kanye, too, is happy his fellator brings along a friend, and he ever so thoughtfully makes sure that his lovers are old enough to drink before poking their faces. 18

I got seniority with the sorority
So, that explains why I love college
Getting brain in the library 'cause I love knowledge
When you use your medulla oblongata
And give me scoliosis until I'm comatose-is
And do it while I'm asleep, yeah, a little osmosis
And that's my commandment, you ain't gotta ask Moses

Not even Moses could likely explain how a woman would get off from sucking the dick of a sleeping man, or where (in between passing out from his own orgasm in the library and getting sucked off in his bed) Kanye would be reciprocating those orgasms. Finally, there's Common, who raps that his consort's oral skills "was gooder than the music," and invites womankind to "get your head right and get up on this conscious dick." It's quite the invitation—that is, if a woman seems solely interested in proving her oral-sex skills and doesn't mind if her partner has no pressing need to prove the same to her. 19

It was starting to seem that for each woman who made it onto the hip-hop and R&B charts and demanded sexual reciprocation, appreciation, and even fidelity, male artists would go just a little further in graphically describing what women could and should enjoy doing to them. Did they stop to consider that their female contemporaries were speaking to an audience increasingly receptive to the idea that giving a blow job to a man who considered her a sex object might not be the ultimate in get-down pleasure? 20

But while Kid Cudi and crew were making their way up the hip-hop charts in the summer of 2009 with women going down, Jeremih had been offering his girlfriend (and female listeners) something just a little different for her birthday since March. 21

First I'm gonna take a dive into the water deep
Until I know I pleased that body
Or girl without a broom
I might just sweep you off your feet
And make you wanna tell somebody

Granted, it's an annoying earworm of a song that no one wanted to admit they liked. Between the slow, pulsating beat and the narrator's almost subservient desire to please his partner without asking anything for himself, it was the kind of thing those fellatio-focused hip-hop artists might have looked down upon. But its phenomenal crossover success was impossible to ignore. 22

And the response was, at a minimum, telling. First up to challenge Jeremih as number-one loverman was Trey Songz, who released "I Invented Sex" in October 2009 and was joined on a remix by Usher and Keri Hilson in December. In the initial version, Trey told his lover that when they got back to his house, he would put some Usher on the stereo and make her orgasm so hard that she would think he invented sex. Usher and Hilson weren't willing to let that stand. In the remix. Usher led off: 23

Leave that teddy on
Take them panties off

Like Trey say "I Can't Help But Wait"
Got that oven preheated
Trey invented sex, but he ain't teach you how to eat it
On ya back now, spread it out now

In his competition with Trey, Usher is offering to prove that he is better at performing oral sex than his competition—kind of a radical departure from competing at who could get more women to do it to them. Later in the remix, Keri and Trey discuss how the missionary position isn't good enough for either of them, and offer to explore more than just how a woman can please a man. 24

While Trey and Hilson span both the R&B and hip-hop genres, the inclusion of Usher in the remix pushed the song well into the realm of R&B, where the idea of sex with women's pleasure in mind wasn't quite so foreign. And Trey hasn't stopped exploring the idea that fucking a woman well is more pleasurable that simply fucking her, as his newest single released in March 2010 "Neighbors Know My Name" indicates. 25

Girl your legs keep shakin'
I swear we breakin' our new headboard, headboard
And the love we make it feels so good, girl, you know I'm proud
Lookin' in your lovely face, scream my name, you do it so loud

Even Snoop Dogg—one of the elder statesman of rap—got in on the game with his late 2009 track. "Gangsta Luv," a title which mirrors the Eve song from earlier in the decade. Seven years after she rapped about wanting a gangsta who still respected her independence. Snoop Dogg took her up on the offer: 26

I won't stop 'til you're finished
but you ain't felt love 'til a gangsta get up in it

Given the history of hip-hop artists calling themselves gangstas and demanding, as a result of their status, blow jobs, performative sex acts, and a level of subservience, defining "gangsta luv" as sex that is intended to last until the woman gets offhand that it's better than the sex a woman might have had with other men—is setting a rather high bar for Snoop's fellow rappers, even if it's a rather low one for a true Don Juan. But, given where women started the decade, it's hardly a bad thing. 27

CAN THE NEW TREND OUTLAST THE COLD?

The real question for male rappers and the women they want to entice to both buy their albums and share their beds is whether the female-focused sex jams of 2009 will continue into the summer of 2010. Women 28 have the market power to demand more from their music, as well as the self-esteem and options to demand more from their lovers—and it seems like the historically male-dominated music industry may finally be realizing that. Chris Brown's arrest sent a shocking signal to female consumers that an artist their money was supporting might well be behaving just as his songs said he was—and they responded by not buying his music. And after years of assuming, often correctly, that women would shell out money for music without paying too much attention to the message, labels took notice.

Ideally, treating women respectfully shouldn't have to be a conscious business decision, but in an industry that's selling, first and foremost, an image, this particular one—women getting off and men wanting them to—is a big step forward. Like the more misogynist music before it, the recent bump in songs about doing right by the ladies sets up a self-reinforcing paradigm of what men should want and what women should get. And like the men of my dad's generation who used Barry White or Marvin Gaye to set a mood, Jeremih, Trey, Usher, Snoop, and their cohorts aren't just interested in getting women to listen. They want—they need—men to open their mouths, not just to do the deed, but to spread the word. 29

Examining the Text

1. Early in this article, the author says that this decade "saw a sea change in how male hip-hop artists addressed female sexuality." According to author Carpentier, how has the portrayal of female sexuality in hip-hop and/or popular music generally changed in recent years? Do you agree with this assertion? Whether your answer is yes or no, provide evidence from your own knowledge of popular music lyrics to back up your point of view.

2. What were the characteristics of "The Dark (and Orgasm-Free) Ages," in popular music lyrics, in Carpentier's opinion? What evidence does she cite to back up her thematic points; can you add additional concrete support from your own excellent recollection of song lyrics? What, according to the author was "dark" (i.e., negative and/or ignorant) about these portrayals?

3. Continuing her historical retrospective of portrayals of female sexuality in popular songs, Carpentier moves into the "Diva Age," in which, she says, nothing improved in these portrayals. What does she mean by the Diva Age, and who are the central artists during this period that might qualify as divas? In what way(s) did the situation not improve, in the author's opinion? Relate any personal knowledge of music and artists during this period to support or disprove Carpentier's central points here.

4. In her concluding section, Carpentier argues, "Like the more misogynist music before it, the recent bump in songs about doing right by the ladies sets up a self-reinforcing paradigm of what men should want and what women should get." Without going into more detail than you are comfortable with, what is this paradigm? That is, what should men want, and what should women get, in the view of this author? Do you agree or disagree with her assertion that there has been a recent upswing in the number of songs that reinforce these antimisogynist values?

5. *Thinking rhetorically:* We have never had an article that was quite so graphic and explicit as this one, and we—both authors and editors—went back and forth about the propriety of including it in the latest revision of *Common Culture.* In the end, we decided that it was smart, articulate, and definitely presented a coherent, focused, and well-supported point of view that had great potential for generating stimulating animated class discussion and lively writing in response. For a brief writing exercise, assume the role of a television or movie script writer and write two pages of dialogue in which authors and editors sit around a conference table and debate the merits of including this article in their popular and universally beloved and respected textbook.

For Group Discussion

Break your class into small groups. In these groups of three or four, attempt to come to some consensus regarding the author's main points in the above essay: what is she saying about the way rap lyrics have changed through time in portraying the sexual roles of women? Next, reassemble the class as a whole, and have one member for each group report on the central themes embodied in this article. Having heard from each group on the subject, engage in a full-class evaluation of these central points: do you agree or disagree with the assertions that the author makes throughout the article? Are there some arguments that ring true and others that seem to stretch credibility, or does the whole article seem on target . . . or uniformly off-base in its interpretations and conclusions? As you engage in the latter discussion, be sure to draw upon your own knowledge of rap lyrics and media portrayals of women to provide concrete examples that support your own arguments.

Writing Suggestion

While dealing with a frankly sexual subject that usually is not discussed in polite society or most college textbooks, the article "The Year Hip-Hop Invented Sex" is nevertheless a social science–based example of media studies scholarship that discusses a sociosexual subject with which you might be familiar . . . either anecdotally, and/or in your actual relationship experience, and/or through your exposure to these ideas through media exposure. Drawing upon the latter of these listed phenomena, in a research essay of four to six pages, consider the ways in which this same subject might have been dealt with openly in various media outlets, by artists *other* than rap singers, as is discussed here. For instance, sexual techniques, gender differences, and stereotyping are issues often raised by contemporary stand-up comedians, certain "shock jock" radio personalities, "reality" television programs, and so forth. In developing your essay, you may want to use the above text as a model for discussing a somewhat taboo topic in a light and humorous way while still exploring the issue in a great deal of intellectual depth . . . not an easy balance to achieve!

The Miseducation of Hip-Hop

EVELYN JAMILAH

In this article, the author points to criticisms currently being leveled at rap music and hip-hop culture from within the community of African American educators. No one would deny that rap culture enjoys unprecedented popularity among young people. Nevertheless, many of these observers believe that while the themes embodied in rap music may reflect real-life situations within America's inner cities, rap's influence may be ultimately counterproductive, causing Black students to perform worse in school—which, in turn, will perpetuate the negative economic and social conditions that rappers dramatize in their lyrics. Some observers go so far as to insist that young African American students turn away from this popular artform, while others suggest that some university courses focus their attention on rap, to make some connections between this popular form and the work of Black historians, sociologists, urban psychologists, and so forth.

***As you read** this article, attempt to determine the author's own stance toward this topic. Does she play the role of dispassionate observer, merely recording journalistically the arguments swirling around this hotly debated topic, or can you detect a certain agenda, a rhetorical stance underlying her reportage? Note also your own reactions to points raised during this piece. The commentators presented in this article will probably cause you to have some emotional reaction; try to set your emotions aside momentarily, make note of specific points of agreement or disagreement as they arise.*

When Jason Hinmon transferred to the University of Delaware two years ago from Morehouse College in Atlanta, the 22-year-old senior says he almost dropped out his first semester. 1

He says that for financial reasons, he came back here to his hometown. But in many ways, he had never felt so abandoned. 2

"I came to class and my professors didn't know how to deal with me," he says, between bites of his a-la-carte lunch. "I could barely get them to meet with me during their office hours." 3

Dark-hued, dreadlocked and, well, young, he says many of his mostly White professors figured they had him pegged. 4

"They took one look at me and thought that I was some hip-hop hoodlum who wasn't interested in being a good student," he says. 5

But if Hinmon represents the "good" students with grounds to resent the stereotype, there are faculty who profess there's no shortage of young people willing to live up—or down—to it. 6

"You see students walking on campus reciting rap lyrics when they should be reciting something they'll need to know on their next test. Some of these same students you won't see back on campus next semester," says Dr. Thomas Earl Midgette, 50, director of the Institute for the Study of Minority Issues at historically Black North Carolina Central University. 7

"These rap artists influence the way they dress," he continues. "They look like hoochie mamas, not like they're coming to class. Young men with pants fashioned below their navel. Now, I used to wear bell-bottoms, but I learned to dress a certain way if I was negotiating the higher education maze. I had to trim my afro." 8

The difference between today's students and their parents, faculty and administrators is marked, no doubt. Technology's omnipresence—apparent in kids with little patience for anything less than instant meals, faster Internet information and cellular ubiquity—is certainly at play when it comes to explaining the divide. 9

But what causes more consternation among many college and university officials is a music form, a culture and a lifestyle they say is eating away at the morals, and ultimately the classroom experience, of today's college students. 10

Hip-hop—brash, vulgar, in-your-face hip-hop—is indisputably the dominant youth culture today. Its most controversial front men floss mad ice (wear lots of diamonds and other expensive jewelry), book bad bitches (usually scantily clad, less than the take home kind of girl), and in general, party it up. Its most visible females brag about their sexual dexterity, physical attributes, and cunning tactics when it comes to getting their rent paid. 11

With college completion statistics at an embarrassing low and the Black–White achievement gap getting wider by the semester, perhaps it's time to be concerned whether the culture's malevolent message is at play. 12

But can atrocious retention rates really be linked to reckless music? Or do university officials underestimate their students? Is it that young folk today have no sense of history, responsibility and plain good manners? Or are college faculty a bunch of old fogies simply more comfortable with Marvin Gaye's "Sexual Healing" than Little Kim's sexual prowess? 13

Is this no different than the divide we've always seen between young people and their college and university elders? Or do the disparities between this wave of students and those charged with educating them portend something more disparaging? 14

THE GAP

At the heart of the rift between the two groups is a debate that has both 15
sides passionately disturbed.

Young people say they feel pigeonholed by an image many of 16
them don't support. They say the real rub is that their teachers—Black and White—believe the hype as much as the old lady who crosses the street when she sees them coming.

And they'd like their professors to consider this: They can listen 17
to the music, even party to it, but still have a response just as critical, if not more so, than their faculty and administrators.

Others point out that the pervasiveness of hip-hop's immoral 18
philosophies is at least partly rooted in the fact that the civil rights movement—the older generation's defining moment—surely did not live up to all its promises for Black America.

And further, they say it's important to note that not all hip-hop is 19
irresponsible. In fact, some argue that it's ultimately empowering, uplifting and refreshing. After all, when was the last time a biology professor sat down with a Mos Def CD? How many can even pronounce his name?

Older faculty, administrators and parents alike respond that the 20
music is downright filth. And anyone associated with it ought to have their mouths and their morals cleansed.

There's a real problem when a marijuana-smoking ex-con named 21
Snoop Doggy Dog can pack a campus auditorium quicker than Black historian John Hope Franklin; when more students deify the late Tupac Shakur and his abrasive lyrics than have ever read the great Martin Luther King Jr.'s "I Have a Dream" speech; when kids decked out in sweats more pricey than their tuition complain that they can't afford a semester's books; when the gains they fought so hard for are, in some ways, slowly slipping away.

"I think what causes us the most grief is that hip-hop comes 22
across as heartless, valueless, nihilistic and certainly anachronistic if not atheistic," says Dr. Nat Irvin, president of Future Focus 2020, an urban futures think tank at Wake Forest University in North Carolina. "Anyone who would argue with that needs to take a look for themselves and see what images are prevalent on BET and MTV."

"But I don't think there's any question that the disconnect comes 23
from the fact that old folks don't have a clue. They don't understand technology. The world has changed. And there's an enormous age gap between most faculty on college campuses and the rest of America," he says.

More than 60 percent of college and university faculty are over 24
the age of 45. Meanwhile, nearly 53 percent of African Americans are under 30 and some 40 percent are under 20.

25 That means more than half of all Blacks were born after the civil rights movement and the landmark *Brown vs. Board of Education* case.

26 "There's no big puzzle why these kids are coming with a different ideology," Irvin, 49, says.

THIS IS WHAT BLACKNESS IS

27 It is universally acknowledged that rap began in New York City's Bronx borough nearly 30 years ago, a mix of Jamaican reggae's dancehall, America's funk music, the inner city's pent-up frustrations and Black folks' general propensity to love a good party.

28 Pioneering artists like the The Last Poets, The Sugar Hill Gang, Kurtis Blow and Run-DMC combined creative genius and street savvy to put hip-hop on the map.

29 Its initial associations were with graffiti and party music, according to Dr. Robin D. G. Kelley, professor of history and Africana studies at New York University.

30 "Then in the late '80s, you begin to see more politicized manifestations of that. BDP, Public Enemy. . . . In essays that students wrote that were not about rap music, but about the urban condition itself, they would adopt the language. They would quote Public Enemy lyrics, they would quote Ghetto Boys," says Kelley, 38.

31 "This whole generation of Blacks in particular were trying to carve out for themselves an alternative culture," he continues. "I saw a whole generation for the first time say, 'I don't want to go to corporate America. I don't want to be an attorney. I don't want to be a doctor. I don't want to get paid. I want to make a revolution.'"

32 "The wave that we're in now is all over the place," he explains.

33 But even hip-hop's fans stop short at endorsing some of the themes prevailing in today's music and mindset.

34 Kevin Powell, noted cultural critic and former hip-hop journalist, says the biggest difference between the music today and the music at its onset is that "we don't own it."

35 "Corporate America completely commodified hip-hop," he says. "We create the culture and corporate America takes it and sells it back to us and tells us, 'This is what Blackness is.'"

36 And while Powell, 34, says he is disappointed in some of the artists, especially the older ones who "should know better," many students are their staunchest defenders.

37 Caryn Wheeler, 18, a freshman at Bowie State University, explains simply that "every day isn't about love." Her favorite artists? Jay-Z, OutKast, Biggie Smalls, Tupac and Little Kim, many of whom

are linked to hip-hop's controversial side. "We can relate because we see what they are talking about every day," she says.

Mazi Mutafa, 23, is a senior at the University of Maryland College Park and president of the Black Student Union there. He says he listens to jazz and hip-hop, positive artists and those who capture a party spirit. "There's a time to party and have fun, and Jay-Z speaks to that," he says. "But there needs to be a happy medium." 38

Interrupting, senior Christine Gonzalez, 28, says a lot of artists like Jay-Z tend to be revered by younger students. "As you get older, you tend to tone down your style and find that happy medium," she says. "It's all a state of mind." 39

"People have to understand that Jay-Z is kind of like a 100-level class—an intro to hip-hop. He brings a lot of people into its fan base," Mutafa chimes in. "But then you have groups like The Roots, which are more like a 400-level class. They keep you engaged in the music. But one is necessary for the other." 40

Erick Rivas, 17, a freshman also at the University of Maryland, says he listens to Mos Def, Black Star, Mobb Deep, Wu-Tang Clan and sometimes other, more mainstream acts like Jay-Z. "Hip-hop has been a driving force in our lives. It is the soundtrack to our lives," he explains. 41

KEEPIN' IT REAL

But if hip-hop is the soundtrack to their lives, it may also mark the failure of it. 42

De Reef Jamison, a doctoral candidate who teaches African American history at Temple University in Philadelphia, surveyed 72 Black male college students last summer for his thesis. Then a graduate student at Florida, A&M State University, Jamison was interested in discovering if there are links between students' music tastes and their cultural identity, their grades and other key indicators. 43

"While the lines weren't always so clear and distinct, I found that many of the students who had a low African self-consciousness, who overidentified with a European worldview and who were highly materialistic were often the students who listened to the most 'gangster' rap, or what I prefer to call reality rap," he explains. 44

As for grades, he says the gangster rap devotees' tended to be lower than those students who listened mostly to what he calls more conscious rap. Still, he's reluctant to draw any hard and fast lines between musical preference and student performance. 45

"I'd recommend that scholars take a much closer look at this," he says. 46

Floyd Beachum, a graduate student at Bowling Green State University in Ohio, surveyed secondary [school] students to try to ascertain if there was a correlation between their behavior and the music they listened to. 47

"The more hyper-aggressive students tended to listen to more hardcore, gangster rap," he says. "Those who could identify with the violence, the drive-by shootings, the stereotypes about women—many times that would play out in their lives." 48

But Beachum, who teamed up with fellow Bowling Green graduate student Carlos McCray to conduct his research, says he isn't ready to draw any sweeping conclusions either. 49

"Those findings weren't across the board," he says, adding that he believes school systems can play a role in reversing any possible negative trends. 50

"If hip-hop and rap influence behavior and you bring all that to school, then the schools should create a very different environment and maybe we'll see more individuals go against the grain," he says. 51

Even undergraduates say they must admit that they see hip-hop's squalid influence on some of their peers. 52

"It upsets me when some young people complain that they can't get a job but when they go into that interview, they refuse to take off their do-rags, their big gold medallion and their baggy pants," says Kholiswa Laird, 18, a freshman at the University of Delaware. "But for some stupid reason, a lot of them feel like they're selling out if they wear proper clothes." 53

"That's just keepin it real," explains Davren Noble, 20, a junior at the University of Delaware. "Why should I have to change myself to get a job? If somebody wants to hire me but they don't like my braids, then either of two things will happen: They'll just have to get over it or I just won't get the job." 54

It's this kind of attitude that many in higher education see as the crux of the problem. 55

"We're not gonna serve them well in the university if we don't shake their thinking about how dress is going to influence job opportunities," says Central's Midgette. 56

Noble, from Maplewood, N.J., is a rapper. And he says that while he grew up in a posh suburb, he often raps about violence. 57

"I rap about positive stuff too, but as a Black person in America, it's hard to escape violence," he explains. "Mad Black people grew up in the ghetto and the music and our actions reflect that." 58

For sure, art has been known to imitate life. Hip-hop icon Sean "Puffy" Combs—who two years ago gave $750,000 to his alma mater, Howard University—is currently facing charges on his involvement 59 in a Manhattan nightclub shooting last December. Grammy-winning rapper Jay-Z also was connected with a night club dispute that ended with a record company executive being stabbed last year.

A BAD RAP?

A simple explanation for the boldness of much of rap's lyrics is that "artists have always pushed the limits," Kelley says. 60

But what's more, there is a politically conscious, stirring, enriching side of hip-hop that many of its fans say is often overlooked. 61

"Urban radio stations play the same songs every day," says Powell, a former reporter for *Vibe* magazine. "The media is ghettoizing hip-hop. They make it look passé." 62

Those often included in hip-hop's positive list are Lauryn Hill, Common, Mos Def, Dead Prez, Erykah Badu, Talib Kweli and other underground acts. Indeed, many of them have been active in encouraging young people to vote. Mos Def and other artists recently recorded a song in memory of Amadou Diallo, "Hip-Hop for Respect." 63

This is the side of hip-hop many young people say they'd like their faculty to recognize. This is also the side that some people say faculty must recognize. 64

"There are scholars—I've seen them do this before—who will make a disparaging remark about a whole genre of music, not knowing a doggone thing," NYU's Kelley says. "That's the same thing as saying, 'I've read one article on rational choice theory and it was so stupid, I dismissed the whole genre.'. . . People who are trained in their own fields would never do that with their own scholarship and yet they are willing to make these really sweeping statements." 65

"And they don't know. They don't have a critical understanding of the way the music industry operates or the way in which people engage music," he says. "But they are willing to draw a one-to-one correlation between the students' failure and music." 66

Some professors argue that another correlation should be made: "My most serious students are the die-hard hip-hop fans," says Dr. Ingrid Banks, assistant professor of Black Studies at Virginia Tech. "They are able to understand politics because they understand hip-hop." 67

Banks says that more of her colleagues would be wise to better understand the music and its culture. "You can't talk about Reagan's policies in the '80s without talking about hip-hop," says the 30-something scholar. "If you start where students are, they make these wonderful connections." 68

CURRICULAR CONNECTIONS

If the augmentation of hip-hop scholarship is any indication, academe just may be coming around to at least tolerating this formidable medium. 69

Courses on hip-hop, books, essays and other studied accounts of the genre are being generated by a pioneering cadre of scholars. And while many people see that as notable, there's not yet widespread belief that academe has completely warmed to the idea of hip-hop as scholarship. 70

Banks, who has taught "Race, Politics and Rap Music in Late Twentieth Century America" at the Blacksburg, Va., school, says she's experiencing less than a speedy response to getting her course included into the department's curriculum. 71

"I understand that it usually takes a while to get a course approved, but there have been courses in bio-history that were signed off on rather quickly," she says. 72

But if academe fails to find ways to connect with hip-hop and its culture, then it essentially will have failed an entire generation, many critics say. 73

"What's happening is that administrators and teachers are faced with a real crisis. And that crisis they can easily attach to the music," Kelley says. "It's the way they dress, the way they talk. The real crisis is their failure to educate; their failure to treat these students like human beings; their failure to come up with a new message to engage students." 74

"Part of the reason why there is such a generational gap is because so few educators make an effort to understand the times in which they live. You can't apply '60s and '70s methods to teaching in the new millennium. You can't apply a jazz aesthetic to hip-hop heads," says Powell, who lectures at 70 to 80 colleges and universities a year. "You have to meet the students where they are. That's the nature of education. That's pedagogy." 75

And while Wake Forest's Irvin says he would agree with that sentiment, he also sees a role that students must play. 76

"What I see as being the major challenge that these kids will deal with is the image of young, urban America," Irvin says. "Young people need to ask themselves, 'Who will control their identity?'" 77

"If they leave it up to the media to define who they are, they'll be devastated by these images," he says. "That's where hip-hop is killing us." 78

Examining the Text

1. What judgment does Dr. Thomas Earl Midgette of North Carolina Central University make about students he sees on campus? What judgment do you make about Dr. Midgette—that is, do you agree with his belief that hip-hop attitude and fashion might somehow contribute to academic and/or social failure?

2. The article alludes to "technology's omnipresence." Describe this concept and cite some concrete examples to support its validity. What effect does technology have on young people, according to this article, and how does Jamilah associate technology with the generation gap that exists within school systems?

3. Where did rap music originate, according to the author? How did it come about, and how did it evolve through subsequent decades? What form(s) does rap take today?

For Group Discussion

Jamilah asks the question concerning hip-hop styles and attitude, "Is this no different than the divide we've always seen between young people and their college and university elders?" Based upon your own experience as a member of the hip-hop generation (even if you're not a rabid fan of hip-hop), attempt to answer this question: Are the styles and behaviors of today the same as the bell-bottoms and Afros to which Dr. Midgette refers near the beginning of this article, or is there something more insidious in hip-hop culture and its effect on students?

Writing Suggestion

Write an essay in which you comment on Jamilah's statement, "There's a real problem when a marijuana-smoking ex-con named Snoop Doggy Dogg can pack a campus auditorium quicker than Black historian John Hope Franklin; when more students deify the late Tupac Shakur and his abrasive lyrics than those have ever read the great Martin Luther King Jr.'s 'I Have a Dream' Speech." As you formulate a thesis, decide first whether you agree with this statement by the author. Next, spend some time freewriting on the topic, letting your mind range over a wide range of points of contention or agreement. Having accomplished this activity, begin to cut and paste those supporting points into an order that has a coherent logical development, and then fill in that framework with supporting paragraphs that contain concrete evidence and examples from your experience, reading, and music listening.

Music and Contemporary Culture

The Money Note: Can the Record Business Be Saved?

JOHN SEABROOK

The music business has always embraced the latest recording technology. Over the decades, music has changed with the tide of technical innovation: from sheet music to mechanical cylinders to 78 rpm records to 8-track and cassette tapes and, most recently, to CDs and MP3s. In the following article originally published in the New Yorker *magazine, author John Seabrook explains how the recorded music business moved from pressing long-playing records to issuing music on compact discs, the latter representing a technology that held promise of more resilience than easily scratched vinyl records and reduced production costs.*

However, while the medium on which music is recorded has changed over the years, the process of selecting and marketing talent has altered little since World War II. According to Seabrook, "a few guys still determine the fate of many." By "the few," he means the artist and repertoire (A&R) men celebrated as heroes by recording-industry insiders for recognizing and promoting the performers who go on to become stars. Yet, the success rate of the A&R specialists is no greater than ten percent: for every one success, there are nine failures, a rate that is less successful than a computer program developed by scientists in Barcelona to determine pop music successes. Although A&R men like the one profiled in Seabrook's article still retain a high importance in the music industry, their ability to help propel future stars to huge record sales has been dented by the ability of consumers to copy CDs for sharing via the Internet. Seabrook says that young people in particular no longer think of purchasing music when it can be copied for free from the Internet.

As you read, *pay special attention to ways in which the author's descriptive language conveys the visceral experiences involved in listening to music, while at the same time informing the reader about popular music history and economic trends.*

When he was a teen-ager, growing up in New York City in the nineteen-seventies, Jason Flom wrote songs, sang, and played guitar for two rock bands, which he named Relative Pleasure and Selective Service. But Flom's dreams of rock stardom ended around the time he 1 started working at Atlantic Records, in 1979, when he was nineteen, and began redirecting his energies into making other people stars. Now forty-two, he is one of the most successful record men of the past twenty years, scoring hits in genres as varied as heavy metal (Twisted Sister), Celtic pop (the Corrs), and rock (Matchbox 20, Sugar Ray). Altogether, his artists have sold more than a hundred million CDs.

In an era when many of the top-selling acts have "flava"—the edgy sound of hip-hop artists and R&B singers and rap-metal groups, who emerge from niches and achieve broad recognition—Flom has continued to have success with pop music, that sweet, beguiling, never-too-challenging sound which has been a record industry staple from Bing Crosby to Doris Day to Britney Spears. Flom's specialty is delivering "monsters"—records that sell millions of copies and become rainmakers for everyone else in the record business, because they bring fans into the music stores. Successful record men are commonly said to have "ears," but prospecting for monsters requires eyes for star quality as well as a nose for the next trend. You have to be able to go to thousands of sweaty night clubs, and sit through a dozen office auditions each week, and somehow not become so jaded that you fail to recognize a superstar when you encounter one. Like the night in 1981 when Clive Davis, then the head of Arista Records, happened to go to a New York supper club and hear a nineteen-year-old gospel singer who was Dionne Warwick's cousin—Whitney Houston. Or the day when Bruce Lundvall, the head of Blue Note Records, had a routine office audition from a singer recommended by an employee in the accounting department—Norah Jones. Or the time in 1997 when Flom met Kid Rock, then an obscure m.c. who had made a couple of records that "stiffed" (sold poorly), in the basement of a Detroit disco at two-thirty in the morning. It is necessary to recognize that ineffable quality a great pop star communicates (Flom calls it "the thing"), but it isn't always necessary to love the way the music sounds. Chris Blackwell, who founded Island Records, told me that he didn't especially like listening to U2 when he first heard them play, in the early nineteen-eighties, but "I could see that they had something," and so he signed them to his label. 2

Why should the latent capacity for superstardom in pop, which is perhaps the most egalitarian of art forms, be obvious to only a gifted few like Jason Flom—those great A&R (artist-and-repertoire) men whom the record industry celebrates as its heroes? (And they are invariably male.) After all, even the great record men are wrong much more often than they are right about the acts they sign (nine misses for each hit is said to be the industry standard). One wonders how much of the art of hit-making is just dumb luck. Scientists in Barcelona say they have created a computer-based "Hit Song Science" that picks hits 3 much more efficiently than a human can. There's even a Web site, hitsongscience.com, where aspiring pop stars can test themselves on a hit-o-meter.

American Idol, the popular *Star Search*–style Fox TV show, in which the viewers pick their own stars by voting over the telephone, is considered a "reality show," but the democratic process is not the way stars are actually discovered. In the record business, a few guys still determine the fate of many. 4

One day last October, I was sitting with Flom in his office at Atlantic, which is part of the Warner Music Group, at Sixth Avenue and Fifty-first Street, when he played me a song by a new artist he had recently signed to his label, Lava Records. (Flom began the label as a joint venture with Atlantic, and then sold his share to the company two years ago, for a reported fifty million dollars.) Lava has a roster of twenty-three artists, and Flom can afford to take "a big bet," as he puts it, on two or three new artists a year. The artist's name was Cherie, he explained, and she was a young French singer whose specialty was the sweeping pop ballad. She was a "belter," as they say in the business—one of those singers who don't hold back. 5

Flom often has a startled expression in his eyes, as if he were waiting for something to go wrong—a look of disappointed optimism, the feeling that anyone who makes a career out of betting on talent must routinely suffer. But today he looked positively grim as he talked about the record business. Sales of recorded music in the United States have dropped by more than a hundred million units in the past two years, falling well below seven hundred million. The eighteen-year-old Canadian singer Avril Lavigne is the idol of ten-year-old girls across the country, but her debut album, "Let's Go," sold far fewer records in its first six months (four million) than did Alanis Morissette's debut album, "Jagged Little Pill" (seven million), which was released in 1995. Around the globe, the record business is sixteen per cent smaller than it was in 2000. Record labels blame the fans, for lacking the long-term loyalty to pop acts which record buyers used to have, and for engaging in wholesale "piracy" of music, either by copying CDs or by downloading music illegally from the Internet. "There is no precedent for what's happening now in the music business," Flom said. "What would happen if groceries suddenly became free, or hotels—do you think those businesses would survive?" 6

However, Flom brightened at the prospect of playing Cherie's demo CD. "I guess you'd call her a diva," he said. "She's seventeen, and she's classically trained, but she sings these pop ballads—and she is phenomenal." He was excitedly hunting for the demo amid the stacks of disks that cover every surface in his office. "I honestly believe she is one of the most important artists I've ever signed." Seeing the skeptical 7 look on my face—a French pop star?—Flom quickly said, "She's also Jewish, and there aren't too many of them left in France, if you know what I mean, so it's a little different from being just French. And," he added, "she doesn't sound French when she sings."

8 Flom lacks the star quality that he divines in other people. He is neither tall nor physically imposing, and he seems more like a laid-back lawyer than like a record man (his father is Joseph Flom, a patriarch of the New York law firm Skadden, Arps, Slate, Meagher & Flom). He is a friend of Bill Clinton's, and a generous supporter of the American Civil Liberties Union. He is not wild and crazy, although his office, like the offices of most record executives, is full of photographs of him posing with wild and crazy guys such as Kid Rock, who usually has his middle finger extended in the picture. During the nineteen-eighties, Flom tried living like a rock star, but when he was twenty-eight he checked into the Hazelden clinic, in Minnesota, for thirty days of rehab, and he hasn't had a drink or a line since. Now he lives with his wife and their two kids on the Upper West Side.

9 He had never heard Cherie sing before she and her manager, Jeff Haddad, turned up in his office the previous February, on Valentine's Day, for an audition. Haddad had given Flom his pitch, which, Haddad told me later, included this question: "There are maybe twenty people in the world who can deliver a song the way Faith Hill sings the Diane Warren song that is the theme in the movie 'Pearl Harbor,' and out of those people how many can do it in four different languages?" Then Cherie performed two songs, one in French and the other in English; her only accompaniment was the noisy heating system in Flom's office. On the basis of that half-hour meeting, and Flom's gut feeling that the girl, whose real name is Cindy Almouzni, had that special quality which can move a massive amount of product, Flom signed her to a million-dollar, five-album contract, and was prepared to do everything that a major label like Warner can do to make an artist a big star—"Whatever it takes to put her over," Flom told me. He declined to say how much that would cost, but David Foster, another top hitmaker with Warner Music, told me, "It's basically a five-million-dollar bet. It might cost only five hundred thousand dollars to make the record, but it's so expensive to promote it. If you get on the *Today* show, you've got to get a band together, fly everyone in and put them up, and by the time you're done it has cost you fifty thousand dollars."

10 Last year, the *Wall Street Journal* ran a story about an unknown eighteen-year-old Irish singer named Carly Hennessy, whose debut CD, from Universal, was the subject of a $2.2-million marketing campaign yet wound up selling only three hundred and seventy-eight copies in its first three months. "If that happens to me," Flom said, "a lot of people are going to look at me funny." For the artist, the stakes were

higher. "This is her shot. It's very rare for an artist to get a buildup like this and then, if things don't go well, come back from it and reinvent herself."

The song Flom played for me that day in his office, "My Way 11
Back Home," is a love ballad written for Cherie by the Canadian singer-songwriter Corey Hart, who has also composed songs for Celine Dion. The lyrics are solidly within the convention of self-help, which is one of the main tropes of the popular love ballad. The singer is finding her way through the darkness, and, in spite of winter storms, bitter cold, and loneliness, manages to reach high and touch the sky, and to find . . . My Way Back Home. It was a surprising choice from the man who gave the world Twisted Sister's "We're Not Gonna Take It," although perhaps this is Flom's genius—understanding how a conventional love ballad and a heavy-metal anthem stimulate the same adult-contemporary emotions. As Doug Morris, the head of Universal Music Group, who was Flom's mentor when Morris ran Atlantic, said to me, "The basic thing is you've got a singer, and you've got a song, and you put them together and it makes people feel good. And if they feel good enough they buy it! That's what it's all about! And it's a beautiful thing when you see it happen—the singer up there singing his song and all the fans are screaming for him. It makes me wanna cry, when I see it."

And Cherie's voice was remarkably appealing. She had the 12
vocal power of Whitney Houston and the feel-good-around-the-edges shimmer of Shania Twain. But she wasn't a screamer; she could sustain the note at the end of a phrase without resorting to vibrato. She hit the high notes effortlessly, could soar from tragedy to triumph in a single breath, and seemed to inhabit the lyrics with complete sincerity. As the chorus rolled around for the second time, I sensed that the song was building toward an emotional climax that people in the record business sometimes refer to as "the money note"—that moment on the record which seems to have an almost involuntary effect on your insides. (According to researchers at Dartmouth who recently studied the brains of people listening to music, the brain responds physiologically to dramatic swoops in range and pitch.) The money note is the moment in Whitney Houston's version of the Dolly Parton song "I Will Always Love You" at the beginning of the third rendition of the chorus: pause, drum beat, and then "Iiiiiieeeeeeiiieeii will always love you." It is the moment in the Celine Dion song from *Titanic,* "My Heart Will Go On": the key change that begins the third verse, a note you can hear a hundred times and it still brings you up short in the supermarket and transports you from the price of milk to a world of grand romantic gesture—"You're here/There's nuthing I fear."

David Foster, the producer of "I Will Always Love You," who is 13
among the contemporary masters of the pop ballad (he has written

and produced songs for Natalie Cole and Toni Braxton, among others), says that he came up with the expression during a session with Barbra Streisand. "Barbra had hit this high note, and she wanted to know how it sounded, because although you'd think Barbra was real confident she's not," he told me. "And I said, 'That sounds like money!'" He added, "And I don't mean money in the crass sense of that will make a lot of money, although that's certainly part of it. I mean expensive. It sounds expensive."

Cherie hit the money note with full force—"When I cry I'm weak/I'm learning to fly." As her voice went up on "fly," an electric guitar came floating up with it, and the tone was so pure that a chill spread over my shoulders, prickling the skin. Flom pumped his fist when the moment hit, lifted his leg a little, and grimaced. 14

When the song ended, he asked me what I thought, and I admitted that I had found the money note shattering. But would it produce the reaction Flom was looking for—the effect he had mimed for me earlier, by taking an imaginary wallet from his back pocket, fingering an imaginary bill, and slapping it down on an imaginary counter? What was to stop people from taking the money notes for free? 15

Flom pointed out that Cherie's music, like that of Norah Jones, should appeal to older people, who are less likely to download music from the Internet. "But who knows?" he said. "It's difficult to compete with free. All I know is what I know—if the star is big enough, people will buy the album, because it's like a piece of the artist. But if the star doesn't have that kind of irresistible appeal then people just say, 'What the heck, I'll download the good songs.' So we just have to figure out how to make her a big star." 16

Five global music companies control more than eighty-five per cent of the record business. (The remaining fifteen per cent is divided among some ten thousand independent labels.) Universal Music Group, which is owned by Vivendi Universal, is the dominant player among the majors; then comes the Warner Music Group, a division of AOL Time Warner; Sony Music Entertainment; the Bertelsmann Music Group (BMG); and the EMI Group. From the early seventies to the mid-nineties, Warner was the leading company in the record industry, but by the end of 2002, with a sixteen-per-cent share of the domestic market, the company had fallen behind Universal, which had a twenty-nine-per-cent share. 17

The story of Warner Music is a parable for the music industry—a tale of corporate dyssynergy. Over the course of the rock era, which began almost fifty years ago, virtually all the original record companies have been bought by larger media corporations. The industry has changed from an art-house business run by the founders of the labels—men with ears, like Ahmet Ertegun, a founder 18 of Atlantic; Chris Blackwell, of Island Records; and Jerry Moss, the co-founder, with Herb Alpert, of A&M Records—into a corporate enterprise run by managers, who in addition to making records have to worry about quarterly earnings and timely results.

Atlantic Records was co-founded in 1947 by the Turkish-born 19
Ertegun, with money borrowed from the family dentist. He began by recording artists like Ray Charles and the New Orleans juke-joint bluesman Professor Longhair. In the nineteen-fifties, Ertegun, working with his partners—his brother Nesuhi and Jerry Wexler, a writer for *Billboard*—had a string of hit records with singers like Ruth Brown and Big Joe Turner, before the dominant power in the music business, CBS Records (now owned by Sony), discovered the commercial possibility of black R&B music. In the mid-sixties, Atlantic expanded into pop (Bobby Darin, Sonny and Cher) and, later, into rock (Buffalo Springfield). In 1968, Ertegun sold the label to Warner-Seven Arts, and the following year Steve Ross's Kinney National bought that company, creating Warner Communications. During the nineteen-seventies, the collection of Warner labels assembled by Ross, and run by the legendary record man Mo Ostin (including Atlantic, Warner Bros., Reprise, Elektra, and Asylum), eclipsed those of CBS, and Warner became the leader of the record industry. Its acts included the Grateful Dead; Crosby, Stills, Nash & Young; the Eagles; Fleetwood Mac; and the Doobie Brothers. "Steve Ross never got involved in anything we did," Ertegun, who continued to run Atlantic after its sale, told me. "He was just happy to see the results." But as Warner Communications grew—it merged with Time, in 1990, and AOL, in 2001—the music business faltered. Ross, who might have been able to run the labels effectively, died in 1992, and Gerald Levin took over.

The business rationale behind the record companies' role in these 20
huge conglomerations was that their corporate owners would use the cash generated by monster hits to pay for other parts of their operations, and the companies would be able to survive the stiffs, thanks to their corporate backing. Corporate ownership also gave record men like Ertegun the financial resources to compete for expensive established acts, like the Rolling Stones, whom he signed in the nineteen-seventies. However, it gradually became apparent that the corporate culture might not provide the best environment for nurturing new talent. Chris Blackwell, who sold Island to PolyGram in 1989 (he now has another independent label, Palm Pictures), told me, "I don't think the music business lends itself very well to being a Wall Street business. You're always working with individuals, with creative people, and the people you are trying to reach, by and large, don't view music as a commodity but as a relationship with a band. It takes time to expand that relationship, but most people who work for the corporations have

three-year contracts, some five, and most of them are expected to produce. What an artist really needs is a champion, not a numbers guy who in another year is going to leave."

Moreover, the kind of controversy that often helps sell records is not good for the corporate image. In the mid-nineties, Warner was well positioned to control the exploding rap market, through its half ownership of Interscope, a label that had been developed by the producer Jimmy Iovine and had recently signed Tupac Shakur. Interscope was allied with Death Row Records, the label run by Dr. Dre and Marion (Suge) Knight, which recorded seminal gangsta-rap acts like Snoop Doggy Dogg. But bad publicity from these acts was hurting Time Warner's other businesses and straining the political connections that the corporation needed in Washington. In 1995, Levin made the decision to sell the company's half share of Interscope, and it eventually became part of Universal. Iovine went on to amass a remarkable streak of hits, including records by Eminem and the rapper 50 Cent. Warner missed out on the rap boom almost entirely. 21

In the past three years, under the leadership of Roger Ames, a suave, cigarette-smoking, fifty-two-year-old Trinidadian, who took over the Warner Music Group in 1999, the company has had major hits with Linkin Park, Enya, and Faith Hill. Ames has also cut costs to improve profits. However, Warner is fourth among the majors in sales of new music and did not have a record on the list of Top Ten-selling albums in 2002: 22

1. "The Eminem Show"/Eminem, 7.6 million (Interscope).
2. "Nellyville"/Nelly, 4.9 million (Universal).
3. "Let's Go"/Avril Lavigne, 4.1 million (Arista, a BMG label).
4. "Home"/Dixie Chicks, 3.7 million (Sony).
5. "8 Mile"/Soundtrack, 3.5 million (Interscope).
6. "Missundaztood"/Pink, 3.1 million (Arista).
7. "Ashanti"/Ashanti, 3.09 million (Murder Inc., Universal).
8. "Drive"/Alan Jackson, 3.05 million (Arista Nashville).
9. "Up"/Shania Twain, 2.9 million (Universal).
10. "O Brother, Where Art Thou?"/Soundtrack, 2.7 million (Universal).

But is a winner-take-all strategy the best way to run a record company—for any of the majors? Hit-making is an imprecise method of doing business. Of thirty thousand CDs that the industry released last year in the United States, only four hundred and four sold more than a hundred thousand copies, while twenty-five thousand releases sold fewer than a thousand copies apiece. No one seems to be able to predict which those four hundred and four big sellers will be. 23

The chairman of BMG, Rolf Schmidt-Holtz, told *Billboard* in December, "We need reliable calculations of returns that are not based solely on hits because the way people get music doesn't go with hits anymore." He added, "We have to get rid of the lottery mentality."

I asked Flom whether he thought hits might become less important to the record business. "That ain't gonna happen," he said. "If anything, hits can be more important than ever, because you can make stars on a global scale now. If the star is big enough, people will want to buy the CD." When I repeated what Schmidt-Holtz had said, Flom looked momentarily stunned. Then he said, "Something must be getting lost in the translation there, because the day we stop seeing hits is the day people stop buying records." 24

When Cindy Almouzni was eight, in 1992, the video of the Whitney Houston song "I Will Always Love You" came out, accompanied by shots of the singer playing opposite Kevin Costner in the film *The Bodyguard*. Cindy was the youngest of three children in a religious household in Marseilles. Her parents are Sephardic Jews from North Africa. As a child, her father fled during the Algerian war, and met his wife years later in France. When Cindy's mother was too busy to watch her, she would put her in front of music videos on TV. Cindy learned "I Will Always Love You," exactly the way Whitney sings it—the breathing, the key change in the third chorus—and she sang it over and over again. At first, she sang the song to herself, then to her family, and then in school. The summer that she was nine, she sang "I Will Always Love You" for several hundred people at a campground where the Almouznis went during August. 25

Her parents sent her to singing school, and after that she received private lessons. She learned the songs of Jacques Brel and Edith Piaf, but she also continued to sing "I Will Always Love You." At fourteen, she won a local karaoke contest and went to Paris for a national competition. There, she met a record producer, who invited her to his studio to record a song he had written called "I Don't Want Nobody (Telling Me What to Do)." The vocals were remixed, and the song became a dance track, which wound up in the hands of Jeff Haddad, a languid, affable Californian. "I heard her sing, and she blew me away, and I thought, Let's do what we can to make this happen," Haddad told me. He flew to France to meet her parents, and they agreed to let him try to make their daughter a star. 26

Haddad is a manager, but, like many other people in the music industry—producers, songwriters, engineers, lawyers—he functions as a filter between undiscovered talent and a major-label deal. He and Dave Moss, the owner of a small record label, put out a single of Cindy's dance song, and it became an international hit for Cherie Amore, as they decided to call her, back in 2000, when there was a 27 vogue for French house music. On the strength of that success, Haddad commissioned a British songwriter and producer named Paul Moessl to create a pop ballad for Cherie. Moessl wrote a song called "Older" ("My love is older than my years/It's wiser than your fears"). There was considerable interest in the demo, and Haddad scheduled a week of office auditions in L.A. and a week in New York, with people like Tommy Mottola, who was then the head of Sony Music. It was cold in New York, and people were coughing and sneezing while Cindy sang. Jason Flom was the last record guy they saw. "Within thirty seconds of hearing her sing," he said, "I just knew." In Cherie, Flom encountered a singer whose artistic sensibility was derived from the kind of commercial music that record men like Flom produce—her flava was pop. He signed her within a week.

The traditional course in star-making is to begin with a local fan base and gradually grow to global renown. Flom was proposing to market Cherie the other way around—she would appear on the scene as a "worldwide artist," with campaigns in France, Italy, England, and Spain, as well as in the United States. Although the music industry more or less invented the hit, it has struggled to make songs and artists into the kind of global properties that movies have become. (The recent film *X2* opened simultaneously in ninety-five countries.) Music is supposed to be the universal language, but pop depends on regional associations, and on language, which is why the charts in France and Spain and Germany are so different from the pop charts in the United States. 28

Last summer, Flom presented his future star at the Warner Music Group summit meeting, held in Barcelona and attended by affiliates from more than a hundred and thirty countries. ("There were some affiliates from countries I didn't even know they had records in," Flom said.) Cherie was a hit, and Flom and Haddad decided that she should sing several of the tracks on her debut album in Spanish and French, as well as in English. They solicited songs from successful pop songwriters, like Kara Dioguardi and Paul Barry, and they hired producers who had scored hits in European and South American countries to work on possible singles for those countries. 29

Flom told me that in some ways Cherie's youth and obscurity were advantages in making her into a worldwide sensation. Stars often balk at travelling to other countries to perform, and don't want to keep up the relentless schedule of public appearances which is necessary to sustain a hit record. "The nice thing about Cherie is she's portable," Flom said. "She'll go places and do stuff if we think she should do it." 30

But, if Cherie truly is an extraordinary artist, why not build her career more slowly? "In an era like this," Flom said, "when the audience has more distractions than ever, you have to reach critical mass to put an artist over. And the outlets you need to do that, the Teen 31

Peoples and whatever, are not going to take you seriously unless they know you are putting a major push behind it."

Of course, it was possible that Flom was wrong about Cherie's talent. Perhaps she wasn't a great artist; maybe she was merely a great karaoke singer, and the audience would be able to tell the difference. On the other hand, maybe the current pop scene is a "karaoke world"—the phrase that the pop impresario Malcolm McLaren uses to describe contemporary pop culture—in which all the great artistic statements have already been made, and the newer artists are merely doing karaoke versions of their predecessors. 32

In November, I attended a marketing meeting in Flom's spacious corner office to draw up an outline for launching Cherie's career, or, as they say in the business, "blowing her up." Seven Lava staff members were in attendance: Richard Bates, creative; Nikki Hirsch and Lee Trink, marketing; Aaron Simon, product management; Doug Cohen, video promotion; Janet Stampler, new media; and Lisbeth Cassaday, publicity. Before the meeting started, Aaron Simon told the others about the experience of having Cherie sing for him, in the office. "I was, like, 'Do you want me to close the door?'" he reported. "And she was, like, 'No, it's cool.' And she just did it right there. And it was, like—chills." 33

Flom began by saying that they hoped to take the first single, probably a mid- to up-tempo dance number, to American radio in June, 2003. When record guys hear fans complaining that pop music has become too commercial, they are often quick to blame radio. Radio doesn't play as much new music as it used to, they argue, and the music that is played has to fit into a certain format, which is based on research about what people like to listen to—or, at least, will tolerate. Many stations also carry between fifteen and twenty minutes of commercials an hour. ("If anyone said we were in the radio business, it wouldn't be someone from our company," Lowry Mays, the founder and CEO of Clear Channel, which is the country's largest radio-station operator, with some hundred million listeners nationwide, told *Fortune* in March. "We're not in the business of providing well-researched music. We're simply in the business of selling our customers products.") 34

Cherie's music fits almost perfectly into the adult-contemporary format, radio's largest; Flom thought that Cherie was tailor-made for New York's WLTW 106.7 Lite-FM, the city's most popular music radio station, which is owned by Clear Channel. Jim Ryan, a programming executive there, told me that when Flom played "My Way Back Home" for him, along with two other songs, during a car ride home from an industry event, he said, "Jason, I want to quit my job at Clear Channel and sign up on the Cherie bandwagon." 35

With luck, Flom went on, Cherie's first single would be a hit, and would cross over from the light-FM stations to the Top Forty stations. At that point, Lava would release the second single, a ballad. Flom was also looking at other ways to promote Cherie. One was a Time Warner DVD, a Batman movie called *Batman: Mystery of the Batwoman*; Cherie was being animated in the film as a sexy singer whom Batman encounters in a late-night *boite*, and who sings a song called "Betcha Neva" (a song that would be on Cherie's album). He added that there had been tremendous interest in Cherie from "the soundtrack community," especially from makers of animated films, and reminded everyone that Celine Dion's big break came with the theme song from the Disney movie *Beauty and the Beast*. "I'm not saying she's another Celine, but there's a road map there." 36

The group then discussed the possibility of getting Cherie a product-endorsement deal with a company like Revlon. As the expense of blowing up an artist increases, and the prospective payoff in record sales becomes ever more in doubt, the industry is shifting the cost of promoting artists onto advertisers. Sting's 1999 album, "Brand New Day," an Interscope release, sold sluggishly until the artist was featured in a Jaguar commercial singing music from the album—and then sales took off. 37

The staff addressed the subject of "imaging" Cherie—what kind of look the artist should affect. Cherie's personal style was a work in progress. She was not a dressy kind of girl: she was partial to jeans. Richard Bates, the art director, said that in examining the images of current pop stars he had noticed that there was a middle ground between Britney Spears and Shania Twain, which no one was trying to fill. "The older singers are very polished and classy, and then it jumps down to young and trashy—which we don't want her to be," he said. The danger was that in trying to strike a balance between these extremes you might wind up with nothing at all. In photos from Cherie's first shoot, the artist, dressed in a sleeveless jersey and neat jeans, well scrubbed, her long hair pushed back from her face, looked as if she were ready for a college interview. 38

Lee Trink talked about making Cherie a keyword on AOL Time Warner's Internet service, and launching a "Who Is Cherie?" instant-messaging campaign. 39

The staff was undecided on the use of what Lisbeth Cassaday referred as "the 'd' word." Cassaday thought it was best not to call Cherie a diva; Flom wasn't so sure. "I mean, she is a diva, right?" he said. It was a conundrum. Operatic divas inhabit classic dramatic roles like Tosca and *Madame Butterfly*, but pop divas, one way or another, have to play themselves, which may be why pop divas wear out faster than operatic divas. The constant blowing up they require eventually causes them to explode. 40

Once the album went platinum—hit a million in sales—Flom 41
said, they would go to the media with the story of Cherie's life. Flom reminded everyone that the artist was Jewish. He had heard that her synagogue in Marseilles was burned recently, and, "while this should obviously be treated as a very sensitive subject, we could go to Oprah and pitch her as an artist who has suffered violence in her life as a result of her religion."

Everyone nodded. 42

"You know. It's a story line." 43

In 1983, the president of PolyGram, Jan Timmer, introduced what 44
he hoped would become the new platform for the sale of recorded music—the compact disk—at a recording-industry convention in Miami. Technically, CDs were a big advance over vinyl and tape. On a CD, music takes the form of digital strings of ones and zeros, which are encoded on specially treated plastic disks. If the disk is properly cared for, there is no "fidelity degradation"—none of those hisses and pops that vinyl develops over time. The high-tech allure of the CD would allow the industry to raise the cost of an album from $8.98 to $15.98 (even though CDs were soon cheaper to manufacture than vinyl records), and the record companies would get a larger share of money, because the industry would persuade artists not to raise royalty rates, arguing that the extra money was needed to market the new format to customers.

Timmer's group was booed by record men in the audience that 45
day. This may have been because the co-inventors of the CD—Philips, which was a corporate partner of PolyGram, and Sony—wanted a patent royalty on the disks. The booing, however, also reflected the music industry's long history of technophobia. A hundred years ago, music publishers were trying to sue player-piano makers out of existence, fearing that no one would ever buy sheet music again. In the nineteen-twenties, the music industry sued radio broadcasters for copyright infringement. Although history has repeatedly shown that new technologies inevitably bring opportunities and create new markets, the industry's attitude toward new technology remains hostile. (Technophobia is also rampant in the film industry: in 1992, when movie studios were suing Sony over the Betamax, claiming that it was a threat to the film business, Jack Valenti, the president of the Motion Picture Association of America, said, "The VCR is to the American film producer and the American public as the Boston Strangler is to a woman alone." Fortunately for the movie industry, it lost the Betamax case: today, videos and DVDs account for more than fifty per cent of a studio's revenues.)

The CD, of course, turned out to be extremely popular with record 46
buyers. Many fans who already owned music on vinyl dutifully replaced their records with CDs. By 1986, CD sales had climbed to a hundred mil-

lion worldwide, and by the early nineties hit albums on CD were selling in greater numbers than hit albums on vinyl had sold. In 1999, in what now looks like hubris, the industry's trade organization, the Recording Industry Association of America (RIAA), created a super-platinum prize with which to honor the new megahits—the Diamond Award, bestowed on records that sell more than ten million copies. (Flom has two Diamond Awards, for Matchbox 20's "Yourself or Someone Like You" and for Kid Rock's "Devil Without a Cause.") CDs also turned out to be a brilliant way of repackaging a label's "catalogue"—all the recordings that were no longer in production on vinyl. CDs spawned a generation of record executives whose skill was in putting together compilations of existing music, rather than in discovering new artists. Through the stock market crash of 1987 and the recession of the early nineties, the CD market grew steadily, until sales abruptly declined in 2001, by six per cent, and then dropped nine per cent in 2002.

Lyor Cohen, the head of Island Def Jam, which is owned by Universal, thinks that the record industry would have been better off without the CD. "The CD kept the whole business on artificial life support," he told me. Without it, the old record industry would have died in the early eighties, and a new, more modern industry would have replaced it. But the CD preserved the status quo. "The record business became a commodity business, not a content-and-creation business," Cohen said. He rubbed his fingertips together. "What was lost was secchie—it means 'touch.'" 47

Unlike Jason Flom, who has always worked at a record label, Cohen got his start as an artist's representative; he co-managed the Beastie Boys and Public Enemy. Now forty-three, he is tall and speaks with a slight Israeli accent. On the morning I visited Cohen in his office, in Manhattan, he was dressed in jeans and an expensive-looking dress shirt and was puffing on a cigar. He propped his size-13 New Balance sneakers up on his desk as he spoke. 48

"The A&R guys at the record companies had gotten a little older and didn't feel like standing in the back of some filthy hole to listen to a new band," he said. "So, instead, they started repackaging stuff from when they were younger. We got the theme album—'Summer of Love,' 'Splendor in the Grass,' whatever—and by the end of the eighties most of the industry's profits were in catalogue." 49

Finally, CDs made piracy possible, by making music much easier to copy. Had the platform never shifted from vinyl, the piracy problem wouldn't be nearly so bad. The zeal with which the labels flogged their catalogues on CD insured that a large amount of previously recorded music was rendered into digital form—almost none of it protected from copying. "None of us wondered what the digitizing of sound waves would mean to our business," Stan Cornyn, a longtime Warner 50 marketing man, wrote in *Exploding*, a recent history of Warner Music. "How fidelity degradation, which had held back some from making free tape copies, would no longer be a factor once sound waves got turned into digits. . . . Digital sound, being so casually accepted into our world, was free to cause an epidemic. It would make data copying easy, clean, free, and something that felt about as immoral as killing an ant."

During the past decade, virtually every piece of popular music 51
ever recorded on CD has been "ripped," converted into a compressed digital file known as an MP3 (short for Moving Picture Experts Group Layer Three), and made available online, where anyone with a computer can get it. Once a song is converted into an MP3, it can be copied millions of times without any fidelity degradation. New music is ripped from CDs and uploaded as soon as the records come out (often before they come out, by studio technicians or by music journalists who receive advance copies). Music fans, who used to hear a song they liked on the radio, go to the record store, and buy the album, now hear a song they like on the radio, go to the Internet, and help themselves to it for free. Teen-agers who were once the labels' best customers are now their worst enemies. "Younger fans, at whom pop music is aimed, tend to be comfortable with computers, which is why downloading hurts the best-selling hits more than other kinds of music," I was told by Hilary Rosen, the departing CEO of the RIAA. "As a result, records that might have sold eight million copies now sell five. Unfortunately, these blockbuster sales pay for the development of new artists—Kid Rock pays for all the others." In 2002, the industry shipped 33.5 million copies of the year's ten best-selling albums, barely half the number it shipped in 2000.

Whether or not the record business figures out how to make 52
money from MP3s, the format is here to stay. Just as CDs replaced vinyl, so will MP3s replace CDs. But, whereas CDs made the record business extraordinarily lucrative, MP3s are making it extraordinarily painful—a gigantic karmic correction that may lead to a bigger music business one day, although not before things get worse. Daniel Strickland, a twenty-three-year-old student at the University of Virginia, told me recently, "Maybe it's because I'm in college and I have an eighteen-year-old sister and a ten-year-old brother, but, let me tell you, nobody I know buys CDs anymore. My sister—she just gets on her computer, and she knows only two things, file sharing and instant messaging. She and friends go online, and one instant-messages the other, and says, 'Oh, there's this cool song I just found,' and they go and download it, play it, and instant-message back about it. My brother has never even seen a CD—except for the ones my sister burns."

Napster, the first widely used music-sharing software, appeared 53
in 1999. It was based on a program developed by a nineteen-year-old

college student named Shawn Fanning. Later that year, the RIAA charged Napster with copyright infringement, and, after a hearing in San Francisco, a California federal judge ruled against Napster and eventually closed the service down. But that action did almost nothing to diminish the availability of free music online; people simply began to use other file-sharing programs, like KaZaA, Morpheus, Grokster, and LimeWire. Unlike Napster, these programs, which operate on what are known as P2P (peer-to-peer) computer networks, have no central computer that keeps an index of all the files on the system. Instead, any computer using one of these programs can search and share files with any other computer using the same software. The number of people downloading music files over P2P networks today is thought to be many times greater than the number of people who used Napster at its height; by some estimates, fifty million Americans have downloaded music illegally.

The music industry has launched alternatives to the P2P 54 networks—legal, online music services like Emusic, Pressplay, and Rhapsody. But so far these have failed to attract many fans, partly because they require users to pay monthly subscription fees, rather than selling individual songs and albums. Sony and Universal recently sold Pressplay to Roxio, a software company, which is expected to give its service a new, sexier-sounding name—Napster. Apple's iTunes Music Store, which was launched in April, selling downloadable songs for ninety-nine cents and albums for ten dollars, is the best-designed and best-stocked of the legal services, and the company sold three million songs in the first month of operation. Although sales have fallen sharply, other companies, including Microsoft, are reportedly planning similar services. Meanwhile, the labels are quietly beginning to harvest the marketing data on songs and artists that the illegal networks offer. Warner Music Group worked with Big Champagne, a company that mines data from the P2P networks, but Big Champagne's CEO, Eric Garland, isn't allowed to talk about it. "We are still very much the mistress," he told me.

In 2001, the RIAA joined the film industry in bringing a 55 copyright-infringement suit against some of the larger P2P networks, including Morpheus and Grokster. But suing peer-to-peer networks isn't as easy as suing Napster; for one thing, there's no one to sue. (KaZaA is based on software that was commissioned by two Scandinavian businessmen. The programmers are Estonian. The right to license the program was acquired by Sharman Networks, an Australian company that has no direct employees and is incorporated in the Pacific island nation of Vanuatu.) Also, P2P networks offer a wide range of legitimate applications for research and businesses. In April, a federal judge in Los Angeles ruled that, because Morpheus and

Grokster can be used for both legal and illegal purposes, the companies that distribute the software can't be sued for copyright infringement.

Last fall, several Microsoft programmers released a study of some 56
of the social implications of P2P. They foresaw the networks converging into what the authors called "the Darknet"—a vast, illegal, anarchic economy of shared music, TV programs, movies, software, games, and pornography which would come to rival the legitimate entertainment industry. Unless the government does something about P2P, our entertainment industry could one day resemble China's, where piracy is endemic. With no means of support, many artists would be forced to stop working, and a cultural dark age would ensue. The movie industry, which is a bigger and more politically powerful force than the record business, has yet to see its profits eroded by illegal downloading, but it may be only a matter of waiting until DVD burners become the standard item in PCs that CD burners are now. Unlike the music industry, the film industry is incorporating copy protection into its digital recordings, but the Darknet is full of bright hackers determined to prove their mettle by breaking through the most robust encryption.

In the face of the recent legal setbacks in the RIAA's campaign 57
against the P2P networks, the organization's war on piracy has shifted toward the people who steal music. In April, the RIAA named four university undergraduates in a multimillion-dollar claim for copyright infringement, forcing them to pay between twelve thousand and seventeen thousand dollars each in fines. The day before the RIAA lost in the Grokster case, it won an important victory in a legal action against Verizon, when a federal judge in New York upheld a ruling that Verizon was required, under the 1998 Digital Millennium Copyright Act, to turn over to the RIAA the names of customers whom the record industry suspected of illegally sharing music files. (Verizon, which is in the business of selling broadband Internet connectivity, does not want to discourage potential customers, even if downloading music illegally is what they want broadband for.) Last week, the RIAA announced that it would begin preparing hundreds of lawsuits against individuals, charging the defendants up to a hundred and fifty thousand dollars per song. "It's easy to figure out whose computer is doing it," Hilary Rosen told me.

The record industry has also engaged in less conventional ways 58
of harassing people who use P2P networks, including posting music files that are corrupt or empty, and has explored the legality of using software that temporarily "locks up" any computer that downloads it. Orrin Hatch, the chairman of the Senate Judiciary Committee, when asked a couple of weeks ago whether he favored passing legislation that would override federal anti-hacking laws, said that if other means of stopping illegal downloaders failed, "I'm all for destroying their

machines. If you have a few hundred thousand of those, I think people would realize the seriousness of their actions."

59 Sir Howard Stringer, the chairman of the Sony Corporation of America, calls downloaders "thieves." "That's a reasonably polite way of saying it," he observed recently. "A shoplifter is a thief. That actress wandering around Hollywood helping herself, she was a thief. She should have adopted the Internet defense—'I was downloading music in the morning, downloading movies in the afternoon, and then I thought I'd rustle a few dresses out of the local department store. And it's been a good day, and all of a sudden I'm arrested. How is that fair?'" Many people I met within the record industry seem to regard today's music fans with disapproval. Tom Whalley, the head of Warner Bros. Records, said, "I think the audience is less loyal today than it used to be. The artist has to prove him- or herself with every new album; it feels like you're starting over each time." Fans I spoke to had, for their part, almost nothing good to say about the record industry. "I think the record companies are greedy pigs," said Oliver Ignatius, a fourteen-year-old music fan who lives in Brooklyn, and who knows as much about pop music as anyone I know. Ignatius is the type of fan a record guy would kill for: he downloads, but he also uses file-sharing services to discover new music and to research previously recorded material, and if he likes what he hears he buys the CD. He keeps his CDs in scrapbook-size folders, like a collection of stamps or baseball cards. Oliver thinks that the price of a CD should be six dollars. The industry is currently drawing the line at ten dollars—the price of downloading an album from Apple's iTunes Music Store.

60 One could argue that the record industry has helped to create these thieving, lazy, and disloyal fans. By marketing superficial, disposable pop stars, labels persuade fans to treat music as superficial and disposable. By placing so much emphasis on hit singles that fit into the radio formats, the record industry has created a fan who has no interest in albums. And the values of the people who share music illegally over P2P networks are, after all, rock-and-roll values: freedom, lack of respect for authority, and a desire for instant gratification—the same values that made so many people in the record business rich.

61 Still, one of the most galling things about the piracy problem, if you happen to be in the record business, is that not only are the fans gleefully and remorselessly taking the hits you make; they are doing so because they think you deserve it—it's your payback for ripping off artists with years of "plantation accounting." "I hope it all goes down the crapper," Joni Mitchell said of the record industry in *Rolling Stone* last year. "I would never take another deal in the record business. . . . I'll be damned if I'll line their pockets." The following month, in *W*, she called the record industry a "corrupt cesspool," saying that

she was leaving the major-label system because "record companies are not looking for talent. They're looking for a look and a willingness to cooperate." (Mitchell's most recent album came out on Nonesuch, a Warner label.) As Malcolm McLaren observed to me, "The amazing thing about the death of the record industry is that no one cares. If the movie industry died, you'd probably have a few people saying, 'Oh, this is too bad—after all, they gave us Garbo and Marilyn Monroe.' But now the record industry is dying, and no one gives a damn."

In December, I went to Los Angeles to visit the recording studio 62
where work on Cherie's album was under way, and to meet the artist. Cherie had moved there in June, shortly after finishing school in France. The label had found her a house in Beverly Hills, and she was living there by herself, although Haddad was keeping a close watch over her. Her mother had come to help her settle in, but she had returned home to Marseilles.

Haddad briefed me on Cherie's schedule in L.A. "Her routine is 63
very intense, and it's all about her," he said. "She gets up early, and she works out at home, sometimes with her trainer, then she does her voice lessons, and she does her English lessons, and if she's recording she spends afternoons and evenings at the studio, and if she isn't she meets with agents and movie producers and a bunch of other people who are interested in her."

Westlake Studios is in Hollywood, in a one-story building with 64
blackout windows, at the corner of Santa Monica and Poinsettia. It's an expensive, state-of-the-art studio. These days, almost all the effects that were once only possible to create in a professional studio like this can now be achieved on a home computer with a software program. (A program called Pro Tools will even correct your voice when you sing off key.) Flom's reason for spending the money anyway, as I understood it, was: Anyone can make a record these days, but only a major label can make a really expensive record. This is what economists call "retreating upmarket," which is the classic response of an entrenched industry threatened with a disruptive technology.

Inside, Cherie, who had recently turned eighteen, was behind 65
a glass wall that separated the recording area from the control room. She was singing "pickups"—the bits of the song in which the vocal needed work. Most of the pickups were the "U" sounds, where Cherie sounded most French.

At the controls of an immense mixing board was Humberto 66
Gatica, a producer of hits by, among others, Celine Dion and Michael Jackson. Gatica had silver hair, a slight Spanish accent (he was born in Chile), and a voluble manner. Beside him, co-producing, was the songwriter Paul Moessl, who had written Cherie's original demo, "Older," and was the co-writer of the song they were working on now, "Fool."

The musicians had already recorded their parts—the label had bought the services of the best studio musicians, including the rock star Beck's father, David Campbell, who specializes in arrangements for strings. Moessl estimated that there were fifty thousand dollars' worth of strings on the record. Now Gatica was mixing everything together on the hundred-and-twenty-track system.

Moessl, who was in his early thirties and had lank blond hair, said, "Did you pull down the crunchy loop?" referring to part of the complicated percussion mix. 67

"No," said Gatica, not taking his eyes off the flashing lights on the console. "I just took a little pressure off the snare." 68

Moessl turned his attention to a volume on his lap, which was entitled *The Book of Positive Quotations*. He was looking for ideas for lyrics for a new song he was writing with Cherie. 69

"If you are writing an artistic song, you write from inside yourself," he said. "You say, oh, I don't know, 'My dog died today,' or something like that. But if it's a commercial song you look for uplifting things." 70

The recording of the album had not been going as smoothly as Flom had hoped. For one thing, the songwriters were having trouble creating the right up-tempo number for Cherie—the song that would become the all-important first single. "Ballads are about love," Flom explained to me, "but, at least for the last twenty years, most dance songs are about sex. But Cherie doesn't sing about sex. She sings about love. So we need a dance song about love. 'Push Push in the Bush' is not the right song for Cherie." 71

Gatica, his back stiff from bending over the mixing board, seemed to have become temporarily confused by all the sonic possibilities at his fingertips. He paused from his work, sat down with his head in his hands, and remained that way in silence for a minute or so. Cherie waited patiently for him to recover. Finally, he sat up and said, "I was riding in the car the other day, and an Annie Lennox song came on, from ten years ago or so—and, man, it was brilliant. Brilliant production. But now the kids don't want that sound anymore." He threw his hands in the air. "They want simple! Like it's made in a garage! So you do an expensive production like this one, made in a facility like this that costs many thousands of dollars a day, and then you end up grunging it up so that it sounds like it was made in a garage." 72

Cherie finished her pickups and emerged from the recording room. She wore a navy turtleneck, Levi's, black boots with pointed toes and stiletto heels, and silver bracelets on each wrist, which she twisted with her long, thin fingers. She wasn't as sultry as the animated Cherie in the Batman movie, but she was much more beautiful than she appeared in the label's first photo shoot, with dramatic cheekbones and striking dark eyes. When she smiled, her mouth went up in the middle but turned 73 down at the corners, in a way that looked French. Her English was passable, and when she was stuck for a word Haddad supplied it. She seemed like a nice, modest girl who was trying hard to please.

We went to a room at the back which was used as a place to hang out between sessions. There were candles burning, and plants, and low, comfortable furniture. Cherie said that she had never been interviewed before, but if she was nervous it added to her charm. I asked her about the feeling she is able to put into a song, adding that Flom had described it as "the thing." Cherie, her eyes bright, responded, "Yes! This is eet! It is the thing. That is exactly what it is—it's just this thing." She gestured toward her chest. "I don't know where it comes from, just comes from inside you—the thing." 74

As we were talking, I could hear Gatica shouting in Spanish as he worked on the word "learn," which sounded particularly Gallic, playing it over and over again, adding what were to me inaudible effects, and shouting some more. 75

"So now I will sing for you, it's O.K.?" Cherie asked. She stood up and launched into her lucky song—a Jacques Brel belter called "Quand on n'a que l'amour." The money note is the last note in the piece, and Cherie hit it perfectly, arms reaching to embrace her amour. Chills. 76

Flom arrived, wearing a suit, and hugged his star. They walked back into the control room, where Gatica was at work. The producer played the song. Flom listened with his head inclined downward, rocking with the beat back and forth, his fist cocked, ready to punch the air when he heard the money note. 77

But the note never came. When the song ended, Flom looked crestfallen. He said he missed some of the simplicity of the earlier demo. 78

"Right," Gatica said. "I am combing it now. The idea is to keep it fresh—transparent. Today, records are simpler. People will say this sounds like Whitney Houston. Well, it is a ballad. But we have to make it for a new generation." 79

They played the song again. "We have been very, very careful not to let the accent get in the way," Gatica said. 80

"Though you can still tell she's French," Flom said. 81

"You can tell?" the producer said, sounding alarmed. 82

"It's not that that's bad," Flom said. "She's French. Hey—it is a Romance language, after all." 83

Flom departed and Gatica went back to work. Hours later, when I left, he was still at it. 84

On the subject of whether the record industry will survive, there are optimists and pessimists. The optimists think record companies will eventually figure out how to sell music over the Internet, and when that happens, the market for music will be three times bigger 85 than it is now. The pessimists say that the industry has missed a crucial opportunity to control the new distribution platform and that unless the government intervenes, the recording industry will disappear, and the music business will return to what it was in the nineteenth century, when publishing and performing were the main sources of revenue. Chris Blackwell thinks the online music business will be a boon to independent labels because manufacturing and distribution costs will be much cheaper; Ahmet Ertegun says, "Yes, but independents still have to get people to buy their records." And, with so much music out there, artists will need more blowing up than ever.

Historically, popular music has been heavily influenced by its format. In the nineteenth century, before Edison invented the phonograph, the music business was a publishing enterprise in which sheet music was the primary commodity. People performed the music themselves, at home, usually on the piano. Songs were made into hits by the popular performers who travelled around the country putting on concerts and musicals. The length of the songs varied. It was a singles business. When recorded music became popular, early in the twentieth century, and the format changed to the shellac 78-r.p.m. disk, popular songs became about three minutes long, which was as much time as a disk could hold. The invention of the LP—the 33-r.p.m. long-playing record—in the late nineteen-forties, created the market for albums. For the record companies, albums cost about the same as singles to produce, but they could be sold for much more. In the CD era, the record industry all but killed off the singles business. 86

MP3s might revive that business. For artists, this will mean that, instead of making grand artistic statements with an album released once every three or four years, they will focus their talent on individual songs, which they will release every month or so. Moby, the popular recording artist, told me he thought this would be a terrible development for artists, "because an album is so much more interesting artistically than a song." Fans will buy this music in part because it will include goods and services like concert tickets and merchandise. Traditionally, record labels have earned money only from the sale of recorded music, but increasingly record companies may make deals like the one EMI made last year with the British pop star Robbie Williams, in which the label paid the artist some eighty million dollars to become a full partner in all of Williams's earnings—from publishing, touring, and merchandise, as well as from record sales. 87

As with CDs, MP3s will probably cause a boom in catalogue sales. At the moment, because of traditional retailing constraints, only a small fraction of a label's catalogue is for sale. In an online music store, everything can be offered. Niche markets could become much more important, and artists with small but loyal followings, who are not economically viable in a winner-take-all market, might hold more appeal. 88

Danny Goldberg, a former president of Warner Bros. Records, who is a founder of the independent Artemis Records, told me, "The Internet will be good for Latin music, jazz, world, and anything that sells five to ten thousand." The singer-songwriter Jimmy Buffett, who decided to leave the major-label system and put out music on his own label, Mailboat Records, told me that he thinks that more artists will go into the music business for themselves. "At Mailboat, we have three people, and we take care of our customers, and we handle the shows, and everyone has a good time—it's just like the old record business," he said.

Arguably, the most important function that record-industry pro- 89
fessionals perform—the task that people like Jason Flom, Jeff Haddad, David Foster, Lyor Cohen, Humberto Gatica, and Paul Moessl are all engaged in, one way or another—is filtering through the millions of aspiring artists who think they can sing or play and finding the one or two who really can. Record men of the future might not need to do A&R; they might not even make records. They may prepare monthly playlists of new songs or artists that will be beamed wirelessly to your portable MP3 player. But their essential task—filtering—will remain the same.

Everything depends on getting people to pay for recorded music 90
that they now get for free. When radio threatened the music business in the nineteen-twenties and thirties, the broadcasters agreed to pay a fee to the various rights holders for the music they played, based on an actuarial accounting system. Rights holders' societies like Ascap administered those payments. Some have argued that a similar system should be adapted to the Internet, but many users would refuse to pay their share, and would go on taking music for free. It may make more sense to address the P2P problem with a government-imposed, statutory license, such as many countries in Europe impose on TV owners. Anyone with an Internet connection would be charged a few dollars a month, regardless of whether he downloaded music or not. That money would be distributed to the rights holders, based on an online sampling system. As Jim Griffin, a former executive at Geffen Records and a digital-rights visionary, explained the concept to me, "You monetize anarchy. Charge them five dollars a month to be thieves."

As the music business shifts online, the hitmakers may give way 91
to people who understand the financial restructuring that's needed. In January, Sir Howard Stringer replaced Tommy Mottola, the head of Sony Music, with Andrew Lack, an executive from NBC with no previous experience in the record industry. The uber bosses of the record labels aren't even necessarily from the entertainment industry. Universal Vivendi is now run by Jean-René Fourtou, an ex-pharmaceuticals executive; and the head of Bertelsmann is Gunter Thielen, who formerly ran the company's printing and industrial operations. In some ways, the record business of the future sounds more like a public utility than like a music company. It also doesn't sound like as much fun.

In April, Flom decided to postpone Cherie's record. Instead of coming out this summer, it will be released sometime during the first quarter of next year. "It's just taking them a lot longer in the studio than we had anticipated," he told me, and I had a vision of Gatica, the producer, driving himself to distraction with the crunchy loops. 92

I said that it seemed as though worldwide politics had given the lie to the idea of a "worldwide artist," especially if the artist is French. "They're not going to boycott the fucking album because she's French," Flom replied. Still, it was perhaps not the ideal time to break a worldwide artist named Cherie. 93

The last time I saw Flom, the numbers for the first quarter of 2003 had just come in, showing that the record industry's downward spiral was continuing. Sales were even lower than those of the first quarter of the disastrous previous year. The top-selling album in the country was a collection of songs sung by Kelly Clarkson, Fox's first *American Idol* winner, who has been discovered and blown up without much help from a record label—television made her a star. (Before too long, the United States' pop charts could begin to resemble Spain's, where seven of the spots on the Top Ten charts were recently occupied by reality-show contestants, causing real recording artists to complain that they aren't getting a fair shake.) And there was talk of a merger between BMG and Warner Music, which could mean that the man who called for the end of Flom's type of "lottery mentality," Rolf Schmidt-Holtz, could be Flom's boss. 94

Still, on this warm, springlike day, Flom seemed to be in a sunnier mood about the future than he had been when we first met, six months earlier. He had recently signed a new, all-girl country-rock group called Antigone Rising, whom he expected to be huge. And he was happily immersed in looking for the right song that would be the first single for Cherie, confident that sooner or later the perfect up-tempo love song would present itself. Jerry Wexler, one of Ertegun's partners at Atlantic, once said that artist-and-repertoire was just a fancy expression for putting a singer together with a song, and in this respect the record business does not seem to have changed at all. 95

Flom said he had even thought about trying to write a song for Cherie himself. But this idea hadn't got very far. 96

"I can't imagine writing a song today," he said. "I don't know where I'd start." 97

Can the record business survive? 98

Examining the Text

1. Beyond the implications of new technology and the recording industry's response to it, what other issues does the author address in this article? On reflection, do you believe that illegal downloading is the main issue confronting the recording industry? Why, or why not?

2. Author Seabrook quotes Jason Flom making the above statement: "If the star is big enough, people will buy the album, because it's like a piece of the artist. But if the star doesn't have that kind of irresistible appeal then people just say, 'what the heck, I'll download the good songs.' So we just have to figure out how to make her a big star." Looking back on recently successful bands and singers, how much of their popularity do you think is owed to this kind of "blowing up" by recording-industry executives like Flom? Using some of your own favorite musicians as examples, examine whether you think Flom's statement is accurate: can record sales be driven by record companies' marketing efforts?

3. Examine the quote from Clear Channel CEO Lowry Mays, who says: "We're simply in the business of selling products." What does this imply about the role of commercial radio and other media in the development and dissemination of your favorite music? When you listen to a radio station that plays current songs (as opposed to hits from the past), do you notice how many get frequent plays? Do you ever consider that record companies might be influencing what gets played on the radio; if so, do you object to such "manipulation"?

4. *Thinking rhetorically:* Based on the title, what sorts of information and themes did you expect from the article? After reading it, did the article meet your expectations? What specific persuasive techniques does the writer employ with this article? By the end of the article, did these techniques alter your views on whether or not the record business can be saved? If so, how; if not, why not? Might the author have approached the subject using different rhetorical strategies and still attained the same result for you?

For Group Discussion

By now, everyone knows that downloading copyrighted music from the Internet is illegal, yet people still do it. Knowing that it is legally wrong has not dissuaded the majority of Americans who still download music, seemingly unconcerned about the ethical issues involved. In light of what you've read in the article, discuss what would have to change in order for people to stop downloading music. Are there steps that the recording industry should take? Should universities and other providers of high-speed Internet connections be held responsible when users download music illegally? Alternatively, take a pro-downloading position and defend the rights of MP3-sharers to access music freely and without legal consequence.

Writing Suggestion

Imagine you are a record label executive faced with declining sales of CDs as a result of downloading from the Internet. Write a letter to the New Yorker magazine in which you defend recent efforts to sue networks like Napster as well as individual heavy users of file-swapping networks. Address how you're trying to win the battle in the court of public opinion as well as legally.

*How to Save the Music Business**

PAUL MCGUINNESS

The previous article by John Seabrook discusses the numerous economic problems facing the popular music industry primarily from the perspective of a music industry insider, with intimate knowledge of the complex fiscal goings-on of that specialized world. The next article pairs nicely with the previous one, as it discusses some of the same problems, but from the perspective of the recording artist and others involved in the creative endeavor of creating music and getting it out for the listening public to appreciate. Paul McGuinness has been U2's manager since 1978 and therefore has a near-lifetime of experience as a middle person, representing the interests of recording and performing artists to executives within the music industry. In this article written recently for Rolling Stone, *the popular music magazine, McGuinness argues that more than a decade of online piracy has devastated the recording industry . . . and with that point very few observers would take serious exception. However, U2's manager contends that there's a relatively simple solution to save the music industry; he outlines that platform in the article after first providing some historical background, based upon his personal experience and wide knowledge of the field, as contextualizing information.*

While we won't divulge the details of his solutions in this headnote (if we did, then you wouldn't bother to read the article, would you?), we will promise that his solutions are reasonable and compelling. However, don't take our word for it; therefore, **as you read,** *consider carefully the changes proposed by Paul McGuinness. Outline them carefully as you take notes and decide for yourself whether you agree that his proposals will indeed resolve the current fiscal crisis in the music industry . . . or at least make the situation a bit better.*

Even after three decades managing the world's biggest rock band, I have a lifetime hero as far from the world of U2 as you could ever get. He was a feisty French 19th-century composer of light orchestral music. His name was Ernest Bourget. It was Bourget who in 1847, while enjoying a drink in a Paris restaurant, suddenly heard the orchestra playing one of his own compositions. He was startled—of course he had not been paid or asked permission for this. So he resolved the problem himself: He walked out of the restaurant without paying his bill. 1

Bourget's action was a milestone in the history of copyright law. The legal wrangling that followed led to the establishment of the first revenue-collecting system for composers and musicians. The modern music industry has a lot to thank him for. 2

I was thinking of Ernest Bourget on a January day two years ago when, in a conference hall packed with some of the world's best-known music managers, gathered at the seafront Palais des Festivals in Cannes, France, I plunged into the raging debate about Internet piracy and the future of music. 3

I had been invited to speak there by the organizers of the Midem Music Convention, where the music industry's great and good debate the Big Question that today dominates our business: How are we going to fund its future? 4

My message was simple—and remains so today. We are living in an era when "free" is decimating the music industry and is starting to do the same to film, TV and books. Yet for the world's Internet Service Providers, bloated by years of broadband growth, "free music" has been a multibillion-dollar bonanza. What has gone so wrong? And what can be done now to put it right? 5

Well-known artists very seldom speak out on piracy. There are several reasons for this. It often isn't seen as cool or attractive to their fans—Lars Ulrich from Metallica was savaged when he criticized Napster. Other famous artists sometimes understandably feel too rich and too successful to be able to speak out on the issue without being embarrassed. 6

Then there is the backlash from the bloggers—those anonymous gremlins who wait to send off their next salvo of bilious four-letter abuse whenever a well-known musician sticks their head above the parapet. When Lily Allen posted some thoughtful comments about how illegal file-sharing is hurting new developing acts, she was ravaged by the online mob and quite understandably withdrew from the debate. Even Bono has stepped into the argument. Quite unprompted by me, he wrote an op-ed piece in the *New York Times*—and he pulled no punches: "A decade's worth of music file-sharing and swiping has made clear that the people it hurts are the creators . . . and the people this reverse Robin Hooding benefits are rich service providers, whose swollen profits perfectly mirror the lost receipts of the music business." Bono is a guy who, when he decides to support a cause, does so with enormous passion. But even he was amazed by the backlash when he was mauled by the online crowd. 7

It is more than two years since my Cannes speech. Some things are better in the music world, but unfortunately the main problem is still just as bad as it ever was. Artists cannot get record deals. Revenues are plummeting. Efforts to provide legal and viable ways of making 8 money from music are being stymied by piracy. The latest industry figures, from IFPI, show that 95 percent of all the music downloaded is illegally obtained and unpaid for. Indigenous music industries from Spain to Brazil are collapsing. A study endorsed by trade unions says Europe's creative industries could lose more than a million jobs in the next five years. Finally, maybe the message is getting through that this isn't just about fewer limos for rich rock stars.

9 Of course, this isn't crippling bands like U2, and it would be dishonest to claim it was. I've always believed artists and musicians need to take their business as seriously as their music. U2 understood this. They have carefully pursued careers as performers and songwriters, signed good deals and kept control over their life's work. Today, control over their work is exactly what young and developing artists are losing. It is not their fault. It is because of piracy and the way the Internet has totally devalued their work.

10 So how did we get here? How is it that in 2010, in a world of iTunes and Spotify, of a healthy live-music scene and hundreds of different legal sites, making money fairly from recorded music remains so elusive?

11 It is facile to blame record companies. Whoever those old Canutes were—the executives who wanted to defend an old business model rather than embrace a new one—they left the business long ago. Last year, more than a quarter of all the music bought globally was sold via the Internet and mobile phones. The record companies know they have to monetize the Internet, or they will not survive.

12 If you had to encapsulate the crisis of the music industry in the past decade, it would be in one momentous word: "free." The digital revolution essentially made music free. For years we (and by "we" I mean the music business, musicians, creative industries, governments and regulators) have grappled with this new concept of "free." One minute we have fought it like a monster, the next we have embraced it like a friend. As consumers, we have come to love "free"—but as creators, seeking reward for our work, it has become our worst nightmare. In recent years, the music business has tried to "fight free with free," seeking revenues from advertising, merchandising, sponsorship—anything, in fact, other than the consumer's wallet. These efforts have achieved little success. Today, "free" is still the creative industries' biggest problem.

13 The good news, I think, is that we have woken up to the issue. In the early years of the decade, it felt almost like heresy even to question the mantra of "free content" on the Internet. But attitudes have changed. Today we take a far more sober view as we see what damage "free" has done to the creative industries, above all to music.

14 Numerous strategies have tried to deal with "free." Many believe music subscription is the Holy Grail that will bring money flowing

back into the business. I agree. A per-household monthly payment to Spotify for all the music you want seems to me a great deal. I support the idea of subscription packages like Sky Songs too (available in the U.K.). These surely point the way to the future where music is bundled or streamed and paid for by usage rather than by units sold. Why should the prices paid not correspond to the number of times the music is "consumed"?

There are clever minds working out how the business model of 15
"music access" is going to work. Perhaps this year Steve Jobs, the genius behind Apple, will finally join in. Steve is a man of decisiveness and surprise. Bono and I did a deal with him, sitting in his kitchen in Palo Alto, California, to launch the U2 iPod in 2004—I still have the notes I scribbled down in the back of my diary. Jimmy Iovine was there too, and I remember he said of iTunes, "This may be the penicillin!" Sadly it turned out not to be. Steve is the guy who has always magically known what the consumer wants before the consumer ever knew it. I wish he would put that great mind and that great corporation of his to work to devise a model that allows artists and creators to get properly rewarded for their work. Maybe he's working on it right now. I hope so.

Newspapers and magazines are trying to reinvent their busi- 16
nesses to deal with "free." It started as a honeymoon: Mainstream titles opened up websites and attracted vast numbers of online readers. But the honeymoon has come to a miserable end. Newspaper circulation and advertising revenues have fallen sharply. Rupert Murdoch is reintroducing the pay wall for some of his flagship newspaper titles. Murdoch has great influence: his empire straddles all the businesses with stakes in the debate, from the social network MySpace to The Wall Street Journal to 20th Century Fox movie studios and the broadcaster Sky. I'm disappointed that he didn't take a closer look at the music industry's experience and see the dark side of "free" earlier.

It was with this mixture of semi-successful and failed strategies 17
to fight "free" in mind that I took to the stage in January 2008. I felt the music industry had to unite around a stronger position on the whole issue. Managers of well-known bands generally do not like to do this—like their artists, they worry about alienating fans. Many managers I know have the coziest private relationships conceivable with record companies, yet publicly will refuse to acknowledge that music piracy is a problem. Great artists need great record companies. They can be big or small.

So what's the answer to "free"? I think it starts by challenging 18
a big myth—the one that says free content is a just and inexorable fact of life brought on by the unstoppable advance of technology. It is not. It is in fact part of the commercial agenda of powerful technology and telecom industries. Look at the figures as the free-music boom

helped drive an explosion of broadband revenues earlier in the decade. Revenues from the "Internet access" (fixed line and mobile) business quadrupled from 2004 to 2009 to $226 billion. Passing them on the way down, music-industry revenues fell in the same period from $25 billion to $16 billion. Free content has helped fuel the vast profits of the technology and telecom industries. Persistent rumors circulate that Internet "freedom" campaigners and lobbyists are supported financially by large tech corporations. Of course they are.

Let's get real: Do people want more bandwidth to speed up their e-mails or to download music and films as rapidly as possible? I'm sure the people running ISPs are big music fans. But their free-music bonanza has got to stop. That will happen in two ways: first by commercial partnership with deals like Sky Songs; and second by ISPs taking proportionate responsible steps to stop their customers illegally file-sharing on their networks. 19

I've done a lot of debating on this issue in the past two years. I have learned about the vast resources of the telecom industry's lobbying machinery and encountered frightening naïveté about the basics of copyright and intellectual-property rights from politicians who should know better. More than once I have heard elected representatives describe paying for music as a "tax." 20

I have become convinced that ISPs are not going to help the music and film industries voluntarily. Some things just have to come with the force of legislation. President Nicolas Sarkozy of France understood that when he became the first head of state to champion laws that require ISPs to reduce piracy in France. In Britain, the major political parties have understood it too. Following the passage of new anti-piracy measures in the Digital Economy Act in April, Britain and France will now have some of the world's best legal environments for rebuilding our battered music business. 21

At the heart of the approach France and Britain are taking is the so-called "graduated response," by which ISPs would be required to issue warnings to serious offenders to stop illegal file-sharing. This is the most sensible legislation to emerge in the past decade to deal with "free." It is immeasurably better than the ugly alternative of suing hundreds of thousands of individuals. 22

Two years into my odyssey into this whole debate, I find a curious mixture of optimism and pessimism about the future of recorded music. I was back at the music industry's annual Cannes shindig in January—this time in the audience, listening to luminaries like Daniel Ek, the quiet-spoken 26-year-old Swedish dynamo who runs the subscription service Spotify. Spotify could be the future mode, but they will have to demonstrate that not only can they collect revenue from their users and advertisers, but that they will fairly pass on those sums 23 to the artists and labels and publishers. The fact that some of the labels are shareholders in Spotify makes it an urgent priority that these transactions be transparent.

So what does a bright future for the music industry look like? 24
Here is my vision: Music subscriptions will be the basic access route, but by no means the only one. Households will pay for a subscription service like Spotify, or they will pay for a service bundled into their broadband bill to an ISP. But many customers will also take out more expensive added-value packages, with better deals including faster access to new releases. There will also be a healthy market in downloads to own and premium albums.; iTunes will be fighting its corner in the market, probably with its own subscription service. And a significant minority will still buy CDs, coveting the packaging, the cover designs and the sense of ownership.

Sound quality will once again emerge as a huge issue. People are 25
cottoning to a dark secret of the digital age—MP3 files sound terrible. The online "lossless" audiophile movement is gathering strength, with one label, Interscope, creating a new master source file that will ensure the efforts of musicians and producers in the recording process are not wasted when the sound gets to the listener. Jimmy Iovine and his team at Interscope/Beats Audio sound solutions hope this superfile will become ubiquitous. They are also working on a variety of headphones and better sound chips in HP computers to improve the listener experience. Most listening nowadays is on tiny earbud headphones.

In the wonderful future I envisage every piece of music will be 26
licensed to be available at any time on any device. All music will be transferable between computer and portable device.

ISPs will be reporting significant revenues from their "content 27
ventures." These are the added-value businesses that over time they must move into as their flat-rate broadband business reaches a saturation point. This is not fantasy: A survey by Ovum recently predicted that ISPs in the U.K. could earn more than £100 million in digital-music revenues by 2013. In the beautiful future of my dream, every record label and every ISP will be joined in commercial partnership, sharing revenues and strategies to get their music to as many millions of people as possible. If the potential of digital were to be harnessed creatively, it would be possible to process the billions of microtransactions that occur when fans listen to tracks, and the artists, the songwriters, the labels and the publishers all get paid. The ISP or telecom gets paid too for being the retailer and the distributor.

We have some way to go until my dream comes true. But we're 28
making progress. Governments, not just in France and Britain, but in South Korea, Taiwan and New Zealand, are tackling piracy. The mindset about free music is changing. Managers and artists I meet take the

issue far more seriously than they did before. Newspaper editors no longer think the problems of music are from another world—they actually ask our advice on how to address them. More artists are talking about piracy hurting their lives. Filmmakers and actors can see that they are next.

I think we are coming to understand that "free" comes with a price—and in my business that means less investment in talent and fewer artists making a living from music. If this point really is sinking in, then we are making headway. It may be that the crisis for music has now gotten so bad that the issue of "free" is really being properly understood for the first time. 29

If the engineers who built the iPhone, if the geniuses who made Google reach every home in the world in less than a decade, if the amazing talents behind Facebook were to apply themselves to our problems and help, what a wonderful world it would be. Great work being made, distributed efficiently and everyone in the value chain being fairly paid. 30

Examining the Text

1. Early in this piece, the author comments on the current state of popular music economics, "Some things are better in the music world, but unfortunately the main problem is still just as bad as it ever was." He goes on to catalog a number of problems causing the financial crisis in today's music. To what, specifically, does he attribute the problem? To this list of ailments, can you add some additional difficulties that might be contributing to the precipitous downturn in musical revenues?

2. A bit later in the article, the author remarks on the proliferation of free music downloads and other musical giveaways, "Numerous strategies have tried to deal with 'free.' Many believe music subscription is the Holy Grail that will bring money flowing back into the business." What does he mean by "musical subscription?" Cite some current examples of this phenomenon, and describe any experience you, or people you know, have had with musical subscription. Why is the author in favor of this partial solution to popular music's fiscal crisis?

3. McGuinness elaborates on the points raised by the previous question, asserting, "So what does a bright future for the music industry look like? Here is my vision: Music subscriptions will be the basic access route, but by no means the only one." In addition to the subscription solution posited in the previous question, by what other means might consumers gain access to the music they want to hear while allowing artists to gain the revenue they deserve, according to the author?

4. Toward the end of the article, author McGuinness notes that the same financial problems that have plagued the music industry in recent years have also spread to other areas of the media as well. What other kinds of media does he see as having problems similar to those of the popular music industry? How does he see a coalition of these media outlets combining forces to help solve the economic problems that are facing the entire spectrum of mass media?

5. *Thinking rhetorically:* Since he is the manager of U2, a band that has remained popular and financially successful for decades, one would predict that the author would reveal certain biases as he discusses the financial problems of the pop music industry and proposes what he considers to be reasonable solutions to the problem. In your opinion, does he make an attempt to maintain a certain objectivity as he develops his central thematic points in this article, or is he too close to the artists' point of view to be able to consider the issues clearly and fairly? Cite specific examples from the text to support your conclusions about the author's rhetorical stance in this article.

For Group Discussion

Arbitrarily break up your class into three groups: one-third of the class will consist of recording artists, such as rap musicians, heavy metal guitarists, professional crooners, Las Vegas lounge lizards, barefoot folk-rock composers, and other assorted and not necessarily stereotypical creative types. The second group will be recording industry executives, such as record producers, A&R people, investors, recording engineers, promoters, iTunes specialists visiting from Apple Corporation in Cupertino, California, and members of the crumbling brick-and-mortar record store contingent. A third group will consist of management persons such as the author of the McGuinness article: managers and such folk who are not themselves artists, but who have a stake in making sure that "their" talent pool gets its share of the musical income pie. First, get together with your group and discuss a coherent platform of several cogent and persuasive points you plan to bring to the table when the three groups get together. Having accomplished this, bring all three groups together, have each group present its platform in either a measured, reasoned way, or a strident and hysterical way—or something in between—and then attempt to come to some agreement about some concrete ways to improve the financial situation of the recording industry to the benefit of all three contingents.

Writing Suggestion

As mentioned in the headnote to this piece, this article, and the previous one by John Seabrook examine financial problems facing the music industry from two distinctly different perspectives: the first, from the point of view of an industry insider; the second from the perspective of one who works intimately with the artists who create the music for our listening pleasure and who deserve to be remunerated for their efforts . . . at least in McGuinness's view. The one perspective that's missing in these two articles is that of the music consumers, the ones who shell out bucks—sometimes hundreds or thousands of dollars—for the privilege of enjoying music on their iPods, car stereos, and home entertainment system . . . or who avoid shelling out bucks by finding ways to access that music for free. Write a persuasive essay similar to that of Seabrook and/or McGuinness, but from the perspective of the consumer. What are the economic problems you face as a consumer and listener of music, and what remedies might you posit for solving the crisis in the music industry today? Some of your solutions may overlap those presented by Seabrook or McGuinness; others may directly contradict them. Your only inviolable requirement as you construct your arguments for this essay: be honest in your assessment of the problem from the consumer's perspective, and don't hesitate to take a controversial stance that skirts the bounds of legality as you attempt to come up with answers that will allow you to listen to your favorite music without going broke in the process.

Sex and Drugs and Rock 'n' Roll: Urban Legends and Popular Music

IAN INGLIS

Urban legends are tales circulated widely in modern societies. While, in previous historical periods, such narratives were usually transmitted orally, nowadays many are discovered and disseminated by the mass media and are told as "true stories" that contain astounding, sensational, or bizarre details. Many urban legends achieve an enviable longevity: there are very few people in the Western world who have not heard of the vanishing hitchhiker, the alligators lurking in the sewers, the funeral ashes mistakenly used as spices, or the babysitter terrorized by the madman upstairs. Popular music has proved to be an especially fertile ground for the propagation of such stories. Whether by word of mouth, through fanzines, or across the Internet, the often dramatic urban legends of popular music have been, and continue to be, generated to ever wider audiences. By examining some of the more familiar urban legends of popular music, the author of this essay aims to illustrate the roles that their persistent repetition perform, and to assess the social and cultural functions they fulfill.

As you read, *note the deliberate formal structure and organization of this piece, characteristic of media studies scholarship. In his introductory section, Inglis introduces the topic of urban legend generally, and then he "downshifts" to a focused and assertive thesis statement regarding urban legends in the popular music sphere. [Note about thesis statements: while you may sometimes want to avoid Inglis's blunt "I propose to" or "I shall" type of thesis declaration in your own academic essays, and instead favor an explicit assertion of your essay's main points, this is a perfectly legitimate and time-honored form of academic writing and has the advantage of letting the reader know exactly where the essay is heading.] Furthermore, the* *author breaks his supporting paragraphs into lists of qualities and characteristics, which lends specificity and credibility to his developing arguments and aids readers by providing discrete "packets" of information to digest as the arguments unfold.*

Within contemporary communities where opportunities to engage in social interaction and technologies to assist such interaction have multiplied rapidly in recent years, rumor and gossip remain routine components of daily conversation. The development of the Internet has ensured that these exchanges are no longer limited to the interpersonal; stories are now transferred between sites rather than between acquaintances. In addition, the media's active promotion of the cult of celebrity allows for the public recognition of many more individuals about whom stories may be told and information exchanged. 1

The proliferation of sensational or dramatic or bizarre tales about those defined as "celebrities" falls into the general category of "urban legends." While it is true that the majority of traditional legends, or myths, have tended to be general in nature, difficult to source, and impossible to verify, there nonetheless exists a substantial collection of tales which are specific, detailed, and, at least in theory, open to verification. In order to illustrate these processes, I propose to explore one particular arena in which such tales have flourished—the world of popular music. I shall examine the nature of the legends themselves, the motivations of those who relate them, and the social functions that their circulation serves. 2

THE URBAN LEGENDS OF POPULAR MUSIC

Urban legends have been defined as stories that "belong to the subclass of folk narratives, legends believed, or at least believable" (Brunvald 3). Furthermore, these narratives are told and retold over years; they achieve an enviable longevity, despite the denials of the actors themselves or the accumulation of counter-evidence. Indeed, denials are often incorporated into the supporting evidence for many of these tales, via the argument that they are merely attempts to conceal an embarrassing truth; ironically, every additional denial only serves to extend the life of the story. Consider the following examples: 3

- *Led Zeppelin, the Shark and the Groupie.* While staying at the Edgewater Inn in Seattle in 1969 on their North American tour, Led Zeppelin and their road crew are visited in their hotel room by a red-haired, 17-year-old groupie named Jackie. She is tied to a bed and members of the group rape her with a live mud shark they caught while fishing from the balcony.

- *Paul Is Dead*. In the winter of 1966, at the pinnacle of the Beatles' success, Paul McCartney is killed in a car crash and replaced by an actor named William Campbell. The Beatles are able to continue their career (with the imposter) for several years, but provide numerous clues about the circumstances of Paul's death—on their album covers, in the lyrics of their songs, in films and photographs of the group.
- *The Rolling Stones, Marianne Faithfull and a Mars Bar*. In May 1967, the police raid Keith Richards's home in Sussex and arrest Richards, Mick Jagger and art gallery owner Robert Fraser on drug charges. During the raid, the police discover a naked Marianne Faithfull lying across the sofa, while Jagger eats a Mars Bar that is protruding from her vagina.
- *Elvis Presley and the Rubber Hose*. In the early years of his career in the mid-1950s, Elvis Presley inserts a length of rubber hose down the front of his trousers before each stage performance in order to exaggerate the overtly sexual nature of his performance.
- *Bob Dylan's Unannounced Visit*. On a trip to London in the late 1980s, Bob Dylan contacts Dave Stewart of the Eurythmics, who invites him to use his studio. However, Dylan goes to the wrong address, the house of a plumber whose name is also Dave. When the plumber returns from work, his wife greets him with the words, "Bob Dylan's here to see you . . . he's in the kitchen, having a cup of tea."
- *The Ohio Players and the Murder in the Studio*. When the Ohio Players are recording their 1976 hit single "Love Rollercoaster," someone is murdered in the studio during the recording sessions. The death scream is inadvertently captured on tape, and can be clearly heard during the track's percussion break.
- *The Dark Side of the Moon and The Wizard of Oz*. Pink Floyd's 1973 album *The Dark Side of the Moon* is composed, constructed, and recorded as a deliberate and calculated soundtrack to MGM's 1939 musical The Wizard of Oz. If played together, the music on the album and the action on the screen are perfectly synchronized.
- *The Beatles' Lost Album*. Shortly before the release of *Abbey Road* in September 1969, the master tapes of another planned album by the Beatles (*Hot as Sun*) are stolen from the home of producer George Martin and from the offices of EMI and Apple and are held to ransom. The ransom is paid, but two of the tapes are destroyed and the third is accidentally erased while passing through the X-ray security equipment at Heathrow airport.
- *Elvis Presley's Faked Death*. Elvis Presley's apparent death at his Graceland home in August 1976 is a cleverly contrived deception. Disillusioned with the stresses and strains that accompany his

position as the world's most famous entertainer, and unhappy with the circumstances of his personal life, Elvis fakes his own death and escapes into anonymity.

- *Stevie Nicks's Cocaine Habit*. By the mid-1980s, after years of cocaine addiction, Fleetwood Mac's Stevie Nicks has caused such severe damage to her septum that she is unable to inhale the drug nasally. The only way she can now satisfy her habit is via an enema and she engages a full-time employee to perform this duty for her.
- *Ozzy Osbourne and the Live Bat*. During Ozzy Osbourne's 1981 "Night of the Living Dead" tour, a member of the audience in Des Moines, Iowa, throws a live bat onto the stage. Stunned, it lies motionless, and Osbourne, believing it to be a rubber toy, bites off its head. He's rushed to hospital and treated for rabies.
- *Motley Crue and the Replacement Nikki Sixx*. During the mid-1980s, Motley Crue's bassist, Nikki Sixx, is forced to quit the group for an extensive programme of drugs rehabilitation. The unknown Matthew Trippe is hired to secretly replace him and does so for several years, even writing some of the group's most successful songs during this period. When Sixx returns, Trippe is sacked, with no reward, recognition or acknowledgement.
- *Keith Richards and His Father's Ashes*. When Keith Richards's father, Bert, dies in 2002, his body is cremated. Later, Richards adds cocaine to the ashes, inhales the mixture, and announces "I snorted my father."

In form and content, these tales are distinguished by three 4 recurring characteristics that relate to their structural, ideological, and occupational dimensions.

First, unlike many of the more traditional urban legends, which 5 are largely unattributed, these are precise and detailed accounts. "The vanishing hitchhiker," "the alligators roaming through the sewers," "the spider in the beehive hairstyle," "the funeral ashes mistakenly used as seasoning," and "the babysitter terrorized by the madman on the upper floor" are among the most recognizable and repeated urban legends, but lack any specific information about time, place, and person. In contrast, the myths of popular music come laden with details—dates, settings, addresses, names, ages, descriptions. And the details remain constant with each telling: the confectionery enjoyed by Jagger and Faithfull is always a Mars, never a Hershey or Kit-Kat bar; Paul McCartney's replacement is identified by name; Bob Dylan's visit is to a plumber, never to any other kind of tradesman; Led Zeppelin's groupie (always Jackie) visits them at the Edgewater Inn in Seattle, and never at any other location; it is only Stevie Nicks and never any other performer who suffers the indignities of a cocaine enema. In this sense, these stories have, over several decades, become more or less convincing replicas of historical truth, or "factoids."

Second, many of the tales exhibit a continuing fascination with the perceived excesses of the rock and roll lifestyle. Musicians have long prided themselves on their bohemian tradition, their identification and exclusion of "squares," and their refusal to adopt conventional modes of behavior (Becker). In such circumstances, a stereotyped ideology of "sex and drugs and rock 'n' roll" lends itself to stories of the fantastic, the outrageous, the unruly, and the shocking. The challenges issued to socially approved norms are illustrated by the declarations contained in many of its anthems: "Hope I die before I get old" (The Who), "Feel like letting my freak flag fly" (Crosby, Stills, Nash & Young), "Don't know what I want but I know how to get it, I wanna destroy" (The Sex Pistols) and "Rock 'n' roll is here to stay, better to burn out than to fade away" (Neil Young) are just a few of the many examples in which a hedonistic and confrontational stance has been knowingly articulated by musicians themselves. 6

Third, the accounts are plausible. They may be unlikely, improbable, even incredible . . . but their events are at least possible and the stories cannot therefore be dismissed out of hand. Within a 50-year history "almost as unruly as the music itself, which is saying a lot" (R. Palmer 11) there have been more than enough recorded examples of financial ruin, sexual excess, violence, imprisonment, drug addiction, alcoholism, premature death, suicide, and mental illness to justify the frequent connections noted between the creative personality and emotional instability or psychological disturbance (Wills and Cooper 16–18). Given this history, the kind of stories discussed above tend to be greeted with less skepticism when told about popular musicians (individually and collectively) than would be the case if they were told about members of other professional groups. Put simply, they would not be believed elsewhere. Thus, the continuing generation and circulation of these tales both contributes to and benefits from a general perception that "undoubtedly rock 'n' roll attracts some seriously unbalanced and deranged people, damaged and unstable" (Shapiro 213). 7

THE STORYTELLERS

It has been argued that: 8

> whatever the origins of urban legends, their dissemination is no mystery . . . groups of age-mates, especially adolescents, are an important channel . . . other paths of transmission are among office workers and club members, and among religious, recreational and regional groups. (Brunvald 4–3)

Informal, face-to-face exchanges of news and information, in casual conversations between peers, at home, in work or school, have been the major routes along which stories have been told and retold, and have also provided the basis for the "word of mouth" evaluations seen as so crucial to commercial success within all areas of the entertainment industry (Kent 40–77). 9

In a more stabilized form, but operating in much the same way, fanzines have become additional vehicles of transmission. Localized, defiantly independent, often highly idiosyncratic, they emerged, as part of a democratization of cultural resources through the 1970s and 1980s, as ideal mediums for the publication of novel, alternative, or "unofficial" readings. Occupying a cultural terrain that lies "somewhere between a personal letter and a magazine" (Duncombe 10), they provide opportunities for narratives to be introduced to, and tested by, a potentially sympathetic audience. 10

However, both of these have been overtaken (but not yet rendered obsolete) since the 1990s through the Internet's capacity to allow its users to go beyond mere interpersonal and subcultural exchanges to instigate global, instantaneous transfers of ideas and information. The character of communication and contact in "the network society" (Castells) has, as a result, been fundamentally reconstituted, with important consequences for the transmission of contemporary myths. 11

> In the past, rumoring has been discussed as a type of communication that was only possible with people who were already involved in the same social network or by way of direct physical contact. The Internet has changed the ways rumoring can happen, and has made possible rumoring between people who have never met or communicated before. (Fisher 159)

Nonetheless, whatever combination of storytelling styles is employed—verbal, in print, online—the motivations of those who engage in such discussions lie at the heart of any attempts to understand the stories' continued circulation. With this in mind, I wish to propose a fourfold typology of storytellers. 12

1. *The Believer*. This is the person who genuinely believes—or, at the very least, hopes—that the legend is true. Denials, often from the protagonists themselves, are dismissed as evidence of a conspiracy theory to prevent the truth from being allowed to surface; the believer's goal is to reveal that truth. There is a familiar literature—both fictional (Lurie) and academic (Festinger, Riecken, and Schachter)—which explores the consequences for believers who refuse to modify their beliefs, even in the face of apparently incontrovertible evidence. In exactly the same way that attempts to question accounts of alien abduction and 13

imminent UFO invasion, or the many reported sightings of Bigfoot and the Loch Ness Monster, only add to the vigor with which those claims are defended, so too within popular music suggestions that believers may be mistaken or misguided typically result in a consolidation of the beliefs in question. The enduring belief that Elvis Presley did not die, as demonstrated in the frequent and persistent alleged sightings of the singer over 30 years, presents the most succinct example of this kind of response (Marcus; Denisoff and Plasketes; Rodman). And, on the other hand, the enduring belief that Paul McCartney did die continues to be upheld to this day by those believers who, for 40 years, claim to have discovered clues, mistakes, and incongruities to support their conclusion (Reeve; Patterson).

2. *The Cynic*. Conversely, the cynic knows or believes the story to be false. In telling the story, he/she intends to illustrate the absurdity of the myth, ridicule its logical inconsistencies, and emphasize the gullibility of those who subscribe to it. Such attacks stem from a perception of believers as irrational and obsessive. They are seen as trying to: 14

> compensate for a perceived personal lack of autonomy, absence of community, incomplete identity, lack of power and lack of recognition . . . someone who is making up for some inherent lack. He or she seeks identity, connection and meaning via celebrities . . . [and] has fragile self-esteem, weak or non-existent social alliances, a dull and monotonous "real" existence. (Jenson 17–18)

Thus, the cynic's retelling of a myth frankly and deliberately undermines a believer's retelling of the same myth. This cynicism illustrates a persistent, and largely negative, approach in the historical analysis of audiences' consumption of popular music that has expressed itself through the adoption of varying degrees of elitist commentary. Adorno's suggestion that pre-war listeners to popular music were "not merely turned away from more important music, but confirmed in their neurotic stupidity" (41) and Hoggart's description of the post-war audience for rock and roll in the United Kingdom as "a depressing group . . . most of them are rather less intelligent than average . . . they have no aim, no protection, no belief" (248–49) may merely be two of the more familiar observations that are routinely reinforced by the storytelling motivations of the cynics. 15

3. *The Entertainer*. For the entertainer, the story is nothing more than a diverting or unusual tale to be told to others; it is related in the same way that a joke is told. From the jongleurs and jesters of medieval Europe to the screen comedians of the contemporary age, a special status has been enjoyed by those persons with an ability to entertain and amuse others. This is as true in routine social interactions as it is in 16

formalized encounters between performers and audiences: "laughter and smiling are actively used as resources in the course of social interaction . . . [they] are built into social life by participants in an intricate manner and are exchanged as part of a collaborative process" (Mulkay 107). Popular music, because of its familiarity and accessibility, thus provides an unusually broad, and continually expanding, range of topics around which such exchanges can happen and from which the entertainer can make his/her selection. In addition, the characteristic narrative form and the allegedly factual content of urban legends—as opposed to other comedic modes, including the one-liner, the "shaggy dog" story, the pun—is particularly attractive to the entertainer, since it reflects a basic property of comedy.

> Much comedy, no matter how funny, commonly uses a narrative form which is not essentially dissimilar from realist narrative in general . . . [it] has an outline, a narrative skeleton, which follows the norms of realism in the minimal sense that the characters progress from point a to point b for a reason . . . [and] the spatial relationships between the two points are portrayed in a way roughly consistent with the laws of the known universe. (J. Palmer 113)

4. *The Expert.* For the expert, each retelling of a story increases the stock of "cultural capital" he/she possesses. In particular, the apparent access to knowledge or information or tastes not shared by others lends the expert a mark of distinction and, as Bourdieu has noted, "nothing more infallibly classifies than tastes in music" (18). The definition, offered by Jones, which sees urban legends as "tales circulated widely in modern society . . . generally transmitted orally . . . [and] told as 'true stories,' often attributed to a friend of a friend" (439) is appropriate here, since it lends support to the way in which distinction is further increased if the expert can claim (as is often the case) a more personal association with the source, or the subject, of the story. Such moments of association are rare. 17

> The relationship between celebrities and fans is typically mediated through representation. Despite the increasing profusion of celebrities in society . . . encounters are comparatively rare. Stage, screen, audio transmission and print culture are the main institutional mechanisms that express the various idioms of celebrity culture. Each presupposes distance between the celebrity and the audience. (Rojek 46)

Because of their rarity, narratives in which the expert may appear to play a central role—by dint of intimacy, presence, or "insider" status—may work to increase the prestige he/she gains with each repetition of the tale, since, in effect, they reduce the distance between 18 the subjects of a story and the tellers of a story, between celebrities and their audiences. This is true of all celebrity types, but particularly of celebrities in popular music.

> More than any other form of celebrity, the popular music celebrity . . . demonstrates the rapidity of dissipation of the power and influence of a public personality. The reason for part of this dissipation is the way in which the popular music industry has helped to construct itself as a symbol of change and transformation . . . the succession of apparent new images and sounds constitutes the representation of change that is often used by the culture at large as a representation of the vitality of the entire culture. (Marshall 183)

Thus, the continued distribution of urban legends within and around popular music derives from a variety of storytelling sources, each of which brings its own motivations (which may vary in intensity) and takes away its own rewards (which may vary in size and scale). The classifications of believer, cynic, entertainer, and expert are not mutually exclusive and, moreover, may be adopted and adapted for specific occasions: the same person may believe that Stevie Nicks's well-documented cocaine addiction did lead to its bizarre consequences, dismiss the claim that a real murder was captured on a U.S. chart-topping single by the Ohio Players, enthusiastically relate Bob Dylan's visit to the unsuspecting plumber as a whimsical joke, and use the detected synchronicities between *The Dark Side of the Moon* and *The Wizard of Oz* as evidence of his/her musical expertise. Furthermore, there is, of course, no guarantee that the audience to whom these myths are told will understand them in the way they are explained by the storyteller: what may be presented as a joke may be perceived as a fact; what is told as an example of expert knowledge may be simply disbelieved. 19

THE SOCIAL FUNCTIONS OF POPULAR MUSIC'S URBAN LEGENDS

In the preceding section, I offered an analysis of the specific factors influencing those storytellers actively involved in the generation of popular music's urban myths. Alongside their personal motivations, it is equally important to consider the functions that the legends serve within the popular music community, and also within society as a whole. 20

First, in a very simple way, such stories provide conversational topics to assist in the establishment and maintenance of social relationships via interaction and communication. Earlier in this discussion, I referred to the ways in which rumor and gossip are routine 21 components of daily interaction. By bracketing them together, I may have implied that the two are identical. This is not strictly true.

> Gossip is like gossip anywhere else in the world. Men and women say things about other men and women; accuracy is beside the point. Rumour-mongering is different. Rumours arise out of social situations containing affective alternatives: the accuracy or truth of the matter is important because . . . [it] will affect future thought and action. (Burridge 130–31)

In this sense, the urban legends discussed above tend to be, in the main, examples of gossip. Although individual storytellers may vociferously defend or attack the reliability of the accounts they present, ultimately any attempts to "prove" or "disprove" the allegations are irrelevant, since their "truth" or "untruth" is relatively unimportant. So too are the value judgments listeners may choose to impose on the stories they hear: the "revelations" about Elvis Presley's use of a rubber hose may be interpreted as a playful prank or offensive or lewd behavior; Stevie Nicks's anal intake of cocaine may invite sympathy or outrage. Fundamentally, both episodes exist as bizarre and sensational tales, readily incorporated into patterns of gossip that allow audiences to exchange intimate and idiosyncratic details of a celebrity's life. They satisfy some of the recurring needs which guide our use of the media and media-related activities—surveillance, personal identity formation, and the establishment of social relationships. Further, their longevity and the absence of a consistent "preferred reading" in response to the events they depict support the general assertion that "the purpose of gossip about celebrities is not to elevate or idealise them as exemplary individuals. The choice of figures about whom gossip will be exchanged is as likely to include those regarded with resentment or derision as those regarded as heroic" (Turner 107). 22

Second, these tales can be seen as modern variants of the deeper, often religious, myths about legendary places, people, and texts—Camelot, El Dorado, Atlantis; Jesus Christ, Confucius, Muhammad, Gautama Siddhartha; the Dead Sea Scrolls, the Holy Grail, the Gnostic Gospels. Whichever we choose to follow or explore, all contain a common characteristic: "It will be always the one, shape-shifting, yet marvellously constant story that we find, together with a challengingly persistent suggestion of more remaining to be experienced than will ever be known or told" (Campbell 3). If this inclination to seek guidance and enlightenment, to experience more, often from the discovery of hidden truths or lost documents, has been historically present in many spiritual communities, it is no less present across the terrain of contemporary popular culture. The remarkable success of Peter Jackson's 2001–2003 film trilogy of Tolkien's *The Lord of the Rings* and the global impact of 23

The Da Vinci Code (Brown) indicate the presence of a significant audience for whom the intersections between myth and reality, legend and logic, the known and the unknown, are central cultural foundations.

Popular musicians have been quickly accommodated into these, and similar, discourses. The pilgrimage (there is no other word) made by hundreds of thousands of fans each year to Graceland reproduces many of the expectations and obligations that a Catholic will take to Lourdes, a Hindu to the Ganges, a Druid to Stonehenge, or a Muslim to Mecca. The transposition of the Beatles from pop stars to spiritual messiahs and the sanctification of Bob Dylan by those of his fans who regard him not merely as a singer-songwriter, but as a philosopher-king are, perhaps, the two most pressing examples of this tendency. And, clearly, some of the urban myths relate to these changes of status very directly. The account of the Beatles' "missing" album, *Hot as Sun*, is less a tale of a few mislaid songs than it is of a legendary text whose truths and insights can never be recaptured. Dylan's arrival at the door of an unsuspecting plumber becomes a pseudo-Biblical parable in which we learn that any of us—however undeserving or unlikely—might one day meet our savior. 24

It may not be accidental that the rise of mass-mediated forms of entertainment (including popular music) has coincided with the decline of secular religion. Rojek's recognition of "inescapable parallels with religious worship, reinforced by the attribution by fans of magical or extraordinary powers" (53) is borne out by the repetition of urban legends in which popular music's people, texts, and places perform functions that are elevated far beyond the confines of mundane reality. 25

Third, there is a considerable number of urban legends whose primary social function is to allow for members of the public to engage in vicarious identification with the named protagonists and elements of their lifestyle. This should not be taken to mean that storytellers would wish to emulate the precise activities detailed in the stories, many of which are, after all, unpleasant, uncomfortable, and dangerous. Instead, the stories reflect an envy for the social and professional environment they describe—particularly for the freedom from constraints (material and behavioral) that wealth and fame allow popular musicians to enjoy. Performers thus become representatives of the communities constructed by their followers: "the musician becomes a blank slate on which the fans project their own desires, hopes, frustrations and unfulfilled pleasures" (Shapiro 216). 26

In this sense, it is not surprising that the largest single category of urban legends in popular music is about examples of sexual behavior; their popularity may be seen as evidence for the theory of catharsis, which argues that exposure to media depictions of sex or violence will act as a form of displacement therapy, by providing a relatively 27 harmless, fantasy outlet for potentially aggressive impulses that would otherwise remain unsatisfied (Feshbach).

So, while it is unlikely that many would wish to mimic Led Zeppelin's participation in a sexual assault that uses a mud shark, or would want to copy Marianne Faithfull and Mick Jagger in their consumption of a Mars bar, it may be more likely that these tales evoke a sense of envy for an unconventional and permissive lifestyle that is beyond scarcity and in which such behaviors are tolerated, even celebrated. And, within the world of urban legends, such behavior is not isolated; there are so many tales told of popular music and sexual excess that it has become one of the central components in the contemporary stereotype of the "rock star." In addition, and crucially, popular music's tacit encouragement of such behavior is not meaningless. 28

> By communicating certain meanings, or structures of meanings, it offers its audiences ways of seeing the world, of interpreting experiences; it offers them values that have a profound impact on the ways they respond to particular situations and challenges. (Grossberg 154)

In short, these stories allow for the construction of a homologous relationship between the real world of the storyteller (and listeners) and the perceived world that urban legends describe. 29

Fourth, some tales are employed individually to perform important political functions. Specifically, an urban legend may emerge to cope with an immediate and ideologically damaging situation. The clearest example of this is the recurring assertion that Elvis Presley faked his death, and is alive and well. Presley's life illustrated both the optimism of "the American dream" and the tragedy of "the American nightmare." Born in impoverished circumstances in Tupelo, Mississippi, the Memphis truck driver became the world's most celebrated entertainer and one of the iconic figures of the 20th century. His career—on record, in movies, in cabaret—provided a ringing endorsement of the belief that, in the land of opportunity, nothing was impossible for those with talent, hard work, and a degree of good luck. When he died in 1977, drug-damaged, bloated, and obese, face down in a pool of vomit on the floor of his bathroom, his death seemed to be an equally emphatic demonstration of the poisonous and corrupting repercussions of his success as a popular musician. 30

To admit the circumstances of his death is therefore to undermine the legitimacy of a national ideology that promotes ambition, possession, and wealth—for what good are such attributes if they lead to a lonely and miserable end? But by choosing to deny his death and prolonging "the liberatory celebration of his life" (Gottdeiner 200), which 31 is "confirmed" by the many reported sightings of him, that ideology is protected. In this case, although it clearly overlaps with the type of myth which functions as a religious/spiritual fable (in that Elvis, like Jesus, is "resurrected"), the urban legend is less about the extraordinary nature of Presley himself, and more about the maintenance of a political philosophy to which the singer himself, and many of his fans, fully subscribed.

Fifth, in their position as cultural texts, the materials of popular 32
music (songs, performances, recordings) continually offer themselves for interpretation. "Meaning," however defined, is contingent, malleable, transitory, and reached only through subtle negotiation. The idea that any text, musical or otherwise, possesses a single, absolute "meaning" is difficult to sustain, since it rests on an assumption that it contains a deliberate message, which is decoded by the reader in the way it was encoded by the producer, and which is accepted uncritically. Texts generate multiple meanings; "alternative readings" are equally valid. In the context of popular music, where, as indicated above, "word of mouth" reports, comparisons, and evaluations play a major role in the politics of consumption, this has helped to create a discourse in which not only alternative meanings, but alternative narratives, explanations, and histories are readily found. And the locations in which we come across many of these alternative accounts are in its urban legends.

Wolff has argued that "the reader, viewer or audience is actively 33
involved in the construction of the work of art . . . without the act of reception/consumption, the cultural product is incomplete" (95). Thus, the discovery that the scream during the percussion break in the Ohio Players' "Love Rollercoaster" is the sound of a murder completes the listeners' understanding of the track. The revelation that the Beatles' album covers from *Rubber Soul* to *Let It Be* contain visual and verbal clues that confirm Paul McCartney's death adds to our knowledge of the group's musical output in those years. And the disclosure that in *The Dark Side of the Moon* Pink Floyd fashioned a precise musical soundtrack to accompany *The Wizard of Oz* increases our estimation of the group's musical virtuosity.

> The reader is always right, and no one can take away the freedom to make whatever use of a text which suits him . . . the right to leaf back and forward, to skip whole passages, to read sentences against the grain, to misunderstand them, to reshape them, to embroider them with every possible association, to draw conclusions from the text of which the text knows nothing. (Enzensberger 11)

Popular music's capacity to sustain this type of urban legend 34
provides the setting and the opportunity for an escape from the tyranny of imposed meaning, in which misunderstanding, reshaping, embroidery—"textual poaching" (Jenkins)—can take place.

CONCLUSION

In the detailed telling of the stories themselves, in the motivations of 35
the storytellers, and in the social functions they serve, the urban legends of popular music differ from other kinds of urban folklore. Those tales are essentially tales of warning: they are direct descendants of the traditional fairy tale, whose main function is to allow members of a community (particularly the young) to access the wisdom and experience of past generations in order to learn of the risks that exist in the wider world. The dangers faced by Little Red Riding Hood, Snow White, and Hansel and Gretel are exactly the same dangers awaiting today's unsuspecting youngsters; thus, the encounter with a vanishing hitchhiker teaches us to be wary of strangers; the fate of the young babysitter reminds us to be vigilant at all times; the eating of the funeral ashes tells us to avoid impulsive actions.

By contrast, popular music's urban legends contain little in the way 36
of warning or guidance; they stand by themselves as independent narratives, told to amuse, to shock, to impress, rather than to educate. Indeed, they bear a remarkable similarity to the traditional tales, or "oral histories," related by storytellers in the communities of North Africa. Alongside the snake-charmers, acrobats, dancers, and other entertainers in Jemaa El Fna, the main square in Marrakech, the practice continues today:

> They're the most skilled of the entertainers . . . their themes are love, death, conquest: the more melodramatic the better. Once a story's been declaimed, it's taken up by another teller and passed on to an ever-growing audience: a verbal chain letter, registering new shifts of emphasis each time it's retold. (Gladstone-Thompson 197)

In addition, they reflect the nature of popular music itself and 37
its social and professional practices, in which chaos and hedonism are routinely presented as equal partners:

> By any definition, being a professional musician can be a crazy way to make a living . . . between bursts of hyperactivity can be periods of cataclysmic boredom. It takes a special effort to avoid this potentially hazardous rollercoaster. (Shapiro 213)
> No matter how one uses the music—the ultimate escape, soothe the pain, liberate the spirit, contemplate life, have fun, make passionate love—it remains an integral part of our lifescripts. (Friedlander 295)

Within an environment that (apparently) values risk, excess, 38
sensuality, and flamboyance and rejects a philosophy of deferred gratification in favor of the pursuit of immediate rewards, accounts of behaviors that display restraint and caution are therefore deemed

inappropriate. In short, the urban legends of popular music effectively manipulate the (stereo)typical characteristics of performers and their associated lifestyle into convenient and familiar narrative forms that are generated and circulated by its followers and fans.

Whether they are accurate or inaccurate is irrelevant; whether 39
they are believed or disbelieved is unimportant. However disruptive, however contrived, however fanciful they may appear, their real significance lies therefore not in their particular details, but in their general role as sources of images, ideas, and information which run counter to, undermine, and challenge "official" discourses. In creating their own narratives, interpretations, and explanations, those previously confined to roles as consumers of cultural texts are, individually and in collaboration with others, demonstrating their ability to also act as producers and distributors of cultural texts.

WORKS CITED

Adorno, Theodor W. *The Culture Industry*. London: Routledge, 1991.

Becker, Howard. *Outsiders*. New York: The Free Press, 1963.

Bourdieu, Pierre. *Distinction*. New York: Routledge, 1985.

Brown, Dan. *The Da Vinci Code*. New York: Bantam, 2003.

Brunvald, Jan Harold. *The Vanishing Hitchhiker: American Urban Legends and their Meanings*. New York: Norton, 1981.

Burridge, Kenelm. "Cargo." *Mythology*. Ed. Pierre Maranda. Harmondsworth: Penguin, 1972. 127–35.

Campbell, Joseph. *The Hero with a Thousand Faces*. Princeton, NJ: Princeton UP, 1949.

Castells, Manuel. *The Rise of the Network Society*. Oxford: Blackwell, 1996.

Denisoff, R. Serge and George Plasketes. *True Disbelievers: Elvis Contagion*. Somerset, NJ: Transaction, 1995.

Duncombe, Stephen. *Notes from Underground: Zines and the Politics of Alternative Culture.* London: Verso, 1997.

Enzensberger, Hans Magnus. *Mediocrity and Delusion: Collected Diversions*. London: Verso, 1992.

Feshbach, Seymour. "The Drive Reducing Function of Fantasy Behaviour." *Journal of Abnormal and Social Psychology* 50 (1955): 3–11.

Festinger, Leon, Henry W. Riecken, and Stanley Schachter. *When Prophecy Fails.* Minneapolis: U of Minnesota P, 1956.

Fisher, Dana R. "Rumoring Theory and the Internet: A Framework for Analyzing the Grass Roots." *Social Science Computer Review* 16.2 (1998): 158–68.

Friedlander, Paul. *Rock and Roll: A Social History*. Boulder, CO: Westview, 1996.

Gladstone-Thompson, Anthony. "The City in the 1960s." *Marrakech: The Red City*. Ed. Barnaby Rogerson and Stephen Lavington. London: Sickle Moon Books, 2003.

Gottdeiner, Mark. "Dead Elvis as Other Jesus." *In Search of Elvis*. Ed. Vernon Chadwick. Boulder, CO: Westview, 1997. 189–200.

Grossberg, Lawrence. "Rock and Roll in Search of an Audience." *Popular Music and Communication*. Ed. James Lull. London: Sage, 1992. 152–75.

Hoggart, Richard. *The Uses of Literacy*. London: Chatto & Windus, 1957.

Jenkins, Henry. *Textual Poachers: Television Fans and Participatory Culture*. New York: Routledge, 1992.

Jenson, Joli. "Fandom as Pathology: The Consequences of Characterization." *The Adoring Audience: Fan Culture and Popular Media*. Ed. Lisa A. Lewis. London: Routledge, 1992. 9–29.

Jones, Alison. *Dictionary of World Folklore*. Edinburgh: Larousse, 1995.

Kent, Nicholas. *Naked Hollywood*. London: BBC Books, 1991.

Lurie, Mison. *Imaginary Friends*. London: Heinemann, 1967.

Marcus, Greil. *Dead Elvis: A Chronicle of Cultural Obsession*. New York: Doubleday, 1991.

Marshall, P. David. *Celebrity and Power: Fame in Contemporary Culture*. Minneapolis: U of Minnesota P, 1997.

Mulkay, Michael. *On Humour*. Cambridge: Polity, 1988.

Palmer, Jerry. *Taking Humour Seriously*. London: Routledge, 1994.

Palmer, Robert. *Rock & Roll: An Unruly History*. New York: Harmony, 1995.

Patterson, R. Gary. *The Walrus Was Paul*. Nashville, TN: Dowling Press, 1996.

Reeve, Andru J. *Turn Me On, Dead Man*. Ann Arbor. MI: Popular Culture Ink, 1994.

Rodman, Gilbert B. *Elvis after Elvis: The Posthumous Career of a Living Legend*. New York: Routledge, 1996.

Rojek, Chris. *Celebrity*. London: Reaktion Books, 2001.

Shapiro, Harry. *Waiting for the Man: The Story of Drugs and Popular Music*. London: Helter Skelter, 1999.

Tolkien J. R. R. *The Lord of the Rings*. London: Allen & Unwin, 1955.

Turner, Graeme. *Understanding Celebrity*. London: Sage, 2004.

Wills, Geoff and Cary L. Cooper. *Pressure Sensitive: Popular Musicians under Stress*. London: Sage, 1988.

Wolff, Janet. *The Social Production of Art*. London: Macmillan, 1981.

Examining the Text

1. How does the author define the term "urban legend" for the purposes of this article? What are some social factors contributing to the rise in urban legend lore in contemporary society, according to the author?

2. What are the three key "recurring characteristics" that, in their form and content, relate to the structural, ideological, and occupational dimensions of popular music-centered urban legends? What qualities do these pop-musical tales share with more "traditional" urban legends, and what traits distinguish rock and hip-hop urban legends with nonmusical ones?

3. In this article, the author proposes a "fourfold typology of storytellers"—that is, a breakdown of the characteristics of different groups responsible for creating and disseminating music-based urban legends. What are the personality qualities and motivations of each group of storytellers, and how does each go about contributing to the ever-growing body of urban legend?

4. Along with his analysis of pop-musical storytellers' personal dynamics, the author states that it is "important to consider the functions that the legends serve within the popular music community, and also within society as a whole." The author then lists and explains five functions that rock-centered legends might serve, either socially or psychologically, or both. Explain these functions, and consider their validity, based upon your own experience and observation.

5. *Thinking rhetorically:* This article falls squarely within the genre of academic discourse called media studies. What is the author's intention of picking this topic in the first place, and what does he intend to prove by analyzing the subject in such exhaustive detail? By what methods does he achieve this result?

For Group Discussion

What are some of the "traditional" urban legends within the sphere of popular music, as presented by the author of this article? If you have heard any of these legends, feel free to amplify them in the small-group discussion setting, filling in any additional narrative material or "gory details" you may have heard. Next, add to this list any pop-musical urban legends *not* covered by Inglis in this piece, and relate that story with as much descriptive detail as you can. Finally, feel free to go beyond the sphere of popular music, relating any other urban legends that support—or perhaps even disprove—the author's assertions in this essay. After reassembling as a full class, have each group report its additional facts and stories and discuss the ways in which class members acquired this knowledge: did this material arrive in the ways predicted by Inglis in this piece, or are there additional ways of disseminating urban legends that the author may not have considered?

Writing Suggestion

Based upon the lists generated in group discussion (see above) choose one of the dozens of pop-musical urban legends circulating on the Web and/or by word of mouth, and write a mini-research or "I-search" essay on it. The I-Search paper has a slightly different voice than the standard academic research paper, as modeled by the essay "Urban Legends and Popular Music." Where the writer of the standard research paper assumes a relatively detached and objective stance, as Ian Inglis did for this essay, the I-Search paper encourages you to assume a more visible role in the presentation. You might consider structuring your paper through several related sections: an introduction, in which you explain your reason for choosing the particular urban legend for analysis; information you already know, or assumptions you have already made, about the legend in question; your search for additional information;

and a summary of the new information you discovered. In the "search" section, you will pursue information about the urban legend mainly by searching the Web, but friends and acquaintances may serve as resources as well. As you write your essay, describe your search in the form of a narrative in which you highlight the key information you have found, and then conclude your essay by comparing your original knowledge and assumptions about the legend with the facts you finally revealed. If you were surprised and/or illuminated by any of your discoveries, you might describe that reaction in detail, in order to lend closure to your essay's conclusion.

ADDITIONAL SUGGESTIONS FOR WRITING ABOUT POPULAR MUSIC

1. Americans receive a great deal of information about important issues—for example, presidential elections, gender-role attitudes, the legalization of drugs—from popular music and the media that purvey it. Write an essay in which you examine the representation of one important social issue or problem through music. For instance, you might focus on how the United States' environmental policy, or inner-city poverty, or the health-care crisis, or the effects of religious fundamentalism, or the threat of international terror, is represented in recent song lyrics, on AM and FM radio stations, and in videos on YouTube.

2. Write an essay in which you first construct a detailed description of a band or an individual performer whose music you know very well, and then analyze the themes embodied in that band's songs. Discuss the effects your band's or individual artist's music has on its listeners and some possible reasons for that band/artist's popularity or lack thereof with mainstream listeners.

3. Imagine that you've recently arrived in the United States from China or any other country that has a very restrictive Internet access policy. You surf the Web freely for the first time and find yourself watching several hours' worth of music clips on YouTube. Based upon this initial viewing, write a description of the interests, attitudes, lifestyles, and customs of young Americans. Try to include information that you gather from everything you've seen during that hour—the videos, game shows, advertisements, promos for upcoming shows, and so on—and make sure that you render your descriptions in vivid detail, so that somebody from another country might visualize all the elements you describe.

4. Write an essay in which you discuss the relative advantages and disadvantages of several primary sources of popular music: television, radio, downloaded songs, record albums or compact discs, and videos—either on YouTube or on artists/bands' MySpace or other Web sites. Which of the these media outlets do you think most effectively conveys the messages intended by contemporary recording artists, and why? Which source do you think trivializes the music, turning it into a popular product without redeeming social relevance? What are the advantages and disadvantages of each pop-music source?

Internet Activities

1. Visit the Web sites of some diverse musicians (possible options are available on the *Common Culture* Web site). Write an essay describing these sites. What features do these Web sites offer? What differences/similarities can you note in the presentations of the different musical genres? How would you account for these differences/similarities? For instance, is there anything offered on a Web site devoted to a rock group that isn't available on a jazz Web site? Are the Web site's features indicative of the genre in any way; that is, do the form/appearance/layout of the site mirror the musical genre it presents?

2. With the advent of various forms of media on the Web, such as streaming radio broadcasts and YouTube videos, music has a new forum to reach an immediate, worldwide audience. Explore some sites that offer music from across the country and the world (options are available at the *Common Culture* Web site). Once you have sampled a diverse selection of music, write an essay categorizing and/or describing your findings. How is the availability of music on the Web changing how listeners access music and what they listen to? What type of music is available? Are any musical types represented more heavily than others? Are any music genres woefully lacking, in your opinion? How would you account for this representation (or lack thereof)?

Reading Images

Write an essay in which you compare and contrast the images of the two popular musicians, Tupac Shakur and Lady GaGa, as illustrated on pages CI-4 and CI-3 in the color section of this book. In this type of essay, you want to spend some time describing each image, so that the reader has a sense of the key visual features of each. Next, you might explore the ways in which the superficial appearances of both illustrations are similar or different (depending on your "reading" of the pictures, following the directions toward the end of Chapter 1). Finally, you will want to show how the images' other elements (coloration, composition, text, and so forth, also as described in Chapter 1 of this book) work in similar or different ways to put forth the images' messages, which may be subtly implied or blatantly "in-your-face."

The problem with this kind of essay is one of organization. Since a comparison/contrast essay by its nature involves looking at both similarities and differences, make sure that you structure your paper so that you don't have to jump back and forth too much from issue to issue, point to point. While many writers, when writing comparison/contrast-type pieces, sometimes favor this approach, you might want to experiment with discussing *all* the elements of the Tupac image and *then* going on to the GaGa, pointing out all its areas of likeness and dissimilarity. Ideally, your paper will flow smoothly and progress logically, while still covering all elements of likeness and dissimilarity.

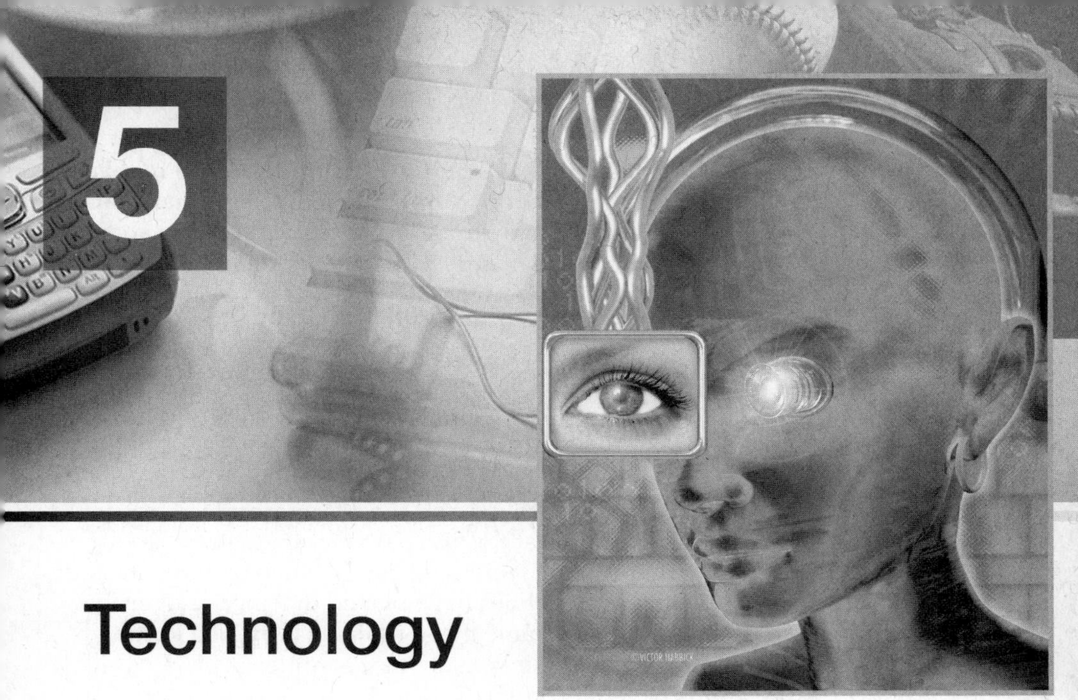

5

Technology

The image above seems to be clearly drawn from the realm of cyborgs and science fiction. After all, our eyeballs are not and could never be attached to a set of wires, or our eye sockets replaced with cybernetic implants. Or could they be? Although this computer-generated image is still a fiction, at least one real-life experiment comes pretty close to it. Steve Mann, a professor of electrical engineering at the University of Toronto, has designed a device called the EyeTap, a very high-tech set of computerized eyeglasses that cause the eye to function as if it were a digital camera. This eye/camera feeds images back into a computer, which can then process the images and can actually alter what the user sees (http://www.eyetap.org). Mann has also designed other kinds of wearable computers, devices that allow humans to change how they interact with their environments and to live in a computer-mediated reality.

The cyborg image and the EyeTap system may both seem extreme, but how far are they really from other technologies that we use every day to enhance our lives and mediate our interactions with the world? Just thinking of our sense of sight, the technologies we commonly use range from simple eyeglasses and sunglasses to contact lenses and LASIK surgery. A wearable computer like the EyeTap is perhaps just the next logical step, one that harnesses the power of the computer in order to augment and alter the capabilities of the human eye. Why wouldn't a cybernetic implant be the next step after that? And after you have the computer implanted in your eye, how about attaching your earphones permanently to your ears, or sticking your cell phone earbud permanently onto your skull? As the technologies in our lives become smaller, faster, and better suited to our needs, it's increasingly important for us to decide on their appropriate uses and be aware of their limitations.

In a wide range of ways, technologies shape our everyday activities, augment our capabilities, and help define who we are individually and as a society. Indeed, like the other subjects in *Common Culture*, technology exerts a profound and mostly unexamined impact on our lives. Historians tell us that this has always been the case, and so we start the chapter with an engaging overview, written by John Steele Gordon, of the role that automobiles have played in America over the past century. Following that is a more theoretical article by Neil Postman that provides a framework for thinking about the influence of any technology, assessing its benefits and its drawbacks. The second section of the chapter offers four articles on the most influential technology of our current times, the computer. Authors weigh in on the computer's impact on our personal, social, and professional lives as well as its potential for changing (for better and for worse) our psychological well-being and our mental processes. Altogether, these readings enact the basic premise of this chapter: that technology demands our sustained critical attention, and that by looking carefully at the machines that human use, we can get a better sense of where our species is headed.

Engine of Liberation

JOHN STEELE GORDON

Although computers may be the technology of our times, automobiles have certainly had a major impact on America over the past century. In the article that follows, John Steele Gordon describes the physical, economic, and social consequences of the automobile and shows the range of ways in which this technology has shaped our country and our lives—for instance, by bringing into existence suburbs, credit cards, motels, billboards, and of course, drive-in movies and drive-through restaurants. Americans have a particularly strong relationship with cars; Gordon writes that America is "a country that loves its cars almost as much as it loves its liberty." Indeed, from NASCAR to Disney/Pixar's Cars *to MTV's* Pimp My Ride, *cars figure largely in popular American culture. A very practical technology that's an essential (and unexamined) part of our everyday lives, cars also have potent symbolic meanings, for individuals and for our entire culture.*

Gordon wrote this article for American Heritage *in 1996.* ***As you read,*** *consider whether any fundamental changes in automobile technology (electric cars?) or in the contemporary world (pollution? traffic?) would cause you to modify Gordon's assessment of the impact of automobiles today.*

The automobile is not an American invention. But an industry capable of manufacturing automobiles in vast numbers at prices the common man can afford most certainly is. And it is this invention that changed the world. 1

To get some idea of just how much, let's do a thought experiment. Imagine it is six o'clock in the afternoon of a late August day in the year 1900. We are standing at the corner of Forty-second Street and Fifth Avenue in the heart of New York City. On the southwest corner rises the great ivy-clad receiving reservoir of the city's water supply. Now empty, it will soon be torn down to make way for the New York Public Library. 2

On the northeast corner stands the house of Levi P. Morton, international banker, former Vice President of the United States, and former governor of New York. Northward the mansions of the nation's other superrich line both sides of the avenue as far as Central Park and, on the east side of the thorough-fare, far beyond. The temperature is ninety; the humidity is not much lower. Cloud banks building in the west promise rain, and perhaps relief, in an hour or two. 3

Listen for a second. What do you hear? 4

You hear the horses. In the greatest metropolis of the Western 5
Hemisphere there are nearly as many horses as there are people, perhaps two million animals throughout the five boroughs. The thousands of vehicles plunging up and down the avenue and the nearby cross streets in the gathering rush hour are almost all pulled by one or more of them. Their iron shoes clang on the Belgian paving blocks at every step; their harnesses and bells jingle with every movement; their snorts and whinnies and occasional screams punctuate the background noise.

You take a deep breath. What do you smell? 6

You smell the horses. It is an odor as overwhelming and pervasive 7
as the smell of cheese in a cheese factory. To be sure, the inhabitants of that world do not notice it. They have smelled it all their lives, and their brains, in self-defense, have long since ceased to bring it to conscious attention. But we, brief visitors from the future, are almost gagged by it.

You look about you. What do you see? 8

You see the horses. Far worse, you see what the horses do to the 9
streets. Many are sweating profusely, their tongues lolling out of their foam-beslobbered mouths as they labor in the heat. All are urinating and defecating frequently. Each horse produces about two gallons of urine a day and twenty pounds of excrement. That's twenty thousand tons a day in New York City, greater than the weight of a battleship of the time. House sparrows, imported in the 1850s, ate the seeds in the droppings and help break them up to be more easily washed away. Nourished by this inexhaustible food supply, the birds breed in enormous numbers and excrete in their turn.

And horses die. The more unfortunate, which pull not the car- 10
riages of the rich but the drays of ordinary commerce, often die in harness, and their bodies are left by the sides of the streets, to be dragged off by private contractors paid by the city. Perhaps an average of twenty-five a day drop dead on the streets of Manhattan, more in the heat and stress of high summer. The bodies are cleared quickly from so busy and fashionable a corner as Forty-second and Fifth, but in the side streets and less elegant parts of town their remains can lie for days, swelling and stinking in the August sun, a mecca for flies, before they are carted off and disposed of.

In 1996, however, they are all gone, except for a few dozen car- 11
riage horses that haul tourists at extravagant prices in nice weather. Today the swish of tires over asphalt and the hum of engines provide the background music for the city's streets, rather than the clip-clop of horses. The horn blast of an angry driver has replaced the shriek of a suddenly terrified animal.

The next time you read an article on the horrors of automobile 12
pollution, you might remember your brief visit to another time and another place, a place and time where the pollution of horses lay underfoot as thick as fallen snow and filled the air as thick as fog.

Then, perhaps, you'll give a silent thank-you to Henry Ford and his brethren for freeing us from the tyranny of the horse, which, after all, was exactly what they set out to do in the first place.

Of course, those men did much more than that. It was the cheap automobile, far beyond any other invention, that transformed the daily life of the nineteenth century into that of the twentieth, especially in America, a country that loves its cars almost as much as it loves its liberty. 13

Let's be clear though. For all its importance the automobile was not a fundamental invention. Such an invention must be something completely new under the sun, and the automobile, when all is said and done, is still just a horseless carriage. Fundamental inventions overturn the cultures that created them and bring forth whole new ones in their place. Twelve thousand years ago agriculture doomed the hunter-gatherer way of life and, in a few millenniums, created civilization. The printing press brought the Middle Ages to a crashing halt in only a few decades. Three centuries later the steam engine ended the primacy of land as the basis of wealth and made possible the triumph of capitalism and democracy. In our own day the computer in the form of the microprocessor is, right before our eyes, remaking the world once again in ways that as yet we only dimly perceive. 14

But if the automobile did not overturn nineteenth-century civilization, it greatly enlarged its possibilities and strengthened numerous trends already under way—and, as we have seen, made the world a much nicer place. In doing so, it put its stamp on this country, visually, economically, and socially, even artistically, as no other invention—including that great transformer of the nineteenth century, the railroad—ever has. 15

First, let's look at the visual. One need only compare a nineteenth-century city, such as Chicago, with an essentially twentieth-century one, such as Houston or Los Angeles, to see how profound has been the impact of the automobile on the urban landscape. It has had an equally profound effect on the rural one. 16

In 1900 there were only some two hundred miles of paved roads in the entire country outside of cities. There was little need for them because only 4,000 cars were manufactured in the United States that year. A decade later, however, 187,000 cars were produced in a single year, and the demand for good roads was growing as quickly as the nation's auto fleet. The Bronx River Parkway, begun in 1907 in New York, was the first limited-access highway, intended as much for "outings" as for actually getting somewhere. By the 1920s a system of interstate highways was beginning to take shape, one that would be completely replaced by another, far grander, starting in the 1950s. 17

The commerce along these new thoroughfares was from the outset affected by the automobile. The new cars needed gasoline. At first this could be purchased at general stores, bicycle shops, or smithies 18 trying to reverse an irreversible decline. Then in 1905 the first purpose-built gas station opened, in St. Louis, Missouri. In 1913 the big oil companies, sensing opportunity, began opening their own stations. Soon there were hundreds of thousands.

But the new gas stations faced a problem. At the speed of a horse, 19
about six miles an hour, people had time to look ahead and see what they were approaching. At thirty and soon forty miles per hour, however, that was much more difficult. So signs grew larger, and corporate logos became important for the first time because they could be grasped in an instant. The wordy style of nineteenth-century advertising started to disappear, not just from billboards but from newspapers and magazines, as the old sort of ad began to seem antiquated. The new punchy, visual style, of course, was perfectly pre-adapted to what would become the dominant advertising medium by the 1950s, television.

The new advertising style soon affected American literature as 20
well, as did the automobile directly. For instance, the Philip Marlowe novels of Raymond Chandler—set in the already auto-besotted Los Angeles of the 1930s and 1940s—are unlike anything written in the nineteenth century.

The need to grab the attention of the passerby in an instant also 21
led to numerous minor American art forms, such as buildings in the shape of ducks, tepees, Paul Bunyan, and heaven only knows what else. There was even a new kind of poetry. In 1925 a retired insurance salesman named Clinton Odell began manufacturing a brushless shaving cream. He sought to find a new way to bring it to the public's attention, and it was his son, Allan, who found it. He suggested using a series of small billboards, each with one line of a jingle on it and the last with the name of the product: WITHIN THIS VALE/OF TOIL/AND SIN/YOUR HEAD CROWS BALD/BUT NOT YOUR CHIN—USE/BURMA-SHAVE.

It virtually demanded the attention of the passing motorist (and, 22
perhaps especially, any child passengers), and the result was immediate commercial success for Burma-Shave and a national craze for jingle writing. By the 1940s there were as many as seven thousand different Burma-Shave jingles lining the nation's highways, and the company paid a hundred dollars for every one sent in and accepted. Today the Burma-Shave campaign lives only in the advertising hall of fame (if there is such a thing), but perhaps an echo can be seen in a latter-day minor art form, the vanity license plate, which also commands close attention from passersby. (My favorite was on a Rolls-Royce Corniche convertible spotted on Sutton Place in Manhattan. Its license plate: "2ND CAR.")

Soon hotels were forced to evolve to satisfy the needs of motorists. 23
Motels (the word dates to 1925) sprang up, surrounded by ample parking and with each guest's room only a few feet from his vehicle. Restaurants

soon began catering to motorists, many of them in a hurry. Unfortunately the spread of franchising in the 1960s and 1970s much diminished the regional diversity of American highway cuisine. Today a hamburger in Seattle is likely to be indistinguishable from one in Georgia, right down to the shape, size, and color of the bag the french fries come in.

But it was only after World War II that the automobile made 24 its biggest impact on the American landscape by making possible the modern suburb. Suburbs were created in the first instance by the railroads. The editor Horace Greeley used to commute to New York in the summer from his farm in Chappaqua, forty miles north of the city. These suburbs were very limited, however, because once the passengers disembarked from the train, they were again reduced to the speed of a horse. (Even worse, they had to wait to be picked up at the station. A horse can't sit in a parking lot all day long.) So a demographic map of an American city in 1900 would have looked a bit like a daddy longlegs, with a dense core of population in the city center and only thin streaks of population running outward along the railroad and trolley tracks. All the rest was deep country.

The automobile allowed a completely different pattern. To- 25 day there is often a semi-void of residential population at the heart of a large city, surrounded by rings of less and less densely settled suburbs. These suburbs, primarily dependent on the automobile to function, are where the majority of the country's population lives, a fact that has transformed our politics. Every city that had a major-league baseball team in 1950, with the exception only of New York—ever the exception—has had a drastic loss in population within its city limits over the last four and a half decades, sometimes by as much as 50 percent as people have moved outward, thanks to the automobile.

In more recent years the automobile has had a similar effect on the 26 retail commercial sectors of smaller cities and towns, as shopping malls and superstores such as the Home Depot and Wal-Mart have sucked commerce off Main Street and into the surrounding countryside.

But the automobile has had as great an effect on the country's 27 "economy as on its landscape. Nineteenth-century industry was largely dedicated to making industrial products, such as steel, products not bought by individuals. But the twentieth century's economy has been increasingly consumer-oriented. The automobile was the first great industrial consumer product and did much to generate that sector of the economy. A trivial part of the American economy in 1900, the automobile industry was by the 1920s the country's largest, as it remains to this day. For the automobile industry is not just the manufacture of automobiles. It encompasses as well the maintenance, servicing, and fueling of cars. Their garaging and parking are major industries in large cities. More, cars must be insured. Traffic must be policed. There are now magazines devoted solely to the sound systems in cars. Auto racing is no small affair. Highway building is a major component of the construction industry. Automobiles account for a very large percent of the gross domestic product.

Indirectly, the economic effect of the automobile has been equally profound. The vast growth of the petroleum, glass, and rubber industries, among others, in this century was largely fueled by the automobile. The drastic decline in the horse population resulted in vast amounts of agricultural land being switched from forage crops to human food, greatly reducing the cost of the latter as the supply increased. The twentieth-century advertising and hotel and tourism industries were built upon the automobile. 28

So was commercial credit. The automobile remains the most expensive major consumer product, an average-price car costing a very substantial fraction of average annual income. Banks in the early twentieth century dealt mostly with business and the very affluent, not the average worker. So automobile manufacturers set up their own credit organizations (such as the General Motors Acceptance Corporation) to help finance automobile purchases. 29

The idea of ordinary citizens borrowing money to buy the wherewithal of a better life was radically new in the early twentieth century, when most Americans still did not even have bank accounts or own their homes. But once it was established by the automobile, it was, inevitably, soon applied to other expensive consumer products, such as household appliances. Credit has been moving outward ever since to encompass more and more of the American economy. Today's near-universal use of credit cards to purchase even such minor items as meals is, in a very real sense, a product of the automobile. 30

The automobile's impact on the American economy also had a vast influence on the ebb and flow of geopolitics in this century. During the Second World War the American automobile industry, by orders of magnitude the largest in the world, produced a grand total of 139 cars. Instead, that huge industrial capacity had been transformed into the "arsenal of democracy," turning out, in breathtaking volumes, the matériel that allowed the Allies to win the war. The Ford Motor Company alone had more military production than the entire Italian economy in the war years. 31

But it is socially, perhaps that the automobile has had its greatest impact on American civilization. For much of its history America was a lonely place. Europe was rich in people, poor in land. European farmers usually lived in villages. They walked out to the surrounding fields (usually owned by someone else) to work and back to the close proximity of their friends and neighbors at night. 32

But this country abounded in land, and its people were spread thinly upon it. The isolated farmhouse, set upon the family's own land, 33 quickly became the norm here, rather than the village. Many a pioneer family came to grief when one or more of its members could not cope with the lack of society. Until the automobile, there was no solution. The railroad had made rapid long-distance movement relatively easy, but local movement remained at the speed of the horse.

So if the nearest town was a mere five miles away, a visit to it would require virtually an entire day to accomplish, an expenditure of time that few farm families could afford very often. Even a visit to a nearby farm could be a considerable undertaking. The horses had to be hitched to a wagon or buggy, a matter that took several minutes even if the horse was in a cooperative mood, which was by no means guaranteed. Then, when the family returned, the horses had to be unhitched, cooled down, and cared for. Then, as now, horses were delicate and expensive means of transportation and required very high maintenance. Unless the family was affluent enough to hire people to handle these chores for them, they often had no real choice but to stay home. 34

The automobile, of course, changed that. Now a trip to town might take no more than an hour, a trip to a neighbor's place for a cup of coffee only a few minutes. The stifling isolation of American farm life began to lift. So did the isolation of the individual towns and the cozy local monopolies of bank and general store. Now families could easily get to the next town if they didn't like the service or the prices available in their own. 35

Another aspect of social life that the automobile changed was courting. Before the automobile, courting had to be largely accomplished in front of families and the watchful eyes of chaperons and was largely confined to one's closest neighbors. Now real privacy and a far wider selection was possible. The "date," once available in large measure only to city dwellers (a minority of the population in the nineteenth century), spread rapidly through the small towns and farms of rural America. 36

The automobile also gave women much more mobility and freedom. The skills needed to handle horses with confidence are difficult to acquire, but driving a car is easy. Once the electric starter removed the need for physical strength (and the device was commonplace by 1916), women began to move. It was the automobile as much as the Second World War that liberated women. American society, long the most fluid and thus the most dynamic in the world, has seen a quantum leap in that fluidity in the twentieth century, thanks to the automobile. And this evolving change has by no means played itself out. 37

Needless to say, much of this change did not come easily. The shift in agriculture caused by the automobile resulted in the squeezing out of marginal farmers and contributed in no small way to the onset of the Great Depression. The Joad family in Steinbeck's *The Grapes of Wrath* were forced to migrate to California (in, of course, an automobile) when their drought-suffering farm could no longer sustain them. 38

Americans had to learn, all too often at first hand, the power of half a ton or more of metal, glass, and rubber moving at forty miles an hour. Because the number of cars in the early days was small compared with later, the number of deaths was relatively low. But the slaughter on a vehicle-mile basis was awesome; in 1921 the rate was 24 per hundred million miles of travel. It began to decline as people became better drivers (most states did not require driver's licenses until the 1930s), roads improved, and cars became more ruggedly constructed. The year 1972 proved the worst in terms of highway deaths when 54,589 people died on the nation's highways, not much lower than the number who lost their lives in the entire Vietnam War then raging. 39

Since then the rate has dropped more or less steadily, thanks to far better-designed cars and highways (padded bridge abutments, for instance) and a decline in alcohol consumption. In 1995 the death rate per hundred million vehicle miles was only 1.7. 40

The mechanics and tinkers banging away in basements and carriage sheds at the turn of the century—men with names like Ford, Durant, Leland, Chrysler, Dodge, and Olds—weren't trying to change the world. Many looked no further than just getting their latest designs to work. Most hoped only to make a buck out of what they were doing, and many of course did so, some in huge amounts. 41

But unintentionally they also gave American civilization, and thus the world in this "American Century," their twentieth-century character, their very nature. That's why when people a hundred years from now imagine themselves standing at the corner of Forty-second Street and Fifth Avenue on a hot August day in the year 2000, they will have to conjure up the automobile—its sounds, its smells, its shapes—to bring the scene to life. 42

Examining the Text

1. How does Gordon define a "fundamental invention" in paragraph 14? What reasons does Gordon give for claiming that the automobile is *not* a fundamental invention? Do you agree with his reasoning?

2. According to Gordon, what are the major ways in which automobiles changed the landscape of America?

3. What have been the key social impacts of the automobile, according to Gordon? In his view, have these social changes been primarily positive or negative?

4. *Thinking rhetorically:* Why do you think Gordon begins his article with a "thought experiment"? In what ways does visualizing a New York City street scene in a pre-automobile era set the stage for the rest of Gordon's discussion? What impact do the sensory details that Gordon includes have on you as a reader?

For Group Discussion
Gordon deals fairly quickly with a wide range of ways in which the automobile has impacted American society over the past century. In a group with several other students, select one of the three main areas Gordon discusses: the physical landscape, the economy, or social life. Make a list of the items Gordon mentions in his discussion. Then add to this list, based on your own reading or observation, other ways that the automobile has impacted this aspect of American life. What general conclusions can you draw about the relative merits of the automobile based on your list of its consequences? That is, do you think the automobile has had a mostly positive or negative impact in the area that your group is discussing?

Writing Suggestion
Gordon considers the broad impact of the automobile on our country and the unique relationship Americans have historically had with automobiles. In this writing assignment, assess your own history with automobiles and their impact on you individually. What importance have specific cars or driving in general had as you grew up? What value do automobiles have for you currently? Identify any economically or symbolically important moments in your life that are associated with automobiles. What role do you see automobiles playing in your future?

The Judgment of Thamus

NEIL POSTMAN

If you've read Gerald Erion's article in Chapter 3, then you're already familiar with Neil Postman, the author of the following article. Erion's title—"Amusing Ourselves to Death with Television News"—is a direct reference to Postman's classic Amusing Ourselves to Death *(1985). In that book, Postman, who was a professor of "media ecology" at New York University, outlines the detrimental effects of television, on children as well as adults. Erion uses Postman's analysis to gain insight into the particular criticisms of television offered by Jon Stewart on* The Daily Show.

The article that follows comes from one of Postman's later books— Technopoly *(1992)—in which he extends his critique beyond the television screen to look more broadly at how technology influences our society. Although Postman was accused of being a technophobe, his argument here is more balanced: "Every technology is both a burden and a blessing; not either-or but this-and-that." Moreover, Postman believes that technological change is "ecological" in the sense that "One significant change generates total change." For Postman, the stakes are high when a new technology is introduced into a culture, and it is important that we think critically about technology if we are to live well with it.*

One reason we chose this article for Common Culture *is that we admire Postman's style of writing; we think that he crafted some particularly delightful phrases and sentences in this article.* **As you read,** *underline any segments of Postman's writing that you find especially pleasing to your stylistic sensibilities.*

You will find in Plato's *Phaedrus* a story about Thamus, the king of a great city of Upper Egypt. For people such as ourselves, who are inclined (in Thoreau's phrase) to be tools of our tools, few legends are more instructive than his. The story, as Socrates tells it to his friend Phaedrus, unfolds in the following way: Thamus once entertained the god Theuth, who was the inventor of many things, including numbers, calculation, geometry, astronomy, and writing. Theuth exhibited his inventions to King Thamus, claiming that they should be made widely known and available to Egyptians. Socrates continues: 1

> Thamus inquired into the use of each of them, and as Theuth went through them expressed approval or disapproval, according as he judged Theuth's claims to be well or ill founded. It would take too long to go through all that Thamus is reported to have said for and against each of Theuth's inventions. But when it came to writing, Theuth declared, "Here is an accomplishment, my lord the King, which will improve both the wisdom and the memory of the Egyptians. I have discovered a sure receipt for memory and wisdom." To this, Thamus replied, "Theuth, my paragon of inventors, the discoverer of an art is not the best judge of the good or harm which will accrue to those who practice it. So it is in this; you, who are the father of writing, have out of fondness for your off-spring attributed to it quite the opposite of its real function. Those who acquire it will cease to exercise their memory and become forgetful; they will rely on writing to bring things to their remembrance by external signs instead of by their own internal resources. What you have discovered is a receipt for recollection, not for memory. And as for wisdom, your pupils will have the reputation for it without the reality: they will receive a quantity of information without proper instruction, and in consequence be thought very knowledgeable when they are for the most part quite ignorant. And because they are filled with the conceit of wisdom instead of real wisdom they will be a burden to society."[1]

I begin my book with this legend because in Thamus' response there are several sound principles from which we may begin to learn how to think with wise circumspection about a technological society. In fact, there is even one error in the judgment of Thamus, from which we may also learn something of importance. The error is not in his claim that writing will damage memory and create false wisdom. It is 2 demonstrable that writing has had such an effect. Thamus' error is in his believing that writing will be a burden to society and *nothing but a burden*. For all his wisdom, he fails to imagine what writing's benefits might be, which, as we know, have been considerable. We may learn from this that it is a mistake to suppose that any technological innovation has a one-sided effect. Every technology is both a burden and a blessing; not either-or, but this-and-that.

Nothing could be more obvious, of course, especially to those 3
who have given more than two minutes of thought to the matter. Nonetheless, we are currently surrounded by throngs of zealous Theuths, one-eyed prophets who see only what new technologies can do and are incapable of imagining what they will *undo*. We might call such people Technophiles. They gaze on technology as a lover does on his beloved, seeing it as without blemish and entertaining no apprehension for the future. They are therefore dangerous and are to be approached cautiously. On the other hand, some one-eyed prophets, such as I (or so I am accused), are inclined to speak only of burdens (in the manner of Thamus) and are silent about the opportunities that new technologies make possible. The Technophiles must speak for themselves, and do so all over the place. My defense is that a dissenting voice is sometimes needed to moderate the din made by the enthusiastic multitudes. If one is to err, it is better to err on the side of Thamusian skepticism. But it is an error nonetheless. And I might note that, with the exception of his judgment on writing, Thamus does not repeat this error. You might notice on rereading the legend that he gives arguments *for* and *against* each of Theuth's inventions. For it is inescapable that every culture must negotiate with technology, whether it does so intelligently or not. A bargain is struck in which technology giveth and technology taketh away. The wise know this well, and are rarely impressed by dramatic technological changes, and never overjoyed. Here, for example, is Freud on the matter, from his doleful *Civilization and Its Discontents*:

> One would like to ask: is there, then, no positive gain in pleasure, no unequivocal increase in my feeling of happiness, if I can, as often as I please, hear the voice of a child of mine who is living hundreds of miles away or if I can learn in the shortest possible time after a friend has reached his destination that he has come through the long and difficult voyage unharmed? Does it mean nothing that medicine has succeeded in enormously reducing infant mortality and the danger of infection for women in childbirth, and, indeed, in considerably lengthening the average life of a civilized man?

Freud knew full well that technical and scientific advances are not 4
to be taken lightly, which is why he begins this passage by acknowledging them. But he ends it by reminding us of what they have undone:

> If there had been no railway to conquer distances, my child would never have left his native town and I should need no telephone to hear his voice; if travelling across the ocean by ship had not been introduced, my friend would not have embarked on his sea-voyage and I should not need a cable to relieve my anxiety about him. What is the use of reducing infantile mortality when it is precisely that reduction which imposes the greatest restraint on us in the begetting of children, so that, taken all round, we nevertheless rear no more children than in the days before the reign of hygiene, while at the same time we have created difficult conditions for our sexual life in marriage. . . . And, finally, what good to us is a long life if it is difficult and barren of joys, and if it is so full of misery that we can only welcome death as a deliverer?[2]

In tabulating the cost of technological progress, Freud takes a 5
rather depressing line, that of a man who agrees with Thoreau's remark that our inventions are but improved means to an unimproved end. The Technophile would surely answer Freud by saying that life has always been barren of joys and full of misery but that the telephone, ocean liners, and especially the reign of hygiene have not only lengthened life but made it a more agreeable proposition. That is certainly an argument I would make (thus proving I am no one-eyed Technophobe), but it is not necessary at this point to pursue it. I have brought Freud into the conversation only to show that a wise man—even one of such a woeful countenance—must begin his critique of technology by acknowledging its successes. Had King Thamus been as wise as reputed, he would not have forgotten to include in his judgment a prophecy about the powers that writing would enlarge. There is a calculus of technological change that requires a measure of even-handedness.

So much for Thamus' error of omission. There is another omis- 6
sion worthy of note, but it is no error. Thamus simply takes for granted—and therefore does not feel it necessary to say—that writing is not a neutral technology whose good or harm depends on the uses made of it. He knows that the uses made of any technology are largely determined by the structure of the technology itself—that is, that its functions follow from its form. This is why Thamus is concerned not with *what* people will write; he is concerned *that* people will write. It is absurd to imagine, Thamus advising, in the manner of today's standard-brand Technophiles, that, if only writing would be used for the production of certain kinds of texts and not others (let us say, for dramatic literature but not for history or philosophy), its disruptions could be minimized. He would regard such counsel as extreme naïveté. He would allow, I imagine, that a technology may be barred entry to a culture. But we may learn from Thamus the following: once a technology is admitted, it plays out its hand; it does

what it is designed to do. Our task is to understand what that design is—that is to say, when we admit a new technology to the culture, we must do so with our eyes wide open.

All of this we may infer from Thamus' silence. But we may learn even more from what he does say than from what he doesn't. He points out, for example, that writing will change what is meant by the words "memory" and "wisdom." He fears that memory will be confused with what he disdainfully calls "recollection," and he worries that wisdom will become indistinguishable from mere knowledge. This judgment we must take to heart, for it is a certainty that radical technologies create new definitions of old terms, and that this process takes place without our being fully conscious of it. Thus, it is insidious and dangerous, quite different from the process whereby new technologies introduce new terms to the language. In our own time, we have consciously added to our language thousands of new words and phrases having to do with new technologies—"VCR," "binary digit," "software," "front-wheel drive," "window of opportunity," "Walkman," etc. We are not taken by surprise at this. New things require new words. But new things also modify old words, words that have deep-rooted meanings. The telegraph and the penny press changed what we once meant by "information." Television changes what we once meant by the terms "political debate," "news," and "public opinion." The computer changes "information" once again. Writing changed what we once meant by "truth" and "law"; printing changed them again, and now television and the computer change them once more. Such changes occur quickly, surely, and, in a sense, silently. Lexicographers hold no plebiscites on the matter. No manuals are written to explain what is happening, and the schools are oblivious to it. The old words still look the same, are still used in the same kinds of sentences. But they do not have the same meanings; in some cases, they have opposite meanings. And this is what Thamus wishes to teach us—that technology imperiously commandeers our most important terminology. It redefines "freedom," "truth," "intelligence," "fact," "wisdom," "memory," "history"—all the words we live by. And it does not pause to tell us. And we do not pause to ask. 7

This fact about technological change requires some elaboration, and I will return to the matter in a later chapter. Here, there are several more principles to be mined from the judgment of Thamus that require mentioning because they presage all I will write about. For instance, Thamus warns that the pupils of Theuth will develop an undeserved reputation for wisdom. He means to say that those who cultivate competence in the use of a new technology become an elite group that are granted undeserved authority and prestige by those who have no such competence. There are different ways of expressing the interesting implications of this fact. Harold Innis, the father of modern communication studies, repeatedly spoke of the "knowledge monopolies" created 8 by important technologies. He meant precisely what Thamus had in mind: those who have control over the workings of a particular technology accumulate power and inevitably form a kind of conspiracy against those who have no access to the specialized knowledge made available by the technology. In his book, *The Bias of Communication*, Innis provides many historical examples of how a new technology "busted up" a traditional knowledge monopoly and created a new one presided over by a different group. Another way of saying this is that the benefits and deficits of a new technology are not distributed equally. There are, as it were, winners and losers. It is both puzzling and poignant that on many occasions the losers, out of ignorance, have actually cheered the winners, and some still do.

Let us take as an example the case of television. In the United States, 9
where television has taken hold more deeply than anywhere else, many people find it a blessing, not least those who have achieved high-paying, gratifying careers in television as executives, technicians, newscasters, and entertainers. It should surprise no one that such people, forming as they do a new knowledge monopoly, should cheer themselves and defend and promote television technology. On the other hand and in the long run, television may bring a gradual end to the careers of schoolteachers since school was an invention of the printing press and must stand or fall on the issue of how much importance the printed word has. For four hundred years, schoolteachers have been part of the knowledge monopoly created by printing, and they are now witnessing the breakup of that monopoly. It appears as if they can do little to prevent that breakup, but surely there is something perverse about schoolteachers being enthusiastic about what is happening. Such enthusiasm always calls to my mind an image of some turn-of-the-century blacksmith who not only sings the praises of the automobile but also believes that his business will be enhanced by it. We know now that his business was not enhanced by it; it was rendered obsolete by it, as perhaps the clearheaded blacksmiths knew. What could they have done? Weep, if nothing else.

We have a similar situation in the development and spread of 10
computer technology, for here too there are winners and losers. There can be no disputing that the computer has increased the power of large-scale organizations like the armed forces or airline companies or banks or tax-collecting agencies. And it is equally clear that the computer is now indispensable to high-level researchers in physics and other natural sciences. But to what extent has computer technology been an advantage to the masses of people? To steelworkers, vegetable-store owners, teachers, garage mechanics, musicians, bricklayers, dentists, and most of the rest into whose lives the computer now intrudes? Their private matters have been made more accessible to powerful institutions. They are more easily tracked and controlled; are

subjected to more examinations; are increasingly mystified by the decisions made about them; are often reduced to mere numerical objects. They are inundated by junk mail. They are easy targets for advertising agencies and political organizations. The schools teach their children to operate computerized systems instead of teaching things that are more valuable to children. In a word, almost nothing that they need happens to the losers. Which is why they are losers.

It is to be expected that the winners will encourage the losers to be enthusiastic about computer technology. That is the way of winners, and so they sometimes tell the losers that with personal computers the average person can balance a checkbook more neatly, keep better track of recipes, and make more logical shopping lists. They also tell them that their lives will be conducted more efficiently. But discreetly they neglect to say from whose point of view the efficiency is warranted or what might be its costs. Should the losers grow skeptical, the winners dazzle them with the wondrous feats of computers, almost all of which have only marginal relevance to the quality of the losers' lives but which are nonetheless impressive. Eventually, the losers succumb, in part because they believe, as Thamus prophesied, that the specialized knowledge of the masters of a new technology is a form of wisdom. The masters come to believe this as well, as Thamus also prophesied. The result is that certain questions do not arise. For example, to whom will the technology give greater power and freedom? And whose power and freedom will be reduced by it? 11

I have perhaps made all of this sound like a well-planned conspiracy, as if the winners know all too well what is being won and what lost. But this is not quite how it happens. For one thing, in cultures that have a democratic ethos, relatively weak traditions, and a high receptivity to new technologies, everyone is inclined to be enthusiastic about technological change, believing that its benefits will eventually spread evenly among the entire population. Especially in the United States, where the lust for what is new has no bounds, do we find this childlike conviction most widely held. Indeed, in America, social change of any kind is rarely seen as resulting in winners and losers, a condition that stems in part from Americans' much-documented optimism. As for change brought on by technology, this native optimism is exploited by entrepreneurs, who work hard to infuse the population with a unity of improbable hope, for they know that it is economically unwise to reveal the price to be paid for technological change. One might say, then, that, if there is a conspiracy of any kind, it is that of a culture conspiring against itself. 12

In addition to this, and more important, it is not always clear, at least in the early stages of a technology's intrusion into a culture, who will gain most by it and who will lose most. This is because the changes wrought by technology are subtle, if not downright mysterious, one might even 13 say wildly unpredictable. Among the most unpredictable are those that might be labeled ideological. This is the sort of change Thamus had in mind when he warned that writers will come to rely on external signs instead of their own internal resources, and that they will receive quantities of information without proper instruction. He meant that new technologies change what we mean by "knowing" and "truth"; they alter those deeply embedded habits of thought which give to a culture its sense of what the world is like—a sense of what is the natural order of things, of what is reasonable, of what is necessary, of what is inevitable, of what is real. Since such changes are expressed in changed meanings of old words, I will hold off until later discussing the massive ideological transformation now occurring in the United States. Here, I should like to give only one example of how technology creates new conceptions of what is real and, in the process, undermines older conceptions. I refer to the seemingly harmless practice of assigning marks or grades to the answers students give on examinations. This procedure seems so natural to most of us that we are hardly aware of its significance. We may even find it difficult to imagine that the number or letter is a tool or, if you will, a technology; still less that, when we use such a technology to judge someone's behavior, we have done something peculiar. In point of fact, the first instance of grading students' papers occurred at Cambridge University in 1792 at the suggestion of a tutor named William Farish.[3] No one knows much about William Farish; not more than a handful have ever heard of him. And yet his idea that a quantitative value should be assigned to human thoughts was a major step toward constructing a mathematical concept of reality. If a number can be given to the quality of a thought, then a number can be given to the qualities of mercy, love, hate, beauty, creativity, intelligence, even sanity itself. When Galileo said that the language of nature is written in mathematics, he did not mean to include human feeling or accomplishment or insight. But most of us are now inclined to make these inclusions. Our psychologists, sociologists, and educators find it quite impossible to do their work without numbers. They believe that without numbers they cannot acquire or express authentic knowledge.

I shall not argue here that this is a stupid or dangerous idea, only 14
that it is peculiar. What is even more peculiar is that so many of us do not find the idea peculiar. To say that someone should be doing better work because he has an IQ of 134, or that someone is a 7.2 on a sensitivity scale, or that this man's essay on the rise of capitalism is an A– and that man's is a C+ would have sounded like gibberish to Galileo or Shakespeare or Thomas Jefferson. If it makes sense to us, that is because our minds have been conditioned by the technology of numbers so that we see the world differently than they did. Our understanding of what is real is different. Which is another way of saying that embedded in every tool is an ideological bias, a predisposition to construct the

world as one thing rather than another, to value one thing over another, to amplify one sense or skill or attitude more loudly than another.

This is what Marshall McLuhan meant by his famous aphorism "The medium is the message." This is what Marx meant when he said, "Technology discloses man's mode of dealing with nature" and creates the "conditions of intercourse" by which we relate to each other. It is what Wittgenstein meant when, in referring to our most fundamental technology, he said that language is not merely a vehicle of thought but also the driver. And it is what Thamus wished the inventor Theuth to see. This is, in short, an ancient and persistent piece of wisdom, perhaps most simply expressed in the old adage that, to a man with a hammer, everything looks like a nail. Without being too literal, we may extend the truism: To a man with a pencil, everything looks like a list. To a man with a camera, everything looks like an image. To a man with a computer, everything looks like data. And to a man with a grade sheet, everything looks like a number. 15

But such prejudices are not always apparent at the start of a technology's journey, which is why no one can safely conspire to be a winner in technological change. Who would have imagined, for example, whose interests and what world-view would be ultimately advanced by the invention of the mechanical clock? The clock had its origin in the Benedictine monasteries of the twelfth and thirteenth centuries. The impetus behind the invention was to provide a more or less precise regularity to the routines of the monasteries, which required, among other things, seven periods of devotion during the course of the day. The bells of the monastery were to be rung to signal the canonical hours; the mechanical clock was the technology that could provide precision to these rituals of devotion. And indeed it did. But what the monks did not foresee was that the clock is a means not merely of keeping track of the hours but also of synchronizing and controlling the actions of men. And thus, by the middle of the fourteenth century, the clock had moved outside the walls of the monastery, and brought a new and precise regularity to the life of the workman and the merchant. 16

"The mechanical clock," as Lewis Mumford wrote, "made possible the idea of regular production, regular working hours and a standardized product." In short, without the clock, capitalism would have been quite impossible.[4] The paradox, the surprise, and the wonder are that the clock was invented by men who wanted to devote themselves more rigorously to God; it ended as the technology of greatest use to men who wished to devote themselves to the accumulation of money. In the eternal struggle between God and Mammon, the clock quite unpredictably favored the latter. 17

Unforeseen consequences stand in the way of all those who think they see clearly the direction in which a new technology will take us. Not even those who invent a technology can be assumed to be reliable 18 prophets, as Thamus warned. Gutenberg, for example, was by all accounts a devout Catholic who would have been horrified to hear that accursed heretic Luther describe printing as "God's highest act of grace, whereby the business of the Gospel is driven forward." Luther understood, as Gutenberg did not, that the mass-produced book, by placing the Word of God on every kitchen table, makes each Christian his own theologian—one might even say his own priest, or, better, from Luther's point of view, his own pope. In the struggle between unity and diversity of religious belief, the press favored the latter, and we can assume that this possibility never occurred to Gutenberg.

Thamus understood well the limitations of inventors in grasping the social and psychological—that is, ideological—bias of their own inventions. We can imagine him addressing Gutenberg in the following way: "Gutenberg, my paragon of inventors, the discoverer of an art is not the best judge of the good or harm which will accrue to those who practice it. So it is in this; you, who are the father of printing, have out of fondness for your off-spring come to believe it will advance the cause of the Holy Roman See, whereas in fact it will sow discord among believers; it will damage the authenticity of your beloved Church and destroy its monopoly." 19

We can imagine that Thamus would also have pointed out to Gutenberg, as he did to Theuth, that the new invention would create a vast population of readers who "will receive a quantity of information without proper instruction . . . [who will be] filled with the conceit of wisdom instead of real wisdom"; that reading, in other words, will compete with older forms of learning. This is yet another principle of technological change we may infer from the judgment of Thamus: new technologies compete with old ones—for time, for attention, for money, for prestige, but mostly for dominance of their world-view. This competition is implicit once we acknowledge that a medium contains an ideological bias. And it is a fierce competition, as only ideological competitions can be. It is not merely a matter of tool against tool—the alphabet attacking ideographic writing, the printing press attacking the illuminated manuscript, the photograph attacking the art of painting, television attacking the printed word. When media make war against each other, it is a case of world-views in collision. 20

In the United States, we can see such collisions everywhere—in politics, in religion, in commerce—but we see them made most clearly in the schools, where two great technologies confront each other in uncompromising aspect for the control of students' minds. On the one hand, there is the world of the printed word with its emphasis on logic, sequence, history, exposition, objectivity, detachment, and discipline. On the other, there is the world of television with its emphasis on imagery, narrative, presentness, simultaneity, intimacy, immediate gratification, and quick emotional response. Children come to school having been 21 deeply conditioned by the biases of television. There, they encounter the world of the printed word. A sort of psychic battle takes place, and there are many casualties—children who can't learn to read or won't, children who cannot organize their thought into logical structure even in a simple paragraph, children who cannot attend to lectures or oral explanations for more than a few minutes at a time. They are failures, but not because they are stupid. They are failures because there is a media war going on, and they are on the wrong side—at least for the moment. Who knows what schools will be like twenty-five years from now? Or fifty? In time, the type of student who is currently a failure may be considered a success. The type who is now successful may be regarded as a handicapped learner—slow to respond, far too detached, lacking in emotion, inadequate in creating mental pictures of reality. Consider: what Thamus called the "conceit of wisdom"—the unreal knowledge acquired through the written word—eventually became the pre-eminent form of knowledge valued by the schools. There is no reason to suppose that such a form of knowledge must always remain so highly valued.

To take another example: In introducing the personal computer to the classroom, we shall be breaking a four-hundred-year-old truce between the gregariousness and openness fostered by orality and the introspection and isolation fostered by the printed word. Orality stresses group learning, cooperation, and a sense of social responsibility, which is the context within which Thamus believed proper instruction and real knowledge must be communicated. Print stresses individualized learning, competition, and personal autonomy. Over four centuries, teachers, while emphasizing print, have allowed orality its place in the classroom, and have therefore achieved a kind of pedagogical peace between these two forms of learning, so that what is valuable in each can be maximized. Now comes the computer, carrying anew the banner of private learning and individual problem-solving. Will the widespread use of computers in the classroom defeat once and for all the claims of communal speech? Will the computer raise egocentrism to the status of a virtue? 22

These are the kinds of questions that technological change brings to mind when one grasps, as Thamus did, that technological competition ignites total war, which means it is not possible to contain the effects of a new technology to a limited sphere of human activity. If this metaphor puts the matter too brutally, we may try a gentler, kinder one: Technological change is neither additive nor subtractive. It is ecological. I mean "ecological" in the same sense as the word is used by environmental scientists. One significant change generates total change. If you remove the caterpillars from a given habitat, you are not left with the same environment minus caterpillars: you have a new environment, and you have reconstituted the conditions of survival; the same is true if you add caterpillars to an environment that has had none. This is how the ecology of media works as well. A new technology does not 23 add or subtract something. It changes everything. In the year 1500, fifty years after the printing press was invented, we did not have old Europe plus the printing press. We had a different Europe. After television, the United States was not America plus television; television gave a new coloration to every political campaign, to every home, to every school, to every church, to every industry. And that is why the competition among media is so fierce. Surrounding every technology are institutions whose organization—not to mention their reason for being—reflects the world-view promoted by the technology. Therefore, when an old technology is assaulted by a new one, institutions are threatened. When institutions are threatened, a culture finds itself in crisis. This is serious business, which is why we learn nothing when educators ask, Will students learn mathematics better by computers than by textbooks? Or when businessmen ask, Through which medium can we sell more products? Or when preachers ask, Can we reach more people through television than through radio? Or when politicians ask, How effective are messages sent through different media? Such questions have an immediate, practical value to those who ask them, but they are diversionary. They direct our attention away from the serious social, intellectual, and institutional crises that new media foster.

Perhaps an analogy here will help to underline the point. In speaking of the meaning of a poem, T. S. Eliot remarked that the chief use of the overt content of poetry is "to satisfy one habit of the reader, to keep his mind diverted and quiet, while the poem does its work upon him: much as the imaginary burglar is always provided with a bit of nice meat for the house-dog." In other words, in asking their practical questions, educators, entrepreneurs, preachers, and politicians are like the house-dog munching peacefully on the meat while the house is looted. Perhaps some of them know this and do not especially care. After all, a nice piece of meat, offered graciously, does take care of the problem of where the next meal will come from. But for the rest of us, it cannot be acceptable to have the house invaded without protest or at least awareness. 24

What we need to consider about the computer has nothing to do with its efficiency as a teaching tool. We need to know in what ways it is altering our conception of learning, and how, in conjunction with television, it undermines the old idea of school. Who cares how many boxes of cereal can be sold via television? We need to know if television changes our conception of reality, the relationship of the rich to the poor, the idea of happiness itself. A preacher who confines himself to considering how a medium can increase his audience will miss the significant question: In what sense do new media alter what is meant by religion, by church, even by God? And if the politician cannot think beyond the next election, then *we* must wonder about what new media do to the idea of political organization and to the conception of citizenship. 25

To help us do this, we have the judgment of Thamus, who, in the way of legends, teaches us what Harold Innis, in his way, tried to. New technologies alter the structure of our interests: the things we think *about*. They alter the character of our symbols: the things we think *with*. And they alter the nature of community: the arena in which thoughts develop. As Thamus spoke to Innis across the centuries, it is essential that we listen to their conversation, join in it, revitalize it. For something has happened in America that is strange and dangerous, and there is only a dull and even stupid awareness of what it is—in part because it has no name. I call it Technopoly. 26

NOTES

[1]Plato, p. 96.

[2]Freud, pp. 38–39.

[3]This fact is documented in Keith Hoskin's "The Examination, Disciplinary Power and Rational Schooling," in *History of Education*, vol. VIII, no. 2 (1979), pp. 135–46. Professor Hoskin provides the following story about Farish: Farish was a professor of engineering at Cambridge and designed and installed a movable partition wall in his Cambridge home. The wall moved on pulleys between downstairs and upstairs. One night, while working late downstairs and feeling cold, Farish pulled down the partition. This is not much of a story, and history fails to disclose what happened next. All of which shows how little is known of William Farish.

[4]For a detailed exposition of Mumford's position on the impact of the mechanical clock, see his *Technics and Civilization*.

Examining the Text

1. What are the two errors made by Thamus that Postman notes in the beginning of the article? Why do you think Postman begins by drawing attention to Thamus's errors?

2. What do you think of Postman's argument in paragraphs 10–11 that "the masses of people" are "losers" in the development and spread of computer technology? Are any of the repercussions he lists at the end of paragraph 10 demonstrably false? Given the fact that this article was written more than 15 years ago, do you think Postman's observations are more or less true today?

3. In what ways is the practice of assigning grades in school a kind of "technology"? In what ways is grading "ideological"? What reasons does Postman give in paragraphs 13–15 for objecting to this practice, and what do you think of his argument here?

4. Postman argues in paragraphs 19–20 that the television and the personal computer collide and conflict with traditional models of education by encouraging children to develop different skills and approaches than they typically learn in the classroom. What do you think of his claims? If they're true, then how do you think television and computers should be effectively integrated into the classroom, if at all?

5. *Thinking rhetorically:* Why do you think Postman begins with the anecdote about King Thamus and extends this anecdote throughout the article? What is the effect of the repeated references to Thamus, Theuth, and Plato? Do these references help to bolster Postman's argument? Do his references to Freud, Thoreau, Gutenberg, and other famous thinkers and scholars serve a similar function?

For Group Discussion

Choose a technology that everyone in the group agrees is either mostly a blessing or mostly a burden. You might think of technologies related to travel (e.g., bicycle, airplane), household tasks (e.g., vacuum cleaner, microwave), health (e.g., eyeglasses, x-ray), communication (e.g., radio, Internet). After you've chosen the specific technology, make a list of all of its "burdens and blessings." Does Postman's belief in the two-sided impact of technology hold true with the technology you're discussing? What can you learn about this technology by looking at both its positive and negative effects?

Writing Suggestion

Postman argues that "technology imperiously commandeers our most important terminology. It redefines 'freedom,' truth,' 'intelligence,' 'fact,' 'wisdom,' 'memory,' 'history'—all the words we live by. And it does not pause to tell us. And we do not pause to ask." For this writing assignment, choose one of these terms, or another similarly important and broad term, and explore the ways in which technology has changed its definition.

Here are several prewriting activities that can help you begin this assignment:

- Make a list of all the different types of technology that may impact the definition of the term; consider how technologies related to communication, entertainment, medicine, travel, education, politics, and family life, for example, cause us to differently define the term you've chosen.
- Write about how you imagine the term was defined in the nineteenth century (or earlier) before the advent of many of the technologies that strongly impact our lives today.
- Think of the way your own understanding of this term has evolved during your life. Have any of the technologies that you use frequently caused you to think differently about this term?

After completing these prewriting activities, compose an essay with a thesis that states both how the term you've chosen is currently defined and how technologies have influenced this definition. Support your argument with specific examples, drawn from your prewriting activities.

Computers, the Internet, and You

Breaking Down Borders: How Technology Transforms the Private and Public Realms

ROBERT SAMUELS

One important premise of Common Culture *is that the culture all around us is worthy of investigation. Indeed, we believe that paying attention to the activities we are involved in every day is particularly important because these activities are highly likely to influence who we are, what we do, and what we value. Robert Samuels, a lecturer in the Writing Programs at UCLA, takes precisely this approach in the article that follows. Samuels reports on a mundane, everyday sort of event: a trip to his local Borders café. But in describing and analyzing what he sees at the café, he is able to draw conclusions about larger changes and challenges in our culture. Specifically, Samuels focuses his attention on the different technologies used by people at the café, and he analyzes how the use of technologies blurs the borders between public and private and between work and play.*

Before you read, *make a list of the technologies you use on a regular basis, particularly those associated with media, communication, and culture: cell phone, computer, MP3 player, TV, VCR, DVD player, remote control, and other technologies like these. How do you think the technologies you regularly use have influenced the way you live your life? What would your everyday life be like without these technologies?*

It's a Tuesday morning and I'm walking through the Borders café just south of the UCLA campus in Westwood, CA. My plan is to find a table, drink my coffee, and read some of the novel that I just bought in the bookstore section. As I head for one of the few empty chairs, I pass by a man sitting at a table, the sports section of the *L.A. Times* spread out in front of him, a cup of coffee and a blueberry muffin to one side, his cell phone close at hand on the other side. He's wearing a t-shirt and shorts, but he might as well be in pajamas and slippers; it's as if he's in his own kitchen, reading his paper and having his breakfast, just following his morning routine. 1

I move past breakfast-man and notice a twenty-something woman sitting in one of the five or six comfy upholstered chairs that Borders provides its customers. She's curled up cozily in the chair with 2 one foot stretched out and resting on a matching upholstered footstool. Actually, the foot isn't resting; it's wagging back and forth in time, I assume, to the music that's coming through the headphones attached to her ears and her iPod. Keeping time to the music, she taps her yellow highlighter pen against the textbook that she's ostensibly reading. As I watch, she begins to hum out loud—it sounds like a wildly out-of-tune version of "Dancing Queen"—and then she abruptly looks up and stops humming, a bit startled, remembering that she's in Borders and not in her living room.

I sit at my own table with my coffee and novel, but I don't get past the first page before I'm distracted by a woman at the table to my left who's talking on her cell phone. I see that she's also got her laptop computer open on the table and a magazine on her lap, but it's her phone conversation that's getting all of her attention—and, of course, the attention of everyone around her. We learn that she's terribly sorry but she has to cancel her job interview that Friday because of a doctor's appointment; our dismay is quickly alleviated when, in her next call, she tells a friend that, yes, the trip to Las Vegas that weekend is back on. The café, it seems, is her personal office. 3

Each of these people seems to have carved a little semi-private, personalized space out of the larger public, commercial space of Borders café. As people come and go, these spaces change, so that a time-lapse video of Borders café would have to show it as not just one space but rather as an aggregate of small, shifting living rooms, kitchens, and offices (no bedrooms—yet!). And of course it's not just Borders; this kind of activity goes on at bookstores and coffee shops across the country. These new commercial public squares have become shared spaces that are neither private nor public. In fact, they compel us to redefine what private and public mean. The cell phone woman, for example, seems to have no problem sharing her Las Vegas plans with everyone sitting around her. But then I look around again and notice that I'm one of the few people who can actually hear her. Most of the other people here have headphones on and they're listening to their own iPods or MP3 players, perhaps precisely in order to avoid having to listen to conversations that should be private in the first place. 4

What I see at Borders convinces me that there are new rules for how to act in public places and for how to socialize with and around one another. It's clear, as well, that none of these changes would have occurred without new technologies helping to break down borders. For instance, the telephone used to be firmly located in the private realm, physically attached to the kitchen wall or set on a desk in an office. Now, however, cell phones allow for a high level of mobility and access, and thus they help us transform any public place into a setting for a private conversation. The laptop, too, has not only transformed 5 the desktop computer but has also reinvented the desktop itself as any table or flat surface. Indeed, your very own lap becomes a desktop of sorts when you put your laptop computer on it.

With wireless technology, laptops and cell phones not only help 6
us cross back and forth between the public and the private, but they also function to undermine the distinction between work and play. For instance, people often jump quickly from doing work on their computers to emailing their friends and playing video games. Likewise, cell phones can combine work functions and play functions, incorporating games as well as digital cameras, video, and, of course, sound clips for ring tones. Some critics of new communication technologies argue that cell phones, laptops, iPods, and the other devices we take with us throughout our day encourage a high level of multitasking and prevent us from concentrating on any single activity. Thus, they argue, people not only become more superficial, but the constant switching between work and leisure activities creates a fragmented sense of self and gives everyone a bad case of attention deficit disorder.

However, another way of looking at these new technologies is to 7
see how they allow people to re-center their sense of self by creating what can be called "personal culture." In other words, instead of seeing culture as a social and public activity, like going to a concert hall, devices like iPods and laptops allow people to take culture with them wherever they go. More importantly, instead of having to let the radio station tell them what to listen to or the newspaper limit their choice of news sources, people are able to personalize their own media and decide on their own what culture they want to consume.

Personal culture derives much of its power from the fact that 8
many of the new media devices are highly immersive: people on cell phones and laptops can become so involved in their own mediated worlds that they forget where they actually are and what they are supposed to be doing. Some states have laws now against driving while talking on a cell phone, but in addition to the physical danger there also may be a social cost. After all, we are social beings who live in public worlds, and therefore we cannot simply forget that other people exist. As I look around me at the people who have temporarily transformed Borders café into a set of small personal spaces, I realize that although we're all together here there's very little chance that we'll interact with one another. Most of us are plugged in to technologies that, while allowing us to personalize our environment, also effectively isolate us from our neighbors.

But is there really anything wrong with that? We adapt to our new 9
technologies and to the new spaces these technologies create; we adapt, in fact, by using more technologies. To tune out the cell phones, we put on our headphones. There seems to be no way of escaping from a

technologically mediated environment, even in a place devoted to selling those old-fashioned, low-tech items called books. But, in Borders, at least, on this sunny Tuesday morning, we seem to be coping well enough even as the borders all around us are shifting and transforming.

Examining the Text

1. Why do you think Samuels begins his article with the detailed descriptions of three people he sees at Borders café? What do you learn from these descriptions? How does this opening strategy help Samuels introduce his argument?
2. What does Samuels mean by "personal culture"? According to Samuels, how do technologies help us create "personal culture"?
3. Reread the last two paragraphs of the article. What do you think is Samuels's opinion of technology's influence on our culture?
4. *Thinking rhetorically:* Who do you think are the target readers of Samuels's article? And what do you see as its overall purpose? Point to specific features of the article that help you determine its audience and purpose.

For Group Discussion

Samuels discusses two different borders in this article: the border between public and private, and the border between work and play. In your group, choose one of these borders, and make a list of all the technologies that contribute to breaking down this border. You can begin with the technologies that Samuels himself describes; for instance, he discusses how the cell phone helps to break down the border between public and private as well as the border between work and play. Be sure to continue your list with examples of other technologies. Then list any technologies that you think help to maintain or increase the border. As a group, try to come to some general conclusions about the role of technology in the particular border area you're discussing.

Writing Suggestion

Samuels acts as an amateur anthropologist in this essay in the sense that he goes to a particular place, observes how people act there, and records and analyzes his observations in an article. Your assignment is to do something similar. Choose a place where people congregate: a coffee shop, a dorm lounge, an outdoor park or playground, a living room. Ideally the place you choose will be somewhere where you can sit and observe and take notes without being too distracted and without distracting others. Spend an hour or two at the place, watching to see what technologies people use and how the people interact with each other. Then write an essay modeled after Samuels's article. Begin the essay with a couple of detailed descriptions of specific people or activities you observed. In the body of the essay, discuss and analyze the ways that you saw technologies influence people's interactions. You might want to cite Samuels's article in your essay, perhaps in order to argue for or against the conclusions he draws.

The Data-Driven Life

GARY WOLF

If you've ever stepped on a scale or tried to balance your checkbook, you've gathered data about yourself. But self-tracking of the kind that Gary Wolf describes in the following article is data gathering of a different magnitude. Wolf writes about people who use technologies of various kinds to methodically track and record their behavior, with the ultimate goal of learning about themselves. As Wolf puts it, "numbers are infiltrating the last redoubts of the personal. Sleep, exercise, sex, food, mood, location, alertness, productivity, even spiritual well-being are being tracked and measured, shared and displayed." Because of technological advances such as small electronic sensors, mobile devices, and cloud computing, we're now able to track, record, and analyze aspects of our lives relatively easily. Of course, whether or not this is good for us is another issue. What can we learn about ourselves through self-tracking? How do these insights compare to what we might have learned through more traditional means such as psychology? Wolf's article begins to answer these questions through specific anecdotes of people who've taken up self-tracking and through a more general discussion of its possibilities and problems.

***Before you read,** visit Quantified Self (http://quantifiedself.com/), a Web site about self-tracking that Wolf and others maintain. Read through some of the most recent entries there to get a sense of the "community" of self-trackers and the issues they're currently discussing.*

Humans make errors. We make errors of fact and errors of judgment. 1 We have blind spots in our field of vision and gaps in our stream of attention. Sometimes we can't even answer the simplest questions. Where was I last week at this time? How long have I had this pain in my knee? How much money do I typically spend in a day? These weaknesses put us at a disadvantage. We make decisions with partial information. We are forced to steer by guesswork. We go with our gut.

That is, some of us do. Others use data. A timer running on 2 Robin Barooah's computer tells him that he has been living in the United States for 8 years, 2 months and 10 days. At various times in his life, Barooah—a 38-year-old self-employed software designer from England who now lives in Oakland, Calif.—has also made careful records of his work, his sleep and his diet.

A few months ago, Barooah began to wean himself from coffee. 3 His method was precise. He made a large cup of coffee and removed 20 milliliters weekly. This went on for more than four months, until barely a sip remained in the cup. He drank it and called himself cured. Unlike his previous attempts to quit, this time there were no headaches, no extreme cravings. Still, he was tempted, and on Oct. 12 last year, while distracted at his desk, he told himself that he could probably concentrate better if he had a cup. Coffee may have been bad for his health, he thought, but perhaps it was good for his concentration.

Barooah wasn't about to try to answer a question like this with guesswork. He had a good data set that showed how many minutes he spent each day in focused work. With this, he could do an objective analysis. Barooah made a chart with dates on the bottom and his work time along the side. Running down the middle was a big black line labeled "Stopped drinking coffee." On the left side of the line, low spikes and narrow columns. On the right side, high spikes and thick columns. The data had delivered their verdict, and coffee lost. 4

He was sad but also thrilled. Instead of a stimulating cup of coffee, he got a bracing dose of truth. "People have such very poor sense of time," Barooah says, and without good time calibration, it is much harder to see the consequences of your actions. If you want to replace the vagaries of intuition with something more reliable, you first need to gather data. Once you know the facts, you can live by them. 5

Five years ago, Ben Lipkowitz, who is now 28, was living with some friends in Bloomington, Ind., and he found himself wondering how much time he spent doing one of his roommates' dishes. Lipkowitz had a handheld electronic datebook that he purchased on a trip to Tokyo, and on May 11, 2005, at 2:20 P.M., he started using it to keep a record of his actions. Instead of entering his future appointments, he entered his past activities, creating a remarkably complete account of his life. In one sense this was just a normal personal journal, albeit in a digital format and unusually detailed. But the format and detail made all the difference. Lipkowitz eventually transferred the data to his computer, and now, using a few keyboard commands, he can call up his history. He knows how much he has eaten and how much he has spent. He knows what books he has read and what objects he has purchased. And of course, he knows the answer to his original question. "I was thinking I was spending an hour a day cleaning up after this person," Lipkowitz says. He shrugs. "It turned out it was more like 20 minutes." 6

Another person I'm friendly with, Mark Carranza—he also makes his living with computers—has been keeping a detailed, searchable archive of all the ideas he has had since he was 21. That was in 1984. I realize that this seems impossible. But I have seen his archive, with its million plus entries, and observed him using it. He navigates smoothly between an interaction with somebody in the present moment and his digital record, bringing in associations to conversations that took place years earlier. Most thoughts are tagged with date, time 7 and location. What for other people is an inchoate flow of mental life is broken up into elements and cross-referenced.

These men all know that their behavior is abnormal. They are outliers. Geeks. But why does what they are doing seem so strange? In other contexts, it is normal to seek data. A fetish for numbers is the defining trait of the modern manager. Corporate executives facing down hostile shareholders load their pockets full of numbers. So do politicians on the hustings, doctors counseling patients and fans abusing their local sports franchise on talk radio. Charles Dickens was already making fun of this obsession in 1854, with his sketch of the fact-mad schoolmaster Gradgrind, who blasted his students with memorized trivia. But Dickens's great caricature only proved the durability of the type. For another century and a half, it got worse. 8

Or, by another standard, you could say it got better. We tolerate the pathologies of quantification—a dry, abstract, mechanical type of knowledge—because the results are so powerful. Numbering things allows tests, comparisons, experiments. Numbers make problems less resonant emotionally but more tractable intellectually. In science, in business and in the more reasonable sectors of government, numbers have won fair and square. 9

For a long time, only one area of human activity appeared to be immune. In the cozy confines of personal life, we rarely used the power of numbers. The techniques of analysis that had proved so effective were left behind at the office at the end of the day and picked up again the next morning. The imposition, on oneself or one's family, of a regime of objective record keeping seemed ridiculous. A journal was respectable. A spreadsheet was creepy. 10

And yet, almost imperceptibly, numbers are infiltrating the last redoubts of the personal. Sleep, exercise, sex, food, mood, location, alertness, productivity, even spiritual well-being are being tracked and measured, shared and displayed. On MedHelp, one of the largest Internet forums for health information, more than 30,000 new personal tracking projects are started by users every month. Foursquare, a geo-tracking application with about one million users, keeps a running tally of how many times players "check in" at every locale, automatically building a detailed diary of movements and habits; many users publish these data widely. Nintendo's Wii Fit, a device that allows players to stand on a platform, play physical games, measure their body weight and compare their stats, has sold more than 28 million units. 11

Two years ago, as I noticed that the daily habits of millions of people were starting to edge uncannily close to the experiments of the most extreme experimenters, I started a Web site called the Quantified Self with my colleague Kevin Kelly. We began holding regular meetings 12 for people running interesting personal data projects. I had recently written a long article about a trend among Silicon Valley types who time their days in increments as small as two minutes, and I suspected that the self-tracking explosion was simply the logical outcome of this obsession with efficiency. We use numbers when we want to tune up a car, analyze a chemical reaction, predict the outcome of an election. We use numbers to optimize an assembly line. Why not use numbers on ourselves?

But I soon realized that an emphasis on efficiency missed something important. Efficiency implies rapid progress toward a known goal. For many self-trackers, the goal is unknown. Although they may take up tracking with a specific question in mind, they continue because they believe their numbers hold secrets that they can't afford to ignore, including answers to questions they have not yet thought to ask. 13

Ubiquitous self-tracking is a dream of engineers. For all their expertise at figuring out how things work, technical people are often painfully aware how much of human behavior is a mystery. People do things for unfathomable reasons. They are opaque even to themselves. A hundred years ago, a bold researcher fascinated by the riddle of human personality might have grabbed onto new psychoanalytic concepts like repression and the unconscious. These ideas were invented by people who loved language. Even as therapeutic concepts of the self spread widely in simplified, easily accessible form, they retained something of the prolix, literary humanism of their inventors. From the languor of the analyst's couch to the chatty inquisitiveness of a self-help questionnaire, the dominant forms of self-exploration assume that the road to knowledge lies through words. Trackers are exploring an alternate route. Instead of interrogating their inner worlds through talking and writing, they are using numbers. They are constructing a quantified self. 14

Until a few years ago it would have been pointless to seek self-knowledge through numbers. Although sociologists could survey us in aggregate, and laboratory psychologists could do clever experiments with volunteer subjects, the real way we ate, played, talked and loved left only the faintest measurable trace. Our only method of tracking ourselves was to notice what we were doing and write it down. But even this written record couldn't be analyzed objectively without laborious processing and analysis. 15

Then four things changed. First, electronic sensors got smaller and better. Second, people started carrying powerful computing devices, typically disguised as mobile phones. Third, social media made it seem normal to share everything. And fourth, we began to get an inkling of the rise of a global superintelligence known as the cloud. 16

Millions of us track ourselves all the time. We step on a scale and record our weight. We balance a checkbook. We count calories. But when the familiar pen-and-paper methods of self-analysis are enhanced by sensors that monitor our behavior automatically, the process of self-tracking becomes both more alluring and more meaningful. Automated sensors do more than give us facts; they also remind us that our ordinary behavior contains obscure quantitative signals that can be used to inform our behavior, once we learn to read them. 17

"When you have small, distributed battery-powered sensors, you want to collect all biometric data," says Ken Fyfe, one of the pioneers of wearable tracking devices. In the mid-'90s, Fyfe was teaching engineering at the University of Alberta in Edmonton, where his specialty was acoustics and vibration. He was also a runner, in a family of runners. His sons were national competitors at 400 and 800 meters. At the time, runners who wanted to know more about the mechanics of their performance—their stride, their cadence, the way their motion changed as they grew tired—had to go into a lab and be filmed. "You would run in a room on a treadmill with reflective stickers on your hips, knees, ankles and feet," Fyfe recalls. 18

Taking video of people in motion, and then analyzing the video, seemed like a roundabout way to get data. Why not use an accelerometer, which can directly measure changes in speed and direction? Accelerometers had long been used in industry and cost several hundred dollars each. Then accelerometers were developed to trigger the air bags in cars. Massive purchases in the automotive industry drove the cost down. The size and power demands shrank, too. Suddenly, it seemed less crazy to put an accelerometer on your body. 19

Fyfe guessed that there would be plenty of interest in something like a personal speedometer, a wearable instrument that displayed how far you'd gone and your average speed. So he tried to invent one. "I worked on it every weekend for three years," Fyfe says. He put accelerometers into a molded plastic insert. The insert fit into a shoe, and data were transmitted wirelessly to a sports watch. But there was a problem. The numbers produced by a motion sensor don't necessarily say anything about a runner's pace and distance. They give you the acceleration of a runner's foot—that's all. Some method—a formula or algorithm—is needed to translate the data into the information you want, and the method must work for almost everybody under a wide range of conditions: stopping and starting, jumping over a curb, limping because of an injury. Developing these algorithms took up most of Fyfe's time during the years he perfected his system. 20

Thanks to faster computers and clever mathematical techniques, Fyfe and other inventors are turning messy data from cheap sensors into meaningful information. "The real expertise you need is signal 21 processing and statistical analysis," says James Park, the chief executive and co-founder of Fitbit, a company that makes a tracker released late last year. The Fitbit tracker is two inches long, half an inch wide and shaped like a thick paperclip. It tracks movement, and if you wear it in a little elastic wristband at night, it can also track your hours of sleep. (You are not completely still when sleeping. Your pattern of movement, however, can be correlated with sleeping and waking, just as the acceleration of a runner's foot reveals speed.) Park and his partner, Eric Friedman, first showed their prototype at a San Francisco business conference in the summer of 2008. Five weeks later, Park and Friedman, who are both 33, had $2 million in venture capital, and they were flying back and forth to Singapore to arrange production. Last winter they shipped their first devices.

At nearly the same time, Philips, the consumer electronics company, began selling its own tiny accelerometer-based self-tracker, called DirectLife, which, like the Fitbit, is meant to be carried on the body at all times. Zeo, a company based in Newton, Mass., released a tracker contained in a small headband, which picks up electrical signals from the brain, and uses them to compile the kind of detailed record of light sleep, deep sleep and REM sleep that, until now, was available only if you spent the night in a sleep-research clinic. Lately I've been running into people who say they wear it every night. And Nike recently announced that its Nike+ system, one of the first personal speedometers, has been used by more than 2.5 million runners since its release in 2006. 22

Ken Fyfe's accelerometer-based tracking system is used with sports watches by Adidas and Polar. In 2006 he sold his company, Dynastream, for $36 million to Garmin, which makes navigation equipment commonly used in cars and airplanes and which is now branching out into personal tracking. Fyfe's former company stayed in Alberta, where it continues to sell tracking components. A low-power data-transmission protocol they invented is in new blood-pressure cuffs, glucose monitors, blood-oxygenation sensors, weight scales and sleep monitors, all of which are aimed at the consumer market. 23

Web entrepreneurs like to talk about democratizing communication. Fyfe's dream is to democratize objective research on human subjects. "Until we came up with this technology, you couldn't do this kind of analysis unless you could get into a lab," he says. "Now you can." 24

At the center of this personal laboratory is the mobile phone. During the years that personal-data systems were making their rapid technical progress, many people started entering small reports about their lives into a phone. Sharing became the term for the quick post to a social network: a status update to Facebook, a reading list 25 on Goodreads, a location on Dopplr, Web tags to Delicious, songs to http://www.last.fm/Last.fm, your breakfast menu on Twitter. "People got used to sharing," says David Lammers-Meis, who leads the design work on the fitness-tracking products at Garmin. "The more they want to share, the more they want to have something to share." Personal data are ideally suited to a social life of sharing. You might not always have something to say, but you always have a number to report.

This is how the odd habits of the ultrageek who tracks everything 26
have come to seem almost normal. An elaborate setup is no longer necessary, because the phone already envelops us in a cloud of computing. This term, "the cloud," has some specialized meanings among software architects, but fundamentally the cloud is just a poetic label for the global agglomeration of computer resources—the processors, hard drives, fiber-optic cables and so on—that allow us to access our private data from any Internet connection. We entrust all kinds of things to the cloud: our mail and our family photographs; the places we go and the list of people we call on the phone. When Jeff Clavier, the founder of SoftTech VC, a Silicon Valley venture capital firm, invested in a small financial company called Mint (now part of Intuit), he was warned that ordinary people were unlikely to trust their bank passwords and credit-card details to the cloud. "About 1.5 million people did it," Clavier says.

One of the reasons that self-tracking is spreading widely beyond 27
the technical culture that gave birth to it is that we all have at least an inkling of what's going on out there in the cloud. Our search history, friend networks and status updates allow us to be analyzed by machines in ways we can't always anticipate or control. It's natural that we would want to reclaim some of this power: to look outward to the cloud, as well as inward toward the psyche, in our quest to figure ourselves out.

Sophie Barbier, a 47-year-old teacher in Palo Alto, is a cyclist who 28
regularly logs her time, distance and heart rate during a ride. "Training logs have been around forever," she told me. "But the more variables I added, the more curious I got." Along with her cycling stats, Barbier began scoring her mood, sleep and ability to focus, as well as her caffeine consumption, and noting the days her menstrual cycle began and ended.

After surgery for a back problem, Barbier had trouble sleeping. 29
On CureTogether, a self-tracking health site, she learned about tryptophan, a common amino acid available as a dietary supplement. She took the tryptophan, and her insomnia went away. Her concentration scores also improved. She stopped taking tryptophan and continued to sleep well, but her ability to concentrate deteriorated. Barbier ran the test again, and again the graph was clear: tryptophan significantly

increased her focus. She had started by looking for a cure for insomnia and discovered a way to fine-tune her brain.

It is tempting to dismiss reports of such experiments as trivial anecdotes, or the placebo effect. I took Barbier's results to a friend of mine, Seth Roberts, an emeritus professor of psychology at the University of California, Berkeley, and an expert on self-experimentation. "There is a large difference between what Barbier did and the minimal story of somebody who takes a pill looking for a certain effect and then finds it," he pointed out. "First, she wrote the numbers down, so the results are not subject to memory distortion. Second, she changed the conditions several times. Every switch is a test of her original theory." 30

Roberts told me about his own method of measuring mental changes, a quick test he programmed on his computer that involves 32 easy arithmetic problems. The test takes about three minutes, and he has found that it can detect small changes in cognitive performance. He has used his self-tracking system to adjust his diet, learning that three tablespoons daily of flaxseed oil reliably decreases the amount of time it takes him to do math. Consuming a lot of butter also seems to have a good effect. 31

Self-experiments like Barbier's and Roberts's are not clinical trials. The goal isn't to figure out something about human beings generally but to discover something about yourself. Their validity may be narrow, but it is beautifully relevant. Generally, when we try to change, we simply thrash about: we improvise, guess, forget our results or change the conditions without even noticing the results. Errors are possible in self-tracking and self-experiment, of course. It is easy to mistake a transient effect for a permanent one, or miss some hidden factor that is influencing your data and confounding your conclusions. But once you start gathering data, recording the dates, toggling the conditions back and forth while keeping careful records of the outcome, you gain a tremendous advantage over the normal human practice of making no valid effort whatsoever. 32

I recently received an e-mail message from a 26-year-old filmmaker named Toli Galanis, who keeps track of about 50 different streams of personal data, including activities, health, films watched and books read, the friends he talks with and the topics they discuss. While Galanis acknowledged that he gets pleasure from gathering data and organizing it intelligently, it was a different aspect of his report that caught my attention. "I know that immediately after watching a bad movie I am more apt to be negative about my career prospects as a filmmaker," he wrote, explaining that tracking has made him better able to detect the influence of seemingly trivial circumstances on his mood and decisions. 33

The idea that our mental life is affected by hidden causes is a mainstay of psychology. Facility in managing the flow of thought and emotion is a sign of happiness and good adjustment. But how is it done? Nearly every therapeutic prescription involves an invitation to notice, to pay attention. Once we have a notion in our sights, we can attack it with an arsenal of tools: cognitive, psychoanalytic, even spiritual. But none of these will tell us if we've missed something. You may simply have failed to notice a debilitating habit, a negative correlation, a bad influence. 34

Galanis's realization that bad movies subject him to professional discouragement is the type of insight that will seem accessible to anybody blessed with a modest amount of self-awareness; finding it is no more difficult than catching sight of a dollar in the street and picking it up. But for every one you grab, how many do you overlook? 35

It's not only the context of our thoughts that escapes us. Our actions do, too. Since 2004, Terry Paul, an educational entrepreneur and philanthropist, has been working on a digital device that tucks into specially designed toddlers' clothing and can be used to predict language development through tracking the number of conversational exchanges a child has with adults. It cost Paul $32 million to perfect the system that takes the noisy sounds of a baby's environment and translates it into reliable data. As a commercial enterprise, it was unsuccessful. His device, called the LENA monitor, is used for academic research but never took off as a consumer product. When I tell parents about it, most of them are horrified. They imagine a nightmare of surveillance and an inducement to neurotic competition: who wants a digital recorder that grades you on how you talk to your kid? 36

Were we to submit to such a test, however, many of us would fare poorly. Parents, in fact, overestimate how much they talk to their preverbal children. Users of the LENA monitor can be awkwardly surprised. A mother I spoke with recently began monitoring after her daughter was prescribed a seizure medication that was associated with language delays. "It became very clear to us that my husband's words were less than mine," she said. He needed to try to talk to his daughter more. Until he saw the data, he had no idea that his attention was wandering. 37

Of course, sometimes we fail to notice what we do because we are motivated not to notice it. We are ashamed of ourselves, so we lie to ourselves. Shaun Rance started tracking his drinking two years ago, after his father was given a diagnosis of end-stage liver disease. He didn't pledge to stop drinking; he didn't do a searching moral inventory; he just started counting, using the anonymous Web site drinkingdiary.com. He found that his externalized memory was very powerful. Having a record of every drink he took sharpened his awareness and increased 38 his feeling of self-mastery—and reduced his drinking. Because his tally is held by a machine, he doesn't feel any of the social shame that might make him, consciously or not, underestimate his drinking. "I don't lie to the diary," he says. After all, it is silly to posture in front of a machine. The tracking system is an extension of a basic faculty of Rance's consciousness, there to remind him where he stands, and it does its work without emotion. As far as he's concerned, that's a virtue.

There may be new domains of our biology that we can incorpo- 39
rate into our sense of self. "We know about asleep, awake, hungry, depressed, cold, drowsy, nauseous," says Dave Marvit, a vice-president at Fujitsu Laboratories of America, where he is leading a research project on self-tracking. "But what about hypoxic, anemic, hyperglycemic?" If we had a gentle signal about how much sugar was in our blood, would we change how we ate? Would it change how we feel? Drinking. Talking. Being discouraged by a movie. Giving a moment's attention to a feeling of anger or elation, a small surge of energy or a metabolic dip. These are the materials of daily life. They barely stand out against the background of what we take for granted, and yet picking up these weak signals gives us leverage. Margaret Morris, a clinical psychologist and a researcher at Intel, recently ran a series of field trials using a mobile phone for tracking emotion. At random times, the phone rang and quizzed its owner about his or her mood. A man in one of Morris's studies reviewed the trends in his data and noticed that his foul mood began at the same time every day. He had a rushed transition from work to home. While unfinished tasks were still on his mind, new demands crowded in. The stress followed him for the rest of the evening. The data showed him where the problem was. With help, he learned to take a short mental break right there. He was much relieved.

The contrast to the traditional therapeutic notion of personal 40
development is striking. When we quantify ourselves, there isn't the imperative to see through our daily existence into a truth buried at a deeper level. Instead, the self of our most trivial thoughts and actions, the self that, without technical help, we might barely notice or recall, is understood as the self we ought to get to know. Behind the allure of the quantified self is a guess that many of our problems come from simply lacking the instruments to understand who we are. Our memories are poor; we are subject to a range of biases; we can focus our attention on only one or two things at a time. We don't have a pedometer in our feet, or a breathalyzer in our lungs, or a glucose monitor installed into our veins. We lack both the physical and the mental apparatus to take stock of ourselves. We need help from machines.

Watch out for those machines, though. Humans know a spe- 41
cial trick of self-observation: when to avert our gaze. Machines don't understand the value of forgiving a lapse, or of treating an unpleas-

ant detail with tactful silence. A graph or a spreadsheet talks only in numbers, but there is a policeman inside all of our heads who is well equipped with punishing words. "Each day my self-worth was tied to the data," Alexandra Carmichael, one of the founders of the self-tracking site CureTogether, wrote in a heartfelt blog post about why she recently stopped tracking. "One pound heavier this morning? You're fat. Skipped a day of running? You're lazy. It felt like being back in school. Less than 100 percent on an exam? You're dumb." Carmichael had been tracking 40 different things about herself. The data she was seeing every day didn't respect her wishes or her self-esteem. It was awful, and she had to stop.

Electronic trackers have no feelings. They are emotionally neu- 42
tral, but this very fact makes them powerful mirrors of our own values and judgments. The objectivity of a machine can seem generous or merciless, tolerant or cruel. Designers of tracking systems are trying to finesse this ambivalence. A smoking-cessation program invented by Pal Kraft, a Norwegian researcher at the University of Oslo, automatically calls people who are trying to quit, asking them every day whether they've smoked in the last 24 hours. When the answer is yes, a recorded voice delivers an encouraging message: *All is well, take it easy, try again*. This mechanical empathy, barely more human than a recorded voice on the customer-service line, can hardly be expected to fool anybody. But a long line of research in human-computer interaction demonstrates that when machines are given humanlike characteristics and offer emotional reassurance, we actually do feel reassured. This is humbling. Do we really feel better when a computer pats us on the back? Yes, we do.

Jon Cousins is a 54-year-old software entrepreneur and former ad- 43
vertising executive who was given a diagnosis in 2007 of bipolar affective disorder. Cousins built a self-tracking system to help manage his feelings, which he called Moodscope; now used by about 1,000 others, Moodscope automatically sends e-mail with mood-tracking scores to a few select friends. "My life was changed radically," Cousins told me recently in an e-mail message. "If I got the odd dip, my friends wanted to know why." Sometimes, after he records a low score, a friend might simply e-mail: "?" Cousins replies, and that act alone makes him feel better. Moodscope is a blended system in which measurement is supplemented by human sympathy. Self-tracking can sometimes appear narcissistic, but it also allows people to connect with one another in new ways. We leave traces of ourselves with our numbers, like insects putting down a trail of pheromones, and in times of crisis, these signals can lead us to others who share our concerns and care enough to help.

Often, pioneering trackers struggle with feelings of being both 44
aided and tormented by the very systems they have built. I know

what this is like. I used to track my work hours, and it was a miserable process. With my spreadsheet, I inadvertently transformed myself into the mean-spirited, small-minded boss I imagined I was escaping through self-employment. Taking advantage of the explosion of self-tracking services available on the Web, I started analyzing my workday at a finer level. Every time I moved to a new activity—picked up the phone, opened a Web browser, answered e-mail—I made a couple of clicks with my mouse, which recorded the change. After a few weeks I looked at the data and marveled. My day was a patchwork of distraction, interspersed with valuable, but too rare, periods of focus. In total, the amount of uninterrupted close attention I was able to muster in a given workday was less than three hours. After I got over the humiliation, I came to see how valuable this knowledge was. The efficiency lesson was that I could gain significant benefit by extending my day at my desk by only a few minutes, as long as these minutes were well spent. But a greater lesson was that by tracking hours at my desk I was making an unnecessary concession to a worthless stereotype. Does anybody really believe that long hours at a desk are a vocational ideal? I got nothing from my tracking system until I used it as a source of critical perspective, not on my performance but on my assumptions about what was important to track.

People are not assembly lines. We cannot be tuned to a known standard, because a universal standard for human experience does not exist. Bo Adler, a young computer scientist at Fujitsu Laboratories of America, is one of the most committed self-trackers I've ever met: during his most active phase he wore a blood-pressure cuff, pulse oximeter and accelerometer all day long, along with a computer on a harness to collect the data. Adler has sleep apnea, and he is trying to figure it out. When he became too self-conscious going to the gym in his gear, he wore a Google T-shirt to throw people off. Maybe he was a freak, but at least people could mistake him for a millionaire freak. 45

"Here's what they told me was the normal surgical course of treatment," Adler explained. "First they were going to cut out my tonsils, and if that didn't work, they would break my jaw and reset it to reposition my tongue, and finally they would cut out the roof of my mouth. I had one question: What if my case is different? They said, 'Let's try the standard course of treatment first, and if that doesn't work, then we'll know your case is different.' " Adler recognized what this proposal meant: it meant that his doctors had no cure for different. They wanted to see him as a standard case, because they have treatments for the standard cases. Before Adler underwent surgery, he wanted some evidence that he was a standard case. Some of us aren't standard, after all; perhaps many of us aren't. 46

Adler's idea that we can—and should—defend ourselves against the imposed generalities of official knowledge is typical of pioneering self-trackers, and it shows how closely the dream of a quantified self resembles therapeutic ideas of self-actualization, even as its methods are startlingly different. Trackers focused on their health want to ensure that their medical practitioners don't miss the particulars of their condition; trackers who record their mental states are often trying to find their own way to personal fulfillment amid the seductions of marketing and the errors of common opinion; fitness trackers are trying to tune their training regimes to their own body types and competitive goals, but they are also looking to understand their strengths and weaknesses, to uncover potential they didn't know they had. Self-tracking, in this way, is not really a tool of optimization but of discovery, and if tracking regimes that we would once have thought bizarre are becoming normal, one of the most interesting effects may be to make us re-evaluate what "normal" means. 47

"My girlfriend thinks I'm the weird person when I wear all these devices," Bo Adler says. "She sees me as an oddity, but I say no, soon everybody is going to be doing this, and you won't even notice." 48

Examining the Text

1. What do you think Wolf means when he writes that "we tolerate the pathologies of quantification—a dry, abstract, mechanical type of knowledge—because the results are so powerful"? What other reasons does Wolf provide to explain why people are drawn to tracking and quantifying their behavior?

2. In what ways is self-tracking similar to and different from psychology and psychoanalysis? According to Wolf, what are the relative strengths and weaknesses of these two approaches toward self-knowledge? What do you think of Wolf's discussion of these different approaches?

3. According to Wolf, what are the four key factors that have enabled self-tracking to become more prevalent and more effective? How is each one used in personal data collection?

4. *Thinking rhetorically:* Wolf includes many specific examples of people who have tracked various aspects of their behavior. What is the effect of these specific examples and anecdotes? In what ways do they help to strengthen Wolf's argument? Did you find any one of the examples more interesting or important than the others?

For Group Discussion

In a group of your peers, create a table with three columns. In the first column, list elements of a person's behavior that could be tracked over the course of one or two weeks. In the second column, describe how that behavior could be tracked; what variables would need to be isolated, and what technologies might be used to help with the record keeping. In the third column, describe what you think a person could learn about himself or herself by tracking that element of his or her behavior. Based on your list and commentary, discuss what you and your peers see as the limits and opportunities of self-tracking.

Writing Suggestion

Following up on both Wolf's article and the Group Discussion question above, choose one element of your own behavior to track over the course of several days or a week. Try to choose an element that is practical and manageable; for instance, rather than tracking how you spend every minute, track major activities of each hour. Before you begin self-tracking, consider whether there are technologies you currently own that might help you track this behavior, and whether some of the Web sites that Wolf mentions might be useful to you. Consider also what you anticipate learning about yourself from this undertaking. After you've completed the task, write a brief report that includes both the "hard data"—that is, the actual numbers related to what you tracked—and your interpretation of this data. What did you learn about yourself from this self-tracking exercise? Can you draw any broader conclusions about the benefits and drawbacks of self-tracking?

Is Google Making Us Stupid?

NICHOLAS CARR

Different studies cite varying statistics about the amount of time Americans spend online and the exact nature of our online activities. But regardless of which study you read, it's clear that we're spending more time on the Internet, and that young Americans in particular are spending more of their free time online. "Radio's Future II: The 2010 American Youth Study," for instance, indicates that during an average day, Americans aged 12–24 spend two hours and 52 minutes on the Internet, making it the preferred media format for most young Americans. What are the consequences of all the time we spend online? How does it affect our behavior, our thoughts, our relationships? As Nicholas Carr notes in the following article, "of all that's been written about the Net, there's been little consideration of how, exactly, it's reprogramming us." Carr begins his discussion of the Internet's effect by charting changes in his own mental functioning; he describes his difficulty reading long stretches of prose, and he sees the Internet "chipping away at my capacity for concentration and contemplation." Broadening his view and drawing on anecdotes and studies, Carr goes on to suggest that by diminishing our skill for "deep reading" and sustained attention, our Internet use is changing how our brains work and what our culture values. ***Before you read,*** *consider your own leisure reading habits: how often do you read longer articles, stories, or books? Do you find it difficult to* *sustain your concentration when you read longer pieces? Do you think that the time you spend online has any influence over what and how you read?*

"Dave, stop. Stop, will you? Stop, Dave. Will you stop, Dave?" So the supercomputer HAL pleads with the implacable astronaut Dave Bowman in a famous and weirdly poignant scene toward the end of Stanley Kubrick's *2001: A Space Odyssey*. Bowman, having nearly been sent to a deep-space death by the malfunctioning machine, is calmly, coldly disconnecting the memory circuits that control its artificial "brain." "Dave, my mind is going," HAL says, forlornly. "I can feel it. I can feel it." 1

I can feel it, too. Over the past few years I've had an uncomfortable sense that someone, or something, has been tinkering with my brain, remapping the neural circuitry, reprogramming the memory. My mind isn't going—so far as I can tell—but it's changing. I'm not thinking the way I used to think. I can feel it most strongly when I'm reading. Immersing myself in a book or a lengthy article used to be easy. My mind would get caught up in the narrative or the turns of the argument, and I'd spend hours strolling through long stretches of prose. That's rarely the case anymore. Now my concentration often starts to drift after two or three pages. I get fidgety, lose the thread, begin looking for something else to do. I feel as if I'm always dragging my wayward brain back to the text. The deep reading that used to come naturally has become a struggle. 2

I think I know what's going on. For more than a decade now, I've been spending a lot of time online, searching and surfing and sometimes adding to the great databases of the Internet. The Web has been a godsend to me as a writer. Research that once required days in the stacks or periodical rooms of libraries can now be done in minutes. A few Google searches, some quick clicks on hyperlinks, and I've got the telltale fact or pithy quote I was after. Even when I'm not working, I'm as likely as not to be foraging in the Web's info-thickets' reading and writing e-mails, scanning headlines and blog posts, watching videos and listening to podcasts, or just tripping from link to link to link. (Unlike footnotes, to which they're sometimes likened, hyperlinks don't merely point to related works; they propel you toward them.) 3

For me, as for others, the Net is becoming a universal medium, the conduit for most of the information that flows through my eyes and ears and into my mind. The advantages of having immediate access to such an incredibly rich store of information are many, and they've been widely described and duly applauded. "The perfect recall of silicon memory," *Wired*'s Clive Thompson has written, "can be an 4 enormous boon to thinking." But that boon comes at a price. As the media theorist Marshall McLuhan pointed out in the 1960s, media are not just passive channels of information. They supply the stuff of thought, but they also shape the process of thought. And what the Net seems to be doing is chipping away my capacity for concentration and contemplation. My mind now expects to take in information the way the Net distributes it: in a swiftly moving stream of particles. Once I was a scuba diver in the sea of words. Now I zip along the surface like a guy on a Jet Ski.

I'm not the only one. When I mention my troubles with reading 5
to friends and acquaintances—literary types, most of them—many say they're having similar experiences. The more they use the Web, the more they have to fight to stay focused on long pieces of writing. Some of the bloggers I follow have also begun mentioning the phenomenon. Scott Karp, who writes a blog about online media, recently confessed that he has stopped reading books altogether. "I was a lit major in college, and used to be [a] voracious book reader," he wrote. "What happened?" He speculates on the answer: "What if I do all my reading on the web not so much because the way I read has changed, i.e., I'm just seeking convenience, but because the way I THINK has changed?"

Bruce Friedman, who blogs regularly about the use of comput- 6
ers in medicine, also has described how the Internet has altered his mental habits. "I now have almost totally lost the ability to read and absorb a longish article on the web or in print," he wrote earlier this year. A pathologist who has long been on the faculty of the University of Michigan Medical School, Friedman elaborated on his comment in a telephone conversation with me. His thinking, he said, has taken on a "staccato" quality, reflecting the way he quickly scans short passages of text from many sources online. "I can't read *War and Peace* anymore," he admitted. "I've lost the ability to do that. Even a blog post of more than three or four paragraphs is too much to absorb. I skim it."

Anecdotes alone don't prove much. And we still await the long- 7
term neurological and psychological experiments that will provide a definitive picture of how Internet use affects cognition. But a recently published study of online research habits , conducted by scholars from University College London, suggests that we may well be in the midst of a sea change in the way we read and think. As part of the five-year research program, the scholars examined computer logs documenting the behavior of visitors to two popular research sites, one operated by the British Library and one by a U.K. educational consortium, that provide access to journal articles, e-books, and other sources of written information. They found that people using the sites exhibited "a form

of skimming activity," hopping from one source to another and rarely returning to any source they'd already visited. They typically read no more than one or two pages of an article or book before they would "bounce" out to another site. Sometimes they'd save a long article, but there's no evidence that they ever went back and actually read it. The authors of the study report:

> It is clear that users are not reading online in the traditional sense; indeed there are signs that new forms of "reading" are emerging as users "power browse" horizontally through titles, contents pages and abstracts going for quick wins. It almost seems that they go online to avoid reading in the traditional sense.

Thanks to the ubiquity of text on the Internet, not to mention the popularity of text-messaging on cell phones, we may well be reading more today than we did in the 1970s or 1980s, when television was our medium of choice. But it's a different kind of reading, and behind it lies a different kind of thinking—perhaps even a new sense of the self. "We are not only *what* we read," says Maryanne Wolf, a developmental psychologist at Tufts University and the author of *Proust and the Squid: The Story and Science of the Reading Brain*. "We are *how* we read." Wolf worries that the style of reading promoted by the Net, a style that puts "efficiency" and "immediacy" above all else, may be weakening our capacity for the kind of deep reading that emerged when an earlier technology, the printing press, made long and complex works of prose commonplace. When we read online, she says, we tend to become "mere decoders of information." Our ability to interpret text, to make the rich mental connections that form when we read deeply and without distraction, remains largely disengaged. 8

Reading, explains Wolf, is not an instinctive skill for human beings. It's not etched into our genes the way speech is. We have to teach our minds how to translate the symbolic characters we see into the language we understand. And the media or other technologies we use in learning and practicing the craft of reading play an important part in shaping the neural circuits inside our brains. Experiments demonstrate that readers of ideograms, such as the Chinese, develop a mental circuitry for reading that is very different from the circuitry found in those of us whose written language employs an alphabet. The variations extend across many regions of the brain, including those that govern such essential cognitive functions as memory and the interpretation of visual and auditory stimuli. We can expect as well that the circuits woven by our use of the Net will be different from those woven by our reading of books and other printed works. 9

Sometime in 1882, Friedrich Nietzsche bought a typewriter—a 10
Malling-Hansen Writing Ball, to be precise. His vision was failing, and keeping his eyes focused on a page had become exhausting and painful, often bringing on crushing headaches. He had been forced to curtail his writing, and he feared that he would soon have to give it up. The typewriter rescued him, at least for a time. Once he had mastered touch-typing, he was able to write with his eyes closed, using only the tips of his fingers. Words could once again flow from his mind to the page.

But the machine had a subtler effect on his work. One of Ni- 11
etzsche's friends, a composer, noticed a change in the style of his writing. His already terse prose had become even tighter, more telegraphic. "Perhaps you will through this instrument even take to a new idiom," the friend wrote in a letter, noting that, in his own work, his "'thoughts' in music and language often depend on the quality of pen and paper."

"You are right," Nietzsche replied, "our writing equipment takes 12
part in the forming of our thoughts." Under the sway of the machine, writes the German media scholar Friedrich A. Kittler, Nietzsche's prose "changed from arguments to aphorisms, from thoughts to puns, from rhetoric to telegram style."

The human brain is almost infinitely malleable. People used to 13
think that our mental meshwork, the dense connections formed among the 100 billion or so neurons inside our skulls, was largely fixed by the time we reached adulthood. But brain researchers have discovered that that's not the case. James Olds, a professor of neuroscience who directs the Krasnow Institute for Advanced Study at George Mason University, says that even the adult mind "is very plastic." Nerve cells routinely break old connections and form new ones. "The brain," according to Olds, "has the ability to reprogram itself on the fly, altering the way it functions."

As we use what the sociologist Daniel Bell has called our "intel- 14
lectual technologies"—the tools that extend our mental rather than our physical capacities—we inevitably begin to take on the qualities of those technologies. The mechanical clock, which came into common use in the 14th century, provides a compelling example. In *Technics and Civilization*, the historian and cultural critic Lewis Mumford described how the clock "disassociated time from human events and helped create the belief in an independent world of mathematically measurable sequences." The "abstract framework of divided time" became "the point of reference for both action and thought."

The clock's methodical ticking helped bring into being the sci- 15
entific mind and the scientific man. But it also took something away. As the late MIT computer scientist Joseph Weizenbaum observed in his 1976 book, *Computer Power and Human Reason: From Judgment to*

Calculation, the conception of the world that emerged from the widespread use of timekeeping instruments "remains an impoverished version of the older one, for it rests on a rejection of those direct experiences that formed the basis for, and indeed constituted, the old reality." In deciding when to eat, to work, to sleep, to rise, we stopped listening to our senses and started obeying the clock.

The process of adapting to new intellectual technologies is reflected in the changing metaphors we use to explain ourselves to ourselves. When the mechanical clock arrived, people began thinking of their brains as operating "like clockwork." Today, in the age of software, we have come to think of them as operating "like computers." But the changes, neuroscience tells us, go much deeper than metaphor. Thanks to our brain's plasticity, the adaptation occurs also at a biological level. 16

The Internet promises to have particularly far-reaching effects on cognition. In a paper published in 1936, the British mathematician Alan Turing proved that a digital computer, which at the time existed only as a theoretical machine, could be programmed to perform the function of any other information-processing device. And that's what we're seeing today. The Internet, an immeasurably powerful computing system, is subsuming most of our other intellectual technologies. It's becoming our map and our clock, our printing press and our typewriter, our calculator and our telephone, and our radio and TV. 17

When the Net absorbs a medium, that medium is re-created in the Net's image. It injects the medium's content with hyperlinks, blinking ads, and other digital gewgaws, and it surrounds the content with the content of all the other media it has absorbed. A new e-mail message, for instance, may announce its arrival as we're glancing over the latest headlines at a newspaper's site. The result is to scatter our attention and diffuse our concentration. 18

The Net's influence doesn't end at the edges of a computer screen, either. As people's minds become attuned to the crazy quilt of Internet media, traditional media have to adapt to the audience's new expectations. Television programs add text crawls and pop-up ads, and magazines and newspapers shorten their articles, introduce capsule summaries, and crowd their pages with easy-to-browse info-snippets. When, in March of this year, *The New York Times* decided to devote the second and third pages of every edition to article abstracts, its design director, Tom Bodkin, explained that the "shortcuts" would give harried readers a quick "taste" of the day's news, sparing them the "less efficient" method of actually turning the pages and reading the articles. Old media have little choice but to play by the new-media rules. 19

Never has a communications system played so many roles in our lives—or exerted such broad influence over our thoughts—as the Internet does today. Yet, for all that's been written about the Net, there's been little consideration of how, exactly, it's reprogramming us. The Net's intellectual ethic remains obscure. 20

About the same time that Nietzsche started using his typewriter, an earnest young man named Frederick Winslow Taylor carried a stopwatch into the Midvale Steel plant in Philadelphia and began a historic series of experiments aimed at improving the efficiency of the plant's machinists. With the approval of Midvale's owners, he recruited a group of factory hands, set them to work on various metal-working machines, and recorded and timed their every movement as well as the operations of the machines. By breaking down every job into a sequence of small, discrete steps and then testing different ways of performing each one, Taylor created a set of precise instructions—an "algorithm," we might say today—for how each worker should work. Midvale's employees grumbled about the strict new regime, claiming that it turned them into little more than automatons, but the factory's productivity soared. 21

More than a hundred years after the invention of the steam engine, the Industrial Revolution had at last found its philosophy and its philosopher. Taylor's tight industrial choreography—his "system," as he liked to call it—was embraced by manufacturers throughout the country and, in time, around the world. Seeking maximum speed, maximum efficiency, and maximum output, factory owners used time-and-motion studies to organize their work and configure the jobs of their workers. The goal, as Taylor defined it in his celebrated 1911 treatise, *The Principles of Scientific Management*, was to identify and adopt, for every job, the "one best method" of work and thereby to effect "the gradual substitution of science for rule of thumb throughout the mechanic arts." Once his system was applied to all acts of manual labor, Taylor assured his followers, it would bring about a restructuring not only of industry but of society, creating a utopia of perfect efficiency. "In the past the man has been first," he declared; "in the future the system must be first." 22

Taylor's system is still very much with us; it remains the ethic of industrial manufacturing. And now, thanks to the growing power that computer engineers and software coders wield over our intellectual lives, Taylor's ethic is beginning to govern the realm of the mind as well. The Internet is a machine designed for the efficient and automated collection, transmission, and manipulation of information, and its legions of programmers are intent on finding the "one best method"—the perfect algorithm—to carry out every mental movement of what we've come to describe as "knowledge work." 23

Google's headquarters, in Mountain View, California—the Googleplex—is the Internet's high church, and the religion practiced inside its walls is Taylorism. Google, says its chief executive, Eric Schmidt, is "a company that's founded around the science of measurement," and it is striving to "systematize everything" it does. Drawing on the terabytes of behavioral data it collects through its search engine and other sites, it carries out thousands of experiments a day, according to the *Harvard Business Review*, and it uses the results to refine the algorithms that increasingly control how people find information and extract meaning from it. What Taylor did for the work of the hand, Google is doing for the work of the mind. 24

The company has declared that its mission is "to organize the world's information and make it universally accessible and useful." It seeks to develop "the perfect search engine," which it defines as something that "understands exactly what you mean and gives you back exactly what you want." In Google's view, information is a kind of commodity, a utilitarian resource that can be mined and processed with industrial efficiency. The more pieces of information we can "access" and the faster we can extract their gist, the more productive we become as thinkers. 25

Where does it end? Sergey Brin and Larry Page, the gifted young men who founded Google while pursuing doctoral degrees in computer science at Stanford, speak frequently of their desire to turn their search engine into an artificial intelligence, a HAL-like machine that might be connected directly to our brains. "The ultimate search engine is something as smart as people—or smarter," Page said in a speech a few years back. "For us, working on search is a way to work on artificial intelligence." In a 2004 interview with *Newsweek*, Brin said, "Certainly if you had all the world's information directly attached to your brain, or an artificial brain that was smarter than your brain, you'd be better off." Last year, Page told a convention of scientists that Google is "really trying to build artificial intelligence and to do it on a large scale." 26

Such an ambition is a natural one, even an admirable one, for a pair of math whizzes with vast quantities of cash at their disposal and a small army of computer scientists in their employ. A fundamentally scientific enterprise, Google is motivated by a desire to use technology, in Eric Schmidt's words, "to solve problems that have never been solved before," and artificial intelligence is the hardest problem out there. Why wouldn't Brin and Page want to be the ones to crack it? 27

Still, their easy assumption that we'd all "be better off" if our brains were supplemented, or even replaced, by an artificial intelligence is unsettling. It suggests a belief that intelligence is the output 28 of a mechanical process, a series of discrete steps that can be isolated, measured, and optimized. In Google's world, the world we enter when we go online, there's little place for the fuzziness of contemplation. Ambiguity is not an opening for insight but a bug to be fixed. The human brain is just an outdated computer that needs a faster processor and a bigger hard drive.

The idea that our minds should operate as high-speed data- 29 processing machines is not only built into the workings of the Internet, it is the network's reigning business model as well. The faster we surf across the Web—the more links we click and pages we view—the more opportunities Google and other companies gain to collect information about us and to feed us advertisements. Most of the proprietors of the commercial Internet have a financial stake in collecting the crumbs of data we leave behind as we flit from link to link—the more crumbs, the better. The last thing these companies want is to encourage leisurely reading or slow, concentrated thought. It's in their economic interest to drive us to distraction.

Maybe I'm just a worrywart. Just as there's a tendency to glo- 30 rify technological progress, there's a countertendency to expect the worst of every new tool or machine. In Plato's *Phaedrus*, Socrates bemoaned the development of writing. He feared that, as people came to rely on the written word as a substitute for the knowledge they used to carry inside their heads, they would, in the words of one of the dialogue's characters, "cease to exercise their memory and become forgetful." And because they would be able to "receive a quantity of information without proper instruction," they would "be thought very knowledgeable when they are for the most part quite ignorant." They would be "filled with the conceit of wisdom instead of real wisdom." Socrates wasn't wrong—the new technology did often have the effects he feared—but he was shortsighted. He couldn't foresee the many ways that writing and reading would serve to spread information, spur fresh ideas, and expand human knowledge (if not wisdom).

The arrival of Gutenberg's printing press, in the 15th century, set 31 off another round of teeth gnashing. The Italian humanist Hieronimo Squarciafico worried that the easy availability of books would lead to intellectual laziness, making men "less studious" and weakening their minds. Others argued that cheaply printed books and broadsheets would undermine religious authority, demean the work of scholars and scribes, and spread sedition and debauchery. As New York University professor Clay Shirky notes, "Most of the arguments made against the printing press were correct, even prescient." But, again, the doomsayers were unable to imagine the myriad blessings that the printed word would deliver.

So, yes, you should be skeptical of my skepticism. Perhaps those who dismiss critics of the Internet as Luddites or nostalgists will be proved correct, and from our hyperactive, data-stoked minds will spring a golden age of intellectual discovery and universal wisdom. Then again, the Net isn't the alphabet, and although it may replace the printing press, it produces something altogether different. The kind of deep reading that a sequence of printed pages promotes is valuable not just for the knowledge we acquire from the author's words but for the intellectual vibrations those words set off within our own minds. In the quiet spaces opened up by the sustained, undistracted reading of a book, or by any other act of contemplation, for that matter, we make our own associations, draw our own inferences and analogies, foster our own ideas. Deep reading, as Maryanne Wolf argues, is indistinguishable from deep thinking. 32

If we lose those quiet spaces, or fill them up with "content," we will sacrifice something important not only in our selves but in our culture. In a recent essay, the playwright Richard Foreman eloquently described what's at stake: 33

> I come from a tradition of Western culture, in which the ideal (my ideal) was the complex, dense and "cathedral-like" structure of the highly educated and articulate personality—a man or woman who carried inside themselves a personally constructed and unique version of the entire heritage of the West. [But now] I see within us all (myself included) the replacement of complex inner density with a new kind of self—evolving under the pressure of information overload and the technology of the "instantly available."

As we are drained of our "inner repertory of dense cultural inheritance," Foreman concluded, we risk turning into "'pancake people'—spread wide and thin as we connect with that vast network of information accessed by the mere touch of a button." 34

I'm haunted by that scene in *2001*. What makes it so poignant, and so weird, is the computer's emotional response to the disassembly of its mind: its despair as one circuit after another goes dark, its childlike pleading with the astronaut—"I can feel it. I can feel it. I'm afraid"—and its final reversion to what can only be called a state of innocence. HAL's outpouring of feeling contrasts with the emotionlessness that characterizes the human figures in the film, who go about their business with an almost robotic efficiency. Their thoughts and actions feel scripted, as if they're following the steps of an algorithm. In the world of *2001*, people have become so machinelike that the most human character turns out to be a machine. That's the essence of Kubrick's dark prophecy: as we come to rely on computers to mediate our understanding of the world, it is our own intelligence that flattens into artificial intelligence. 35

Examining the Text

1. In describing the change in his relationship to research and information, Carr says, "Once I was a scuba diver in the sea of words. Now I zip along the surface like a guy on a Jet Ski." In your own words, explain what Carr means by this comparison. Do you get a sense that he thinks one mode (scuba diving or jet skiing) is superior to the other?

2. Carr cites Maryanne Wolf's quote that "We are not only *what* we read, . . . we are *how* we read." What does it mean to say that "we are *how* we read"? Why is this an important point for Carr's argument?

3. According to Carr, what are "intellectual technologies"? Why does he think that the Internet is an intellectual technology? What are the consequences of the Internet's absorption of other intellectual technologies?

4. How does Carr define Taylorism? Why does he think it is relevant in a discussion of the Internet's effects on our ways of thinking?

5. *Thinking rhetorically:* The focus of Carr's analysis is the Internet broadly rather than Google specifically, yet his title asks directly whether Google (rather than the Internet or computers) is making us stupid. Why do you think Carr puts Google in his title? And why does he choose the word "stupid" to describe the potential outcome? What is the overall effect of the title on you as a reader?

For Group Discussion

Toward the end of his article, Carr sounds quite similar to Neil Postman, whose "Judgment of Thamus" is included earlier in this chapter. Carr, like Postman, discusses the blessings and burdens of technologies, the way that a new technology redefines old terms, and the difficulty people have in foreseeing the ultimate consequences of a new technology. For this group discussion, have one group member play the role of Nicholas Carr and another play the role of Neil Postman. What topics would they discuss? What would be their key points of agreement and disagreement?

Writing Suggestion

"Is Google Making Us Stupid?" generated a lot of discussion when it was first published by Nicholas Carr in *Atlantic Monthly* in the summer of 2008. The article has its own Wikipedia page—http://en.wikipedia.org/wiki/Is_Google_Making_Us_Stupid%3F—that summarizes the discussion and points to several key responses to Carr's assertions. Clay Shirky (the author of an article on the future of television in Chapter 3 of this book) responded to Carr, and this initiated a discussion of sorts, with Carr replying to Shirky and Shirky replying back to Carr. Follow the links below to read this discussion:

"Why Abundance Is Good: My Reply to Nick Carr," by Clay Shirky http://www.britannica.com/blogs/2008/07/why-abundance-is-good-a-reply-to-nick-carr/

"Why Skepticism Is Good: My Reply to Clay Shirky," by Nicholas Carr http://www.britannica.com/blogs/2008/07/why-skepticism-is-good-my-reply-to-clay-shirky/

"Why Abundance Should Breed Optimism: A Second Reply to Nick Carr," by Clay Shirky http://www.britannica.com/blogs/2008/07/why-abundance-should-breed-optimism-a-second-reply-to-nick-carr/

After reading the responses and replies of Shirky and Carr, write an essay in which you summarize their key points of agreement and disagreement. You can devote one paragraph to each of these key points, first stating the point and then providing evidence in the form of direct quotations and paraphrases from Carr's and Shirky's responses and replies. At the end of your essay, explain which author makes the strongest points, in your opinion. Whose argument do you find more compelling, and why?

Meet Your iBrain

GARY SMALL AND GIGI VORGAN

In the previous article, Nicholas Carr comments that "we still await the long-term neurological and psychological experiments that will provide a definitive picture of how Internet use affects cognition." The next article begins to provide this kind of information, as it reports on current research regarding the Internet's effects on the brain. The article was originally published in Scientific American *in 2008; it was drawn from the book* iBrain: Surviving the Technological Alteration of the Modern Mind, *co-authored by Dr. Gary Small, a researcher on memory and aging at UCLA, and Gigi Vorgan. Small and Vorgan write that "Daily exposure to high technology . . . stimulates brain cell alteration and neurotransmitter release, gradually strengthening new neural pathways in our brains while weakening old ones." In short, they argue that our use of the Internet and other technologies is physically altering our brains. Moreover, they provide evidence that this is taking place through recaps of a range of scientific studies.* ***As you read*** *about these studies, keep in mind your own experience as a user of the Internet and other technologies. What aspects of the research confirm or contradict the knowledge you've developed from your own experience?*

You're on a plane packed with other businesspeople, reading your electronic version of the Wall Street Journal on your laptop while downloading files to your BlackBerry and organizing your PowerPoint presentation for your first meeting when you reach New York. You 1 relish the perfect symmetry of your schedule, to-do lists and phone book as you notice a woman in the next row entering little written notes into her leather-bound daily planner. You remember having one of those . . . What? Like a zillion years ago? Hey, lady! Wake up and smell the computer age.

You're outside the airport now, waiting impatiently for a cab along with dozens of other people. It's finally your turn, and as you reach for the taxi door a large man pushes in front of you, practically knocking you over. Your briefcase goes flying, and your laptop and BlackBerry splatter into pieces on the pavement. As you frantically gather up the remnants of your once perfectly scheduled life, the woman with the daily planner book gracefully steps into a cab and glides away. 2

The current explosion of digital technology not only is changing the way we live and communicate but also is rapidly and profoundly altering our brains. Daily exposure to high technology—computers, smart phones, video games, search engines such as Google and Yahoo—stimulates brain cell alteration and neurotransmitter release, gradually strengthening new neural pathways in our brains while weakening old ones. Because of the current technological revolution, our brains are evolving right now—at a speed like never before. 3

Besides influencing how we think, digital technology is altering how we feel, how we behave. Seven out of 10 American homes are wired for high-speed Internet. We rely on the Internet and digital technology for entertainment, political discussion, and communication with friends and co-workers. As the brain evolves and shifts its focus toward new technological skills, it drifts away from fundamental social skills, such as reading facial expressions during conversation or grasping the emotional context of a subtle gesture. A 2002 Stanford University study found that for every hour we spend on our computers, traditional face-to-face interaction time with other people drops by nearly 30 minutes. 4

DIGITAL NATIVES

Today's young people in their teens and 20s, who have been dubbed "digital natives," have never known a world without computers, 24-hour TV news, Internet and cell phones—with their video, music, cameras and text messaging. Many of these natives rarely enter a library, let alone look something up in a traditional encyclopedia; they use Google, Yahoo and other online search engines. The neu- 5 ral networks in the brains of these digital natives differ dramatically from those of "digital immigrants," people—including most baby boomers—who came to the digital/computer age as adults but whose basic brain wiring was laid down during a time when direct social interaction was the norm.

Now we are exposing our brains to technology for extensive periods every day, even at very young ages. A 2007 University of Texas at Austin study of more than 1,000 children found that on a typical day, 75 percent of children watch TV, whereas 32 percent of them watch videos or DVDs, with a total daily exposure averaging one hour and 20 minutes. Among those children, five- and six-year-olds spend an additional 50 minutes in front of the computer. A 2005 Kaiser Family Foundation study found that young people eight to 18 years of age expose their brains to eight and a half hours of digital and video sensory stimulation a day. The investigators reported that most of the technology exposure is passive, such as watching television and videos (four hours daily) or listening to music (one hour and 45 minutes), whereas other exposure is more active and requires mental participation, such as playing video games (50 minutes daily) or using the computer (one hour). 6

We know that the brain's neural circuitry responds every moment to whatever sensory input it gets and that the many hours people spend in front of the computer—including trolling the Internet, exchanging e-mail, video conferencing, instant messaging and e-shopping—expose their brains to constant digital stimulation. Our research team at the University of California, Los Angeles, wanted to look at how much impact this extended computer time was having on the brain's neural circuitry, how quickly it could build up new pathways, and whether we could observe and measure these changes as they occurred. 7

GOOGLE IN YOUR HEAD

One of us (Small) enlisted the help of Susan Bookheimer and Teena Moody, U.C.L.A. experts in neuropsychology and neuroimaging. We planned to use functional magnetic resonance imaging to measure the brain's activity during a common Internet computer task: searching Google for accurate information. We first needed to find people who were relatively inexperienced and naive to the computer. 8

After initial difficulty finding people who had not yet used PCs, we were able to recruit three volunteers in their mid-50s and 60s who were new to the technology yet willing to give it a try. To compare the 9 brain activity of these three naive volunteers, we also recruited three computer-savvy volunteers of comparable age, gender and socioeconomic background. For our experiment, we chose searching on Google for specific and accurate information on a variety of topics, ranging from the health benefits of eating chocolate to planning a trip to the Galápagos.

Next, we had to figure out a way to perform MRIs on the volunteers while they used the Internet. Because the study subjects had to be inside a long, narrow tube of an MM machine during the experiment, there would be no space for a computer, keyboard or mouse. To re-create the Google-search experience inside the scanner, we had the volunteers wear a pair of special goggles that presented images of Web site pages. The system allowed the volunteers to navigate the simulated computer screen and make choices to advance their search by pressing one finger on a small keypad, conveniently placed. 10

To make sure that the fMRI scanner was measuring the neural circuitry that controls Internet searches, we needed to factor out other sources of brain stimulation. To do this, we added a control task in which the study subjects read pages of a book projected through the specialized goggles during the MM. This task allowed us to subtract from the MM measurements any nonspecific brain activations that resulted from simply reading text, focusing on a visual image or concentrating. 11

We wanted to observe and measure only the brain's activity from those mental tasks required for Internet searching, such as scanning for targeted key words, rapidly choosing from among several alternatives, going back to a previous page if a particular search choice was not helpful, and so forth. We alternated this control task—simply reading a simulated page of text—with the Internet-searching task. We also controlled for nonspecific brain stimulations caused by the photographs and drawings that are typically displayed on an Internet page. 12

Finally, to determine whether we could train the brains of Internet-naive volunteers, after the first scanning session we asked each volunteer to search the Internet for an hour every day for five days. We gave the computer-savvy volunteers the same assignment and repeated the fMRI scans on both groups after the five days of search-engine training. 13

BRAIN CHANGES

As we had predicted, the brains of computer-savvy and computer-naive subjects did not show any difference when they were reading the simulated book text; both groups had years of experience in this mental task, 14 and their brains were quite familiar with reading books. In contrast, the two groups showed distinctly different patterns of neural activation when searching on Google. During the baseline scanning session, the computer-savvy subjects used a specific network in the left front part of the brain, known as the dorsolateral prefrontal cortex. The Internet-naive subjects showed minimal, if any, activation in this region.

One of our concerns in designing the study was that five days 15
would not be enough time to observe any changes. But after just five days of practice, the exact same neural circuitry in the front part of the brain became active in the Internet-naive subjects. Five hours on the Internet, and these participants had already rewired their brains. The computer-savvy volunteers activated the same frontal brain region at baseline and had a similar level of activation during their second session, suggesting that for a typical computer-savvy individual, the neural circuit training occurs relatively early and then remains stable.

The dorsolateral prefrontal cortex is involved in our ability to 16
make decisions and integrate complex information. It also is thought to control our mental process of integrating sensations and thoughts, as well as working memory, which is our ability to keep information in mind for a very short time—just long enough to manage an Internet-searching task or to dial a phone number after getting it from directory assistance.

In today's digital age, we keep our smart phones at our hip and 17
their earpieces attached to our ears. A laptop is always within reach, and there's no need to fret if we can't find a landline—there's always Wi-Fi (short for wireless fidelity, which supplies a wireless connection to the Internet) to keep us connected.

Our high-tech revolution has plunged us into a state of "con- 18
tinuous partial attention," which software executive Linda Stone, who coined the term in 1998, describes as continually staying busy—keeping tabs on everything while never truly focusing on anything. Continuous partial attention differs from multitasking, wherein we have a purpose for each task and we are trying to improve efficiency and productivity. Instead, when our minds partially attend, and do so continuously, we scan for an opportunity for any type of contact at every given moment. We virtually chat as our text messages flow, and we keep tabs on active buddy lists (friends and other screen names in an instant message program); everything, everywhere, is connected through our peripheral attention.

Although having all our pals online from moment to moment 19
seems intimate, we risk losing personal touch with our real-life relationships and may experience an artificial sense of intimacy as compared with when we shut down our devices and devote our attention to one individual at a time.

TECHNO-BRAIN BURNOUT

When paying continuous partial attention, people may place their brain in a heightened state of stress. They no longer have time to reflect, contemplate or make thoughtful decisions. Instead they exist in a sense of constant crisis—on alert for a new contact or bit of exciting news or information at any moment. Once people get used to this state, they tend to thrive on the perpetual connectivity. It feeds their ego and sense of self-worth, and it becomes irresistible. 20

Neuroimaging studies suggest that this sense of self-worth may protect the size of the hippocampus—the horseshoe-shaped brain region in the medial (inward-facing) temporal lobe, which allows us to learn and remember new information. Psychiatry professor Sonia J. Lupien and her associates at McGill University studied hippocampal size in healthy younger and older adult volunteers. Measures of self-esteem correlated significantly with hippocampal size, regardless of age. They also found that the more people felt in control of their lives, the larger the hippocampus. 21

But at some point, the sense of control and self-worth we feel when we maintain continuous partial attention tends to break down—our brains were not built to sustain such monitoring for extended periods. Eventually the hours of unrelenting digital connectivity can create a unique type of brain strain. Many people who have been working on the Internet for several hours without a break report making frequent errors in their work. On signing off, they notice feeling spaced out, fatigued, irritable and distracted, as if they are in a "digital fog." This new form of mental stress, what Small terms "techno-brain burnout," is threatening to become an epidemic. Under this kind of stress, our brains instinctively signal the adrenal gland to secrete cortisol and adrenaline. In the short run, these stress hormones boost energy levels and augment memory, but over time they actually impair cognition, lead to depression, and alter the neural circuitry in the hippocampus, amygdala and prefrontal cortex—the brain regions that control mood and thought. Chronic and prolonged techno-brain burnout can even reshape the underlying brain structure. 22

Research psychologist Sara C. Mednick, then at Harvard University, and her colleagues were able to induce a mild form of techno-brain burnout in volunteers experimentally; they then were able to reduce its impact through power naps and by varying mental assignments. Their study subjects performed a visual task: reporting the direction of three lines in the lower left corner of a computer screen. The volunteers' scores worsened over time, but their performance improved if the scientists alternated the visual task between the lower left and lower right corners of the computer screen. 23

This result suggests that brain burnout may be relieved by varying the location of the mental task.

The investigators also found that the performance of study sub- 24
jects improved if they took a 20- to 30-minute nap. The neural networks involved in the task were apparently refreshed during rest; however, optimum refreshment and reinvigoration for the task occurred when naps lasted up to 60 minutes—the amount of time it takes for rapid-eye-movement (REM) sleep to kick in.

THE NEW, IMPROVED BRAIN?

Whether we're digital natives or immigrants, altering our neural net- 25
works and synaptic connections through activities such as e-mail, video games, Googling or other technological experiences does sharpen some cognitive abilities. We can learn to react more quickly to visual stimuli and improve many forms of attention, particularly the ability to notice images in our peripheral vision. We develop a better ability to sift through large amounts of information rapidly and decide what's important and what isn't—our mental filters basically learn how to shift into overdrive. In this way, we are able to cope with the massive amounts of data appearing and disappearing on our mental screens from moment to moment. Initially the daily blitz that bombards us can create a form of attention deficit, but our brains are able to adapt in a way that promotes rapid processing.

According to cognitive psychologist Pam Briggs of Northumbria 26
University in England, Web surfers looking for facts on health spend two seconds or less on any particular site before moving on to the next one. She found that when study subjects did stop and focus on a particular site, that site contained data relevant to the search, whereas those they skipped over contained almost nothing relevant to the search. This study indicates that our brains learn to swiftly focus attention, analyze information and almost instantaneously decide on a go or no-go action. Rather than simply catching "digital ADD," many of us are developing neural circuitry that is customized for rapid and incisive spurts of directed concentration.

Digital evolution may well be increasing our intelligence in the 27
way we currently measure and define IQ. Average IQ scores have been steadily rising with the advancing digital culture, and the ability to multitask without errors is improving. Neuroscientist Paul Kearney of Unitec in New Zealand reported that some computer games can actually improve cognitive ability and multitasking skills. He found that volunteers who played the games eight hours a week improved multitasking skills by two and a half times. Other research at the University

of Rochester has shown that playing video games can improve peripheral vision as well. As the modern brain continues to evolve, some attention skills improve, mental response times sharpen and the performance of many brain tasks becomes more efficient.

While the brains of today's digital natives are wiring up for rapid-fire cyber searches, however, the neural circuits that control the more traditional learning methods are neglected and gradually diminished. The pathways for human interaction and communication weaken as customary one-on-one people skills atrophy. Our U.C.L.A. research team and other scientists have shown that we can intentionally alter brain wiring and reinvigorate some of these dwindling neural pathways, even while the newly evolved technology circuits bring our brains to extraordinary levels of potential. 28

All of us, digital natives and immigrants, will master new technologies and take advantage of their efficiencies, but we also need to maintain our people skills and our humanity. Whether in relation to a focused Google search or an empathic listening exercise, our synaptic responses can be measured, shaped and optimized to our advantage, and we can survive the technological adaptation of the modern mind. 29

Examining the Text

1. According to Small and Vorgan, how do technological skills affect social skills? In other words, what are some of the ways that digital technology alters how we feel and behave, according to the authors?

2. What significant findings do Small and Vorgan report from the UCLA study? What differences did they discover in their computer-savvy and computer-naïve subjects, and how did those differences change over time and with additional Internet exposure?

3. According to Small and Vorgan, what is "continuous partial attention"? How does it differ from "multitasking"? What effects do they believe maintaining a state of "continuous partial attention" has on us?

4. *Thinking rhetorically:* Small and Vorgan use an opening strategy that's akin to the strategy used by John Steele Gordon in the first article of this chapter. Go back and read Gordon's first 11 paragraphs and then re-read Small and Vorgan's first two paragraphs. What similarities and differences do you see in the openings of these two articles? Which opening do you think is more effective, and why?

For Group Discussion

With your peers, reexamine the details of the UCLA fMRI study that Small and Vorgan report on. Take notes of the specific features of the study: how many participants were there; what characteristics did these participants have; what tasks were they given to complete; how were their actions measured? In your group, discuss what you see as strengths and weaknesses of this study.

Barbie and Ken
Branding
Photographer: Aaron Goodman

"Conversion Barbie," by Kimmy McCann

"Absolute End," by Adbusters Media Foundation

Jon Stewart and Stephen Colbert
"The Rally To Restore Sanity"

Lady Gaga

Tupac Shakur
Getty Images/Time Life Pictures

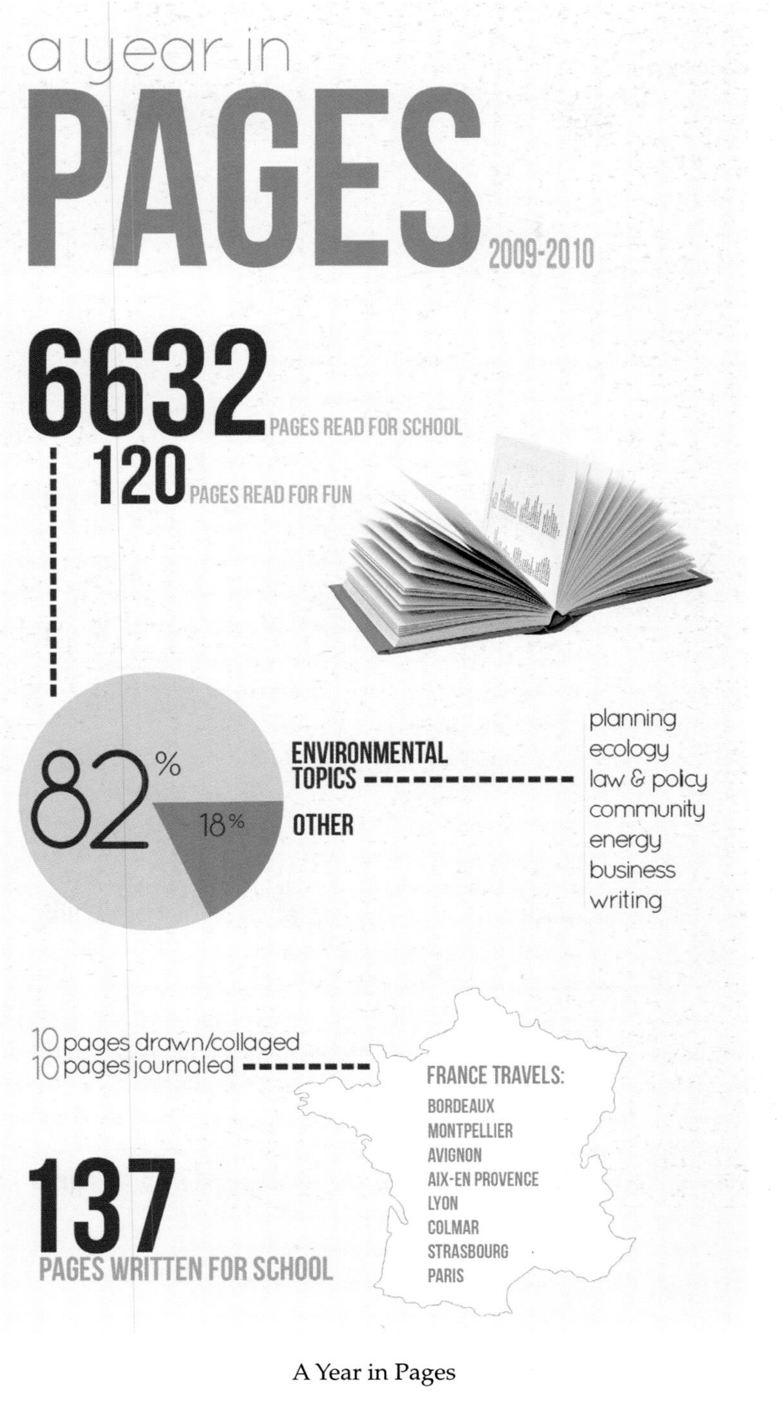

a year in
PAGES
2009-2010

6632 PAGES READ FOR SCHOOL

120 PAGES READ FOR FUN

82%
18%

ENVIRONMENTAL TOPICS

OTHER

planning
ecology
law & policy
community
energy
business
writing

10 pages drawn/collaged
10 pages journaled

FRANCE TRAVELS:
BORDEAUX
MONTPELLIER
AVIGNON
AIX-EN PROVENCE
LYON
COLMAR
STRASBOURG
PARIS

137
PAGES WRITTEN FOR SCHOOL

A Year in Pages

A Week of Water

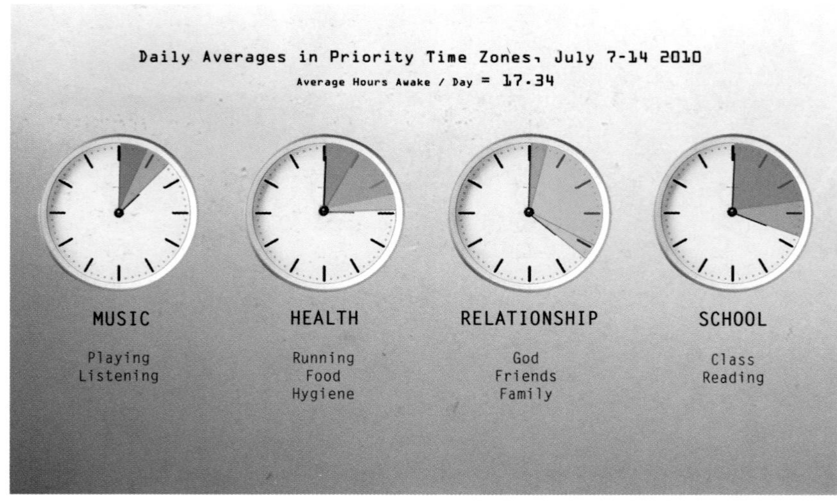

Daily Averages in Priority Time Zones

High school student after scoring a touchdown

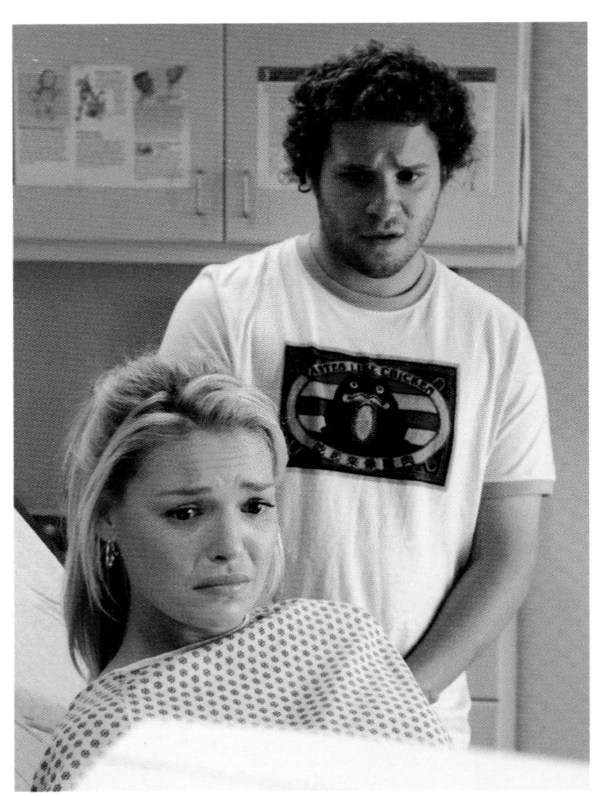

"Knocked Up," 2007. Katherine Heigl and Seth Rogen.
Directed by Judd Apatow.
Suzanne Hanover/Universal; Picture Desk, Inc./
Kobal Collection

Are there limitations to the study that make you hesitant to draw broad conclusions from it? If you had time and funding, what kind of follow-up study would you design to help you test the validity of the UCLA study?

Writing Suggestion

This article provides a useful overview of current scientific research on how technology use affects our brains and other aspects of our personalities. Small and Vorgan report on a number of studies in which researchers measure different variables and come to different conclusions. For this writing assignment, create a chart in which you list and summarize these studies. Use four columns for your chart: in the first column, state the name and institutional affiliation of the researcher(s) and the date of the study (if it's provided); in the second column, briefly describe the study itself; in the third column, list the findings or results of the study; and in the fourth column, describe your response to the study. After you've created this chart, write a one-paragraph analysis of what you see as the most important findings in recent research on technology and the brain.

ADDITIONAL SUGGESTIONS FOR WRITING ABOUT TECHNOLOGY

1. Postman argues that technologies have important and fairly unpredictable impacts on society, and he provides several brief examples to support this claim. Write a research-based report in which you describe the history of a particular technology, emphasizing the impact that this technology has had on popular culture or on a specific subculture. You might use Gordon's article on the history of cars as a model for your own structure and approach in this essay.

To choose a technology for your research topic, think in terms of categories; there are, for instance, technologies associated with music, movies, entertainment, health and medicine, science, communication, sports, cooking, cleaning, and so on. Once you've chosen a category that interests you, it should be easier to choose a specific technology. Do research both in the library and on the Web in order to find out when the technology was invented, how it evolved through the years, when its popularity grew and declined, and, most importantly, what impact it has had on the people who have used it. You might end your research report with speculations about the future of this technology: what new developments are in store for it, and in what new ways do you imagine will people use it in the future?

2. Samuels is concerned with the ways in which technologies redefine borders: between public spaces and private spaces, and between work and play. Write an essay in which you state your own opinion about technology's impact on one of these or on another border area—for instance, human/machine, child/

adult, male/female. What are the key technologies that have helped to shape your understanding of these supposedly opposite terms? What technologies change the way you understand the distinction between these terms?

Drawing from the articles, you can use quotations that you agree with to support claims that you make, and you can also use quotations that you disagree with in order to provide you with material to argue against. Try to draw as well on your own experiences and observations with the technologies you're discussing.

3. This is a tough assignment: go and play a video game. Actually, the tough part comes next: write an essay in which you analyze the video game you played. To prepare for this assignment, give some thought to the video game you choose to play. You might want to choose a game with which you're very familiar, so that you have a complete understanding of its characters, rules, scenarios, and strategies. On the other hand, you might want to choose a game that's entirely new to you so that you come to it from a fresh perspective.

After you've chosen a video game to play, go ahead and play—but as you're playing, pay attention to both the game and your reactions to it. This may require that you play the game more than once! Ultimately you want to walk away from the experience with something to say about the underlying premises of the game as well as about how playing the game affected you. After playing, be sure to jot down some notes about the most salient and interesting features of the game; you can use these notes as you develop your essay.

In writing your analysis of the video game you played, begin with a specific claim about the game, and use evidence from the game and from your experience of playing it to support the claim you make.

Internet Activities

1. As a means of exploring the phenomenon of social networking on the Internet, take a look at a project by Jonathan Harris and Sep Kamvar, entitled "We Feel Fine" (http://www.wefeelfine.org/). This interactive site explores the world of social networking in a visualization of data drawn from a range of social networking sites (e.g., MySpace, LiveJournal, Flickr). This assignment asks you to visit "We Feel Fine," explore it in detail, and write a response to it.

As you'll see when you visit the site, Harris and Kamvar focus on sentences having to do with feelings (i.e., sentences that contain the phrase "I feel" or "I am feeling"); they present multiple ways to view these sentences along with data about the people who have written the sentences. Be sure to explore the different ways of viewing the data as well as to read the descriptions of the project in the Missions, Movements, Methodology, and Findings sections. You might also take a look at another visualization project by Harris and Kamvar that explores the world of online dating: "I want you to want me" (http://iwantyoutowantme.org/).

Once you've thoroughly explored the site, write a response that addresses the following questions: What does "We Feel Fine" tell you about social networking in general? In the Mission section, Harris and Kamvar describe "We Feel Fine" as "an exploration of human emotion on a global scale"; does this seem to you to be an accurate description? How do the different ways of viewing the data contribute to your understanding of social networking and self-representation on the Internet?

In the response that you write to these questions, consider including one or more screenshots from "We Feel Fine" to help you illustrate specific points.

2. Many blogging sites on the Internet provide open-ended forums for writing about yourself, your interests, your witty observations, and your unique experiences. This assignment asks you to give blogging a try yourself. Visit Blogger (http://www.blogger.com) or one of the other free blogging sites on the Web and follow the directions there to start your own blog. If you have questions or run into problems setting up your blog, services like Blogger have excellent Help functions to guide you along.

Once you've got your blog set up, what should you write? Your teacher might have some specific suggestions for you, but we'd suggest that you start with the filter-style blog. That is, write an entry that has a link to a site on the Web that you find interesting or important or surprising or otherwise worthy of note. Along with the link, write a paragraph or two with your commentary on this link: why have you chosen it? Why should people visit the site you're linking to? After you've written one filter-style entry, try writing another one; perhaps you could write one filter-style entry each day for a week or two. You might conclude your blog-writing adventure by writing an entry analyzing your experience: what do you find worthwhile or problematic about writing in a blog? How is it different from writing for print? Do you think you might continue blogging in the future?

Reading Images

The images on pages CI5-CI6 are information visualizations created by students in Madeleine Sorapure's multimedia writing course at the University of California at Santa Barbara. Before they created these images, students had read Gary Wolf's "The Data-Driven Life" and had responded to an assignment very similar to the Writing Suggestion on page 336. Jennifer Verhines accessed information she had already collected about her reading habits over the past year; Nik Edlinger tracked his water consumption for a week; and Lauren Carr recorded the amount of time she spent on different activities during a week. The students then created visualizations of their data, using images, colors, and other visual elements to highlight their key findings from the data they had gathered.

Choose one of these images and look at it carefully. Write a brief (one-paragraph) description of the most important information that the visualization conveys. Then devote several paragraphs to an analysis of *how* the visualization effectively conveys this information, keeping in mind that the students made very specific, intentional choices about all elements of their visualizations. Consider the color, size, and font choice for text included; the use of colors elsewhere in the image; the placement of elements in the image; and, the visual metaphors (e.g., a clock) to signify certain meanings. Finally, conclude your analysis with an assessment of the visualization: in what ways is it effective, and where could it be improved.

After viewing these visualizations of personal data, you might also consider creating one of your own.

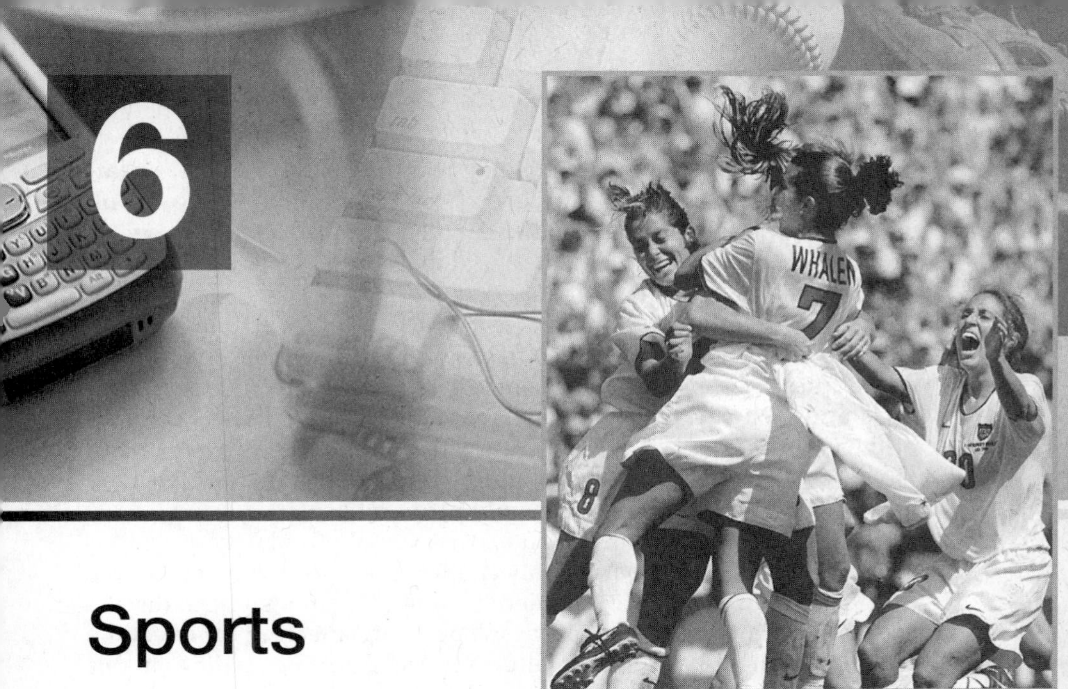

6

Sports

The United States seems to be a nation obsessed with sports, an obsession nowhere more evident than in some fans' virtual addiction to sports statistics. Somewhere there's a statistics maven who knows the number of foot faults in the final 1956 Davis Cup match or the most triples by a left-handed batter during Tuesday afternoon World Series games. Fans crave statistics, no matter how minute, as a way of measuring the achievements of their favorite athletes and teams—and perhaps also as a way of holding the memory of never-to-be-repeated athletic performances.

It's not difficult to find further evidence of America's preoccupation with sports. Most daily newspapers allocate an entire section to sports reports and statistics; a number of national weekly and monthly publications concentrate exclusively on sports. Special sporting events such as the Super Bowl are consistently among the most highly rated TV broadcasts, and several cable networks are devoted solely to sports twenty-four hours a day. Americans play sports trivia games, call sports telephone hotlines, and participate in a multibillion dollar sports gaming industry; they display team logos on T-shirts, sweatshirts, baseball caps, and countless other articles of clothing. Many colleges and universities capitalize on the prominence of their sports programs to increase enrollments and donations.

Sports can affect fans in surprisingly intense ways. We all probably know people whose moods fluctuate with the fortunes of their favorite team, who might "bleed Dodger blue," as they say. Indeed, entire cities rejoice when their team brings home a championship, and our national mood lifts when an American underdog takes a medal at the Olympics or when the "Dream Team" squashes an opponent. Given this obsession, it's no wonder that professional athletes are among our most revered—and highly paid—citizens.

How can we explain the almost universal popularity of sports? The essays in the first part of this chapter offer views about the role of sports in American life in general, along with an insightful discussion of the ways in which American sports are affecting (or *in*fecting, in the opinion of some critics) cultures worldwide. The readings in this section focus on one extremely popular sport—football—and discuss some recent traumatic events and controversies concerning the sport.

Obviously, sports and games can influence the way we speak and the way we feel, our notions of teamwork and individuality, success and failure, and male and female roles. From sports and games we learn how to deal with pressure, adversity, and physical pain and we discover models of grace, skill, and style. As you read the essays in this chapter, think of the sports you play and watch, of the athletes, the gamers, the physical risk-takers you admire, of the role sports and games play (or have played) in your life.

Sport and Society

The Roar of the Crowd

DAVID P. BARASH

In the Music chapter of this edition of Common Culture, *you encountered an article from* Bitch Magazine, *a delightfully opinionated and much respected feminist journal. A recent piece in that same journal contains an article titled, "Top Ten Reasons Why This Feminist Is a Sports Fan," in which the author proclaims, ". . . folks, I still love sports and I love being a sports fan. Sports are community-building . . . sports celebrate physical intelligence . . . sports are one of the few realms where adults play." The author concludes that sports fans are inherently optimistic folk, noting that "hope and faith are elevated in the sports fan. In the bleachers, you come to hone your sense of the possible and impossible. 'Believe,' say so many signs in the stands during a team's sports season. 'Do you believe in miracles?' rang one of the most memorable sportscasts of all time, and then, a second later, when the 1980 U.S. Olympic hockey team of amateur college players improbably won a game over the Soviet team of pros—which had clobbered them 10–1 in an exhibition game a week before—the voice rang again in answer to his own question, 'YES!'"*

While many fans echo this resounding praise for sports fandom, others are not so sanguine, as the following article illustrates. David P. Barash, a professor of psychology at the University of Washington, has a new book, How Women Got Their Curves and Other Just-So Stories, *co-written with Judith Eve Lipton, coming out with Columbia University Press. In response to the ringing "YES!" Dr. Barash utters a somewhat grumpier "No," or at best a qualified "Maybe." He admits to a certain confusion as to why so many people identify with groups of athletes with whom they have no personal connection, and he wonders why people idolize sports stars more than, say, notable scholars, scientists, and so forth.* ***As you read*** *this article, consider the source: the article appeared not in a magazine such as* Sports Illustrated *or* Sporting News, *but in a professional journal for educators, which may explain, at least in part, his attitude, rhetorical stance, and core points. Nevertheless, the arguments he makes are cogent and well articulated, and certainly worth your consideration, whether or not you ultimately agree with them.*

Marx was wrong: The opiate of the masses isn't religion, but spectator sports. What else explains the astounding fact that millions of seemingly intelligent human beings feel that the athletic exertions of 1 total strangers are somehow consequential for themselves? The real question we should be asking during the madness surrounding, for instance, the current collegiate basketball championship season, is not who will win . . . but why anyone cares.

Not that I would try to stop anyone from root, root, rooting to his or her heart's content. It's just that such things are normally done by pigs, in the mud, or by seedlings, lacking a firm grip on reality—fine for them, but I am not at all sure this is something that human beings should do. In desperation, if threatened with starvation, I suppose that I would root—for dinner. But for the home team? Never. 2

More than a decade ago, a baseball strike canceled the season and the World Series. The first time ever, we were told in hushed tones. A national trauma. Baseball had survived world wars, cold wars, hot dogs—even night games, the designated hitter, and Astroturf—only to succumb to a labor dispute between spoiled millionaire players and even-more-spoiled billionaire owners. How could it be summer without baseball, the pundits pouted? Most portentous, how could we be us without our spectator fix? 3

But wait. Here is heresy indeed: Was it really such a disaster? Or is it a disaster that our current paragons have been revealed to be hormonally enhanced and ethically challenged? Or if a college team is denied a bowl slot? Is life so pale, dull, and unsatisfying that it must be experienced vicariously in order to be savored? You might try reading a book, talking with your family, going for a walk, wrestling with the dog, listening to some music, smelling a flower, making love. 4

Let me be clear: It is not the doughty doing of sports that is so ill-conceived, but the woeful watching, the ridiculous rooting, the silly spectating. Nor is it a uniquely American affliction. Spectator sports may be a true "cross-cultural universal," in which the soccer ball has the kind of global salience to which Esperanto once unsuccessfully aspired, although the details of spectatorship owe much to local flavoring: Among Canadians, hockey worship is so pervasive that the running joke when the 2005 season was canceled was that sell-out crowds would still show up, just to watch the ice-resurfacing machines go around the empty rinks. In Afghanistan, the rage—except for brief banishment under the Taliban—has long been buzkashi, a violent and tumultuous game seemingly devoid of rules, in which thousands of onlookers go berserk while hundreds of mounted riders try to carry off the decapitated corpse of a goat. 5

I have no quarrel with vigorous participation, pursuing an activity for its own sake, for the exercise, the camaraderie, the joy of simply doing it. That appeal is in fact so strong that the Dutch historian Johan Huizinga seriously proposed 70 years ago that the human species be renamed *Homo ludens* (man the player). 6

Maybe there is a primitive, deep-seated wisdom in our penchant for play generally, and for athletics in particular. "We run," according to the first four-minute miler, Roger Bannister, "not because we think it is doing us good but because we cannot help ourselves." But if we run—or jump, throw, catch, kick, or bat—because we cannot help ourselves, do we also watch others do so for the same reason? Are we compulsive voyeurs? 7

For one thing, we get identification from our sports frenzy, the experience of seeing ourselves in the exploits of another. In his novel A Fan's Notes, Frederick Exley depicted the New York Giants' star running back Frank Gifford accomplishing with a football all those things the narrator failed to achieve in love and work: "It was very simple, really. Where I could not, with syntax, give shape to my fantasies, Gifford could, with his superb timing, his great hands, his uncanny faking, give shape to his." Earlier in the novel, the narrator—in a mental hospital—told a friend: "He may be the only fame I'll ever have!" 8

Maybe it is time to rework Andy Warhol's observation that in the future, everyone will be famous for 15 minutes: Thanks to spectator sports, each of us can know fame for most of our lives, so long as we are satisfied with the ever-shifting, warmed-over shadow of someone else's. Youngsters seem especially prone to that delusion, desperate as they are for heroes, and craving the opportunity to bask in another's glory. And so when children avidly pore over vacuous images and vital statistics, or traipse enthusiastically to the local (or even distant) stadium, it is easy to make allowances. Indeed, there is something touching about such fresh-faced yearning for exemplars, even though the constellations they see may not be notable for the content of their characters, intelligence, compassion, decency, or creativity, but rather for an uncommon and sometimes downright freakish ability to hit, throw, catch, roll, or bounce a ball, to jump high or punch hard, or to bump into other people in such a manner as to knock them down and/or avoid being knocked down themselves. Small wonder everyone ends up disappointed when those luminaries are revealed to be moral dwarfs. 9

"Say it ain't so, Joe. Say it ain't so," a young child is supposed to have pleaded with Shoeless Joe Jackson, the Chicago White Sox baseball star who helped "throw" the 1919 World Series in return for a payoff from gamblers. But it was so, and none but the most naïve of children and the most ardently deluded of adults should have been surprised. What is remarkable is not that athletes so often fail to be admirable people or to lead exemplary lives off the field, but that anyone would ever expect it to be otherwise. 10

For every youngster who admires the likes of Einstein, Gandhi, Jonas Salk, or Alice Walker, there are probably tens of thousands who 11 wind up adoring and seeking to emulate Ty Cobb, known as a racist, or drunkards and gluttons like Babe Ruth, compulsive womanizers like Wilt Chamberlain, gamblers like Pete Rose, or steroid abusers like . . . (fill in the blank).

Of course, there have been athletes who were admirable, even off the field. On balance, however, the probability is that successful athletes number among themselves more than their share of alcoholics, misogynists, sociopaths, and violence-prone dimwits and miscreants. After all, these are adults paid to play children's games, and there is simply no reason why the ability to do remarkable things with one's body—things that are generally quick and violent—should make someone worth emulating in any other way, and probably good reasons why the opposite is more likely. 12

Add to the primal passion for identification another natural tendency—the yearning to be part of a group—and the result is a potent brew. Spectator sports offer quick and easy entree into an instant community. Never mind that it is ersatz. It is there for the joining; no need to "make the team." Instead, just buy a ticket, a T-shirt, or turn on the television or radio. The would-be applicant is immediately taken in . . . in more ways than one. 13

It makes sense that an athlete's family and friends (at least some of them) might want to watch him or her compete. But surely not the many thousands who cram into our arenas this month. One possibility is that these observers, neither family nor friends of the athletes, are in some way deceived into imagining themselves family or friends. 14

The sports audience is complicit in its own deception, downright eager to be thus misled. As to why, let's consider the basic biology of Homo sapiens, as well as some general traits that we appear to share with other living things. Take, for starters, our basic inclination to affiliate into groups. Nothing abnormal here; it is one of the most appropriate human needs. Both developmentally and evolutionarily, it pays human beings to be group-loving, aggregative creatures. 15

The human fondness for groups begins early; namely, at birth. Each of us enters the world utterly dependent on someone else, most of the time a mother who provides nurturance and, specifically, milk, as with other mammals. As we grow, we expand our circle of connectedness, becoming part of an ever-growing "team" consisting of siblings, other relatives, close friends and associates, and so forth. In all probability, our Pleistocene ancestors affiliated into like subgroups within each tribe, and when it came to encounters between tribes, they made sure, first, that they were members of one tribe or another (to be unaffiliated was, in most cases, to be soon dead), and second, when the choice presented itself, to be part of the bigger—hence, stronger—one. 16

The issue was survival and reproduction versus failure and extinction, à la Darwin. "The more the merrier," we often tell ourselves, and for good reason: Even though two is company and three a crowd, we have always spent much more time trying to survive and prosper than courting or making love. 17

For tens of thousands of years during our early evolutionary history, there was safety in numbers, just as there is today for ants, horses, or chimpanzees. A single herring, swimming fearfully in the cold Atlantic, or a lonely wildebeest tramping its solitary way over the African savannah, is vulnerable to a hungry tuna or lion. But that herring or wildebeest can make itself somewhat safer by sidling up close to another herring or wildebeest, if only because a potential predator might choose the neighbor instead. Better yet, get yourself near a pair of herrings or wildebeests, or a dozen, or a hundred. For their part, the other group members aren't feeling "used," since they have been figuring the same way. They positively invite you to join because your presence makes them safer, too. Very likely such evolutionary factors were operating among our ancestors. Groups also provided the opportunity for division of labor, made it easier for prospective mates to meet, and provided for the pooling of material resources (like food) and for sharing precious wisdom (where to find water during those once-in-50-year droughts). 18

In addition—and this may well have been especially important for early human beings—we doubtless benefited from group size when we became enemies to each other. Even as affiliative grouping undoubtedly contributed to our survival and success, it could well have created its own kind of Frankenstein's monster: other groups. Although considerations of efficiency might have meant that our social units sometimes became oversized, it is easy to imagine how the presence of large, threatening bands of our own species pressured us to seek numbers to find safety. 19

When group fought group, the likelihood is that the larger one won; if so, individuals preferring a sizable crowd triumphed at the expense of those less socially inclined. To the primitive wisdom of the infant, seeking connection first to the mother and then to other family members and friends, there would accordingly have been added a related tendency: preferring larger groups to smaller ones. 20

Here we may well detect yet another of our connections to the animal world. Students of animal behavior identify what they call "releasers," signals that induce a seemingly automatic response in another animal. For example, the Nobel Prize–winning ethologist Nikolaas Tinbergen described how male stickleback fish, kept in an aquarium, rushed to attack the image of a red truck whenever one drove by his lab window. Male sticklebacks themselves have red breasts, and 21 apparently a patch of red serves to "release" the fishes' aggression. Not only that, but the larger the patch, the more the aggression. So there are exaggerated stimuli in the animal world that evoke exaggerated responses.

Consider the American oystercatcher, a shorebird about the size of a crow, with black back, white belly, and a stunning orange bill and feet. This bird lays eggs that are appropriate to its size; it then incubates them, as behooves most birds. The oystercatcher can also be fooled, however, induced to sit on artificial eggs made of plaster or papier-mâché, so long as the models are painted with the appropriate pattern of blotches that signals "egg" and releases incubation behavior in this species. 22

Things get especially interesting for our purposes when the oystercatcher is presented with a hugely oversized model egg, as big as a watermelon, but adorned with the correct releasing pattern. Oystercatchers are positively entranced by such a supernormal releaser and contentedly perch upon it in preference to their own eggs. There is something absurd about a small bird, earnestly incubating an "egg" that is perhaps 20 times its body volume, although the preference becomes understandable in terms of the oystercatcher's biologically appropriate inclination to hatch its own eggs. Give the unsuspecting animal an oversized model, and we get an oversized response. 23

Human beings, fortunately, are not as vulnerable as oystercatchers. We do not dangle helplessly at the end of strings pulled by releasers. On the other hand, we seem to have certain preferences that whisper deep within us. And so women are inclined to exaggerate the redness of their lips, the lushness of their hair, or the size of their breasts, in efforts to enhance their appeal to men, just as men might seek to enhance their apparent height, or the breadth of their shoulders, hoping to evoke a larger-than-ordinary response from women. Could we be similarly susceptible to the blandishments of large groups? 24

Certainly we can be bamboozled, induced to sit atop our various self-identified groups in an orgy of affiliation that makes the oystercatcher seem downright insightful. But it feels good because as we perch there, we satisfy a deep craving, indulging the illusion of being part of something larger than ourselves and thus nurtured, understood, accepted, enlarged, empowered, gratified, protected. 25

The observer of spectator sports cannot help but confront the odd underbelly of this passion: the yearning to be someone else, or at least, a very small part of something else, so long as that something else is Something Else, large and imposing, impressive and thus 26 irresistible. That dark desire for deindividuation was felt for millennia by the herring and the wildebeest, and perfected by human beings centuries ago: interestingly, not by sports franchises but by the world's military forces.

To the psychologically naïve, it may seem a peculiar anachronism that military boot camps prescribe close-order drill for young recruits and conscripts. After all, the days of the British square are long gone. But drill sergeants the world around know something important about the impact of repetitive, closely coordinated and choreographed movements, performed in synchrony by large numbers of people. The originating genius of that practice was Maurice of Nassau, a Dutchman living from 1567 to 1625. The historian William H. McNeill once commented on why modern armed forces still use Maurice's techniques, nearly five centuries after he introduced them: "When a group of men move their arm and leg muscles in unison for prolonged periods of time, a primitive and very powerful social bond wells up among them. This probably results from the fact that movement of the big muscles in unison rouses echoes of the most primitive level of sociality known to humankind." 27

It is no great distance from the mesmerizing impact of close-order drill to the stimulating consequence of shared chanting and cheering, the waving of arms (military or civilian) in unison. The Wave, which many fans say originated in my hometown of Seattle, is a good example. Even though they don't get to swing a bat, throw a pass, or sink a three-pointer, fans have been inventive in providing themselves with ritualized, shared movements that further embellish the allure as well as the illusion of being part of the larger, shared whole, tapping into that primitive satisfaction that moves at almost lightning speed from shared, ritual action to a tempestuous sense of expanded self. One becomes part of a great beckoning, grunting, yet smoothly functioning, and, presumably, security-generating Beast. And for those involved, it apparently feels good to be thus devoured whole and to live in its belly. 28

In his book *The Ghost in the Machine*, Arthur Koestler noted that "the glory and the tragedy of the human condition both derive from our powers of self-transcendence." Koestler went on to point out that there was an important difference between primitive identification (fish in a school, birds in a flock) that results in a homogenous, selfless grouping, and the higher level of integration that produces a heterogeneous assemblage whose members retain their individuality. In the first case—which includes the rabid sports fan—there is a surrender of personal identity and responsibility. In the second—that of the reader or theatergoer—the escape from the self is always conditional, transient, and within control. 29

Sometimes the rapport of identification can be harmless, not uncommonly resulting in giggles, laughter, yawning. Sometimes it is more sinister. As Koestler emphasized, the acts of greatest human violence and destructiveness have arisen not from personal aggressiveness or nastiness, but from self-transcendence in the form of seductive, mindless identification with a group. Think of Rwanda's Hutus and Tutsis, Bosnian Serbs and Muslims, Nazis and Jews, Irish Catholics and Protestants, Armenians and Azerbaijanis, Israelis and Palestinians. 30

It is not even necessary to be physically present in the belly of the beastly group in order to be swallowed up by it. As Koestler put it, "One can be a victim of group mentality even in the privacy of one's bath." How about the privacy of one's box seat? Although some studies have shown that players may be a bit less aggressive after a game—probably because they are physically exhausted—fans are not. Thus when spectators were assessed as to their degree of hostility before and after attending various athletic events, the researchers found, if anything, a slight tendency for aggressiveness to be higher after witnessing the spectacle. In that sense, watching sports it is not altogether different from watching other forms of violence. As hooliganism after soccer games repeatedly demonstrates, it can literally evoke violence as well. 31

Our predisposition for large groups has also given birth to one of the most grotesque happenstances of human history: nationalism. When ardent nationalists convince themselves that a highly arbitrary conglomeration of tens of millions of human beings is somehow biologically or socially "real" and deeply consequential enough to give up their lives and shed the blood of those associated with other nations—you can bet that something deep in the human psyche is being touched. Sports fans may simply be the comic sidekicks of nationalists. 32

Come and sit here, they are told. And eagerly, they do. They think it is a seat in a stadium, or by their television set, but really they are incubating an oversized egg. 33

Dazzled by the prospect of being part of a group, fans eagerly wear the group's insignia or team colors. They get to "know" the team members, "up close and personal," as sports journalists like to boast, inducing many spectators to believe that they are personally important to "their" team's success. In Japan, where baseball is the national passion as well as pastime, the illusion is carried even further: Thousands show up at every game fully dressed in their team's uniform, as though just waiting to be called to the plate. In America there is always the occasional scramble to get a ball hit into the stands, although in reality the only real "participation" permitted major-league baseball fans is standing up for the national anthem 34 and then the seventh-inning stretch. (Not that the latter should be disparaged; for many avid fans, after all, it is closest thing to exercise they are likely to get.)

"We're No. 1!" chant the crowds. "We have them now, only two innings to go." "If we can only hold on for another quarter." As Tonto pointedly asked the Lone Ranger in the old joke: "What you mean 'we,' white man?" 35

By we, the fan means the whole deliciously desirable, immensely seductive group. He means that he is no longer just little old himself, but something larger, grander, more impressive, more important, and thus, more appealing. Sports fans, in this view, are nationalists writ small. Or oystercatchers writ human, which is to say, moved by inclinations less distinct and less automatic than the rigidly stereotyped response to releasers and the obedient superresponse to supernormal releasers that are found among many animals, but inclined to some sort of response nonetheless. There is nothing unusual about it, although even now, I must admit, the whole business perplexes me. 36

But an oystercatcher would understand perfectly. 37

Examining the Text

1. Author Barash asks, "Is life so pale, dull, and unsatisfying that it must be experienced vicariously in order to be savored?" He then goes on to suggest, "You might try reading a book, talking with your family, going for a walk, wrestling with the dog, listening to some music, smelling a flower, making love." In this passage, what thematic point is being posited assertively and sarcastically? What is your emotional and/or intellectual response to this central point?

2. After making clear his confusion regarding human beings' fascination with watching other people engage in sporting activities, the author posits some possible reasons for rampant fandom: "For one thing," he says, "we get identification from our sports frenzy, the experience of seeing ourselves in the exploits of another." How might this vicarious participation in athletic activity enhance sports fans' lives, in the view of the author? Do you agree or disagree with this partial explanation of people's identification with sports teams and players?

3. Barash, writing in a journal written and read mainly by educators, notes, "For every youngster who admires the likes of Einstein, Gandhi, Jonas Salk, or Alice Walker, there are probably tens of thousands who wind up adoring and seeking to emulate Ty Cobb, known as a racist, or drunkards and gluttons like Babe Ruth, compulsive womanizers like Wilt Chamberlain, gamblers like Pete Rose, or steroid abusers like . . . (fill in the blank)." What point is this professional educator making about the hero preferences of the mass population? What is your own opinion about this point?

4. The author makes a central issue of comparing sports fandom to political nationalism. Does he see this similarity as a positive phenomenon, or another instance of perplexing and problematic human behavior? Do you consider this an apt comparison, supported by evidence in the essay, or did this comparison seem unconvincing to you?

5. *Thinking rhetorically:* At the beginning of this article, the author comments, "Not that I would try to stop anyone from root, root, rooting to his or her heart's content. It's just that such things are normally done by pigs, in the mud, or by seedlings, lacking a firm grip on reality—fine for them, but I am not at all sure this is something that human beings should do." How would you characterize the tone Barash establishes early in the article? And if you are a sports fan, how do you feel initially at being compared to a pig in the mud? Why would the author make the rhetorical choice of potentially alienating a significant portion of his audience? Does he soften this position as the piece progresses, so that sports fans end up not feeling compared to filthy swine?

For Group Discussion

In our previous experience discussing this article in class, the students have split pretty evenly in their opinions about the piece's central theme(s). At the beginning of this class discussion activity, take a vote on who agrees fundamentally with the points made by Barash in this piece, and those students who take great exception with his assertions. Having broken the class into two groups, have each group meet separately and come up with a platform statement, summarizing the specific reasons why they agree or disagree with Barash's thematic points. Having accomplished this initial subgroup task, reassemble the class as a whole, and engage in a lively and spirited debate, with members of each group presenting those specific platform points assertively and coherently. It may not be possible to resolve these polar differences in opinion, but—if possible—at least make an attempt to arrive at some areas of compromise and even agreement.

Writing Suggestion

The author of his piece looks at the phenomenon of sports fandom from a number of theoretical/ disciplinary lenses, including the anthropological, the psychological, the sociological, and even the biological. In a personal essay, discuss your own experience as a sports fan. If you are one of those pig-like dedicated rooters, attempt to explain in your essay why you love your team or teams to the high degree that you do. If your experience with sports fandom has been largely negative, describe with descriptive detail and personal reflection the specific ways in which sports as a popular phenomenon has had primarily a negative effect upon the quality of your life in some significant (or mildly irritating) way.

*Life on the Edge**

WILLIAM DOWELL ET AL. (*TIME* MAGAZINE)

Fewer Americans are getting together for relaxed games of touch football or slow-pitch softball, and professional team sporting events are no longer attracting the large audiences of the past. Meanwhile, however, participation in high-risk extreme sports is on the rise. Increasing numbers of healthy, seemingly sane men and women are risking life and limb on a Sunday afternoon by jumping from a bridge or cliff or by climbing up a steep, sheer mountain face.

In this article, the authors examine the increasing popularity of extreme sports such as BASE jumping, paragliding, and so on, arguing that our current interest in dangerous sports stems from the fact that most Americans are living comfortable, safe lives. We seek out risk because it no longer seeks us—as in past eras when risks came routinely from war, famine, disease, and wild animals. In support of this argument, the authors point out the prevalence of other types of risk-taking behavior, which are common outside of sports, such as playing the stock market or engaging in unprotected sex.

***As you read,** think about the legitimacy of the authors' argument. Is there necessarily a connection between the popularity of extreme sports and risky behavior in other areas of social life? Is it fair to connect these behaviors to our generally comfortable lives? Can you think of other possible reasons for the rise in risky sporting behavior? Or are you persuaded by the connections these authors make?*

"Five . . . four . . . three . . . two . . . one . . . see ya!" And Chance McGuire, 25, is airborne off a 650-ft. concrete dam in Northern California. In one second he falls 16 ft., in two seconds 63 ft., and after three seconds and 137 ft. he is flying at 65 m.p.h. He prays that his parachute will open facing away from the dam, that his canopy won't collapse, that his toggles will be handy and that no ill wind will slam him back into the cold concrete. The chute snaps open, the sound ricocheting through the gorge like a gunshot, and McGuire is soaring, carving S-turns into the air, swooping over a winding creek. When he lands, he is a speck on a path along the creek. He hurriedly packs his 1

*William Dowell et al., "Adventure: Life on the Edge" from Time, September 6, 1999.

chute and then, clearly audible above the rushing water, lets out a war whoop that rises past those mortals still perched on the dam, past the commuters puttering by on the roadway, past even the hawks who circle the ravine. It is a cry of defiance, thanks and victory; he has survived another BASE jump.

McGuire is a practitioner of what he calls the king of all extreme sports. BASE—an acronym for building, antenna, span (bridge), and earth (cliffs)—jumping has one of the sporting world's highest fatality rates: in its 18-year history, 46 participants have been killed. Yet the sport has never been more popular, with more than a thousand jumpers in the U.S. and more seeking to get into it every day. It is an activity without margin for error. If your chute malfunctions, don't bother reaching for a reserve—there isn't time. There are no second chances. 2

Still, the sport's stark metaphor—a human leaving safety behind to leap into the void—may be a perfect fit with our times. As extreme a risk taker as McGuire seems, we may all have more in common with him than we know or care to admit. Heading into the millennium, America has embarked on a national orgy of thrill seeking and risk taking. The rise of adventure and extreme sports like BASE jumping, snowboarding, ice climbing, skateboarding and paragliding is merely the most vivid manifestation of this new national behavior. Investors once content to buy stocks and hold them quit their day jobs to become day traders, making volatile careers of risk taking. Even our social behavior has tilted toward the treacherous, with unprotected sex on the upswing and hard drugs like heroin the choice of the chic as well as the junkies. In ways many of us take for granted, we engage in risks our parents would have shunned and our grandparents would have dismissed as just plain stupid. 3

More than 30% of U.S. households own stocks of some form or another, whether in investment accounts, mutual funds or retirement plans, up from 12% just 10 years ago. While an ongoing bull market has lulled us into a sense of security about investing, the reality is we are taking greater risks with our money than any other generation in American history. Many of us even take this a step further, buying "speculative growth," i.e., highly risky Internet and technology stocks, breezily ignoring the potentially precipitous downside. 4

We change jobs, leaping into the employment void, imagining rich opportunities everywhere. The quit rate, a measure of those who voluntarily left their most recent job, is at 14.5%, the highest in a decade. Even among those schooled in risk management, hotshot M.B.A.s who previously would have headed to Wall Street or Main Street, there is a predilection to spurn Goldman Sachs and Procter & Gamble in order to take a flyer on striking it rich quickly in dot.com land. "I didn't want someone in 20 years to ask me where I was when the Internet took off," says Greg Schoeny, a recent University of Denver M.B.A. who passed up opportunities with established technology firms like 5

Lucent to work at an Internet start-up called STS Communications. Schoeny is a double-dare sort who also likes to ski in the Rockies' dangerous, unpatrolled backcountry.

A full 30% of this year's Harvard Business School graduates are joining venture-capital or high-tech firms, up from 12% just four years ago. "The extended period of prosperity has encouraged people to behave in ways they didn't behave in other times—the way people spend money, change jobs, the quit rate, day trading, and people really thinking they know more about the market than anyone else," says Peter Bernstein, an economic consultant and author of the best-selling *Against the Gods: The Remarkable Story of Risk*. "It takes a particular kind of environment for all these things to happen." That environment—unprecedented prosperity and almost a decade without a major ground war—may be what causes Americans to express some inveterate need to take risks. 6

There is a certain logic to it: at the end of a decade of American triumphalism abroad and prosperity at home, we could be seeking to upsize our personalities, our sense of ourselves. Perhaps we as a people are acting out our success as a nation, in a manner unfelt since the postwar era. 7

The rising popularity of extreme sports bespeaks an eagerness on the part of millions of Americans to participate in activities closer to the metaphorical edge, where danger, skill and fear combine to give weekend warriors and professional athletes alike a sense of pushing out personal boundaries. According to American Sports Data Inc., a consulting firm, participation in so-called extreme sports is way up. Snowboarding has grown 113% in five years and now boasts nearly 5.5 million participants. Mountain biking, skateboarding, scuba diving, you name the adventure sport—the growth curves reveal a nation that loves to play with danger. Contrast that with activities like baseball, touch football and aerobics, all of which have been in steady decline throughout the '90s. 8

The pursuits that are becoming more popular have one thing in common: the perception that they are somehow more challenging than a game of touch football. "Every human being with two legs, two arms is going to wonder how fast, how strong, how enduring he or she is," says Eric Perlman, a mountaineer and filmmaker specializing in extreme sports. "We are designed to experiment or die." 9

And to get hurt. More Americans than ever are injuring themselves while pushing their personal limits. In 1997 the U.S. Consumer Products Safety Commission reported that 48,000 Americans were admitted to hospital emergency rooms with skateboarding-related injuries. That's 33% more than the previous year. Snowboarding E.R. visits were up 31%; mountain climbing up 20%. By every statistical measure available, Americans are participating in and injuring themselves through adventure sports at an unprecedented rate. 10

Tony Hawk

11 Consider Mike Carr, an environmental engineer and paraglider pilot from Denver who last year survived a bad landing that smashed 10 ribs and collapsed his lung. Paraglider pilots use feathery nylon wings to take off from mountaintops and float on thermal wind currents—a completely unpredictable ride. Carr also mountain bikes and climbs rock faces. He walked away from a 1,500-ft. fall in Peru in 1988. After his recovery, he returned to paragliding. "This has taken over many of our lives," he explains. "You float like a bird out there. You can go as high as 18,000 ft. and go for 200 miles. That's magic."

12 America has always been defined by risk; it may be our predominant national characteristic. It's a country founded by risk takers fed up with the English Crown and expanded by pioneers—a word that seems utterly American. Our heritage throws up heroes—Lewis and Clark, Thomas Edison, Frederick Douglass, Teddy Roosevelt, Henry Ford, Amelia Earhart—who bucked the odds, taking perilous chances.

13 Previous generations didn't need to seek out risk; it showed up uninvited and regularly: global wars, childbirth complications, diseases and pandemics from the flu to polio, dangerous products and even the omnipresent cold war threat of mutually assured destruction. "I just don't think extreme sports would have been popular in a ground-war era," says Dan Cady, professor of popular culture at

California State University at Fullerton. "Coming back from a war and getting onto a skateboard would not seem so extreme."

But for recent generations, many of those traditional risks have been reduced by science, government or legions of personal-injury lawyers, leaving boomers and Generations X and Y to face less real risk. Life expectancy has increased. Violent crime is down. You are 57% less likely to die of heart disease than your parents; smallpox, measles and polio have virtually been eradicated. 14

Combat survivors speak of the terror and the excitement of playing in a death match. Are we somehow incomplete as people if we do not taste that terror and excitement on the brink? "People are [taking risks] because everyday risk is minimized and people want to be challenged," says Joy Marr, 43, an adventure racer who was the only woman member of a five-person team that finished the 1998 Raid Gauloises, the granddaddy of all adventure races. This is a sport that requires several days of nonstop slogging, climbing, rappelling, rafting and surviving through some of the roughest terrain in the world. Says fellow adventure racer and former Army Ranger Jonathan Senk, 35: "Our society is so surgically sterile. It's almost like our socialization just desensitizes us. Every time I'm out doing this I'm searching my soul. It's the Lewis and Clark gene, to venture out, to find what your limitations are." 15

That idea of feeling bracingly alive through high-risk endeavor is commonly echoed by athletes, day traders and other risk takers. Indeed, many Silicon Valley entrepreneurs are extreme-sports junkies. Mike McCue, 32, CEO and chairman of Tellme Networks, walked away from millions of dollars at his previous job to get his new company off the ground. It's his third start-up, and each time he has risked everything. In his spare time, McCue gets himself off the ground. He's also an avid rock climber. "I like to feel self-reliant and independent," he says. "And when I'm up there, I know if I make a knot wrong, I die." 16

Even at ground level, the Valley is a preserve of fearless entrepreneurs. Nirav Tolia passed up $10 million in Yahoo stock options to start Epinions.com, a shopping-guide Web site. "I don't know if I would call it living dangerously," he says. "At Yahoo I realized that money was not the driver for me. It's the sense of adventure." 17

Psychologist Frank Farley of Temple University believes that taking conscious risk involves overcoming our instincts. He points out that no other animal intentionally puts itself in peril. "The human race is particularly risk taking compared with other species," he says. He describes risk takers as the Type T personality, and the U.S. as a Type T nation, as opposed to what Farley considers more risk-averse nations like Japan. He breaks it down further, into Type T physical (extreme 18 athletes) and Type T intellectual (Albert Einstein, Galileo). He warns there is also Type T negative, that is, those who are drawn to delinquency, crime, experimentation with drugs, unprotected sex, and a whole litany of destructive behaviors.

All these Type Ts are related, and perhaps even different aspects of the same character trait. There is, says Farley, a direct link between Einstein and BASE jumper Chance McGuire. They are different manifestations of the thrill-seeking component of our characters: Einstein was thrilled by his mental life, and McGuire—well, Chance jumps off buildings. 19

McGuire, at the moment, is driving from Hollister to another California town, Auburn, where he is planning another BASE jump from a bridge. Riding with him is Adam Fillipino, president of Consolidated Rigging, a company that manufactures parachutes and gear for BASE jumpers. McGuire talks about the leap ahead, about his feelings when he is at the exit point, and how at that moment, looking down at the ground, what goes through his mind is that this is not something a human being should be doing. But that's exactly what makes him take that leap: that sense of overcoming his inhibitions and winning what he calls the gravity game. "Football is for pansies," says McGuire. "What do you need all those pads for? This sport [BASE jumping] is pushing all the limits. I have a friend who calls it suicide with a kick." 20

Bungee jumping at the X Games

When a BASE jumper dies, other BASE jumpers say he has "gone in," as in gone into the ground or gone into a wall. "I'm sick of people going in," says Fillipino. "In the past year, a friend went in on a skydive, another drowned as a result of a BASE jump, another friend went in on a jump, another died in a skydiving-plane crash. You can't escape death, but you don't want to flirt with it either." It may be the need to flirt with death, or at least take extreme chances, that has his business growing at a rate of 50% a year. 21

The jump today from the Auburn bridge, which Fillipino has done dozens of times, is about as routine as BASE jumping can be. But Fillipino is a veteran with 450 BASE jumps to his credit. For McGuire, who has just 45, every jump is still a challenge. And at dawn, as he gets his gear ready, stuffing his chute and rig into a backpack so it won't be conspicuous as he climbs the trestles beneath the bridge (jumping from this bridge, as from many other public and private structures, is illegal), he has entered into a tranquil state, as if he were silently preparing himself for the upcoming risk. 22

When our Type T traits turn negative, though, there is a disturbing, less serene element to America's being the risk nation. One chilling development is the trend of "barebacking," a practice in which gay men have unprotected sex with multiple partners. Jack, an avid proponent of barebacking, argues that the risk of becoming HIV positive is outweighed by the rush of latex-free passion—especially in an era when, in his view, protease inhibitors are on the verge of turning AIDS from a fatal disease into a chronic illness. "It's the bad boy in me getting off," he admits. "One thing that barebacking allows is a certain amount of control over the risk. In sex, we have the ability to face the risk and look it in the eye." 23

The Stop AIDS Foundation surveyed some 22,000 gay men in San Francisco between 1994 and 1997, and during this period, the number of men who reported they always used condoms fell from 70% to 61%. "For some gay men, there is a sense of inevitability of becoming infected," says Michael Scarce, 29, a doctoral student in medical sociology who has been researching the barebacking phenomenon for the past two years. Scarce says that rather than living in fear and wondering when their next HIV test is going to return positive, some men create an infection ritual. "It really is a lifestyle choice," he says. "It comes down to quality of life vs. quantity of life." 24

This consequences-be-damned attitude may also be behind some disquieting trends that surfaced in a report issued last week by the Substance Abuse and Mental Health Services Administration stating that the number of Americans entering treatment centers for heroin surged 29% between 1992 and 1997. "I'm seeking the widest possible range of human experience," says a recent Ivy League graduate about his heroin use. 25

The most notorious example of negative thrill seeking may have been when the Risk Taker in Chief, Bill Clinton, engaged in unprotected sex in the Oval Office. Experts point out that many people were forgiving of Clinton in part because they could identify with his impulsiveness. "Risky behavior has been elevated to new heights," argues Cal State's Cady. "There was never so much value put upon risk as there is now." 26

The question is, How much is enough? Without some expression of risk, we may never know our limits and therefore who we are as individuals. "If you don't assume a certain amount of risk," says paraglider pilot Wade Ellet, 51, "you're missing a certain amount of life." And it is by taking risks that we may flirt with greatness. "We create technologies, we make new discoveries, but in order to do that, we have to push beyond the set of rules that are governing us at that time," says psychologist Farley. 27

That's certainly what's driving McGuire and Fillipino as they position themselves on the Auburn bridge. It's dawn again, barely light, and they appear as shadows moving on the catwalk beneath the roadway. As they survey the drop zone, they compute a series of risk assessments. "It's a matter of weighing the variables," Fillipino says, pointing out that the wind, about 15 m.p.h. out of the northwest, has picked up a little more than he would like. Still, it's a clear morning, and they've climbed all the way up here. McGuire is eager to jump. But Fillipino continues to scan the valley below them, the Sacramento River rushing through the gorge. 28

Then a white parks-department SUV pulls up on an access road that winds alongside the river. Park rangers are a notorious scourge of BASE jumpers, confiscating equipment and prosecuting for trespassing. Fillipino contemplates what would happen if the president of a BASE rig company were busted for an illegal jump. He foresees trouble with his bankers, he imagines the bad publicity his business would garner, and he says he's not going. There are some risks he is simply not willing to take. 29

Examining the Text

1. What do the authors mean in paragraph 3 when they state that the "stark metaphor" of BASE jumping "may be a perfect fit with our times"?

2. In contrast to all the risk taking mentioned in this article, as a society we also engage in a lot of risk minimizing. Paradoxically, these efforts to ensure safety may be helping to spawn more thrill-seeking activities. Discuss examples of safety measures and risk minimizing in which we as a culture engage—both on the personal as well as on a political or public level.

3. Explain why the authors state that risk taking is perhaps America's "predominant national characteristic." Do you agree or disagree, and why? If this assertion is true, what are the positive and negative consequences of this characteristic for us as country?

4. *Thinking rhetorically:* An article on extreme sports could be written in a likewise extreme tone, attempting to keep readers' interest and inflame their passions with lavish turns of phrase, lurid descriptions, and gruesome examples. How would you characterize the rhetorical stance of this article's authorial/editorial team? If you find the article sensationalistic, provide evidence to support this belief; if, on the other hand, the article seems to avoid such excesses, cite some examples of a more measured approach to the topic at hand.

For Group Discussion

While this article focuses on the risky characteristics of extreme sports—and uses this element of these sports to make connections to the larger cultural climate in America—another characteristic of extreme sports is noteworthy: nearly all of the sports discussed in this article are individual in nature. The rock climber, for example, tests her own individual abilities against the challenges posed by nature. Interestingly, the increasing popularity of these individual sports corresponds with the declining interest in playing and watching team sports. Use these ideas to theorize, as a group, about the possible significance of this shift from team to individual sports. Just as the *Time* article makes connections between sports and other cultural phenomena, ultimately using all of it to comment upon human nature as it appears in America today, can you think of other cultural phenomena that might relate to this issue of individualism? Does this lead you to theorize some ideas about where we are or where we seem to be headed?

Writing Suggestion

It has been described here and elsewhere that an increasing number of Americans are choosing "the leisure pursuit of danger," spending their free time climbing slick rocks, steep mountains, and frozen waterfalls; paragliding; whitewater rafting; or even turning moderately dangerous sports such as downhill skiing into life-threatening endeavors such as extreme skiing. Conventional theories of personality suggest that these people might be acting on a "death wish," while others offer a more positive view of high-risk activities. For example, some researchers suggest that courting peril and undertaking potentially dangerous challenges are actually essential for the progress of societies and for the development of confidence, self-awareness, and a stronger sense of identity in an individual. In an essay, examine your own risk-taking behavior. Even if you're not a high-risk taker by any reliable psychological measure, you've undoubtedly taken a few risks in your life; for the purposes of this essay, risking might be defined as "engaging in any activity with an uncertain outcome," such as asking someone for a date or taking on a new and difficult challenge. To begin this writing assignment, recall a time when you took a risk, and describe that event in concrete detail, as though you were writing a short story. Next, make a smooth transition into a section in which you reflect upon and assess both the positive and negative effects of this experience. From this examination you should arrive at some conclusions regarding the ways in which this event revealed your own degree of risk-taking behavior, and/or helped to shape you as an individual. Finally, go back and construct an opening paragraph, using that conclusion as the basis for your essay's thesis statement. *Voilà!* You have written an autobiographical narrative essay.

Fixing Kids' Sports

PETER CARY, RANDY DOTINGA, AND AVERY COMAROW

The following article was originally published in the journal Science & Society. *In it, the authors explore the changing face of children's team sports in the United States. The authors document the increasing seriousness applied to youth sports such as baseball, soccer, basketball, and softball, and contrast this with a corresponding decline in family activities like dinners together and vacations.*

In addition to the emergence of "select" and "elite" programs designed to tap the most talented youngsters in a particular sport, the authors also note that children are specializing in just one sport, playing more frequently and spending large amounts of time (as well as money) traveling to distant tournaments and competitions. As a result, the article states, children are becoming injured, disillusioned and, ultimately, abandoning sports they formerly enjoyed. Experts, including a pediatrician, a parks administrator, a sports director, and others lend support to the authors' position on what's happening to kids' sports. They also use former professional player Cal Ripken, Jr., who has expertise both as a player and a sports parent, in support of the article's central theme.

As you read, *notice the writers' technique of using statistics to establish the legitimacy of claims they make in the article. Also, note how the quotes used at the beginning of the article signal clearly to the reader the direction the article will take. Quotes used throughout the story underscore the particular slant of the article, which urges readers to agree with the premise that youth sports in the United States need a new approach. Consider your own response to these techniques: did you appreciate the wealth of hard evidence, or did you feel as though you were being positioned or manipulated by the authors to agree with their position?*

Fred Engh has seen it all. A wiry former college wrestler and father of seven, Engh has been a baseball dad, a coach, an athletic director, and, for nearly 30 years, an evangelist out to fix youth sports. Mention any ugliness at a kids' sporting event, and Engh, the founder of the National Alliance for Youth Sports, can counter with tales even worse. There's the father telling the kid, "You little bastard, you could never get anything right." Or the beefy guy, captured on video, telling his young baseball player, "I'm gonna get you tonight because you let me down, buddy." Or the one that started Engh on his crusade, the kid pitching in a local recreation league, who, after every pitch, grabbed his elbow and winced. When the umpire stopped the game, the boy's father and coach came out to the mound. "What's wrong?" he asked the boy. "It's my arm; it hurts," said the child, crying. "Son," said the coach, "this is a man's game. Now stay in there and pitch." 1

Cal Ripken Jr., the former Baltimore Orioles star shortstop and a father of two, has his own catalog of youth sports at their worst. He has seen coaches use what he calls the "loopholes" just to get wins. They will, in the younger leagues, tell players not to swing the bat because of the likelihood that the pitcher will throw more balls than strikes. Soon the bases are loaded. "So," Ripken continues, "you exploit the base-running, and you create an environment that is frustrating to the defensive team, especially the pitcher. He starts crying. He's thinking, 'How terrible that all these kids are crossing the plate on passed balls and wild pitches and they are stealing on me. It's not fair; it's not fair.' And they break the kids down emotionally, and that's how you win." 2

On a plane not long ago, Ripken read Engh's *Why Johnny Hates Sports* and found himself highlighting passage after passage. "I was struck by how the things he wrote about were things I cared about," Ripken recalls. He arranged to meet with Engh, and last week they got together again to talk. The topic: How to give kids' sports back to the kids. 3

That Ripken, a perennial all-star, would find common ground with Engh, a 68-year-old grandfather of 13, isn't quite as surprising as it may sound. Just about anyone who has spent time around youth sports these days has had a bad experience or has heard of plenty more. A survey of 3,300 parents published in the January/February issue of *SportingKid* magazine last year found that 84 percent had witnessed "violent parental behavior" toward children, coaches, or officials at kids' sports events; 80 percent said they had been victims of such behavior. A survey in South Florida in 1999 of 500 adults found 82 percent saying parents were too aggressive in youth sports, and 56 percent said they had personally witnessed overly aggressive behavior. 4

An informal survey of youngsters by the Minnesota Amateur Sports Commission found 45 percent saying they had been called names, yelled at, or insulted while playing. Twenty-two percent said they had been pressured to play while injured, and an additional 18 percent said they had been hit, kicked, or slapped while participating. Not surprisingly, the dropout rate of all children from organized sports is said to be 70 percent.

Suffer the family. In the past decade, some disturbing new trends have emerged. Children are starting in sports younger, specializing in one sport earlier, and may play the same sport year-round. The consequences of such activity are not yet fully understood, but sports physicians say stress injuries among kids are way up, and coaches say some of the most talented athletes drop out by their teens. And for many parents the demands of toting kids to practice, travel games, and tournaments are taking a big toll on what used to be called family life. In the past 20 years, says Alvin Rosenfeld, a New York psychiatrist who specializes in adolescents, structured sports time has doubled while family dinners have been cut by a third and family vacations have decreased 28 percent. "There's been a huge growth in youth sports," says Paul Roellig, a Virginia coach and parent. "The question nobody's asking is, is this a good thing?" 5

Perhaps it all began way back in 1929, when the owner of a Philadelphia factory set out to stop neighborhood youths from breaking his windows. He got a friend to organize a youth football league to keep the kids busy. Five years later, they named their club after the legendary Temple University football coach, Glenn Scobie "Pop" Warner. About the same time, in Williamsport, Pa., a sandpaper plant worker named Carl Stotz decided to organize a league for the little kids left out of sandlot play. It came to be called "Little League." The first pitch was thrown on June 6, 1939. 6

From those humble beginnings, kids' sports exploded. Pop Warner Football came to enroll more than 225,000 children in 36 states. Little League has 2.5 million kids playing in 50 states. Babe Ruth League baseball, whose younger divisions now bear Cal Ripken's name, has 945,000 players and, like Little League, a World Series of its own. 7

The real boom in youth sports, however, was driven by soccer. Here was a sport—unlike batting a pitched ball or shooting a basketball through a high hoop—that any tot could play. In 1964, the American Youth Soccer Organization was formed in Torrance, Calif. Its founding principles included the ideas that every kid had to play at least half of every game and that teams had to be balanced in talent to ensure fairness. Soccer leagues grew like kudzu. In 2003, the Sporting Goods Manufacturers Association reported that 6.1 million kids from ages 6 to 17 8 played soccer more than 25 days a year. All told, more than 26 million, or two-thirds of America's youth, play a team sport in America.

The boom in youth sports coincided with the suburbanization 9 of America, but it was stoked by the maturing of the baby boom generation and its unprecedented focus on its children. Parenting became "the most competitive sport in America," says Rosenfeld, the psychiatrist. "Soccer mom," meanwhile, came to conjure up more than just the image of a mother shuttling her kids to and from practice. "It's the culture," says Andrew Holzinger, athletic programs coordinator for Palm Beach County, Fla. "Maybe all I wanted to do was have my daughter kick the soccer ball around because she's driving me crazy. But Soccer Mom gets out to the field, and she has a new personality. She gets to bond with the other parents about the lousy call, or 'Why is this an 11 o'clock game; I told them to schedule it earlier.' Soccer Mom, she gets to have her own sport."

"Child abuse." As parents got more involved, some got *too* in- 10 volved, and things turned ugly. By the mid-'70s, Engh had seen enough. His daughter played on a softball team whose coach was caught urging his girls to shoplift for him, Engh says. And then, coaching his own son's baseball team, he ran into the father who told his boy with the sore elbow to stay in there and pitch. This was nothing more, Engh says, than "legalized child abuse."

He decided to do something about it. By 1980, he began working 11 out of a tiny second-floor office in West Palm Beach, creating a training manual for coaches. The idea: to make team sports less pressurized, safer, and more child friendly. Engh still remembers the day when the bank called and told his wife, Michaele, they were $440 overdrawn. With seven kids to feed, Engh thought it was the end. Then he opened his mail, and in it was his first order for the new manual, a check for $732. He never looked back.

Today, Engh's National Alliance for Youth Sports has certified 2.1 12 million volunteer coaches. But that, he says, isn't enough; everyone in youth sports—administrators, coaches, officials, parents—should be trained and sensitized. Indeed, one evening in February 2000, the Jupiter-Tequesta Athletic Association in Florida packed more than 1,500 parents into a stadium to watch a video on how to be a good sports parent, pick up a handbook, and sign a sportsmanship pledge—or their children could not play. Engh's National Alliance has even created a program to teach basic skills to kids as young as 3, so they can enjoy sports from the start. Near Buffalo, N.Y., the town of Hamburg adopted all of the alliance programs. "The coaches used to show up like, 'We're going to war here,'" says Tim Jerome, president of the junior football league. "It was pretty bad." Verbal abuse, shoving matches, parents misbehaving, it's all "changed dramatically," he says.

"The one thing people need to understand," Engh emphasizes, "is that they don't need to put up with this anymore." Mike Murray agrees. "Here in Northern Virginia," says Murray, a high school coach, teacher, and a director of youth baseball training programs, "you've seen a real cultural shift. All the things you'd want, people policing themselves. I think in large part people have bought into this." Murray is a trainer for another organization, the Positive Coaching Alliance. The alliance shares many of the same goals as Engh's organization—and even some of the same tips—but their approaches are different. Engh's organization wants all volunteers trained and certified; the Positive Coaching Alliance is focused more on the Zen of coaching. 13

The PCA is the brainchild of a soft-spoken former college basketball player named Jim Thompson. While studying at Stanford University Business School in the mid-1980s, he found himself coaching his son's baseball and basketball teams. Seeing too many "negative interactions" between coaches and players, he recalled his earlier experiences working at the Behavioral Learning Center in St. Paul, Minn. There he had learned the power that positive reinforcement had on severely disturbed children. He wrote a book called *Positive Coaching*, which stressed some basic principles: Athletes perform best when they feel good about themselves. The way to keep them confident is with positive comments. Athletes so motivated will be confident, try hardest, take chances, and play "over their heads." And when that happens, the team wins. 14

Thompson's manuscript made its way to Phil Jackson, then the head coach of the Chicago Bulls. Jackson, recalling his own trying years in youth sports, was struck: "It fused a lot of my thinking," he said. He decided to test Thompson's theory at the pro level. At the time, Jackson was riding one of his players, Horace Grant, pretty hard, and their relationship had fallen apart. Jackson tried the positive approach, and things turned around. Jackson, now with the Los Angeles Lakers, became the PCA's national spokesman. 15

Its influence has been sizable. The PCA's 65 trainers have run workshops for 400 youth sports organizations, training an estimated 60,000 coaches and parents. "I can tell you the first year we ran PCA programs the number of coaches being ejected from games was cut drastically," says Tim Casey, former vice president of Chicagoland Pop Warner football conference. The Dallas Parochial League, with 3,500 fifth to eighth graders enrolled in 11 sports, began offering PCA workshops to all coaches. In basketball, "our most volatile sport," says athletic director B. J. Antes, technical fouls dropped from over 100 to 26 in three years. This year, PCA workshops will no longer be optional, Antes says. "It's too darned important not to make it mandatory." 16

Coaches say they like the PCA's "dual goal" approach: striving to win, but using sports to teach life lessons. PCA workshops stress "honoring the game," mastering sports skills, and shrugging off mistakes. "The way I see the world of youth sports," Thompson says, "is that the win-at-all-costs mentality is the root of all evil."

Studies confirm this. A survey last summer at the National PTA Convention in Charlotte, N.C., found 44 percent of parents saying that their child had dropped out of a sport because it made him or her unhappy. These parents were not wimps. In fact, 92 percent of the respondents said sports were either important or very important to the overall development of their children. But 56 percent said that youth sports were too competitive, nearly half said that organized youth sports need to be completely revamped, and half said if they could change one thing, they would want their coach to be less focused on winning. Many surveys support this conclusion: Most kids would prefer to play a lot on a team that loses than sit on the bench of a team that wins. 17

For all the progress that the Fred Enghs and Jim Thompsons have made, however, they have yet to address a development of the '80s and '90s that has swept up many families. Known as travel teams, they are formed of the best players in a league or a community, may be coached by a volunteer parent or a well-paid coach, and travel to other towns—and sometimes even other states—to play teams of their own caliber. Also known as elite, select, or club teams, they're found in virtually every town in the nation. 18

At their best, travel teams provide young players with professional-level coaching, better competition, and even family bonding. "The clubs get very tight. They like each other; they travel with each other; they go on trips. It becomes much more of a long-term social thing as well as a competitive thing," says Craig Ciandella, California director of United States Specialty Sports Association baseball, which has 1,300 teams. Many young athletes believe their clubs give them the accelerated development they need to make the high school varsity or go beyond. "It's no longer a myth: If your kid wants to make a high school team, he has to play club ball," says Jim Tuyay, a tournament director with the California Beach Volleyball Association. "They're getting the training and the attention that the normal rec leagues are not providing." 19

Pressure. Travel teams can be nothing if not intense. They may practice twice a week and play twice more. They can travel one, two, three hours each way for games, chewing up entire Saturdays or weekends. "It becomes a way of life. It winds up being what you do on weekends. You don't go away; you don't go on vacation; you do baseball. I wouldn't have had it any other way," says Ciandella. And most 20 kids playing on elite teams are encouraged to play the same sport again in one, two, or three more seasons—even if they are playing other sports. Some are told—and believe—that if they don't play, say, soccer year-round, they will fall behind their peers.

One effect is even more pressure in the early years. Children now play travel hockey at the age of 7, and baseball tournaments are organized featuring pitchers as young as 8. "Where we live, travel soccer starts at the U-9 [8-year-old] level," says Virginia father Roellig. If you resist, he says, "you will be told, 'Your kids will quickly fall behind and not make the team when they are 10.' If you want your kid to play in high school, you have to start [travel] at 10, and if you want to travel at 10, you have to play travel at 8." Roellig says his community recently started a U-5 soccer program. Called the "Little Kickers," children can play at age 3 1/2. In 2003 it enrolled 50 kids, he says; now it has more than 150. "It's an arms race," complained one soccer mom in Washington, D.C. 21

Some wonder whether things have not gotten out of hand. Roellig, who coaches soccer, has three children, ages 10, 15, and 16—all involved in sports. His 15-year-old daughter, a high school freshman, plays year-round soccer and two other sports to boot. In the spring, she plays high school and travel soccer. In the summer she attends camps, does a basketball league, and has August soccer practice. In the fall, she has travel soccer and field hockey. And in the winter, she plays indoor travel soccer and basketball. Most nights she gets home at 7:00 or 7:30 from practice, has to eat and do her homework. She may make it to bed by 10 P.M., but she has to get up at 5:40 for school. "What gives is the homework and the sleep," Roellig says, adding that his daughter often looks exhausted. "If I had to do it again as a parent, I'd definitely scale back sports," he says. "I think I'm doing more harm than good." 22

He's not alone. Holzinger, the parks administrator in Palm Beach County, oversees 120 athletic fields and issues permits for their use by 65 different youth organizations. Only 2 to 5 percent of children under the age of 13, he believes, qualify as "elite" athletes. But in his region, the proportion of kids being placed on "elite" teams has grown to 25 to 30 percent of the athletic pool in the area. It's not that more kids have become better athletes; more parents are simply insisting that their kids be enrolled on select teams. "As we see these children as elite players, we stop thinking of them as children," Holzinger says. "You're not a child; you're my defensive line that nobody ever gets through. So if someone gets through, you let me down." The 25 percent of kids who shouldn't be on the select teams, in other words, frustrate the team and the coach. Parents get down on the coach because the team isn't winning, and coaches sometimes take it out on the kids. Or some kids 23 simply ride the bench. "You, the kid," Holzinger explains, "are now becoming frustrated with a sport, and it's a sport you loved. Past tense."

Much of the problem, Holzinger and others say, stems from coaches. "You'd be surprised," Holzinger says, "by how many parents are really impressed when a coach tells them, 'I'll have your child in a scholarship; stick with this program.'" What parents don't understand, and what the coaches don't tell them, are the real numbers. Dan Doyle, a former collegiate basketball player and head coach, is the executive director of the Institute for International Sport at the University of Rhode Island. For his forthcoming book, *The Encyclopedia of Sports Parenting* (to be published in September 2005), Doyle's research team surveyed young basketball players. Using data from nationally affiliated basketball leagues, they estimated that the total number of fourth-grade boys playing organized basketball was about 475,000. At the same time, the team found, only 87,000 teens were playing basketball as seniors in high school. Of the 87,000, they say, 1,560 will win Division I college scholarships, 1,350 will get Division II scholarships, and 1,400 more will play at Division III schools. And of those 4,310, about 30 will make it to the National Basketball Association. An additional 130 will play pro ball in Europe. 24

In soccer, the odds are even longer, because so many colleges recruit foreign players. "It's not a worthy objective at the fourth- or fifth- or sixth-grade level," Doyle says, "which is what some of these coaches are telling them. You know, 'If you don't play for me you're not going to get to college.'" And tennis? Doyle found that there are approximately 3 million males between 10 and 18 worldwide aspiring to be top tennis players. How many make money on the pro circuit? 175. "The professional aspiration," he says, "it's just crazy." 25

Equally crazy, experts say, is the idea that child stars can be created by starting early. "It doesn't matter when you start a sport. If you start at 3, it doesn't necessarily help," says Paul Stricker, a pediatric sports medicine specialist in San Diego. "Kids develop sports skills in a very sequential manner, just like they do sitting up and walking and talking. Parents and coaches just don't understand that sequence. They feel that after they're potty trained, if they practice something enough they'll get it." Parents, some coaches say, are often fooled by "early maturers," kids who are big and well-coordinated at a young age. But often it's the late bloomers, who had to work longer and harder at sports, who turn into the stars. 26

Pushing kids to play sports too early and too often can result in pain and worse. Since he began his specialty practice in 1991, Stricker says, "I've had at least a 30 to 40 percent increase in overuse injuries like stress fractures and tendinitis. Those are things we just didn't see much in kids previously." Stress fractures, which occur when kids 27 overtax their bones, are common. "These only come from forces that are repetitive," Stricker explains. "The bone breaks down faster than it can build up." Tendinitis is also common, especially in pitchers and swimmers, because young muscles aren't strong enough yet to keep up with adult training regimens. In young pitchers, Stricker says, "the growth plate gets pulled apart like an Oreo cookie."

The American Academy of Pediatrics has taken note. "Those who participate in a variety of sports and specialize only after reaching the age of puberty," the academy said in a statement four years ago, "tend to be more consistent performers, have fewer injuries, and adhere to sports play longer than those who specialize early." 28

What overeager parents should really worry about, some experts say, is burnout. Jim Perry is director of athletics at La Quinta High School in Westminster, Calif., a public school where club sports are hugely popular. He says he recently read an article about a national powerlifting championship for kids as young as 9. "What 9-year-old gets up in the morning and says, 'I want to be powerlifting'?" he asks. "That came about because of a coach or a parent." Perry says many kids, so pushed, tire of sports by the time they reach high school. "It's not a matter of [club sports] sucking talent away [from high school]. They're driving high-end kids away from athletics in general," he says. "They're sick and tired of playing 135 travel baseball games a year by the time they're 12 years old. They're sick of playing 100 soccer games a year before they ever set foot in high school. They don't need it anymore." 29

Besides, it's not yet proven that year-round play, travel teams, and specialization make better athletes. "Most of today's top professional athletes didn't even think to specialize in just one sport until they were in high school, around the age of 15," says Rick Wolff, chairman of the Center for Sports Parenting at the University of Rhode Island. Cal Ripken, for one, attributes his success on the diamond partly to playing three sports into high school. Soccer taught him footwork and balance, he says. Basketball gave him explosiveness and quick movements. "I think athleticism is developed," he says, "by everything you do." For that reason, he tells his 10-year-old son, Ryan, "put down your glove" when spring baseball is over. 30

All the emphasis on winning, perversely, can make for inferior skills. The Virginia Youth Soccer Association, with 138,000 registered players, recently posted a long note on its website from Technical Director Gordon Miller assailing "overly competitive travel soccer." In their zeal to win games, Miller warned, some Virginia travel teams emphasize the wrong things. Big kids are recruited and taught to kick the ball long down the field instead of being taught to make tight, short passes and ball-handling skills. "You don't encourage flair, creativity, 31 and passion for the game," he says, emphasizing that it is in practice, not games, that young athletes develop their skills. Studies show, Miller says, that in a typical game a player on average has the ball in his or her control for only two to three minutes. "The question is, 'Is playing all of these matches the best way to develop players?'" he asks. "And the answer is, 'No.'"

If we could only start over—that's one of Fred Engh's dreams. 32
Engh has been traveling and speaking abroad, hoping to learn from others and to find countries where it's not too late to fix things. In the course of his travels, he came across the tiny Caribbean nation of Dominica, a place where organized youth sports do not yet exist. The Dominicans agreed to let Engh and his Alliance for Youth Sports start a complete roster of kids' sports there, from scratch. Engh told Ripken of the venture. Ripken says he was intrigued by the idea of starting a youth sports program with the slate entirely clean. "I never thought there was a place on this planet that hadn't played baseball as an organized sport," he says. "Maybe I could help participate in something like that—rebuilding the joy of baseball."

DROPPING OUT

Although the number of kids ages 6 to 17 rose by more than 7 million between 1990 and 2002, the most popular team sports lost significant numbers of players.

(Millions of players)	
Basketball	
1990	20
1998	22
2002	18
Soccer	
1990	12
1998	14
2002	13
Softball	
1990	12
1998	9
2002	6
Baseball	
1990	10
1998	8
2002	7

Source: American Sports Data Inc., Sporting Goods Manufacturers Association

Examining the Text

1. In what ways do the authors appear to support the contention of Fred Engh that youth sports need fixing? Do you think this article is about the mission of Engh to reform kids' sports, or does it represent a broader criticism of youth sports? What role does Engh play in the article? Could it have been written without any mention of him?

2. Look carefully at the statistics the authors quote. What information do they convey? Do you think those statistics provide a complete picture? What other perspectives might benefit by the inclusion of some statistics or other hard data?

3. The technical director of the Virginia Youth Soccer Association is quoted as saying that "overly competitive travel soccer" doesn't encourage "flair, creativity and passion for the game." In your opinion, is it reasonable to draw conclusions about travel soccer based on the comments of one particular technical director? How might the inclusion of several other sports program directors' opinions have altered the tone and/or argumentative position and credibility of this article?

4. *Thinking rhetorically:* Parents seem to come in for much criticism in this article, yet the authors appear to have not spoken to anyone representing parents. Do you think this was a conscious rhetorical choice, a deliberate omission on their part? If so, why? If not, do you think hearing from parents would have altered your perception of the article? Based on the way the authors wrote the story and the emphasis given in the article, do you believe they have succeeded in addressing the source of the problem? Does the article offer a viable solution to the problems it highlights?

For Group Discussion

How many people in your group played sports regularly as kids? How many do so now? If, as the authors of this article predict, a significant number of your group members have stopped playing organized sports, discuss whether the reasons cited by the author match the reasons put forward by members of your group. In the opinion of your group members, are there other reasons why youngsters stop playing baseball, soccer, and other team sports?

Writing Suggestions

As an exercise in critical thinking and writing, develop an essay that counters the arguments put forth in this article. You might begin by making a list of all the statistics the authors use in their story about kids' sports, noting what categories they fall into. You might proceed to conduct some research via the library and the Internet, trying to find statistics that contradicts the statistics used in the article. For example, one survey by the Minnesota Amateur Sports Commission reportedly found that forty-five percent of participants had been called names, yelled at, or insulted while playing for a youth team. The explicit goal of this assignment will be to conduct research and write a persuasive essay in which you defend the role of competitive team sports. Explain why you think there are benefits for children from specializing at a young age, practicing frequently, and taking part in tournaments. Use the statistics you find to support your arguments.

Champion of the World

MAYA ANGELOU

Maya Angelou is a well-known poet, novelist, and performer. Born in 1928 and raised in the segregated South, Angelou persevered through countless hardships to become one of the country's most revered authors and cultural leaders. Angelou read her poem, "On the Pulse of Morning," at the 1993 inauguration of President Bill Clinton.

The selection which follows is from Angelou's first volume of autobiography, I Know Why the Caged Bird Sings *(1969). She relates an important recollection from childhood about the night in the 1930s when world heavyweight champion Joe Louis, nicknamed the "Brown Bomber," defended his boxing title against a White contender. Much of Angelou's narrative is made up of the words and feelings of the local Black community gathered in her Uncle Willie's store to listen to the broadcast of that highly publicized match. Angelou shows how her neighbors' hopes and fears and their image of themselves as a people were intimately connected to the fortunes of Louis, one of a very few Black heroes of the day. Her narrative reveals that a "simple" sporting event can be of intense significance for a group of people who see it as a symbol of personal victory or defeat.*

***Before you read,** recall any experience you've had or heard about in which a sporting event took on an emotional power and significance far greater than the event itself would seem to warrant. Whether this event is one that you participated in, watched, or read about, think about how and why sports can have such an intense influence on people's lives.*

The last inch of space was filled, yet people continued to wedge themselves along the walls of the Store. Uncle Willie had turned the radio up to its last notch so that youngsters on the porch wouldn't miss a word. Women sat on kitchen chairs, dining-room chairs, stools, and upturned wooden boxes. Small children and babies perched on every lap available and men leaned on the shelves or on each other. 1

The apprehensive mood was shot through with shafts of gaiety, as a black sky is streaked with lightning. 2

"I ain't worried 'bout this fight. Joe's gonna whip that cracker like it's open season." 3

"He gone whip him till that white boy call him Momma." 4

At last the talking finished and the string-along songs about razor blades were over and the fight began. 5

"A quick jab to the head." In the Store the crowd grunted. "A left to the head and a right and another left." One of the listeners cackled like a hen and was quieted. 6

"They're in a clinch, Louis is trying to fight his way out." 7

Some bitter comedian on the porch said, "That white man don't mind hugging that niggah now, I betcha." 8

"The referee is moving in to break them up, but Louis finally pushed the contender away and it's an uppercut to the chin. The contender is hanging on, now he's backing away. Louis catches him with a short left to the jaw." 9

A tide of murmuring assent poured out the door and into the yard. 10

"Another left and another left. Louis is saving that mighty right. . . ." The mutter in the Store had grown into a baby roar and it was pierced by the clang of a bell and the announcer's "That's the bell for round three, ladies and gentlemen." 11

As I pushed my way into the Store I wondered if the announcer gave any thought to the fact that he was addressing as "ladies and gentlemen" all the Negroes around the world who sat sweating and praying, glued to their "Master's voice." 12

There were only a few calls for RC Colas, Dr. Peppers, and Hires root beer. The real festivities would begin after the fight. Then even the old Christian ladies who taught their children and tried themselves to practice turning the other cheek would buy soft drinks, and if the Brown Bomber's victory was a particularly bloody one they would order peanut patties and Baby Ruths, also. 13

Bailey and I laid coins on top of the cash register. Uncle Willie didn't allow us to ring up sales during a fight. It was too noisy and might shake up the atmosphere. When the gong rang for the next round we pushed through the near-sacred quiet to the herd of children outside. 14

"He's got Louis against the ropes and now it's a left to the body and a right to the ribs. Another right to the body, it looks like it was low. . . . Yes, ladies and gentlemen, the referee is signaling but the contender keeps raining the blows on Louis. It's another to the body, and it looks like Louis is going down." 15

My race groaned. It was our people falling. It was another lynching, yet another Black man hanging on a tree. One more woman ambushed and raped. A Black boy whipped and maimed. It was hounds on the trail of a man running through slimy swamps. It was a white woman slapping her maid for being forgetful. 16

The men in the Store stood away from the walls and at attention. Women greedily clutched the babes on their laps while on the porch the shufflings and smiles, flirtings and pinching of a few minutes before were gone. This might be the end of the world. If Joe lost we were back in slavery and beyond help. It would all be true, the accusations that we were lower types of human beings. Only a little higher than apes. True that we were stupid and ugly and lazy and dirty and, unlucky and worst of all, that God Himself hated us and ordained us 17 to be hewers of wood and drawers of water, forever and ever, world without end.

We didn't breathe. We didn't hope. We waited. 18

"He's off the ropes, ladies and gentlemen. He's moving towards 19
the center of the ring." There was no time to be relieved. The worst might still happen.

Joe Louis, Champion of the World

"And now it looks like Joe is mad. He's caught Carnera with a 20
left hook to the head and a right to the head. It's a left jab to the body and another left to the head. There's a left cross and a right to the head. The contender's right eye is bleeding and he can't seem to keep his block up. Louis is penetrating every block. The referee is moving in, but Louis sends a left to the body and it's an uppercut to the chin and the contender is dropping. He's on the canvas, ladies and gentlemen."

Babies slid to the floor as women stood up and men leaned to- 21
ward the radio.

"Here's the referee. He's counting. One, two, three, four, five, six, 22
seven. . . . Is the contender trying to get up again?"

All the men in the store shouted, "NO." 23

"—eight, nine, ten." There were a few sounds from the audience, but 24
they seemed to be holding themselves in against tremendous pressure.

"The fight is all over, ladies and gentlemen. Let's get the micro- 25
phone over to the referee. . . . Here he is. He's got the Brown Bomber's hand, he's holding it up. . . . Here he is. . . ."

Then the voice, husky and familiar, came to wash over us—"The winnah, and still heavyweight champeen of the world. . . . Joe Louis." 26

Champion of the world. A Black boy. Some Black mother's son. 27

He was the strongest man in the world. People drank Coca-Colas like ambrosia and ate candy bars like Christmas. Some of the men went behind the Store and poured white lightning in their soft-drink bottles, and a few of the bigger boys followed them. Those who were not chased away came back blowing their breath in front of themselves like proud smokers. 28

It would take an hour or more before people would leave the Store and head home. Those who lived too far had made arrangements to stay in town. It wouldn't do for a Black man and his family to be caught on a lonely country road on a night when Joe Louis had proved that we were the strongest people in the world. 29

Examining the Text

1. Unlike the other selections in this chapter which offer fairly objective analyses of sport, Angelou relates a personal recollection. What conclusions about the influence of sports on culture, and specifically on African American culture in the 1930s, can you draw from her story? Has that influence changed significantly over the last sixty years?

2. In paragraphs 16 and 17 Angelou describes her own thoughts about the prospect of Louis losing the match. After rereading these paragraphs, what do you think they contribute to the overall meaning and drama of the story? How are they connected to the final paragraph?

3. What is the effect of the concluding paragraph in the story? How would Angelou's message be different if she had not ended it this way?

4. *Thinking rhetorically:* As writers and editors, we are always challenged by the notion of including a popular culture piece from a bygone era . . . the concern being, of course, that readers will find the material dated and no longer relevant. As you read and eventually finished reading this piece, what was your feeling regarding this concern? What might have been our rhetorical intention in deciding to include the piece, despite its age? Are there elements of the story that are relevant today? If so, enumerate and discuss.

For Group Discussion

Angelou's recollection demonstrates in vivid detail how a sporting event can take on much larger significance, how people can invest a great deal of emotion in the performance of an athlete or team. In your group, list some other specific examples of sporting contests that have taken on intense emotional significance and meaning for an individual or a group of fans. As a class, discuss the advantages and disadvantages of the strong influence sports has on its fans.

Writing Suggestion

In her narrative, Angelou describes how Joe Louis was an inspiration and sign of hope for African Americans in the 1930s. Choose another athlete who you think has similarly been an inspiration to his or her fans or has served as a role model. In an essay discuss the qualities that make that person a particularly good model. At the same time, if you think that athlete has negative qualities, you may cite these as well in analyzing how he or she has influenced fans.

Football: A Gridiron Case Study

The Boy Who Died of Football

THOMAS LAKE

Three days after he collapsed from heatstroke at practice in 2008, fifteen-year-old Max Gilpin became one of 665 boys since 1931 to die as a result of high school football; it's possible that number is significantly higher, but that is the "official" high school football–related death toll. However, here's what made his case different than most such cases historically: In this case, the Commonwealth of Kentucky tried to prove that Max's coach had a hand in killing him. The following article by Thomas Lake, senior writer for Sports Illustrated, *relates the story in detail, attempting to assess what parties might be responsible for this and similar deaths and injuries, and perhaps suggesting some potential responses to the situation.*

This article was, for a time, widely circulated and many people responded to it with great depth of feeling, along with numerous suggestions for changes in high school sports generally, and in football particularly. For instance, a commentator on the CBS mega–Web site observed, "To be honest, I'm not sure how I feel about it other than feeling sorry for the family, the team and the school. The article got me thinking about my high school football experience. I remember many times (especially during hell week) of players throwing up on the side during conditioning and of coaches making the time honored statement, 'We're gonna run 'til somebody quits.' 'Heck,' I remember thinking, 'maybe I'll quit just so we can stop.'" Of course, and especially for adolescents, there is a great deal of peer pressure not *to quit, and this is precisely why Max died.* ***As you read,*** *then, consider the question of culpability: who, if anybody, is to blame in this situation, either legally or morally or both? As another Web site commentator concluded, this story should, if nothing else, "show the seriousness of this deal, and bring those who contributed to the end of this boy's life to an account, if only for the purposes of illustrating to others that this should not happen again."*

On the day Max Gilpin ran himself to death before nearly 140 witnesses, he did almost nothing but what he was told. He began complying an hour before dawn, when he stumbled out of bed at his father's command, and he continued through the morning and afternoon behind the brick walls of his school as the August sun parched the 1 valleys of Kentuckiana. After school he surrendered to the will of his football coach, a man he loved as he loved his father, and he hoped this surrender would be enough to please them both.

This is a story about obedience, the kind that gives football and religion their magnetic power. Max Gilpin was an obedient boy. He was, to borrow a word from his adoring mother, a pleaser, and if he misbehaved, he had four parents to set him straight. They had family meetings, four against one, mother and stepfather and father and stepmother. Max's mother told him to obey his stepmother, and his father told him to obey his stepfather. So he did. And although he hated the Adderall pills—although they flattened his personality, made him smile less, made him want to hurl them off the deck into the backyard—he took them, usually, because they also made him stare at the teacher instead of the ceiling fan. 2

Max had a girlfriend named Chelsea Scott, a cheerleader with green eyes and shining auburn hair. They were sophomores at Pleasure Ridge Park High in Louisville, and they'd been a couple barely 48 hours. It should have been much longer, but Max couldn't muster the courage to ask her out. Fortunately Chelsea was a modern woman. Since the end of their freshman year she had kept a picture of Max on her phone, with the caption MY BABY, and over the summer, on MySpace, she had asked for and received his cell number. Still he needed encouragement. Finally Chelsea wrote Max a love note, delivered by her best friend, and he understood. That was Monday. Today was Wednesday. He had never taken Chelsea on a date. Instead they commiserated in the halls between periods, and Max complained about football. 3

In middle school Max's mother, Michele, struggled with Max to put his pads on. He was on the verge of quitting until Michele (head cheerleader, Western High) called his father, Jeff, and put Max on the line, and when the conversation was over, Max was no longer quitting. He did manage to sit out for a couple of years, but at the start of high school Max told his father he was going to play football. And his father (offensive lineman, Butler High) taught him power cleans and leg presses and rhythmic breathing. He bought Max protein shakes, and his mother bought him the muscle-building substance creatine. Max tried to quit again that year, but his parents talked him out of it, and gradually he came to embrace football. By August 2008, just after his 15th birthday, he stood 6′2″ and weighed 216 pounds. He had gained about 26 pounds in six months and had begun wearing sleeveless shirts to show off his muscles. 4

One thing stood in the way of Max Gilpin and football greatness. Football demands a certain brutality, a hunger to smash the other guy's face, and Max had no such hunger. He liked to fix things—decks, 5 porch swings, BMX bikes—and he talked about opening a mechanic's shop on Miami Beach. He didn't want to smash anything, even though he was an offensive tackle and his job was knocking people down. The coaches told him to get angry, get mean, use that helmet, quit being so nice. Max tried very hard, and his father saw him improving by the day, but he had a long way to go. In practice, as the linemen took turns facing off to improve their skills, Max stepped aside and let others go in front of him. His girlfriend from freshman year said Max was a true Christian, and this sounds about right. If Jesus had played football, He might have played like Max Gilpin.

Max's football coach also believed in Jesus and lived his life in relentless pursuit of heaven. His name was Jason Stinson, and he sat in the balcony on Sunday mornings at Valley View Church in southwest Louisville with a bible called God's Game Plan on a lap whose wide expanse would barely fit between the door and the center console of his Toyota Camry. Coach Stinson was 6'4" and 300 pounds, and he had been such a fearsome offensive lineman at Louisville that he got an NFL tryout with the Giants before being cut in the preseason of 1996. Now he was 35 years old, with a wife and two children, and he saw the 104 boys on the Panthers' football team as sons of a different kind. They came to him for money when they couldn't afford lunch, counsel when their girlfriends turned up pregnant, new shoes when their old ones wore out. And although his coaching job paid only $20 a day on top of his salary as a Web design teacher, he never turned them away, because he knew God was watching. The coach liked to say he wasn't making football players; he was making good daddies, good citizens, good taxpayers. So he was more surprised than anyone when his conduct at football practice on Aug. 20, 2008, became the subject of one of the largest investigations in the history of the Louisville Metro Police Department. 6

It was a miserable practice. The temperature hit 94° that day, and the boys, after staying up late all summer, came in exhausted from a new routine that had them out of bed long before sunrise. Around 5:30 that afternoon, after team stretching and individual drills, Coach Stinson called the 22 varsity starters to join him near the center of the field. This is how he remembers it: 7

"Offense, huddle up!" he said. "Defense, put your skivvies on!" (Skivvies in this case were jerseys of an alternate color.) The boys either ignored him or didn't hear. 8

"OFFENSE, HUDDLE UP! DEFENSE, PUT YOUR SKIVVIES ON!" 9

Still they did not come. Perhaps they were distracted by the girls' soccer game beginning on the next field. 10

"OFFENSE, HUDDLE UP! DEFENSE, PUT YOUR SKIVVIES ON!" 11

Only four or five boys obeyed. Later, several witnesses would use the words mad and angry to describe Stinson's reaction. But Stinson insisted he was not angry. He was just disappointed, and now he needed a new plan. 12

"ON THE LINE!" he bellowed. "IF WE'RE NOT GONNA PRACTICE, WE'RE GONNA RUN." 13

The command applied to everyone, not just the starters, and the boys got on the line. They knew what was coming. In helmets and pads they would run across the field and back and across the field and back again, a total of about 220 yards, or one eighth of a mile. Each of these runs counted as a single gasser, and today the boys were starting the gassers earlier and running them longer than usual. Yes, it was good preparation for the hard running they would do in games. But this early running was also widely seen as a punishment. Max Gilpin was not a varsity starter and therefore not one of those who had misbehaved. He was, however, a poor runner. And so he quietly accepted a punishment he had not earned, which fell harder on him than on those who deserved it. 14

The events of the next 50 minutes are a case study in the limits of eyewitness testimony. No video footage surfaced in the police investigation, and the roughly 140 spectators told stories that ranged from the plausible to the mathematically impossible. They couldn't even agree on whether Stinson was wearing a whistle that day. Nevertheless, a parade of witnesses said they heard the coach say one thing that set the tone for the gassers. It seems strange that Stinson still denies saying it to the runners, because it wasn't just soccer parents who said they heard it. It wasn't just assistant coaches and disgruntled players. In the opening statement at Stinson's trial for the reckless homicide of Max Gilpin, the coach's own defense attorney acknowledged, "Jason said it." 15

And what Jason Stinson said to his players, according to many people, was this: "WE'RE GONNA RUN TILL SOMEBODY QUITS." 16

Football coaches have a long and rich tradition of daring their players to quit. It probably didn't start with Bear Bryant, the most revered college coach of all time, but he did it as well as anyone. Bryant believed any boy who quit on him in practice would quit on him in the fourth quarter, and he did horrible things to make sure no quitter ever got the chance. In 1954, his first year with Texas A&M, he led 111 young men to a thorn-infested wilderness camp in Junction, Texas, and proceeded to nearly kill them. Bryant didn't believe in injuries, because he'd once played a whole game on a broken leg, and he didn't believe in water breaks, because he thought his boys would be tougher without them. His radical expectations are described in the following passage from Jim Dent's 1999 book, *The Junction Boys*. 17

18 "All of these boys need some time off," [trainer Smokey Harper] said. "Some got bad injuries in there, Coach. Joe Boring can barely walk with that bum knee, and another boy looks like he's got a fractured ankle. "

19 Bryant nodded and said nothing. Then he swung open the screen door and marched into the trainers' room. He jabbed at the air with his index finger and shouted, "You, you, you, you, you, you, and you! Get your butts dressed for practice. Be on the field in ten minutes. I want no more excuses out of you candy asses!"

20 So the boys limped out for more punishment. Players who collapsed from heat exhaustion had to crawl to the sideline or be dragged off by student assistants. When a boy fell face-first to the ground from heatstroke, Bryant kicked his fallen body. Sure enough, he ran off all the quitters. Seventy-six boys quit during those 10 days, and another 10 were too badly hurt to play in the opener. The Aggies went 1-9 that season, but two years later they went undefeated and finished fifth in the national rankings. The survivors of Bryant's hell camp discovered that nothing in life could stop them. They became doctors, lawyers, engineers, chief executives. By the time of their team reunion 25 years later, many were millionaires.

21 In the genealogy of football coaches, you can draw a line from Bear Bryant straight down to Jason Stinson. Bryant begat Howard Schnellenberger (he played tight end for the Bear at Kentucky in the 1950s and served as his assistant coach at Alabama from '61 to '65), and Schnellenberger coached Stinson at Louisville in the early 1990s. In '89 Schnellenberger recruited a lineman named Thomas Sedam. According to Sedam, water was never available at practices. Schnellenberger, who declined to comment for *SI*, made his boys run gassers, just as Bryant had and Stinson would, and when thirsty players took mouthfuls of the ice that was kept to cool down injuries, coaches forced them to spit it out. One day Sedam collapsed from heatstroke after running too much. He spent almost a month in the hospital and later sued Schnellenberger for negligence. They settled out of court.

22 After Louisville, Schnellenberger went to Oklahoma. He resigned at the end of a mediocre season during which two players quit because of heat illness. One of them, defensive tackle Brian Ailey, nearly died of heatstroke. He filed his own lawsuit, but Schnellenberger said water was not restricted at his practices, and a federal judge threw the case out for lack of evidence. According to a 1996 *Tulsa World* story, "Schnellenberger dismissed Ailey's incident as unfortunate but insisted his coaching techniques were not out of line. He points out that he had been doing business like that for years." Schnellenberger, who coached Miami to a national championship in 1983, is still doing business, at 76, as coach at Florida Atlantic.

Sedam played for Schnellenberger before Jason Stinson did; Ailey played after. You might expect Stinson to tell stories similar to theirs. He will not. He says the coach was demanding but never abusive and always provided sufficient water at practice. He says he would play for Schnellenberger again. And if this is hard to understand, remember that the Junction Boys—that is, the ones who survived Junction—would almost certainly play for Bear Bryant again. They wore those 10 days like a badge of honor for the rest of their lives. Jason Stinson says his father made him a man. But when Stinson left the care of Howard Schnellenberger, he considered himself even more of a man. 23

In the '60s at Southern High in Louisville there was another football coach who didn't believe in injuries. When a player broke his thumb and said, "Coach, I broke my thumb," and it was all swollen and purple, the coach told him to spit on it and get back in the game. Around that time a boy named David Stengel decided to tend his horses instead of attending the coach's unofficial spring practice, and when the coach punished him that fall by giving him old equipment and shoes that didn't fit, David quit. 24

Nearly 50 years later, after David Stengel became Louisville's chief prosecutor, after he had Jason Stinson indicted for the death of Max Gilpin, he would say Stinson reminded him of his old football coach. And when Stengel got e-mails from around the world telling him what a "sissy" he was, going after a football coach for doing nothing but coaching football, well, Stengel begged to differ. In his younger days he could bench-press 370 pounds, and he kept a picture of the Mohawk OV-1A in which he flew 127 combat missions over the Ho Chi Minh Trail, including one in which he was shot down. Football is a pale imitation of war. Sissy? David Stengel would love to see you walk through this door and say that. 25

About a month after the fatal practice, under questioning by the police, Coach Stinson made a casual remark that explains quite a lot about Max Gilpin's collapse. "Now, but Max is the kind of kid," he said, "if you don't see him, you wouldn't notice him." Even though he was 6'2" and 216 pounds, Max was not a commanding presence. He could be almost invisible. And visibility made a crucial difference on that sweltering afternoon. 26

The boys were allowed to run at their own pace, but they had an incentive to run as hard as they could. It went beyond merely impressing the coaches. If Stinson noticed a boy giving extraordinary effort, he might dismiss him from the running and let him cool off in the shade. One of the team's best runners was Antonio Calloway, a safety who also sprinted for the track team, and Antonio ran angry that day. First he was angry at the other boys for goofing off, and then he was angry 27 at Stinson for not rewarding him with a license to quit. At some point the soccer spectators heard a horrible sound, something deep and strange and very loud, which turned out to be Antonio Calloway gasping for breath. His reward for blind obedience was a precautionary trip to the hospital.

The boys ran on. They took turns. The smaller players ran while the big boys (including Max) rested, and then they switched. Most players agree that Max ran hard, but there is a wide range of stories about how the running affected him. Some say he had no trouble breathing. Others say he vomited, fell to his knees, struggled for breath. There were many reports of players vomiting, and one boy said he heard others crying. None of this was enough to make Stinson call off the drill. "If we stop the drill every time somebody got hurt," he said later in a deposition for the wrongful-death suit filed by Max's parents, "we wouldn't have any drills left to do." 28

Michael Cooper, Plaintiff's Attorney: Well, let's say that we have players, one or more, that are vomiting—

Stinson: No, sir.

Cooper: —would you stop a drill?

Stinson: No, sir.

Cooper: One or more players that are vomiting, another player had to quit the drill because he had passed out.

Stinson: No, sir.

Cooper: Players vomiting, passing out, they want water, do you quit the drill?

Stinson: No, sir. I mean, you can keep building on this all day long and keep adding up, and eventually, yes, you quit the drill, but it's not to the point of if a child is vomiting do we stop the drill, no, sir.

Cooper: I'm just trying to figure out, is there something you as head coach can tell me if I saw these events occur with my players I would stop the drill because I think they're getting overheated. Can you give me any scenario where that would occur?

Stinson: Not that I can think of.

In any case, Stinson had other things to worry about. Some boys were running and some were not. Understand: This was not an elite squad. If you wanted to play football at Pleasure Ridge Park High, you just showed up and took the physical. You might not get playing time, but at least you'd get a jersey, and some boys just wanted that jersey. They were called the jersey-wearers, and they had no intention of overworking themselves. As one of them later told the police, 29

"We wasn't really runnin' for real, we was walkin' and laughin' and stuff, 'cause we wasn't about to run for no hour in the sun." (Not that it was even an hour; the best estimates put the running at 35 to 40 minutes.)

30 Those boys demanded attention, and Stinson gave it to them. He called them away from the group and supervised them in a drill called up-downs, which involved running in place and then dropping to the ground and then running in place some more. Even at this they performed badly, which, according to the court transcript, led the coach to say something like, "We're gonna do 'em right or we're gonna do 'em until somebody quits." Today the coach says that this statement might have been misconstrued as applying to all the players, including the ones still running gassers. He claims to have said at the beginning of gassers, "If you don't want to do what we're asking you to do, please feel free to quit. We'll still be friends, we'll still high-five you in the hallway, but you can't play football." All this may be true, but there is a loose consensus that the boys running the gassers believed Stinson was telling them to keep running until someone quit the team.

31 Which someone did.

32 Now, a word about quitting. Stinson believed that if you quit in practice, you wouldn't just quit in the fourth quarter. You would quit in life. Bear Bryant actually wanted the boys to quit—that is, he wanted the quitters to quit—but Stinson, despite appearances, actually wanted to keep them. If they stayed on the football team, he kept his leverage. He could make sure they made good grades and behaved in class. He could keep trying to mold them into good daddies, good citizens, good taxpayers. And if they really did quit—if they called his bluff—he lost that leverage. Which is why he tried to bring them back. A player named David Englert had quit three times, and Stinson always talked him into returning. Sure enough, he was in the up-down group, the incorrigible group, and sure enough, he quit again. And sure enough, a few days later he was back on the team. (Not long after that, he quit for the last time.) Later he wrote Stinson a letter that read, in part, "You have always been there for me in everything I do. I haven't been able to sleep for the past couple of days, I walk around with a lump in my throat. . . . I love you. . . . Please pray for me as I pray for you."

33 Jason Stinson didn't believe in quitting on anyone. After all, Jesus never quit on the dying thief.

34 But there is another way to see David Englert, and in this light he needs neither mercy nor forgiveness. What he deserves is a round of applause. "I congratulated the child for quitting the team," a soccer spectator named Timothy Moreschi testified at Stinson's trial. "I said, 'You're the only man out on that field.'"

35 Take a moment now to go with Max Gilpin as he runs the last mile of his life.

36 Early in the running, before the damage is irreversible, he can look to the right through the face mask of his steaming helmet and see his father watching him. And this sight must give him the courage to run harder. Max is a pleaser, remember, and he wants to make his father proud. His father played lineman too, for Butler High, class of '80, and Butler won the Kentucky Class 4A championship his senior year. But his father quit football before that season and missed his chance at immortality.

37 Max has a shot at starting for the jayvee, and what he lacks in meanness he can try to make up in determination. At a scrimmage just last Friday, his father saw him take on a powerful defensive end from another school and play better than he'd ever played: "Max shut this kid down. He knocked him down two or three times. He turned him. He got under him. This kid never made another tackle or another play that I saw. In fact, Max played so well that they put him on defense. He's never played defense on a high school level. He didn't even know the plays. They just told him to go for the ball."

38 Later, when presented with Jeff Gilpin's account of that scrimmage, Stinson will refuse to confirm it. ("Didn't see it happen, didn't hear about it and didn't have any film to review.") Which will leave two ways to interpret the story. Either Jeff Gilpin is imagining things or Coach Stinson is oblivious. And both possibilities leave Max with the same mandate. Either he must close the gap between his actual performance and his father's vision of his performance, which means he must work even harder; or he must play so surpassingly well that Coach Stinson finally takes notice—which means he must work even harder.

39 Like most sons, Max regards his father with a blend of love and fear. Jeff will later say Max was his best friend. He will talk about driving Max to guitar lessons, about missing the way Max laughed so deeply that his eyes nearly shut. And while both Jeff and Michele want Max to go to college, Max would rather be an auto mechanic just like his father. But in other ways Max is nothing like Jeff. There is some indication that Jeff is capable of violence and coercion. In 1999, when Max was five and his parents had separated, Jeff was arrested and charged with aggravated assault after allegedly punching and bruising his live-in girlfriend. (Records of the case's outcome are no longer on file at the courthouse.) Max's stepmother, Lois Gilpin, will later say Jeff used to slap Max on the back of the head and drag him around by the ear. Jeff will deny all this, but Lois will not be the only one to say Max saw Jeff as a bully. She and Katlin Reichle, who dated Max during freshman year, will say Jeff monitored Max's performance at football

practice and, if Max didn't play well enough, left him there and made someone else pick him up. Lois will say Jeff sent Max text messages to express shame in Max's performance. Katlin will say Max told her, "I'm trying my best, but I don't know what more I can do."

All around him now on this August afternoon, Max's teammates 40
find ways to get out of running. Fast ones are dismissed for good effort. Freshmen are dismissed because they're freshmen. Some of the fat kids are barely running. The goof-offs are pulled out to do up-downs. Max is a slow runner, of course, so running hard doesn't make him stand out more. It makes him stand out less. It puts him closer to the middle of the pack. It ensures that he will run the maximum distance at maximum effort. And if he shows signs that something is wrong—if he vomits or falls to his knees or stands up only with the help of his teammates, as witnesses will later testify at the trial—Stinson doesn't notice. He's distracted by the jersey-wearing goof-offs who can't even do the up-downs right.

Max's temperature is rising to catastrophic levels, to 105°, 107°, 41
perhaps 109°. The cells in his body are melting. And so, when his father sees him cross the finish line on the last sprint, fall on all fours, stand again, stagger and fall for the last time, there's no telling whether Max hears Stinson say the mystifying line that marks the end of practice. The Panthers have run until someone quit, and the quitter is not Max Gilpin. "DING, DING, DING!" the coach yells as David Englert quits once again. "WE HAVE A WINNER!"

Looking back on the practice two years later, the coach noticed 42
a major coincidence. David Englert quit at nearly the precise moment that Max's group finished what was always going to be the last sprint. Neither event caused the other, Stinson said. He insisted that practice would have ended regardless, because everyone knew that the activity bus was on a fixed schedule and many of the boys had to ride it home.

Then, more coincidences. The coach wasn't looking when Max 43
collapsed. Nor did he notice anything was wrong when Max's father ran onto the field, or when at least three assistant coaches hustled to Max's side, or when the athletic director drove toward Max on a John Deere utility cart. A lot was happening right then, with nearly 100 players leaving the field and a soccer game proceeding a few feet away. The coach was busy. He had a team meeting to conduct, but first he had several goof-offs to yell at once again. They'd gone straight to the water, which was forbidden until after the meeting, and he had to round them up. And then he had to yell at everyone for the terrible practice and tell them they didn't deserve to be Panthers, which half of them probably didn't. All this time Max's cells were melting. Numerous soccer parents turned around to witness the practice, because Stinson was

loud and the soccer game was boring. Some saw fit to inform the local newspaper, *The Courier-Journal*, whose reporting led to the criminal investigation.

There followed a series of natural disasters that coincided with milestones in the investigation. On Sept. 14, the day Stinson gave his statement to the police, rare winds battered Louisville with hurricane force and caused four deaths from falling timber. The following January, just after Stinson was indicted for reckless homicide, an ice storm came upon Kentucky and deprived nearly half a million homes and businesses of electricity; at least 55 people were killed. And on Aug. 4, 2009, the day Stinson was indicted for wanton endangerment in the same case, many residents of Louisville fled to their rooftops to escape a rising flood. Stinson worked with his church to ease the suffering of the victims. Nevertheless he saw these events as acts of a God who cared enough to keep him off the front page. 44

In general the people of Pleasure Ridge Park took Stinson's side. They knew him to be a good Christian man and trusted him with their boys because their boys loved Coach Stinson. They held a silent auction to help pay for his legal defense, and Howard Schnellenberger donated an autographed football. A barbecue joint called Mark's Feed Store promised to donate a portion of its profits over several nights to Stinson's cause, and so many people showed up that one night the place had to shut down because the food was all gone. Stinson's friend Rodney Daugherty wrote a well-researched book—*Factors Unknown: The Commonwealth of Kentucky vs. David Jason Stinson & Football*—that redirected blame from Stinson to the prosecutors who brought the case. Pleasure Ridge Park High principal David Johnson (free safety, Louisville) summed up the feeling of many others when he said he knew Stinson did nothing wrong because "I know what kind of person he is." 45

It wasn't just that Stinson did nothing wrong. Stinson could do nothing wrong. Max's mother said that Stinson's wife told her around the time of Max's funeral that the coach was on "suicide watch." Not possible, according to Stinson, because he didn't blame himself for Max's death, and he would never consider suicide—that would be quitting. A soccer mom swore at the trial that Stinson said something to the boys during the running that no one else seemed to remember: "Come on, who's going to be the sacrificial lamb?" No way, Stinson says. He would never say that, because he knows of only one sacrificial lamb. And that lamb's name is Jesus. 46

But football is America's game, and more than 1,000 boys and men have been killed since 1931 as a direct result of playing football. No other team sport comes close. The National Center for Catastrophic Injury Research measured catastrophic injuries in all high school 47 fall sports from 1982 to 2009 and found that 97.1% of them occurred in football. And it must be no coincidence that in an '08 Gallup poll, more Americans chose football as their favorite sport to watch than chose baseball, basketball, hockey, soccer, auto racing, golf and tennis combined. We can say we watch for the precision of the quarterbacks, the grace of the receivers, the speed of the running backs, but this is only part of the truth. We watch because football players are warriors, because they are brave, because all that throwing and catching and running is done under threat of lethal violence. There is such a thing as touch football, and such a thing as flag football. Both are safe. No one pays to watch them.

You've got a man looking at prison time for being a football 48
coach," defense attorney Alex Dathorne (cornerback, Miami Palmetto Senior High) said in his closing argument on Sept. 17, 2009. "Jason Stinson on August the 20th of 2008 did absolutely nothing different than every coach in this county, in this Commonwealth, in this country, was doing on that day."

This was part of the reason Dathorne and his law partner, Brian 49
Butler (rabid fan, Notre Dame), two of the best defense attorneys in Louisville, took Stinson's case at a discounted rate. They believed the game of football was on criminal trial and a loss would be disastrous. Coaches would quit by the hundreds for fear of prosecution. The media coverage already had them terrified. During jury selection, one potential juror (a coach, apparently of another sport) said, "Literally every practice, if we're running, I make a point of telling the kids up front so people can hear me, 'You can stop, you can go on or you can do whatever you want on your own.'"

Before the trial Stengel put his chance of winning a conviction at 50
less than 10%, based on how the people of Louisville felt about football. "Football coaches," he said, "are right up there with the Father, Son and Holy Ghost." This is why, during jury selection, his assistants did their best to identify football bias. They asked all fantasy football players to raise their hands. They tried to weed out college football season-ticket holders. They tried-and failed miserably-to stock the jury with women. And women might not have helped them anyway. Max's girlfriend's mother, Misty Scott, had marinated so long in football culture that she could stand in her driveway one afternoon and say about Louisville coach Bobby Petrino's departure: "Louisville football went down the drain so fast that we're still washing the red out of the sink."

More to the point, the commonwealth had a fragile case. Stinson 51
would later look back at the 13 days of the trial and decide his attorneys had racked up 12 wins, no losses and one tie. So why did Stengel prosecute a case he knew he would lose? There are two prevalent

theories, and Stengel denies them both. One says he got the indictment before he understood the science of what happened to Max, and by that time it was too late to back out because the national media had descended. The other theory says the prosecution was a kind of public-service announcement intended to make coaches be more careful. Which it did. Some coaches reconsidered their use of negative motivation, and the state passed regulations that required more first-aid training and better education on heat illness.

The prosecutors tried to prove that Stinson withheld water that 52 day, but one player after another said he'd taken several water breaks, including one right before the sprints. Besides, dehydration wasn't a factor in Max's death. Three doctors said so: Bill Smock, who usually testifies for the prosecution in Louisville; George Nichols, who founded the state medical examiner's office in Kentucky; and Dan Danzl, a coauthor of the hallowed textbook *Rosen's Emergency Medicine.* The best the prosecution's kidney expert could do was to conclude from the records that Max was just dehydrated enough to be thirsty.

When the commonwealth attacked Stinson for his failure to help 53 Max, the defense was ready. Stinson's attorneys showed that several other people quickly came to Max's aid and did the same things—applying ice packs, dousing him with water, removing his socks, calling 911 after a few minutes—that Stinson would have done if he'd been there. Both sides agreed that the presence of a certified athletic trainer might have improved Max's chances, but trainers are expensive, and the school was not required to have one at the practice.

The doctors agreed that Max died of complications from exertional heatstroke. This, of course, raised a crucial question: Why was 54 Max the only player to die? The defense proposed an answer.

Tests from the hospital showed amphetamines in Max's system. 55 They were most likely from the Adderall, the drug Max reluctantly took for better focus in school. And while it's impossible for Adderall alone to have caused Max's collapse—he'd been taking it for a year, and other boys at the practice also took Adderall—it could have slightly raised his body temperature.

There was also the creatine. It's not a banned substance, but the 56 NCAA forbids colleges to distribute it to athletes. Max's mother said she hadn't bought it for him since March or April, but a friend testified that he saw Max taking creatine a week or two before his collapse. While scientists disagree on the possibility of side effects, a 2002 article in the journal *Neurosurgery* said there is credible evidence that creatine might contribute to heatstroke in some people.

But Max had probably been on both Adderall and creatine at 57 other practices, some of them hotter than 94°. Something had to be different on Aug. 20.

The prosecutors had a theory. The difference was Coach Stinson. 58
He lost his temper and forced the boys to run much harder than usual.

Except they weren't running for that long. Many football teams 59
practice twice a day in the summer. There was just one practice that day, and it was a short one. The boys ran sprints for no more than 40 minutes; actually it was much less, because they were in two alternating groups. Each group ran for about 20 minutes. Some boys gave implausibly high estimates for the number of 220-yard sprints they ran in that time period—as many as 32. It probably seemed like 32, but Coach Stinson always said it was 12, and the math works in his favor. No one was allowed to start running until everyone in the other group had finished, including the players who were barely running; that would mean Max ran about a mile and a half, the majority of it in helmet and pads.

What was extraordinary, then, about Aug. 20? The defense had 60
another answer: By the time he got to practice, Max was already sick.

Here the medical experts fought to a draw. They argued over his 61
white blood cells, his elevated lymphocytes, but it all came down to guesswork. The numbers neither proved nor disproved that he had a viral infection. They could be made to support either belief.

That left eyewitnesses, who were also problematic because of 62
their vested interests in the outcome. Max's parents, who said he wasn't sick that day, were seeking more than $19 million in a wrongful-death suit. Some of Stinson's players, who said Max was dragging along and complaining that he didn't feel well, felt a powerful loyalty to their coach. Two girls who knew Max contradicted each other, even though they were best friends: One, who was friends with Max's mother at the time of the trial, said he had seemed all right at lunch; the other, whose parents openly supported Stinson, said Max was obviously sick after school.

The truth was in there somewhere. 63

The defense called Lois Gilpin. 64

You should know a few things about Lois, the stepmother who 65
saw Max before school on the day of his collapse. She and Jeff Gilpin had gone through an unpleasant separation. A judge granted her a restraining order against him after she said Jeff had threatened to drag her out of the house by her hair. She was also attending Stinson's church, Valley View, and she had accepted $700 from its benevolence fund to help pay her mortgage.

But when a prosecutor suggested that Lois had pulled a new 66
story out of thin air to help Stinson, there was evidence to suggest otherwise. Two days after Max was hospitalized, a doctor wrote in the record, "New history, that patient may not have been feeling well on day of collapse." Lois swore that her story had remained the same all along, and the doctor's note seemed to corroborate it.

This is the story Lois Gilpin told under oath about Max's last morning at home: "I asked him if he wanted juice. He was to take his medicine, his Adderall that morning. And he was cranky. And I leaned over and I kissed his head, and he told me he had a headache and he was sick and he was hot. Jeff walked in and told him, 'We're going to be late, you need to get up; you need to get your butt in gear and you need to get to school.' 67

"He just said he didn't feel good, he had a headache. He didn't talk back to his dad. You know, when I kissed him, I told him he was hot. You know, I imagine he would have liked to have stayed home. I wish he would have stayed home. But he did what his dad said." 68

Later, when he looked back at his son's last practice, Jeff Gilpin was filled with pride and wonder. "I underestimated this kid, big-time," he said. "His heart. Can you imagine the fortitude it took to keep running out there?" 69

It is almost unimaginable. Never mind how long Max actually ran. What matters is that he ran far longer than he should have, despite what must have been terrible pain, even though quitting would have saved his life. And in dying he probably saved the lives of several boys who might otherwise suffer the same fate. 70

Cold blue twilight, Salvation Army parking lot. A very large man stands by a folding table, digging for clean underwear in a cardboard box. When he finds the white briefs, he holds them up, like a merchant or an auctioneer, until a poor man steps out of the crowd to claim them. 71

"Got a large sweater! Anybody? Anybody?" The large man's voice carries across the parking lot. "Long-sleeve, flannel! Nah, we're outta socks right now. Still lookin'. All right, brother. You have a good one." 72

All right, brother. This is how the men of Valley View Church talk. They come downtown every Monday night to feed and clothe the needy, and Jason Stinson comes with them because he is a free man. To him this is an act of godly obedience, not atonement, because Stinson is not guilty of anything. The jury said so. It took less than 90 minutes to decide. 73

When the giving is done, Stinson walks into the Texas Roadhouse off Dixie Highway, less than a mile from Max Gilpin's grave, and orders an eight-ounce sirloin, medium, and a baked potato with butter and sour cream. Every few minutes a high school girl comes over to smile and say hello. While he was under indictment, Stinson was placed in an administrative position away from children. But he is back in the classroom now, coaching basketball this fall. He plans to coach football again. Another man might have moved to another 74 school or even another town, but that would be quitting. Anyway, there was no need. Stinson's stature in Pleasure Ridge Park is probably greater now than it was before. His supporters rose up with him for victory.

"We busted 'em in the teeth," Stinson says, referring to the crimi- 75
nal trial, by way of saying he and his lawyers would have done the same thing in the civil trial if it had gone that far. It was the school's insurance companies that insisted on the $1.75 million settlement in September with Max Gilpin's parents, he says. Purely a business decision. No one admitted anything.

During a bench conference at the criminal trial, Stinson's own 76
attorney, Dathorne, said to the judge, "I think you can almost take judicial notice that Jason Stinson was being a jerk that day. Everybody said that." Now, at the roadhouse, when Stinson is asked to acknowledge the truth of this statement, he refuses. "I don't know what Alex meant by that," he says. "You'd have to ask him."

After interviews with more than 125 witnesses, the Jefferson 77
County Public Schools (JCPS) delivered their own report on the Max Gilpin incident. It was so favorable to Stinson that Stengel called it "the biggest cover-up since Watergate." Nevertheless, school superintendent Sheldon Berman had a few things to say about Stinson's conduct:

"While the evidence did not reveal any violation of . . . JCPS 78
rules, I am extremely troubled—actually I am outraged—by the statement made that day by head coach Jason Stinson—that the running would end when someone quit the team. While this kind of negative motivation may be used in some amateur and even professional sports, that kind of culture has absolutely no place in JCPS' athletic programs."

The superintendent established an annual seminar that trains 79
coaches not to motivate their players the way Stinson did that day. Stinson has attended it twice. Now, at the roadhouse, when asked to acknowledge that the seminar is a result of what he did on Aug. 20, 2008, he seems genuinely unaware of the connection. And if this is hard to believe, consider the story he gave in his civil deposition about a brief encounter with Max Gilpin after Max had finished the running that killed him.

At the trial, one of Stinson's own witnesses said Max leaned over 80
and breathed heavily after the running. Another defense witness said Max fell and beat the ground in anger. Other players said Max couldn't even finish the running and had to be propped up. One of them said he returned from the final sprint to find Max on his hands and knees. Soon after that, he said, Max appeared to be foaming at the mouth, and

his face was pale blue. But in the civil deposition, Stinson gave this account:

> *Stinson:* Yes, sir. He had finished conditioning and was headed where he was needed to go.
> *Plaintiff's Attorney:* He really wasn't in any distress as far as you could see?
> *Stinson:* As far as I could tell.

For a few minutes on that Wednesday, after school and before football practice, no one told Max Gilpin what to do. And what he did was a total surprise. He was walking to the bus with Chelsea Scott, the green-eyed cheerleader who became his girlfriend through sheer will and persistence, and he was wearing one of his favorite outfits: a pair of yellow plaid shorts and a butter-yellow Aeropostale T-shirt that nicely set off the tan of his arms. He may have done what he did because he knew she wanted it, but perhaps this one time he decided to do what he wanted, just because. Anyway, he bent down and hugged her, close enough to smell the vanilla in her Victoria's Secret perfume, and then he kissed her mouth, for at least two seconds, as if he knew exactly what he was doing. It was their first kiss, and of course their last: a glimmer of the man Max Gilpin was becoming. 81

Then he walked toward the locker room and returned to obedience. He never stopped obeying, not even at the hospital. He hung on for three days, never fully conscious, as his body fell apart from the inside. His best friend, Zach Deacon, told him, "Hang in there. Keep fighting. I love you." And Max kept fighting. His heart rate seemed to rise when people prayed. A nurse asked him to squeeze her hand, which he did, and said, "Max, if you can hear me, wiggle your toes." And he did. 82

Toward the end he had blood in his mouth and tears on his cheeks, and he finally got permission to quit. His mother whispered into his ear, "It's O.K., Max. You can let go." A minute later he was gone. 83

Examining the Text

1. The author relates a certain amount of "back story" about a number of characters in this tragic story, including the football coach. ". . . The coach liked to say he wasn't making football players; he was making good daddies, good citizens, good taxpayers. So he was more surprised than anyone when his conduct at football practice on Aug. 20, 2008, became the subject of one of the largest investigations in the history of the Louisville Metro Police Department." In your opinion, does the author ultimately depict Coach Stinson as a positive or negative "character" in the story, or does he take care to describe him with impeccable journalistic objectivity?

2. Lake reports, "Before the trial," the prosecutor in this case, "put his chance of winning a conviction at less than 10%." What social, political, and historical factors, according to the prosecutor and the author of this article, contributed to the unlikelihood that the coach would be found guilty of any legal wrongdoing in the death of Max Gilpin?

3. The author reports that, after interviews with more than a hundred witnesses, the Jefferson County Public Schools delivered their own report on the Max Gilpin incident. It was so favorable to Stinson that the prosecutor in the case called it "the biggest cover-up since Watergate." To what specific elements of cover-up is prosecutor Stengel referring? After reading the article, would you tend to agree that a number of incriminating facts were overlooked and/or buried, or do you get the sense that the investigation and subsequent trial events were conducted fairly and impartially?

4. The author concludes the article this way: "Toward the end he had blood in his mouth and tears on his cheeks, and he finally got permission to quit. His mother whispered into his ear, 'It's O.K., Max. You can let go.' A minute later he was gone." In doing so, author Lake purposely does not end with an essay-like conclusion in which he moralizes about the coach's behavior specifically, or high school football generally. Why does he choose to end the article in this way, and how does this ending make you feel and/or think about the issues raised by this article?

5. *Thinking rhetorically:* Rather early in this article, the author writes, "Max . . . was on the verge of quitting until Michele (head cheerleader, Western High) called his father, Jeff, and put Max on the line, and when the conversation was over, Max was no longer quitting. He did manage to sit out for a couple of years, but at the start of high school Max told his father he was going to play football. And his father (offensive lineman, Butler High) taught him power cleans and leg presses and rhythmic breathing. He bought Max protein shakes, and his mother bought him the muscle-building substance creatine." While author Lake never comes out and points the finger of blame at anyone in this passage, what is the implied message here? Lake uses this technique a number of times throughout the article; scan it carefully, and see if you can find other instances in which culpability, if not overtly expressed, is skillfully and subtly implied. What is your gut reaction as you read this passage? It is likely that you are not having that reaction by accident: an artful writer can play on readers' emotions like Yo Yo Ma on a cello or Jack White on a Stratocaster.

For Group Discussion

The author at one point in this article delivers the offhand remark, "Football demands a certain brutality, a hunger to smash the other guy's face." Based upon your knowledge of football—either from having played it, watched it on television, attended a game, participated as a cheerleader on the sidelines, or had friends/family who were dedicated football players and/or fans, debate the validity of this assertion. Does football require as much hunger to smash another guy's face as a more obvious example, such as boxing, as was related earlier in Maya Angelou's article about Joe Louis, or does football fall in some kind of violence-related "gray area," somewhere between mixed martial arts and, say, table tennis?

Writing Suggestion

Following upon the question posed in the For Group Discussion prompt above, if football indeed demands a certain kind of brutality, what is its mass pop-cultural appeal? Some have argued that human beings' evolutionary history has left us with a certain degree of hard-wired physical aggressiveness, and that sports such as football are actually civilizing forces, channeling those aggressive impulses away from more egregious forms of brutality and into a "relatively" save game that has had "only" six hundred deaths at the high school level in the past century or so. Do a bit of research to uncover various observers' theories concerning the role of football and other violent sports in civilized society, with the goal of finally arriving at a thesis that reflects your own conclusions after doing this research: do you feel that violent sports serve a civilizing function in society, or do they reinforce and perpetuate a hypothetically innate tendency toward brutality?

Does Football Have a Future?

BEN MCGRATH

The author of the previous reading, "The Boy Who Died of Football," concluding his article by purposely not *exploring the physical dangers associated with football as one of the most popular sports—both for fans and players—in America today. We mention this rhetorical choice by the author in the apparatus following that reading, and it's a particularly important point, since the following article by Ben McGrath takes a completely different editorial direction in his examination of football. McGrath, a staff writer for the* New Yorker *magazine since 2003, looks at a similar phenomenon in football as does Thomas Lake—namely its inherent violence and the risks associated with that harsh reality—but he moves from the amateur ranks to the highest—and perhaps most brutal—level of the sport: namely the game as played in the National Football League (NFL).*

Where Lake mainly narrated a story with journalistic objectivity, McGrath conducts a more lengthy and in-depth study of the physical dangers associated with football at the professional level. Specifically, this article discusses head injuries and concussions among NFL players, along with a gradually rising public awareness of the dangers associated with violence in the sport. McGrath consults a number of authorities and specialists in the field in order to bring to light specific and prevalent dangers. For example, the author devotes much attention to a journalist named Alan Schwarz, who has brought media and public attention to football-related injuries such as chronic traumatic encephalopathy. ***As you read*** *this article, consider this along with the many other subtopical issues raised by McGrath, such as potential reforms to the game, suggested alterations to the rules, controversies regarding helmet technology, and, ultimately, the very future of the NFL itself.*

I still remember my first football game. It was 1983. I was six. My father 1
took me to our local high school, in northern New Jersey, and we sat on the home team's side, but it wasn't long before my allegiance began to waver. The opponents, from a town called Passaic, were clearly superior—or, rather, they had a superior player whose simple talents were easy to identify in a game so complex and jumbled-seeming that even lifelong fans do not fully understand it. He wasn't the biggest person on the field, and probably not the fastest, but he was strangely fast for a big person and unusually big for a fast person. He played both sides of the ball: running back and linebacker. He was also the kicker, and he returned punts. In my memory, he scored a touchdown, kicked a field goal, and sacked the quarterback for a safety. 12–0. As my father and I searched for his name in the program, a man seated a couple of rows in front of us spun around and said, "They call him Ironhead." I was smitten.

Ironhead, whose given name was Craig Heyward, went on to 2
become a star at the University of Pittsburgh and then a pro with several N.F.L. teams, although he was probably more famous for his nickname and for his physique than for his accomplishments on the field. He was strictly a running back after high school, but he looked more like a lineman: a "bread truck with feet," as one writer called him. Heyward did not run sweeps. He ran up the middle: into, through, and over, but seldom around, defenders. His style of play embodied Newton's second law of motion: force equal to mass times acceleration. I think of him every time I see the Old Spice commercial in which the Baltimore Ravens star Ray Lewis emerges from the shower naked except for a suit of fake soapsuds, because Ironhead, as a spokesman for Zest body wash, in the mid-nineties, was a pioneer of the genre. He was that crucial thing in the marketing of football: a cuddly warrior.

It's easier to marvel at the gladiatorial nature of the game when the participants appear to be laughing about something as trivial as personal hygiene.

"He would lower his head into opponents' stomachs, and one opponent said it hurt so much that Heyward's head had to be made of iron:" that explanation for the name that made him my favorite player appeared in Heyward's obituary in the *Times*, in 2006. The anecdote referred to his habit while playing "street football," without a helmet, as a "wayward" boy in Passaic. He was only thirty-nine when he died, from a brain tumor. Even the hardest of heads is vulnerable to disease. I've never read or heard any suggestions that the cancer was related to Heyward's football career, but when the executives at the N.F.L.'s headquarters, in Manhattan, talk about "changing the culture" of the sport, as they have been doing with increasing urgency in the past few months, in response to growing public concern over concussions, the use of the head as a battering ram, with or without a helmet, is near the top of the list of things they'd like to disown. 3

I thought of Ironhead last month as well, while standing in the lobby of the InterContinental Hotel, where a special meeting of the league's Head, Neck, and Spine Injury committee was convening in one of the function rooms. Bert Straus, an industrial designer with a background in bathroom fixtures, dental-office equipment, and light-rail vehicles, was showing off a prototype of a new helmet called the Gladiator, whose primary selling point is that it has a soft exterior. A colleague of Straus's handed me a pamphlet titled "Collision Physics for Football Helmets." This stuff goes way beyond Newton: elastic versus inelastic collisions, "Complex Modulus = f (Rate of deflection, Young's modulus, % compression)." I picked up the helmet. It felt awfully heavy. It also didn't feel very soft. The Gladiator is made of reaction-molded polyurethane, like the bumper on your car. Truly soft shells run the risk of causing friction, which is bad for the neck. 4

Colonel Geoffrey Ling, a neurologist with the Defense Department, had come to the InterContinental to share some of the government's research with the N.F.L.'s medical brain trust. (Concussions among the men and women returning from Iraq and Afghanistan, one doctor told me, could be "the next Agent Orange.") "If you look historically, what really hurts our soldiers from blasts is artillery shells, mortar shells," Ling said. "The combat helmet was designed particularly for mitigation of fragments. It does have some ballistic protection. You could shoot at the thing point blank with a 9-millimetre pistol, and you won't penetrate it. That's pretty doggone good. I'm surprised New York City policemen aren't wearing the doggone thing. But, like, I wouldn't play football with the thing. It ain't *that* good." 5

Was Ironhead a role model for a sport with no future? 6

We've been here before, historians remind us, and we have the pictures to prove it: late-nineteenth-century newspaper and magazine illustrations with captions like "The Modern Gladiators" and "Out of the Game." The latter of those, which appeared in *Harper's Weekly* in 1891, describes a hauntingly familiar scene, with a player kneeling by his downed—and unconscious—comrade, and waving for help, as a medic comes running, water bucket in hand. It accompanied an essay by the Yale coach Walter Camp, the so-called Father of American Football, whose preference for order over chaos led to the primary differentiating element between the new sport and its parent, English rugby: a line of scrimmage, with discrete plays, or downs, instead of scrums. 7

Camp viewed football as an upper-class training ground, not as a middle-class spectator sport. But the prevalence of skull fractures soon prompted unflattering comparisons with boxing and bullfighting. Another image, which ran in the New York *World*, depicted a skeleton wearing a banner labelled "Death," and was titled "The Twelfth Player in Every Football Game." Campaigns in Chicago and Georgia to outlaw the sport were covered breathlessly in the New York dailies. That was in 1897, "the peak of sensationalized football violence," as Michael Oriard, a former offensive lineman for the Kansas City Chiefs who is now an associate dean at Oregon State University, explains in "Reading Football: How the Popular Press Created an American Spectacle." 8

The crisis surrounding football's brutality at the turn of the twentieth century was so great that it eventually inspired Presidential intervention. Greg Aiello, the N.F.L.'s present-day spokesman, told me, "You should research Teddy Roosevelt's involvement in changing the game in 1905." Roosevelt, whose son was then a freshman football player at Harvard, summoned college coaches to the White House to discuss reforming the sport before public opinion turned too far against it. Eighteen people had died on the field that year. The idea, or hope, was to preserve the game's essential character-building physicality ("I've got no sympathy whatever with the overwrought sentimentality that would keep a young man in cotton-wool," Roosevelt wrote) without filling up the morgue. The next year, the forward pass was legalized, thereby transforming football from a militarized or corporatized rugby to something more like "contact ballet," as Oriard calls it. 9

Aiello's point was that the game goes on; you reform it as needed. Dave Pear, a retired Tampa Bay Buccaneer, brought up the same example with the opposite lesson in mind. "Look at the historicity of football and Heisman," he said, referring to John Heisman, who was 10 among the leading advocates of the forward pass in 1906. "Football almost ended in the early nineteen-hundreds." Pear's view is that the game always has been "hazardous to your health, like smoking cigarettes," and that trying to remove violence from football, as the N.F.L. now seems bent on doing, is like trying to remove the trees from a forest. "Now it's not an instant death," he said. "Now it's a slow death." You could say that Dave Pear holds a grudge: he has a minuscule pension, is uninsurable, and estimates that he has spent six hundred thousand dollars on surgeries and other medical issues (fused disks, artificial hip, vertigo) related to his football career. "I'm not trying to end football," he said. "It's not that I don't like football." But: "I wish I had never played."

Introducing the forward pass may have saved the sport from marginalization, or even banishment, but it did not resolve the inherent tension in our secular religion. With increased professionalization, in the middle decades of the last century, came specialization within the sport, and the demise of players who covered both offense and defense. And with specialization came increased speed and intensity, owing, in part, to reduced fatigue among the players, as well as skill sets and body types suited to particular facets of the game. "Savagery on Sunday" was the headline on a *Life* story in 1955. Walter Cronkite produced a half-hour special, "The Violent World of Sam Huff," about a New York Giants linebacker who had declared, "We try to hurt everybody." 11

The increased attention—football was on its way to surpassing baseball as the nation's favorite spectator sport—brought more reforms, many of them related to equipment: chinstraps, the rubber bar, full-on face masks. "Even as the discussion of the game's violence was at its shrillest, the sport was becoming safer," Michael MacCambridge writes in "America's Game: The Epic Story of How Pro Football Captured a Nation." But, even as the game was becoming safer, through better equipment and further tweaking of the rules (calling a play dead as soon as a knee touched down, say, to limit bone-crunching pileups), it was evolving in such a way that it also became more dangerous, as players, comfortably protected by their face masks, learned to tackle with their heads instead of with their arms and shoulders. When Michael Oriard played for the Chiefs, in the early nineteen-seventies, he weighed two hundred and forty pounds; his counterpart on today's Chiefs roster weighs about three hundred and ten, and is probably no slower. Players didn't obsessively lift weights in Oriard's day. 12

From all these developments, we got smash-mouth football and, later, the spectacularly combustive open-field collisions that seem to leave players in a state of epileptic seizure nearly every weekend 13 now. "We had a lot of discussions right after I became commissioner about this subject," Paul Tagliabue, who served as the N.F.L.'s chief executive from 1989 until 2006, told me recently. "And one by-product of that was the question of whether defensive players were acquiring a sense of invulnerability, and playing the game with a level of abandon and recklessness that was not warranted. We created a committee with Mel Blount and Willie Lanier and some others. They raised the idea that it was no longer tackle football. It was becoming collision football. The players looked like bionic men. Whatever was the violence of Sam Huff, I don't think he felt invulnerable, like a bionic man."

Throughout most of the Super Bowl era, football was understood to be an orthopedic, an arthroscopic, and, eventually, an arthritic risk. This was especially obvious as the first generation of Super Bowl heroes retired and began showing up at reunions and Hall of Fame induction ceremonies walking like "Maryland crabs," as a players'-union representative once put it. But a couple of incidents early in Tagliabue's tenure left him with a sense of foreboding. "In 1991, my second season, Mike Utley went down," he said, alluding to the paralysis of a Detroit Lions offensive lineman. "A year later, Dennis Byrd went down. Once you see two injuries like Mike Utley's and Dennis Byrd's, you begin to see that there are long-term consequences to injuries on the football field." He meant long-term consequences of a sort that you can't joke about, while patting your fake knee or hip and complaining that you can no longer navigate stairs or play with your grandkids. Byrd, who was a defensive lineman for the Jets, gradually taught himself to walk again, after being given a prognosis of partial paralysis, and delivered a rousing pep talk to the Jets before their upset victory over the Patriots in the conference semifinals, earlier this month. Utley's moral is a grimmer one. As he was being carried off the field on a stretcher, he didn't yet know that he was paralyzed from the chest down. He stuck his thumb up, and the fans applauded. 14

What was missing from this picture was the effect of all that impact on the brain. You got your "bell rung," they used to say. You're "just a little dinged up." This was not merely macho sideline-speak; it was, as recently as a decade and a half ago, the language of the N.F.L.'s leading doctors. Elliot Pellman, who served until 2007 as the Jets team physician, once told a reporter that veteran players are able to "unscramble their brains a little faster" than rookies are, "maybe because they're not afraid after being dinged." 15

Chronic traumatic encephalopathy, or C.T.E., is the name for a condition that is believed to result from major collisions—or from the accumulation of subconcussions that are nowhere near as noticeable, including those incurred in practice. It was first diagnosed, in 16

2002, in the brain of the Pittsburgh Steelers Hall of Fame center Mike Webster, who died of a heart attack after living out of his truck for a time. It was next diagnosed in one of Webster's old teammates on the Steelers' offensive line, Terry Long, who killed himself by drinking antifreeze. Long overlapped, at the end of his career, with Justin Strzelczyk, who was also found to have C.T.E. after he crashed, fatally, into a tanker truck, while driving the wrong way down the New York Thruway.

Credit for the public's increased awareness of these issues must go to the *Times*, and to its reporter Alan Schwarz, whom Dr. Joseph Maroon, the Steelers' neurosurgeon and a longtime medical adviser to the league, calls "the Socratic gadfly in this whole mix." Schwarz was a career baseball writer, with a heavy interest in statistics, when, in December of 2006, he got a call from a friend of a friend named Chris Nowinski, a Harvard football player turned pro wrestler turned concussion activist. Andre Waters, the former Philadelphia Eagles safety, had just committed suicide, and Nowinski was in possession of his mottled brain. The earliest cases of C.T.E. had been medical news, not national news. Nowinski's journalist contacts, as he recalls, were in "pro-wrestling media, not legitimate media." He needed help. 17

Schwarz, acting more as a middleman than as a journalist pitching a hot story, set up a meeting between Nowinski and the *Times'* sports editor, Tom Jolly, for whom Schwarz had been writing Sunday columns about statistical analysis on a freelance basis. Rather than assign the story to one of his staffers, Jolly suggested that Schwarz write it. The result, "Expert Ties Ex-Player's Suicide to Brain Damage from Football," wound up on the front page, on January 18, 2007. It described Waters's forty-four-year-old brain tissue as resembling that of an eighty-five-year-old man with Alzheimer's, and cited the work and opinions of several doctors whose research into the cumulative effect of head trauma was distinctly at odds with that of the N.F.L.'s own Mild and Traumatic Brain Injury committee (M.T.B.I.), which had been created by Tagliabue. "Don't send them back out on these fields," Waters's niece told Schwarz, referring to young would-be football players. 18

Ted Johnson, a recently retired New England Patriots linebacker, read the Waters piece and called Schwarz. He was thirty-four-years old and had been locking himself in his apartment with the blinds drawn for days at a time. He believed that his problems had started in 2002, when, he said, his coach, the sainted Bill Belichick, ignored a trainer's recommendation that Johnson practice without contact while recovering from a concussion. Schwarz accompanied Johnson to a meeting with his neurologist, Dr. Robert Cantu, who said, "Ted already shows the mild cognitive impairment that is characteristic of 19 early Alzheimer's disease." Two weeks after the Waters piece, Schwarz landed another freelance submission on A1: "Dark Days Follow Hard-Hitting Career in N.F.L."

Schwarz's phone kept ringing. Several of the callers were the mothers and wives of football's damaged men. They represented a readership far less likely to have come across, say, the annual men's-magazine features about mangled knees, wayward fingers, and back braces, which had hardened almost into a sportswriting trope. In March, Schwarz published another front-pager: "Wives United by Husbands' Post-N.F.L. Trauma." Glenn Kramon, an assistant managing editor at the *Times* who oversees long-term, Pulitzer-worthy projects, read this piece and decided to intervene. Schwarz was given a full-time position, with no responsibilities other than to broaden his new beat's focus beyond the N.F.L. to the more than four million amateur athletes who play organized football. Although Schwarz was assigned to the sports desk, the *Times* framed the story as a matter of public health, akin to tobacco, asbestos, and automobile safety. Schwarz covered high schools, helmets, workmen's comp, coaching, and so on, earning the nickname Alan Brockovich among friends. "You can imagine how many lawyers I hear from," he once told me. 20

Schwarz's expansive focus, as he reiterated it, one piece at a time, threatened to affect the so-called pipeline, the future sons of football, whose non-sports-fan mothers were reading his accounts. The reaction of the football establishment, both at the league office and at stadiums around the country, was not warm. "I remember hearing voices within the game, at the club level: 'We don't need this muckraking reporter doing this,' " Michael MacCambridge told me. 21

"Their initial reaction was 'This guy's out to get football,'" Gregg Easterbrook, the author of ESPN's popular "Tuesday Morning Quarterback" column, said. "I felt a little of that myself." 22

Schwarz may not have been out to get football, but he was clearly less emotionally invested in it than most of his predecessors and peers, who had helped build the sport into the de-facto national pastime with romantic coverage of heroic sacrifice. He was not a fan. "I'd been pitching this to reporters for years," Nowinski told me, of the head-injury problem in general. "People in football told me, point blank, 'I don't want to lose my access.' It literally took a baseball writer who did not care about losing his access, and didn't *want* the access, to football." 23

Schwarz's math background came in handy, too, as he batted away the statistical objections about the unknown incidence of C.T.E. from skeptical doctors. And Schwarz had the backing of a news organization that did not see itself as having any symbiotic ties to the game's economic engine. (ESPN, which drives the national conversation on sports, invests more than a billion dollars a year in football 24 broadcasting.) "There's certainly been a lot of tension between Alan and the N.F.L., and the N.F.L. and our editors," Jolly said. "Their communications people made it clear that they were not happy with the reporting. Some of their folks were pretty brusque and not particularly eager to work with Alan."

What we now know, from reading Schwarz, is that retired N.F.L. players are five to nineteen times as likely as the general population to have received a dementia-related diagnosis; that the helmet-manufacturing industry is overseen by a volunteer consortium funded largely by helmet manufacturers; and that Lou Gehrig may not actually have had the disease that bears his name but suffered from concussion-related trauma instead. (Since 1960, fourteen N.F.L. players have had a diagnosis of amyotrophic lateral sclerosis, which is about twelve more than you would expect from a random population sample.) In the manner of Elisabeth Kübler-Ross, Dr. Maroon has delineated four stages in the N.F.L.'s reaction to the reality of brain damage: active resistance and passive resistance, shifting to passive acceptance and, finally, in the past few months, active acceptance. "What we're seeing now is that major cultural shift, and I think Alan took a lot of barbs, and a lot of hits, initially, for his observations," Maroon said. 25

When I ran into Schwarz in the lobby of the InterContinental Hotel, last month, he mentioned that his story tally on the beat was at "a hundred and twenty-one and counting." We were both there for the meeting of the N.F.L.'s Head, Neck, and Spine Injury committee, a newly rebranded version of the M.T.B.I. group, which had come in for so much Schwarz criticism from the beginning. Several of the old doctors, including the Jets' Elliot Pellman, were gone. Some of the new committee members were longtime sources of Schwarz's. 26

The meeting was closed to the press. Although Schwarz told me he'd heard from various participants that they were advised not to speak with him, he'd been getting live updates on his cell phone from sources inside the room. The gadfly was enjoying his moment. During a midday break in the proceedings, five doctors, including Robert Cantu, Ted Johnson's neurologist, emerged to take questions. About two dozen journalists had showed up. By my count, twelve questions were asked, eight of them by Schwarz. 27

"They may never give Alan himself credit, but he's done the work of angels," Easterbrook said. 28

"There's no question that HD television is remarkable," Art Rooney II, the president of the Pittsburgh Steelers, said, the week before Thanksgiving. "But it also, at times, may give us a view of something that we didn't always have before, and in some cases it may be shocking to people, I guess." Rooney was sitting in his office at the team's practice facility, on the south side of the Monongahela River, 29 and reflecting on the state of pro football, a Rooney family business since 1933. His Steelers, who are among the most successful and beloved franchises in all of professional sports, had recently drawn better ratings for a midseason Sunday-night matchup against the New Orleans Saints than had Game Four of the World Series. They had also become a focal point in football's culture war. "I mean, we had the one weekend where we had three or four hits that some may have overreacted to," Rooney went on. "But in general, from what I've been able to observe, it's been a robust debate."

On the weekend in question, which one writer called Black and 30
Blue Sunday, and which fell in the middle of October, at least eleven N.F.L. players were concussed, about one or two more than average. A few of the hits were cringe-worthy—helmet-knockers that lent themselves especially well to modern replay technology, where the elasticity of the human neck is on full display. What's more, they followed on the heels of a tragic accident that was still fresh in the news from the day before, involving a Rutgers student who was paralyzed while defending a kick return at New Meadowlands Stadium, the home of the Giants and the Jets. If the reaction of the league—levying a hundred and seventy-five thousand dollars in fines on three hard hitters and threatening suspensions for future infractions—could be considered excessive, then so, certainly, were the inevitable gripes that followed, about putting pink skirts on the players. October is a month in which the N.F.L. has taken to courting female fans by celebrating breast-cancer awareness. A number of players, victims and offenders alike, were already wearing pink accessories (gloves, cleats, chinstraps) in honor of the cause.

A couple of the concussive hits that Rooney referred to had been 31
delivered by the Steelers' linebacker James Harrison, a onetime Defensive Player of the Year, who made the mistake, in the locker room afterward, of being honest about his understanding of football, which was, after all, the same as Sam Huff's: "I try to hurt people." Successfully hurting people hadn't earned him any penalty flags in this particular game, and a photograph of him flattening one of his victims was briefly available as a souvenir for sale through the N.F.L.'s Web site, the next day. But he was villainized in the national press, and fined seventy-five thousand dollars, anyway, and it left him at a loss. "What we saw Sunday was disturbing," Ray Anderson, the N.F.L.'s executive vice-president of football operations, said. "We're talking about avoiding life-altering impacts." The rules remained the same; the league just seemed to want them enforced differently, and with an eye toward outcome and appearance as much as technique. Harrison took a day off and contemplated retirement ("James is very concerned about how to play football," his agent said), while his teammates rallied around him

and joked about how they might have to start tweeting opponents before tackling them, as a precautionary measure. If there were to be no more "devastating hits," as Anderson had indicated, and if "defenseless" receivers were to be somehow protected by their opponents, then was this really football?

"I understand our players when they say they're not sure what they can do at this point," Rooney said, cautiously. "We are asking a lot of our defensive players, in terms of watching where they hit somebody, when everything's happening so fast out there. What we're asking them to do is not easy. That's in addition to the fact that we're also asking them to do something different from what they've been trained to do over the years." 32

Two generations ago, the Rooney men were boxers. They are now lawyers and diplomats, the civic paragons of Pittsburgh, and also of the N.F.L. They epitomize what family-run businesses can mean to a place, because of the implied trust and moral responsibility involved. The so-called Rooney rule, under which N.F.L. teams are required to interview at least one minority candidate for all head coaching and G.M. jobs, is named after Art's father, Dan, the team's chairman emeritus and also our Ambassador to Ireland. (His public endorsement of Barack Obama, during the most recent Presidential campaign, was a major event in coal country.) Here was a man who is revered by progressive, charitably minded people, not your typical asbestos-plant manager. The Steelers had been the first team to keep a neurosurgeon with them on the sidelines, and the first to introduce any kind of objective measurement of cognitive function. It wasn't enough, and the norms of polite society were shifting underneath Rooney. 33

In the month following Black and Blue Sunday, the Steelers found it more useful to view themselves as victims of a different kind of culture war, between the suits on Park Avenue and the grunts in Pittsburgh. Their coach, Mike Tomlin, had objected to efforts by the league to demonstrate that Harrison was changing his behavior to comply with the new mandate. The previous week, against New England, the Steelers' captain, Hines Ward, had left the game with what the team at first described as a neck injury, which would allow reëntry at the player's discretion, instead of a concussion, which, as of last year, forbids it. But a concussion it was. "It's my body," Ward complained afterward. "I feel like if I want to go back out there I should have the right." 34

"Hines would go back in the game with a broken leg, so that's just the kind of player he is," Rooney said. "I do think that there's been a connection between our team and our region, let's say, that is based on a blue-collar-work-ethic-type approach to life, and certainly people that grew up working in the mill were tough people that had to work hard and had to work tough jobs. And so I think the reason football 35 became so popular here in western Pennsylvania was because of that—because the area was populated by people who were accustomed to and appreciated hard work and tough work, and wanted their football team to reflect that." He mentioned that Harrison, a man who earns several million dollars a year for his toughness, had been receiving unsolicited donations from Steelers fans to help pay his fines. "So I think our fans want to see our players continue to play football the way they understand football should be played," he said.

The robust debate over how football should be played is further 36
complicated by a contentious labor situation that threatens to result in the cancellation of the 2011 season. The league and the owners would prefer an eighteen-game schedule. The players, naturally, have tried to characterize this as hypocrisy: if the game has become disturbingly dangerous, why play more? They doubt that anyone has ever really had their long-term interests in mind, and maintain a deeply felt sense that fans and owners can't begin to appreciate how hard football is, and how tenuous the line is between fearlessness and vulnerability.

"I don't think there's enough of them up there that have actu- 37
ally played the game," James Harrison said, of the league executives in Manhattan, when I visited the Pittsburgh locker room after a big win against the Oakland Raiders, late in the season. "You got Merton Hanks that, you know, played the game so many years ago. I mean no disrespect, but the game's a lot faster than it was when he played. When we're right there, and it's bang-bang, you don't have time to adjust." Hanks, who is the N.F.L.'s director of game operations, was an All-Pro safety for the San Francisco 49ers. He retired in 1999, which hardly seems like that many years ago, but twelve years is four times the average length of a professional football career.

Up in the press box, I'd noticed a casual disdain for the initial ef- 38
forts to sanitize the game as the referees tossed yellow flag after yellow flag. "Apparently, you can't tackle the quarterback now," one writer mused, after one of Harrison's fellow-linebackers was called for roughing the passer. "Unbelievable!" another said, after a personal foul on Harrison—who had landed with the full force of his body weight on the QB—negated a Steelers interception. The Steelers had wound up with more penalty yards in this game than in any previous game, and the writers saw this as an opportunity to highlight the differences between the league and the team.

When I brought up the call for change with the Steelers' Troy 39
Polamalu, an All-Pro safety who plays with brilliant abandon, and mentioned that the sport's popularity seemed to be unflagging, he cut me off. "Is that your opinion? That it doesn't need to be changed?" He later added, "This game's on the verge of getting out of hand," and defended the refs, who, he said, were "just trying to protect it."

This from a guy who, a few weeks earlier, had complained that there was "a paranoia that is unneeded," and that if people wanted to watch soccer they could and would.

"In the past, it was a style of ball that was three yards and a cloud 40
of dust, so you didn't see too many of these big hits, because there wasn't so much space between players," Polamalu said. "I mean, with the passing game now, you get four-wide-receiver sets, sometimes five-wide-receiver sets. You get guys coming across the middle, you get zone coverages. You know, there's more space between these big hits, so there's more *opportunity* for these big hits." The *Times*, in 1906, celebrated the dawn of the forward-passing era as an opportunity to "open up the game," and to showcase speed and skill instead of mere brute strength. Bill Walsh, the late 49ers coach, and the man most often credited with popularizing the passing-dominated approach to offense that Polamalu was describing, was committed to changing the sport's militaristic culture. "Too many high-school coaches, in his opinion, were veterans who viewed football like preparing for combat," Paul Tagliabue recalled.

Troy Polamalu is about as dynamic an athlete as I have ever seen, 41
and as soft-spoken in person as anyone I have ever met. He is football's Dalai Lama. He has had at least seven concussions. "Honestly, it hurts both players, you know, and, whenever you see those big hits, it's not just offensive guys lying on the ground," he said. The statistics bear this out: defensive backs were the most extensively concussed group of players on the field this N.F.L. season, followed by wide receivers. Contact ballet can kill.

The fastest running on a football field often occurs during kick- 42
offs and punts, when some members of the defending team are able to build up forty or more yards of head-on steam before a possible point of impact. (The forty-yard dash, the standard measurement for judging the speed of potential draft picks, is so named because it was thought to be the distance a player would have to sprint to catch up with a punt.) One proposed reform that I've heard about would involve removing this element from the game, through automatic fair catches, or at least neutering it, by shortening the distance travelled by the kicking team. The most frequent head-butting on a football field, meanwhile, occurs at the line of scrimmage, where linemen often begin in what's known as a three-point stance: crouching and leaning forward on one hand, and then exploding upward in a meeting of crowns. Another suggestion: banning the stance and requiring linemen to squat, sumo style. And then, more important, there's simply teaching proper tackling technique. As one recently retired player put it to me, "Instead of telling a kid to knock the snot out, you say, 'Knock the wind out of him.'"

43 "The reality is you're going to need about twenty fixes that reduce risk by a couple of percentage points each," Chris Nowinski said. "There's still going to be four downs. Still going to be a football. Still going to be eleven guys on the field—and touchdowns. Other than that, everything's in play."

44 Technology, naturally, is another big component of the discussion. The agenda for the Head, Neck, and Spine meeting was dauntingly ambitious and impressive, with presentations on subjects like "Finite element modelling in determining concussion thresholds" and "On-field testing of impact biomechanics." Telemetric feedback from accelerometers may soon give trainers on the sidelines a more objective, real-time perspective on the abuse that each player is suffering, which could prove valuable in quickly diagnosing concussions. Yet, in the absence of a concussion-proof helmet, which is not looming, and will likely never arrive, there is perhaps as much to be gained from using technology to help address the necessary abstraction that allows fans to view their football heroes as characters rather than as people with families. (Ironhead Heyward led a troubled life off the field, with alcohol-abuse issues and sporadic run-ins with the police; the news accounts somehow only made me more fascinated.) Markus Koch, a defensive lineman for the Washington Redskins in the nineteen-eighties, asked me whether it might not be more valuable to communicate real-time information about the physicality of the game to the people at home on their sofas, happily consuming Budweiser and buffalo wings. "So maybe you'd have a mouth guard that registers the impact they're getting on the field, and at certain g-forces the helmet shell would crack and explode and leak gray matter and blood," Koch said, only half kidding. "Or what about a whole pneumatic suit that a fan could step into, and that would be telemetrically linked to a player on the field, at seventy per cent or fifty per cent—you could adjust the dial to your liking—and actually have the fan experience what the player is going through?" Koch broke his lumbar vertebrae in his third season, and, because he was otherwise in such good shape, continued to play for three more years. He now suffers from depression, and is sometimes unable to get out of bed for extended periods. His legs go numb if he stands for too long.

45 Two weeks after Black and Blue Sunday, on October 28th, an honor student in Spring Hill, Kansas, returned to the sidelines after making an interception at his high school's homecoming game and told his coach that his head was hurting. Soon afterward, he fell to the ground, suffered a subdural hematoma, and died. The next week, Jim McMahon, the ex-quarterback, confessed at a twenty-fifth reunion of the 1985 Super Bowl champion Chicago Bears that his memory is "pretty much gone," and that he often walks into a room

without knowing why. "It's unfortunate what the game does to you," he said. I was reading about McMahon during a commercial break in the "Monday Night Football" game between the Steelers and the Cincinnati Bengals—a commercial break that included a surprising Toyota promotion involving football. It began with a woman discussing her worries, as a mother, about her son playing the sport: "Which is why I'm really excited, because Toyota developed this software that can simulate head injuries in an accident. . . . So, you know, I can feel a bit better about my son playing football."

A few days later, a Cleveland Browns linebacker collapsed at his 46
locker-room stall, after practice, in the presence of reporters, and was taken to the hospital. Shortly after that, two high-school players died on the same day—one on the field, in Massachusetts, of a heart stoppage, and the other, in North Carolina, by suicide, five weeks after suffering a season-ending concussion. The same week, two Division I college players announced their retirement, out of concerns relating to concussions, and team doctors at the University of Utah "medically disqualified" a sophomore from continuing his career.

This kind of anecdotal momentum is inherently distorting, of 47
course. Jim McMahon added that he has no regrets, and that football "beats the hell out of a regular job." (The fallen Brown later attributed his condition to anxiety over the impending birth of his son.) But I didn't exactly have to go digging for it. "Now, with the Internet, we're all talking to each other, and this is the league's worst nightmare," Dave Pear, the ex-Buccaneer, told me. Pear publishes a blog for "independent football veterans," where, in addition to railing against the N.F.L.'s treatment of retired players, he tracks the sport's latest gloomy news. I've also begun reading the Concussion Blog, which is written by a high-school athletic trainer in Illinois named Dustin Fink, who was moved to devote his life to the cause of player safety and awareness after suffering depression that he attributes to "many" concussions. From Fink's research, for instance, I know that the rate of reported concussions in the N.F.L. did not decline after the stern warnings in October; it increased. Some of this may be attributable to greater conscientiousness on the part of players and medical staffs, which is a good thing, but the "disturbing" hits, as the league's Ray Anderson called them, were just as prevalent, if not more so, as the season wore on. When I called Fink, he told me about a friend of his who plays in the N.F.L., a longtime taxi-squad member who had finally caught on as a starter. Earlier this season, the friend showed up in the concussion database that Fink compiles from news reports and other sources. "I texted him and asked how it happened," he said. "He texted back, 'I'm always concussed, they just caught me this week.'"

Fink was an offensive lineman in high school, but his own injury history clouds the picture somewhat. "I trace my first one back to fourth grade, in 1986," he said. "I hit my head on one of the basketball uprights while playing touch football in the recess yard." He got another one in a fight with a classmate, in eighth grade, and still another as a high-school sophomore, when he was struck by a batted baseball while standing on the pitcher's mound. "My most recent one was in 2006," he said. "While I was helping out at basketball practice, I fell back and hit my head pretty hard." His depression set in late in 2008. Only one of his concussions, as far as he knows, came from playing tackle football. So what do we blame, other than bad luck and a larger society that was slow to recognize the fragility of the human head? 48

In fact, reading the Concussion Blog exposes you to a steady drip of news that is not so good for your anterior insula, the part of the brain associated with worry. Rugby, lacrosse, baseball: concussions are seemingly epidemic everywhere. The problem with having access to better information about the risks we all take is that most leisure pursuits start to seem inherently irresponsible. What are we to do about skiing, bicycling, sledding? 49

"Hockey, by the way, has a higher incidence of concussions than football," Dr. Maroon told me. This is true of women's college hockey, at least, which doesn't even allow body-checking. (Women, in general, seem substantially more prone to concussions, and explanations vary, from weaker necks to a greater honesty in self-diagnosis.) And in December, 2009, Reggie Fleming, a New York Rangers defenseman in the nineteen-sixties who was known more for his fighting than for his scoring, became the first pro hockey player to be given a diagnosis of C.T.E. Hockey may now have a concussion crisis on its hands, with the N.H.L.'s best and most marketable player, Sidney Crosby, having been blindsided during the sport's annual Winter Classic; attempting to play again, four days later, he was drilled into the boards, and he hasn't played since. I play hockey twice a week myself, and was once concussed, or so I now believe, while skating outside, on a frozen pond, without a helmet. 50

Troy Polamalu suggested soccer as an alternative for squeamish fans. But soccer players collide sometimes, too (Taylor Twellman, a forward with the New England Revolution, recently retired because of ongoing symptoms from a neck injury sustained in 2008), and the ball is harder than you think. The g-forces involved in most headers are equivalent to minor car crashes. "Twenty-five years from now, I wouldn't be surprised to see everybody on a soccer field wearing some kind of headgear," Michael MacCambridge said. 51

Still, there is an element of protesting too much on the part of football defenders when it comes to citing the risk factors of other sports. Between 1982 and 2009, according to the National Center for Catastrophic Injury Research, two hundred and ninety-five fatalities directly or indirectly resulted from high-school football. From 1977 to 2009, at all levels, three hundred and seven cervical-cord injuries were recorded. And between 1984 and 2009 there were a hundred and thirty-three instances of brain damage—not slowly accruing damage, as in the case of C.T.E., but damage upon impact. The injury incidence is far lower in most sports. And in the case of similarly treacherous activities, like gymnastics and boxing, far fewer people participate. 52

Some of the most effective proposed reforms seem to involve limiting contact during practice, and forbidding children to tackle until adolescence or beyond. (Developing brains are vulnerable to "second-impact" syndrome.) "Seventy-five per cent of the hits are in practice," Nowinski said. "You could drop the exposure by fifty per cent without changing the game at all." You could, perhaps, but it does also make you wonder about a game whose preservation is couched largely in terms of reducing the frequency with which people really play it. The sport as it stands requires fifty men on a side just to be able to field a team once a week, for a competition that involves a mere ten or eleven minutes of live action; and the news cycle between games is dominated by questions surrounding which players are "probable," which "questionable," and which definitively out of commission. 53

"What happens if football players become like boxers, from lower economic classes with racially marginalized groups?" the ex-Chief Michael Oriard wondered. "If it gets to the point where it's rich white guys cheering on hits by black guys and a Samoan or two, Jesus, I hate to imagine we're indifferent to that." 54

And yet we are, for the most part, already indifferent to that. Two-thirds of N.F.L. players are African-American, and the white players do not typically come from New Canaan. The sport has long had a heavy underclass or, at least, working-class strain. "Football was something you tried to play to get out of the mill," Dan Rooney once said. The people most inclined to ask the question "Would you let your kid play football?" did not play football themselves growing up, because their parents were put off by the sport's brutish culture, regardless of any understanding of brain science. "Any parent who has let their child play football in the past fifty years and claimed never to have understood the risks involved was either kidding himself or an idiot," Buzz Bissinger, the author of "Friday Night Lights," wrote last week in the Daily Beast. Dustin Fink, on the other hand, told me that he would 55 have no problem allowing his five-year-old boy to play, given the current level of medical awareness.

How many of the men on the field in the Super Bowl will be playing with incipient dementia? "To me, twenty per cent seems conservative," Nowinski said. C.T.E., as of now, can be observed only with an autopsy. The ability to detect it with brain scans of living people is at least a couple of years off. "It's not going to be five per cent," Nowinski went on. "The reality is we've already got three per cent of the brains of people who have died in the last two years confirmed, and that's not alarming enough to people. What number is going to be the tipping point? People are O.K. with three per cent. They may look sideways at ten per cent. Maybe it needs to be fifty per cent." 56

A race to collect cadaver brains is now under way, with Bennet Omalu, the original discoverer of C.T.E., leading one group, out of West Virginia University. Ann McKee, a co-director of Boston University's new Center for the Study of Traumatic Encephalopathy, is a leader of the other group. The Boston University center, which is aligned with Nowinski's Sports Legacy Institute, received a million-dollar donation from the N.F.L. last spring, and Nowinski returned the favor by honoring the league's commissioner, Roger Goodell, with an "Impact" award last October, three days after Black and Blue Sunday. Omalu is from Biafra, and has no personal connection to football. He is often the more strident critic, and prone to making antagonistic remarks about his fellow-doctors for their slowness to accept his findings. McKee, on the other hand, is "a longtime football fan," as Malcolm Gladwell noted in these pages in 2009. Each group sees its relationship to the game as a plus: true independence, on the one hand, and a connection to the people who can make the biggest difference, on the other. Competition, in any case, is always good. 57

Like nearly everyone else I talked to, Nowinski, the former wrestler, made sure to absent himself from any moral determination about the game's future. "I used to go through tables for a living from the top ropes," he said. "I'm a firm believer that adults should be able to decide for themselves." Dustin Fink's Concussion Blog comes with a disclaimer—"IN NO UNCERTAIN TERMS DO I BELIEVE THAT WE SHOULD OUTLAW OR 'WUSS DOWN' CONTACT SPORTS!!!"—that begs a question few people are really willing to ask. The campaign to ban boxing has been going on for decades—the *Times* endorsed the idea in 1967, and the American Medical Association lobbied for it in 1983—to no avail. Boxing has a bigger problem: it has slipped into cultural irrelevance. 58

As for football's fate, "I don't think it'll be driven by public opinion, but by lawyers and insurance companies," David Meggyesy, who played linebacker for the St. Louis Cardinals in the nineteen-sixties, 59 told me. Meggyesy was put off by the sport's cultural overlap with American imperialism, as he saw it, and wrote a book, "Out of Their League," that served as football's "Ball Four": a startling exposé that reads, a generation later, as largely unsurprising. He wrote, "When society changes the way I hope it will, football will be obsolete." He also mentioned to me in an e-mail, not long ago, that he had reacted with "big pride" when his rugby-playing daughter confessed to him, "You know, Dad, I really love to hit." The tension is within us all. But with new medical evidence may come new legal risk and liability, and recalibrated insurance premiums, for schools as well as for individuals. "Football may go the way of gymnastics, where these private entities will come forward and have teams," Meggyesy said, envisioning a scenario in which the social pecking order at American high schools is not driven by quarterbacks and their doting cheerleaders.

"There's a potential lawsuit out there that's devastating," the Steelers Hall of Fame quarterback Terry Bradshaw said on Fox's pregame show, the weekend after James Harrison threatened retirement. I know of two groups of lawyers preparing class-action suits, on behalf of recent players, against the N.F.L., with an eye toward filing in the first six months of this year. At issue is what the league knew and when, and, ultimately, what responsibility it has to its players, with a likely focus on the difference between two documents that were distributed in locker rooms as safety guidelines. The first, a pamphlet written in 2007, left open the question of whether "there are any long-term effects of concussion in N.F.L. athletes," while the second, a poster that was introduced before the start of this season, mentioned that "concussions and conditions resulting from repeated brain injury can change your life and your family's life forever." Trial lawyers, tort reform, the nanny state: this is no small part of football's future. 60

The N.F.L.'s idea of a "good football story," to judge from the Twitter feed of Greg Aiello, the league's spokesman, is one that calls attention to the uptick in passing touchdowns this year: more points, fewer hits. The league is nothing if not serious about its messaging. It was unhappy with the Toyota commercial that aired during "Monday Night Football," and urged the automaker to alter the spot. (Toyota complied, and excised a scene dramatizing a helmet-to-helmet collision.) Earlier this month, the league also issued warnings to several teams about midweek trash talking, of the "His days are numbered" variety. 61

Buzz Bissinger, who came away from his yearlong experience reporting "Friday Night Lights," in Odessa, Texas, in 1988, with a strong sense that the priorities of football culture were warped, 62 declared in his Daily Beast column that he had since changed his mind. "It may be time for the *Times* to move on," he wrote. "Violence is not only embedded in football; it is the very celebration of it. It is why we like it. Take it away, continue efforts to curtail the savagery, and the game will be nothing, regardless of age or skill." Tiki Barber, the former Giants running back, and a man who boasted, in his playing days, of listening to the BBC, voiced a surprisingly similar sentiment when I spoke with him last fall. "They can't try to do more," he said. "They can't afford to change what it is: an aggressively fast, physically brutal game." He added that he believes he will die with traces of C.T.E. in his brain tissue; he now views C.T.E. as "a necessary side effect of contact activity. . . . It's scary."

I'm not so convinced that violence fully explains football's popularity as a spectator sport, or that the language of war that suffuses the game (blitz, bomb, sack) is meaningfully connected any longer to actual, rather than notional, bloodlust. The game is more narrative than any other. It unfolds at a pace that is at once slow enough for us to unpack (we spend more time watching replays than watching the live action) and fast enough, in bursts, to rattle our nerves. Go to YouTube and search for "Austin Collie 3rd Concussion." Look at the faces of the fans, many of them with their hands instinctively covering their mouths, as medics attend to the felled Indianapolis Colts wide receiver. Those aren't expressions of morbid curiosity. They reflect a guilty fear that, one of these days, millions of us are going to watch a man die on the turf. 63

To my mind, the most exciting moment in this football season was not a demonstrative QB sack or a bruising, Ironhead-like run, or even a perfectly executed Hail Mary, but a punt return. The recipient of the punt was the Eagles' DeSean Jackson, one of the most flagrant victims of Black and Blue Sunday, and the victim, a year earlier, of a concussion that sidelined him for a week. There were fourteen seconds left on the clock in a tie game against the Giants, in December. That the Eagles were still in the game at all was an almost miraculous testament to the acrobatic exploits of their quarterback, Michael Vick, who had led them forward from a twenty-one-point deficit with only eight minutes left in the game. (Vick's season-long redemption after going to jail for promoting dogfighting was the uplifting counterweight to Concussiongate.) The Giants meant to kick the ball out of bounds, but somehow didn't. Jackson bobbled the ball at his own thirty-five-yard line, and you winced with instinctual worry; he is, at a hundred and seventy-five pounds, one of the smallest men in the N.F.L. The Giants' gunners—so named because their job is, in essence, to impersonate speeding bullets—were closing in. 64

Instead of falling on the ball—the safer option—Jackson picked it up, and quickly retreated to the thirty before turning to face upfield again, with a fraction of a second's worth of room to accelerate away from trouble. The first defender dived at his feet and missed. Then Jackson cut right. Another dive. Another miss. He found a seam running diagonally toward the sideline. Suddenly, as he hit the fifty, the field opened up in front of him. Could this really be happening? The only question now involved the clock: would he reach the end zone before it expired, thereby requiring his own team to kick back the other way for an encore? Jackson raised the ball in the air and began to slow down. Finally, just to make sure, he made a sharp left in front of the goal line and began running parallel to it, indulging the stalling maneuver for long enough so that it could no more be thought shrewd. This was hubris, of the sort that ends up getting a small man hurt. 65

It's all there in the replay: the exuberant Jackson hurling the ball twenty rows deep into the stands; the angry Giants coach, Tom Coughlin, throwing his headset in disgust and tearing into his dumbfounded rookie punter; the blocked tacklers lying on the field like fallen soldiers. Setting aside regional partisanship, you don't root for the man carrying the ball to be tackled at moments like this. You stop breathing and root for the near-miss. Averted danger is the essence of football. 66

But what if he'd been clobbered? And what if some of those blocked tacklers whom we laugh at are hearing bells and are too ashamed to admit it? 67

Examining the Text

1. Author McGrath opens this article with a lengthy discussion of a running back whom he saw as a child, and whose career he continued to follow as he moved through the college ranks, and finally into the NFL. For what thematic reason does McGrath begin this analytical article with such a lengthy description of a single football player who goes by the nickname of "Ironhead?" (Note: We include this question as a friendly reminder that, even in some of your most objective, analytical essays, it may be a good idea to draw the reader in with something that would pique their personal interest, such as a brief narrative, as the author does here.)

2. McGrath follows up the Ironhead narrative with the provocative statement that gets to the thematic heart of his article: "Was Ironhead a role model for a sport with no future?" He goes on to provide a brief history of historical attempts to confront the sometimes lethal physical dangers inherent in the game of football. Summarize the most salient examples of proposed changes to football, as enumerated by the author. What was the ultimate result of these attempts at "humanizing" the sport, in McGrath's view?

3. What is chronic traumatic encephalopathy, as related in this text? Briefly describe the physical characteristics of the condition, the reasons why a human being might suffer this condition, and the reasons why McGrath spends so much time talking about it in this article.

4. After some discussion of various football rules "fixes" currently being proposed, in addition to the historical ones proposed in question ones, McGrath mentions, "A race to collect cadaver brains is now under way." Toward what hopefully positive ends are researchers collecting and studying the brains of dead football players? What changes in the game could potentially emerge from such study, in the view of researchers?

5. *Thinking rhetorically*: What role does *Times* reporter Alan Schwarz play in the development of this article? What new information about potential physical effects of football did Schwarz bring to light in his writing? What effects have his investigations had on the current state of the sport, if any? What attitude and/or rhetorical position does McGrath reveal as he relates the history of Alan Schwartz? Does he seem to be siding with Schwarz as he proceeds with his investigations and allegations, or does he attempt to maintain a journalistic objectivity in relating this portion of the article?

For Group Discussion

Engage in a spirited in-class debate on concussions in football. On one side of the debate might be those who believe that football is no more dangerous than most contact sports, and who can cite evidence from this article to back up that contention. Proponents of this position might argue that a certain amount of risk is to be expected in sports, and that part of living a full and rich life is confronting (and usually surviving) such risk, which makes us stronger and more able to confront life off the field or outside the ring. At the polar opposite end of the opinion spectrum might be classmates who argue that there are plenty of sports that do not entail significant, sometimes life-threatening physical risk, such as tennis and swimming, and that the more violent sports should either be outlawed, or at least regulated much more stringently in a society that calls itself civilized. As this discussion winds down, attempt to arrive at some tentative agreement regarding what might be done about the problems McGrath raises in this article: a consensual middle ground that most of the class members can accept.

Writing Suggestion

Toward the end of this article, McGrath reports, "In fact, reading the Concussion Blog exposes you to a steady drip of news that is not so good for your anterior insula. . . . Rugby, lacrosse, baseball: concussions are seemingly epidemic everywhere. The problem with having access to better information about the risks we all take is that most leisure pursuits start to seem inherently irresponsible. What are we to do about skiing, bicycling, sledding?" McGrath goes on to mention a number of other sports that are concussion-prone. Using McGrath's article as a model, write a research essay about the physical dangers inherent in a sport other than football. You may choose a sport from those listed by McGrath in this article, or you might choose another one with which you have more familiarity and/or interest, such as skateboarding or tae kwon do. Whatever sport you choose, make sure to provide a thorough discussion of the sport's physical injury potential, historical attempts to make the sport safer, the current state of safety in the sport, any current controversies raging in the mainstream news and the blogosphere regarding safety-related issues concerning this sport, and some conclusions about what concrete steps to take to improve the safety of the sport—if any such "fixes" are feasible and practicable.

The Unbeautiful Game

ADAM GOPNIK

A student journalist for a Tennessee college newspaper recently posted an article with the provocative title, "What's Wrong with the NFL?" In it, the writer pointed to the transgressions of a number of players—from Michael Vick's dog-fighting scandal to "Tank" Johnson's firearms convictions—and went on to conjecture about the reasons why many pro footballers have become so degraded. The college reporter concluded that salaries were to blame: some players have contracts of over one hundred and fifty million dollars, which in their minds gives them license to behave in increasingly outrageous ways, while other players misbehave out of a deep resentment because they are working just as hard as—or harder than—the multi-millionaire players but are earning the league minimum salary. The following article, from the New Yorker *magazine, draws similar conclusions about the relationship between money and the degradation of pro football but takes the college newspaper posting several steps further. Gopnik examines the ways in which football has become "unbeautiful," but does so from the point of view of spectators and fans. Using a game between the New York Jets and the Houston Texans as a backdrop, Gopnik observes that the attitude of those who watch pro football has soured in recent years. To support this contention, he analyzes his own experience and also reviews a number of books that have been written about pro football in the past several decades, including John Feinstein's* Next Man Up: A Year Behind the Lines In Today's NFL, *and* Moving the Chains: Tom Brady and the Pursuit of Everything *by Charles P. Pierce, along with several others.*

As you read, *notice the way in which the author interweaves his present experience watching the Jets game, his reflections on his experience as a fan, and his reportage on the books he brings in as evidence. Because this is an example of magazine journalism and not a piece of academic research, the author can synthesize a number of secondary sources without having to employ citation conventions such as the MLA and APA styles. Furthermore, he can bring in his personal experience to a degree that one rarely sees* *in academic research papers. Nevertheless, the author brings to bear on his subject a wealth of analysis, critical thinking, and organizational skill in developing his thematic points about the ways in which football has changed, and, ultimately, the ways that watching football still provides meaning for its millions of fans.*

Joe Namath is late. Promised for a twelve-thirty press "availability" in the lounge of the press box at Giants Stadium, in East Rutherford, New Jersey—that vital place where the fulcrum of the First Amendment, free food, is celebrated by reporters for hours on end every Sunday morning when the Giants or the Jets are in town—Namath finally wanders into the noiseless, sealed-glass press box around one-fifteen, when the Jets' game against the Houston Texans is already under way. The crowd in the press box has to decide whether to stick with the dullish game or go out and meet the greatest superstar (O.K., the only superstar) this hexed team has ever produced. A small line of reporters hisses out of the press box toward the lounge, like helium leaking from a balloon. 1

The tiny, intent circle gathers around Namath, who, at sixty-three, has aged into a cartoon version of his younger self. His schnoz, always notable, has become more so; he now looks weirdly like Joe Pepitone, that other, lesser New York swinger of the sixties. His salt-and-pepper hair is swept back, his face, after years in Florida, is leathery, and he wears oversized chestnut-tinted sunglasses, right out of a disco movie. His slouch has become a full question mark of a slump, but his genial, barracuda smile is intact, as are the elaborate schoolboy manners that lead him to refer to the men who mentored him by both their names and their nicknames. "I think that, after my family, Coach Paul 'Bear' Bryant was the biggest influence on me," he says, or, "I think the credit for creating that image"—of the quarterback as playboy—"has to go to Sonny Werblin. I mean, David A. 'Sonny' Werblin." 2

Joe talks for a bit about his new autobiography, one of two he has published. ("I certainly had help with it, but I wrote most of it myself this time.") But the reporters are looking elsewhere. 3

"What do you think of Eli?" one asks. 4

"Well, I think Eli has everything going for him except maybe his facial expressions and the way he carries himself, " Namath jokes. (Eli Manning, the Giants' talented, inconsistent quarterback, has an unfortunate wide-eyed, golly-gee look for all occasions, like Opie, on the old Andy Griffith show, if he were to see Floyd the barber in a Halloween mask.) 5

"You don't think he has a leadership look?" the reporter says, leaning in eagerly. 6

"Now, I didn't say that." Namath laughs, seeing the approaching headline clearly and ducking it. "I think he's got all the talent—I just said maybe people misinterpret the way he looks." 7

I've been a Jets fan for forty years, and it's hard for me to believe this full hand of good fortune. Namath, beyond reason or even the bonds of fandom, got me through some bitter bits of my mixed-up adolescence. I loved him, we all loved him, not just for his famous upset win in Super Bowl III but for his slouch and his white shoes and his quick release—that upper body torquing around to shoot the ball out to George Sauer, Jr., never needing to have the back foot planted—and for the mildly Homeric drama of his career. Crippled early in his football life by bad knees of a kind the surgeons just don't make anymore, he would disappear for half a season, reappear to throw for four hundred yards and four or five touchdowns, and then disappear again into a welter of missed games and interceptions. As with Bobby Orr, his great on-ice contemporary, his fragility was part of his resonance. 8

Someone asks Namath if he believes that Chad Pennington is in a slump. Pennington, the Jets' current and gallant incumbent, is recovering from two shoulder surgeries and has had a couple of off games. Namath is suddenly intent. "No, he's a good quarterback," he says seriously. "I've only watched him this year as a fan, on television. I haven't had a chance to break down the passing game to see if Chad's going to the right spots or going to the wrong receiver." You sense that the distinction the old quarterback is making—between watching as a fan and actually watching—is, for him, larger than he can quite explain. It isn't just that he hasn't watched as attentively as he might have; watching "as a fan, on television," means that he hasn't really watched at all. 9

Pennington, it turns out, after everyone has traipsed back to the warm silence of the press box, is breaking out of his slump, courtesy of the slow-footed Houston secondary. Pennington throws—well, not strikes, exactly, but something like special-delivery messages, rising up on his toes to send them spinning nicely, dartlike, into his receivers' arms. The Jets pull out to a twenty-point lead. 10

Yet, astonishing as that is, what is really astonishing is to be reminded again of how different this game looks depending on where you see it from, on where you're standing (or sitting) while you watch it. When you watch a pro football game from the Crimean War general's viewpoint of the press box, you can see what's going to happen. On television, the quarterback peers out into the distance within the narrowed frame of the midfield camera and for a moment everything seems possible; the viewer can't know if there's a 11 wide-open man fifty yards deep or if there is nothing ahead of Pennington but despair—four men crowding two receivers, who aren't even bothering to wave their arms. The drama of the game on TV lies in finding out.

On the field, the quarterback backpedals, rolls right and takes a look, and what is available—or not—is, within half a second, pitifully evident. If you're watching live, Namath's point comes home; on television you see free will instead of a series of forced choices, mostly bad. The quarterback, the gallant general, peering out, in command, becomes, in reality, a stitch in the pattern already woven, his fate nearly sealed before he gets to fiddle with it. (Which is why coaches always refer to heroic quarterbacks as though they were mere middle-management executives, making "good" and "bad" decisions in the pocket.) 12

The real excitement of the game on the field lies in the sudden moments of frenzied improvisation, most often by the linebackers and especially by the safeties, who on television mainly appear at the end of the play to make a hit or swipe vainly at a pass. The Jets' safety Kerry Rhodes, for instance, whose excellence is much cited but mostly invisible to one at home in front of the set, becomes the most entertaining player to watch—racing the width of the field to cover an open receiver, running like a man chasing his hat as it blows down the street on a windy day, not running in tandem but running to get there, before it's gone. Now, on a routine pass, Pennington is brought down hard, and writhes on the ground in agony. The entire stadium goes silent. But then he is bouncing up again, ready to go, and pumping his fists to excite the crowd. 13

After the game, which the Jets hold on to win, 26–11, there is relief in the locker room; Pennington is fine. The players, naked and seminaked, hold forth on the game, a ritual that we normalize (gotta beat those deadlines) but in which any half-awake anthropologist would spot something significant: the reporters being put in their place by the players' sheer physicality, and the players being put in their place by the reporters' being able to enforce their availability. Pete Kendall, the Jets' left guard, is talking about Pennington's near-miss. "Let's say, he was intently verbalizing," he says, sumo wrestler's body jiggling and eyes ever so slightly alert. "Did I see it? No, I had no idea what was happening. That's good for an offensive lineman. If you can watch what's happening to your quarterback, you're not doing your job." He smiles, tightly and pointedly, and goes back to putting on his pants. 14

All sports change depending on your point of view, but perhaps none change so much as pro football. There is the familiar Sunday-afternoon television—quarterback-centered, replete with instant replays, each play a brief drama of courage and determination, a family entertainment, the original reality television. There is the actual 15 game, seen on the field, where the offensive and defensive lines meet in a pit that is a kind of black hole of heaving, battling bodies—who knows exactly what's going on in there. Rumors of fingers broken and eyes gouged come back, and it is hard not to believe them. (In his new book about football, *The Blind Side*, Michael Lewis explains that one of the most famous images in football memory—Lawrence Taylor's wild gesturing for help after breaking Joe Theismann's leg in two places—came about less from L.T.'s unexpected empathy for a stricken colleague than from his fear of getting caught in the pileup himself.) And there is the game as it has been presented, magnificently, by Ed Sabol and his family at N.F.L. Films, all caped Darth Vader-ish heroes, steam rising from mouths in the Green Bay winter; dramatic orchestral music and slow-motion long passes arcing lazily over and over in the midafternoon sky before they come racing to earth in someone's outstretched, praying hands. (A moment that in the stadium would just whiz by, unmusically.)

This makes pro football the original silly putty of the big media, 16 reshaped each year to entice an ever-larger audience—and at the same time sporadically mysterious, alluring, a weird mixture of violence, showman's calculation, and some kind of intense, medieval-tournament-like heraldry (those capes! those helmets! those cheerleaders!) and gallantry. Even when you try to be hardheaded about the game, some bit of color springs out. Alan Yost, a meat-and-potatoes financial journalist who writes most often for the *Wall Street Journal*, points out, in his new book about the finances of the sport, *Tailgating, Sacks and Salary Caps*, and with magical correctness, that the success of "Monday Night Football" derived in part from its lighting: all those shadowless fields and gleaming helmets. But when you try to be romantic about pro football its reality comes back: the snapping sound of Theismann's fibula, the nearly parodic corporatism that infects the game. The N.F.L. actually employs a special squad of sidelines watchers—"clothes Nazis," the players call them—to be sure that no coach ever strays from wearing officially sanctioned merchandise, right down to the skin, at game time. (Coaches can no longer wear a suit on the sidelines.)

Anything this self-consciously dressed up is asking to be 17 dressed down. And there was a time when pro football, seen from inside the locker room, offered the material for a kind of affable, blue-collar comedy, as an alternative to the nostalgic pieties of baseball and the urban realism that seems to halo basketball. It played the same role that its daddy sport, rugby, still plays throughout the world: the funny, dirty one. George Plimpton's 1966 *Paper Lion* and its even better sequel, *Mad Ducks and Bears*, like Dan Jenkins's roughly contemporary novel *Semi-Tough*, are not just funny. They are about being funny, about the N.F.L. as a place where one is able to be funny. It's the laughter and the conversation, Plimpton explains to a baffled friend at one point about his love for the company of pro football players.

There's no laughter now. John Feinstein's new book on Brian Billick and the Baltimore Ravens, *Next Man Up: A Year Behind the Lines in Today's NFL*, employs the same premise as the best of all books about pro football, Roy Blount, Jr.'s *About Three Bricks Shy of a Load*, an account of the 1973 season of the young Pittsburgh Steelers, the year after the Immaculate Reception game but before they won a Super Bowl. Feinstein takes the Ravens and their 2004 season as his subject, and the cast of characters is remarkably similar. There's an oppressed proletariat of special-teams players, a hard-pressed and overpaid first-round-draft-pick quarterback (Terry Bradshaw in Blount, Kyle Boller in Feinstein), a bunch of struggling linemen, and a tight-lipped, humorless, defensive-minded coach (Chuck Noll for the Steelers). 18

Blount's account of a year within an N.F.L. team thirty years ago was essentially festive and high-spirited; Feinstein's is unrelievedly gloomy, tense, and depressing. "Next Man Up" refers to the cavalier cry of the coaches when yet another player goes down with a severe injury, and his tales are all of players belittled, bruised, and generally beleaguered, hoping to hang on long enough—five years is the run-up time to free agency these days—for a major payday. (And the paydays are major; twenty-five- and forty-million-dollar contracts come and go in his pages.) In part, of course, this difference in tone reflects a difference in taste. Blount saw what he wanted to see and didn't see what he didn't want to see; there are no prizes on Parnassus for fair play. By his own account, he missed the fact that "Jefferson Street" Joe Gilliam, the Steelers' third-string quarterback, was not a free spirit but a heroin addict, and that the Steelers, at least by retrospective legend, were pioneers in steroid abuse. Feinstein, on the other hand, sees what a diligent, intelligent, yet mainly humorless reporter is likely to see: a tangle of ambitions, injuries, and extremely short career expectancies, interrupted by sudden onsets of very big money. The closest thing to a hero in Feinstein's book is the offensive coordinator, Matt Cavanaugh, who, we know from almost the first page, is going to be fired at the end of the season for failing to do enough for the Ravens' offense, not that there is much he could have done. Cavanaugh is a sympathetic and unostentatious man, and, knowing his fate as we do, we wince with Feinstein every time this decent guy comes onstage to get kicked around one more time by the radio talk-show hosts and the owner and the other coaches. 19

It doesn't sound like fun, you figure out in the end, because it isn't fun. Where it seemed natural for Blount to identify with the players, and be warily sympathetic to the coach, Feinstein identifies with 20 the owner and the coaches and is warily sympathetic to the players. He empathizes with them sufficiently to defend, at length, the linebacker Ray Lewis from the charge of murder, during a melee in Atlanta after the 2000 Superbowl, when in fact he was no more than a reluctant witness, but it's obvious that the culture of the players is alien to him, as it would be to most outsiders. The atmosphere is closed, guarded, and immensely knowing about the media; the artless charm with which Bradshaw or Dwight White confided in Blount would just not be possible now. With the best will in the world, there is very little you can squeeze out of the players that has not been pasteurized first by the agents and the league and the players' entourage, and by the players' understanding, essentially true, that the reporter is on nobody's side but his own. "Hang-around time," the old journalists' and sportswriters' favorite, is rarely part of the game now.

It is the owners, curiously, who are more eager to have their struggles and dramas narrated. Feinstein has the obnoxious Redskins' owner, Dan Snyder, drop into the narrative from time to time like Snidely Whiplash, to sneer and roll his mustache, while the Ravens' owner, Steve Bisciotti, who let Feinstein into the locker room, is very nearly made the hero of the book. Though Bisciotti does seem like a more levelheaded man than most N.F.L. owners, at one moment Feinstein relates a ritual and needless bit of humiliation that Bisciotti inflicted on Billick, shortly after he became the sole owner of the team. "You have some bad habits," he says to him. "For example, you always address me as 'young man' when you see me, and my wife as 'young lady.' . . . I'm about to become the owner of this team—your boss—and you greet me the same way you greet some kid coming up to you for an autograph. That's disrespectful." The insolence of wealth will creep out, as Dr. Johnson said. 21

The sour tone of so much of Feinstein's book isn't peculiar to Feinstein. Charles P. Pierce, a Boston sportswriter, who has the tools to pull a Blount, and the desire to do it, too, has written his own year-long, hang-around account, this one about the Patriots and their star quarterback, Tom Brady—*Moving the Chains: Tom Brady and the Pursuit of Everything*—but his book, though better written, isn't much more fun than Feinstein's, mostly because Pierce has to write around his hero rather than through him. Brady is no Alex Karras. "I always figured that being a little dull was part of being a pro," Johnny Unitas is quoted as saying (in a new biography, *Johnny U.*, by the former *Time* sportswriter Tom Callahan). "Win or lose, I never walked off a professional football field without first thinking of something boring to say." Brady resembles Unitas in this as in so much else. At one point, Pierce actually has to admit, "What Brady said reads more banal than it sounded at the time." The Patriots' coach, Bill Belichick, meanwhile, 22 is so buttoned-up and close-mouthed that he makes both Chuck Noll and Brian Billick sound like Shecky Greene. (Belichick on Brady: "He does a lot of things well. He makes a lot of good plays. He makes a lot of good throws.")

23 Even books not precisely about the N.F.L. but about the path to getting there have something strained and unhappy in them. In *The Blind Side*, Michael Lewis, an expert storyteller, can stop telling stories long enough to make a case for a complicated point in a convincing way, and one of the points he is making here is about the narrowed focus that football demands. His protagonist, a poor black kid named Michael Oher, is discovered to have "ideal" left-tackle potential, and he's taken in by an evangelical family who help nurture him—the story is basically *Gigi* without Louis Jourdan or the song: "Thank Heaven for Very Big Boys." But where, for this football-loving reader, Lewis's baseball book was enlivening and cheering, his football book—about the making of a behemoth who may or may not get to the N.F.L.—is oddly sad. (The story of Gigi, who probably wouldn't have made starting courtesan, either, is a pretty sad one, too.)

24 Partly what drains the joy from the inner game of pro football these days is the same as what drains the joy from much of American life: there's a lot of money to be made by a few people, and a lot less for everybody else. The money in pro football comes in two flavors: more than you can imagine and less than you might think. The base pay for players is much higher, of course, than it is in the real world—the minimum for a rookie is almost three hundred thousand dollars—but the disproportion is real, too, and though the players maybe ought to be grateful for having as much as they do, like the rest of us they can't help being resentful for not having as much as they might. For every Chris McAlister, a shut-down cornerback making eight million a year, there is a Mike Solwold, a long snapper who after three seasons in the N.F.L. has already been cut or waived six times by four teams, and who has the bad luck in the Ravens camp to recover from an injury before he gets cut. (If he had still been injured, the Ravens would have had to pay him compensation.)

25 Feinstein reminds the reader that this here-today, gone-tomorrow rule is part of life in the N.F.L.; there is no, or very little, "guaranteed" money in pro football—the players work, and can be fired, "at will"—and, while a few upper-crust performers get to keep their signing bonus, most players are a snapped knee ligament away from street clothes. (Pierce reports that seventy-eight per cent of N.F.L. players are unemployed, bankrupt, or divorced within two years of leaving the game, and those are the guys who make it.) Billick says grimly, about cutting players, "Whenever I have to make these cuts, I always think about what Clint Eastwood said in *Unforgiven*: 'When you kill a man,

you not only are ending his life, you're taking away everything he ever had or is going to have.'" The unhappiness that you feel among the players in all these books is hardly the misery of the oppressed, but it is something more familiar these days, the rancor of the near-miss. Why them and not us? is a radical question. Why the guy at the next locker and not me? a bitter one.

26 One way of dealing with the difference between the players and their experience—and, occasionally, their income—and everyone else's is to advance into a world of abstract manipulation where the players are best appreciated as lines of numbers or as groupings of pixels. The kids do it through Electronic Arts Sports and its video games, where they make up their own teams and even their own players, and have as much allegiance to the dancing dots as we did to Joe Namath and Matt Snell. The grownups achieve the same effect, deep participation at a precarious distance, by becoming obsessed with the statistical analysis of sports. It is no accident, probably, that, as baseball salaries get bigger, a good deal of baseball writing has become more decorously removed from actual baseball into the numbers world (although Bill James, who started it all, has moved at last into management).

27 Pro football, however, has traditionally resisted statistical analysis. Again and again, someone, like the fine sportswriter Allen Barra, has tried to match Bill James and write a football abstract, and, again and again, the enterprise has failed. One might think that the betting interest in pro football—which Yost estimates at more than a billion dollars per season—would lead to an ever more avid appetite for numbers, but the kind of analysis that Barra et al. are able to do is, although powerfully suggestive, weakly predictive. Football analysis is trickier than the baseball kind because football really is a team sport: every baseball act is colored by the context in which it takes place—the stadium and the situation—but football acts are the context in which they take place. A running back whose team wins every time he runs for a hundred yards is almost certainly busy running out the clock in the second half; he runs for a hundred yards because his team has already won. Unlike in baseball, all eleven guys on the field are involved in every play, and who deserves the credit or blame is harder to know than it looks.

28 Now, though, intricate analysis seems to have come to pro football, through the good offices of the Internet and its capacity for the micro-niche, and the Web site Footballoutsiders has thrown off a book, the annual *Pro Football Prospectus*, which is apparently catching on. Football analysis has triumphed by combining the kind of detached statistical crunching that James pioneered with close amateur breakdowns of Namath's "films." The two things taken together—the actual visual pattern of each play and the numerical representation of it—enable one to

escape the contexts and "grade" the individual acts of the ballplayers to get a sense of who is doing what how well on every play.

The point of statistical analysis has never been to crunch numbers but to challenge the conventional wisdom about how teams win and lose, and the football analysts are doing that now. Their conviction (much simplified) is that in the N.F.L. you pass to win and run to sustain a victory—though the average running play nets four yards, the median nets only three—and that most of the more conservative, hard-nosed football strategies, like the one-run, bunt-and-sacrifice strategies in baseball, look canny and play dumb. There is even a strong, heretical movement under way against automatically punting on fourth down. (The irony of sophisticated analysis is that, while it tends to run counter to what the shouting heads on television pontificate about, it tends, ultimately, to go along with what the ignorant fans in the stands are screaming for: swing for the fences, go for it on fourth, etc.) 29

People within the game, though, still talk about brute physical effort, and how much it matters. The two-yard runs, after all, are being played not in a video game but in a real world where the energy and will to get beaten up is a capital sum reduced by expenditure; those two-yard runs expend it. So the closeup view, emphasizing physical domination, isn't necessarily false, though it may be badly argued. The insiders may miss the pattern and still get the point. (Bill James himself has said—half as a joke, but only half—that he thought what brought the Red Sox back in 2004 was "veteran leadership." In the pure world of analysis, veteran leadership was long thought to be an explanatory principle on a par with water sprites and the rotation of the zodiac.) 30

As our efforts to explain and predict are baffled, we retreat into pure pleasure. Then the question becomes: Enjoy what, how? Fortunately, a new book helps lead us back to becoming the armchair aesthetes we were all along. *In Praise of Athletic Beauty*, by Hans Ulrich Gumbrecht, who is a professor of comp lit at Stanford, is the book, and football the central game. Much of the book sounds like the kind of guide to the aesthetic of sports that would be written by someone named Hans Ulrich Gumbrecht; long passages improve by being read in a light German accent. "Looking at empty stadiums," he remarks of his love of Stanford Stadium, "I suspect that stadiums 'stage' or 'make present' what Martin Heidegger once identified as the most elementary philosophical question: why there is something at all, opposed to nothing? On many levels and in multiple settings stadiums materialize, and make us part of, this ultimate ontological contrast." 31

Nonetheless, Gumbrecht really is a fan, and he is trying to make sense of a fan's experience. Instead of focussing on the easy cases—everybody can admire divers and gymnasts and the lacier 32 kind of ice skaters—he takes for his subject the aesthetic of ballgames, which, he points out, began to become central to Western life as spectator sports only a century ago. His central thesis, to round it out a little crudely, is that we watch sports not out of identification with the players but out of a kind of happy absorption in someone else's ability: "The euphoria of focused intensity seems to go hand in hand with a peculiar quietness. I am at peace with the impression that I cannot control and manipulate the world around me. So intensely quiet do I become and so quietly confident, at least during the seconds when my favorite football team is talking through its next play in the huddle, that I feel I can let go and let come (or not) the things that I desire to come."

In other words, when we watch Joe Namath or Chad Pennington or even Eli complete a pass what we feel isn't pathetic and vicarious but generous and authentic: we give up a bit of ourselves in order to admire another. We're broadened, not narrowed, by our fandom. Our connection with our heroes is through an act of imagination, and the act of imagination, not the connection, is what is worth savoring and saving. (Stephen Dubner, before he struck gold with *Freakonomics*, wrote a book about going in search of the Steelers' star runner Franco Harris that made exactly this point; so did Frederick Exley's *A Fan's Notes*, for that matter, where the narrator's obsession with Frank Gifford helped him discover himself.) 33

These sentiments are what our grandfathers would have called noble and manly, and certainly have something to do with what makes us fans, whether the kind who tailgate in the cold or the kind who compile stats in the overheated apartment. But is it possible to divorce, or elevate, our aesthetic and imaginative interest so entirely from our tribal and rooting interest? We can't be aesthetes without also being fans. Even in the press box, many of us aren't really football fans; at least some of the time we're Jets fans or Giants fans or Seahawks fans, and the connection between the team's fate and the fan's fate isn't quite so beautifully disinterested as the formula suggests. My ideal game is not one in which the Jets and the Patriots are engaged in a sterling contest where Pennington and Brady trade coups and the final score is determined in overtime by an inspired play. It's one in which the Jets pull ahead, 35–0, in the first quarter and then coast to victory on a muddy field, as Brady slips and falls. This may be many things, some of them forgivable, but generous and broadening it isn't. 34

What makes the bald rooting interest forgivable, maybe, is the near-certainty that the ideal game is never, or almost never, going to happen. The essential experience of watching sports is experiencing loss; anyone who has consoled a twelve-year-old after a Jets loss, or been a twelve-year-old in need of consolation, knows this. Since loss and disappointment are the only fixed points in life, maybe the best we can say is that pro football, like anything else we like to watch, gives us 35 a chance to organize those emotions into a pattern, a season, while occasionally giving us the hope of something more. The Jets don't always lose—just nearly always. When they do better, we feel better. That's the margin, or sideline, on which we live.

Examining the Text

1. This article begins with a long description of an encounter with professional football legend Joe Namath, and this encounter leads to the author's expressing a significant thematic point regarding the difference between watching football live versus on television. In what ways do the two viewing experiences differ, in Gopnik's opinion?

2. The author of this article calls pro football "the original silly putty of the big media." How does this image of a children's toy—a flesh-colored silicone plastic blob that can be molded into a variety of shapes and lift newsprint off a sheet of paper—relate to the venerable American game of football, in Gopnik's view?

3. One of the subthemes of this article is that the image of football has changed over time. In a previous era, notes the author, football carried a connotation of being a somewhat quirky alternative to other sports. How does the author describe football's former identity in this article, and how has that identity changed, in his opinion?

4. Toward the end of this article, Gopnik provides some reasons why statistical analysis of professional football games is a less than satisfying pursuit—unlike baseball, which provides a wealth of enjoyable material for "stats geeks." However, the author ends this article on an upbeat note, positing a point of view that explains the real "beauty" in watching a variety of sporting activities, including football. On whose writing does he base this exaltation of sports fandom, and what are the specific propositions of this viewpoint?

5. *Thinking rhetorically:* This article's author contends that football in contemporary America is, on balance, "less fun"—and correspondingly more "unbeautiful"—than it was in previous eras. Examining the techniques with which he develops this persuasive position, what sorts of evidence does Gopnik provide to support this key thematic point? How does this mass of evidence add up to a convincing explanation for the decline in professional football's fun quotient?

For Group Discussion

Gopnik concludes this article by proposing that an essential experience sports fandom is "experiencing loss." In this he seems to echo the Buddhist notion that every human life includes a certain experience of sickness, loss, and ultimately death—his point being that being a sports fan give one practice in coping with these issues. Says, Gopnik, "Since loss and disappointment are the only fixed points in life, maybe the best we can say is that pro football, like anything else we like to watch, gives us a chance to organize those emotions into a pattern, a season, while occasionally giving us the hope of something more." Discuss your own experience as a sports fan: what affective (i.e. emotional, psychological, and even spiritual) functions has being aligned with a certain team provided for you?

Writing Suggestion

In your experience in grammar through high school, you undoubtedly had the wonderful opportunity to write one, if not literally hundreds of book reports: short documents in which you proved to your teacher that you actually read a certain text, by summarizing the contents of the book and perhaps doing some rudimentary analysis as well. This article by Adam Gopnik might be seen as a kind of glorified—or at least extended—book report, in that he folds into his discussion a description of several books, all of them dealing with sports fandom generally, and professional football specifically. However, he goes *way* beyond your typical middle school book report, because he summarizes and analyzes these texts in service of a larger purpose: namely, to understand historical changes in professional football, and to arrive at some conclusions about emotional rewards and challenges of watching sports. This assignment asks you to undertake a similar task: in a piece of writing that transcends the traditional book report, choose and develop a sport-related topic and find several texts to help you explore and develop that hypothesis. Since you probably won't have time to read a wheelbarrow full of books, feel free to find shorter texts on the Web and through electronic journals on library databases. In some ways your writing will resemble an academic research essay, in that it will synthesize secondary sources; however, unlike an academic research paper, though, this synthesis will appear more informal and journalistic, and might incorporate more elements of personal experience, as Gopnik does. Also, you are excused from using MLA or APA documentation formats for the purposes of this assignment, although you will still, of course, need to identify and attribute your sources rigorously, as Gopnik does.

ADDITIONAL SUGGESTIONS FOR WRITING ABOUT SPORTS

1. Using Maya Angelou's "Champion of the World" as a model, write a narrative in which you tell of a past experience with sports, either as a spectator or as a participant, that had a significant effect on your life. Perhaps this experience revealed something about yourself that you didn't realize, helped you better understand someone else, taught you an important lesson, or corrected a misconception that you had. Or perhaps you're not certain what effect the experience had, and can use this assignment to speculate on its significance.

2. Attend a local sporting event, and bring a notebook and, if possible, a tape recorder or video camera. Observe and take notes about how the people

around you behave, what they do and say, what they wear, how they relate to one another, what interests or bores them, when they seem satisfied or disappointed. Note also how their behavior is different from what it would likely be in other contexts. Try to be an impartial observer, simply recording what you see in as much detail as possible. From your notes, write an extended description of one or several typical spectators, and then draw some conclusions about why people enjoy watching sports. You may also want to discuss the psychological benefits and/or harm that being a spectator might cause.

3. Choose a sport or a game with which you're very familiar, either because you play it or watch it regularly. Reflect on your experience playing or watching this sport/game, and write down some of your recollections. Think about what you've learned from this activity, and how it has affected other areas of your life. Next, write an essay in which you show how this particular sport has influenced your beliefs, attitudes, and values. Be as specific as possible and try to show precisely how and why the sport/game has influenced you.

4. Many of the writers in this chapter discuss the impact of professional sports on individuals and on society as a whole. Referring to essays in this chapter, construct your own argument about the influence of professional sports. As a prewriting exercise, make lists of the beneficial and the detrimental influences of professional sports on our society. Try to come up with specific examples to illustrate each of the items on your lists. Working from those lists, develop a persuasive argument about the influence of sports on our society.

Internet Activities

1. Professional athletes are often role models in our society. As a prewriting exercise for this assignment, list some of the reasons why this is so, especially for young people. Also list the ways in which athletes might be good role models, as well as some of the reasons other professionals (for example, teachers or government leaders) might actually be better role models.

Next, visit the links to information about professional athletes, provided at the *Common Culture* Web site, to official and unofficial homepages of individual athletes. After browsing through these links, choose an athlete who you think is either a good or a bad role model. Do further research on this athlete, looking up interviews and articles about him or her in the library. From this information, write a brief biography of the athlete, focusing on the kind of role model he or she is.

2. Professional sports teams are in the business of making money, and the World Wide Web is increasingly becoming a venue for advertising and marketing. It's no surprise, then, that all of the major professional sports teams now have their own Web sites. Go to the *Common Culture* Web site for links that you can follow to visit the homepages of professional teams in baseball, football, men's basketball, women's basketball, and hockey. Choose a Web site for one team and read the site carefully and completely. Make a list

of the information that the site offers, including statistics, pictures, news and "inside information," schedules, and so on. Then analyze the ways in which the information offered at the site is intended to promote or "sell" the team. Is the site addressed to current fans of the team, or is it intended to cultivate new fans? How effectively do you believe the Web site is in advertising and marketing the team it represents?

Reading Images

The high school student shown in the photo on page CI-7 is enjoying a moment of unbridled exuberance after scoring a touchdown. Football players at all levels of accomplishment report there is no greater feeling than scoring a goal—especially the winning touchdown, but *any* touchdown will do. In so doing, it's natural to express one's joy of accomplishment with a bit of what the cartoon character Snoopy used to call "happy feet." Over the years, dancing in the end zone after a touchdown became more and more elaborate, especially at the pro ranks, where some players devised elaborate ritual dances involving choreographed hip-hop moves, crowd dives, and goalpost slam dunks. In fact, such displays in recent years became so prevalent, extravagant, and time-consuming that the NFL, in an attempt to restrict celebrations severely, actually changed the rules of the game in 2006 to include a mandatory fifteen-yard penalty against any player who jumps for joy or uses a prop such as a towel or a football to engage in this kind of display. The penalty has come to be known commonly as "excessive celebration."

Write an essay in which you "read" the images of the celebrating boy in this text. Google the phrase "touchdown celebration," to see other images and read about other instances of "excessive celebration." Your goal in retrieving this material will be to uncover and discuss the sociocultural messages they contain. Look carefully at all elements of the graphics. Discuss possible meanings implicit in the colors and the central images of the players involved. However, don't be content merely to focus on the central images: study the background "negative space" as well, to ascertain how the entire composition combines to create meaning. Note also the juxtaposition of image and text, along with messages contained in the text itself. The central question you should be asking yourself is whether this display seem truly excessive, or if the NFL being excessively restrictive in its recently enacted policy.

If you wish, you may take this discussion a step further by addressing a central issue raised by the pictures: namely, the unnecessary taming of sport. Some longtime fans and commentators believe that sports are tainted by excessive rules. They might therefore point to the rules against excessive celebration and charge that by condemning this pure moment of sport-centered bliss, the spirit of competition is reduced in its emotional impact and mass appeal. Consider this idea, examining your own feelings about the pros and cons of ritualistic exuberance in football and other sports, and then develop a thesis that takes a persuasive stance with regard to this issue.

7 Movies

It's Friday night. You park in an exhaust-filled subterranean garage or a vast asphalt lot surrounding a mall. You make your way into the neon-lit megaplex, where you and a companion or two pay half a day's salary for tickets, an industrial-size bucket of popcorn, and a couple of ten-gallon sodas. You wind your way through a maze of corridors to the theater of your choice, where a psychedelic montage filling the screen is soon replaced by the first of an interminable series of quick-cutting previews, as you bathe in rolling quadraphonic surround sound. You sink into your space-age stadium plastic seat and kick back, surrendering to the waves of sound and images. . . .

Such is moviegoing in the new millennium. Gone are the nickel matinee and the discount double feature, newsreels, cartoons, and comic short subjects, and the drive-in, where many a pair of teenagers learned human anatomy in the back seat of a Chevy.

The external trappings of the moviegoing experience may have changed, but the reasons people go are still pretty much the same: to get out of the house and escape the routine of their daily lives; to be part of a communal group sharing an experience; to find a romantic setting where conversation is at a minimum; to indulge, for one night, in an orgy of junk food; and, above all, to be entertained and, perhaps, touched emotionally. So strong is the draw of motion pictures that Americans fork over billions of dollars a year on domestic movies alone, despite the increasing availability of home entertainment through DVD rental services such as Netflix.

As there are many reasons for going to the movies, so there are many ways of explaining their popularity and studying their influence within the fabric of contemporary culture. From a sociological perspective, movies can reflect, define, or even redefine social norms, and—in the work of politically focused filmmakers such as Michael Moore—depict urgent social problems within the relative safety of the big screen. From a psychological perspective, viewers identify with the character and project their own feelings into the action, giving them a deep emotional connection to a protagonist along with feelings of tension and, ultimately release. From a literary perspective, movies can be interpreted in terms of genres—horror movies, or crime dramas, or menaced-female stories—or in terms of plot, characterization, imagery, and so forth. From an economic perspective, movies may be seen primarily as a consumable product, defined solely by the marketplace. To the cultural critic, this economic influence might seem to be negative, reducing a potentially powerful artistic form to the lowest common denominator. The capitalist observer might see such forces as positive, however, because they encourage the worldwide spread of American cultural values. Finally, from a semiological perspective, movies are ripe with symbolic imagery, from the multiple associations possible in a character's name to the way images are juxtaposed in the editing.

This chapter introduces film criticism arising from several of these views. The first readings focus on the social impacts and implications of film. The second part of this chapter looks closely at two moviemakers who have had a tremendous impact not only on the film scene, but on modern culture as well. The first, Judd Apatow, gained critical acclaim through his short-lived television series *Freaks and Geeks,* and went on to produce some of the most popular comedies of our time, including *The 40-Year-Old Virgin, Knocked Up,* and *Superbad,* all of which reflect to a high degree the preoccupations of Americans in this unique period in history. The second contemporary filmmaker, Tyler Perry, has given us the unforgettable character of Madea in a series of films that includes *Diary of a Mad Black Woman, Madea's Family Reunion, Meet the Browns, Madea Goes to Jail, I Can Do Bad All by Myself,* and most recently, *Madea's Big Happy Family*, arguably the most popular, financially successful, and therefore culturally influential—and controversial—African American-centered films of the postmodern era. While the films of these two individuals couldn't be more different in style and content, they are nevertheless related, since each tells us much about ideas, fears, concerns, and impulses deeply implanted in American culture as we move into the new millennium.

Film and American Culture

The Way We Are

SYDNEY POLLACK

If anyone knew American moviemaking, it was Sydney Pollack. A director of more than sixteen films—including The Way We Were, Tootsie, Out of Africa, *and* The Interpreter, *starring Nicole Kidman and Sean Penn—a producer of numerous films, including* The Reader, *and an occasional actor (including, for you trivia buffs, an appearance on the television megahit* The Sopranos*), Pollack had an unparalleled opportunity to observe the changing tastes of the American viewing public and the movie industry's response to those changes. In the following article, a transcript of an address Pollack delivered at a conference about the influence of the popular media on American values, Pollack suggested that changes in the moral fabric of our society are responsible for the kinds of movies we see today, not vice versa.*

In its examination of contemporary America, Pollack's analysis notes a conspicuous lack of the "kind of scrupulous ethical concern for the sanctity of life" that prevailed in past decades and was reflected in motion pictures of the time, when there were less frequent and less graphic scenes of violence, when characters were esteemed for their humility and personal integrity, and when explicit sexuality was found only in "stag" films, not in mainstream theaters. Many people today, Pollack notes, are nostalgic for the "old values" and believe that movies should encourage the return of these values rather than reflecting current values. Pollack disagrees, however, pointing out that, although screenwriters and directors may want their movies to reflect some moral content, the economics of the industry require first and foremost that movies be entertaining, and therefore, they must appeal to a buying audience whose values may be very different from those of the reformers.

***As you read,** consider whether you agree with Pollack's notions of artistic integrity, especially his assertions that a filmmaker's prime goal should be to entertain an audience and that movies simply reflect the surrounding society. Is it possible that, in responding to their audience's changing tastes, filmmakers also "construct" public attitudes toward violence, sexuality, and so forth by pushing their explicitness further and further?*

Six weeks ago, I thought I was going to be happy to be a part of this 1 conference, which shows you how naive I am. The agenda—for me at least—is a mine field. Normally, I spend my time worrying about specific problems and not reflecting, as many of you on these panels do. So I've really thought about this, and I've talked to anyone who would listen. My colleagues are sick and tired of it, my wife has left for the country and even my agents—and these are people I pay—don't return my phone calls. By turns, I have felt myself stupid, unethical, a philistine, unpatriotic, a panderer, a cultural polluter, and stupid. And I've completely failed to solve your problems, except in one small way. You have delayed by at least six weeks the possibility of my contributing further to the problems you see.

I know your concerns have to do with American values and whether those values are being upheld or assaulted by American entertainment—by what I and others like me do. But which values exactly? 2

In the thirties, forties, and fifties, six men in the Valley, immigrants really, ran the movie industry. Our society was vastly different. The language of the movies was a language of shared values. If you put forward a virtuousness on the part of your hero, everybody responded to it. 3

When Sergeant York, played by Gary Cooper, refused to endorse a breakfast cereal, knowing he'd been asked because he'd won the Medal of Honor, he said: "I ain't proud of what I've done. You don't make money off of killing people. That there is wrong." We expected him to behave that way. 4

But society's values have changed. That kind of scrupulous, ethical concern for the sanctity of human life doesn't exist in the same way, and that fact is reflected in the movies. There's a nostalgia now for some of the old values, but so many people embrace other expressions of values that it's hard to say these other expressions aren't reality. 5

Their idea of love, for example, is a different idea of love. It's a much less chaste, much less idealized love than was depicted in the earlier films. We are seeing some sort of return to the ideal of marriage. There was a decade or two when marriage really lost its popularity, and while young people are swinging toward it again, I don't believe one could say that values have not changed significantly since the thirties, forties, and fifties. 6

Morality, the definitions of virtue, justice, and injustice, the sanctity of the individual, have been fairly fluid for American audiences in terms of what they choose to embrace or not embrace. 7

Take a picture like *Dances with Wolves*. You could not have made it in the thirties or forties. It calls into question every value that existed in traditional Westerns. It may not reflect what everybody thinks now, but it expresses a lot of guilty reevaluation of what happened in the West, the very things shown in the old Westerns that celebrated the frontier. 8

If we got the movies to assert or talk about better values, would that fix our society? Well, let me quote Sam Goldwyn. When he was told by his staff how poorly his studio's new—and very expensive—film was doing, Sam thought a minute, shrugged, and said, "Listen, if they don't want to come, you can't stop them." 9

Now that's as close to a first principle of Hollywood as I can come. It informs everything that we're here to discuss and it controls every solution that we may propose. 10

OUT OF HOLLYWOOD

Before they can be anything else, American movies are a product. This is not good or bad, this is what we've got. A very few may become art, but all of them, whatever their ambitions, are first financed as commodities. They're the work of craftsmen and artists, but they're soon offered for sale. 11

Whether we say that we're "creating a film" or merely "making a movie," the enterprise itself is sufficiently expensive and risky that it cannot be, and it will not be, undertaken without the hope of reward. We have no Medicis here. It takes two distinct entities, the financiers and the makers, to produce movies, and there is a tension between them. Their goals are sometimes similar, but they do different things. Financiers are not in the business of philanthropy. They've got to answer to stockholders. 12

Of course, the controlling influence in filmmaking hasn't changed in 50 years: it still belongs to the consumer. That's the dilemma and, in my view, what we're finally talking about. What do you do about culture in a society that celebrates the common man but doesn't always like his taste? 13

If you operate in a democracy and you're market-supported and driven, the spectrum of what you will get is going to be very wide indeed. It will range from trash to gems. There are 53,000 books published in this country every year. How many of them are really good? Tired as I may be of fast-food-recipe, conscienceless, simple-minded books, films, TV, and music, the question remains, who is to be society's moral policeman? 14

Over the course of their first 30 or 40 years, the movies were a cottage industry, and the morality that was reflected in them was the morality of the early film pioneers. Now, film studios are tiny divisions of multinational corporations, and they feel the pressure for profits that happens in any other repeatable-product business. They look for a formula. Say you get the recipe for a soft drink and perfect it; once customers like it, you just repeat it and it will sell. More fortunes have 15 been lost than made in the movie business pursuing such a formula, but unfortunately today, more junk than anything else is being made pursuing it. And film companies are folding like crazy.

Since we are in the democracy business, we can't tell people what they should or shouldn't hear, or support, or see, so they make their choices. The market tries to cater to those choices, and we have what we have. 16

MAKING FILMS

Are American films bad? A lot of them surely are, and so are a lot of everybody else's, the way a lot of anything produced is bad—breakfast cereals, music, most chairs, architecture, mail-order shirts. There probably hasn't been a really beautiful rake since the Shakers stopped making farm implements. But that is no excuse. 17

I realize that I am a prime suspect here, but I'm not sure that you really understand how odd and unpredictable a business the making of films actually is. It just doesn't conform to the logic or rules of any other business. It's always been an uneasy merger of two antithetical things: some form of art and sheer commerce. 18

If the people who make films get the money that is invested in them back to the people who finance them, then they'll get to make more. We know that the business of films is to reach as many people as possible. That works two ways; it's not just a market discipline. You have to remember that most of us who are doing this got into it for the romance, the glory, the applause, the chance to tell stories, even to learn, but rarely for the money. The more people you reach, the greater your sense of success. Given the choice, I'd rather make the whole world cry than 17 intellectuals in a classroom. 19

But, paradoxically, if you are the actual maker of the film—not the financier—you can't make films and worry about whether they'll reach a large audience or make money, first, because nobody really knows a formula for what will make money. If they did, I promise you we would have heard about it, and studios would not be going broke. Second, and much more practically, if you spent your time while you were making the film consciously thinking about what was commercial, then the real mechanism of choice—the mechanism that is your own unconscious, your own taste and imagination, your fantasy—would be replaced by constant reference to this formula that we know doesn't work. 20

So the only practical approach a filmmaker can take is to make a film that he or she would want to see. This sounds arrogant, but you try to make a movie for yourself, and you hope that as many people 21 as possible will like it too. If that happens, it's because you've done something in the telling of the story that makes people care. One of the things that makes a film distinct from other American business products is this emotional involvement of the maker. A producer of auto parts can become pretty emotional about a sales slump, but it isn't the same thing. His product hasn't come from his history; it isn't somehow in the image of his life; and it lacks mystery. It is entirely measurable and concrete, which is certainly appropriate in the manufacture of auto parts. I wouldn't want to buy a carburetor from a neurotic, mixed-up auto manufacturer.

Fortunately for those of us in film, no such standards apply. Quite the contrary, in fact. No matter what his conscious intentions are, the best part of what the filmmaker does—the part, when it works, that makes you want to see the film—doesn't come from a rational, consciously controllable process. It comes from somewhere inside the filmmaker's unconscious. It comes from making unlikely connections seem inevitable, from a kind of free association that jumps to odd or surprising places, conclusions that cause delights, something that creates goose pimples or awe. 22

This conference has suggested a question: While you're actually making the movie, do you think about whether or not it will be doing the world any good? I can't answer it for filmmakers in general. For myself, candidly, no, I don't. 23

I try to discover and tell the truth and not be dull about it. In that sense, the question has no significance for me. I assume that trying to discover the truth is in itself a good and virtuous aim. By truth I don't mean some grand, pretentious axiom to live by; I just mean the truth of a character from moment to moment. I try to discover and describe things like the motives that are hidden in day-to-day life. And the truth is rarely dull. If I can find it, I will have fulfilled my primary obligation as a filmmaker, which is not to bore the pants off you. 24

Most of us in this business have enormous sympathy for Scheherazade—we're terrified we're going to be murdered if we're boring. So our first obligation is to not bore people; it isn't to teach. 25

Most of the time, high-mindedness just leads to pretentious or well-meaning, often very bad, films. Most of the Russian films made under communism were of high quality in terms of craft, but they were soporific because their intent to do good as it was perceived by the state or an all-knowing party committee was too transparent. 26

I'm sure that you think the person in whose hands the process actually rests, the filmmaker, could exert an enormous amount of control over the film's final worthiness. The question usually goes like this: Should filmmakers pander to the public, or should they try to elevate public taste to something that many at this conference would 27 find more acceptable? Is the job of an American filmmaker to give the public what it wants or what the filmmaker thinks the public should have? This doesn't leave much doubt as to what you think is the right answer.

28 But framing your question this way not only betrays a misunderstanding of how the filmmaking process works but also is just plain wishful thinking about how to improve society. I share your nostalgia for some of those lost traditional values, but attempting to reinstall them by arbitrarily putting them into movies when they don't exist in everyday life will not get people to go to the movies or put those values back into life. I wish it were that simple.

ENGAGING AN AUDIENCE

29 This conference is concerned with something called popular culture and its effect on society, but I am concerned with one film at a time and its effect. You are debating whether movies corrupt our souls or elevate them, and I'm debating whether a film will touch a soul. As a filmmaker, I never set out to create popular culture, and I don't know a single other filmmaker who does.

30 Maybe it's tempting to think of Hollywood as some collective behemoth grinding out the same stories and pushing the same values, but it's not that simple. Hollywood, whatever that means, is Oliver Stone castigating war in *Born on the Fourth of July* and John Milius celebrating it in *The Wind and the Lion*. It's Walt Disney and Martin Scorsese. It's Steven Spielberg and Miloš Foreman. It's *Amadeus* and *Terminator* and hundreds of choices in between.

31 I don't want to defend Hollywood, because I don't represent Hollywood—I can't, any more than one particular writer can represent literature or one painter art. For the most part, the impulse toward all art, entertainment, culture, pop culture, comes from the same place within the makers of it. The level of talent and the soul, if you'll forgive the word again, is what finally limits it.

32 At the risk of telling you more than you need to know about my own work, I make the movies I make because there is in each film some argument that fascinates me, an issue I want to work through. I call this a spine or an armature because it functions for me like an armature in sculpture—something I can cover up and it will support the whole structure. I can test the scenes against it. For me, the film, when properly dramatized, adds up to this idea, this argument.

33 But there are lots of other ways to go about making a film, and lots of other filmmakers who do it differently. Some filmmakers begin knowing exactly what they want to say and then craft a vehicle that

contains that statement. Some are interested in pure escape. Here's the catch. The effectiveness and the success of all our films is determined by exactly the same standards—unfortunately, not by the particular validity of their message but by their ability to engage the concentration and emotions of the audience.

Orson Welles in *Citizen Kane*

Citizen Kane is an attack on acquisition, but that's not why people go to see it. I don't have any idea if the audience that saw *Tootsie* thought at any conscious level that it could be about a guy who became a better man for having been a woman; or that *The Way We Were*, a film I made 20 years ago, may have been about the tension between passion, often of the moment, and wisdom, often part of a longer view; or that *Out of Africa* might be about the inability to possess another individual and even the inability of one country to possess another. That's intellectual and stuffy. I just hope the audiences were entertained. 34

I may choose the movies I make because there's an issue I want to explore, but the how—the framing of that issue, the process of finding the best way to explore it—is a much more mysterious, elusive, and messy process. I can't tell you that I understand it; if I did, I would have a pep talk with myself and go out and make a terrific movie every time. 35

I would not make a film that ethically, or morally, or politically trashed what I believe is fair. But by the same token, I feel an obligation—and this is more complicated and personal—to do films about arguments. I try hard to give each side a strong argument—not because I'm a fair guy but because I believe it's more interesting. Both things are going on. 36

I do the same thing on every movie I make. I find an argument, a couple of characters I would like to have dinner with, and try to find the most fascinating way to explore it. I work as hard as I can to tell the story in the way I'd like to have it told to me. 37

What is really good is also entertaining and interesting because it's closer to a newer way to look at the truth. You can't do that consciously. You can't start out by saying, "I am now going to make a great film." 38

The virtue in making a film, if there is any, is in making it well. If there's any morality that's going to come out, it will develop as you begin to construct, at every moment you have a choice to make. You can do it the honest way or you can bend it, and the collection of those moments of choice is what makes the work good or not good and is what reveals morality or the lack of it. 39

I've made 16 films. I've had some enormous successes and I've had some colossal failures, but I can't tell you what the difference is in terms of what I did. 40

AN AMERICAN AESTHETIC?

In some circles, American films suffer by comparison with European films precisely because a lot of our movies seem to be the product of little deliberation and much instinct. It's been said of European movies that essence precedes existence, which is just a fancy way of saying that European movies exist in order to say something. Certainly one never doubts with a European film that it's saying something, and often it just comes right out and says it. 41

American films work by indirection; they work by action and movement, either internal or external, but almost always movement. Our films are more narratively driven than others, which has a lot to do with the American character and the way we look at our lives. We see ourselves and our lives as being part of a story. 42

Most of our movies have been pro the underdog, concerned with injustice, relatively anti-authority. There's usually a system—or a bureaucracy—to triumph over. 43

More often than not, American movies have been affirmative and hopeful about destiny. They're usually about individuals who control 44 their own lives and their fate. In Europe, the system was so class-bound and steeped in tradition that there was no democratization of that process.

There's no prior education required to assimilate American mov- 45
ies or American culture. American culture is general, as opposed to the specificity of Japanese or Indian culture. America has the most easily digestible culture.

Our movies seem artless. The best of them keep us interested 46
without seeming to engage our minds. The very thing that makes movies so popular here and abroad is one of the primary things that drives their critics to apoplexy, but seeming artlessness isn't necessarily mindlessness. There's a deliberate kind of artlessness in American movies that has come from a discipline or aesthetic long ago imposed by the marketplace. Our movies began as immigrants' dreams that would appeal to the dreams of other immigrants, and this aesthetic has led American films to transcend languages and cultures and communicate to every country in the world.

THE FILMMAKER'S RESPONSIBILITY

It has been suggested to some extent in this conference that I ought to 47
study my own and American filmmakers' responsibilities to the public and to the world. I realize I have responsibilities as a filmmaker, but I don't believe that they are as a moralist, a preacher, or a purveyor of values. I know it's tempting to use filmmaking as such, but utility is a poor standard to use in art. It's a standard that has been and is still used by every totalitarian state in the world.

My responsibility is to try to make good films, but "good" is a 48
subjective word. To me at any rate, "good" doesn't necessarily mean "good for us" in the narrow sense that they must elevate our spirits and send us out of the theater singing, or even that they must promote only those values that some think are worth promoting.

Good movies challenge us, they provoke us, they make us an- 49
gry sometimes. They present points of view we don't agree with. They force us to clarify our positions in opposition to them, and they do this best when they provide us with an experience and not a polemic.

Somebody gave the okay to pay for *One Flew over the Cuckoo's* 50
Nest, Driving Miss Daisy, Stand by Me, Moonstruck, Terms of Endearment, and *Amadeus,* and despite conventional wisdom that said those films could not be successful, those decisions paid off handsomely because there are no rules. Studio executives and other financiers do exceed themselves. They take chances. They have to, and we have to hope that they'll do it more often.

What we see in movie theaters today is not a simple reflection of today's economics or politics in this country but is a sense of the people who make the movies, and they vary as individuals vary. So what we really want is for this very privileged process to be in the best hands possible, but I know of no force that can regulate this except the moral climate and appetites of our society. 51

What we're exporting now is largely a youth culture. It's full of adolescent values; it's full of adolescent rage, love, rebelliousness, and a desire to shock. If you're unhappy with their taste—and this is a free market—then an appetite has to be created for something better. How do we do that? Well, we're back to square one: the supplier or the consumer, the chicken or the egg? Let's not even ask the question; the answer is both. 52

Of course filmmakers ought to be encouraged toward excellence, and audiences ought to be encouraged to demand it. How? That's for thinkers and social scientists to figure out. I have no idea. But if I had to play this scene out as an imaginary dialogue, I might say that you must educate the consumer first, and the best places to start are at school and at home. And then you would say that that is my job, that popular entertainment must participate in this education. And I would say, ideally, perhaps, but I do not think that will happen within a system that operates so fundamentally from an economic point of view. On an individual basis, yes, one filmmaker at a time; as an industry, no. An appetite or market will have to exist first. 53

That's not as bad as it sounds, because in the best of all possible worlds, we do try to satisfy both needs: entertain people and be reasonably intelligent about it. It can be done, and it is done more often than you might think. It's just very difficult. 54

It's like the two Oxford dons who were sitting at the Boarshead. They were playwrights, grousing because neither one of them could get produced, neither one could get performed. One turned to the other and said, "Oh, the hell with it. Let's just do what Shakespeare did—give them entertainment." 55

Examining the Text

1. Pollack says there "probably hasn't been a really beautiful rake since the Shakers stopped making farm implements" (paragraph 17). What does his point say in terms of questioning whether American films are "bad"? Do you find his analogy persuasive?

2. When Pollack asserts that he'd "rather make the whole world cry than 17 intellectuals in a classroom" (19), what is he implying about his—and other filmmakers'—motivations? Do you think most creative people feel this way?

3. Pollack describes his interest in making "films about arguments" and giving "each side a strong argument" (36). What does he mean? Do you think movies that balance two sides of an "argument" are "more interesting" than those with clear-cut "good guys" and "bad guys"?

4. *Thinking rhetorically:* What is Pollack's point in paragraph 8? How does *Dances with Wolves* "call into question every value that existed in traditional Westerns," and how does it reflect a change in society's values? Is *Dances with Wolves* a good example of the kind of movie that critics would say contributes to the decline in American values? What do you think is Pollack's rhetorical intention—that is, his persuasive purpose—in mentioning this so early in his speech?

For Group Discussion

Pollack himself did not make the kinds of graphically violent movies that critics claim have a negative influence on American society. Nonetheless, he argues that "scrupulous, ethical concern for the sanctity of human life doesn't exist in the same way [it did in the past], and that fact is reflected in the movies." As a group, list examples from current events and recent films that demonstrate this lack of concern for human life. As a class, consider whether, based on these examples, you agree with Pollack that movies only reflect the values of society and do not contribute to their creation.

Writing Suggestion

Rent and watch one or more of Pollack's films (titles other than those mentioned in the headnote include They Shoot Horses, Don't They?, Three Days of the Condor, and The Electric Horseman). In an essay, analyze Pollack's work as a reflection of contemporary American life. What themes or messages do you discover beyond his aim to tell a good story? Does he succeed in his stated goal of presenting an "argument," as he mentions in the above article?

Fight Club: *A Ritual Cure for the Spiritual Ailment of American Masculinity*

JETHRO ROTHE-KUSHEL

Some social observers believe that corporate, consumer life has visited a loss of masculinity upon American males. Absent the hard labor that earlier times required in order to survive, men have lost their strength and toughness. In the process, according to these social critics, society has lost the containment and support of ritualized passages that transition boys into manhood. In this article, the author analyzes these broad social issues raised by the movie Fight Club *(1999).*

Fight Club *stars Edward Norton as Jack, an aimless, contemporary American male who seemingly lives the American dream in a home furnished from a catalog. He meets his alter-ego, Tyler, played by Brad Pitt, a rugged, risk-taking individual who is everything that Jack is not. Together, the two form Fight Club: a kind of men's support group without the drumming circles or manly hugs. The men in Fight Club engage in physical therapy, otherwise known as punches, kicks, and brute violence. The club's goal is to help men find their inner hooligan using a modified set of the Marquess of Queensberry rules that normally govern boxing. Naturally, things spin out of control.*

In the following article, the author/film critic scans the movie through a sociological lens to find references to masculinity and meaning in the postindustrial, consumer-driven society that is modern America. The author turns to Freud and Jung and other psychoanalysts to understand such concepts as the ego and symbols of masculinity. The problem, Rothe-Kushel concludes, is that Jack and Tyler are confused. Their lack of clarity about what it means to be a man mirrors the confusion in the wider society. By setting up the Fight Club and going to blows to save the soul of their masculinity, the movie's characters reveal a darker side of American culture, where violence, lawlessness, and rage are glorified and, ultimately, seen as redemptive. Tyler is the violent foil to Jack's tenderness, the rage against Jack's tears, the absent father to Jack's solicitous mother.

As you read, *notice how the author parallels the film's use of cinematic effects with the ultimate breakdown of the Fight Club into Project Mayhem. The audience sees a disintegration of the film stock—or at least a deliberate diminishment in visual quality—as the concept of seeking violence in search of masculinity begins to unravel. What does the filmmaker want to achieve by tying a plot device to a visual effect?*

"Motion Pictures are going to save our civilization from the destruction which has successively overwhelmed every civilization of the past. They provide what every previous civilization has lacked—namely a means of relief, happiness, and mental inspiration to the people at the bottom. Without happiness and inspiration being accessible to those upon whom the social burden rests most heavily, there can be no stable social system. Revolutions are born of misery and despair."

—Mary Gray Peck, General Federation of Women's Clubs, 1917

"Hollywood is the nearest thing to 'hell on earth' which Satan has been able thus far to establish in this world. And the influence of Hollywood is undermining the Christian culture and civilization which our fathers built in this land."

—Dan Gilbert, Chairman of the Christian Newspaper Men's Committee to Investigate the Motion Picture Industry, 1994

INTRODUCTION

When I first saw *Fight Club*, I had just returned from a workshop in Oregon entitled "Men: Born to Kill?" The program was a four-day workshop for about thirty men in which we learned to hold hands and "discharge." It was the first time since infancy I had been given a forum in which to touch other men and cry together with no discomfort or judgment. In the privacy of this idyllic setting, we discussed the ways in which we use women for touch and to hold us emotionally because we are too afraid to use other men for this purpose. 1

As a filmmaker and a man, I had been told *Fight Club* was one of those movies I would like. I tend not to enjoy violent films, but with the new energy from the workshop I thought I would give it a chance. I was not sure how I felt about the movie then and I'm not sure now, but I felt. 2

SYNOPSIS

Directed by David Fincher, written for the screen by Jim Uhls, and based on a novel by Chuck Palahniuk, *Fight Club* was released to Americans recovering from the Columbine school shootings in the fall of 1999. From the beginning, the film examines consciousness itself. We hear a gun cock and watch the sound as an electrical impulse inside the psychoneurotic center of the protagonist's brain. "The electricity that's running through it is like photo-electrical stimuli. . . . These are fear-based impulses. We're changing scale the whole time so we're starting at the size of a dendrite and we pull through the frontal lobe." Our narrator, Jack, is a product of American problems of meaning. America may promise freedom, especially to the white man, but Jack's life is anything but free. He lives in indentured servitude to his corporate copying office job and his IKEA catalogues. He is on a spiritual[1] train straight to nowhere. But when he sees a doctor for a diagnosis of his spiritual death, the doctor assures him, "No, you can't die from insomnia. . . . You want to see pain?" mocks the doctor. "Swing by Meyer High on a Tuesday night and see the guys with testicular cancer. Now that's pain!" 3

The testicular cancer support group gives Jack the kind of emotional attention he needs. Here people "really listen" and he can cry and feel for the first time. The testicular cancer group inspires him to join support groups for lymphoma, tuberculosis, blood parasites, brain parasites, organic brain dementia, and ascending bowel cancer. He becomes a support group addict, with a different group each day of the week—all for a condition he does not have. Accustomed to regarding people as packages, he meets a perfect "single-serving friend" who 4 sits next to him on a business flight. Tyler Durden (Brad Pitt) is everything the narrator wishes he could be. Tyler is a walking, talking, cultural commentator. He is cynical, strong, and forthright. This chance encounter with Tyler Durden leads our narrator to his drastic change of "lifestyle." When the narrator's IKEA-furnished house burns down, he moves in with Tyler Durden. Together, they start Fight Club, a new kind of support group for men that encourages them to sock and punch and tear at each other in order to feel saved. The fights are primal, brutal, and bloody. This is an honorable group with its own codes and ethics. But Fight Club aggression spins out of control into Project Mayhem. When the narrator finally confronts Tyler about the project, he comes to the realization that he is Tyler Durden. The narrator confronts the inner psychological split by placing a gun in his own mouth. He shoots himself to kill off his alter-ego, but it is too late. Project Mayhem ends where it began, at "ground zero," with bombs exploding and corporate skyscrapers crumbling.

CULTURAL AND ARCHETYPAL MYTH

Fight Club comments profoundly on America's problems of meaning (e.g., indentured servitude to capitalism in a land of freedom, violence in a land of justice, consumer Darwinism in a land of community, meaning in a post-modern reality that understands all meaning as a relative cultural construct, etc.). In sociological terms, Jack, a white male, could represent the hierarchical leadership of the American patriarchy. "I was the warm little center that the life of this world crowded around." America seems to love him, but he feels hurt and betrayed by his culture and the dulled-down consumerist dreams he has inherited. 5

> We're consumers. We're by-products of a lifestyle obsession. Murder, crime, poverty—these things don't concern me. What concerns me is celebrity magazines, television with five hundred channels, some guy's name on my underwear. Rogaine, Viagra, Olestra.

But according to Fincher, "We're designed to be hunters and we're in a society of shopping. There's nothing to kill anymore, there's nothing to fight, nothing to overcome, nothing to explore. In that societal emasculation this everyman is created."[2] Where does Jack go to discuss his problems? What community exists to support him emotionally and spiritually? 6

Seeking guidance, Jack stumbles into a group for men with testicular cancer. He finds that a weekly catharsis between Bob's breasts rids 7 him of his insomnia by allowing him to feel. But this apparent solution produces a new dilemma for Jack—crying men.

> *Bob:* We're still men.
> *Jack:* Yes. We're men. Men is what we are.
> *Jack (V.O.):* Bob cried. Six months ago, his testicles were removed. Then hormone therapy. He developed bitch tits because his testosterone was too high and his body upped the estrogen. That was where my head fit—into his sweating tits that hang enormous, the way we think of God's as big.

Jack's masculinity has been reduced to undifferentiated tears. But from these tears, he finds "strength." Despite the temporary relief he feels from his catharsis, Jack quickly returns to his initial dilemma: 8

> You are here because the world
> As you know it no longer makes sense.
> You've been raised on television
> To believe we'll all be
> Millionaires and movie gods and
> Rock stars—but we won't.
> You pray for a different life.[3]

If Jack is not allowed to express his creativity as a "movie god" or "rock star," he can create his own god in the theater of his mind that will grant him permission to feel in a more lasting way. 9

Carl Gustav Jung (1875–1961), a disciple of Sigmund Freud, believed that his mentor had neglected the soul and religion in his understanding of human psychology. For this reason, Jung left Freud and spent years of research in religious iconography and mythical stories. His findings suggest that archetypal stories exist cross-culturally and that each individual psyche has the potential for two opposing personalities: ego and shadow. Ego controls the psyche, but when ego is disrupted (through Tyler's cutting frames into the film) or weakened through sleep loss or an emotional void (in Jack's case), the shadow creeps in to take control. The ego is constructed around societal norms and the desire for behavior which "fits into society." However, Post-Modernity challenges these social norms as simply one narrative or structure which is no better than any other structured narrative. The destruction of Jack's ego also parallels the destruction of American hegemony. 10

Tyler Durden, Jack's alter-ego creation, forces Jack to create binary oppositions (love/fear, ego/shadow, etc.) which perhaps necessitate post-modern "queering" for any resolution. 11

> Howard Teich calls The Solar/Lunar Twin-Ego, "a universal theme that is documented in nearly all cultural histories. Rivalrous pairs such as Romulus and Remus, Jacob and Esau, may be most familiar to us, but examples of amicable solar/lunar Twins abound as well. It is for example, seldom recalled that even our superhero Hercules was born with a twin named Iphicles. Together the Twins represent a balanced, complete energetic principle of the masculine, partaking of both light and dark influences."[4]

It is this "balanced, complete energetic principle of the masculine" which Jack strives to be. Without Tyler, Jack is a spineless, volumeless, emotionless, placid, and flaccid half-man. Jack's creation of Tyler Durden allows him to reclaim his masculinity amidst a culture of post-feminist, cathartic, "self"-help groups. 12

Eugene Monick, a contemporary of Jung, wrote a recent book entitled *Phallos: Sacred Image of the Masculine*, in which he explains a concept of Phallos which Jung neglected in his research and writings. According to Monick, masculine identity in the American patriarchy is often taken for granted as dominant; therefore it is neglected. Monick suggests that in a post-feminist America, masculine identity may have become a larger enigma for men than feminine identity for women. He also explains that in his own practice of analysis more men are coming to therapy to correct a psychological situation in which they "feel something is missing." Men often find themselves in a quandary about their violent and sexual urges and tend either to act on them and feel guilty, or to suppress them and remain unfulfilled. Nothing has been written on the archetypal basis of masculinity since Erich Neumann's *Origins and History of Consciousness* in 1995.[5] Monick explains: 13

> Phallos is subjective authority for a male, and objective for those who come into contact with him. This is what makes phallus archetypal. No male has to learn phallos. It presents itself to him as a god does.[6]

With his addiction to self-help groups, Jack attends a leukemia group and experiences a guided meditation. When he is told to meet his power animal in one meditation, he finds a penguin in a snowy cave who speaks like a child—a poignant image of Jack's lonely and docile masculinity. In an article entitled "What Men Really Want," Robert Bly captures this over-emphasized docility: 14

> When I look out at my audiences, perhaps half the young males are what I'd call soft. They're lovely, valuable people—I like them—and they're not interested in harming the earth, or starting wars, or working for corporations. There's something favorable toward life in their whole general mood and style of living. But something's wrong. There's not much energy in them. They are life-preserving but not exactly life-giving.[7]

In a culture that's been robbed of its masculine principle, Jack finds himself only accepting his masculinity through tears and the estrogen-enriched breasts of another man who completes him. 15

Jack (V.O.): The big moosie, his eyes already shrink-wrapped in tears. Knees together, invisible steps. Bob takes Jack into an embrace.
Jack (V.O.): He pancaked down on top of me.
Bob Two grown kids . . . and they won't return my calls.
Jack (V.O.): Strangers with this kind of honesty make me go a big rubbery one. Jack's face is rapt and sincere. Bob stops talking and breaks into sobbing, putting his head down on Jack's shoulder and completely covering Jack's face.
Jack (V.O.): Then, I was lost in oblivion—dark and silent and complete. Jack's body begins to jerk in sobs. He tightens his arms around Bob.
Jack (V.O.): This was freedom. Losing all hope was freedom.

Crying for Jack seems to be one way to address his masculinity and disappointment with a spiritless life. In contemporary America, it seems that an increasing number of men are turning to tears as a way of emoting. Bly discusses these catharsis-obsessed American males. 16

> Often the younger males would begin to talk and within five minutes they would be weeping. The amount of grief and anguish in the younger males was astounding! The river was deep. . . . They had learned to be receptive, and it wasn't enough to carry their marriages. In every relationship something fierce is needed once in a while; both the man and the woman need to have it.[8]

Monick suggests that the fierceness excluded from the masculine crying model comes with the re-integration of the shadow. Monick devotes the sixth chapter of his book to the shadow of phallus, called chthonic phallus: 17

> . . . characterized by its grossness, brutality and carelessness. It can be characterized by its unmitigated power needs, by a kind of mad drivenness, by the mayhem of war and ruthless competition it occasions. Life is replete with examples of its stupid and devastating behavior, "the man eater," as Jung's mother called it in his childhood dream.[9]

Though Freud and Jung saw the mother as the primary relationship for any child, Monick suggests that for a man, religion helps fill the void neglected by his father. "Psychoanalytic theory, whether 18

Freudian or Jungian, gives singular primacy to the mother as the basis of life. This is an error."[10]

19 The argument could be made that Freud, Jung, and Monick all cater to perhaps outdated gender roles that have no place in a post-modern scholarship where all gender roles are merely conditioned identities to maintain social control. Judith Butler, among others, argues that to speak of gender in any way is to speak of mere conceptual binaries that have been mistakenly mapped onto the human body. Perhaps I am stuck in an outdated paradigm that does not take into account the plurality of roles a human can play for a child and the plurality of circumstances in which a child can be raised, but this writer still finds psychological gender theories interesting if not useful.

20 Monick claims an individuating spirit cannot become complete until it incorporates the shadowed Other—the darker side of masculinity.

> The issue of chthonic phallus is important to men who have a strong spiritual component in their lives and/or a dominant solar masculinity. What do they do with the sweaty, hairy, animal phallos represented by Iron John?[11]

21 Monick suggests that in the ideal nuclear family, the individuating spirit can grow under the guidance of a mother and a father. But like most American families, Jack's family was anything but ideal:

> *Jack:* My mother would just go into hysterics. My Dad. . . . Don't know where he is. Only knew him for six years. Then, he ran off to a new city and married another woman and had more kids. Every six years—new city, new family. He was setting up franchises. Tyler smiles, snorts, shakes his head.
>
> *Tyler:* A generation of men raised by women. Look what it's done to you.

22 With households across the country either consisting of or dominated by women, young men seem to have trouble finding guidance on the integration of the darker sides of masculinity. Monick claims mothers cannot teach their sons about chthonic phallus.

> It is not only the mother's desire to keep her son close and compatible with her style of life that damages chthonic phallos. The father participates, as the king did in the fairy tale. The father who has lost the power and raw energy of chthonic phallos would also deny it to the son. In practical terms, this may become manifest in the abrogation of

the father's masculine authority, which by default goes to the mother. And often when the father experiences the return of phallic energy, he leaves the domestic scene to act it out. In such cases, the son is left to fend for himself in a maternal—and often hostile-environment, with no male role-model.[12]

With the lack of a male role-model, all that is left for the American boy without a father is the consumer "product." When there is no other solution, Jack turns to a "modern versatile domestic solution" to fill the void: 23

Jack flips the page of the catalogue to reveal a full-page photo of an entire kitchen and dining room set.
Jack (V.O.): I would flip and wonder, "What kind of dining room set *defines* me as a person?"

Jack wants out of his dead end corporate job and his IKEA furnished "lifestyle." Jack, who does not have enough courage of his own, creates a shadow that has enough nerve to break free and enough audacity to become his own true individual. Jack creates Tyler Durden as a mentoring father figure who will help him integrate his shadow in relationship with sex and violence and bring Jack closer to the Other. 24

Tyler: Shut up! Our fathers were our models for God. And if our fathers bailed, what does that tell you about God?

Increasingly American boys are raised by their mothers with a lack of any strong male role model in their life. Tyler becomes such a role model for Jack who paradoxically holds all of Jack's rage and all of his love simultaneously. The fighting itself becomes an act of love through which they can relate to one another. However, Tyler Durden, like Iron John, is only a temporary experience. 25

The young prince must go into the forest to live for a time with Iron John. A gentleman must know that he is also a beast and know the appropriate times to become that beast—that is the integration of shadow chthonic phallos. The prince must of course emerge from the forest, but with his eyes open to the duality of his nature.

The last scene of the film illuminates Jack's final encounter with Tyler. With a gun to Jack's head, Tyler begins the last scene where the film began. 26

Tyler: 3 minutes. This is it. Here we are at the beginning. Ground zero. Would you like to say a few words to mark the occasion?

Jack is at a loss for words, but realizes he no longer craves the destruction Tyler wants. "I don't want this!" But it is too late. Vans loaded with "blasting gelatin" are set to detonate and destroy urban phallic skyscrapers in a matter of minutes. Jack realizes the only way to stop his alter-ego gone awry is to point the gun at himself. Tyler dies when Jack shoots himself in the mouth, but Jack remains a spirit to bear witness to "ground zero."[13] The last image of the film is framed as a vista from within a glass skyscraper. Jack and his lover, Marla Singer, hold hands at the "theater of mass destruction." Two tall towers crumble to the ground. Premiered years before September eleventh, the film serves as chilling prophecy even more profound and ripe with cultural and historical mythic elements than even this author had expected. 27

FIGHT CLUB AS SACRED

But how can a film with such a dark and violent conclusion be classified as sacred? The French anthropologist, René Girard, suggests that sacred violence is an inherent component of any well functioning society throughout history. Girard classifies violence into pure and impure violence. Impure violence is uncontained and lawless and warrants retaliation from the victim's fellowship. Such violence is ultimately destructive to the community because its results are interminable. However, pure violence is contained through a lawful sacrifice in which the victim and his fellowship understand the death as sacred. Such a sacrifice satisfies the cultural need for violence while maintaining order and purpose. *Fight Club* becomes such a structure wherein violence is contained within a particular communal order. It is worth noting that all participants in *Fight Club* are white males, kings of American hegemony, who have no scapegoat for their problems but themselves and the corporations. The sacrificial victim becomes a scapegoat by which to purge the society of its anger and hatred. The scapegoat allows the community to project all of its anger onto the victim, thereby eliminating its anger at itself. By sacrificing the scapegoat the community relinquishes itself from its anger. Girard suggests that the scapegoat is both fatherless and randomly chosen so that he will not be avenged after his death. The ideal scapegoat is a king or hero who has achieved success in the community, but is destroyed by destiny. "God giveth and God taketh. The best of scapegoats is thus a dethroned idol, a broken idol marginalized from the society he once ruled. And this is exactly what the action hero is."[14] Tyler Durden is such an action hero—fatherless as Jack is his only creator, and a model of the ultimate American idol, popular icon and movie star Brad Pitt himself. While Tyler Durden 28 becomes a scapegoat for Jack, corporate buildings become a scapegoat for Tyler as the "Demolitions Committee" of "Project Mayhem." The demolition of Brad Pitt and about seven skyscrapers leaves the viewer with a sense of peace leaving the theater.[15] *Fight Club*, the film, and Fight Club, the cult within the film, becomes the reclamation of American sacred violence.

I would argue *Fight Club* is avant-garde sublime art. However, categorizing the film in artistic terms negates the highest measurement of sacredness in America: box-office success. As with most American endeavors that afford some power, the projected image does not come for free. Film is the most costly and time-consuming art form.[16] Production on such a grand and costly scale will both comment on culture and affect culture profoundly. If money is not sacred in America, what is? The American dollar dictates American values, and by that measure, *Fight Club* is irrevocably sacred. 29

FORMATIVE MYTH AND ITS MEDIUM

But what is the impact of this violent myth on the community? The space of the movie theater is a sacred ritual arena that few scholars have analyzed as such. Martin discusses the lack of scholarly work linking film and religion: 30

> Scholars engaged in prevailing modes of film criticism have had almost nothing to say about religion. And scholars who study religion have had almost nothing to say about Hollywood film. Instead of encountering an ongoing and stimulating dialogue about religion and film, I encountered silence.[17]

The viewer experiences a cognitive shift when he steps into the movie theater. *Fight Club* as a cultural artifact has the ability to affect individual and collective consciousness. But how do we measure this effect? In oral traditions, the communication of sacred stories is confined to a specific time and place. However, with a text, cultural effects can be analyzed through critical literary faculties that human consciousness has developed over hundreds of years. The impact of the classic text on its culture is also easily discussed from the privileged temporal position of having a distance of many years with which to measure cultural change. However, discussing the impact of a contemporary film on its community is a much more daunting task for which scholars have only the most archaic tools. 31

The French philosopher, Emmanuel Levinas, suggests that a significant cognitive distinction exists between the experience of 32 reading a text and the experience of viewing an image. The linearity of the textual narrative empowers its consumer in a way that the image does not. The literary text is only reconstructed through the critical faculties of its reader. Thus, the textual consumer is empowered with ultimate control over his or her interpretation. However, the viewer of the image is instantaneously seduced into an uncontrollable holistic experience. The image dominates its viewer, requires a fundamental passivity, and denies the viewer the freedom of interpretation. Levinas has an abhorrence of images. He critiques the artist whose compulsion for expressing truth supercedes the responsibility of the consequences of such an expression. The question remains: does the artist influence the culture or does the culture merely influence the artist? When people remarked that Gertrude Stein did not look like Picasso's portrait, Picasso replied, "She will." In a similar way, when *Fight Club* was first released in 1999, many critics were upset by its violence, voicing the concern that the film itself creates a violence that does not exist within the culture. However, five years later, the last image of two buildings crumbling confirms the film's prophetic power as young American men come together to fight a new scapegoat—Islamic fundamentalists.

The visual arts bring us to a safe place where we can experience extreme emotion. Film can have the effect of a formative religious experience more so than the most sublime texts. However, such a film experience is more dangerous; text depends on critical faculties whereas the film requires passive vulnerability. 33

Film belongs in both the critical worlds of text and image. The rapid projection of twenty-four 35mm photographs every second is reconstructed only in the viewer's memory using both narrative critical faculties and image domination. There becomes a temporal quality to the image that allows the mind to re-create a holistic experience. And sound only complicates this ultimately inarticulatable experience. 34

Film can seduce and indoctrinate the viewer urging him or her to confront his or her own emotion. Also, film can have a stronger emotional draw than even theater (assuming the audience chooses to accept the film as a reality) by permitting the viewer to suspend critical judgment. The safety of the movie setting allows the viewer to make himself more vulnerable and be affected in emotionally deeper ways. Consumers move from a "normal" sphere to a sphere in which they allow alternative realities to be presented. In this act, the consumer suspends his or her control of how reality "should" operate. Artaud, the French poet, essayist, playwright, and actor conceptualized cinema as "literally a stimulant or narcotic, acting directly and materially on the mind."[18] Artaud's film work combats 35 the medium, attempting to "tear the image from representation and position it in proximity within the viewer's perception/interpretative sensorium."[19] In his work, Artaud interrupts the narrative itself so the audience can become conscious of its existence. He theorized that "raw cinema" would come from eliminating film's narrative qualities and therefore relying solely on the indoctrination of the image. *Fight Club* moves in this direction.

That the film has its viewers blindly accept a new value structure which undermines and subverts most "normal" values of right and wrong, is a stunning testament to film's ability to create a separate reality within the confines of the theater space. 36

> That the film promotes this idea and wins our involvement, before completely undermining itself and the exercise, displays a clever, highly manipulative comment on the influence of a film to persuade its viewers into accepting a new set of values. . . .[20]

The film's ability to persuade its viewer to accept a moral relativity has some frightening implications: 37

> It's a modern, cerebral world, and these characters go away and be macho not to re-claim some latent untapped masculinity, but to revel in the absurdity of doing so, and thus the absurdity of being cerebral; the power of its world that ropes us in and that we take for granted has us in chains.[21]

The film which exists apart from conventional reality can provide an ecstasy—an ex stasis allowing the viewer to be taken outside of the domain of normal consciousness and into a reality that is probably most similar to the passive experience of the unconscious dream mixed with conscious memory. The film exists within the inner life of Jack: 38

> *Jack:* Listen to this. It's an article written in first person. "I am Jack's medulla oblongata, without me Jack could not regulate his heart rate, blood pressure or breathing!" There's a whole series of these! "I am Jill's nipples." "I am Jack's Colon."

From such statements about the inner body of Jack stem further meditations by Jack about his own inner life: "I am Jack's smirking revenge." "I am Jack's cold sweat." "I am Jack's broken heart." 39

What may be unique about *Fight Club* is its self-consciousness about its own medium. The breakdown of Jack's ego is manifest through the breakdown of cinematic form itself. *Fight Club* itself is a radical meditation on film form and language. 40

Tyler appears to Jack about six times before the audience becomes conscious of the encounter. This is accomplished through a technique that may be truly unique by which Tyler is introduced to single frames in the film. Ironically, Tyler works as a projectionist who cuts in singular frames of pornography into family films. In the last scene of the film a single frame of a naked penis is cut into the film just before the crumbling buildings fade to black. The splice acts as a formal reminder of our journey with "chthonic phallos." 41

Fight Club also examines the temporal quality of film itself creating a unique stream-of-consciousness experience. Computer concepts like RAM (random access memory) seem to influence Fincher's understanding of time. 42

> We take the first forty minutes to literally indoctrinate you in this subjective psychotic state, the way he thinks, the way he talks about what's behind the refrigerator. . . . It's gotta move as quick as you can think. We've gotta come up with a way that the camera can illustrate things at the speed of thought. And that's one of the things that was interesting to me, how much can you jump around in time and go: Wait, let me back up a little bit more, okay, no, no, this is where this started, this is how I met this person. . . . So there's this jumping around in time to bring you into the present and then leaping back to go, let me tell you about this other thing. It's almost conversational. It's as erratic in its presentation as the narrator is in his thinking. I think maybe the possibilities of this kind of temporal and freedom points to a future direction for movies.[22]

In addition to temporality, Fincher manipulates the medium itself dirtying the film through specific processing. "When we processed it, we stretched the contrast to make it kind of ugly, a little bit of underexposure, a little bit of re-silvering, and using new high-contrast print stocks and stepping all over it so it has a dirty patina."[23] The processing of the film is apparently similar to Fincher's last film, *Seven* (1995). "The blacks become incredibly rich and kind of dirty. We did it on *Seven* a little, just to make the prints nice. But it's really in this more for making it ugly." The deconstruction of the film chemistry itself and Fincher's homage to his own formal past indicates the layers of complexity that contribute to the experience of the film. Gavin Smith positions *Fight Club* and its form in relation to other contemporary cinema: 43

> Is *Fight Club* the end of something in cinema, or the beginning? Zeitgeist movie or cult item? Whether you find the state-of-the-art cinematic values of this current moment liberating or oppressive, radical or specious, of lasting significance or entirely transitory, as the little girl in Poltergeist says: they're here.

The speed with which film is produced makes a conscious inter-textual dialogue difficult—or at least undermines the ability of the critic to place himself within a contemporary dialogue about film form. 44

A performance is only ritualized by its repetition, and only cult viewers naturally watch a movie multiple times. Thus, *Fight Club* as a film can only become ritualized by its small but growing cult watching public. 45

AFTER THE THEATER

When an individual steps into a church, how much do they expect of their experience to follow them out? Great art changes our experience of reality and challenges us to take that experience home with us. Is this great art? 46

> *Tyler:* 3 minutes. This is it. Here we are at the beginning. Ground zero. Would you like to say a few words to mark the occasion?

The film effectively holds up a mirror to the male viewer and suggests that the real story begins at "ground zero" in "three minutes" as the film fades out, the end credits begin, and the audience exits the theater. Most of us are confused when we leave a movie theater and enjoy reveling in the passivity of the experience. However, the film maintains a moral ambiguity which challenges the viewer to "say a few words to mark the occasion." One informant says of his experience, "It didn't let me be a white, middle-class American male, ages 18–24, the most powerful person in the world, and remain comfortable in my seat."[24] During an interview at Yale University, Edward Norton confirmed this reaction as intentional: 47

> I hope it rattles people. I hope it dunks very squarely in your lap because I think one of the things we strove very specifically to do with this was on some levels retain a kind of moral ambivalence or a moral ambiguity—not to deliver a neatly wrapped package of meaning into your lap. Or in any way that let you walk away from the film like this, comfortable in having been told what you should make of it.[25]

But what words can Americans say to "mark the occasion?" Howard Hampton expresses his anger towards an American public that received the film with no noticeable "kamikaze act[s] of homage": 48

> . . . *Fight Club* generated no noticeably baleful side effects whatsoever. Are left-wing critics and right-wing politicians the only ones left who believe in the potency of "transgression"? What is the world coming to when a

> movie featuring charismatic performers reveling in anti-social behavior and a host of semi-subliminal advertisements for the joys of chaos can't incite a single unbalanced loner to commit a kamikaze act of homage?[26]

Unfortunately, in the wake of September 11th terrorist attacks, *Fight Club*'s moral aloofness has become less clear. A more courageous cultural critic might argue that the film encouraged Americans to create an alter-ego (Islamic Fundamentalists) which could ignite a new kind of *Fight Club*-war. However, I would not be so courageous. 49

While the collective effects of the film remain ephemeral, the individual responses are easier to attain. For example, Alexander Walker of the *London Evening Standard* is quoted as attacking *Fight Club* as "an inadmissible assault on personal decency and on society itself."[27] Kenneth Turan of the *Los Angeles Times* (1999, pg. 1) suggests that, "What's most troubling about this witless mishmash of whiny, infantile philosophizing and bone-crunching violence is the increasing realization that it actually thinks it's saying something of significance. That is a scary notion indeed." Edward Norton challenges dismissing *Fight Club* because of its violence or moral ambiguity. 50

> My feeling is that it is the responsibility of people making films and people making all art to specifically address dysfunctions in the culture. I think that any culture where the art is not reflecting a really dysfunctional component of the culture, is a culture in denial. And I think that's much more intensely dangerous on lots of levels than considered examinations of those dysfunctions through art is dangerous. I don't believe that it's the chicken and the egg question, I do think there is violence in the culture. I think there always has been violence in our culture in one form or another. I think that it's a very appropriate discussion to ask what are the ways in which the presentations of violence effect us.[28]

After interviewing a dozen American male college students, I feel confident that I have attained some sense of the emotional response it may have warranted from its intended audience (American males age 18–24). Though the sample size was relatively small, the informants included a cross-section of socio-economic and cultural backgrounds. Though the specifics varied, all males interviewed felt something. One informant was "anesthetized": 51

> I guess I felt shock in response to all this destruction, yet the visual image was so beautiful that I was seduced by it and gave myself over to scopophilic consumption. When I left the theater, I felt numb. I was anesthetized.[29]

Others similarly describe the anesthesia of *Fight Club* as "stress release," "peace," and "liberating." 52

> I felt violated, but not really violated. Like I was tricked into seeing something I shouldn't see. Like taken advantage of. It was a stress release.[30]
>
> It was jarring, I guess, because he shoots himself. But there's a sense of peace in the destruction. He's sitting there holding her hand, and it's just kind of peaceful. It's kind of a defiant peace. It was definitely one of those moments where you're like, "Whoa! Dude! Like Jesus Christ. I got to think about it."[31]
>
> Liberating. As unjustified as it was, the buildings were tolerable. You'd expect a feeling of regret for the antagonist to accomplish destruction. But there was a liberating feeling somehow.[32]

Jack, the character, has a similar experience to the informants when he finishes his fight.

> *Jack (V.O.):* Fight Club was not about winning or losing. It wasn't about words. The Opponent recovers, throws a headlock on Jack. Jack snakes his arm into a counter headlock. They, wrestling like wild animals. The crowd CHEERS maniacally.
>
> *Jack (V.O.):* The hysterical shouting was in tongues, like at a Pentecostal church. The onlookers kneel to stay with the fight, cheering ever louder. The Opponent smashes Jack's head into the floor, over and over.
>
> *Jack:* Stop. Everyone moves in as the Opponent steps away. They lift Jack to his feet. On the floor is a BLOOD MASK of Jack's face—similar to his TEAR MASK on BOB'S SHIRT, seen earlier. EXT. BAR — NIGHT Everyone files out of the bar, sweating, bleeding, smiling.
>
> *Jack (V.O.):* Nothing was solved. But nothing mattered. Afterwards, we all felt saved.

The screening of *Fight Club* itself can become the classic salvation experience for its audience by which an icon (in this case the screen or television) serves as a scapegoat which asks to become an object onto which the viewer can manifest his own darkness. The salvation experience in the Greco-Roman tradition of the Cults of Metamorphosis operates through the re-integration of the self with something lost. The self is saved through sacred violence from a self-alienation it is suffering. The same process governs the Christian cross, an object that materializes and owns human sin. The weight of the human experience is somehow saved, enlightened, or made more peaceful by the 53 presence of a sullied sacred icon. One informant describes the film as such an icon:

> I thought it was like destruction, but cathartic destruction. That's what people need at times. . . . I get frustrated . . . and feel a subconscious or latent desire to react against it all. . . . I don't feel like I have a place to vent my destructive behavior. It eats at my conscience. . . . I also appreciated the scenes where he went to those self-help sessions. . . . I probably wouldn't do anything like that—go and cry and hug and stuff. . . . It might help some people, even me, but it didn't influence me to do anything like that. When I want to cry, I go to my family at home—two older brothers, an older sister, and a mother. My dad's not around.[33]

CONCLUSION

Fight Club, the movie, exists to solve the very problems of meaning it poses. It holds a mirror up to young white males and says, "This is who you are." And the very act of holding up that mirror allows the film to own a dark part of the culture which cannot be experienced within the culture. 54

Fight Club frames America lacking a public venue to integrate the emotional component of white male identity. When there is a communal or cultural void, history suggests that violence can complete that lack. *Fight Club* exposes the void and offers three solutions: crying, violence, and movies. *Fight Club* asks the question, what do you want to do with the Jacks of our country—those unwanted children of America who were raised on cultural action hero myths and yearn to live those stories? We can send them to support groups to mourn the impossibility of living this dream, send them to war to partake in the battle, or send them to experience the "Fight Club" of American cinema. 55

AFTERWARD

Since the initial conception and transcription of my argument, I have been given reason to revisit a concern of many critics addressed in an article by Gary Crowdus: "They felt scenes served only as a mindless glamorization of brutality, a morally irresponsible portrayal, which they feared might encourage impressionable young male viewers to set up their own real-life Fight Clubs in order to beat each other senseless."[34] 56

Since my interest in *Fight Club* has blossomed, I have been informed on numerous occasions of accounts of real-life Fight Clubs formed in honor of the film. In one Ivy League college, fraternity 57 brothers gather weekly in the name of their "Fight Club." On at least one occasion they were seen engaged in a ritual taken directly from the film—pouring lye on each other and burning holes in their brothers' skin. Another informant confesses:

> I thought it was very confusing. I was definitely surprised by the ending. I also felt a weird urge to be like the guys in the movie. That is, I wanted to be able to participate in that type of violence except that I knew that I was too scared to do that. I did not feel brave enough to participate in that even though I kind of wanted to. Too afraid of hurting myself. . . . Although at one point a friend of mine and I started punching each other in the head to progressively toughen ourselves. We stopped when we thought of what happened to Mohamed Ali. I also know of a guy whose frat (not here) had a Fight Club like the one in the movie.[35]

One female college student in Mexico informs me that she engages regularly in "fight club" with her brothers after having watched the film in which they bruise each other for the fun of it. 58

One African-American informant who detested the film offers perhaps the most simple and sober solution: 59

> I thought, "Just great! This is what America needs. Another 'the-solution-to-our-deteriorating-white-male-crisis is violence and rebellion and stuff.' . . . just replacing one problem with another. The solution is to be honest. Admit how you feel. Love. And feel however it is you feel. The support groups were weird. I was like, "What's this guy doing?" and "What's this all about?" I'm still trying to find a place to feel. I like to think that it takes being alone and by yourself a lot of times so you can truly hear yourself and find out what truly is the problem that's bothering you. I don't want to say that it can't be done with other people, but it's just a very personal thing. To really understand and accept what's happening inside you, it takes getting in touch with the part of you that people tried to kill even before you could speak—when you knew you wanted to cry, but they told you that wasn't okay. You had to sublimate that to exist in this world. So the problem is trying to get back into it. But they've had you sublimate it so long, that you don't even know what the problem is any more. The movie didn't solve anything for me. It just re-confirmed my ideas that society is really wrong.[36]

These examples further problematize my claim that *Fight Club* the film does in fact solve the problems it poses—or at least that it does so neatly and non-violently without consequences. Herein lies the moral ambiguity of both my argument and the film that I submit to the reader and future scholars for further reflection. 60

NOTES

[1]For the purposes of this paper, I am defining spiritual as that experience of wholeness or oneness classically found in religion which is relegated in modern America to the confines of the individual.

[2]David Fincher as quoted in Gavin Smith, "Inside out," *Film Comment*. New York; Sep/Oct 1999; Vol. 35, Iss. 5, 58–66.

[3]Jim Uhls, *Fight Club, "The Shooting Script,"* February, 16, 1998.

[4]M. Greene, 2000.

[5]Erich Neumann, Translation by R. F. C. Hull, *The Origins and History of Consciousness* (Mythos Books) (New Jersey: Princeton University Press, 1995).

[6]Eugene Monick, "Studies in Jungian Psychology," *Phallos: Sacred Image of the Masculine*, 9.

[7]Quoted by Keith Thompson in "What Men Really Want: A New Age Interview with Robert Bly," 32.

[8]Bly, 23.

[9]Monick, 94.

[10]Monick, 96.

[11]Monick, 95.

[12]Monick, 95.

[13]The definition of "ground zero," *http://dictionary.reference.com/*, expands on the rich depth of meaning of the term in relation to recent events in America and the film itself: **ground zero n**. 1) The target of a projectile, such as a missile or bomb. 2) The site directly below, directly above, or at the point of detonation of a nuclear weapon. 3) The center of rapid or intense development or change: "The neighborhood scarcely existed five years ago, but today it is the ground zero from which designer shops and restaurants radiate" (Robert Clark). 4) The starting point or most basic level: My client didn't like my preliminary designs, so I returned to ground zero.

[14]J. David Slocum, *Violence and American Cinema*. "Passion and Acceleration: Generic Change in the Action Film," by Rikke Schubart. New York: Routledge, 2001, 194.

[15]See section entitled "After the Theater" for a chronicle of peaceful feelings and reactions upon leaving the theater.

[16]This statement is made solely from the rationality of the author. With the possible exception of rare public architecture, I cannot think of an art form that costs many millions of dollars to produce like the Hollywood film.

[17]Joel W. Martin and Conrad E. Ostwalt, Jr., *Screening the Sacred: Religion, Myth, and Ideology in Popular American Film* (Boulder: Westview Press, 1995), p. 2.

[18]Adrian Gargett. *Doppelganger: Exploded States of Consciousness in Fight Club, http://www.disinfo.com/pages/article/id1497/*, 2001, 7.

[19]Gargett, 7.

[20]Adrian McOran-Campbell, "Recent Incarnations: Generation X-Y," *Postmodern Science Fiction and Cyberpunk: The "New Edge" as Cultural and Evolutionary Leap*. Version of dissertation submitted for degree-level English Literature (Chester, UK, May 2000), 25.

[21]McOran-Campbel, 26.

[22]Smith, 58.

[23]Smith, 60.

[24]American male college student, personal interview, March 10, 2003.

[25]Edward Norton, interview printed on *Fight Club* DVD disc 2, "Special Features."

[26]Howard Hampton, "Blood and Gore Wars," *Film Comment* (New York, Nov/Dec 2000, Vol. 36, Iss. 6) 30.

[27]"How to Start a Fight," *Fight Club* DVD, 200, 14.

[28]Edward Norton, Interview printed on *Fight Club* DVD disc 2, "Special Features."

[29]American male college student, interview, March 10, 2003.

[30]American male college student, personal interview, March 10, 2003.

[31]American male college student, personal interview, March 10, 2003.

[32]American male college student, personal interview, March 10, 2003.

[33]American male college student, personal interview, March 12, 2003.

[34]Gary Crowdus, "Getting Exercised over Fight Club," *Cineaste* September 2000 (25:4), 47.

[35]American male college student, personal interview, March 8, 2003.

[36]American male college student, personal interview, March 9, 2003 and March 12, 2003.

BIBLIOGRAPHY

Althusser, Louis. *For Marx*. New York: Vintage Books, 1970.

Arthur, Chris. "Media, Meaning and Method in Religious Studies" in *Rethinking Media, Religion, and Culture*, Ed. S. Hoover and K. Lundby. Thousand Oaks, London, New Delhi: Sage, 1996.

Bellah, Robert N. "Civil Religion in America," in *Daedalus*, 1967.

Bryant, M. Darrol. "Cinema, Religion, and Popular Culture," in *Religion in Film*, Ed. by John R. May and Michael Bird. Knoxville: University of Tennessee Press, 1982.

Carolyn, Marvin, and David W. Ingle. "Blood Sacrifice and the Nation: Revisiting Civil Religion," in *Journal of the American Academy of Religion*, 1996.

Cavell, Stanley. *The World Viewed: Reflections on the Ontology of Film*. Cambridge: Harvard University Press, 1979.

Clark, J. Michael. "Faludi, *Fight Club* and Phallic Masculinity: Exploring the Emasculating Economics of Patriarchy," in *Journal of Men's Studies*. 11(1):65–76, 2002.

Crowdus, Gary, "Getting Exercised over *Fight Club*," *Cineaste* September 2000 (25:4), 46–48.

Deacy, Christopher. "Redemption and Film: Cinema as a Contemporary Site of Religious Activity," in *Media Development* XLVII (1), 2000, 50–54.

Deacy, Christopher. "Integration and Rebirth through Confrontation: *Fight Club* and American Beauty as Contemporary Religious Parables," in *Journal of Contemporary Religion*. London: Carfax Publishing, 2002.

Deren, Maya. "Cinematography: The Creative Use of Reality." *Daedalus, the journal of the American Academy of Arts and Sciences*. Boston, Massachusetts: The Visual Arts Today, 1960.

Dreyer, Richard. *Heavenly Bodies: Film Stars and Society*. New York: St. Martin's Press, 1986.

Durkheim, Emile. *The Elementary Forms of Religious Life*. New York: The Free Press, 1995.

Eliade, Mircea, *The Sacred and the Profane; the Nature of Religion*. Trans. from the French by Willard R. Trask. New York: Harcourt, Brace, 1959.

Gargett, Adrian. *Doppelganger: Exploded States of Consciousness in Fight Club*. *http://www.disinfo.com/pages/article/id1497/*, 2001.

Girard, René (tr. Patrick Gregory). *Violence and the Sacred*. Baltimore, London: John Hopkins, 1977.

Graham, David John. "The Uses of Film in Theology," in *Explorations in Theology and Film: Movies and Meaning*, eds. C. Marsh and G. Ortiz. Oxford: Blackwell, 1997.

Hampton, Howard. "Blood and Gore Wars," *Film Comment*. New York, Nov/Dec 2000, Vol. 36, Iss. 6.

Hoover, Stewart M. "Media and the Construction of the Religious Public Sphere," in *Rethinking Media, Religion, and Culture*, ed. S. Hoover and K. Lundby. Thousand Oaks: Sage, 1996.

Hoover, Stewart M. "Religion, Media, and the Cultural Center of Gravity," in *Religion and Popular Culture: Studies on the Interaction of Worldviews*, Ed. Daniel A. Stout and Judith M. Buddenbaum. Ames, Iowa: Iowa State University Press, 2001.

Hoover, Stewart M. and Shalini S. Venturelli. "The Category of the Religious: The Blindspot of Contemporary Media Theory?," in *Critical Studies in Mass Communication*, 1996.

Jarvie, Ian Charles. *Movies and Society*. New York: Basic Books, 1970.

Jarvie, Ian Charles. *Towards a Sociology of the Cinema: A Comparative Essay on the Structure and Functioning of a Major Entertainment Industry*. London: Routledge & K. Paul, 1970.

Jowett, Garth. *Film: The Democratic Art*. Boston: Little, Brown, 1976.

Lévi-Strauss, Claude. *Myth and Meaning*. New York: Schoken Books, 1995.

Levinas, Emmanuel. Ed. Seán Hand. *The Levinas Reader*. "Reality and Its Shadow" and "The Transcendence of Words." Malden Massachusetts: Blackwell Publishers, Inc., 1989.

Marsh and Ortiz. *Explorations in Theology and Film: Movies and Meaning*. Malden, MA: Blackwell Publishers, 1997.

Martin, Joel W. and Conrad E. Ostwalt, Jr. *Screening the Sacred: Religion, Myth, and Ideology in Popular American Film*. Boulder, CO: Westview Press, 1995.

Marx, Karl. *The Marx-Engels Reader*. New York: W. W. Norton & Company, 1978

McOran-Campbell, Adrian. *Postmodern Science Fiction and Cyberpunk: The "New Edge" as Cultural and Evolutionary Leap*. "Recent Incarnations: Generation X-Y." Version of dissertation submitted for degree-level English Literature, Chester, UK, May 2000.

Miles, Margaret R. *Seeing and Believing: Religion and Values in the Movies*. Boston: Beacon Press, 1996.

Neumann, Erich. Translation by R. F. C. Hull. *The Origins and History of Consciousness* (Mythos Books). New Jersey: Princeton University Press, 1995.

Nietzsche, Friedrich Wilhelm. 1974. *The Gay Science*. Translated by Walter Kaufmann. New York: Random House.

Palahniuk, Chuck. *Fight Club*. London: Vintage Books, 1997.

Scott, Bernard Brandon. *Hollywood Dreams and Biblical Stories*. Minneapolis, MN: Fortress Press, 1994.

Smith, Gavin. "Inside out," *Film Comment*. New York, Sep/Oct 1999, Vol. 35, Iss. 5, 58–66.

Smith, Warren, and Debbie Leslie. "Fight Club." *International Feminist Journal of Politics*.

Steimatsky, Noa. "Pasolini on Terra Sancta: Towards a Theology of Film." *The Yale Journal of Criticism*, 1998.

Tarkovsky, Andrey. *Sculpting in Time: Reflections on the Cinema*. New York: Knopf, 1987.

Turner, Bryan S. *Religion and Social Theory*. Thousand Oaks: SAGE Publications, 1991.

Tremblay, Robert. *Canada: DIS (Hons)* IV, Carleton University, 1999–2000.

Turner, Victor. *The Ritual Process: Structure and Anti-Structure*.

White, David Manning. *Sight, Sound, and Society; Motion Pictures and Television in America*. Boston: Beacon Press, 1968.

Wilson, Charles Reagan. "The Religion of the Lost Clause: Ritual and Organization of the Southern Civil Religion, 1865–1920," in *Religion and American Culture: A Reader*, Ed. D. Hackett. New York and London: Routledge, 1995.

Examining the Text

1. In this article, the author argues that American culture has been robbed of its masculine principle. What does he mean by this assertion, and do you agree with his position? Cite specific examples in the text that the author uses to support his contention.

2. Identify the ways in which the author relates the idea of sacredness to the themes in *Fight Club* and movies in general. What does the word "sacred" mean to you? What do you think of the author's use of this word in the context of a film about a bunch of guys beating the holy daylights out of each other?
3. The author initially describes *Fight Club* as "avant-garde sublime art," yet seems to concede that the real measure of a film's value is its box-office success. What do you think the author is implying when he discusses these issues of sacredness and money? What comment might he be making about the preoccupation with money and material value in American society?
4. The author states, "When an individual steps into a church, how much do they expect of their experience to follow them out? Great art changes our experience of reality and challenges us to take that experience home with us. Is this great art?" (line 46). Examine this passage from the article again. In what ways might art change our perceptions and beliefs? Based on your knowledge of the film gleaned from the article, as well as your own experience as a filmgoer, does *Fight Club* fall into the category of great art?
5. *Thinking rhetorically*: What sources does the author use to provide evidence for his assertions in this essay? Does the author's use of a variety of sources, ranging from the familiar to the obscure, enhance the clarity and depth of the article? What does the use of such diverse references suggest about the article's intended audience? On a more personal note, do the references increase your own understanding of the article? What risks might be posed when writers quote from sources that are not commonly known and are not explained in the article?

For Group Discussion

In a full-class discussion, engage in a debate over the question: Do men in American society lack rituals that mark their entry into manhood? Do rituals already exist that might support the passage of contemporary American males into adulthood? Short of organizing mutual-mayhem groups, as happens in the film, what other means can you imagine for boys to become "real" men? Discuss ways in which the enactment of such rituals might support or detract from author Rothe-Kushel's thesis in this piece.

Writing Suggestion

The author of this essay acknowledges that he may be "stuck in an outdated paradigm that does not take into account the plurality of roles a human can play?" (line 19). Using libraries and the Internet, write an essay that responds to the article from a feminine perspective. Be sure to address both the underlying themes of the movie as well as the text of the article itself. For example, examine carefully the author's contention that households across the country are dominated by women, and that young men are left without adequate models of masculinity. Do you agree that men need male role models or are women equally suited to raising sons who are comfortable and clear about their masculinity?

From Chick Flicks to Millennial Blockbusters: Spinning Female-Driven Narratives into Franchises

ASHLEY ELAINE YORK

The English language is a fluid medium, always evolving and expanding to add new words and phrases as their usage becomes common within the broader culture. While some of those new words have to do with technologies that never existed before, others include slang that becomes so much of everyday language that they get their own listing in the dictionary. So it is with the phrase "chick flick." A decade or two ago, you would not have found this phrase in your library's thick and dusty Webster's, but today it appears on the Merriam-Webster Web site, defined as "a motion picture intended to appeal especially to women." Whether such films have always existed since the beginning of silent films and "talkies" and/or whether there has been a proliferation of such films in recent years—prompting the creation of a new dictionary listing to describe the films—is a matter of debate. In fact, this very question lies at the heart of the following article, which presents an analysis of major motion pictures targeted at female audiences. Beyond the usual films aimed primarily toward women, there has been an upswing in the number of movies described in the industry as "blockbuster chick flicks," such as The Devil Wears Prada *and* Mamma Mia!

In this article, author Ashley Elaine York provides a brief overview of the evolution of films produced primarily for female audiences, beginning in the 1940s, as the "chick flick" genre evolved. York, a true expert in this field, is the first Corus Entertainments PhD Fellow in Television Studies at The University of Alberta and the 2009 William E. Brigman Journal of Popular Culture Award–Winner. Her previous publications include magazine, newspaper, and webzine articles and photo essays, and her current research examines the role that contemporary woman-centered dramas play in American pop culture. ***As you read,*** *consider your own experience with so-called chick flicks: have you, in your movie-viewing experience, noticed an increase in the number of such movies—including large-scale, large-budget films directed at female audiences? Likewise, have you noticed an increase in "chick flick" sequel franchises, merchandising, and marketing, as is discussed in York's article?*

In 2004, *Variety* editors Dade Hayes and Jonathan Bing noticed a change in the way Hollywood was doing business. A film's box office could no longer be defined as a theater venture, or even a domestic, 1 action-adventure, or male-dominated domain. Rather, Hollywood had evolved beyond the walls of the theater to the "story of the architectural and retail infrastructure into which the studios plug their product." Even today, film branding starts at the conception of a pitch and ends years after the theatrical release, when ancillary products have flooded the market, texts have been repurposed up and down the conglomerate food chain, and series, sequels, and spin-offs are in the pipeline. A critically lauded film is not noteworthy if it opens with a box office whimper. Neither is a film that blows up on opening weekend, but does not have legs, secondary products, sequels, or tie-ins to back it up. With the box office affected by and managed in tandem with style and iconography, celebrity and star, music, fashion, and the entire global commercial complex, women's films have a chance in the new millennium to compete for success among the grosses and the rankings. Women's genres of yesteryear, forties' "weepies," seventies' romances, eighties' heroine action adventures and contemporary chick flicks have heretofore concentrated on the domestic market and catered to a small niche group. The new women's blockbuster competes on bottom line and overnight has turned a genre filled with sleepers or domestic hits into global powerhouses.

The new women's film is defined by a combination of elements of women's films from over the decades; for example, they continue to touch on topics of consumerism, romance, beauty, and escape; however, overriding this subject matter is a theme of validation. In addition to a change in subject matter, this new genre is marketed in the same way that all blockbusters have been in the past: with spectacle aesthetics and a focus on ancillary marketing and foreign box office. This newfound women's genre represented by such films as *The Devil Wears Prada* (2006), *Sex and the City* (2008), and *Mamma Mia!* (2008) are no longer promoted as standalone texts solely marketed to women consumers. Rather, they are advertised in a manner similar to *Jaws* (1975), *Independence Day* (1996), and *Titanic* (1997) and often compete with and eclipse male-driven, big-budget vehicles in their total earnings. In 2008, *Mamma Mia!* and *Sex and the City* outperformed *The Incredible Hulk, Get Smart,* and *Journey to the Center of the Earth* in the worldwide revenue (boxofficemojo.com, December 16, 2008), changing the Hollywood moviemaking formula and affecting the types of women's films that are produced in the future. This new breed of women's giants may best be described as "women's blockbusters" and touted as the newest conglomerate trend; however, fat bottom lines and climbing industry rankings aside, they are, as yet, cited as neither. Nevertheless, it is clear that the film industry is busy spinning female-driven narratives into gold. Whatever new front this 2 indicates on the global filmic landscape, the study of the millennial women's blockbuster deserves careful consideration and adequate study among contemporary industry scholars.

HISTORY OF WOMEN'S FILMS

Movies have become more than stories; they connote lifestyles that 3
foreign and domestic audiences both appreciate and aspire to. Nearly overnight, the commercial push of women's films has helped chick flicks move out of the niche project category and catapult up the grosses and the rankings. From *The Devil Wears Prada* to *Mamma Mia!* and *Sex and the City*, this new brand of women's film is successfully competing with male-driven action and superhero tales in terms of both box office and global franchise success. In 2008, the number of women-headlined movies among the top 100 worldwide grossers is fifteen, including *Mamma Mia!* at number six and *Sex and the City* at number ten. In 2006, *The Devil Wears Prada* ranked twelfth on that list. Now, with a category of women's film consistently competing among the short list of sure-fire winners, not only is Hollywood's box office affected, but the way women's films are made and distributed are also impacted in two main ways. First, films like *Sweet Home Alabama* (2002), *13 Going on 30* (2004), and *Working Girl* (1988)—one-offs that make a nice domestic run yet have no impact outside the text—do not represent the blockbuster-styled storyline and marketing package of *Sex and the City* or *Mamma Mia!* In the future, films such as these may be bypassed in favor of women's films with franchise and ancillary marketing potential. Second, in synergizing the theme, aesthetics, and marketing of global women's hits, the texts themselves have changed. No longer sad or complicated storylines that appeal to a domestic few, today's women's blockbuster present a focused package of image, advertising, and text beyond the chick flick audience of 18- to 34-year-old heterosexual women. Therefore, such films appeal to a wide demographic that brings older and younger heterosexual women, lesbians and gays, heterosexual men, and transnational viewers together to transform what was once a small domestic following into a large, sutured, global audience.

Like blockbusters of all genres, millennial women's blockbust- 4
ers adhere to certain characteristics that mold them into success cases. First, women's blockbusters are high concept. Their storylines can be summed up in single sentences that easily translate across cultures and borders. Second, they offer a millennial women's theme of validation, physically reaffirming this message in product placements, commercial

tie-ins, cross-promotions, and the general culture of consumerism that is shepherded around these projects. Third, women's blockbusters, like all high-concept commodities, need only be tweaked with a shift in emphasis or attached to a different star to be refashioned into novel vehicles over and over again. However, the real drive behind the success of this category of women's films is a new push in the direction of ancillary marketing and foreign box office. By marketing them as blockbusters from their conception, the women's films of today offer something beyond story; that is, they offer a millennial-themed narrative together with blockbuster aesthetics and a global marketing complex that drive them to newfound levels of success.

In addition, the new women's blockbuster stands differentiated 5
from women's films of the past in the various components included in its recipe for success. It is nevertheless important to look at the historical significance of the films that preceded it, as many successful elements have been borrowed or updated from the past. Hollywood first marketed films to women consumers in the 1940s with the advent of the Women's Film. These "weepies," movies such as *Mildred Pierce* (1945), *Letter from an Unknown Woman* (1948), and *Now Voyager* (1942), evolved as a marketing strategy and a tie-in to consumerism. Meant to inspire the material ambitions of a generation just past two world wars and the Great Depression, these films symbolized the possibility of a better life, but on the backs of a class of women positioned and represented as either afflicted or that of self-sacrificing mothers, leaving little room for women protagonists no less women consumers to negotiate space outside the categories of wife, mother, and victim. Within thirty years, newfound economic promise, the "free love" generation, and the women's liberation movement encouraged Hollywood to take a turn toward the romantic, and the prime-time soap opera was born, first with ABC's Peyton Place (1964–1969) and in the 1980s with many successful series, including *Dallas, Dynasty, Knot's Landing,* and *Falcon Crest*. In the 1980s and early 1990s, female action-adventure heroines moved droves of women to the box office. But *Titanic* (1997), the number one grossing film of all time, changed Hollywood and the complexion of the women's film forever. This sea-changing film, which to date has grossed $1.8 billion, garnered widespread appeal among female fans the world over; moreover, it met with equal success among male moviegoers. The mix of narrative style, thematic elements, spectacle aesthetics, and concentrated effort on the franchise is an approach to women's film that was not conceived of before that time. Henceforth, the success of *Titanic* would serve as an indicator to Hollywood of the true potential of the franchised women's picture. After Titanic, Hollywood dabbled in creating a new formula. Setting the dramatic category to the side, Hollywood's initial attempts at turning chick flicks into mainstream

hits met with only lukewarm success. *Miss Congeniality* (2000), *Bridget Jones's Diary* (2001), *My Big Fat Greek Wedding* (2002), and, most importantly, *Legally Blonde* (2001) were some of the first women's films of the new millennium to cross the $100 million mark; yet all but *Bridget Jones's Diary* made most of its money in the United States. Even though each of these films met with limited franchise success, *Legally Blonde* is one of the first chick flicks built around a limited franchise and also one of the first to break free of a niche style of Hollywood production. In contrast to the women's films of the past, *Legally Blonde* put forth the theme of wish fulfillment. As part of its positive message, it conveyed a theme that anyone could achieve Elle Wood's level of success. The movie, nevertheless, fell short of becoming a blockbuster. Although its ancillary devices were successful, including campaigns such as National Blonde Day, tie-ins to free makeovers at salons across the country, and the *Cosmopolitan* magazine contest to turn ten women into "blonde bombshells," the movie itself failed to cash in on its potential foreign box office, earning just 31% of its worldwide box office overseas. Thus, when the potential sitcom was dropped from its television development deal, the fate of *Legally Blonde* was sealed. Although *Legally Blonde* did not become a women's blockbuster, it is noteworthy that by 2001, four years after *Titanic*, the chick flick had gone mainstream and done well at least domestically. In *Film Theory Goes to the Movies*, industry scholar Tom Schatz describes the qualities that turn feature films into mass market successes. "Mainstream hits are where stars, genres, and cinematic innovations invariably are established, where the 'grammar' of cinema is most likely to be refined, and where the essential qualities of the medium—its popular and commercial character—are most evident. These blockbuster hits are, for better or worse, what the New Hollywood is about, and thus are the necessary starting point for any analysis of contemporary American Cinema" (10–11). With the success of precursors *Titanic* and *Legally Blonde,* today's chick flicks have the potential to go beyond even Schatz's imaginings and turn mainstream hits into global box office sensations. In a constantly evolving industry, in which power has shifted to the dealmakers who can package talent around individual projects on a film-by-film basis, blockbusters of any genre—women's or otherwise—are the "mainstream" films of the future.

THE WOMEN'S FILM INCORPORATES BLOCKBUSTER ELEMENTS

One of the tenets of filmmaking in the new millennial Hollywood is 6
spending more and more money on fewer and fewer films, thereby requiring big budget features to recoup not only their costs but also the

outlay of the studio's flops. Hollywood has long evolved past the film text as the sole resource necessary in the war over box office; more than any other ingredient today, the key to global success is the franchise. As Dade Hayes and Jonathan Bing, editors of *Variety*, duly note in *Open Wide: How Hollywood Box Office Became a National Obsession,* the new, New Hollywood is about the infrastructure that surrounds and supports the movie industry. This essay argues that the twenty-first century women's film is the women's blockbuster, and that it profoundly impacts the infrastructure of which Hayes and Bing speak. Any assessment of contemporary entertainment should take into consideration this new category as a change agent to both millennial women's pictures and the current Hollywood industry.

The millennial women's blockbuster contains three key characteristics that set it apart from women's films of the past. First, its story is high concept, and its narrative is easy to translate. Additionally, it offers a theme not of affliction or of sadness or even primarily of romance, but rather of affirmation that viewers too can "have it all." Second, this category of films, like all blockbusters, uses art cinema aesthetics to simultaneously relay style and story. Finally, there is a newfound focus on the franchise. Like the male-dominated powerhouses to come before, women's blockbusters also maximize potential ancillary marketing efforts, from the soundtrack to the foreign box office, in order to gain more momentum and develop an infrastructure that reaches further and wider to lure potential moviegoers the world over and thus increase the total lifetime intake of the franchise. Three key characteristics define this new women's blockbuster and thereby set it apart from the various women's genres that came before. First and foremost, women's blockbusters are high-concept vehicles. From *Jaws* to *Titanic* to *Sex and the City,* Hollywood has utilized the strategy encapsulated as "the look, the hook, and the book" to market and sell franchises the world over. In characterizing the difference between these and other Hollywood films, industry scholar Justin Wyatt writes, "High concept films are differentiated within the marketplace through an emphasis on style and through integration with their marketing" (23). The image, narrative, and advertising are conceived, pitched, and marketed in one fell swoop: in a single-sentence catchphrase that easily translates among cultures and across borders. For example, "where *Sisterhood of the Traveling Pants* meets *Grease*" could convey *Mamma Mia!* to an industry insider, as well as a Japanese patron. "The slapstick, fish out of water story of a recent, nerdy Northwestern journalism graduate who takes a job as the second assistant to a fashion editor the likes of Anna Wintour" would successfully explain *The Devil Wears Prada* to its core target audience. And, finally, the *Sex and the City* TV series is such a well-known commodity that simply describing the movie version as 7 "where *Sex and the City* meets one of the Dreamgirls" would amply describe the logline to Carrie Bradshaw fans at every port.

In addition to high-concept storytelling, women's blockbusters 8 rely on genre and story elements that have immediate and wide-reaching appeal. For example, *Mamma Mia!* incorporates dance numbers reminiscent of the movie musical genre of the 1930s and 1940s. *The Devil Wears Prada* interweaves two genres (i.e., the fish out of water story with the Cinderella complex). *Sex and the City* is tied into consumerism. Thus, when mixed with a dash of slapstick humor reminiscent of screwball comedies past, this millennial women's blockbuster out of New Hollywood produces an explosive recipe of hybrid-genre success. Further, the global setting of all three of the texts discussed herein is also appealing. In *Sex and the City* and *The Devil Wears Prada,* the protagonist goes to the big city; in *Mamma Mia!,* it comes to her. But an even more critical characteristic of the recent success of women's blockbusters is found in their themes, which appeal to international consumers. Not only do all three films represent popular dramas across the globe with the genres of the movie musical, Cinderella complex, and romantic comedy, each film also smartly matches the appropriate star/s to its property. These key features in combination allow women's blockbusters to be replicated and successfully repackaged over and over again.

Beyond genre and star/vehicle match-up, women's blockbust- 9 ers offer material that is both temporal and in vogue. As of late, the world of fashion and fashion magazines are very popular; however, as always, escape from the city to a place like Greece—a beautiful country that represents freedom from technology and deadlines—is always a good idea. Second, each of these films represents a hot trend inspired by either movie musicals, for example, Hairspray (2007) and *High School Musical 3* (2008), or fashion television, for example, *Stylista, Project Runway, America's Next Top Model,* and *The Victoria's Secret Fashion Show.* Third, all three films present myriad attractive characters in fun and interesting jobs; thus, audience members enjoy ample opportunities to fantasize about their favorite character's experiences and imagine them to be their own.

Although relying on set identities is an important component in 10 the success of the women's blockbuster, this high-concept formula also requires that franchises bring something new to the table with each successive film text. These three films discussed herein certainly offer that added dimension. For example, a girl with three potential dads summoned together for the first time just before her wedding day is an unusual premise to say the least. So too is a graduate of the number one journalism program in the country who takes a job as not the first, but rather the second assistant to the vixen boss of a fashion magazine empire. These novel touches differentiate among mainstream hits. However, an ever more crucial characteristic of their success is their ability to tap into the pulse of the global consumer: that is, to sell their movies based on properties that are well known among peoples and cultures the world over. Part of their feat is owed to genre conventions, surely; however, in addition, much is owed to a slate of international stars who drive audiences from one vehicle to another. For example, Meryl Streep as a headliner most assuredly factors into the bottom line successes of both *The Devil Wears Prada* and *Mamma Mia! Parade* recently named her one of the five most popular American stars (4–5). And, *Elle* magazine, in its annual survey of Hollywood, includes both Streep and Sarah Jessica Parker in their illustrious gang of the twenty-five most influential women stars (110–20). Such wide-reaching appeal can only propel their films to blockbuster status. Anne Hathaway similarly transfers her *Princess Diaries* fans over to *The Devil Wears Prada* franchise. And, the four protagonists of the *Sex and the City* television series not only carry over, but indeed build upon their hugely loyal fan base generated over the six seasons of the award-winning HBO series. *Mamma Mia!* similarly draws existing mega-fans, for example the ABBAphiles and the aficionados of the Tony Award–nominated musical, to their big-screen version. In this high-concept formula for success, globally appealing stars and genre work hand in hand to increasingly build upon the prior achievements of the franchises and conglomerates they represent. Thus, the idea of high concept then denotes an intersection where commercial orientation meets star persona and marketing genius. *The Devil Wears Prada, Mamma Mia!,* and *Sex and the City* each bring this concept to bear in achieving heretofore unparalleled levels of success for films within the women's genre.

Beyond high concept, a second feature of the women's blockbuster is their millennial theme of validation, which was missing in many women's films of yesteryear. No longer relegated to messages of self-sacrifice or affliction, or held hostage to love (and a male star) or action-adventures that altogether deprive them of romantic possibilities, heroines of women's blockbusters live out their fantasies in all respects and come out on top in each and every case. In *Mamma Mia!,* for example, Meryl Streep's character, Donna Sheridan, is not sitting around waiting for love. She abandoned it—three times, actually—to live her life and raise her daughter as a single parent. As *Mamma Mia!* opens, the audience finds her struggling to cope with a dilapidated inn that is rarely to never rented, while mentally preparing to lose her only daughter Sophie to marriage. As fits within the new formula of women's films, Sophie never marries; instead, she seeks validation in her own right and by searching for her father hopes to find herself. Although these women are involved in love stories, these serve as 11 subplots rather than main storylines in their respective texts. This millennial theme of validation also holds true for Andy Sachs in *The Devil Wears Prada*. Played by Anne Hathaway, the protagonist is primarily looking for work. After graduating from college and moving to New York City, Andy lands a job as the second assistant to a fashion editor. The position, however, is far from perfect, although it is the vehicle through which she ultimately secures both self-knowledge and personal validation by the end of the film. Andy Sachs proves that she is more than a second assistant. She comes to understand her own moral code, and more importantly, what she can and must give up in order to stay true to herself. Furthermore, in each of the three discussed texts, love comes and goes. It is part of life, but only that much. Millennial women's blockbusters champion validation as their main theme, as well as other themes of modern female life: bad relationships, cheating, divorce, weight gain, growing older, hair loss, getting cancer, growing up without a father, deciding to delay marriage to first discover who you are, transitioning from college to career, or from career to motherhood and back again. Put simply, these texts are the screen versions of women's own lives. They explore the gamut of human emotions, from anger to joy and from loneliness to ultimate satisfaction, while encouraging moviegoers to laugh and cry over the lot of it with characters confronting similar demons along life's pathways. In this way, women's films of the twenty-first century construct a new space for women viewers in three important ways. First, they explore the many facets of women's lives in the form of female bonding, mischief, and mayhem as reminiscent of the screwball comedies of the 1930s and 1940s. Second, they recognize sexual difference but no longer serve to marginalize female protagonists in the roles of wife and/or mother, as in the 1940s. Finally, much like male-driven blockbusters from the 1970s to date, millennial women's blockbusters exhibit tremendous hope. The message of "You can do it!" rings loud and clear throughout the texts to the exclamation point in *Mamma Mia!*'s title and situates new types of women protagonists in the process of living their lives in a complex yet hopeful twenty-first-century space.

12 In creating films with greater depth and breadth of setting, storyline, and character, the new women's blockbuster speaks to viewers outside the typical 18- to 34-year-old heterosexual American women's audience. Such storylines include characters of different ages, sexes, and sexual orientations, thus bringing new fans to both their texts and franchises. For example, a fiftyish-year-old woman and a teenage girl dually headline *Mamma Mia!* Further, its cast is made up of women and men of all ages, including a trio of attractive, well-known actors in Pierce Brosnan, Colin Firth, and Stellan Skarsgård. *Sex and the City* also includes myriad virile male characters in the cast who draw not only

women but also male viewers sutured into the stars and/or the characters they portray. All three films also include gay characters among their stellar supporting casts: Stanley Tucci as Nigel in *The Devil Wears Prada,* Colin Firth as Harry Bright in *Mamma Mia!*, and Willie Garson as Stanford Blatch in *Sex and the City*. These characters contribute not only to the development of the narrative but also to the reconstructed family lives of newly situated female protagonists who live far away from "home" and apart from their biological families. Because women outside 18–34 years are also targeted by the millennial women's blockbuster, younger fans of related projects by star or genre (e.g., *The Princess Diaries* and *High School Musical 3*, as well as sexy young-adult novels and television shows such as *Twilight* and *Gossip Girl*, respectively) are brought to the fore as new fans of the franchise as well. Thus, the potential fan base of millennial women's blockbusters has widened to include a bi-gendered, worldwide audience of older and younger men and women, which is necessary to turn a chick flick into a successful global powerhouse.

Instead of shoot 'em up and special effects, women's blockbusters utilize different aesthetics to create their movie spectacles. By using what David Bordwell and Kristin Thompson call "historical poetics" to examine the mise-en-scène, framing, composition, and editing of these modern women's films, scholars can situate the women's blockbuster among the women's genres as well as within contemporary filmmaking practices. As Christian Metz argues in his seminal book, *Film Language,* "It is precisely to the extent that the cinema confront[s] the problems of narration that, in the course of successive groupings, it [comes] to produce a body of specific signifying procedures" (69–70). The aesthetic codes to which Metz refers connote meaning beyond the textual level. Aesthetics have changed over the years from classic Hollywood cinema until today. Now the narrative form and compositional elements of the image reflect both the film school generation's knowledge of hybrid genres and the music video generation's expectations of TV aesthetics: that is, close-up shots, rapidly paced montage, and a deep color saturation that has become more and more common over the past thirty years. To understand the special image qualities that make blockbusters stand out, it is necessary to analyze them in relation to the compositional codes and the norms of their time. 13

The editing styles among all three films analyzed herein reflect a match between the characters and their lifestyle. Close-up glamour shots of the protagonists are intercut with countershots of the material items that are part and parcel of their lives—shoes, bags, laptops, clothing, books, keepsakes, food, sex, eyes, and other body parts—and medium and medium long shots that relay the exotic locals, shopping 14 meccas, throngs of people, and well-apportioned décor around them. When it comes to the millennial women's blockbuster, "style makes up a . . . utopian way of life" (Ewen 42). It "replicates the superior, upscale lifestyles promised in the many ads" (Wyatt 25). In the case of *Mamma Mia!*, although the family of characters is by no means wealthy, they are nevertheless elegantly apportioned. The green water, white mountains, and brown trees of lush Greece surround the leading ladies, who are appropriately donned in flowing, brightly colored peasant dresses. The entire cast to that end lives in a laidback tropical oasis that, at once, promises freedom and extravagance to every sutured viewer. In addition to ornate set decorations and costumes, the performances of these characters are also that of a spectacle. From facial expression and gestures to action and movement, the characters appear animated, theatrical, and larger than life. For example, there is more singing than dialogue in *Mamma Mia!* The large-scale dance numbers present what Tom Gunning would describe as a "theatre of attractions," wherein women dance about in aprons while men play pianos, sit seaside at tables, and applaud them as they go by.

Beyond mise-en-scène, the poetics of popular women's films are 15
also characterized by a style that frames and composes them in close-up, in order to promote compositional motivation and meet the expectations of moviegoers most familiar with the graphic music video images, which leave little to the imagination. As Mark Crispin Miller writes about the adaptation of TV aesthetics to film, "Each shot [in contemporary Hollywood films] presents a content closed and unified, like a fist, [which] makes the point right in your face: big gun, big car, nice ass, full moon, a chase (great shoes!), big crash (blood, glass), a lobby (doorman), sarcasm, drinks, a tonguey, pugilistic kiss (nice sheets!), and so on" (205). Thus, the combination of a highly mobile camera, rapid cutting, and music video-paced montage shots serves the film's compositional qualities by driving both the visuals and the narrative throughout the diegesis.

In the opening sequence of *The Devil Wears Prada*, these charac- 16
teristic aesthetics are made evident. The film opens with a medium close-up of Andy Sachs brushing her teeth; immediately, an intimacy is established between the protagonist and the viewers. After the camera cranes over the metropolis in an establishing shot of the city, the camera cuts to an unknown girl standing in front of a large window many stories high. The camera pans left to a close-up of the girl's back. She puts on a black bra before turning to face the camera. Breaking the fourth wall, the camera cuts to face her, and, in doing so, highlights her well-endowed bosom. In the cutaway, another woman steps into a thong. She is shot at knee level in a medium wide shot that reveals a dozen long-stemmed white roses in a crystal vase set on the

windowsill in the background. Interlaced shots of various unknown women pulling up their glamorous panties and sexy stockings follow. The camera then cuts back to their counterpart, Devil's "everygirl" Andy Sachs. Now postshower and wrapped in a white towel, this protagonist sorts through her neatly organized underwear drawer, filled to the brim with cotton panties of the Hanes or Fruit of the Loom varieties sold in five-pair packs. After much deliberation, she chooses a white pair. In the cutaway, the rest of her outfit—a white button-down shirt, black pants, and a slouching lavender sweater—is revealed in a medium wide shot.

Within a few shots, both her story goal and character traits are revealed to the audience. In close-up, the camera tracks her index finger as it slides down a page of her hand-dated Daytimer. An 8 A.M. appointment with "Elias-Clarke Human Resources" on Monday, March 13th, is revealed. In the cutaway, her bylines glued to black cardstock are unveiled. As she flips through the stack one by one, the titles expose her penchant for writing human interest stories. The camera cuts to a comparison sequence. Andy, who is similarly dressed as before, is juxtaposed with an interlaced series of glamorous women putting the finishing touches on their fashion-forward outfits. The camera cuts to a woman kissing a gorgeous man snuggled beneath high-count white cotton sheets; in the cutaway and in juxtaposition, Andy kisses a man dressed in a rumpled black T-shirt buried under a cheesy striped department store duvet and a sprawling newspaper. "Good luck," he says, and then gets back to his reading. Andy walks out of their apartment and into the next chapter of her life. 17

In the above two-minute montage sequence, the binary opposites of Andy's lifestyle and the world she is about to inhabit are equally illustrated and juxtaposed in a series of close-ups and medium shots edited together in a fast-paced style reminiscent of blockbusters. From these opening scenes, viewers can gather that *The Devil Wears Prada* is a Big Apple fish out of water story about the fashion world and one nerdy journalism student's rub up against it. In this and the other films mentioned herein, style serves as an additional layer of text within the diegesis. Indeed, for high-concept women's blockbusters in general, the characters' styles often drive the stories they tell. Not always reflective of designers and Fifth Avenue, in *Mamma Mia!*, an adherence to style is represented by the characters' free-flowing dresses and hair as they dance about and sing their way over the complex and across the beach. In *Sex and the City,* style is represented in the myriad close-ups of women entrenched in various deep hues and framed like magazine covers in medium wide frames. The saturated colors, glossy close-up shots, and montage cutting of contemporary women's films not only exhibit the exotic, exciting, and adventurous lifestyles the 18 tales promote, but also serve as their answers to the "shoot 'em up," "save the planet," and "discover the holy grail" visual environments of men's blockbusters of the past three decades.

CASE STUDIES OF THESE FILMS AS FRANCHISES

As important as high-concept narrative, spectacle aesthetics, and mil- 19
lennial themes are to the creation of the women's blockbuster, what most sets it apart from women's films past is its focus on the franchise. Having recognized the potential of global box office success in the case of *Titanic*, but meeting with delimited domestic success in the case of *Legally Blonde*, in the last couple of years, Hollywood has taken a global step forward in applying the rudiments of the male-driven action films to the successful making and marketing of women's blockbusters. To date, *The Devil Wears Prada* has earned $326 million in global revenue (61% abroad), *Sex and the City* $415 million (63% abroad), and *Mamma Mia!* $571 million and counting (74% abroad). These cases serve as testimonies to the success of this new marketing formula (boxfficemojo.com, December 16, 2008).

More so than any other characteristic, ancillary marketing is re- 20
sponsible for the aforementioned global box office achievement, and, in particular, five key marketing characteristics are responsible for their feat. First, blockbuster films utilize the soundtrack as well as the text to make money. Second, the momentum surrounding blockbusters is created long before opening weekend, by which time the buzz is already strong and the distribution environment is already saturated with related products, in addition to the text. Third, in an effort to maximize both vertical integration and content-sharing among their brands, New Hollywood uses all branches of their conglomerate structure to repurpose the product up and down the corporate food chain. Fourth, the high-concept formula that sold the text to the producer and easily conveys the narrative to its viewers is again used to sell the film on a secondary level, through its print advertising and television and radio spots, and in trailers attached to both formal theatrical releases and already released DVD movies. Finally, Hollywood now treats women's blockbusters as franchises rather than the standalone products of chick flicks past. In this way, these filmic texts are tied to the global commercial complex via retail tie-ins and cross-promotions that saturate the infrastructure that surrounds the movie theater and the film. Fully entrenched, these franchises stand perfectly poised with easily translatable themes and texts, international stars, and spectacular images to convey "the good life" in a setting of global consumerism.

Thus, their campaigns amass large global audiences that catapult them to resounding success.

Soundtracks also play a large part in this conglomerate marketing push. No longer a compendium of the film's score, in the world of women's blockbusters, the soundtrack is as stylishly accessorized and earnestly marketed as the movie project. Indeed, the soundtrack's jacket often mimics the graphic design of the one-sheet. The distributors of *Sex and the City*, for example, in an approach similar to the way in which HBO marketed the seasonal DVD releases of the long-running television series, created multiple versions of one-sheets and soundtrack jackets as part of their wide-reaching campaign to promote the movie from the vantage point of all four characters. The jacket cover of Volume 2 of the motion picture soundtrack and a secondary version of the one-sheet, for instance, feature the four female protagonists as they were routinely depicted on the DVDs jackets of the series. The motion picture's original soundtrack jacket and its primary one-sheet, in contrast, feature Sarah Jessica Parker's Carrie Bradshaw alone, with ad copy that reads "Get Carried Away." This example keenly displays the way in which high concept is simply conveyed from pitch to product and illustrated within a streamlined marketing approach from the genesis of the series to the promotion of the movie. 21

In a manner similar to the film that courted foreign box office, the movie's soundtrack was prereleased abroad on May 26, 2008, to coincide with its UK world premiere, and then rereleased in the United States the next day just before the US premiere on May 30, 2008. By releasing the soundtrack early, New Line Records jump-started the Time Warner gravy train. Its prerelease excitement coincided with the rerelease of both the book and the long-running cable series. In an illustration of the powerful effect of vertical integration, the same studio that released the film, Time Warner's New Line Cinema, also produced and distributed the soundtrack via New Line Records. The first single of that much anticipated soundtrack, Fergie's *Labels or Love,* premiered on May 4, 2008, three weeks ahead of the movie, and similarly engaged fans. The *Sex and the City* soundtrack was similarly successful. It debuted at number two on the *Billboard* 200 chart, the highest debut for a multiartist soundtrack since 2005, and to date has sold 55,000 copies (http://en.wikipedia.org/wiki/Sex_and_the_City_(film), December 16, 2008). The sequel, volume 2 of *Sex and the City*, was released on September 23, 2008, coinciding with the DVD release of the film, which further promoted New Line's dedication to and focus on the franchise. The film was thus promoted in a multiplatform viral, virtual, and physical marketing campaign before, during, and after its theatrical release, and included print, television, and radio advertising, one-sheets, 22 trailers, music videos, and merchandise tie-ins and cross-promotions with DVDs of the hit television series. This multifaceted approach created a buzz and intensity that sutured viewers not only to the film but also to its ancillary products, characters, and brand, in short, to the conglomerate franchise as a whole.

Mamma Mia!'s soundtrack, in an even more illustrative example 23
of this process, was released three weeks after the film's debut, on August 8, 2008, but by August 20, 2008, had already become the number one selling iTunes album and the top Internet album of the year. It went on to spend the next two weeks atop the *Billboard* 200 chart, and worldwide to date has sold 2.75 million copies (November 16, 2008). In addition, the film was nominated for a Grammy for best compilation soundtrack album for motion picture, television, or other visual media. New Line promoted the soundtrack separately and alongside the DVD release of the movie in circulars around the country on December 14, 2008. By marketing these two products side by side, the franchise stood to grow at double the rate—and did. Furthermore, because soundtracks are integral to the development of the narrative in women's blockbusters, they serve at a metatextural level to the filmic text, which further builds the momentum surrounding the movie. Music thus works in tandem with the picture to drive fans back and forth between the film, the soundtrack, and other products. Like *Titanic,* contemporary women's films now make use of their soundtracks in combination with other elements of their franchises in wide-reaching ancillary marketing campaigns designed to catapult them to global box office success.

The growth and success of the soundtrack is an example of a 24
critical difference in the promotion of the millennial women's blockbuster. Ancillary products marketed within and separate from the film spur the bottom line of its global franchise value and the retail infrastructure that surrounds it in three main ways: first, by creating a simple and memorable message; second, by generating awareness of the brand; and third, by mapping the way to a loyal, lucrative, and worldwide audience. The *Mamma Mia!* soundtrack was utilized in various commercial tie-ins. RyansIncredibleWorld.com, for example, sold the deluxe edition of the soundtrack with a hard cover booklet, which featured lyrics to the songs, never-before-seen photos, ringtones, and a DVD of additional footage from the recording sessions, commentaries on the making of the film and soundtrack, and interviews with Meryl Streep, Pierce Brosnan, Amanda Seyfried, and original ABBA members Benny Andersson and Bjorn. This special edition was simultaneously released with the DVD in the US on December 16, 2008 . Such multiplatform marketing efforts give fans a second chance to buy the CD and keep alive the franchise in the

minds of consumers. Another key ancillary marketing feature of the women's blockbuster is the franchise's use of the Internet for marketing purposes. Not only did RyansIncredibleWorld.com successfully tie its corporate brand to that of *Mamma Mia!*'s, but the film's official beauty sponsor, Biolage, did as well. The international beauty company ran an essay contest to give one prospective bride a professional wedding day stylist to help her "create the wedding day hairstyle of her dreams." Such ancillary devices tie directly into the wedding theme of *Mamma Mia!*, while cross-promoting the movie with its retail infrastructure. In another example of multilevel and metatextual promotion, *The Devil Wears Prada* presold the Patricia Fields' studded leather bag carried in the movie by Andy Sachs on Amazon.com, weeks before the movie premiered.

Sex and the City is, however, the women's blockbusters' leader in 25
terms of exploiting the opportunities inherent in ancillary marketing campaigns. Not only are Carrie, Samantha, Miranda, and Charlotte model agents for the film as well as the lifestyle it promotes, their longstanding and well-known images presell franchise-endorsed products at every level within the conglomerate structure. From ad campaigns and media buys to the licensing of product placements, these characters came through for the brand every time. Like *The Devil Wears Prada* and *Mamma Mia!*, *Sex and the City* previews and trailers were repeatedly hit upon by the users of YouTube, ComingSoon.net, and Yahoo! Movies. Fans could also post their own versions of trailers and previews on YouTube, by "mashing up" stills and music in unique combinations that both inserted their personalities into the mix of characters and situated them within the filmic worlds.

With regard to blockbusters in general, fan websites act as exem- 26
plary ancillary marketing devices by offering moviegoers the opportunity to write reviews or letters, create fan novelizations of the text, and blog about the movie and its related products on official fan websites as well as those created and managed by the fans themselves (e.g., *The Devil Wears Prada* Hollywood.com Fan Website, *Mamma Mia!* Fans Home). These extratextual devises not only connect viewers on one occasion to one component of the franchise but also serve as mediums to repeatedly draw viewers back to the global product. As such, they have proven especially strong in promoting women's blockbusters, which encourage fans to stay loyal to their products over the ensuring years. At the top of the opening page of *The Sex and the City* Fan Club site, Carrie Bradshaw is quoted as saying, "You shouldn't have to sacrifice who you are just because someone else has a problem with it." This self-reflexive statement not only speaks to the nature of the character and her voice but also to the premise of the text and its theme of validation. This film, like the two others discussed herein, purports

to directly and seamlessly translate a simple message—"You can have it all!"—across ages, genders, cultures, and even borders to a wide-reaching demographic thirsty for all which that connotes.

CONCLUSION

A question to pose at this juncture is whether or not it would have been possible to conceive of the women's blockbuster in any decade before media conglomeratization, because vertical integration and content sharing are such important elements of the franchise success of this hybrid genre. In the case of each of the three texts discussed herein, marketing efforts were carried out by way of a saturation release. For example, both *Sex and the City* and *The Devil Wears Prada* offered book tie-ins; each franchise offered a soundtrack; and all three films came on the heels of other franchise successes, including a long-running cable series in the case of *Sex and the City* and an award-winning musical in the case of *Mamma Mia!* In addition, these films have subsequently sold numerous copies of their DVD versions, and all are in talks for sequels or follow-up projects, with *Sex and the City* already in preproduction. Furthermore, each franchise broke sales records partially due to its soundtrack's success. The original motion picture soundtrack of *Sex and the City,* for example, outperformed all competing multiartist soundtracks since 2005 and scored hits with Fergie's *Labels or Love* and Jennifer Hudson's *All Dressed in Love*. *Mamma Mia!*, an even finer example, has sold nearly three million copies to date, while creating a surge in ABBA CD sales, a resurgence in ABBA singles played on the airwaves, and a Grammy Award–nomination for Meryl Streep and the cast of the hit film. 27

In contemporary times and in relation to what may be described as the New "Hollyworld," the conglomerates' desire for synergy between their companies and the global products with which they are aligned is paramount. Such vertical groupings include film production companies, cable stations, book publishing giants, magazines that promote the franchises, merchandisers, and retail outlets that sell related ancillary products, and online companies that promote each division of the conglomerate over the worldwide superhighway. Furthermore, the infrastructure that surrounds and endorses the film itself is now part and parcel of the franchise as well. This essay thus argues that conglomeration and the infrastructure it promotes have paved the way for a new category of women's films, namely the millennial women's blockbuster. 28

Since the postwar decline in domestic box office, foreign markets have become increasingly important to total corporate revenue. One of the biggest future challenges that trend poses is the need for 29 conglomerates to diversify risk. Partially based on a failed strategy of reliance on advanced sales of foreign rights to bankroll its pictures, New Line, the company behind *Sex and the City,* closed its doors and was folded into Warner Brothers Entertainment on February 28, 2008. This failure serves as a wakeup call to industry insiders that foreign box office is critical to the success of today's features. *The Devil Wears Prada, Mamma Mia!,* and *Sex and the City* each secured nearly two-thirds of their global grosses from foreign box office receipts. Furthermore, the latter premiered in the UK, US. This countermanding of box office conventions unequivocally illustrates the importance of foreign box office to all blockbusters, but especially to millennial women's films as they begin to take off in the "Hollyworld" era.

In adhering to this franchise mode of production, blockbusters 30
naturally court foreign audiences that are easily drawn to translatable themes and narratives, global stars, consumerism, and spectacular images. The millennial women's blockbuster serves up precisely that fare. For the global women's audience, this new hybrid genre opens up myriad possibilities in terms of representing and positioning women in the future. For the first time, women are able to enjoy the rewards of spectacular production in combination with millennial themes and narratives pitched from their own points of view. Standalone women's features are still valuable, of course, and remain the more numerous category of women's films available from global production companies as well as independents. Nevertheless, women's choices have widened. And, because this new category of women's films are made and marketed to women, but speak to a wide, bi-gendered, global audiences, the industry can rely on them to produce, as male blockbusters have done historically, and to resonate outside the narrow chick flick audiences of the past.

WORKS CITED

Bordwell, David, Janet Staiger, and Kristin Thompson. *The Classical Hollywood Cinema: Film Style and Mode of Production to 1960*. London: Routledge & Kegan Paul, 1985. 11–22. Cameron, James. dir. *Titanic.* Paramount 1997. DVD, 1999.

Cowie, Elizabeth. "Storytelling: Classical Hollywood Cinema and Classical Narrative." *Contemporary Hollywood Cinema*. Eds. Steve Neale and Murray Smith. New York: Routledge, 1998. 178–90.

Ewen, Stuart. "Marketing Dreams: The Political Elements of Style." *Consumption, Identity & Style*. Ed. Alan Tomlinson. London: Routledge, 1990.

Frankel, David. dir. *The Devil Wears Prada*. 20th Century Fox, 2006.

Gunning, Tom. "Response to 'Pie and Chase.'" *Classical Hollywood Comedy*. Eds. Kristine Brunovska Karnick and Henry Jenkins. New York: Routledge, 1995. 120–22.

Hayes, Dade, and Jonathan Bing. *Open Wide: How Hollywood Box Office Became a National Obsession*. New York: Hyperion, 2004.

King, Michael Patrick. dir. *Sex and the City*. Warner Bros./New Line, 2008. DVD.

Lloyd, Phyllida. dir. *Mamma Mia!* Universal Pictures, 2008. 16 Dec. 2008, http://en.wikipedia.org/wiki/Sex_and_the_City_(film)i.

Luketic, Robert. dir. *Legally Blonde*. MGM, 2002. DVD.

Mayne, Judith. "The Woman at the Keyhole: Women's Cinema and Feminist Criticism." *Revision*. Eds. Mary Ann Doane, Patricia Mellencamp, and Linda Williams. Los Angeles: American Film Institute, 1984. 49–50.

"Meet the Machers." *Elle*. November 2008: 110–20.

Metz, Christian. *Film Language: A Semiotics of the Cinema*. New York: Oxford UP, 1974.

Miller, Mark Crispin. "Advertising: End of Story." *Seeing Through Movies*. Ed. Mark Crispin Miller. New York: Pantheon Books, 1990. 186–246.

Shatz, Thomas. "The New Hollywood." *Film Theory Goes to the Movies*. Eds. Jim Collins, Hilary Radner, and Ava Preacher Collins. New York: Routledge, 1993. 10–11.

Winter, Jessica. "Who Let the Underdogs Out?" *Village Voice* 10 July 2001. 23 Nov. 2008, http://www.villagevoice.com/2001-07-10/film/who-let-the-underdogs-out/1i.

Wolf, Jeanne. "America's Favorite Stars." *Parade*. 9 Nov. 2008: 4–5.

Wyatt, Justin. *High Concept: Movies and Marketing in Hollywood*. Austin: U of Texas P, 1994.

Examining the Text

1. The core thematic point of this article—its thesis statement, if you will—is this, as stated by the author: "The new women's blockbuster competes on bottom line and overnight has turned a genre filled with sleepers or domestic hits into global powerhouses." By what identifiable steps did this transition from sleeper to megahit take place in the world of movies whose audiences are primarily women? What are some examples of iconic films as this gradual transition has taken place?

2. Early in the article, author York provides some contextualizing definition for her subject, saying, "The new women's film is defined by a combination of elements of women's films from over the decades." What specific elements define women's films historically, according to York? What similarities might the "blockbuster" women's films of today share with those earlier female-centered filmic offerings, and in what ways might the modern, extremely successful "chick flick" differ from those earlier movies, according to research presented by the author?

3. Toward the middle of this article, the author asserts, "By marketing them as blockbusters from their conception, the women's films of today offer something beyond story; that is, they offer a millennial-themed narrative together with blockbuster aesthetics and a global marketing complex that drive them to newfound levels of success." In other words, three key factors contribute to the blockbuster "chick flicks" of today. Explain what the author means by each of these factors—especially the phrases "millennial-themed narrative" and "blockbuster aesthetics." As you consider these factors, list any films that spring to mind as exhibiting these traits.

4. In the section of this essay entitled "The Women's Film Acquires Blockbuster Elements," the author states, "The millennial women's blockbuster contains three key characteristics that set it apart from women's films of the past." She goes on to list those three characteristics, discussing each in some detail. What are the three main characteristics that set the millennial women's blockbuster apart from earlier women's films, as articulated by York in this section of the essay? As you go through your discussion of each element in this list, feel free to add any movies that, in your experience, conform to the elements under discussion.

5. *Thinking rhetorically:* According to York, where mainstream Hollywood blockbuster action movies feature lots of explosions, car chases, computer-generated imagery, and violent confrontations, "Instead of shoot 'em up and special effects, women's blockbusters utilize different aesthetics to create their movie spectacles." What rhetorical techniques does York employ to convince the reader that this assertion is valid and credible? If women's blockbusters can't rely on the tried-and-true elements of action films to achieve the status of spectacle, how do they create the spectacular aesthetic that York says is a requirement for blockbuster chick flicks? Again, provide examples from your own experience, as well as from this article, to illustrate your ideas.

For Class Discussion

The last major section of this essay, before the conclusion, discusses the financial dimension of movie blockbusters. In small groups, discuss the economic factors that combine to make a certain film conform to the industry term "blockbuster." As you engage in this small-group discussion, you may want to define some key terms that York raises in this section and throughout the essay, such as the notion of franchise. Those of you who are business or economics majors might want to lend your disciplinary expertise to this portion of the discussion. Conclude your small-group activity by making a brief list of the characteristics of blockbusters—not just blockbuster "chick flicks," but all blockbusters, whether aimed at males, females, or bi-gendered. Then, when you reassemble for whole-class discussion, compare the lists of each group, noting areas of overlap (and lack thereof) as you attempt to generate a comprehensive list of movie blockbuster attributes. Finally, apply this list of attributes to contemporary women's films of your knowledge and experience, to see if it corresponds to the examples and assertions provided by York in this article.

Writing Suggestion

The author of this article cites the movie *Titanic* as a significant turning point in the evolution of women's movies toward blockbuster status. For the purposes of an analytical essay, watch *Titanic* again (is there anyone who has not seen the movie at least once?), examining it for elements that correspond to points raised by York in this article. In a sense, you will be writing a combination analysis and comparison/contrast, since you will be both looking carefully at the movie itself, and comparing its scenes, characters, aesthetics, and even its marketing with individual points raised by York in this article. For that reason, it may be worth your while to keep two running lists as you construct your essay: one containing the main subtopical points articulated by York in the above essay, and a second list of *Titanic* attributes that correspond to this list, or fail to exhibit such correspondence. After making this comparison, you will derive a thesis that either supports or disagrees with York's claim regarding *Titanic:* in your view, does that movie mark a significant turning point? Is it, in your opinion, the first blockbuster chick flick, or is the movie merely one of many steps in a very gradual evolution?

Raising the Dead: Unearthing the Nonliterary Origins of Zombie Cinema

KYLE BISHOP

The word "zombie," in everyday parlance, evokes a sense of lethargic dullness, as in, "I stayed up 'til three a.m. working on my English essay, and now I feel like a zombie." This connotation, whether we are aware of it or not, derives from its association with a particular brand of movie character: the half-decayed corpse ponderously and mindlessly walking with arms outstretched, seeking human victims to dismember and devour. Zombies shambled into mainstream American popular culture relatively recently, having first been introduced in a 1929 book about life in Haiti, including a tangential reference to a voodoo death cult that is in fact rare in Haiti. Nevertheless, that book's representation of zombies touched a popular nerve in the United States and inspired a string of movies featuring animated corpses with a hunger for human flesh, leading up to the definitive zombie flick: George Romero's 1968 Night of the Living Dead. *This film, with its groundbreakingly gory special effects and implied critiques of U.S. policy in the Vietnam War, became the template for the modern zombie movie, which is the subject of genre critic Kyle Bishop's analysis in the following essay.*

As you read, *observe the theoretical lenses through which Bishop takes an in-depth look at the rise of the zombie as an archetypal figure in contemporary culture. In particular, note the way in which he speculates about the complex appeals of this character, attempting to explain through several approaches, especially the Freudian psychological, the pervasiveness of zombies in modern film, video games, and so forth. Also, pay attention to your own initial preconceptions about certain theories, such as Freud's notions regarding psychosexual development in humans. Understanding that certain readers might somehow have acquired the notion that Freud's concepts are too simplistic in their orientation ("He thinks everything is about sex!" a student in a basic writing class exclaimed recently), in fact there is much to value within the writings of the father of modern psychology. Bishop takes care to present one of Freud's relevant subtheories—that of the uncanny—in a palatable and comprehensible way here.*

The year 2004 saw the theatrical release of three major zombie movies: *Resident Evil: Apocalypse*, a sequel to a movie based on a video game; *Dawn of the Dead*, a remake of a cult classic from the 1970s; and *Shaun of the Dead*, a sometimes funny, sometimes terrifying re-visioning of an established genre. In addition, dozens of low-budget zombie movies were released directly to video or appeared as made-for-television movies. . . . 1

Although creatures such as vampires and reanimated corpses often have been realized by literary means, the traditional zombie story has no direct antecedent in novels or short fiction. In fact, zombies did not really see the light of day until filmmakers began to dig them out of their graves in the 1930s. The "classic" zombie horror film, which is the focus of this investigation, was pioneered by George A. Romero in the late 1960s and features a veritable plague of reanimated corpses that attack and slaughter the living. The established generic conventions of such movies are relatively simple and remarkably consistent: Ordinary characters in ordinary places are confronted with overwhelmingly extraordinary challenges, namely the unexpected appearance of an aggressive horde of flesh-eating ghouls. Zombie cinema is essentially a macabre romp—a live-action comic book brought to the big screen both to horrify and entertain. 2

Much has already been written concerning the more esoteric social commentary offered by zombie movies, but few critics have investigated the unusual origins of these monsters and their horrific stories. Although the cinematic popularity of zombies has certainly 3 made the move to video games and graphic novels, the zombie remains a primarily nonliterary phenomenon. Establishing the folkloric origins of the zombie creature itself will explain this rather singular fact and illustrates its evolution into the more recognizable cinematic horror show developed by Romero. The zombie genre does not exist prior to the film age because of its essentially visual nature; zombies do not think or speak—they simply act, relying on purely physical manifestations of terror. This unique embodiment of horror recalls Sigmund Freud's concept of the uncanny, a phenomenon that finds itself better suited to filmic representations rather than prose renditions.

PREPARING THE POTION: EXHUMING THE VODOUN ZOMBIE

Most classic monsters—from ghosts to vampires to werewolves—have 4
their origins in folklore, and the zombie is no exception. However, whereas those other creatures have cross-cultural mythologies, the zombie remains a purely American monster, born from Vodoun magic and religion. In addition, creatures such as Dracula passed through a literary tradition on their way to the silver screen, but the zombie did not. Zombie scholar Peter Dendle illustrates this point: Although possessing certain thematic characteristics that tie it to the traditions of classical horror, the zombie is "the only creature to pass directly from folklore to the screen, without first having an established literary tradition" (2–3). This singularity makes an investigation of the anthropological roots of the zombie an essential part of understanding the film genre.

According to anthropologist Wade Davis, the modern English 5
word *zombie* most likely derives from the Kimbundu term *nzumbe*, which means "ghost" or "spirit of a dead person" (xii). This concept was brought from Africa to Haiti with the slave trade and was translated into the Creole *zobi*, which was modernized to zombie, a word with a number of accepted meanings, from a mindless automaton to an exotic mixed drink. As far as the traditional cinematic monster is concerned, however, the designation of zombie is reserved for the cannibalistic walking dead: people brought back to life either to serve or to devour the human race. This definition is tied to the Vodoun religion, a mystical practice that supposedly harbors the magic required to strike people down to a death-like state and revive them later from the grave to become virtually mindless servants—the most subordinate of slaves (Davis 42). But, in reality, zombification is the result of pharmacology, the careful administration of powerful neurotoxins.

Davis is the world's leading authority on the zombification ritual, and as a Harvard University ethnobotanist, he traveled to Haiti in 1985 in search of exotic new medicinal drugs. Davis recorded his weird experiences and botanical research in *The Serpent and the Rainbow*. According to this primarily anthropological text, a limited number of powerful and unorthodox Vodoun priests, called *bokors*, possess a keen knowledge of natural drugs and sedatives and have created a "zombie powder"—called *coup poudre*—that renders its victims clinically dead (Davis 90). Davis's interest in the drug was purely scientific at first, but he soon realized that zombies are real creatures within the Vodoun religion. The method of creating such a dangerous substance is naturally a closely guarded secret, controlled by the secret societies of Haiti (Davis 260). 6

Those well versed in the administration of this powder could conceivably create the illusion of raising the dead and, thus, give the zombie legend credibility. The most potent poison included in the *coup poudre* comes from a specific kind of puffer fish, a nerve agent called tetradotoxin (Davis 134). This drug "induces a state of profound paralysis, marked by complete immobility during which time the border between life and death is not at all certain, even to trained physicians" (Davis 142). All major life functions are paralyzed for an extended period, and those suffering from the effects of the drug run the real risk of being buried alive. If the powder is too strong or mixed incorrectly, the victim might die immediately—or suffocate slowly in the coffin (Davis 226). Unfortunately, even those victims lucky enough to be rescued from the grave inevitably suffer brain damage from the lack of oxygen; they are understandably sluggish and dimwitted (Davis 21). 7

These superstitious fears of the walking dead are not limited to Haiti, however; most cultures share a strong psychological response to the concept of death. Bodies of dead friends and family are burned, buried, walled up, or even eaten, but the result is the same: The corpses are hidden from sight and mind. Although statues, portraits, and photographs are treasured as valued reminders of those now dead, no one really wants to see the face of a loved one slowly rot or be reminded of the brutal realities of mortality; such a confrontation would be frightening, to say the least. In psychoanalytical terms, Freud identifies this fear of the once familiar as the *unheimlich*, a complex term that literally means "un-homely" or "un-homey" but is usually translated as "the uncanny." This concept is key to understanding the ability of the zombie to instill fear: Those who should be dead and safely laid to rest have bucked the natural order of things and have returned from the grave. 8

The anthropological origins of the zombie are important to recognize, but what makes zombie narratives unique to cinema are not the shambling foes themselves but rather the stories they tell. 9

Zombie folklore and Vodoun traditions clearly set the stage for the zombie horror movie as it is known and recognized today; poisoning, premature burial, loss of cognition, slavery, the return of the dead, and death itself are all key features of zombie cinema. But the classic zombie movie owes its unique existence to George A. Romero, who Dendle calls the "Shakespeare of zombie cinema" (121). Romero took a rather insipid, two-dimensional creature, married it to an established apocalyptic storyline, and invented an entirely new genre.

ADMINISTERING THE POWDER: CREATING THE MODERN ZOMBIE

Unlike the ancient traditions of the vampire and werewolf, the zombie did not enter Western consciousness until around the turn of the twentieth century. According to Dendle, most Americans were only vaguely aware of Haitian Voudo and zombie lore from nineteenth-century Caribbean travel literature (2). Civilized society probably dismissed such concepts as remote superstitions and pagan fantasies until the publication of William Seabrook's travel book *The Magic Island* in 1929, which brought the romantic exoticism—and possible reality—of the zombie to the attention of mainstream audiences (Dendle 2). Shortly thereafter in 1932, Kenneth Webb produced a play called *Zombie in New York City*, and "the creature fell irrevocably under the auspices of the entertainment industry" (Dendle 2). 10

Hollywood quickly recognized the marketability of the zombie, with the first true zombie movie arriving the same year as Webb's play: Victor Halperin's *White Zombie* (1932). Set in Haiti, Vodou is the central feature of the film, although the tone and style are obviously influenced by Tod Browning's *Dracula* (1931). As the white heroes travel across the countryside at night, their coach driver explains the mysterious figures they pass as "the living dead. Corpses taken from their graves and made to work in the sugar mills" (Halperin). These zombies are slow, dimwitted, and lumbering—but not completely mindless; they can follow commands and perform simple tasks. They are not monsters but rather hypnotized slaves who are still alive and can be saved with the death of the Vodoun priest who enslaved them. The true villain in *White Zombie* is Bela Lugosi's mad bokor Murder Legendre, not the pitiful zombies themselves. 11

A number of similar, if unremarkable, zombie films were made over the next few years—for example, *Revolt of the Zombies* (1936), *King of the Zombies* (1941), and *I Walked with a Zombie* (1943)—but their rather prosaic view of the undead would change gradually over the next few decades with the help of EC Comics. The 1940s and '50s saw 12 a dramatic upswing in all horror media, most notably the publication of *Tales from the Crypt* in 1950. According to book columnist and comic aficionado Digby Diehl, "Horror comics of the 1950s appealed to teens and young adults who were trying to cope with the aftermath of even greater terrors—Nazi death camps and the explosion of the atomic bombs at Hiroshima and Nagasaki" (28). Terror had become a tangible part of daily life, and these early graphic novels brazenly presented images of rotting corpses, stumbling zombies, and gory violence. Film scholar Paul Wells claims the young Romero would have been directly influenced by such comics (82), for a predominately visual narrative format can be seen in his zombie movies, in which the action is presented through a series of carefully framed and largely silent images. Romero confirms this connection himself in a documentary by Roy Frumke, referring to the filming of *Dawn of the Dead* (1978) as "making a comic book."

Romero was likely influenced by popular horror films of the 1950s as well, especially those featuring end-of-the-world scenarios. According to Frumke, Romero's earliest film influence was Christian Nyby's *The Thing from Another World* (1951). This science fiction movie, based on the short story "Who Goes There?" by John W. Campbell, Jr., features a small group of isolated survivors who must fight off a mysterious foe that can take any form and exists only to kill. 13

Film scholar Robin Wood offers another connection, claiming the most obvious antecedent to Romero's zombies to be the pod people in Don Siegel's *Invasion of the Body Snatchers* (1956), based on Jack Finney's 1955 novel (126). This unsettling story posits another view of the apocalypse, in which one's best friends and family members become threatening monsters. The film's ending departs from that of the novel, clearly illustrating the paranoia rampant in cold war America. Horror expert Stephen King writes how critics read Siegel's film as an allegory about "the witch-hunt atmosphere that accompanied the McCarthy hearings," although Siegel claimed it was really about the "Red Menace" itself (308). Either way, fear of the Other was clearly rampant on both sides of the political spectrum. 14

Romero established and codified the zombie horror genre in 1968 with *Night of the Living Dead*. The screenplay was based on Romero's own short story "Night of Anubis," a tale of isolation and supernatural peril that borrowed heavily from Richard Matheson's 1954 novella *I Am Legend* (Martin). Matheson's story features hordes of vampires who rampantly infect and replace the world's population. Richard Neville is essentially the last man on earth, and he must garrison himself inside his home each night to escape the hungry fangs of the vampiric infestation. During his struggle to survive, Neville must fortify his house, scavenge for food and supplies, and kill the monsters his friends and 15 family have become. All of these fundamental plot elements are found in Romero's series of zombie movies and have become firm protocols of the genre.

The situation faced by Matheson's Neville is also seen in Alfred Hitchcock's *The Birds* (1963), based on the 1952 short story by Daphne du Maurier. Film scholar R. H. W. Dillard considers this film the artistic predecessor to Romero's *Night*, pointing out how "in both films, a group of people are besieged by an apparently harmless and ordinary world gone berserk, struggle to defend themselves against the danger, and struggle to maintain their rationality and their values at the same time" (26). *The Birds* explicitly presents the idea of the apocalypse; in fact, the Bodega Bay town drunk warns the protagonists that it is the "end of the world." The birds are an unstoppable collective, and the movie's heroes must board themselves up in a house against their relentless onslaught. 16

The essential motifs and tropes of the classic zombie movie have some thematic and stylistic roots in Haitian travel narratives and the zombie films of the 1930s and '40s, specifically the exoticism of Vodoun zombie folklore, and early horror and science fiction cinema, particularly the end-of-the-world scenario. In addition, the paranoia narratives of the cold war 1950s and '60s would have given Romero some core ideas about his general plot structure, but it was his own imagination and invention that united the zombie legend with these popular stories of the primal struggle for survival. Although such movies as *White Zombie* were first, Dendle points out that "Romero liberated the zombie from the shackles of a master, and invested his zombies not with a function . . . but rather a drive" (6). With the creation of *Night of the Living Dead*, Romero decisively established the structure of the classical zombie movie, and many directors have since followed his lead and conformed to the criteria of the new genre. 17

PERFORMING THE RITUAL: EXPLAINING ZOMBIES' CINEMATIC SINGULARITY

Zombies do not exist in a vacuum, nor did they spring forth fully grown from the head of Romero. In addition to being derived from mythology, legend, and the imagination, zombies also have close ties to other, more literary monsters. They belong to a diverse class of creatures that cross the metaphysical line between life and death, where a strong sense of the uncanny inspires unease and fear. But whereas ghosts, vampires, and golems have been a part of storytelling for thousands of years, the zombie is a relatively modern invention. Their lack of emotional depth, their inability to express or act on human desires, 18 and their primarily visual nature make zombies ill suited for the written word; zombies thrive best on screen.

Freud defines the abstract concept of the uncanny as "that species of the frightening that goes back to what was once well known and had long been familiar" (124). He further points out how "this uncanny element is actually nothing new or strange, but something . . . estranged from [the psyche] only through being repressed" (147). The true manifestation of this fear occurs, therefore, when a repressed familiarity (such as death) returns in a disturbing, physical way (such as a corpse); the familiar (*heimlich*) becomes the unfamiliar or uncanny (*unheimlich*) (Freud 148). Of course, this concept applies to monsters other than zombies as well. As Dillard points out, "the idea of the dead's return to a kind of life is no new idea; it is present in all the ancient tales of vampires and ghouls and zombies, and it has been no stranger to films. . . . All of these tales and films spring from that ancient fear of the dead" (20–21). Dead bodies are not only a breeding ground for disease but also a reminder to the living of their own mortality. For such reasons, creatures that apparently have overcome the debilitating effects of the grave are treated with revulsion and fear—especially when said creatures are hostile, violent, and ambulatory. 19

Freud also claims that ". . . to many people the acme of the uncanny is represented by anything to do with death, dead bodies, revenants, spirits and ghosts" (148). Therefore, it is no surprise that those supernatural creatures able to defy the powers of death are usually at the heart of horror narratives and stories. Perhaps the oldest campfire tale is the ghost story: What is more uncanny than someone returning from the grave to wreak havoc on the living? Ghosts have a firmly established tradition, both orally and literarily, from Homer to Dante to Shakespeare to Dickens. But ghosts are merely spirits, consciousnesses that lack physical form; zombies belong to a much more specific phylum: the corporeal monster. Such unnatural terrors include vampires (demons who constantly cheat death by preying on the living), golems (unnatural creatures reassembled and brought back to life through the means of science), and zombies (mindless automatons fueled by purely animalistic passions). 20

However, when one considers the literary origins of these beasts (specifically in novels and short fiction), the zombie is virtually missing in action. Why are vampires and other supernatural creatures prevalent in horror stories and gothic literature but not the traditional zombie? 21

It is the essentially human behavior that explains the success of such fiends in nineteenth-century literature, and the vampire is the most prolific of these. Although undead, Bram Stoker's archetypical Count acts as though still alive, using his immortality to pursue rather 22 carnal desires. Dracula is mysterious, cunning, and seductive, using his piercing stare and eloquent tongue to beguile young women and readers alike. He appears both attractive and familiar by wearing the guise of youth and vitality, but Dracula is fundamentally an uncanny symbol of mortality. Not only is he decidedly inhuman—he lacks a reflection, which is regarded as a manifestation of the soul (Stoker 31)—he also represents the reality of death itself with his drinking of innocent blood, his propensity to murder women and small children, and his habit of sleeping in the grave.

Similarly, Victor Frankenstein's intriguing monster possesses es- 23
sentially human qualities that make him such a complex literary character; he thinks and feels and speaks with great passion. Contrary to most screen adaptations, Frankenstein's creature is not frightening by himself—he is in fact quite sympathetic and humane. His unnatural state makes him essentially uncanny: He is a collection of dead body parts and stitchery, a creature brought back to life through science, not the supernatural. However, although Dracula and Frankenstein's monster are both fine examples of the uncanny, neither of these classic monsters is technically a zombie; a vampire lives a conscious, basically human existence, and Frankenstein's creature is flesh made living and mortal once more.

In contrast to these monsters, the zombie is completely and 24
thoroughly dead—it is essentially a walking corpse. Zombies are not uncanny because of their humanistic qualities; they are uncanny because they are, in essence, a grotesque metaphor for humanity itself. Like the vampire, the zombie rises from the grave to feed off the living. Like the golem, the zombie has the form of someone familiar, yet monstrous. But the zombie is a much different creature from these established monsters: It does not think or act on reasonable motives—it is purely a creature of blind instinct. The zombie does not recognize individuals or discriminate in its quarry. Zombies have no speech or consciousness—they do not talk to their victims or speculate about their existence; they are essentially superficial, two-dimensional creatures.

Because zombies do not speak, all of their intentions and activi- 25
ties are manifested solely through physical action. In other words, because of this sensual limitation, zombies must be watched. Their primary actions are visceral and violent: They claw, rend, smash, and gnaw. In addition, post-1960s zombie movies are most noteworthy not for violence or horror but for the gore (Dendle 6). Decapitations, disembowelings, and acts of cannibalism are particularly effective on the screen, especially if the audience does not have time to look away. Moreover, the recognition of former heroes as dangerous zombies realizes an uncanny effect, eliciting an instantaneous shock on the part of the film characters and the audience members alike.

Of course, shocking images can be conveyed quite effectively in writing as well. In Stoker's Dracula, the somewhat feckless Jonathan Harker methodically documents a horrific confrontation with the Count: 26

> I raised the lid, and laid it back against the well; and then I saw something which filled ray very soul with horror. There lay the Count, but looking as if his youth had been half renewed, for the white hair and moustache were changed to dark iron-grey; the cheeks were fuller, and the white skin seemed ruby-red underneath; the mouth was redder than ever, for on the lips were gouts of fresh blood, which trickled from the corners of the mouth and ran over the chin and neck. Even the deep, burning eyes seemed set amongst swollen flesh, for the lids and pouches underneath were bloated. It seemed as if the whole awful creature were simply gorged with blood; he lay like a filthy leech, exhausted with his repletion. (53)

Stoker presents quite a visage, but the diachronic nature of prose forces him to describe one aspect of the Count at a time. This gradual, paratactic unfolding of visual detail must necessarily diminish the ultimate shock; it takes time for the audience to read it. Because humans process visual images synchronically, literary texts present an unrealistic form of perception. The cinematic representation is much closer to reality, showing the entire view simultaneously. 27

Aspects of the film zombie may be recognizable in other classic monsters, but no traditionally literary tale conforms to the genre as it has been so firmly established by Romero. Although they were once human, zombies have no real connection to humanity aside from their physical form; they are the ultimate foreign Other. They do not think, speak, or act on passionate or conscious desires as do the monsters found in novels or short fiction—a zombie's essentially silent and shallow nature makes it a fundamentally visual creature instead. The primitive characteristics of these ghouls make them ideal cinematic monsters. 28

RAISING THE DEAD: UNDERSTANDING THE ROMERO FORMULA

The classic zombie story pioneered by Romero, and recognized in so many horror movies since, has a number of specific characteristics that distinguish it from other tales of the supernatural. Zombie movies are always set at the apparent end of the world, where devastating events have rendered the human race all but helpless. Yet, the primary details in Romero's films are in essence bland and ordinary, implying that 29 such extraordinary events could happen to anyone, anywhere, at any time. Zombies confront audiences with stark horror and graphic violence, using the seemingly familiar to present the most unnatural and frightening. A detailed look at the prototypical zombie film—*Night of the Living Dead*—will best illustrate these defining cinematic features and help show the limitations of print.

30 *Night of the Living Dead* is presented on a very pessimistic stage: that of the apocalypse. A strange phenomenon overcomes society, resulting in a literal hell on earth where the dead walk and no one is safe. A space probe has returned from Venus, bearing some kind of unknown radiation. For some unexplained reason, this extraterrestrial fallout causes all recently dead humans to rise and attack the living—no Vodoun rituals here. The ghouls feed on human flesh in blatant disregard of society's cannibalism taboo, and those thus killed are infected as if by a blood-borne virus and soon rise themselves, assuming there is enough flesh remaining for the corpse to become mobile. The dead are mechanical juggernauts, and those left struggling to survive are forced to adopt a much more primordial stance—it is kill or be killed, and average folks are quickly transformed into desperate vigilantes.

31 Society's infrastructure begins to break down, especially those systems associated with the government and technology. Law enforcement is depicted as incompetent and backwater (the local sheriff is a stereotyped yokel with a "shoot first" attitude), so people must fend for themselves instead. The media do what they can, broadcasting tidbits of helpful information and advice by way of radio and television, but the outlook is fundamentally grim: Hide if you can, fight if you have to. In the end, the rigid structure of society proves little help; human survivors are left to their own devices with no real hope of rescue or support. Motley groups are forced into hiding, holing up in safe houses of some kind where they barricade themselves and wait in vain for the trouble to pass.

32 Of course, such a scenario is not necessarily limited to zombie movies: Slasher films and alien-invasion pics often have a similar modus operandi. However, whereas those movies feature either an unrealistic cast of vivacious eye candy, computer-savvy geniuses, or stylized superheroes, zombie cinema pursues the hapless adventures of bland, ordinary (*heimlich*) citizens. As *Night* opens, a rather plain, average young woman and her equally pedestrian brother are traveling to visit the grave of their father in rural Pennsylvania. While they are paying their respects and praying at the gravesite, an innocuous gentleman can be seen shuffling across the background of the frame. Johnny begins to tease his sister about her childish fear of cemeteries, and he uses the passing stranger to feed the fire: "They're coming to get you, Barbara!" he taunts, forcing his sister's disgusted retreat.

As Barbara embarrassingly approaches the man to apologize, the unthinkable happens—he is out to get her! Although the zombie looks like a normal human being (albeit a bit pasty), he attacks Barbara with wanton savagery and kills her ill-fated brother when Johnny tries to intervene.

In the grand tradition of most horror films, Barbara runs away, 33 stumbling and tripping her way to the car. The zombie begins its methodical, if rather slow, pursuit, its every movement highlighted by lightning flashes and dramatic camera angles. Although she makes it to the car, Barbara is thwarted in her escape: The keys are still in Johnny's pocket. Another footrace ensues, and Barbara makes it to the relative safety of a farmhouse. Granted, the former occupants are already dead and partially eaten, but at least her friend from the cemetery is locked outside. Enter Ben, another survivor who has come to the farmhouse in search of refuge and hopefully some gasoline for his truck. At this point, the zombie film establishes another of its defining characteristics: hiding out.

The literal *heimlich* nature of the house quickly becomes some- 34 thing far more *unheimlich*. The farmhouse symbolizes the comforting idea that one's home is a place of security, but this place does not belong to either Barbara or Ben—it is a foreign, unfamiliar environment, and they are indeed strangers in a strange land. Barbara unsettlingly discovers the masticated corpses of the house's former occupants, and Ben must defend her from some zombies that have likewise broken in. Out of desperate necessity, Ben immediately begins a radical home renovation, quickly converting the farmhouse into a fortress. He incapacitates the zombies, tosses the bodies outside, and starts boarding up the doors and windows. Barbara can do little more than sit and stare, bemoaning the loss of her brother in a catatonic state. Although the home continues to possess its physical sense of security, it has lost its power to provide any psychological comfort.

That the seemingly harmless and ordinary would prove to be 35 so life threatening is one of the fundamental precepts of the zombie formula. In addition to the slow-moving ghouls and the common farmhouse, the film's protagonists never become anything spectacular—Barbara is a simple girl, traumatized by the brutal slaying of her brother; Ben is a workaday "everyman"; and the Coopers, soon found hiding in the cellar, are an average middle-class family. This link to normalcy is emphasized by Dillard, who describes the essentially mundane nature of *Night* as "the story of everyday people in an ordinary landscape, played by everyday people who are, for the most part, from that ordinary locale". In his afterword to the graphic novel *Miles Behind Us*, a zombie story told in another primarily visual medium, Simon Pegg points out that the protagonists of zombie movies are not superheroes or professional monster slayers such as Van Helsing—they are common, average folk forced to "step up" and defend themselves.

However, the ordinary by itself is not threatening—it also needs to be rendered as the fundamentally unfamiliar. In his introduction to *Horror Film Reader,* James Ursini writes, "Horror is based on recognizing in the unfamiliar something familiar, something attractive even as it is repulsive. . . . The best horror films are those that evoke that feeling of the uncanny in us most strongly". Ursini refers here to Freud's sense of the uncanny as something that has been repressed (148). This makes the "familiar unfamiliar" (the *heimlich unheimlich*) even more terrifying, for the familiar and recognizable are wrought into the foreign and uncanny. This perspective on the monster is most apropos the zombie movie, in which the threat is not only manifested as a hostile undead human but likely a hostile undead human the victim recognizes as a former intimate. 36

The physical form of the zombie is its most striking and frightening aspect: It was once—quite recently—a living person. The one-time protagonists of the movie become its eventual antagonists; thus, the characters cannot fully trust each other. As Dillard points out, "The living people are dangerous to each other . . . because they are potentially living dead should they die". Night introduces its audience to a number of diverse characters, but these so-called heroes, when infected, rapidly become the most savage and threatening of villains. This stark manifestation of the uncanny is chillingly illustrated when poor Johnny returns near the end of the picture as a zombie, "still wearing his driving gloves and clutching for his sister with the idiotic, implacable single-mindedness of the hungry dead" (King 134). His deceptive familiarity is what ultimately leads Barbara to her doom—she hesitates at the sight of her brother, failing to recognize the dangers of his zombification until it is too late. 37

This terrifying prospect is shown even more graphically when the young Karen Cooper feasts on her own parents. As the battle with the swarming zombies rages upstairs, Karen dies from a zombie bite and succumbs to the effects of the radiation. She then gnaws hungrily on her dead father's arm and brutally attacks her mother with a trowel. Helen Cooper does little more than allow herself to be butchered; shock at seeing her daughter turned into a zombie and a binding sense of love and compassion render her impotent. When Ben eventually retreats to the perceived safety of the cellar, he is forced to kill the zombie versions of the entire Cooper family. Such a visceral shock works so well in a cinematic medium because the audience instantly recognizes the former protagonists in their zombified forms and can intimately relate to the horrified reactions of the survivors. 38

Finally, the zombie monster is ultimately terrifying because in it one sees one's self. Pegg discusses the essential function of the zombie: "Metaphorically, this classic creature embodies a number of our greatest fears. Most obviously, it is our own death, personified. The physical manifestation of that thing we fear the most. More subtly, the zombie represents a number of our deeper insecurities. The fear that deep down, we may be little more than animals, concerned only with appetite." In a very real sense, Night is the story about humanity's struggle to retain its sense of humanity. Ben and the others fight the zombies just to stay alive, but they also clash among themselves. Although he remains uninfected by the zombie plague, Ben's civility suffers and crumbles under the stress of the siege: He strikes Barbara for being hysterical, beats Mr. Cooper for disagreeing with his plans, and eventually shoots and kills Mr. Cooper. Ben is almost as violent and irrational as the zombies themselves, although he is the closest thing the movie has to a real hero. 39

Because anyone can potentially become a zombie, these films deal unabashedly with human taboos, murder, and cannibalism, which Dillard proposes have much to do with the genre's success. The dead are not allowed to rest in peace: Barbara's attempt to honor the resting place of one relative turns into a nightmare in which she vainly combats the remains of another dead relative. Ben becomes a kind of avenging angel, bashing, chopping, and shooting people—he is not only forced to disrespect the sanctity of the dead, but he also becomes a type of mass murderer. The cannibalism taboo is the one broached most blatantly. After dying in an explosion, the bodies of Tom and Judy are mercilessly devoured by the gathered zombies, and Romero pulls no punches in showing charred flesh, ropy intestines, and closely gnawed bones. Karen's cannibalistic act even borders on incest, consuming the very flesh that originally gave her life. 40

Night, as with the zombie movies to follow, fulfills its generic promises with a great deal of gore and violence. This is a major reason film is so successful in telling the zombie story—blood, guts, and gore can be shown instantly with graphic detail. Humans have their intestines ripped out, zombies are cheerfully hunted and butchered, and mad doctors perform unspeakable acts on the reanimated corpses of their former associates. The synchronic nature of cinema allows these shocking images to be suddenly and thoroughly unleashed on the viewing public, resulting in the expected gleeful revulsion. 41

The horror of the zombie movie comes from recognizing the human in the monster; the terror of the zombie movie comes from knowing there is nothing to do about it but destroy what is left; the fun comes from watching the genre continue to develop. Although zombies are technically dead, their cinematic genre is a living, breathing entity 42 that continues to grow and evolve. Zombie-themed video games have spawned such films as *Resident Evil* (2002), and the genre's popularity and longevity have resulted in remakes of both *Dawn of the Dead* and the forthcoming *Day of the Dead* (2006). But the genre is also constantly reinventing itself with revisionist films such as *Shaun of the Dead* and Romero's own *Land of the Dead* (2005). (12) Such overwhelming contemporary evidence firmly establishes zombie cinema as a valued member of genre studies.

WORKS CITED

Davis, Wade. *The Serpent and the Rainbow*. New York: Werner, 1985.

Dendle, Peter. *The Zombie Movie Encyclopedia*. Jefferson, NC: McFarland, 2001.

Diehl, Digby. *Tales from the Crypt: The Official Archives*. New York: St. Martin's, 1996.

Dillard, R. H. W. "Night of the Living Dead: It's Not Like Just a Wind That's Passing Through." *American Horrors*. Ed. Gregory A. Waller. Chicago: U of Illinois P, 1987. 14–29.

Freud, Sigmund. *The Uncanny*. New York: Penguin, 2003.

Frumke, Roy, dir. *Roy Frumke's Document of the Dead*. Synapse Films, 1989. DVD. *Dawn of the Dead Ultimate Edition*. Anchor Bay Entertainment, 2004.

Halperin, Victor, dir. *White Zombie*. Perf. Bela Lugosi. 1932. DVD. The Roan Group, 1999.

Hitchcock, Alfred, dir. *The Birds*. Universal City Studios, 1963. VHS. *The Alfred Hitchcock Collection*. MCA Universal Home Video, 1995.

King, Stephen. *Danse Macabre*. New York: Berkley, 1981.

Martin, Perry, dir. *The Dead Will Walk*. DVD. *Dawn of the Dead Ultimate Edition*. Anchor Bay Entertainment, 2004.

Matheson, Richard. *I Am Legend*. New York: Tom Doherty, 1995.

Nyby, Christian, dir. *The Thing from Another World*. Winchester Pictures Corporation, 1951. DVD. Warner Home Video, 2005.

Pegg, Simon. Afterword. *Miles Behind Us. The Walking Dead* 2. Image Comics, 2004.

Romero, George A., dir. *Dawn of the Dead*. The MKR Group, 1978. DVD. Ultimate Edition. Anchor Bay Entertainment, 2004.

———, dir. *Day of the Dead*. United Film Distribution Company, 1985. DVD. Anchor Bay Entertainment, 2003.

———, dir. *Land of the Dead*. Universal Pictures, 2005.

———, dir. *Night of the Living Dead*. Image Ten, 1968. DVD. Millennium Edition. Elite Entertainment, 1994.

Siegel, Don, dir. *Invasion of the Body Snatchers*. Walter Wanger Productions, 1956. DVD. Republic Studios, 2002.

Skal, David J. *The Monster Show*. New York: Faber, 1993.

Stoker, Bram. *Dracula*. 1897. Ed. Nina Auerbach and David J. Skal. Norton Critical Edition. New York: Norton, 1997.

Ursini, James. Introduction. *Horror Film Reader*. Ed. Alain Silver and James Ursini. New York: Limelight, 2000. 3–7.

Wells, Paul. *The Horror Genre: From Beelzebub to Blair Witch. Short Cuts: Introductions to Film Studies 1*. New York: Wallflower, 2002.

Wood, Robin. "Neglected Nightmares." *Horror Film Reader*. Ed. Alain Silver and James Ursini. New York: Limelight, 2000. 111–27.

Examining the Text

1. By the author's account, the zombie is a "purely American monster." What are the "nonliterary" origins of zombies in contemporary film? What is a zombie, as it appears in non-American and early American folkloric traditions and subsequently in movies, and what are the early stages, both folk-cultural and contemporary-creative, that paved the way for the development of the zombie character we know and love in modern cinema?

2. When did zombies first appear on the "big screen"—that is, in movies? After that point, how did zombie movies evolve into the 1950s, when they became a mainstay of the burgeoning B-movie horror film genre? What was George A. Romero's contribution to the development of zombie movies . . . not only in the '50s, but in modern cinema as well?

3. In his "Performing the Ritual" section of this essay, Bishop introduces the Freudian concept of "the uncanny" as a potential means of entry into understanding zombie films' subconscious appeal to a vast audience. Briefly explain the meaning of "the uncanny" from the Freudian theorist's perspective. How does this concept help explain movie fans' fascination with and/or attraction to zombie films?

4. Bishop argues that the zombie film, as pioneered by Romero and represented by any number of worthy successors, has several specific characteristics that distinguish it from, slasher flicks, monster movies, and other supernatural cinematic renderings. What are the four distinguishing appeals of zombie movies, as enumerated by the author of this essay?

5. *Thinking rhetorically:* This essay's author, a genre theorist by profession, concludes his discussion by stating, "The horror of the zombie movie comes from recognizing the human in the monster; the terror of the zombie movie comes from knowing there is nothing to do about it but destroy what is left; the fun comes from watching the genre continue to develop." By what means does he attempt to convince readers that studying zombie films is a worthy pursuit for academics . . . as well as for students such as yourself?

For Group Discussion

In the fictional world of the zombie film anyone can potentially become a zombified monster, and many people do, over the course of the typical onscreen narrative. Because of this fact, argues Bishop, zombie movies deal "unabashedly with human taboos, murder, and cannibalism, which Dillard proposes have much to do with the genre's success." In group discussion, first consider the validity of this proposition, and list several other reasons why zombie movies may be popular among persons of your generation in particular. Next, consider Bishop's "taboo theory" as manifest in other films: What other specific films, or discrete genres of film, might confront taboo subjects to reach audiences at the basest primal and archetypal levels?

Writing Suggestion

The author concludes this essay by arguing that zombie films are particularly successful because "blood, guts, and gore can be shown instantly with graphic detail. Humans have their intestines ripped out, zombies are cheerfully hunted and butchered, and mad doctors perform unspeakable acts on the reanimated corpses of their former associates. The synchronic nature of cinema allows these shocking images to be suddenly and thoroughly unleashed on the viewing public, resulting in the expected gleeful revulsion." In an essay, discuss your own relationship to the horror film and attempt to propose a psychological theory to explain your particular experience with zombie movies, chainsaw massacre flicks, monster epics such as *Cloverfield* or *War of the Worlds,* and so forth. If you experience the "gleeful revulsion" to which Bishop refers, what might this reveal about your character, your upbringing, your hard-wired excitement threshold, your fears and anxieties, and your concerns about death that is the eventual and unavoidable end for us all? If, conversely, you find yourself not in the least interested in coming face-to-face, gleefully or otherwise, with blood, gore and unspeakably brutal practices on the big screen, what does this reveal about you and your complex personality dynamics?

Judd Apatow and Tyler Perry: Two Contemporary Filmmakers

A Fine Romance

DAVID DENBY

Here's a quick quiz on English diction: What does the word Apatovian mean? No clue? Don't bother looking it up in a dictionary, because you won't find it. However, in constructing this section of the Common Culture movie chapter, we have run across the word no fewer than seventeen times in various movie reviews, cinema Web sites, and blogs. Since it does not yet appear officially in any dictionary, let us hereby put forth our own working definition, which goes something like, Apatovian: adj. of or pertaining to the film comedies of writer/director Judd Apatow. We introduce this contemporary neologism (made-up word) because this section of the Movies chapter introduces two pairs of articles pertaining to modern filmmakers who are having significant impacts on movies specifically, and on broader issues of art and culture as well: Judd Apatow and Quentin Tarantino. There is more on Tarantino at the end of the chapter; meanwhile, turning to Apatow . . . if his name isn't immediately familiar to you, his films certainly are, because you've no doubt seen one—if not all—of his very long list of movie accomplishments, which include: Forgetting Sarah Marshall *(2008) (producer);* Walk Hard: The Dewey Cox Story *(2007) (writer/producer);* Superbad *(2007) (producer);* Knocked Up *(2007) (director/writer/producer);* Talladega Nights: The Ballad of Ricky Bobby *(2006) (producer);* The 40-Year-Old Virgin *(2005) (director/writer/producer);* Anchorman: The Legend of Ron Burgundy *(2004) (producer). In the following essay, film critic David Denby discusses the evolution of the romantic comedy, leading from movies starring Katherine Hepburn and Spencer Tracy, through Woody Allen and Diane Keaton, and finally up to what has been called—sometimes lovingly, sometimes dismissively—slacker romantic comedy . . . Apatow's* Knocked Up *being the prime example.*

As you read, *notice the judicious tone of distance and* open-mindedness *that Denby, the consummately literate film critic, brings to his subject. While clearly an avid fan of the earlier "screwball" comedies and, later, the films of Woody Allen, the author nevertheless acknowledges that Apatovian comedy is "fascinating and funny," even as he offers up some pointed critique of this contemporary form.*

His beard is haphazard and unintentional, and he dresses in sweats, or in shorts and a T-shirt, or with his shirt hanging out like the tongue of a Labrador retriever. He's about thirty, though he may be younger, and he spends a lot of time with friends who are like him, only more so—sweet-natured young men of foul mouth, odd hair, and wanker-mag reading habits. When he's with them, punched beer cans and bongs of various sizes lie around like spent shells; alone, and walrus-heavy on his couch, he watches football, basketball, or baseball on television, or spends time memorializing his youth—archiving old movies, games, and jokes. Like his ancestors in the sixties, he's anti-corporate, but he's not bohemian (his culture is pop). He's more like a sullen back-of-the-classroom guy, who breaks into brilliant tirades only when he feels like it. He may run a used-record store, or conduct sightseeing tours with a non-stop line of patter, or feed animals who then high-five him with their flippers, or teach in a school where he can be friends with all the kids, or design an Internet site that no one needs. Whatever he does, he hardly breaks a sweat, and sometimes he does nothing at all. 1

He may not have a girlfriend, but he certainly likes girls—he's even, in some cases, a hetero blade, scoring with tourists or love-hungry single mothers. But if he does have a girlfriend she works hard. Usually, she's the same age as he is but seems older, as if the disparity between boys and girls in ninth grade had been recapitulated fifteen years later. She dresses in Donna Karan or Ralph Lauren or the like; she's a corporate executive, or a lawyer, or works in TV, public relations, or an art gallery. She's good-tempered, honest, great-looking, and serious. She wants to "get to the next stage of life"—settle down, marry, maybe have children. Apart from getting on with it, however, she doesn't have an idea in her head, and she's not the one who makes the jokes. 2

When she breaks up with him, he talks his situation over with his hopeless pals, who give him bits of misogynist advice. Suddenly, it's the end of youth for him. It's a crisis for her, too, and they can get back together only if both undertake some drastic alteration: he must act responsibly (get a job, take care of a kid), and she has to do something crazy (run across a baseball field during a game, tell a joke). He has to shape up, and she has to loosen up. 3

There they are, the young man and young woman of the dominant romantic-comedy trend of the past several years—the slovenly hipster and the female straight arrow. The movies form a genre of sorts: the slacker-striver romance. Stephen Frears's *High Fidelity* (2000), which transferred Nick Hornby's novel from London to Chicago, may not have been the first, but it set the tone and established the self-dramatizing underachiever as hero. Hornby's guy-centered material also inspired *About a Boy* and *Fever Pitch*. Others in this group include 4

Old School, Big Daddy, 50 First Dates, Shallow Hal, School of Rock, Failure to Launch, You, Me and Dupree, Wedding Crashers, The Break-Up, and—this summer's hit—*Knocked Up.* In these movies, the men are played by Vince Vaughn, Owen Wilson, Adam Sandler, John Cusack, Jimmy Fallon, Matthew McConaughey, Jack Black, Hugh Grant, and Seth Rogen; the women by Drew Barrymore, Jennifer Aniston, Kate Hudson, Sarah Jessica Parker, and Katherine Heigl. For almost a decade, Hollywood has pulled jokes and romance out of the struggle between male infantilism and female ambition.

5 *Knocked Up,* written and directed by Judd Apatow, is the culminating version of this story, and it feels like one of the key movies of the era—a raw, discordant equivalent of *The Graduate* forty years ago. I've seen it with audiences in their twenties and thirties, and the excitement in the theatres is palpable—the audience is with the movie all the way, and, afterward, many of the young men (though not always the young women) say that it's not only funny but true. They feel that way, I think, because the picture is unruly and surprising; it's filled with the messes and rages of life in 2007. The woman, Alison (Katherine Heigl), an ambitious TV interviewer in Los Angeles, gets pregnant after a sozzled one-night stand with Ben (Seth Rogen), a nowhere guy she meets at a disco. Cells divide, sickness arrives in the morning—the movie's time scheme is plotted against a series of pulsing sonograms. Yet these two, to put it mildly, find themselves in an awkward situation. They don't much like each other; they don't seem to match up. Heigl has golden skin, blond hair, a great laugh. She's so attractive a person that, at the beginning of the movie, you wince every time Rogen touches her. Chubby, with curling hair and an orotund voice, he has the round face and sottish grin of a Jewish Bacchus, though grape appeals to him less than weed. At first, he makes one crass remark after another; he seems like a professional comic who will do anything to get a laugh. It's not at all clear that these two should stay together.

6 Authentic as Ben and Alison seem to younger audiences, they are, like all the slacker-striver couples, strangers to anyone with a long memory of romantic comedy. Buster Keaton certainly played idle young swells in some of his silent movies, but, first humiliated and then challenged, he would exert himself to heroic effort to win the girl. In the end, he proved himself a lover. In the nineteen-thirties, the young, lean James Stewart projected a vulnerability that was immensely appealing. So did Jack Lemmon, in his frenetic way, in the fifties. In succeeding decades, Elliott Gould, George Segal, Alan Alda, and other actors played soulful types. Yet all these men wanted something. It's hard to think of earlier heroes who were absolutely free of the desire to make an impression on the world and still got the girl.

And the women in the old romantic comedies were daffy or tough or high-spirited or even spiritual in some way, but they were never blank. What's going on in this new genre? *Knocked Up,* a raucously funny and explicit movie, has some dark corners, some fear and anxiety festering under the jokes. Apatow takes the slacker-striver romance to a place no one thought it would go. He also makes it clear, if we hadn't noticed before, how drastically the entire genre breaks with the classic patterns of romantic comedy. Those ancient tropes fulfill certain expectations and, at their best, provide incomparable pleasure. But *Knocked Up* is heading off into a brave and uncertain new direction.

Shakespeare knew the Roman farces—by Plautus, Terence, and others—in which a scrambling boy chases after a girl and lands her. He varied the pattern. His comedies were rarely a simple chase, and the best American romantic comedies have drawn on the forms that he devised—not so much, perhaps, in the coarse-grained *Taming of the Shrew* but in *Much Ado About Nothing,* with its pair of battling lovers, Beatrice and Benedick. Why is the contact between those two so barbed? Because they are meant for each other, and are too proud and frightened to admit it. We can see the attraction, even if they can't. They have a closely meshed rhythm of speech, a quickness to rise and retort, that no one else shares. Benedick, announcing the end of the warfare, puts the issue squarely: "Shall quips and sentences and these paper bullets of the brain awe a man from the career of his humor? No, the world must be peopled." 7

Romantic comedy is entertainment in the service of the biological imperative. The world must be peopled. Even if the lovers are past child-rearing age or, as in recent years, don't want children, the biological imperative survives, as any evolutionary psychologist will tell you, in the flourishes of courtship behavior. Romantic comedy civilizes desire, transforms lust into play and ritual—the celebration of union in marriage. The lovers are fated by temperament and physical attraction to join together, or stay together, and the audience longs for that ending with an urgency that is as much moral as sentimental. For its amusement, however, the audience doesn't want the resolution to come too quickly. The lovers misunderstand each other; they get pixie dust thrown in their faces. Befuddled, the woman thinks she's in love with a gas-station attendant, who turns out to be a millionaire; an unsuitable suitor becomes a proper suitor; and so on. It's always the right guy in the end. Romantic drama may revel in suffering, even in anguish and death, but romantic comedy merely nods at the destructive energies of passion. The confused lovers torment each other and, for a while, us. Then they stop. 8

The best directors of romantic comedy in the nineteen-thirties and forties—Frank Capra, Gregory La Cava, Leo McCarey, Howard 9

Hawks, Mitchell Leisen, and Preston Sturges—knew that the story would be not only funnier but much more romantic if the fight was waged between equals. The man and woman may not enjoy parity of social standing or money, but they are equals in spirit, will, and body. As everyone agrees, this kind of romantic comedy—and particularly the variant called "screwball comedy"—lifted off in February, 1934, with Frank Capra's charming *It Happened One Night,* in which a hard-drinking reporter out of a job (Clark Gable) and an heiress who has jumped off her father's yacht (Claudette Colbert) meet on the road somewhere between Florida and New York. Tough and self-sufficient, Gable contemptuously looks after the spoiled rich girl. He's rude and overbearing, and she's miffed, but it helps their acquaintance a little that they are both supremely attractive—Gable quick-moving but large and, in his famous undressing scene, meaty, and Colbert tiny, with a slightly pointed chin, round eyes, and round breasts beneath the fitted striped jacket she buys on the road. When she develops pride, they become equals.

The cinema added something invaluable to the romantic comedy: the camera's ability to place lovers in an enchanted, expanding envelope of setting and atmosphere. It moves with them at will, enlarging their command of streets, fields, sitting rooms, and night clubs; rapid cutting then doubles the speed of their quarrels. Out on the road, in the middle of the Depression, Gable and Colbert join the poor, the hungry, the shysters and the hustlers; they spend a night among haystacks, get fleeced, practice their hitchhiking skills. In screwball comedy, the characters have to dive below their social roles for their true selves to come out: they get drunk and wind up in the slammer; they turn a couch in an upstairs room of a mansion into a trampoline; they run around the woods at a country estate—the American plutocrats' version of Shakespeare's magical forest in *A Midsummer Night's Dream,* where young people, first confused and then enlightened, discover whom they should marry. 10

In many of the screwball classics, including *Twentieth Century, My Man Godfrey, The Awful Truth, Easy Living, Midnight, Bringing Up Baby, Holiday, The Philadelphia Story, The Lady Eve*—all made between 1934 and 1941—the characters dress for dinner and make cocktails, and the atmosphere is gilded and swank. The enormous New York apartments, the country houses with porticoes, the white-on-white night clubs in which swells listen to a warbling singer—all this establishes a facade of propriety and manners, a place to misbehave. Except for the Fred Astaire & Ginger Rogers dance musicals, in which evening clothes are integral to the lyric transformation of life into movement, the lovers are no more than playing at formality. The characters need 11 to be wealthy in order to exercise their will openly and make their choices. The screwball comedies are less about possessions than about a certain style of freedom in love, a way of vaulting above the dullness and petty-mindedness of the sticks. (In these films, no matter how rich you may be, you are out of the question if you hail from Oklahoma or Albany—you are Ralph Bellamy.)

Many of the heroines were heiresses, who, in those days, were 12
prized for their burbling eccentricities—Carole Lombard's howl, Irene Dunne's giggle, Katharine Hepburn's Bryn Mawr drawl. Pampered and dizzy, they favored spontaneity over security when it came to choosing a man. As for the men, they came in two varieties. Some owned a factory or a mine, or were in finance—worldly fellows who knew how to float a debenture or hand a woman into a taxi—and others were gently cartooned intellectuals. Innocents preoccupied with some intricate corner of knowledge, they gathered old bones (Cary Grant, in *Bringing Up Baby*), or new words (Gary Cooper, in *Ball of Fire*), or went up the Amazon and discovered unspeakable snakes (Henry Fonda, in *The Lady Eve*). The man is the love object here—passive, dreamy, and gentle, a kind of Sleeping Beauty in spectacles—and the woman is the relentless pursuer. Katharine Hepburn in *Baby* nearly drives Cary Grant crazy with her intrusions into his work, her way of scattering his life about like pieces of lawn furniture. She's attracted by his good looks but also by what's unaroused in him, and she will do anything to awaken him. Equality in these comedies takes a new shape. The man is serious about his work (and no one says he shouldn't be), but he's confused about women, and his confusion has neutered him. He thinks he wants a conventional marriage with a compliant wife, but what he really wants is to be overwhelmed by the female life force. In the screwball comedies, the woman doesn't ask her man to grow up. She wants to pull him into some sort of ridiculous adventure. She has to grow up, and he has to get loose—the opposite of the current pattern.

The screwball comedies were not devoted to sex, exactly—you 13
could hardly describe any of the characters as sensualists. The Production Code limited openness on such matters, and the filmmakers turned sex into a courtship game that was so deliriously convoluted precisely because couples could go to bed only when they were married. The screwball movies, at their peak, defined certain ideal qualities of insouciance, a fineness of romantic temper in which men and women could be aggressive but not coarse, angry but not rancorous, silly but not shamed, melancholy but not ravaged. It was the temper of American happiness.

14 Sometimes the couple in a romantic comedy are already married, or were formerly married, but husband and wife go at each other anyway, because they enjoy wrangling too much to stop. Who else is there to talk to? In a case like that, romance becomes less a dazed encounter in an enchanted garden than a duel with slingshots at close quarters—exciting but a little risky. The most volatile of these comedies was *His Girl Friday,* Howard Hawks's 1940 version of the 1928 Ben Hecht–Charles MacArthur play *The Front Page*. In the original, the star reporter Hildy Johnson is a man. In Hawks's version, Hildy (Rosalind Russell) is a woman who has fled the barbarous city desk and plans to marry a timid businessman (Ralph Bellamy). Her former husband and editor, Walter Burns (Cary Grant), will do anything to get her back to the paper. He doesn't seem drawn to her as a woman, yet he woos her in his way, with scams, lies, and one important truth—that she's the only person good enough to cover the hottest story in town. She knows him as an indifferent and absent husband, yet she's attracted, once again, by the outrageous way this man fans his tail. And, despite her misgivings, she's caught, too, by the great time they have together toiling in the yellow journalism that they both love. Vince Vaughn, in some of his recent roles, has displayed a dazzling motormouth velocity, but he has never worked with an actress who can keep up with him. Rosalind Russell keeps up with Grant. These two seize each other's words and throw them back so quickly that their dialogue seems almost syncopated. Balance between the sexes here becomes a kind of matched virtuosity more intense than sex.

15 If Russell and Grant were exactly alike in that movie, Spencer Tracy, slow-talking, even adamantine, with a thick trunk and massive head, and Katharine Hepburn, slender, angular, and unnervingly speedy and direct, were opposites that attracted with mysterious force. In the classic comedy *Adam's Rib* (1949), their sixth movie together (they made nine), they were an established onscreen married couple, rising, drinking coffee, and getting dressed for work. How can you have romantic comedy in a setting of such domestic complacency? *Adam's Rib,* which was written by a married couple, Garson Kanin and Ruth Gordon, and directed by George Cukor, takes these two through combat so fierce that it can be ended only with a new and very desperate courtship. They become opposing lawyers in a murder case. He prosecutes, and she defends, a woman (Judy Holliday) who put a couple of slugs in her husband when she caught him in the arms of his mistress. As the two lawyers compete in court, and Tracy gets upstaged by Hepburn, the traditional sparring at the center of romantic comedy intensifies, turns a little ugly, and then comes to an abrupt stop with a loud slap—Tracy smacking Hepburn's bottom in a proprietary way

during a late-night rubdown session. The slap is nothing, yet it's everything. The husband has violated the prime rule of mating behavior by asserting a right over his wife physically. The drive for equality in movies can lead to bruising competitions, and in *Adam's Rib* the partnership of equals nearly dissolves. Suddenly anguished, the movie uneasily rights itself as husband and wife make concessions and find their way back to marriage again.

Achieving balance between a man and a woman in a romantic comedy can be elusive. Marilyn Monroe, her tactile flesh spilling everywhere, was either lusted after or mocked, but only Tony Curtis, appearing in Cary Grant drag in *Some Like It Hot,* knew how to talk to her. Rock Hudson and Doris Day, in their films together, were exclusively preoccupied with, respectively, assaulting and defending Day's virtue, and they both seemed a little demented. Tom Hanks matched up nicely with Daryl Hannah and with Meg Ryan, as did Richard Gere and Hugh Grant with Julia Roberts, whose eyes and smile and restless, long-waisted body charged up several romantic comedies in the nineties. 16

In recent decades, however, Woody Allen and Diane Keaton have come closest to restoring the miraculous ease of the older movies. Short and narrow-jawed, with black-framed specs that give him the aspect of a quizzical Eastern European police inspector, Allen turned his worried but demanding gaze on Keaton, the tall, willowy Californian. In their early films together, they seemed the most eccentric and singular of all movie couples; it was the presence of New York City, in *Annie Hall* (1977) and *Manhattan* (1979), that sealed their immortality as a team. Allen, narrating, presented himself as the embodied spirit of the place, sharp and appreciative, but also didactic, overexplicit, cranky, and frightened of lobsters off the leash and everything else in the natural world. The idea was that beauty and brains would match up, although, early in *Annie Hall,* the balance isn't quite there—Keaton has to rise to his level. Initially, she's nervously apologetic—all floppy hats, tail-out shirts, and tremulous opinions—and she agrees to be tutored by Allen, who gives her books to read and takes her repeatedly to *The Sorrow and the Pity*. For a while, they click as teacher and student. If Tracy and Hepburn were like a rock and a current mysteriously joined together, these two neurotics were like agitated hummingbirds meeting in midair. 17

Working with the cinematographer Gordon Willis, Woody Allen created the atmosphere of a marriage plot in conversations set in his beloved leafy East Side streets—his version of Shakespeare's magical forest. But *Annie Hall,* surprisingly, shifts away from marriage. The quintessential New Yorker turns out to be a driven pain in the neck, so insistent and adolescent in his demands that no woman can 18 put up with him for long. And the specific New York elements that Allen added to romantic comedy—the cult of psychoanalysis and the endless opinions about writers, musicians, and artists—also threaten the stability of the couple. Psychoanalysis yields "relationships" and "living together," not marriage, as the central ritual, and living together, especially in the time of the Pill and the easy real-estate market of the seventies, is always provisional. Opinions about art—the way the soul defines itself in time—are provisional, too. In *Annie Hall,* Keaton outgrows Allen's curriculum for her and moves on, and in *Manhattan,* perhaps the best American comedy about selfishness ever made, she returns to the married man she was having an affair with. Allen loses her both times; the biological imperative goes nowhere. *Annie Hall* and *Manhattan* now seem like fragile and melancholy love lyrics; they took romantic comedy to a level of rueful sophistication never seen before or since.

The louts in the slacker-striver comedies should probably lose the girl, too, but most of them don't. Yet what, exactly, are they getting, and why should the women want them? That is not a question that romantic comedy has posed before. 19

The slacker has certain charms. He doesn't want to compete in business, he refuses to cultivate macho attitudes, and, for some women, he may be attractive. He's still a boy—he's gentler than other men. Having a child with such a guy, however, is another matter, and plenty of women have complained about the way *Knocked Up* handles the issue of pregnancy. Alison has a good job, some growing public fame, and she hardly knows the unappealing father—there's even some muttering about "bad genes." Why have a baby with him? Well, a filmmaker's answer would have to be that if there's an abortion, or if Alison has the child on her own, there's no movie—or, at least, nothing like this movie. And this movie, just as it is, has considerable interest and complication as fiction. 20

What's striking about *Knocked Up* is the way the romance is placed within the relations between the sexes. The picture is a drastic revision of classic romantic-comedy patterns. Ben doesn't chase Alison, and she doesn't chase him. The movie is not about the civilizing of desire, and it offers a marriage plot that couldn't be more wary of marriage. *Knocked Up,* like Apatow's earlier *The 40-Year-Old Virgin,* is devoted to the dissolution of a male pack, the ending of the juvenile male bond. Ben and his friends sit around in their San Fernando Valley tract house whamming each other on the head with rubber bats and watching naked actresses in movies. The way Ben lives with his friends is tremendous fun; it's also as close to paralysis as you can get and continue breathing. Apatow, of course, has it both ways. He squeezes 21 the pink-eyed doofuses for every laugh he can get out of them, but at the same time he suggests that the very thing he's celebrating is sick, crazy, and dysfunctional. The situation has to end. Boys have to grow up or life ceases.

Ben and Alison's one-night stand forces the issue. Willy-nilly, the 22
world gets peopled. Yet the slowly developing love between Ben and the pregnant Alison comes off as halfhearted and unconvincing—it's the weakest element in the movie. There are some terrifically noisy arguments, a scene of Rogen's making love to the enormous Heigl ("I'm not making love to you like a dog. It's doggy style. It's a style"), but we never really see the moment in which they warm up and begin to like each other. That part of the movie is unpersuasive, I would guess, because it's not terribly important to Apatow. What's important is the male bond—the way it flourishes, in all its unhealthiness, and then its wrenching end. Alison lives with her sister, Debbie (Leslie Mann), and brother-in-law, Pete (Paul Rudd), and Ben begins to hang out with Alison at the house of the married couple, who are classically mismatched in temperament. Pete is restless, disappointed, and remorselessly funny, and Ben links up with him. Whooping with joy, they go off to Las Vegas, but they don't gamble or get laid. Instead, they hang out and eat "shrooms." They merely want to be together: it's as if Romeo and Mercutio had left the women and all that mess in Verona behind and gone off to practice their swordsmanship. When Ben and Pete get high, crash, and then return, chastened, to the women, the male bond is severed at last, the baby can be born, and life continues. In generic terms, *Knocked Up* puts the cart before the horse—the accidental baby, rather than desire, pulls the young man, who has to leave his male friends behind, into civilization.

As fascinating and as funny as *Knocked Up* is, it represents what 23
can only be called the disenchantment of romantic comedy, the end point of a progression from Fifth Avenue to the Valley, from tuxedos to tube socks, from a popped champagne cork to a baby crowning. There's nothing in it that is comparable to the style of the classics—no magic in its settings, no reverberant sense of place, no shared or competitive work for the couple to do. Ben does come through in the end, yet, if his promise and Alison's beauty make them equal as a pair, one still wants more out of Alison than the filmmakers are willing to provide. She has a fine fit of hormonal rage, but, like the other heroines in the slacker-striver romances, she isn't given an idea or a snappy remark or even a sharp perception. All the movies in this genre have been written and directed by men, and it's as if the filmmakers were saying, "Yes, young men are children now, and women bring home the bacon, but men bring home the soul."

The perilous new direction of the slacker-striver genre reduces the role of women to vehicles. Their only real function is to make the men grow up. That's why they're all so earnest and bland—so nice, so good. Leslie Mann (who's married to Apatow) has some great bitchy lines as the angry Debbie, but she's not a lover; she represents disillusion. As Anthony Lane pointed out in these pages, Apatow's subject is not so much sex as age, and age in his movies is a malediction. If you're young, you have to grow up. If you grow up, you turn into Debbie—you fear that the years are overtaking you fast. Either way, you're in trouble. 24

Apatow has a genius for candor that goes way beyond dirty talk—that's why *Knocked Up* is a cultural event. But I wonder if Apatow, like his fumy youths, shouldn't move on. It seems strange to complain of repetition when a director does something particularly well, and Apatow does the infantilism of the male bond better than anyone, but I'd be quite happy if I never saw another bong-gurgling slacker or male pack again. The society that produced the Katharine Hepburn and Carole Lombard movies has vanished; manners, in the sense of elegance, have disappeared. But manners as spiritual style are more important than ever, and Apatow has demonstrated that he knows this as well as anyone. So how can he not know that the key to making a great romantic comedy is to create heroines equal in wit to men? They don't have to dress for dinner, but they should challenge the men intellectually and spiritually, rather than simply offering their bodies as a way of dragging the clods out of their adolescent stupor. "Paper bullets of the brain," as Benedick called the taunting exchanges with Beatrice, slay the audience every time if they are aimed at the right place. 25

Examining the Text

1. After the general introduction mentioned in Question 5, Denby goes on to provide a brief survey of romantic comedy through history. As the first stop in this comedic time-travel trip, how did playwright William Shakespeare craft his comedies, and what themes and narrative structures emerged from them? What important social function has romantic comedy traditionally served, as discussed in this section of Denby's essay?

2. What social-psychological function did romantic comedies serve in economic Depression-era and post-Depression-era America, according to Denby? How did the visual nature of cinematography contribute to the role played by motion picture comedy—especially that of the "screwball" variety—in early-to mid-twentieth century America?

3. Denby says that the male and female protagonists of the screwball comedy era interact in a way that is exactly "opposite of the current pattern" as exemplified in Judd Apatow's films. What were the specific characteristics of women and men in the earlier romantic comedies, and how might this have contributed to a portrayal of "equality between the sexes" during this earlier period?

4. How did the Academy Award–winning romantic comedies of Woody Allen—especially *Annie Hall* (1977) —update the themes and portrayals of the "screwball" romantic comedies? In what ways did Woody Allen's comedies echo the sentiments evoked by the earlier comedies, and in what ways were his portrayals significantly different, representing a change in the social fabric of America?

5. *Thinking rhetorically:* Denby begins this piece by generally contrasting the male and female protagonists of today's "slacker comedies" with the comedic heroes and heroines of romantic comedies in bygone eras. Denby says that, although the main characters of *Knocked Up* may seem authentic to younger audiences, "they are, like all the slacker-striver couples, strangers to anyone with a long memory of romantic comedy." In what ways do the characters and situations—and implied themes—in contemporary romantic comedy differ from those of earlier romantic comedies, by Denby's account? In terms of structure and rhetorical design, how does this opening paragraph prefigure the discussion that follows in this essay?

For Group Discussion

Denby compares the comedies of Judd Apatow to the earlier romantic comedies this way: ". . . it represents what can only be called the disenchantment of romantic comedy, the end point of a progression from Fifth Avenue to the Valley, from tuxedos to tube socks, from a popped champagne cork to a baby crowning." In what ways does *Knocked Up,* and films like it, represent a deevolution of the romantic genre, in Denby's opinion? In the whole-class setting, discuss the accuracy of the author's critique: do you agree with Denby that in the new romances, "There's nothing in it that is comparable to the style of the classics—no magic in its settings, no reverberant sense of place, no shared or competitive work for the couple to do"? On the other hand, do you find in these movies a shared "magic" that reverberates for individuals of your generation—some set of qualities that Denby, who is older, might be missing? If the latter, what specific qualities might make Apatovian comedy qualify as "enchanting"?

Writing Suggestion

At the beginning of this article, Denby documents a certain kind of character that appears in Judd Apatow's romantic comedies: the contemporary young male. This description includes: "His beard is haphazard and unintentional, and he dresses in sweats, or in shorts and a T-shirt . . . he spends a lot of time with friends who are like him, only more so—sweet-natured young men of foul mouth, odd hair, and wanker-mag reading habits. When he's with them, punched beer cans and bongs of various sizes lie around like spent shells; alone, and walrus-heavy on his couch, he watches football, basketball, or baseball on television, or spends time memorializing his youth—archiving old movies, games, and jokes . . . he's anti-corporate, but he's not bohemian (his culture is pop). He's more like a sullen back-of-the-classroom guy, who breaks into brilliant tirades only when he feels like it. . . . He may not have a girlfriend, but he certainly likes girls. . . . " Using the rhetorical form of comparison–contrast, write an essay of five pages in which you discuss the real-life accuracy of this depiction in your experience: if you're a guy, how does this character resemble you and/or your buds, and in what ways does it completely miss the mark? If you're *not* a guy, in what ways does this characterization resemble guys you know (and love?) and in what ways do the males of your acquaintance differ from the Apatovian stereotype?

Freaks, Geeks, and Mensches: Judd Apatow's Comedies of the Mature

ALEX WAINER

If you happen to have been raised in a home with one or more Jewish parents (as was Judd Apatow, the subject of this article by film critic Alex Wainer), then you probably heard the phrase, "Be a mensch," at some point (or many points) in your development. While the word derives literally from the German, meaning simply "man," in Yiddish the phrase takes on a deep cultural resonance, along with a more moral tone: it refers specifically to a person (usually a male, but occasionally female as well, despite the literal male definition) who does good deeds, and/or is an upright or rigorously decent human being. For example, in the home of this headnote's writer, the phrase, "Be a mensch!" could be heard any time my behavior strayed from the above-given definition, as when I failed to clean my room or made fun of my sister's saddle shoes or shoplifted a ballpoint pen from a local supermarket. Likewise, the term "mensch" appears in the title of the following reading because Judd Apatow's comedies often involve a male protagonist who undergoes a change from a shlub (look it up) to a mensch. As you have read in the previous David Denby article, male protagonists in Apatovian comedies tend—at the beginning of movies such as Knocked Up*—not to be mensches: they are aimless, stoned-out, video game-addicted, and don't clean their rooms . . . and as such are kind of grown-up college freshmen. However, by the end of Apatow's films, the boys shape up and become men—and mensches, in the view of Wainer—taking on responsibilities of job and family. This is both the charm and the redeeming thematic quality* *of Apatovian comedies, in Wainer's opinion: the movies ultimately deliver a message that support traditional family values.*

As you read, *note the way in which two intelligent, well-respected movie critics can have different—if not altogether opposite—"takes" on a movie's value. While David Denby, in the previous reading in this text, takes a mildly critical position regarding the protagonists' shift from slackers to mensches, suggesting that this represents a conformist capitulation to bourgeois middle-class expectations, Wainer seems to praise these resolutions and their moral implications. Each critic brings credible evidence to bear on his thematic conclusions, leading readers to realize that a good work of art allows for a multiplicity of "correct" interpretations, depending upon one's philosophical orientation. It's up to you, the reader, to situate yourself within this dialog, and to decide ultimately which is the interpretation that rings true for you.*

We are currently in the era of the boy-man (or mook). 1

Male character types in popular culture run in cycles: The 1950s square-jawed hero, the '60s rebel, the '70s swinger and the '80s action hero. The early 21st-century male type is shaping up to be the hapless 20-something who is developmentally arrested. Manhood is forestalled by indecision, partying and smoking marijuana from bongs, spending long hours mastering video games, and living in plain fear of growing up. A culture of boy-men characterizes numerous movie types—Adam Sandler, Jack Black, characters in Kevin Smith films, etc. 2

But two recent exceptions take an ethnographic look at the slacker lifestyle and discover characters searching for their escape out of a boy's life and into manhood. Judd Apatow's raucous and insightful film comedies understand that world and these guys, but challenge his characters to act their age. 3

R-RATED MORALITY TALES

The first thing to know: these films aren't made for your church youth group (although I'll bet a few have watched them). They're R-rated and for a reason. Characters talk the way people in this subculture speak—except probably wittier. But like all good dramas and character-based comedies, the screenplay forces them to painfully confront their problems. They have behavior that they must grow out of, but first the audience has to see and hear it to understand the lives the characters live and the challenges they face. 4

In the last two years, Apatow has directed and co-written two films, *The 40-Year-Old Virgin* and *Knocked Up,* where the need to put 5 away childish things and belatedly face responsibilities sets these films apart from other R-rated comedies. Here are brief plot synopses (with spoilers) of these very raunchy films, so you won't need to watch them to understand just how their themes run counter to the cultural flow.

BOYS TO MEN

In *The 40-Year-Old Virgin,* Andy Stitzer works at an electronics superstore where his male co-workers engage in the usual masculine sexual braggadocio. One night during a card game, as the guys are swapping their bawdy tales of female conquest, real or imagined, it becomes quite obvious that the nice but dorky Andy doesn't know what he's talking about and soon has to admit that he is a virgin. When as a youth he'd tried to fornicate—though the flesh was willing—his heart just wasn't in it, and awkwardness led to embarrassing disaster and decades of romantic and sexual solitude. The other guys now make it their mission to initiate Andy into sexual activity. 6

What follows is a hilarious commentary on the misplaced priorities of young males who are mostly still little boys on the inside. In fact, the men in Apatow's stories are terrified of women and can only relate to them as sexual playthings, but though Andy is the most scared of all, he doesn't see women as sex objects, but as individuals. He respects the idea of sexual love with one woman so much that he has never had sex. When he tries to play the swinger, he fails horribly and hilariously. 7

He feels much safer immersed in his house full of hobbies and hundreds of valuable mint-condition (never opened) action figures. Obviously, Andy's had to learn a lot about sublimation. In a scene charged with insightful dual meanings, taking his action figures out of its original packaging becomes a metaphor for the sexual activity everyone is urging on Andy. Unconsciously referring to more than the action figure, Andy says, "It loses its value if you take it out of its packaging." 8

Eventually he meets an attractive woman older than him, Trish, who is already a youthful grandmother. There's good chemistry but, though they date, Andy's virginity is a secret whose revelation he thinks would scare off any woman who learned the truth. Andy finally "confesses" his sexual purity motivated by his desire to commit himself to one woman for life. "For so long I thought that there was something wrong with me . . . because it had never happened, but . . . I realize now that it was just because I was waiting for you." 9

In the biggest surprise of the movie, rather than finally having sex, the two middle-aged sweethearts are married and after the minister tells him he may kiss the bride, he adds to Andy, "And for God's sake, consummate the thing." In a profane and obscene sex comedy, the title character endures decades of abstinence before matrimony allows him to lose his virgin status. A better advertisement for the "True Love Waits" campaign in the real world is hard to imagine. 10

A SECOND TAKE

Last summer saw Apatow's second directorial effort, *Knocked Up*, win similar critical and box office success. Ben Stone, another layabout living off a now-dwindling insurance settlement, spends his days with his stoner buddies planning to create a website that chronicles the nude scenes of Hollywood stars. When he meets a beautiful blonde, Alison, at a club, the two awkwardly drink their way into her apartment and have intoxicated sex that Ben scarcely remembers in the morning. 11

The mismatched couple goes their separate ways until eight weeks later, Alison begins to suspect she is pregnant. Contacting Ben to bring him into the loop, they go to the doctor's office where they view an early sonogram with awe and dismay—indeed, there is an obviously visible tiny life growing inside her. This new and unplanned development has interrupted their lives and they are completely unprepared. Alison's mother gives her this chilling advice: 12

"I cannot be supportive of this. This is a mistake. This is a big, big mistake. Now think about your stepsister. Now, you remember what happened with her? She had the same situation as you and she had it taken care of. And you know what? Now she has a real baby. Honey, this is not the time." 13

Alison refuses to "have it taken care of." Ben's father tells Ben the child is a blessing and he should welcome it. When Alison tells Ben she's keeping the baby, Ben gamely agrees that he should be a part of the child's life and the two begin to work on their relationship. They go shopping for baby clothes and Ben tells her he'll read a stack of child-rearing books to prepare. But it won't be that easy for Ben to change. His friends are his support group and they are arrested adolescents. Ben doesn't really know how to be an adult, and as the months pass, Alison begins to question whether he will be a fit partner in rearing their child. When she discovers that Ben has never even taken those child-rearing books out of the bag, she breaks up with him. 14

Hitting rock bottom, Ben turns to his father, Harris, a thrice-married man, for advice. The only thing Harris can tell his son is, 15

"You can go around blaming everyone else, but in the end, until you take responsibility for yourself, none of this is going to work out."

Ben leaves his druggie pals, moves into his own apartment, and finds a real job. He stays home in the evenings and reads the baby books. He grows up. When Alison goes into labor alone, she calls him and a new side of Ben emerges. He manages to get Alison to the hospital and stand with her through a difficult (but hilariously graphic) birth process. The gestation period has resulted in two births—one of a baby, and the other of an adult male. Ben's whole demeanor has changed from that of a man-child to someone who acts like a husband. The hard-won maturity raises the hope that the couple, once so wildly different, has been transformed by the process into good parents for their baby daughter. 16

Critics were struck at finding such traditional values in an R-rated sex comedy. In the *New York Times*, A. O. Scott remarked, "While this movie's barrage of gynecology-inspired jokes would have driven the prudes at the old Hays Office mad, its story, about a young man trying to do what used to be the very definition of the Right Thing, might equally have brought a smile of approval to the lips of the starchiest old-Hollywood censor." *Time*'s film critic Richard Schickel wrote that Apatow "clearly believes in marriage, family, bourgeois dutifulness." 17

A *New York Times Magazine* profile of Apatow describes his films as having "conservative morals the Family Research Council might embrace—if the humor weren't so filthy." The reporter accompanied the director/writer/producer, his wife, and the *Knocked Up* stars to a chic club on the rooftop of a Las Vegas hotel and noted how uncomfortable Apatow was amidst the glitz and girls. In the same article, a friend reports that Apatow doesn't even like it when he points out attractive women to him. The director confirms this unease: "He's right . . . I'm the guy who gets uncomfortable. That's why I was able to write *The 40-Year-Old Virgin* and *Knocked Up*. I believe in those guys. There's something honorable about holding out for love and not breaking up for the sake of the baby. I see people get divorced, and there is a part of me that thinks, I wonder how hard they tried?" 18

What's striking is finding such morals in what are truly R-worthy comedies. The F-word and other such language flow freely because that is the social world of these nerds and geeks, although, as the *New York Times* review notes, "for all its rowdy obscenity it rarely feels coarse or crude." Although Apatow has a clear affection for his male losers and bong-smoking boys, they serve as a sharp contrast when his protagonists start to break away from their boys club, leaving them looking somewhat pathetic in their immaturity. They will probably never know the joy and satisfaction of Andy and Ben, who traded their action figures and porn sites for commitment and fidelity. 19

This is not to advocate that readers should rush out and rent an Apatow film, but I find their critical and commercial success interesting cultural indicators that even in the midst of an age long past the restraint and taste of yesteryear, there is an underlying attraction to the stability and joy that can come from taking responsibility to act one's age. 20

Can a couple of subversively moral sex comedies reverse the results of the sexual revolution? Media effects theorists argue it takes many exposures to a given message over an extended period of time before attitudes change and behavior is altered. Cultural transformation is a mysterious and complex phenomenon so only the presumptuous would read these films as harbingers of moral regeneration. But we can still marvel when someone like Judd Apatow can make people laugh at themselves while pondering his challenge to be a mensch. 21

Examining the Text

1. Describing his feelings toward the protagonists he created for *40-Year-Old Virgin* and *Knocked Up,* writer/director Judd Apatow says, "I believe in those guys." What personality traits and behavioral patterns make the male leads of those two movies sympathetic in the eyes of their creator?

2. The author comments that, although "these films aren't made for your church youth group," they do contain some implicit suggestions for correct moral/ethical behavior within a civilized society. What qualities of Judd Apatow's comedies render them unfit for the stereotypical "church youth group," and what suggestions for upright citizenship emerge from Apatovian romantic comedy, despite their raunchiness?

3. The author of this article devotes most of his attention to two of Judd Apatow's comedies, *The 40-Year-Old Virgin* and *Knocked Up*. Briefly summarize the author's plot summary of the first of those movies, and explain the themes that emerge from the narrative of *The 40-Year-Old Virgin,* in the opinion of Wainer.

4. Wainer next turns his attention to *Knocked Up,* giving it a similar summary/analysis treatment that he gave to *The 40-Year-Old Virgin.* Report on the significant plot details of *Knocked Up,* as provided by Wainer, and discuss the ways in which the author of this article sees "traditional values" emerging from *Knocked Up:* a movie that contains, once again, a relatively "raunchy" set of circumstances and character portrayals.

5. *Thinking rhetorically:* The author of this article gives a quick rundown of "male character types" in popular movies through several decades. He then goes on to update this list, discussing personality traits of leading men in current romantic comedies. Summarize Wainer's points about male protagonists over the past several decades and then—drawing upon your own history as a movie watcher—test the critic's persuasive points: do his generalizations about these male leads hold up, or do your examples contradict the evidence he provides here, perhaps casting doubt upon his conclusions?

For Group Discussion

At the beginning of this article, author Wainer attempts to set the comedies of Judd Apatow apart from other contemporary R-rated comedies, stating that Apatovian films have a certain moral dimension that the other productions do not. In all cases, Wainer says, "a culture of boy-men characterizes numerous movie types" cast as leads in these films . . . but the non-Apatow-like comedies—films starring Adam Sandler, Jack Black, and characters in Kevin Smith films, for example—do not have the redeeming [at least in Wainer's and Apatow's minds] quality of elevating marriage and societal conformity through their narrative resolutions. In class discussion, and from your own extensive knowledge of films of this type, bring up specific examples of recent romantic comedies, both of the Apatovian and the non-Apatovian variety, in order to test the validity of Wainer's hypothesis here.

Writing Suggestion

Using the comparison/contrast rhetorical form, write an essay discussing this chapter's paired readings on the comedies of Judd Apatow. Each author—David Denby and Alex Wainer—has a unique perspective on these films, both in terms of their quality as satisfying viewing fare, and as indicators of broader societal trends and moral/ethical currents. Each critic finds much to admire in Apatovian film, and yet each arrives significantly different conclusions about the merits and meanings of the movies under scrutiny. To construct your essay, first make an outline of the specific issues of similarity between the two reviewers' points of view, and then outline the reviewers' issues of difference. Next, employing the "point-by-point" method of comparison/contrast, follow your outline in discussing the reviewers' specific areas of likeness and dissimilarity in their "takes" on Apatow's films and their wider implications. Finally, as you move toward your conclusion, attempt to situate yourself within this discussion: what is *your* "take" on the artistic merit of Judd Apatow's movies, and how do *you* believe those movies indicate—and perhaps even construct—societal tastes, ethics, and mores?

Mama's Gun

HILTON ALS

Tyler Perry's movies have grossed over $350 million, thanks mostly to his filmic creation, Mable (Madea) Simmons: a tall, plain-spoken, bong-hitting, middle-aged matriarch who fights verbally (and with her handgun, as mentioned in this article's title) to impose a certain order in her sometimes chaotic world. Madea and her supporting characters have made Perry, at forty, the most financially successful black individual in the history of the American film industry. According to some observers *within the community, before Perry came along, the movie industry had made African Americans experience a certain invisibility by having few leading characters to whom they could relate; likewise, according to the same observers, the movie industry portrayed very negatively the few white figures with whom black audiences could identify, such as President Bill Clinton. However, when Perry arrived on the scene as writer, director, and producer of his own films, he offered a radically different perspective, something akin to what their preachers had been offering every Sunday: an entertainment for hardworking black Christians who wanted, at least for a couple of hours, to be distracted from the truth about their continuing difficulties in advancing economically and socially in their own country.*

Tyler Perry has released eight movies in the past three years, almost all of them reworkings of the themes (and titles) of his plays and from his early days as a live performer. In the following essay from the New Yorker *magazine, Hilton Als—an American theater critic, long-time staff writer for* The Village Voice *and former editor-at-large at* Vibe *magazine—comments that the social factors that drive Madea's actions in her movies frequently consist of other women who try to place themselves above their station in life, in Madea's view. Similarly, Madea finds fault with other black women's exhibiting excessive style, using nonstreet diction, making a good living while living as a single woman, and having relations with a white men. Madea's negative take on ambitious and successful African American women comes up again and again in his movies, leading Hilton Als to question whether this portrayal of Madea isn't ultimately a bit of self-criticism—that is, a sort of penance by Tyler Perry's for having "made it" financially and professionally, while so many others around him have not.* ***As you read,*** *then, consider the criticism that has been leveled at Perry here and elsewhere: namely that, in presenting an idealized conception, he has failed to reflect the African American experience in its profound complexity, instead giving audiences a series of shallow melodramas that render the screen—and the true life of black people—far flatter than they should be. If you have seen any of the Madea films, do these criticisms ring true, or do they seem excessive and unfair? If you haven't seen any of Tyler Perry's films, consider whether Als's discussion in this article makes you interested to delve into Madea's world.*

Mabel (Madea) Simmons, a six-foot-five, homespun, truth-spouting, pot-smoking, politically incorrect middle-aged black matriarch, wears a silver wig, spectacles, and a series of interchangeable floral-print dresses. She lives in the suburbs of Atlanta. There is always a note of complaint in her voice, but who can blame her. As the sometimes 1 beleaguered go-to person for any number of younger relatives who find themselves in bad marriages, broke, or incapable of managing their children, the take-charge Madea busts ass while brandishing her handgun, fighting to impose emotional order in her world. Madea is, of course, the very popular creation of Tyler Perry, the director, writer, and impresario, who is, at forty, the most financially successful black man the American film industry has ever known. Madea, who is played by Perry, has put in appearances in six of his plays and five of his movies, including his 2009 film *I Can Do Bad All by Myself,* which opened in the No. 1 slot last September and grossed fifty-two million dollars. Madea has also shown up on Perry's TV series *Tyler Perry's House of Payne,* and its spinoff, *Meet the Browns.* And she is the author of the 2006 best-seller *Don't Make a Black Woman Take Off Her Earrings:* Madea's *Uninhibited Commentaries on Love and Life.* Perry penned a foreword to the book in his own voice, in which he identifies his creation as a certain type: she is one of those strong older women who preside over inner-city or underprivileged suburban neighborhoods, becoming, in a sense, their moral authority. "Whoever came up with the saying that 'it takes a village to raise a child' must have been thinking of my friend Madea," he writes, adding:

> In the black community, Madea was the head of that village. . . . Madea used to be on every corner in every neighborhood when I was growing up and generations before. . . . She's not politically correct. She doesn't care about anything but what is honest and true. . . . If somebody's child was doing something wrong, Madea got to them and straightened them out or she would go directly to the parents, and the parents straightened the kids out.

Madea was based, Perry notes, on his mother and an aunt, honest women who had relatively uncomplicated relationships to their own authority and who helped him to beat the odds in his own life. Perry grew up, in New Orleans, with little money and a construction-worker father who injured him physically and psychologically. His mother was a preschool teacher. He dropped out of school at sixteen—he later completed his GED.—and worked a variety of low-paying jobs. In 1991, Perry saw an episode of *The Oprah Winfrey Show* that talked about the healing powers of writing. He began to keep a diary, which he then adapted into his first play, *I Know I've Been Changed.* In 1992, using his life's savings of twelve thousand dollars, he made his first attempt to launch himself into the black theatre world, setting up shop in Atlanta—drawn there by the city's large population of successful blacks—and renting a two-hundred-seat hall, in order to stage *I Know I've Been Changed.* The show dealt with child abuse, rape, and other 2 forms of damage, which, in Perry's vision, could be fixed by prayer and by faith, and it had a strong gospel-music element. The play flopped: no one came, and Perry lost his investment.

3 Years passed. He lived in his car and in pay-by-the-week hotels until he understood what had gone wrong and who his audience should be. In 1998, he decided to stage *I Know I've Been Changed* again, this time at a church turned theatre in Atlanta, where it sold out all its performances, before moving to a sold-out run at the much larger Fox Theatre, and then taking to the road. In 1992, Perry had just waited for people to show up, as they would at a "regular" play. In 1998, he saw that he had to take a more direct approach. The audience that he wanted to attract—poor and lower-middle-class Christian blacks like him—thought of theatregoing as a luxury. Churchgoing, on the other hand, was a necessity. Perry resolved to turn his performances into an extension of their faith. He did the rounds of Atlanta's black churches, becoming a spokesman for his play and the values it stood for. He was personable, presentable, and religious; and his play, he made clear, delivered a Christian message—Jesus forgives everything, even poverty and blackness—through characters and situations that audience members would recognize from their own social, cultural, and economic worlds. ("It would be easy to liken this show to Bill Cosby meets the Bible Belt: good clean comedy that somehow is still very amusing and fun to watch," one reviewer wrote of the touring production of *I Know I've Been Changed*.)

4 In short, Perry's vehicle was aspirational, geared toward blacks from backgrounds similar to his, who dreamed of Huxtable-like success and comfort in an imperfectly integrated world. By the time Perry came along, the white world had failed his future fans time and again, both by making them feel invisible (all those ignored ballots in Florida were only a few years away) and by crucifying the few white figures they could identify with, including their first "black" President, Bill Clinton. What Perry's target-audience members lacked onscreen and onstage was a lens through which to see themselves refracted, and a forum in which their religious and political beliefs would be neither challenged nor ignored. Perry offered them something akin to what their preachers offered: entertainment for hard-working black Christians who wanted, at least for a couple of hours, to be distracted from the truth about their failure to advance in their own country.

5 Soon he was doing two to three hundred shows a year, zigzagging around the country on what used to be known as the chitlin circuit (a term that Perry objects to, via Madea: "It's black folks want to see theatre. I don't see no chitlin"), playing to thousands of people at a time, writing, directing, and starring in play after play, from *I Can*

Do Bad All by Myself (1999), which introduced both Madea and her obstreperous brother Joe (also played by Perry), to *Why Did I Get Married?* (2004). Touring, Perry built up the money and the reputation that eventually supported his film studio and his television series. (He also started selling paraphernalia at his shows and online; ever mindful of his audience, he allows his fans to buy his DVDs or his book by filling out a form and mailing in a money order, rather than assuming that they all have credit cards.) It was part of Perry's genius, of course, that he didn't stay on the circuit forever. In his pragmatism, he understood the intimacy of film and television, and the access they offer to those who are less inclined to join in the community aspect of theatre. Communities may crumble and fracture, but everybody goes to the movies. In 2005, he co-produced his first film, *Diary of a Mad Black Woman,* with Lionsgate. The next year, he released Madea's *Family Reunion,* again with Lionsgate. It cost eleven and a half million dollars to make both films. Each opened at No. 1, and together they grossed a hundred and fourteen million.

Perry has released eight movies in the past four years, many 6
of them reworkings of the themes (and titles) of his plays from his days as a live performer. And they almost all follow the basic rules of melodrama. Someone—usually a woman—is in distress. She can't pay her bills or is in an abusive relationship or both. She returns "home," generally to the strong, no-nonsense arms of Madea, who's a relative of some kind. There, the woman meets someone who falls in love with her; after much emotional resistance—she's afraid of getting hurt again—she falls in love with him and marries him, withholding sex until after the wedding. (Madea, who sometimes runs into trouble with the law of the land, has no trouble imposing her own interpretation of the laws of the Lord on her charges.) Mixed in with all this are some craven relatives—along with Madea, they provide the comic highlights—and one or two rousing gospel numbers. The heroes of Perry's movies bear no resemblance to the young white men in search of a sense of purpose in the comedies of, say, Judd Apatow or Adam Sandler. (Madea, of course, would have no truck with the lack of faith in those scenarios, which are driven by the dual forces of white-male power and white-male sexuality, and by the exploitation of a kind of freedom that the blacks in her community can't even dream of.) The white-boy comedies of the past two decades are about the grating, strained emo charm of never growing up, while Perry's films are about the necessity of growing up in a largely segregated world.

None of this qualifies Perry for any prizes in "legit" theatre cir- 7
cles or in the art-house film world; he's interested in showmanship, not

in the vicissitudes of artistic expression or even in a deeper dramatic discussion of faith, of the kind that August Wilson, for one, embarked on. But Perry's work does fill a need, building on the comfortable predictability of such black sitcoms as *Good Times* and *Sanford and Son,* and adding a dose of Christian reassurance. Part of what's satisfying for some audience members in Perry's plays and movies is how Jesus always prevails and the bad guys always get their comeuppance. Perry keeps his plots moving inexorably toward the payoff—which is to show us that black people who live outside the precincts of the white world can still find fulfillment.

In 2008, Perry opened Tyler Perry Studios, which sits on thirty acres in a primarily black neighborhood in southwest Atlanta. The seventy-five-thousand-square-foot building was once the property of Delta Airlines, and had been empty for more than a decade when Perry purchased the lot. It includes five soundstages, a three-hundred-seat theatre, thirty dressing rooms, editing facilities, a gym, and a duck pond. There, Perry films his half-hour television "dramedy" *House of Payne,* which premièred in 2006, and will soon reach its hundred and fiftieth episode. The series takes certain tropes from his plays and films: a working-class, multigenerational Atlanta family muddles through life under one roof. But, instead of Madea, a man, Curtis (Pops) Payne, is at the center of the conflict. Payne (LaVan Davis) works as a fireman and grumbles about all the biscuits his greedy relatives consume. He's a latter-day Ralph Kramden, with a wife, Ella (Cassi Davis), who, like Alice Kramden, makes sense of things for him—and attributes her own clearheadedness to her strong religious beliefs. After Perry spent five million dollars of his own money to produce the first ten episodes of the series, TBS picked up the show in a deal said to be worth two hundred million. Perry still oversees every aspect of the production. 8

Like the pioneering black filmmaker Oscar Micheaux, who wrote, directed, and produced a number of successful "race films" between 1919 and 1948, Perry works in the black American vernacular but presents a vision that is actually far removed from the realities of urban black life. Although he deals with such miseries as domestic abuse, broken homes, alcoholism, and rape, he virtually always shows these obstacles being overcome or defeated by religious feeling. In Perry's universe, the heroines, for the most part, learn to keep their panties on. Responsible adults enforce strict boundaries. The good guys in his films have more than one job; they don't hit on women they don't intend to marry; they play basketball but don't get too sweaty; and they are almost always Christian. The emotional soundtrack to Perry's productions is unthreatening, devoid, for the 9 most part, of the complications that his viewers face in their everyday lives. His message of uplift leaves little room, for instance, for a truthful portrayal of black-white relations in this country. The elements of real life that Perry does underscore are often the comforting ones: the Madeas of the world, mouthy, matriarchal, sexless black women who raised and counselled many of his loyal fans, setting the moral barometer at home, and not only feeding the children but earning the money to do so. (One wonders, though, how many of the real women are as taken with camp irony as Madea is. In *Diary of a Mad Black Woman,* for instance, Madea refers to the "No wire hangers!" line from the film *Mommie Dearest,* and, in his 2009 film Madea *Goes to Jail,* she sends up the "All my life I had to fight" speech from *The Color Purple,* which is one of Perry's favorite films.) Madea, running around taking care of people like a zealous Louise Beavers, is a cartoon version of the real thing, but that is part of the point. Depression-era audiences went to the movies to see Fred and Ginger live a life of glamour; today's black audiences go to Perry's movies to watch Madea—and Perry—impose a feel-good order on an uncertain world.

In *Don't Make a Black Woman Take Off Her Earrings,* Perry allows for some moral and social ambiguity in black communities. He writes, for instance: 10

> I remember a guy on the corner of my neighborhood who wanted to be a Madea. He would come out of his house every morning with curlers in his hair and a bandanna and just look around and see what the kids were doing. He would then run and tell their parents. But he was kind of illegitimate.

In his movies, however, things are far more cut and dried. There is no place in Madea's imagination for that odd-seeming guy in curlers—or for anyone else who can't find social legitimacy, who doesn't fit into the parameters of what she deems proper behavior. Although many of Perry's plots ostensibly revolve around the idea of female self-actualization, his heroines, instead of finding themselves, are bullied by Madea into a kind of social conformity that has little to do with whatever character traits they exhibit. What's most offensive to Madea, in her universe of no-good men and the women who love them because they can't love themselves, are those women who try to catapult themselves above what she sees as their station in life. The most astonishing moment in the otherwise predictable Madea's *Family Reunion* occurs toward the end. A slim, devious relative of Madea's (Lynn Whitfield) arrives at an afternoon party in a silk dress and a picture hat. Madea, sitting on a porch with two plus-sized 11 women, pokes fun at her relative's sartorial pretensions, which, to her, signify an attempt to step up in class—and, by extension, in race. Exhibiting style, using passable diction, earning a good salary as a single woman: to Madea, these are all pollutants to the authentic black woman.

12 This kind of class rage is the central subject of *Daddy's Little Girls* (2007), in which Gabrielle Union plays a successful Atlanta lawyer named Julia. When we first meet her, Julia is wearing a black dress, carrying a briefcase, and speaks in clipped tones. It's clear that she has no faith and is married only to her work. Julia has more money and authority than is rightfully hers; power has made her cold, unyielding. She's less a woman—which is to say, a caring, strong black woman—than a version of the repressed, capricious white women who pop up in the following year's *The Family That Preys* and are in it only to win it. Luckily, there's hope for Julia. It takes her a while to notice her chauffeur, Monty (played by the British-born actor Idris Elba, best known to American audiences for his role in HBO's *The Wire*), a churchgoing single dad who holds down two jobs to support his family. The working-class Monty is Lady Chatterley's lover, trapped in Perry's version of urban blight, which the director shows through décor: all the "poor" characters in his films seem to share the same tacky sofa and old TV. Eventually, Julia is unable to resist her black knight, and falling into his arms authenticates her as a black woman. Under his spell, she becomes maternal, loving, patient—a Mammy of the boardroom and Monty's "little girl."

13 Still, in Perry's oeuvre, dark-skinned black men are not always heroes like Monty. More often, they are buffoons, evil businessmen, or less sexy versions of the chronically unemployed hustler father that John Amos played on the seventies TV series *Good Times*. The romantic interests in Perry's movies are usually light-skinned saviors. April (Taraji P. Henson), the alcoholic night-club singer in *I Can Do Bad All by Myself*, finds redemption in her love for a hardworking immigrant, played by the Hispanic Adam Rodriguez, a star of *CSI Miami*. In *Meet the Browns*, a single mother (Angela Bassett) who recently lost her job finds her angel of hope in a lighter-skinned boyfriend, played by the half-Bahamian half-Italian-Canadian Rick Fox. And in Perry's latest film, *Why Did I Get Married Too?*—which has grossed nearly fifty million dollars since it opened, at the beginning of April—the singer Janet Jackson plays a self-help guru who indirectly causes the death of her violent, dark-skinned husband. Her loss is her friends' gain. She insists that the quarrelling couples around her heal their relationships; time is precious. A year into widowhood, she is rewarded: a colleague sets her up with a worthy

man, played by the light-skinned, half-black half-Samoan Dwayne (the Rock) Johnson.

Perry often uses hair style and skin color to tell us who his characters are, or, more to the point, how he sees them. In his movies, women, unlike men, must be dark-skinned to be authentic. The "real" women often sport dreadlocks or tight curls, and one can generally look to the more "rootsy" sister in a Perry film to speak the virulent "truth" about, say, domestic abuse, while her lighter-skinned sidekick looks on, stunned by the revelations. This simplified view of the color scale smoothes over the complicated feelings that most blacks have about it. A black doctor who came of age during the civil-rights movement once told me that he was surprised to see someone like me, who was so "dark-skinned, liver-lipped, and woolly-haired," doing so well. Perry may share some of that internalized racism. In the world that he puts forward, light-skinned men seem to have more potential—both professional and sexual—than their dark-skinned brothers, and a worthy dark-skinned woman usually needs a high-yellow man to pave her way. 14

Perry's (and Madea's) negative take on ambitious or successful black women comes up again and again, leading one to ask whether it isn't ultimately a bit of self-flagellation—penance for his own enormous ambitions and success, which he sometimes tries to mask with Christian fervor. In 2004, speaking of his sixteen-thousand-square-foot mansion, which he named Avec Chateau, Perry said, "When I built this house . . . everyone asked why a single man, with no family, needed a house this big. But I realized this house was a testament to my religious faith." 15

Madea is currently the nation's most popular black female comedian. (After seeing Madea *Goes to Jail*, Oprah Winfrey said, "I laughed so hard I had to go home and take some Excedrin.") She has long since surpassed her most significant forebears, Whoopi Goldberg and Geraldine, the signature character on Flip Wilson's seventies NBC variety show. Geraldine, a back-talking black woman with a brunet flip, was as fast as anything, and she didn't take any guff from men, particularly those in positions of authority. In short, she was an amalgamation of the male and female forces that had gone into making Flip Wilson—a black boy raised in foster care—taken to the nth degree. Geraldine wasn't, in any way, a type. There was something sexually dangerous about what she presented while addressing the complicated politics of her community: black women's psychological domination of black men and black men's physical and financial domination of black women. 16

Whoopi Goldberg's early work was similarly radical. Her 1983 one-woman show at New York's Dance Theatre Workshop was one of 17 the first real attempts to tell comedic stories from a black female perspective. Goldberg owed something to the nineteen-fifties and sixties comedian Moms Mabley, but she didn't desexualize herself in a house dress or a wig to get her point across: she was a woman that New Yorkers could recognize; she had been on the street long enough to find the poetry in it. Unfortunately, that poetry didn't become epic. Goldberg was quickly ushered to Broadway, where Mike Nichols produced a version of the show. While the material was recognizable, the stakes were higher, and Goldberg and Nichols made the production more general, less intimate. Goldberg became a star, and from then on no banality was too great in the service of her celebrity. Instead of pursuing her talent as a modern, urban black female comedian, Goldberg defected to Hollywood, a brushoff that was driven home to black audiences (to black women, in particular) in 1993, when, at a roast held in her honor, she yukked it up with her former lover, Ted Danson, who wore blackface.

After Wilson's death, in 1998, black female voices in comedy were 18
almost nonexistent. Perry donned drag and stepped into that void. And, unlike Goldberg or, for instance, Eddie Murphy—who, when not in his fat-lady suit, was stopped by police with a transvestite prostitute—he has been smart enough not to mix his personal life with his comedy. Perry lives relatively quietly, far from Hollywood. He hasn't had bad marriages or cultivated a reputation for being difficult. He eschews the largely white, hip comedy world and its fascination with "bad nigger" behavior. His work isn't crossover "intelligent"—that is, white and pretentious. Better to espouse a Booker T. Washington type of dedication, he seems to say. Uplift yourself through the pleasure that can be found in entertaining the society you come from, rather than aspiring to something more. Make your own black world—one that reflects you.

Unfortunately, though, Perry, like several black filmmakers be- 19
fore him, has failed to properly reflect his own world. Like much of Goldberg's recent work, his movies condescend to their audience, conveying lazy cultural stereotypes about blackness. His characters aren't people; they are folksy signposts. They are, like Madea's bosom, put on—what the audience wants to see, rather than what actually is. Perry has been, for some time, virtually critic-proof. No white critic wants to tell a black man what he can or cannot say about his own society. As for black audiences and critics, Perry is just about the only director who actually makes an effort to reach and entertain them; why wouldn't they appreciate that attention? (Spike Lee's turgid films are too filled with agitprop to be aimed at blacks alone.)

Perry is now in preproduction on a film version of Ntozake Shange's *For Colored Girls Who Have Considered Suicide When the Rainbow Is Enuf,* a 1975 chamber piece about the dreams and hopes and tragedies of a group of black women. Given Perry's previous work, there is cause for alarm in this: he will likely emphasize Shange's sentimentality, rather than her force or her feminist radicalism. In Perry's hands, blackness is not a complicated, unresolved fact of American life but an occasion for shallow melodrama that renders the screen far flatter than it should be. 20

Examining the Text

1. How did Tyler Perry create the character of Madea? On what models did he base this recurrent central character in many of his films? How might the knowledge of this creative process undermine critics' assertions that Madea is an unrealistic stereotype?

2. The author of this article observes, "Perry has released eight movies in the past four years, many of them reworkings of the themes (and titles) of his plays from his days as a live performer. And they almost all follow the basic rules of melodrama." This suggests that Tyler Perry's movies follow a certain predictable formula. What are the specific stages and elements of Perry-based melodrama, by author Als's description?

3. After discussing Perry's melodramatic formula that informs the plots of virtually all his movies, Hilton Als comments, "Perry keeps his plots moving inexorably toward the payoff—which is to show us that black people who live outside the precincts of the white world can still find fulfillment." This sounds like a worthwhile payoff; why, then, do some critics—mainly within the African American community—take exception to Perry's portrayals . . . as will be seen in the following article by Svetkey et al.?

4. Als makes the critical observation that throughout Tyler Perry's films, Perry's (and Madea's) "negative take on ambitious or successful black women comes up again and again." What conscious or subconscious reason might Perry have for ridiculing and/or openly condemning successful black women in his movies, according to the author?

5. *Thinking rhetorically:* Through much of this article, Hilton Als treats his subject, Tyler Perry, objectively, describing him and his work to readers who may be unfamiliar with him, discussing the themes and structures of his dramatic creations, and finally taking a critical stance, thus: "Unfortunately, though, Perry, like several black filmmakers before him, has failed to properly reflect his own world. Like much of Goldberg's recent work, his movies condescend to their audience, conveying lazy cultural stereotypes about blackness. His characters aren't people; they are folksy signposts." For what rhetorical purpose does Als structure his essay his way? Why—unlike the next article in this pairing, doesn't Als address these critical concerns from the outset?

For Group Discussion

In a discussion with the entire class, consider the merits of Tyler Perry's work. In this article, the author seems to point to a number of potentially positive attributes in Perry's movies, and yet he also seems to arrive at a negative evaluation. As you discuss, you might first focus only on the positive attributes of Perry's work, perhaps even making a list of artistic and/or social successes in his portrayals and elaborating a bit on each. Having established those more noble goals and qualities as a ground, then look at some of the less admirable qualities of the Madea movies, both in the view of Hilton Als and based upon your own experience as a viewer of Tyler Perry's work, if you have seen one or several of his films.

Writing Suggestion

Describing Tyler Perry's personal history that led to being a phenomenally successful writer and filmmaker, the author of this article relates the following factoid: "In 1991, Perry saw an episode of 'The Oprah Winfrey Show' that talked about the healing powers of writing. He began to keep a diary, which he then adapted into his first play, 'I Know I've Been Changed.'" If you do not already do so, begin keeping a daily diary for the rest of the school term, noting in it your feelings as they pass by like clouds in the sky, your observations of places and people, snatches of dialogue caught on the fly, philosophical insights, unfocused stream-of-consciousness mind-spew, and so forth. After a certain amount of time undertaking this daily practice, reflect upon it and write an essay of three pages in which you describe the process—both the joys and difficulties—and ultimately assess whether, as suggested on the former Oprah show, the regular act of writing was—and might continue to be—therapeutic in your own life. Perhaps some plays and successful movies will even come from it!

*How Do You Solve a Problem Like Madea?**

BENJAMIN SVETKEY, MARGEAUX WATSON, AND ALYNDA WHEAT

In this second section of the Movies chapter of Common Culture, *we have chosen two contemporary filmmakers and provided a pair of articles devoted*

*Svetkey, Benjamin; Watson, Margeaux; and Alynda Wheat, "Tyler Perry: The Controversy Over His Hit Movies" from Entertainment Weekly, Issue #1039, March 20, 2009.

to each of them. In this second such pairing, focusing on the work of Tyler Perry, we have included two pieces that take very different tones. The previous article by Hilton Als was a relatively objectively analysis: a description of the Madea films, aimed primarily at those who have never seen any of Perry's movies; some personal, professional, and creative history of Tyler Perry; a retrospective discussion of his films, specifically leading up to the appearance and great success of the Madea series; and finally, some controversy regarding the impact of his filmic portrayals on the image of African Americans in contemporary culture. The second article, which follows, picks up the latter thread, exploring in greater depth and perhaps with a more inflammatory tone, social/ethnic controversies potentially stirred up by Perry's work.

*Supporters of Perry and his unforgettable characters tend to echo the sentiments of one blogger: "That's why she [Madea] is so loved—she acts the way a lot of us (white and black) would love to act, and she gets away with it! And Madea is very intelligent—probably one of the smartest characters in movies today." On the other hand, detractors wonder whether Perry is reinforcing negative racial stereotypes in his characters' portrayals and actions. In the words of one Yahoo commentator, "*Madea, Meet The Browns, *and* House of Pain *. . . are terrible, filled with black stereotypes. . . .* Madea *is nothing short of a minstrel show, and* House of Pain *is just flat out terrible and unoriginal."* ***As you read*** *the following article, then, please consider both sides of the issue as objectively as possible—the evidence of supportive, empowering portrayals versus the accusations of stereotyping and perpetuating traditional ethnic preconceptions . . . and perhaps view (or re-view) one or several of Tyler Perry's movies as you pursue such consideration.*

If you happened to buy a ticket to Tyler Perry's *Madea Goes to Jail* without knowing what you were getting into, you might think you'd stumbled onto a cheery comedy about an overgrown granny with anger-management issues. A black *Mrs. Doubtfire*, say, with car chases and reefer jokes. You'd never suspect that you had strayed into the midst of a culture war—one that's been simmering inside the African-American community since before blackface. "I loved working with Tyler Perry, but he's a controversial, complicated figure," says Viola Davis, who costarred in *Madea Goes to Jail* and recently snagged an Oscar nomination for *Doubt*. "People feel the images [in his movies] are very stereotypical, and black people are frustrated because they feel we should be more evolved. But there are very few black images in Hollywood, so black people are going to his movies. That's the dichotomy. Tyler Perry is making money." 1

A lot of money. *Jail* has already earned more than $75 million, making it Perry's highest-grossing film to date. And his seven 2 movies—starting with his 2005 big-screen drag debut as Madea in *Diary of a Mad Black Woman*—have grossed more than $350 million combined, putting him on track to join John Singleton and Keenen Ivory Wayans as one of the most successful black filmmakers ever. He may already be the most divisive. At a time when Barack Obama is presenting the world with a bold new image of black America, Perry is being slammed for filling his films with regressive, down-market archetypes. In many of his films there's a junkie prostitute, a malaprop-dropping uncle, and Madea, a tough-talking grandma the size of a linebacker ("Jemima the Hutt," one character calls her). "Tyler keeps saying that Madea is based on black women he's known, and maybe so," says Donald Bogle, acclaimed author of *Toms, Coons, Mulattoes, Mammies, & Bucks: An Interpretive History of Blacks in American Films*. "But Madea does have connections to the old mammy type. She's mammy-like. If a white director put out this product, the black audience would be appalled."

Perry and his supporters disagree, to say the least. "These stories have come out of my own pain and everything I've been through," the director says, referring to his six years of struggle, including three months living in his car in Atlanta, before his plays became such huge hits in Southern black theaters (a.k.a. the chitlin circuit) that even Hollywood couldn't ignore him. "These characters are simply tools to make people laugh," Perry says. "And I know for a fact that they have helped, inspired, and encouraged millions of people." In truth, the films are laced with moral lessons trumpeting forgiveness and personal responsibility. "He's not out there promoting gangster culture," says Vicangelo Bulluck, executive director of the NAACP's Hollywood bureau. "If anything, he's trying to make us think about family values." Nor is every African-American cultural critic up in arms over Perry's caricatures. "Comedy and stereotypes go hand in hand," notes Nelson George, author of *Blackface: Reflections on African Americans and the Movies* and the memoir *City Kid*. "That's why intellectuals have a hard time with humor." 3

But it isn't just the stereotypes in Perry's movies that trouble his detractors. It's also what they consider to be his plantation-era attitudes about class. "All of his productions demonize educated, successful African-Americans," says Todd Boyd, professor of critical studies at USC School of Cinematic Arts. "It's a demonization that has long existed in certain segments of the black community." The schism reaches back to the days of "house" and "field" slaves—when the first African-Americans were segregated even from one another—and persists today in distinctions between light- and dark-skinned blacks. "Tyler Perry is simply reflecting the thinking of a lot of uneducated, working-class African-Americans," Boyd says. 4

In *Madea Goes to Jail*, for instance, the ambitious light-skinned female district attorney (Ion Overman) who puts Madea behind bars is 5 not only a snob but a conniving, corrupt criminal. The most sympathetic character, by contrast, turns out to be a darker-skinned, strung-out prostitute (Keshia Knight Pulliam). The upscale African-Americans who rent a ski cabin together in the drama Tyler Perry's *Why Did I Get Married?* aren't all amoral elitists, but the pattern recurs in Perry's comedies: *In Diary of a Mad Black Woman*, the successful black businessman (Steve Harris) is a wife abuser, and in Tyler Perry's *Madea's Family Reunion*, the social-climbing mother-in-law (Lynn Whitfield) gets sneered at by Madea for committing the ultimate sin of trying to look "bourgie," as in bourgeois.

"Tyler Perry understands that much of his audience is African-American women—the most ignored group in Hollywood—so he's doing movies that speak to them," Bogle says. "You could see these films as parables or fables. There's a black prince figure who shows up for black women who've been frustrated, unhappy, or abused." That's the real reason critics don't like Perry's movies, says Nelson George: They're made for churchgoing, working-class black women, not urban hipsters (or tenured professors). "Tyler Perry speaks to a constituency that is not cool," George says. "There's nothing cutting-edge about the people who like Tyler Perry. So, for a lot of other people, it's like, 'What is this thing that's representing black people all over the world? I don't like it. It doesn't represent me.'" 6

Right now, there are still so few consistent, high-profile representations of African-Americans in film—Will Smith and Denzel Washington are pretty much it—that Perry has a near monopoly on the depiction of American black life on screen. That gives him power beyond the images he puts in his movies; it makes him the top employer of black actors in Hollywood (not to mention Atlanta, where he owns a 200,000-square-foot production house, which also produces his TV sitcom, Tyler Perry's *House of Payne*). In other words, if you're an African-American actor, he's the biggest boss in town, which may explain the reluctance of so many black actors, even those who've appeared in his films, to talk about Perry on the record. Nine of them declined to be interviewed for this story. 7

"There just aren't a lot of roles out there for black actors, and even fewer for black actresses, so if someone is going to give you a job, you're going to do it, even if you think it's substandard," Viola Davis says. Besides, she adds, "the roles for black women in Tyler Perry movies are sometimes better than the roles in higher-quality movies. They're more realized, more fleshed out." Jenifer Lewis, who co-starred in Tyler Perry's *Meet the Browns* and in *Family Reunion*, puts it more directly. "Tyler treats us like queens," she says. "He is so gracious, you have no idea. He's writing about the black experience, and he allows us to express that. He's bringing jobs into the community." 8

Perry himself is keenly aware of the responsibilities resting on his shoulders. And while his critics aren't likely to hurt business—two more movies have just been greenlit by Lionsgate, including a sequel to *Why Did I Get Married?*—the filmmaker also doesn't want to be hemmed in by race. Lately, in fact, he's been taking cues from a certain law professor who recently got a job on Pennsylvania Avenue. "After Obama became president, I realized that black people could not have put him in the White House—it had to be a collective effort of everybody in the country," Perry says. "My fan base crosses all ages, all cultures, all classes. I won't be forced to just do Madea. There's no way I'm going to do that." And that's change that (almost) everyone can believe in. 9

Examining the Text

1. Although this article contains predominantly negative assessments of Tyler Perry's representations of black culture, the author also makes a point of giving a nod to some commentators how have positive things to say about Perry. List the positive opinions that are expressed here and summarize the specific points raised by the purveyors of these opinions.

2. Referring to Tyler Perry's allegedly stereotypical portrayals of African Americans, one of the black commentators cited in this article notes, "If a white director put out this product, the black audience would be appalled." Why would such a reaction occur, in the implication of this statement? How do you respond to this observation; what does it imply about the difference between black and white audiences?

3. Critic Nelson George is quoted in this article as noting, "That's the real reason critics don't like Perry's movies: They're made for churchgoing, working-class black women, not urban hipsters (or tenured professors). Tyler Perry speaks to a constituency that is not cool." In making this observation, George is drawing a distinction between black movie critics (and movie critics in general) and black audiences. Explain the difference, based upon your understanding of both groups, both from your own experience/understanding, along with the discussions in this essay and the previous one by Hilton Als.

4. Why are so many black actors, according to Svetkey et al. in this article, reluctant to say anything critical about Tyler Perry? How might this reluctance affect critics' ability to analyze the sociocultural impact of his films accurately? Likewise, how might that reluctance make it difficult for you, as a student, to tackle the Writing Suggestion assignment below?

5. *Thinking rhetorically:* Todd Boyd, professor of critical studies at USC School of Cinematic Arts, comments at the middle of this article, "All of his [Perry's] productions demonize educated, successful African-Americans. . . . It's a demonization that has long existed in certain segments of the black community." Explain this particular phenomenon and criticism at greater length: what is Boyd's rhetorical purpose in using a purposely loaded term such as "demonization" in this context? What are your feelings/thoughts about the merits of this argument, and the criticism as applied specifically to Tyler Perry?

For Group Discussion

The last paragraph of this essay suggests that Tyler Perry is poised to expand his filmic oeuvre beyond the world of Madea and her compatriots. In class discussion, based upon your knowledge of Perry's work from your reading of the two articles above, along with any experience you might have as a viewer/fan of his films, evaluate the potential success of such a proposed enterprise: how do you feel that Tyler Perry will fare as a "crossover artist," if that is indeed his goal? Use specific examples from both these articles and his movies as evidence for assertions you make during this discussion.

Writing Suggestion

Pick one of Tyler Perry's movies and watch it carefully, keeping in mind the criticisms (and the positive comments as well) leveled at Perry in this article. In an analytical essay, evaluate the movie you watched, considering specifically whether or not it perpetuates negative stereotypes or portrays uplifting role models, or both. To construct this essay, you might first make a comprehensive list of the criticisms and positive qualities delineated in this essay, summarizing each in a paragraph or two. Having generated this list and summary, examine the scenes in the movie you viewed, judging which specific elements of the movie might fit under the headings for each criticism or element of praise. At the end of your essay, you might conclude by deciding whether, on balance, the movie presents a positive or negatively stereotypical depiction of African Americans in contemporary America.

ADDITIONAL SUGGESTIONS FOR WRITING ABOUT MOVIES

1. In this chapter, we presented several articles that focus on a central filmic theme, namely violence. In your own interpretative essay, compare and contrast several movies dealing with a different central theme or issue. For instance, you might compare several films about the Vietnam War, or about the lives of the current generation of "twentysomethings," or about inner-city gangs, or about parent–child relationships. Choose movies that interest you and, ideally, that you can see again. You might want to structure your essay as an argument aimed at convincing your readers that one movie is in some way "better" than the others. Or you might use your comparison of the movies to draw some larger point about popular culture and the images it presents to us.

2. In a research or "I-search" essay, consider the complex relationship between film and social morality. Do you believe that films such as *Fight Club* and zombie flicks tend to encourage audience identification with the villain and help sanction violent behavior . . . or is there a more "sublime" dimension to film violence, as suggested by some of the authors in this chapter? In your research, explore what other experts say about the relationship between real and fictional violence. Can you find specific current events that support your arguments?

3. In a speculative essay that uses Kyle Bishop's article on zombie flicks as a model, explore why audiences crave movies of a certain genre: futuristic techno-thrillers, movies based on television sitcoms and cartoons, chase movies, menaced-female dramas, psychotic-killer stories, romantic comedies, supernatural comedies, and so forth. Choose a type of movie familiar to you so that you can offer as many specific examples as possible. In approaching this assignment, try to answer some of these questions: What is the "fun" of seeing this type of movie? What sort of "psychic relief" does it deliver? Are there specific types of people who are likely to enjoy the genre more than others? Does the genre serve any function for society? In what ways do movies in this genre affect us, changing our thoughts or feelings after we've seen them?

Internet Activities

1. These days, anyone with a Web site has the power to post a movie review. Choose several online reviews—written by both professional movie critics and "regular" moviegoers such as yourself—for a movie you've seen (some options are available on the *Common Culture* Web site). Write an essay in which you note the primary differences between the reviews done by professionals and those done by the regular fan(s). What aspects of the film do the professionals focus on? Are they the same as those of the regular fan or do they vary? Does one group emphasize certain elements, such as the emotions encouraged by the film, the acting, or the cinematography? Which of the reviews most closely reflects your opinion of the movie? Why do you think these reviews are the ones with which you best identify?

2. Visit a Web site for a new film you're interested in seeing and write a review of the site (some options are available on the *Common Culture* Web site). What is offered on the Web site that a potential audience wouldn't get from any other form of media? What do you like best about the Web site? What would you change? Describe the advantages of having a Web site for a new film. Are there any disadvantages? How do you feel movie Web sites will influence which movies we want to watch?

Reading Images

The image on page 578 encapsulates the dramatic (and comedic) tension in Judd Apatow's film *Knocked Up*. As you can see, it depicts actors Seth Rogen

"Knocked Up," 2007. Starring Katherine Heigl and Seth Rogen. Directed by Judd Apatow.

and Katherine Heigl stressing about their mutual predicament, i.e., her pregnancy. After rereading the section in Chapter 1 about how to analyze images, take notes about the particular features of this image—expressions, body composition, the text on Rogen's T-shirt, Heigl's gold earrings—and come to a conclusion about the narrative subthemes it conveys. Then, in an essay, discuss the ways in which this single frame from the movie encapsulates concepts that are raised in Denby's and Wainer's discussions of Apatovian comedy. You might conclude your essay by discussing what effect the image has on you as a reader/viewer, and whether the image—along with situations portrayed within the narrative arc of the film—leads you to conceptualize additional themes within the text of *Knocked Up:* ideas that were not raised by Denby or Wainer but that you find provocative and worth considering.

For Further Reading: A *Common Culture* Bibliography

CHAPTER 2: ADVERTISING

Barthel, Diane. *Putting on Appearances: Gender and Advertising*. Philadelphia: Temple University Press, 1988.

Berger, Arthur Asa. *Ads, Fads, and Consumer Culture: Advertising's Impact on American Character and Society*. Lanham, MD: Rowman & Littlefield, 2000, 2007.

Ewen, Stuart and Elizabeth Ewen. *Channels of Desire: Mass Images and the Shaping of American Consciousness*. 2nd edition. Minneapolis: University of Minnesota Press, 1992.

Fowles, Jib. *Advertising and Popular Culture*. Thousand Oaks, CA: Sage, 1996.

Fox, Roy. *Mediaspeak: Three American Voices*. Westport, CT: Praeger, 2001.

Garfield, Bob. *The Chaos Scenario*. New York: Stielstra Publishing, 2009.

Jones, John Philip. *When Ads Work: New Proof That Advertising Triggers Sales*. Armonk, NY: M. E. Sharpe, 2007.

Kilbourne, Jean, director. *Still Killing Us Softly*. Cambridge, MA: Cambridge Documentary Films, 1992 Videocassette.

———. *Deadly Persuasion: Why Women and Girls Must Fight the Addictive Power of Advertising*. New York: Free Press, 1999.

Klein, Naomi. *No Logo: No Space, No Choice, No Jobs*. New York: Picador, 2002.

Lasn, Kalle. *Culture Jam: The Uncooling of America*. New York: Eagle Brook, 1999.

McQuarrie, Edward F. and Barbara J. Phillips (Eds.). *Go Figure! New Directions in Advertising Rhetoric*. Armonk, NY: M. E. Sharpe, 2008.

Mitchell, Arthur. *The Nine American Lifestyles: Who We Are and Where We're Going*. New York: Warner Books, 1983.

Oglivy, David. *Confessions of an Advertising Man*. New York: Southbank Publishing, 2004.

Quart, Alissa. *Branded: The Buying and Selling of Teenagers*. New York: Basic Books, 2004.

Schor, Juliet. *Born to Buy: The Commercialized Child and the New Consumer Culture*. New York: Scribner, 2004.

Sivulka, Juliann. *Soap, Sex, and Cigarettes: A Cultural History of American Advertising*. Belmont, CA: Wadsworth, 1998.

Twitchell, James. *Twenty Ads That Shook the World: The Century's Most Groundbreaking Advertising and How it Changed Us All*. New York: Crown Publishers, 2000.

CHAPTER 3: TELEVISION

Andrejevic, Mark. *Reality TV: The Work of Being Watched*. Lanham, MD: Rowman & Littlefield, 2003.

Batten, Frank and Jeffrey L. Cruikshank. *The Weather Channel: The Improbable Rise of a Media Phenomenon*. Boston, MA: Harvard Business School Press, 2002.

Cantor, Paul A. *Gilligan Unbound: Pop Culture in the Age of Globalization*. Lanham, MD: Rowman & Littlefield, 2001.

Gitlin, Todd. *Inside Prime Time*. 2nd edition. New York: Pantheon, 1994.

Hartley, John. *Uses of Television*. London: Routledge, 1999.

Heller, Dana (Ed.). *Makeover Television: Realities Remodelled*. London: I. B. Taurus, 2007.

Holt, Jason (Ed.). *The Daily Show and Philosophy: Moments of Zen in the Art of Fake News*. Malden, MA: Blackwell, 2007.

Johnson, Steven. *Everything Bad Is Good For You: How Today's Popular Culture Is Actually Making Us Smarter*. New York: Riverhead, 2005.

Lotz, Amanda. *The Television Will Be Revolutionized*. New York: NYU Press, 2007.

Mander, Jerry. *Four Arguments for the Elimination of Television*. New York: Morrow, 1978.

Miller, Mark Crispin. *Boxed In: The Culture of TV*. Evanston, IL: Northwestern University Press, 1988.

Mittel, Jason. *Television and American Culture*. New York: Oxford University Press, 2009.

Newcomb, Horace. *Television: The Critical View*. New York: Oxford University Press, 2000.

O'Neill, John. *Plato's Cave: Television and Its Discontents*. Cresskill, NJ: Hampton Press, 2002.

Palmer, Shelly. *Television Disrupted: The Transition from Network to Networked TV*. Boston, MA: Focal Press, 2006.

Peterson, Russell L. *Strange Bedfellows: How Late-Night Comedy Turns Democracy into a Joke*. New Brunswick, NJ: Rutgers University Press, 2008.

Postman, Neil. *Amusing Ourselves to Death*. New York: Penguin Books, 1985.

Riegert, Kristina (Ed.). *Politicotainment: Television's Take on the Real*. New York: Peter Lang, 2007.

Spiegel, Lynn and Jan Olsson (Eds.). *Television After TV: Essays on a Medium in Transition*. Durham, NC: Duke University Press, 2004.

Verklin, David and Bernice Kanner. *Watch This, Listen Up, Click Here: Inside the 300 Billion Dollar Business Behind the Media You Constantly Consume*. New York: John Wiley & Sons, 2007.

Watson, Mary Ann. *Defining Visions: Television and the American Experience in the 20th Century*. Malden, MA: Blackwell, 2008.

Williams, Raymond. *Television: Technology and Cultural Form*. New York: Schocken Books, 1975.

CHAPTER 4: POPULAR MUSIC

Cloonan, Martin and Reebee Garofalo. *Policing Pop*. Philadelphia: Temple University Press, 2003.

Colegrave, Stephen and Chris Sullivan. *Punk: The Definitive Record of a Revolution*. Boston, MA: Thunder's Mouth Press, 2001.

Echols, Alice. *Hot Stuff: Disco and the Remaking of American Culture*. New York: W. W. Norton & Company, 2011.

Forman, Murray. *The 'Hood Comes First: Race, Space, and Place in Rap and Hip-Hop*. Middletown, CT: Wesleyan University Press, 2002.

Greene, Bob. *When We Get to Surf City: A Journey through America in Pursuit of Rock and Roll, Friendship, and Dreams*. New York: St. Martin's Press, 2008.

Holt, Fabian. *Genre in Popular Music*. Chicago: University of Chicago Press, 2007.

Joyner, David Lee. *American Popular Music*. New York: McGraw-Hill, 2002.

Krasilovsky, M. William, Sidney Shemel, and John M. Gross. *This Business of Music: The Definitive Guide to the Music Industry*. New York: Billboard Books, 2003.

Krims, Adam. *Rap Music and the Poetics of Identity*. Boston: Cambridge University Press, 2003.

Meizel, Katherine L. *Idolized: Music, Media, and Identity in American Idol*. Bloomington: Indiana University Press, 2011.

Moore, Allan F. *Analyzing Popular Music*. Boston: Cambridge University Press, 2003.

Morgan, Johnny. *Gaga*. New York: Sterling, 2011.

Neal, Mark Anthony. *Soul Babies: Black Popular Culture and the Post-Soul Aesthetic*. New York: Routledge, 2002.

Perkins, William Eric. *Droppin' Science: Critical Essays on Rap Music and Hip Hop Culture*. Philadelphia: Temple University Press, 1996.

Posner, Gerald L. *Motown: Money, Power, Sex, and Music*. New York: Random House, 2002.

Queen Latifah. *Ladies First: Revelations from a Strong Woman*. New York: William Morrow & Company, 1999.

Rose, Tricia. *The Hip Hop Wars*. New York: Perseus Books Group, 2008.

Savage, Jon. *England's Dreaming: Anarchy, Sex Pistols, Punk Rock, and Beyond*. New York: St. Martin's Press, 2002.

Strong, Martin C. and Brendon Griffin. *Lights, Camera, Soundtracks: The Ultimate Guide to Popular Music in the Movies*. New York: Canongate, 2008.

Vogel, Joseph. *Man in the Music: The Creative Life and Work of Michael Jackson*. New York: Sterling, 2011.

Webb, Peter. *Exploring the Networked Worlds of Popular Music: Milieu Cultures*. London: Taylor & Francis, Inc., 2007.

Weisbard, Eric (Ed.). *Listen Again: A Momentary History of Pop Music*. Durham, NC: Duke University Press, 2007.

CHAPTER 5: TECHNOLOGY

Carr, Nicholas. *The Shallows: What the Internet Is Doing to Our Brains*. New York: W. W. Norton, 2010.

Baker, Stephen. *The Numerati*. New York: Mariner Books, 2009.

Bauerlein, Mark. *The Dumbest Generation: How the Digital Age Stupifies Young Americans and Jeopardizes Our Future*. New York: Tarcher Press, 2009.

Chayko, Mary. *Connecting: How We Form Social Bonds and Communities in the Internet Age*. Albany: State University of New York Press, 2002.

Fornas, Johan (Ed.). *Digital Borderlands: Cultural Studies of Identity and Interactivity on the Internet*. New York: Peter Lang, 2002.

Gee, James Paul. *What Video Games Have to Teach Us About Learning and Literacy*. New York: Palgrave Macmillan, 2003.

Gergen, Kenneth. *The Saturated Self: Dilemmas of Identity in Contemporary Life*. New York: Basic Books, 2000.

Gleick, James. *The Information: A History, A Theory, A Flood*. New York: Pantheon Press, 2011.

Holloway, Sarah L. and Gill Valentine. *Cyberkids: Children in the Information Age*. London: Routledge, 2003.

Postman, Neil. *Technopoly: The Surrender of Culture to Technology*. New York: Vintage Books, 1993.

Powers, William. *Hamlet's BlackBerry: A Practical Philosophy for Building a Good Life in the Digital Age*. New York: Harper, 2010.

Shirky, Clay. *Here Comes Everybody: The Power of Organizing Without Organizations*. New York: Penguin, 2008.

Smolan, Rick and Jennifer Erwitt (Eds.). *24 Hours in Cyberspace: Painting on the Walls of the Digital Cave Photographed on One Day by 150 of the World's Leading Photojournalists*. Que(R): Macmillan, 1996.

Turkle, Sherry. *Alone Together: Why We Expect More from Technology and Less from Each Other*. New York: Basic Books, 2011.

CHAPTER 6: SPORTS

Austin, Michael W. *Football and Philosophy*. Fredericksburg: University Press of Kentucky, 2008.

Brisick, Jamie and J. H. Behar. *Have Board, Will Travel: The Definitive History of Surf, Skate, and Snow*. New York: HarperCollins Publishers, 2008.

Eitzen, D. Stanley. *Fair and Foul: Beyond the Myths and Paradoxes of Sport*. New York: Rowman & Littlefield, 2006.

Gerdy, John R. *Sports: The All-American Addiction*. Mississippi: University Press of Mississippi, 2002.

Hanrahan, Stephanie J. *Handbook of Applied Sport Psychology: A Comprehensive Guide*. New York: Routledge, 2010.

Hjorth, Larissa. *Games and Gaming: An Introduction*. New York: Berg, 2011.

McLaughlin, Thomas. *Give and Go: Basketball as a Cultural Practice*. New York: State University of New York Press, 2008.

Miller, Toby. *Sportsex*. Philadelphia: Temple University Press, 2002.

Moran-Miller, Kelli. "Where are the women in women's sports?" *Research Quarterly for Exercise and Sport* 82, no. 1 (March 1, 2011).

Moskowitz, Tobias J. *Scorecasting: The Hidden Influences Behind How Sports Are Played and Games Are Won*. New York: Crown, 2011.Munslow, Alun (Foreword) and Murray G. Phillips (Ed.). *Deconstructing Sport History: A Postmodern Analysis*. New York: State University of New York Press, 2006.

Rinehart, Robert E. and Synthia Sydnor. *To the Extreme: Alternative Sports, Inside and Out*. New York: State University of New York Press, 2003.

Sugden, John and Alan Tomlinson. *A Critical Sociology of Sport*. New York: Routledge, 2002.

Templeton, Brian. "The dangerous territory of sports dominance." *The Skeptic*, January 1, 2011.

Vlasich. James A. (Ed.). *Horsehide, Pigskin, Oval Tracks And Apple Pie: Essays on Sport And American Culture*. McFarland & Company, 2005.

Walker, James R. and Robert V. Bellamy. *Center Field Shot: A History of Baseball on Television*. Lincoln: University of Nebraska Press, 2008.

Whitaker, Matthew C. *African American Icons of Sport: Triumph, Courage, and Excellence*. Westport, CT: Greenwood Publishing Group, 2008.

Wilcox, Ralph C. et al. *Sporting Dystopias: The Making and Meaning of Urban Sport Cultures*. New York: State University of New York Press, 2003.

CHAPTER 7: MOVIES

Beltran, Mary and Camilla Fojas. *Mixed Race Hollywood*. New York: New York University Press, 2008.

Benshoff, Harry M. and Sean Griffin. *America on Film: Representing Race, Class, Gender, and Sexuality at the Movies*. New York: Blackwell, 2003.

Briley, Ron and Deborah A. Carmichael. *All-Stars and Movie Stars*. Fredericksburg: University Press of Kentucky, 2008.

Charyn, Jerome. *Raised by Wolves: The Turbulent Art and Times of Quentin Tarantino*. New York: Thunder's Mouth Press, 2006.

Fuller-Seeley, Kathryn H. *Hollywood in the Neighborhood: Historical Case Studies of Local Moviegoing*. Berkeley: University of California Press, 2008.

Gillis, Stacy and Melanie Waters (Eds.). *Women on Screen: Femininity in Visual Culture*. New York: Macmillan, 2011.

Griffiths, Alison. *Shivers Down Your Spine: Cinema and the History of the Immersive View*. New York: Columbia University Press, 2008.

Hubbert, Julie. *Celluloid Symphonies: Texts and Contexts in Film History*. Berkeley: University of California Press, 2011.

Iton, Richard. *In Search of the Black Fantastic: Politics and Popular Culture in the Post-Civil Rights Era*. New York: Oxford University Press, 2008.

Lindlof, Thomas R. *Hollywood Under Siege: Martin Scorsese, the Religious Right, and the Culture Wars*. Fredericksburg: University Press of Kentucky, 2008.

Linson, Art. *What Just Happened? Bitter Hollywood Tales from the Front Line*. New York: Grove, 2008.

McGowan, Todd. *Real Gaze: Film Theory after Lacan*. New York: State University of New York Press, 2008.

Monaco, James. *How to Read a Film: Movies, Media, and Beyond*. 4th Edition. New York: Oxford University Press, 2009.

Phillips, Kendall R. *Controversial Cinema: The Films That Outraged America*. Westport, CT: Greenwood Publishing, 2008.

Rodriguez, Clara. *Heroes, Lovers, and Others: The Story of Latinos in Hollywood*. New York: Oxford University Press, 2008.

Rueschmann, Eva. *Moving Pictures, Migrating Identities*. Mississippi: University Press of Mississippi, 2003.

Rushton, Richard. *The Reality of Film: Theories of Filmic Reality*. Manchester, UK: Manchester University Press, 2011.

Skal, David. *The Monster Show: A Cultural History of Horror*. Boston: Faber & Faber, 2001.

Tuck, Greg and Havi Carel (Eds.). *New Takes in Film*. New York: Macmillan, 2011.

Credits

TEXT CREDITS

p. 10 From MEN AND OTHER STRANGE MYTHS by Hilary Tham. Copyright © 1994 by Hilary Tham Goldberg. Used with permission by Lynne Rienner Publishers, Inc.

p. 15 Nachbar, Jack. POPULAR CULTURE: AN INTRODUCTORY TEXT, © 1992 by the Board of Regents of the University of Wisconsin System. Reprinted by permission of The University of Wisconsin.

p. 43 Carolyn Muhlstein, "Role-Model Barbie: Now and Forever?." Reprinted with permission of the author.

p. 49 Kalle Lasn, "The Cult You're In." Courtesy of adbusters.org.

p. 54 Jib Fowles, "Advertising's Fifteen Basic Appeals" from Advertising and Popular Culture, © 1996 Sage Publications. Used with permission of Sage Publications; permission conveyed through Copyright Clearance Center, Inc.

p. 73 John E. Calfee, "How Advertising Informs to Our Benefit." Reprinted with permission of the author.

p. 86 Jean Kilbourne, "Jesus is a brand of jeans" from New Internationalist, September 2006. http://www.newint.org/features/2006/09/01/culture/. Reprinted with permission.

p. 93 Interview with Mark Crispin Miller from FRONTLINE website for "The Persuaders," found at http://www.pbs.org/wgbh/pages/frontline/shows/persuaders/interviews/miller.html. From FRONTLINE/WGBH Boston. Copyright © 1995–2011 WGBH Educational Foundation. Reprinted with permission.

p. 101 Bob Garfield, "The Post Advertising Age" from Advertising Age, March 2007. Reprinted with permission.

p. 109 Alice Park, "The Brain: Marketing to Your Mind" in Time, January 19, 2007. Copyright TIME INC. Reprinted by permission. TIME is a registered trademark of Time Inc. All rights reserved.

p. 117 George Gerbner, "Society's Storyteller: How TV Creates the Myths by which we Live." Used with permission of Center for Media Literacy from Media and Values, Issue 61 (Winter 1993), © 1993; permission conveyed through Copyright Clearance Center, Inc.

p. 122 TV Guide Magazine grid listings courtesy of TV Guide Magazine, LLC © 2011.

p. 123 Robert Kubey and Mihaly Csikszentmihaly, "Television addiction Is No Mere Metaphor" from Scientific American 286 (February 2002). Copyright © 2002 by Scientific American, Inc. Reprinted by permission. All rights reserved.

p. 131 Steven Johnson, "Watching TV Makes You Smarter," © Steven Johnson 2005. Article originally published in the New York Times Magazine, adapted from EVERYTHING BAD IS GOOD FOR YOU, Riverhead. Reprinted with permission.

p. 144 Clay Shirkey, "Gin, Television, and Social Surplus" from http://www.shirky.com/herecomeseverybody/2008/04/looking-for-the-mouse.html. Reprinted with permission.

p. 151 Peterson, Russell. Strange Bedfellows: How Late Night Comedy Turns Democracy into a Joke. Copyright © 2008 by Russell Peterson. Reprinted by permission of Rutgers University Press.

p. 168 Gerald J. Erion, "Amusing Ourselves to Death with Television News: Jon Stewart, Neil Postman, and the Huxleyan Warning," in The Daily Show and Philosophy: Moments of Zen in the Art of Fake News by Jason Holt, Ed. © 2007, pp. 5–15. Reproduced with permission of Blackwell Publishing Ltd.

p. 178 Jeffrey P. Jones, "'Fake' News versus 'Real' News as Sources of Political Information: The Daily Show and Postmodern Political Reality," in Politicotainment: Television's Take on the Real. Kristina Riegert, Ed. (New York: Peter Lang, 2007): 129–149. Reprinted with permission.

p. 205 "5 Things that Killed Hip-Hop," J-Zone. Republished from HipHopDX.com and .myspace.com/jzoneoldmaid.

p. 214 Kelefa Sanneh, "Word: Jay_Z's Decoded and the language of hip_hop" from the New Yorker, December 6, 2010, Vol. 86, Issue 39, © 2010. Reprinted with permission of the author.

p. 225 Megan Carpentier, "The Year Hip-Hop Invented Sex" from Bitch Magazine: Feminist Response to Pop Culture, Summer 2010, Issue 47, © 2010, pp. 40–44. Reprinted with permission.

p. 234 Evelyn Jamilah, "The Miseducation of Hip-Hop," from Black Issues in Higher Education 17, December 7, 2000. Reprinted with permission.

p. 243 John Seabrook, "The Money Note: Can the Record Business Be Saved?" from The New Yorker 79:18 (July 2003). Copyright © 2003 by John Seabrook. Reprinted with permission of the author.

p. 268 Paul McGuiness, "How to Save the Music Business," originally published in the August 2010 issue of British GQ, © The Conde Nast Publications Ltd. Reprinted with permission.

p. 276 Ian Inglis, "Sex and Drugs and Rock 'n' Roll": Urban Legends and Popular Music from Popular Music and Society, January 12, 2007, Volume 30, Issue 5. Reprinted by permission of Taylor and Francis Group, http://www.informaworld.com.

p. 297 John Steele Gordon, "Engine of Liberation" from American Heritage Magazine, v. 47, no. 7, November 1996. Reprinted by permission of American Heritage Publishing.

p. 305 Neil Postman, "The Judgment of Thamus," from TECHNOPOLY: THE SURRENDER OF CULTURE TO TECHNOLOGY. Copyright © 1992 by Neil Postman. Used by permission of Alfred A. Knopf, a division of Random House, inc.

p. 319 Robert Samuels, "Beyond Borders." Reprinted by permission of the author.

p. 323 Gary Wolf, "The Data-Driven Life" from The New York Times Magazine, April 2010. © 2010 The New York Times. All rights reserved. Used by permission and protected by the Copyright Laws of the United States. The printing, copying, redistribution, or retransmission of the Material without express written permission is prohibited.

p. 336 Nicholas Carr, "Is Google Making Us Stupid?" from The Atlantic, July/August 2008, © 2008 The Atlantic Monthly. Used with permission of The Atlantic Monthly. Permission conveyed through Copyright Clearance Center, Inc. All rights reserved.

p. 347 Gary Small, M.D. and Gigi Vorgan, Adaptation of text (as appeared in Scientific American, October 8, 2008) from IBRAIN by Gary Small, M.D. and Gigi Vorgan. Copyright © 2008 by Dr. Gary Small and Gigi Vorgan. Reprinted by permission of HarperCollins Publishers.

p. 361 David P. Barash, "The Roar of the Crowd" from Chronicle of Higher Education, March 20, 2009, Volume 55, Issue 28. Reprinted with permission of the author.

p. 371 William Dowell et al., "Adventure: Life on the Edge" from Time, September 6, 1999. Copyright TIME INC. Reprinted by permission. TIME is a registered trademark of Time Inc. All rights reserved.

p. 380 Peter Cary, Avery Comarow and Randy Dotinga, "Fixing Kids' Sports" from U.S. News and World Report, May 2004. Copyright © 2004 by U.S. News and World Report. Reproduced with permission.

p. 391 Maya Angelou, "Champion of the World", copyright © 1969 and renewed 1997 by Maya Angelou, from I KNOW WHY THE CAGED BIRD SINGS by Maya Angelou. Used by permission of Random House, Inc.

p. 396 Reprinted courtesy of Sports Illustrated: Thomas Lake, "The Boy Who Died of Football" from Sports Illustrated, December 6, 2010, Vol. 113, Issue 21, copyright © 2010 Time Inc. All rights reserved.

p. 414 Ben McGrath, "Does Football Have a Future?" from New Yorker, January 31, 2011, Volume 88, Issue 46. Reprinted by permission of the author.

p. 436 Adam Gopnik, "The Unbeautiful Game," from The New Yorker, January 8, 2007. Copyright © 2007 Conde Naste Publications. All rights reserved.

p. 453 Sydney Pollack, "The Way We Are" from Film Comment, September/October 1975. Reprinted with permission.

p. 463 Jethro Rothe-Kushel, "Fight Club: A Ritual Cure for the Spiritual Ailment or American Masculinity" from The Film Journal.

p. 487 Ashley Elaine York, "From Chick Flicks to Millennial Blockbusters: Spinning Female-Driven Narratives into Franchises" from the Journal of Popular Culture, Feb. 1, 2010, © 2010. Reprinted by permission of the publisher (John Wiley and Sons).

p. 507 Kyle Bishop, "Raising the Dead" from Journal of Popular Film and Television, January 1, 2006, Volume 33, Issue 4. Reprinted by permission of Taylor and Francis Group, http://www.informaworld.com.

p. 524 David Denby, "A Fine Romance," from The New Yorker, July 23, 2007. Copyright © 2007 Conde Nast Publications. All rights reserved. Reprinted with permission.

p. 536 Alex Wainer, "Freaks, Geeks, and Mensches" from http://www.breakpoint.org/listingarticle.asp?ID=7282. Reprinted by permission of the author.

p. 542 Hilton Als, "Mamas Gun" from New Yorker, 0028792X, April 26, 2010, Volume 86, Issue 10. Copyright © 2010 Conde Nast Publications. All rights reserved. Reprinted with permission.

p. 553 Svetkey, Benjamin; Watson, Margeaux; and Alynda Wheat, "Tyler Perry: The Controversy Over His Hit Movies" from Entertainment Weekly, Issue #1039, March 20, 2009. Copyright TIME INC. Reprinted by permission. TIME is a registered trademark of Time Inc. All rights reserved.

PHOTO/ILLUSTRATION CREDITS

Chapter 1: p. 1 AP Photo/Dan Krauss

Chapter 2: p. 46 Timex Corporation; p. 54 Courtesy of Adbusters.org; p. 92 Courtesy of the Mary Boone Gallery, New York

Chapter 3: p. 115 Glen Baxter/The New Yorker/Cartoon Bank

Chapter 4: p. 203 Steve Chong/BizOne News EPN/Newscom

Chapter 5: p. 295 Victor Habbick Visions/Photo Researchers, Inc.

Chapter 6: p. 359 AP Photo/Mark J. Terrill; p. 374 John Storey/Time & Life Pictures/Getty Images; p. 376 AP Photo/Matt York; p. 393 AP Photo/Anthony Camerano

Chapter 7: p. 451 Universal City Studios, Inc./Photofest; p. 459 Keystone/Hulton Archive/Getty Images; p. 560 Photos 12/Alamy

Color Insert: p. CI-1a Photo Illustration by Aaron Goodman; p. CI-1b "Conversion Barbie", © 2001 Kimmy McCann, Artist. Private Collection: Ms. Taea Calcut; p. CI-2a Courtesy of Adbusters.org; p. CI-2b SAUL LOEB/AFP/Getty Images/Newscom; p. CI-3 RHA/ZOB/Newscom; p. CI-4 Time Life Pictures/DMI/Time Life Pictures/Getty Images; p. CI-5 Jennifer Verhines; p. CI-6 Nik Edlinger; p. CI-6 Lauren Carr; p. CI-7 FancyVeerSet16/Fancy/Alamy; p. CI-08 Photos 12/Alamy

Index by Author and Title

Index by Academic Discipline

Political Science

Pop Cultural Criticism

Psychology

Sociology/Communications

Gender Studies

Index by Rhetorical Mode

Analysis

Argumentation

Classification/Division

Comparison/Contrast

Definition

Narrative

Illustration